UNITED NATIONS HANDBOOK

on Selected Issues for

TAXATION OF THE
EXTRACTIVE INDUSTRIES

by Developing Countries

United Nations
New York, 2021

For further information, please contact:

United Nations
Department of Economic and Social Affairs
Financing for Sustainable Development Office
United Nations Secretariat
Two UN Plaza, Room DC2-2306
New York, N.Y. 10017, USA
Tel: (1-212) 963-7633 • Fax: (1-212) 963-0443
E-mail: fsdoffice@un.org

Foreword to the Second Edition (2021)

This second edition of the United Nations Handbook on Selected Issues for Taxation of the Extractive Industries by Developing Countries (the Handbook) is an extension to the first edition published in 2017. Considering the importance of natural resources as a source of national revenue and the potential of extractive industries as a driving force for economic activities in many other sectors, the UN Committee of Experts on International Cooperation in Tax Matters created a Subcommittee to study the issue related to taxation of extractive industries in developing countries.

Created in 2013, the first Subcommittee on Extractive Industries Taxation Issues for Developing Countries had the following mandate to consider, report on and propose draft guidance on extractive industries taxation issues for developing countries. To execute its mandate the Subcommittee had to:

- Identify and consider the most pressing issues where guidance from the Committee may most usefully assist developing countries in this area and report to the Committee on such;

- Identify and prioritize such issues on a preliminary basis and included proposals providing policy and administrative guidance for developing countries at a very practical level; and

- Provide draft guidance on such issues as are approved by the Committee at its annual sessions.

The Subcommittee identified a range of issues facing developing countries and other countries endowed in mineral and other natural resources. It developed guidance on many of those issues which was in line with the 2030 Development Agenda and the need to fight tax base erosion to increase domestic resource mobilization for the financing of Sustainable Development Goals (SDGs).

At the end of its term in 2017, the UN Tax Committee had already reviewed and approved guidelines for a set of key issues and decided to publish them in a unique document, the United Nations Handbook on Selected Issues for Taxation of the Extractive Industries by Developing Countries. The Handbook was organized in nine following chapters: 1. Overview; 2. Tax treaty issues; 3. Permanent establishment issues; 4. Indirect transfer of assets; 5. Transfer pricing issues; 6. The tax treatment of decommissioning; 7. The government's fiscal take; 8. Tax aspects of negotiation and renegotiation of contracts; and 9. Value added tax.

The publication of guidance on the issues above was conscientious decision by the Committee even as many other topics not less important were still to be addressed. They made recommendation to the continue the work during the next term (2017-2021) and at its fifteenth Session in October 2017, the Committee, with a new membership, decided to reinstate the Subcommittee on Extractive industries Taxation to continue the work and extend the guidance to other key issues not studied in the previous Handbook due to lack of time.

The new Subcommittee's mandate was as follows:

The Subcommittee is mandated to consider, report on and propose draft guidance on extractive industries taxation issues for developing countries in the form of updates to the United Nations Handbook on Selected Issues for Taxation of the Extractive Industries by Developing Countries ("the Handbook"). This work shall be conducted on the basis that it shall:

- Identify and consider the most pressing issues where further guidance from the Committee may most usefully assist developing countries in this area and initially report to the Committee on such matters at its sixteenth session in 2018;

- Provide draft guidance on such issues as are approved by the Committee at its sessions; and propose other updates and improvements to the Handbook for approval. In undertaking its work, the Subcommittee shall seek to engage with other organizations active in the field. The Subcommittee shall report on its work at each session.

At its sixteenth Session in May 2018, The Committee agreed that the future update of the Handbook would include additional areas of priority for developing countries, such as practical guidance on auditing mining and oil and gas activities, trade mispricing issues (to the extent that they were not transfer pricing issues), the tax treatment of service providers and subcontractors, the tax treatment of financial transactions related to extractive industries, environmental tax issues and tax incentives. Where appropriate, those issues might be analysed in coordination with other relevant Subcommittees.

In seeking consistency, the Subcommittee developed guidelines on new key issues which after discussion and approval by the Committee, were included in the Handbook with a new structure and chapter numbering, and a few chapters were slightly modified to include new data in the extractive industries in light new developments. Chapters reviewed include: Overview, Transfer pricing issues, and The tax treatment of decommissioning. The new chapter structuring is as follows: 1. Overview; 2. The government's fiscal take; 3. Tax aspects of negotiation and renegotiation of contracts; 4. Production Sharing Contracts; 5. Tax Incentives; 6. Tax treaty issues; 7. Permanent establishment issues; 8. Tax Treatment of Subcontractors; 9. Tax Treatment of Financial Transactions in the Extractive Industries; 10. Indirect transfer of assets; 11. Transfer pricing issues; 12. Value added tax; 13. Issues and Best Practices in Auditing Oil, Gas and Mining Activities; 14. The tax treatment of decommissioning.

This Handbook has been the work of many authors, and particular thanks are due to the Members of the Subcommittee on Extractive Industries Taxation Issues for Developing Countries contributing to this work. Participants included the following Members of the United Nations Tax Committee:

Coordinators: Eric Nii Yarboi Mensah (Co-Coordinator and Committee Member); Ignatius Mvula (Co-Coordinator, Zambia); Dang Ngoc Minh (Committee Member); Carmel Peters (Committee Member); Alexandr Smirnov (Committee Member); Elfrieda Stewart Tamba (Committee Member); Abiodun Aina (Nigeria); Gonzalo Arias (International Organization/CIAT); Rodolfo Bejarano (Latindad); Jorge Cabral (Brazil); Hafiz Choudhury (Business); Jan P de Goede (Academia/NGO); Alvaro de Juan Ledesma (Business); Johan de la Rey (South Africa); David Delahay (Business); Michael Durst (Business); Clarence Ellis (Business); Olav Fjellsa (Business); Kenny Hawsey (Business); Michael Kobetsky (Academia); Thomas Lassourd (NGO/Natural Resource Governance Institute); Ross Lyons (Business); Marius Van Oordt (Academia); Nara Monkam (International Organization/ATAF); Andre Nsabimana (Academia); Nana Okoh (Business); Moises Orozco (Mexico); Alexandra Readhead (International Organization/IGF); Jim Robertson (Business); Chris Sanger (Business); Bevon Sinclair (Jamaica); Stig Sollund (Norway); Anna Theeuwes (Business); Christophe Waerzeggers (International Organization/IMF); Tomas Balco (International Organization/OECD); Vy Tran (International Organization/OECD).

Secretarial support for the second edition of the Handbook was provided by Mr. Olivier Munyaneza and Ms. Maria De Azevedo Sodre. We also wish to acknowledge the assistance of Ms. Silvia Yiu, Ms. Kaylin Richards, and Ms. Sheilah Trotta in compiling and editing this publication, as well as the assistance of Ms. Katie Yang. The editing and graphic design were done respectively by Mr. Hafiz Choudhurry and Ms. Carla De Franco.

The Subcommittee especially expresses its gratitude to the relevant ministries and agencies of the governments of Vietnam and Kenya, for generously hosting Subcommittee meetings, and also to the European Commission and the government of India for financially supporting the meetings.

Foreword to the
First Edition (2017)

The United Nations Handbook on Selected Issues for Taxation of the Extractive Industries by Developing Countries (the Handbook) is a response to the need, often expressed by developing countries, for clearer guidance on the policy and administrative aspects of applying taxes to enterprises, including multinational enterprises (MNEs) acting in the extractive industries and other local and international companies accessory to the business. Such guidance should not only assist policy makers and administrators in dealing with complex issues such as the quantification of the fiscal take, the costs of decommissioning, and loss of revenues derived from the indirect transfer of assets, but should also assist taxpayers in their dealings with tax administrations.

The Handbook highlights some of the issues developing countries should bear in mind when negotiating new contracts for the exploration and exploitation of natural and mineral resources within their territories. The Handbook covers the following topics in chapter order: 1. Overview; 2. Tax treaty issues; 3. Permanent establishment issues; 4. Indirect transfer of assets; 5. Transfer pricing issues; 6. The tax treatment of decommissioning; 7. The government's fiscal take; 8. Tax aspects of negotiation and renegotiation of contracts; and 9. Value added tax.

The objective of the Handbook is to focus on specific areas of interest for developing countries. The Handbook, as a product of the United Nations Committee of Experts on International Cooperation in Tax Matters (United Nations Tax Committee), has a special role in reflecting the diversity of the United Nations Membership and placing taxation of the extractive industries in its developmental perspective, by exploring the challenges of taxing an industry that is of particular relevance to developing countries, including the least developed, where extensive natural resources are often located. This recognizes both the importance to development of fair and effective tax systems, but also the fact that foreign investment, on appropriate terms, is seen as an important path to development by most countries.

Helpful guidance in this complex area must, in particular, be geared to the inevitable limitations in some countries' administrations, and deficits in information and skills that many countries are affected by in this area. Issues, in particular, of building and retaining capability as well as the need for focus and efficiency in dealing with limited resources, bear strongly on the approach taken in the Handbook. Practical examples relevant to developing countries have been especially relied upon, because the experiences of other developing countries in addressing the extractives sector are an important way of finding effective solutions that work in their context, and of doing so in the most cost and time effective ways. Examples were also drawn from developed countries, such as Norway and the United Kingdom, due to their first-hand experience in defining some of the policy approaches that are still currently applied to tax the extractive industries, and to charge national rent, also known as fiscal take.

Whereas other intergovernmental organizations have sought to provide guidance on selected tax issues for the extractive industries, such as transparency and transfer pricing approaches, the United Nations Tax Committee felt that there is insufficient analysis of the basic features which should be taken into account by any tax administration when deciding to develop policies or taxation strategies for the extractive industries. The Handbook is therefore quite unique in its aim to provide governments with a basic outline of the challenges they will encounter when seeking to compute the administrative, fiscal, environmental and other related costs of exploring natural resources — so that the economic venture does not occur at the expense of the quality of life of the citizens and environment.

This Handbook is intended to provide guidance only. It seeks to address relevant issues in the extractive industries in a clear form, to raise awareness of potential challenges and opportunities as well as the pros and cons of possible options for countries and agencies in differing positions, and ultimately to assist in making decisions on policy and administration that are informed and reflect country realities and priorities. To the extent of any inconsistency between this Handbook and the United Nations Model Double Taxation Convention between Developed and Developing Countries, the latter prevails.

This Handbook has been the work of many authors, and particular thanks are due to the Members of the Subcommittee on Extractive Industries Taxation — Issues for Developing Countries contributing to this work. Participants included the following Members of the United Nations Tax Committee: Mr. Eric Mensah (Coordinator); Mr. Mohammed Baina (Morocco); Mr. Johan Cornelius de la Rey (South Africa); Mr. El Hadji Ibrahima Diop (Senegal); Ms. Liselott Kana (Chile); Mr. Enrico Martino (Italy); Mr. Ignatius Kawaza Mvula (Zambia); Ms. Carmel Peters (New Zealand); Ms. Pragya S. Saksena (India); Mr. Stig B. Sollund (Norway); Ms. Ingela Willfors (Sweden); and Mr. Ulvi Yusifov (Azerbaijan). Other participants were: Mr. Charles Bajungu (Tanzania Revenue Authority); Mr. Tomas Balco (Ministry of Finance of Slovakia); Mr. Rodolfo Bejarano (Red Latinoamericana sobre Deuda, Desarrollo y Derechos — Latindadd); Ms. Susana Bokobo (Repsol); Mr. Jorge Cabral (Receita Federal, Brazil); Mr. Hafiz Choudhury (M Group); Mr. Michael Durst (Attorney); Mr. Jan de Goede (International Bureau of Fiscal Documentation — IBFD); Mr. Alvaro de Juan Ledesma (Repsol); Mr. Olav Fjellså (Aker BP, Norway); Mr. Kwesi K. Obeng (Tax Justice Network Africa); Mr. Michael Kobetsky (University of Melbourne); Mr. Tomas Lassourd (Resource Governance Institute); Mr. Cephas Makunike (Tax Justice Network Africa); Ms. Nara Monkam (African Tax Administration Forum — ATAF); Ms. Nana Okoh (Gold Fields Ghana Ltd); Mr. Moises Orozco (Servicio de Administración

Tributaria — SAT, Mexico); Mr. Miguel Pecho (Inter-American Centre on Tax Administrations — CIAT); Mr. Richard Stern (World Bank Group); Mr. Chris Sanger (Ernest & Young — EY); Mr. Karl Schmalz (United States Council for International Business); Mr. Brian Twomey (Reverse Engineering Services Ltd); Ms. An Theeuwes (Shell); Mr. Marius van Oordt (African Tax Institute); and Mr. Christophe Waerzeggers (International Monetary Fund — IMF). Chapter 5 of the Handbook, on transfer pricing, was prepared with extensive assistance of Mr. Joe Andrus, Ms. Melinda Brown (OECD), Ms. Monique van Herksen (Simmons & Simmons), Mr. Toshio Miyatake (Adachi, Henderson, Miyatake & Fujita), and Ms. Jolanda Schenk (Shell), all members of the Subcommittee on Transfer Pricing. While consensus has been sought as far as possible, the views expressed in the Handbook may not reflect the understanding of all Subcommittee members.

Secretarial support for the Handbook was provided by Mr. Michael Lennard, Ms. Ilka Ritter, Ms. Tatiana Falcão and Ms. Elena Belletti. We also wish to acknowledge the assistance of Ms. Mary Lee Kortes and Ms. Leah McDavid in compiling and editing this publication, as well as the assistance of Ms. Nathalia Oliveira, Ms. Suzana Hoefle, Ms. Janaina Muller and Mr. Ahtesham R. Khan. The Subcommittee especially expresses its gratitude to the relevant ministries and agencies of the governments of Slovakia, South Africa, United Republic of Tanzania, and Zambia for generously hosting Subcommittee meetings, and also to the European Commission for financially supporting some key meetings.

Finally, it should be noted that this Handbook is conceived as a living work that should be regularly revised and improved, including by the addition of new chapters and additional material of special relevance to developing countries. This will only improve its relevance to users and its significance as a work that can be relied upon in the capacity building efforts of the United Nations and others.

Contents

Chapter 2   The Government's Fiscal Take

Chapter 3   Tax Aspects of Negotiation and Renegotioation of Contracts

Chapter 4   Production Sharing Contracts

Chapter 5   Tax Incentives

Chapter 6   Tax Treaty Issues

Chapter 7   Permanent Establishment Issues

Chapter 8   Tax Treatment of Subcontractors and Service Providers

Chapter 9   Tax Treatment of Financial Transactions the Extractives Industry

Chapter 10   Indirect Transfer of Assets

Chapter 11   Transder Pricing Issues

Chapter 12   Value Added Tax

Chapter 1

Overview

1.1   INTRODUCTION

1.1.1   Executive summary

1.1.1.1   The purpose of this chapter is to give an overview of some of the taxation issues for extractive industries in developing countries and the interactions between them, as well as options available, and the likely effect of choosing such options in particular circumstances. This is intended to assist policy makers and administrators in developing countries as well as to provide information to other stakeholders. The background contained in this chapter will provide a broader context for viewing the overall issue of natural resource development and the specific issues addressed in more detail in additional chapters.

1.1.1.2   The work covered by this and each of the additional specific-issue chapters stems from a mandate given by the United Nations Committee of Experts on International Cooperation in Tax Matters (UN Tax Committee) to the Subcommittee on Handbook on Taxation of Extractive Industries ("the Subcommittee") to consider, report on and propose guidance on extractive industries taxation issues for developing countries, in the form of updates to the UN Handbook on Selected Issues for Taxation of the Extractive Industries by Developing Countries (the Handbook). The Handbook will seek to provide policy and administrative guidance at a very practical level.

1.1.1.3   This chapter is intended to broadly identify issues of taxation of the extractive industries; address several of the most significant ones in short form; help build awareness; and, ultimately, along with the additional specific-issue chapters, assist those faced with these issues to make policy and administrative decisions in relation to them. This publication is an update of the previous version of the Handbook issued in 2018. That publication was a result of work undertaken by the Subcommittee during 2014-2017 and approved by the UN Committee of Experts on International Cooperation in Tax Matters. It contains five new chapters on tax incentives; tax treatment of subcontractors and service providers; production sharing contracts; tax treatment of financial transactions in the extractive industries; and audit. Other chapters have been edited for cross-referencing and accuracy, without amending the underlying principles approved in 2018. In addition, new data has been included where appropriate, especially to take account of the current world-wide humanitarian situation induced by the COVID-19 Pandemic.

1.1.2   Background

1.1.2.1   Since early 2020, the world has been dealing with the COVID-19 pandemic which has put the world economy on its knees. It started as a humanitarian crisis but quickly evolved into a global socio-economic emergency with devastating inter-generational effects unseen since World War II, leaving no country unharmed and almost all social groups affected, with the brunt of the impact falling on the already vulnerable groups. Recent estimates indicate that COVID-19 may have pushed 71 to 100 million people into extreme poverty, erasing any gain recorded since 2017[1]. In developing countries, the COVID-19 crisis is having an immediate and amplified impact on the poorest and most vulnerable regions. Some experts do not hesitate to call what they see as a "lost decade" if the international community does not come together quickly to propose adequate solutions with bold measures commensurate to the magnitude of devastation brought about by the pandemic.

1.1.2.2   It is against this backdrop that the Deputy Secretary-General in collaboration with the Regional Economic Commission have conveyed a series of Regional Roundtables to assess the potential for the extractive industries to be an engine of the recovery and for the rebuilding of the economy especially for natural resource-rich developing countries. Indeed, in a number of countries, keeping the extractives industry operating has been a priority for Governments, due to the heavy reliance on extractive operations in their economies.

1.1.2.3   Extractive industries can support economic growth and employment and can generate substantial revenues for resource-rich countries to be used to accelerate their economic recovery and regain the path to sustainable development by investing in sustainable development goals (SDGs). It is important to note, however, that developing countries endowed with natural resources for various reasons have not always been able to collect the expected level of revenue to finance their development and to invest in safety nets crucial for achieving SDGs.

1.1.2.4   The sector is, to varying degrees, linked to almost all other SDGs as well, for example: i) affordable and clean energy; ii) decent work and economic growth; iii) industry innovation and infrastructure; iv) peace and security; and (v) Partnership for the Goals[2]. As a case in point, it is noteworthy mentioning the extractive industries' dominant economic, social and political role in the lives of 3.5 billion people living in 81 countries, and accounting for a quarter of global GDP.

1.1.2.5   With the right sectoral policy and an effective tax administration, the extractive industries can be an engine for increased foreign direct investment (FDI), a substantial source of public revenue, and foundation for reduced poverty

---

[1] World Bank report (June 8, 2020), Projected poverty impacts of COVID-19 (coronavirus): https://www.worldbank.org/en/topic/poverty/brief/projected-poverty-impacts-of-COVID-19

[2] As set out in SDG 17, partnerships between governments, the private sector and civil society are necessary for the development agenda, built on principles and values, a shared vision and shared goals. Partnerships are required at the global, regional, national and local level.

programs at domestic level. Taking stock of such a potential, resource-rich developing countries can focus their efforts on key areas such as tax policy settings that encourage investment in the industry, sustainable revenue collection and transparency, effective regulatory framework, environmental impact mitigation and rehabilitation, and increased local value and diversification.

1.1.2.6   In the current pandemic-ravaged world economy, all regional Roundtables sought to answer the generic question of how extractives can be leveraged as an engine for economic recovery and sustainable development especially for low- and middle-income countries. A related question is how extractive industries can be aligned with the outcomes of the Financing for Development[3] programme in the era of COVID-19 to use the sector to anchor an economic rebuilding aligned with the SDGs and the Paris Agreement on Climate Change.

1.1.2.7   The Roundtables debated those important questions and raised several key points that need to be addressed if the extractive industries are to play a key role in "building back better." Some of the recommendations were relative to the unique situation of each region but some key takeaways are as follows:

- Domestic policies should be designed to encourage further investment in the sector, including investment in downstream processes which add value to mineral exports;

- Creating a fiscal buffer, through long term savings;

- An adequate and investment-conducive legal framework including the stability and capacity of institutions that implement the framework;

- Technical and capacity-building support to combat illicit financial flows, through traceability and transparency in the value chain;

- Efforts to integrate extractives into the circular economy[4];

- Using extractive industries and revenue to diversify the economy;

- Developing extractive industries in an environmentally-sustainable way (transforming waste into resource recovery, provision for decommissioning activities); and

- Convening stakeholders to create norms, standards, and disclosure frameworks.

1.1.2.8. The final and global Roundtable convened by the Secretary General in May 2021 discussed developing renewable energy technologies and phasing out

---

[3] The Addis Ababa Action Agenda included a new global framework for financing sustainable development aligning financing flows and policies with economic, social and environmental priorities.

[4] The circular economy involves sharing, reusing, repairing and recycling materials and products for as long as possible, extending the life cycle of products.

assets based on fossil-fuels. This would involve phasing out the use of coal; moving subsidies from fossil fuels to renewable energy; promoting technology transfer; development finance support from development banks, the IMF and other institutions; and greater regional and global cooperation to support a sustainable transition.

1.1.2.9   Despite the disruption caused by the COVID-19 pandemic in the global economy, and particularly the mining and oil and gas sectors, the industry outlook remains strong in the long run. Therefore, the analysis and description provided in the previous edition of the Handbook and in the added chapters remain applicable, notwithstanding a clear trend towards the growing importance to manufacture cleaner energy technologies for several key minerals and metals.

1.1.2.10   As the world moves toward containment of the pandemic by immunization, economic activities, including mining and oil and gas, are steadily regaining ground. For instance, according to the International Energy Agency (IEA), under the Stated Policies Scenario (STEPS), which takes into account current policies by governments aimed at greenhouse gas emissions reduction, in 2021 the global oil demand will continue to recover from its historic drop in 2020 and is expected to surpass the pre-crisis level by 2023. Likewise, natural gas will recover quickly from a drop in demand in 2020 as demand rebounds by almost 3% in 2021 to rise by 14% above 2019 levels by 2030[5].

1.1.2.11   Extractive industries are engaged in finding, developing, producing and selling non-renewable natural resources such as crude oil, natural gas and mining products.[6] The extractive industries are an important sector and thus a potentially important revenue base in many developing countries and emerging economies.

1.1.2.12   The IEA, under the STEPS, expects the world energy demand to increase by 9 per cent by 2030 and by 19 per cent by 2040 while oil demand increases by 5 per cent and 6 per cent by 2030 and 2040 respectively. The demand for natural gas is projected to be stronger on the two periods with increases of 15 per cent by 2030 and 30 per cent by 2040. Without a significant technological breakthrough, these non-renewable sources of energy will continue to be the major source of energy in the world by 2040. Combined, oil and gas will represent 53 per cent of global energy demand in 2040.

1.1.2.13   In its October 2020 report, the IEA estimates the investment needed to achieve universal energy access at $40 billion per year between 2021 and 2030, with a large share going to electricity. This is double the annual

---

[5] See International Energy Agency, *World Energy Outlook 2020, Outlook for Energy Demand*. Available at https://www.iea.org/reports/world-energy-outlook-2020/outlook-for-energy-demand#abstract

[6] Crude oil and natural gas are key energy resources, as well as inputs to other worldwide products, such as chemicals, plastics, and fertilizers. Hard minerals comprise a wide variety of products, such as copper, iron, gold, bauxite and numerous rare earth minerals, which are also used as inputs for many essential products, such as steel, aluminum, plastics, and fertilizers.

investment under STEPS but falls far short of the annual investment of $3 trillion that is required by 2030 in the Sustainable Development Scenario (SDS). In fact, the SDS requires an annual increase of 25% from 2021 to 2050. However, the large increase comes from renewable-based power which doubles the current level between 2020 and 2050. This increase in investment will also be partially offset by reduced fuel cost to mitigate the impact on consumers.

1.1.2.14   It is against this backdrop that the IEA reports that the world is not on track to meet the energy-related components of the Sustainable Development Goals (SDGs). With the current trend, three SDGs most related to energy consumption and production, to achieve universal access to energy (SDG 7), to reduce the severe health impacts of air pollution (part of SDG 3) and to tackle climate change (SDG 13), are unlikely to be met.

1.1.2.15   A substantial increase in investment in renewable energy will be needed. In its report on minerals for climate action, the World Bank reports that the production of minerals, such as graphite, lithium and cobalt, could increase by nearly 500% by 2050[7], to meet the growing demand for clean energy technologies. This is a big opportunity for countries endowed in such minerals, especially developing countries, which with the appropriate policies can reap the benefits of their mineral production to fund the SDGs.

1.1.2.16   With minerals playing crucial roles throughout economic sectors, especially in agriculture, construction, energy, transportation, electronics, and medicine, the projections for population, economic and energy growth translate into increased demand for minerals. For example, steel demand could potentially exceed 2010 levels by 120 per cent in 2040, with the greatest increase being in emerging economies. Similar results are projected for copper.[8] The International Council on Mining and Metals (ICMM) has underscored the significance of regions with emerging economies, noting the large investments that were recently undertaken in Latin America, Africa and parts of Asia, and the outlook that these will likely increase in the next 10 years.[9]

1.1.2.17   Against this macroeconomic backdrop political, financial, monetary, and legal stability, as well as a labour market-fiscal stability, are crucial in developing countries' efforts to attract foreign direct investment in the extractive industries to contribute to mobilizing domestic resources for development. While resource development will be needed to meet worldwide energy demand and foster economic growth, the extractive industries are and will increasingly become an important sector in many developing countries and emerging economies.

---

[7] World Bank Group report, "Minerals for Climate Action: "The Mineral Intensity of the Clean Energy Transition."

[8] See K. Keramidas, A. Kitous and B. Griffin, *Future availability and demand for oil gas and key minerals*. p. 45. Available at http://www.eisourcebook.org/cms/February%202016/ Future%20availability%202012.pdf.

[9] See International Council on Mining and Metals, *The role of mining in national economies*. Available at https://www.icmm.com/website/publications/pdfs/social-and-economic-development/romine_1st-edition.

Not only will the direct investment that such industries generate be an important contributor to economic development, it will also continue to provide a broader and potentially important revenue base for additional economic development that countries may wish to pursue.

1.1.2.18   The tax and broader fiscal system that applies to the extractive industries should ensure that the government obtains an adequate and appropriate share of the benefits from its resources—taking into account that extractives are assets owned by the country and once extracted, they are gone—while providing a return commensurate with the risks borne and functions carried out by the parties. Tax laws and regulations that provide legal certainty and stability reduce financial risk, and therefore, aid in attracting investment. In addition, transparent administration of the tax system and the avoidance of double taxation further reduce risks and influence investment decisions in the extractive industries. Governments should seek to balance creating or sustaining a supportive environment for large investment with the country's need for revenue streams that can be applied to their development efforts. Close collaboration among different governmental agencies, including ministries of energy and mining, environment, finance, tax policy and administration, along with those entrusted to govern, manage, or reinvest revenues from natural resource development, is important in arriving at the correct balance at the outset and on an ongoing basis.

1.1.2.19   The extractives industries are unique in many ways: the sector is shaped by high sunk costs in the form of substantial investments that cannot be recouped if a project is unsuccessful; significant up-front construction costs; long lead times from initial investment to project start-up and very long production/project lives; fluctuating costs and commodity prices that in turn influence the profitability of exploration, development and extraction; volatile demand; and environmental impacts, including ultimately 'decommissioning', rehabilitation or reclamation responsibilities.[10] The extractive industries are often located in remote areas, at great distance from their eventual markets. The potential for losses is therefore real. At the same time, companies active in the extractive industries have the potential of substantial earnings in excess of the return on investment required to induce their acceptance of the risks they assume (i.e., windfall gains).[11]

1.1.2.20   Given the large capital investment required to develop and produce natural resources, and the fact that the output is also physically present in the source country, often with world market benchmark prices available, the risk that the product sales value cannot be validated by tax authorities may be lower than for some other non-commodity-based businesses. Similarly, particularly in the petroleum industry where joint ventures are present, goods or services charged

---

[10] For a more complete list of the risk factors investors face, see International Energy Agency, *World Energy Investment Outlook 2014, Special Report*, p. 32, Table 1.4 "Categories of risk facing an energy investment project." Available at https://www.iea.org/publications/freepublications/publication/WEIO2014.pdf.

[11] See L. Burns, Income *Taxation through the Life Cycle of an Extractive Industries Project*, Asia-Pacific Tax Bulletin, vol. 20, no. 6 (18 November 2014), p. 401.

into the venture by the operator are generally required under industry practice to be at cost and subject to audit by the co-venturers.[12] Nevertheless, given the large production values and associated development and production costs, there is an ongoing concern about the erosion of the source country tax base via aggressive tax planning strategies, and thus fiscal regime design and administration procedures and practices should properly address these issues.

1.1.2.21   Governments will likely want to tailor their auditing plans and efforts based on the natural resource activities and parties involved, evaluating the potential risks presented and benefits to be gained from specific enforcement actions. While the challenges of dealing with these issues are the same for all natural resource countries, tax administrations in developing countries may have capacity constraints in dealing with them. They may need augmentation, additional training, and capacity building as extractive industries activities commence, or significantly increase, in order to deal with them effectively. The information and knowledge needed to design and administer appropriate tax rules that apply to the extractive industries may be lacking or very thinly spread locally. Coordination between different parts of the government often proves challenging. Owing to a lack of funding that frequently exists, access to specialists in tax design and administration is often asymmetrical between multinational companies and developing countries.

1.1.2.22   In designing an overall taxation regime and developing its administration, each country will carefully determine its priorities and consider a wide array of choices available to it. There are numerous issues it must deal with, and the approach on any particular issue may not be the same across countries. Ultimately, it is recommended that each country will develop its own set of principles and goals, tailoring these to its specific priorities and to its unique circumstances (including location and quality of the natural resources to be developed, infrastructure, political and economic climate, development needs, and other resources available in the country). Two examples, one from a country and the other from an investor perspective, are shown in boxes 1.B.1 and 1.B.2 to illustrate possible approaches that can be taken in developing principles and development goals. Once a country determines its own set of principles and goals, the choices it makes in its taxation system design, including the structure and administration of taxation, other fiscal terms, and legal/regulatory requirements, should be tested to determine whether they advance and are consistent with those objectives.

1.1.2.23   To summarize, some recurring issues that countries face are summarized below. They underscore the interests that a country will need to balance, such as:

- Attracting new foreign or domestic direct investment to support growth and employment in the extractive industries and encourage expansion of existing operations;

---

[12] Jack Calder, *Administering Fiscal Regimes for Extractive Industries: A Handbook* (Washington, D.C: International Monetary Fund, 2014), p. 80.

- Ensuring the government receives an appropriate share of revenues;

- Weighing timing issues in relation to receipt of revenue;

- Ensuring sound environmental policies and protections exist;

- Fostering the development of local capacity in providing goods and services to the extractive industries;

- Reconciling transparency, and confidentiality; and

- Designing appropriate governance rules for the extractive industries, including capacities to deal with potential corruption.

1.1.2.24   Additionally, as revenues are generated under the fiscal plans, management of such funds over the short and long-term requires planning, diligence, and governance structures.

BOX I.B.1:
Investment principles and goals: country perspective:

Mozambique Natural Gas Master Plan[a]
In June 2014, the Cabinet Council of the Republic of Mozambique adopted a comprehensive plan for the development of its natural gas resources to "maximize the benefits to Mozambican society, in order to improve the living standards of its population, while minimizing the negative environmental impacts"[b].

The Natural Gas Master Plan focuses on three pillars for development: economic and institutional, financing and tax, and environmental and social development, as summarized in the table below.

With respect to the investment environment, the Plan further provides for the Government to "identify the essential elements of the business and investment environment needed to encourage investment in general, in the Mozambican economy, and that need to be in place and maintained in a transparent, stable and lasting way"[c]. It finds that, since "the development of the gas resources will require huge investments, throughout periods that will stretch for decades, it is vital that this environment is sustained and ameliorated as necessary"[d].

Principles of the Natural Gas Master Plan

Regulatory clarity
Clear definition of the responsibilities of regulators. This will have a positive impact on investment decisions, especially in downstream natural gas projects.

Sustainable use of revenues
The gas revenues constitute a clear form of directing the gas use to the economy for the creation of added value for the industry, and expansion of economic development. On the other hand, there would be sufficient revenue for supporting infrastructure and economic development in a number of areas in addition to the natural gas sector.

Identification of needs and coordination of infrastructure
It is necessary to define how the necessary infrastructure for the development—ports, roads, airports—needs to be created based on the gas production and use to meet the needs of communities that will host these gas-oriented enterprises. In addition to the infrastructure for natural gas, there is also a need for coordination with the planning of electricity and the development of other infrastructure.

---

[a] Republic of Mozambique, Cabinet Council, Natural Gas Master Plan, 2014. Available at http://www.inp.gov.mz/en/Policies-Legal-Framework/Policies NATURAL-GAS-MASTER-PLAN2
[b] Ibid, p. 23.
[c] Ibid, p. 28.
[d] Ibid, p. 28

Pillars	Strategic objectives
Economic and institutional aspects	Ensure the availability of gas for the domestic market, facilitating the industrialization of the country.
	Develop and implement a communication plan to increase transparency and manage expectations.
	Maximize national support for the development of natural gas projects.
	Encourage and support the use of natural gas in domestic industries.
	Increase institutional expertise in matters related to gas, including exploration, development and marketing of natural gas.
Financing and tax aspects	Establish and maintain a good business environment.
	Establish a financing mechanism for the development of gas projects and for local development initiatives.
	Improve the existing legal framework regarding natural gas.
	Ensure the Government's share of gas, both in kind and in cash.
Environment and social development	Ensure that the local communities, in particular in the areas of exploration and production, are benefiting from natural gas-related activities.
	Create and/or increase the environmental awareness of local communities.
	Prevent and/or mitigate environmental damage resulting from the production and use of natural gas.
	Strengthen institutional capacity for the implementation of environmental legislation.
	Training and capacity building of the national workforce.

Box I.B.2:
Investment principles and goals: investor perspective

Investor principles for developing country natural resources investment policies.[a]

The overall fiscal and regulatory structure should begin with an alignment on valuing and recovering resources in a manner consistent with the country's framework for economic development, and should

» **Create the greatest overall value from the country's resources**

› Provide revenues for country (including all governmental stakeholders) to reinvest;

› Promote growth in local economies as part of value creation via development of local infrastructure, industries, jobs and training;

› Generate value through maximum life cycle economic recovery of resources consistent with the most efficient, safe and environmentally sound development and decommissioning and restoration.

» **Be equitable to both government and investors**

› Ensure the government, as ultimate steward of the resources, receives for the country an equitable share of the benefit from its resources;

› Provide that investors receive a share reflecting all of their contributions and commensurate with the overall risks they bear;

› Align government and investing companies' interests throughout project life;

› The regime should be responsive such that equitable sharing of value is realized through all stages of the project life cycle and across ranges of outcomes and market conditions;

› Recognize that projects and relationships are long-term and seek ways to promote partnership and mutual trust.

» **Promote a stable and sustainable business environment**

› Country and investors should be able to plan ahead and rely on agreed terms;

> › Investors should be willing to manage and accept business risks (e.g., exploration, technical, project execution and operation), and market conditions (price and costs), and the country should seek to provide maximum possible certainty on rights and economic terms (e.g., rule of law, contract terms, legal framework, and fiscal terms);

> › Investors and the country should operate in good faith to resolve and satisfy potential disputes quickly and efficiently; and adoption of mutually agreed dispute resolution procedures, such as mediation and/or arbitration practices, may promote this goal.

» **Be administratively simple**

> › Provide a clear, practical, enforceable, stable, and non-discriminatory framework for administration of laws, regulations, and agreements;

> › Adopt programmes promoting cooperation and trust between tax administrators and taxpayers.

» **Be competitive**

> › Should attract the widest range of potential investors to ensure the country maximizes competition for its resources;

> › Should strive to be competitive with other countries given relative attractiveness and risks of resource development.

---

[a] This illustration is, with modifications to broaden coverage to all extractives, based largely on a set of investment principles published in the EI SourceBook and developed by the International Tax and Investment Center. Available at http://www.eisourcebook.org/2889_OilGasSpecifics.html.

1.2 INDUSTRY OVERVIEW

1.2.1 Extractive industries structures: life cycle

1.2.1.1 As noted, there are similarities but also many differences between the extractive industries and other industries that should be taken into account when designing and administering a tax regime. In order to better understand the specific problems that may arise in the extractive industries, a diagram of the generalized life cycle of a natural resource project is shown below in figure I.F.1, followed by an overview of the oil and gas and hard minerals industry structures.

1.2.1.2   The life cycle of an extractive industry project has five broad phases, as illustrated below:

Figure I.F.1: Life cycle of an extractive industry project

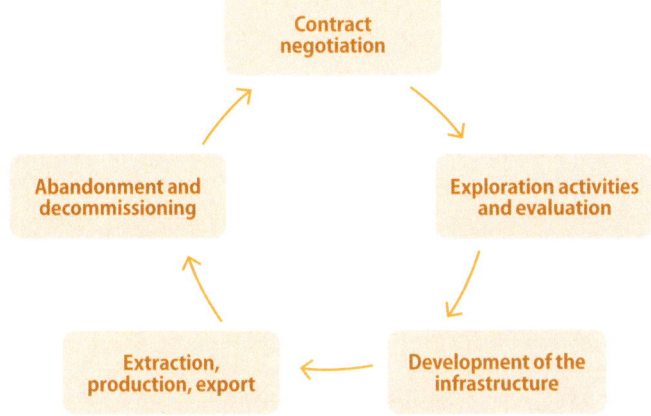

Source: UN/DESA

1.2.2   Extractive industries structures: oil and natural gas

General

1.2.2.1   The oil and gas industry involves exploration, production, transportation, the refining of crude oil and natural gas, manufacturing, distribution and marketing of crude oil and petrochemical products as well as liquefied petroleum gases.

1.2.2.2   In the oil and gas industry, reserve ownership and production are dominated by governments and government-owned or sponsored national companies. The latter are increasingly investing outside of their residence countries and becoming major competitors of publicly traded multinational companies. Government-owned national oil companies (NOCs) control 78 per cent of global oil reserves and 58 per cent of global oil production.[13] In addition to NOCs, international oil companies (IOCs)[14] also supply oil to the market, such that 84 per cent of the world's oil is produced by about 100 companies (NOCs or IOCs).

---

[13] NOCs are, for example, Saudi Aramco (Saudi Arabia), Pemex (Mexico), the China National Petroleum Corporation (CNPC), the Nigerian National Petroleum Corporation (NNPC), and Petróleos de Venezuela, S.A. (PdVSA).

[14] IOCs are integrated companies such as ExxonMobil, BP p.l.c., Royal Dutch Shell or Repsol, and many companies focused purely on exploration and production, such as ConocoPhillips, Apache, Tullow and Ophir Energy.

1.2.2.3   NOCs can encompass various degrees of government involvement, and often operate as government agencies or corporate entities. NOCs operating as an extension of the government mainly aim for macroeconomic goals such as employing residents, furthering a government's domestic or foreign policies, generating long-term revenue to pay for government programmes, and supplying inexpensive domestic energy. By contrast, NOCs with strategic and operational autonomy[15] balance profit-oriented concerns with the well-being of the country as a whole[16].

1.2.2.4   IOCs are investor-owned, market-oriented, and mainly aim to increase shareholder value. Various degrees of size, specialization and integration exist in IOCs. Often, companies specialize in one or more individual industry segments, such as the exploration and production, refining, transportation/distribution or marketing segments[17]. Many of the largest multinational oil and gas companies integrate all businesses, and are referred to as "vertically integrated" oil companies.

1.2.2.5   The oil and gas industry is often considered to have two major parts: the upstream activities — those related to the exploration and production of crude oil and natural gas, and the downstream activities — those related to the transportation, refining and marketing of oil and natural gas and their products.

Upstream

1.2.2.6   The exploration and production activities are the beginning stages of the life cycle and involve large upfront capital investment that carries significant risks in terms of achieving commercially successful results. Lead times from exploration through development to first production are long — often 10 years or more — further increasing project risks.

1.2.2.7   Investors often seek to reduce risks via project diversification, often in cooperation with other partners. The oil and gas industry is characterized by joint ventures (JVs) involving an operator along with several other investing partners that own undivided interests in the project and participate in decisions pursuant to an operating agreement. This approach is (and has traditionally been) the most common way of sharing economic risks. JV partners can also include government bodies or NOCs.

---

[15] NOCs with strategic and operational autonomy are, for example, Petrobras (Brazil) and Statoil (Norway).

[16] See U.S. Energy Information Administration, Oil: *Crude Oil and Petroleum Products Explained—Where our oil comes from.* Available at http://www.eia.gov/energy_in_brief/article/world_oil_market.cfm.

[17] There are independent refining, marketing, pipeline, shipping, and exploration and production companies, as well as major service companies (also referred to as subcontractors) providing seismic, drilling, construction, environment and environmental and other services and technologies for all phases of the international oil and gas industry.

1.2.2.8   The first phase of upstream activities (i.e., the acquisition of exploration rights) can occur via several methods, including participation in companies; entering into a joint venture with other investors to find or to develop resources; international bids (unilaterally or with partners); direct negotiations with governments and/or nationally owned oil companies; and outright purchases of assets or companies.

1.2.2.9   An exploration contract or licence can last for several years, divided into subperiods during which the company commits to a series of investments in geological, geophysical and seismic work and to drill a certain number of exploratory wells.

1.2.2.10   The operation, management, and policymaking procedures of a JV are regulated in a "joint venture" or partnership agreement called a Joint Operating Agreement (JOA). In the JOA, one of the participating companies is designated as the "operator," responsible for the day-to-day management of the activities to be performed, and the implementation of the decisions taken by the partners, including representation vis-a-vis local governments and third-party providers of services and materials.

Photo I.P.1:
Upstream offshore production facility

Source: Currahee/123RF.com

1.2.2.11   The operator assigns its own resources to the project (i.e., a team of technical and administrative support) that are charged at cost to the joint venture and allocated to each party based on its ownership percentage.

1.2.2.12   Non-operator companies are responsible for controlling and over-seeing that the activities performed by the operator are carried out according to quality standards and that the costs are in conformity with the agreement and budget of the consortium.

1.2.2.13   In the case of a commercial discovery, following government approval, the development phase commences, consisting of investments in engi-neering, development drilling, construction of processing facilities, civil works, platforms, well production and control facilities, and oil and gas transportation/offloading systems.

1.2.2.14   The operator forms a development team to conduct the develop-ment project, which involves coordinating with the partners as well as with the numerous subcontractors and service companies involved, and to ensure compli-ance with, and sound administration of, the contracts involved.

1.2.2.15   The development phase can last from a few months to three years or longer depending on the size, location and complexity of the site to be developed.

1.2.2.16   Once the facilities and offloading systems are commissioned and development surveys are completed, the production phase starts. Contractually, this phase usually lasts between 15 and 25 years, provided that the economic limit of the field has not been reached earlier. Throughout time, new and/or improved assisted recovery techniques are applied to maximize production levels and reserve recovery.

1.2.2.17   Throughout the project, the environmental impacts need to be assessed and managed to minimize adverse impacts and, at the end of the proj-ect's life, contracts generally provide for the decommissioning of the structures, and restoration of the site.

Downstream

1.2.2.18   "Downstream" is the term generally given to the transportation of crude oil and natural gas and to the refining, storage, distribution and marketing of crude oil and its derived products. Refining involves conversion of crude oil into industrial and consumer products such as petrol, diesel, liquid petroleum gas, aviation fuel, bunker for marine transport, and chemical feedstock. Marketing can involve retail petrol station activities and other marketing to wholesale or retail customers, including petrochemical manufacturing activities.

1.2.2.19   Activities connecting the pure upstream and downstream functions are sometimes referred to as "midstream," and consist of trading and transporta-tion (by pipeline, rail, barge, tanker or truck) storage, and wholesale marketing of crude oil, natural gas or refined petroleum products. These functions can be performed within integrated companies (where they are also called the Supply and Transportation (S&T) function) or by independent businesses specializing in one or more of these activities.

Photo I.P.2:
Downstream refining complex

Source: photowrzesien/123RF.com

1.2.2.20   An integrated company's S&T function is important since companies often lack sufficient production of their own, in total or in the right locations or specifications, to meet their refining or marketing needs. These constraints are addressed by businesses actively involved in purchasing, exchanging, and/or selling crude oil, intermediate or end products. Additionally, the fact that many producing and refining countries export their production to other markets requires a robust supply and transportation industry.

Liquefied natural gas: an expanding business[18]

1.2.2.21   The liquefied natural gas (LNG) business involves upstream, midstream, and downstream elements in the commercialization of natural gas resources through extracting and processing, liquefying, transporting such liquefied gas in special ships, re-gasifying it in processing facilities, and delivering it to customers.

1.2.2.22   LNG projects involve very large upfront capital investments, with a development phase typically between five and six years. Given the significant upfront capital investment, LNG suppliers typically require revenue certainty by having off-take contracts for a significant portion of the expected LNG production to be in place prior to a final investment decision. Once LNG projects are in the

---

[18] See United States Department of Energy. *Liquefied Natural Gas: Understanding the Basic Facts* (Washington, D.C.: 2005), available at http://energy.gov/sites/prod/files/2013/04/f0/LNG_primerupd.pdf (August 2005); see also *B.C. and Petronas reach LNG agreement paving way for energy giant's proposed $36-billion investment,* Financial Post (May 2015), available at http:// business.financialpost.com/commodities/energy/malaysias-petronas-and-b-c-reach-lng-deal-paving-way-for-companys-proposed-35b-investment/wcm/368d8783-0dc6-4d95-ba93-019db3191e9e.

production phase, they can continue producing for 30–50+ years depending on the size of the gas resource and the investment of additional capital expenditure during the project life.

Photo I.P.3: LNG tanker

Source: photowrzesien/123RF.com

1.2.3   Extractive industry structures: mining

General

1.2.3.1   The mining industry worldwide is often described as having a formal and an informal sector. The formal sector has been estimated to include approximately 6,000 public and state-owned companies. Within this group, the 20 largest companies accounted for some 30 per cent of global output in 2010, and the largest 150, sometimes referred to as the "majors," accounted for approximately 85 per cent of global output.[19]

Photo I.P.4: Large-scale mining project

Source: dennisdvwater/123RF.com

---

[19] See Magnus Ericsson, *Mining industry corporate actors analysis*, POLINARES Working Paper No. 16. Available at http://www.eisourcebook.org/cms/Mining%20industry%20corporate%20actors%20analysis.pdf.

1.2.3.2   The majors are often broken into two categories: global (the largest 50 companies, with asset bases in excess of $10 billion) and senior companies (the next largest 100 companies with asset bases generally in the $3 billion-10 billion range) followed by approximately 350 "intermediates" with lower access to capital but with goals of growing into the major category. Below the intermediates are three categories of so-called junior companies: those large enough to be involved in exploration and production, those only involved in the exploration phase, and, finally, the smallest involving companies that are at the threshold of the formal industry sector and are seeking venture capital to grow within the industry.

1.2.3.3   The informal sector of the industry includes 15 to 20 million firms operating in 30 countries and employing 80 to 100 million people. This compares to the approximately 2.5 million people employed by the formal sector, half of whom are employed by the majors. The formal mining sector operates under legal and fiscal frameworks, but application of such rules and standards in some parts of the informal sector of the industry can be challenging[20]. For some minerals, artisanal and small-scale miners can account for a substantial amount of the value of minerals extracted (e.g., less than 5 per cent of worldwide iron, lead, zinc and copper but 25 per cent or more of gold, tin and tantalum).

Photo I.P.5:
Small-scale mining

Source: sergioz/123RF.com

1.2.3.4   The mining industry life cycle is delineated into four stages: prospecting/exploration, development, production (including processing), and closure/rehabilitation. The period between the production and permanent closure stages may involve a suspension of production where the mine is placed under "care and maintenance." This may become necessary for a number of reasons,

---

20 The informal sector of the industry is made up of small-scale and very small-scale (sometimes described as "artisanal") minors. See International Council on Mining and Metals, *Trends in the mining and metals industry. Mining's Contribution to Sustainable Development* (October 2012). Available at http://www.ibram.org.br/sites/1300/1382/00002639.pdf.

including prevailing economic conditions or unfavourable resource prices, and may continue until fundamentals improve or the operations are otherwise turned around.

1.2.3.5   There is less direct government participation in mining projects as compared with the oil and gas sector, and the mining sector does not have national mining companies comparable to NOCs. But like the oil and gas industry, the use of subcontractors is prevalent throughout many phases of the life cycle of a mine.

Figure I.F.2:
Schematic of underground and surface mining methods

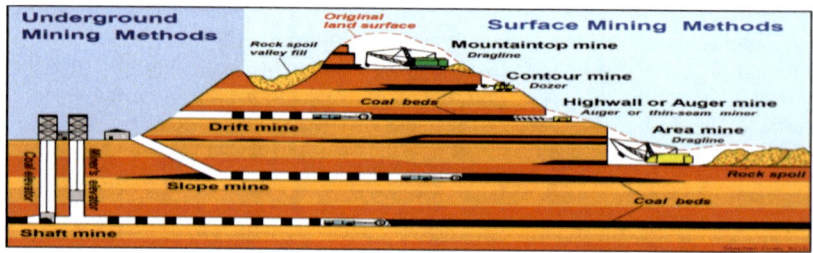

Source: Kentucky Geologic Survey, reprinted with permission. Available from http://www.uky.edu/ KGS/coal/coal-mining.php

Prospecting/exploration

1.2.3.6   The exploration phase, often consisting of reconnaissance and prospecting activities, generally involves the greatest uncertainty. The inherent risks of the exploration stage are similar to those described for the oil and gas industry. Exploration and prospecting activities are undertaken to identify whether mineral deposits exist. Subsequently further work is undertaken to define the mineral deposits (the ore body) — that is, its extent and location as well as its peculiarities.

1.2.3.7   Following the above, a feasibility study is undertaken to determine the commercial and financial viability of the project. Risks and potential upsides are also taken into account at this stage. Significant risks of commercial viability are inherent to exploration as the feasibility and other studies could conclude that a project is not commercially viable based on external market variables as well the mining company's own internal trigger points. The time frames from exploration through development to first production can range from three to ten years, sometimes longer, depending on the point in the commodity price cycle and technical risk associated with developing a project.

Development

1.2.3.8   Once exploration activities have demonstrated that there is a viable mining opportunity, the development phase commences. During the development, detailed geological and geothermal studies are undertaken to map the ore body and to substantiate the economics of the mine. This enables detailed mine planning. The required infrastructure and mine processes are developed at this stage. During the development stage, significant capital investments are made in expectation of eventual income when the mineral is extracted.

1.2.3.9   In addition to the above and in recognition of the socioeconomic and environmental implications of mining, regular studies should be undertaken to determine and properly plan for minimizing the impact of mining on the environment as well as surrounding communities. Once planning is completed, construction commences, requiring significant investment to build the mine and associated infrastructure including processing facilities, utilities such as power and water supplies, and transportation facilities such as roads, rails and ports. For large-scale mines, there can be a number of years from when construction commences to reach production.

Production

1.2.3.10   Physical extraction and processing of the ore, which can be called the production phase of mineral development, makes up the bulk of the mining life cycle. At this stage, due to the detailed development work that has been done, the overall life of the mine, based on current economic and market fundamentals can be estimated.

1.2.3.11   The ore that is mined is generally physically prepared (via crushing, grading, and grinding) and concentrated for further processing so as to extract the raw mineral.

1.2.3.12   Waste and tailings resulting from the processing activities need to be carefully managed at this stage so as to prevent adverse environmental effects.

1.2.3.13   The ore or unrefined mineral product may then be further processed near the mine/mill facility, but is more often transported to an offsite processing facility. Processing can take the form of smelting, leaching or refining, which are value-adding processes that result in the final products being available for sale in the open market.

1.2.3.14   Prospecting/exploration, development, and production are similar to oil and gas upstream activities, and the further processing and transportation are similar to the oil and gas downstream. The terms "upstream" and "downstream" are, however, not as commonly used to describe mining activities as they are for oil and gas. In general, in mining, the "upstream" processes include physical extraction of the ore and initial processing of materials such as crushing and washing, and "downstream" processes involve value adding processes such as refining and smelting, and transport of the product.

1.2.3.15   Similar to the oil and gas industry, sale and transportation of ore, unrefined metals, and ultimately the upgraded and refined metals and metal products globally is an increasingly important aspect of the industry. Many mineral-producing countries export ore or upgraded products to markets around the world. Further, mechanisms to reduce or manage risks—including commodity price risks—are necessary realities of a business undertaking the inherent risks of worldwide mining. Thus, as within the oil and gas business, these logistics and risk management issues need to be addressed by active businesses or functions designed to meet business objectives and optimize processes and costs. The physical production and process activities differ across commodities. The example below depicts the relevant activities for copper.

Figure I.F.3:
Schematic of physical copper mine processing activities[21]

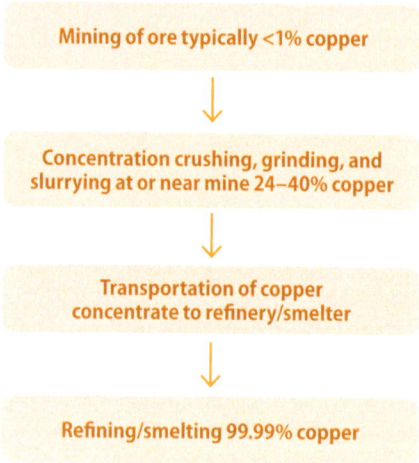

Source: http://investingnews.com/daily/resource-investing/base-metals-investing/copper-investing/copper-refining-from-ore-to-market/

1.3   OVERVIEW OF FISCAL INSTRUMENTS IN THE EXTRACTIVE SECTOR

1.3.1   Overview

1.3.1.1   Specific agreements are a feature of the extractives sector in developing countries. Minerals and oil and gas agreements or contracts often have some unique features and at times are subject to specific legal, tax, and commercial

---

[21] Note that concentrate containing other elements may yield credits (for desired ones such as gold or silver) or financial penalties (for undesired ones such as lead).

requirements. They often are limited to certain geographical areas and may involve a completely different legal, tax and economic regime from general business activities, and even from natural resource contracts covering a different area. Requirements often include separate and independent accounting for each mine or contract area.

1.3.1.2   Fiscal systems governing natural resources generally fit into two broad categories: concession or contract regimes.[22]

1.3.2   Concession regimes

1.3.2.1   Concession regimes are often also described as "tax and royalty" regimes. These are common both to the mining and petroleum industries and are usually prescribed by law.[23] Minerals or oil and gas extracted pursuant to these arrangements belong to the investors, who in exchange for such rights generally pay a royalty on the volumes of resources extracted as well as other payments such as bonuses and delay rentals. In addition, some sort of profit-based taxation is usually due on the profits related to the venture or the exploiting company. Concession regimes may also involve equity participation by host country governments.

1.3.2.2   Application of a regular corporate income tax ensures income is taxed at the corporate level just as in other sectors. However, many countries apply a higher tax rate on mining and petroleum activities, while others have separate income tax regimes addressing sector-specific issues. These may include tax depreciation rules that reflect the high risk and cost incurred at an early stage of investment, and long loss carry forward periods, reflecting the long life of the assets. In contrast to royalties and bonuses, profit taxes are only levied on a profitable investment.

1.3.2.3   Some of the most important profit-based taxes used are corporate income taxes, excess profits (or variable income) taxes, and resource rent taxes. Since such taxes are profit based, in early years of projects, or in low-price environments, they will yield less revenue than some non-profit-based taxes. In high-priced environments, the opposite is generally true.

1.3.2.4   Royalties are generally calculated as a percentage of the gross volume or value of the production (i.e., costs do not reduce the base) and are due

---

[22] For further information about fiscal instruments in the extractives sector, see IMF, *Fiscal Regimes for Extractive Industries: Design and Implementation* (2012), available at https://www. imf.org/external/np/pp/eng/2012/081512.pdf; IMF, *Guide on Resource Revenue Transparency* (2007), available at http://www.imf.org/external/np/pp/2007/eng/051507g.pdf; Philip Daniel, Michael Keen and Charles McPherson (Eds.) *The Taxation of Petroleum and Minerals: Principles, Problems and Practice* (New York, Routledge, 2010) particularly, chapter 4, Carole Nakhle, "Petroleum fiscal regimes: evolution and challenges," p. 89 and chapter 5, Lindsay Hogan and Brenton Goldsworthy, "International Mineral Taxation: experience and issues," p. 122.

[23] For example, in South Africa, permits are issued and rights are granted under national legislation.

once production commences (versus profit-based taxes which are often delayed as production ramps up and cost recovery reduces net profits). They are relatively predictable and ensure some payments in times of low prices and revenues. As the payment of royalties does not require the project to be profitable and are not reduced by production costs, governments seeking revenues early in the project life might choose to impose royalties as one part of their overall fiscal structure.

1.3.2.5   Bonuses can be attractive to governments since they provide early revenue and are easy to administer. Since bonus payments are usually made upfront before knowledge of commerciality, and are unrelated to production, they are generally less attractive to investors. Bonus costs can be recovered, if at all, only from profits.

1.3.3   Contract regimes

1.3.3.1   Contract regimes generally embody three categories: Investment Agreements, Production Sharing Contracts and Risk Service Contracts. Investment Agreements are common in mining and Production Sharing Contracts and Risk Service Contracts are common in oil and gas.

Investment agreements

1.3.3.2   Investment agreements apply to specific projects, and they can often contain the specific tax rules applicable to a project. They are common in the mining sector but may also be used in oil and gas. This may be in the form of specific rules that differ from the general law; or the agreement may provide for stabilization of tax settings under the general corporate tax law. This is essentially a variation on the concession regime. In other words, the contract determines the precise tax and royalty regime applicable to the project.

Production sharing contracts

1.3.3.3   Production sharing contracts (PSCs) are common within the oil and gas industry, but less so in the area of mining. Under such contracts, states share the results of the exploitation with the investors.

1.3.3.4   PSCs generally provide a formula for sharing the production between the investor and the government (or government-owned company). As with the concession arrangements, ownership of the investors' share of such production generally vests with the investors upon production.

1.3.3.5   Normally, but not always, a royalty on gross production is payable, with a certain percentage of the remaining production (usually called "cost oil") allocated to the investor to cover its actual investment and production costs. Recoverable costs exceeding the cost oil allocation for a particular year are generally carried forward. After deducting any royalty amounts and cost oil entitlement, the remaining amount (called "profit oil") is allocated per percentages or formulas in the agreement between the investors (as a return on investment) and the government. Profit oil is generally also subject to the profit-based taxes imposed, which can be variable. Thus, the government obtains its share of profit oil outright, along with a payment or a larger in-kind allocation of the investors' profit oil to cover the investors' income taxes. The profit oil allocation percentage between the investors and the government can also change over time based on overall profitability of the project. Costs recoverable under the cost oil definitions may be different in amount and in timing from those that are deductible under income or profit-based tax rules.

1.3.3.6　　　PSCs are dealt in detail at Chapter 4.

Risk service contracts

1.3.3.7　　　Risk service contracts are found primarily in the oil and gas sector. Under a service contract, the State owns the oil and gas that can be exploited and pays a fee to the investors for the exploration and production services. All production is effectively owned by the State, in contrast to concession regimes and PSCs.

1.3.3.8　　　Risk service contracts can take several forms, but they generally place full investment risk on the contractor/investor in return for a fee (which may be paid in the form of the oil or gas produced). The fee can be subject to profit-based taxes.

1.3.4　　Other fiscal terms

Equity participation

1.3.4.1　　　Governments may also desire an equity stake in a project, as a means of increasing government revenues over time or for non-fiscal motivations such as a desire for direct government ownership, the possibility to participate in decision-making, or a means to promote knowledge transfer. State equity can take different forms.

1.3.4.2　　　Fully paid-up equity on commercial terms puts the government on the same footing as the private investor.

1.3.4.3　　　Where governments do not have, or do not wish to risk, the funds needed to bear the costs on an ongoing basis as a full equity partner, they may request their cost shares to be advanced by the other investors. Under such a "carried interest" arrangement, the government's equity share of exploration and/ or development costs is advanced by the other investors. Recovery of such "carried costs" comes from production, i.e., is repaid by the government through contributing their share of production to the investor, or through repayment of loans from the government's share of profits. This arrangement can delay the time from which the government receives production or dividends from the project.

1.3.4.4　　　Where a government owns an equity share of the project, its

25

interests with respect to that share are well aligned with the other investors; this can promote ongoing cooperation and collaboration.

Table I.T.a1: Types of petroleum rights and contracts

Type of contract	Cost and risk	Exclusive right to operate	Right to production
Licence/concession {or Concession (tax and royalty) Contracts}	Private company	Private company	Private company
Joint venture {or Participation/ Association (or Arrangements)}	Private company	Shared	Shared
Production sharing {or Product Sharing Contract/Agreement (PSC/PSA)}	Private company	State	Shared
Service contract	Private company	State	State

Other taxes and fees

1.3.4.5   A number of other taxes and fees can also be imposed on the natural resources industries. Some of the more common ones are briefly noted below.

1.3.4.6   Broad-based consumption taxes in the form of value added taxes (sometimes referred to as goods and services taxes) and other sales taxes are often levied by countries and are designed as taxes on domestic consumption. They are generally refundable on exports. Since much of the natural resource production in many developing countries is exported, consumption taxes usually do not provide lasting revenues to governments.

1.3.4.7   In the exploration and development stages for the extractives industry, consumption-based taxes can, contrary to their design, represent a cost to the industry. This is because during the exploration and development phases, significant capital expenditure is incurred but no exports or revenues exist. Thus, companies are often faced with negative cash flow impacts from consumption taxes unless refunds are processed in a timely manner. Consumption taxes can put additional strain on tax administrations, as they require significant administrative efforts.

1.3.4.8   In general, sales or other disposition of business assets are frequently subject to income taxation on the net gain from such transfers under a country's tax on ordinary income or in the form of a capital gains tax. The scope of transactions covered by such taxes varies widely.

1.3.4.9   Dividend or other profit distributions, interest, royalties and subcontractor payments to non-residents are common and can be significant. Withholding taxes on these payments, which allow source States to effectively tax this income, are often borne by investors and are another component of the overall fiscal take. Withholding tax rates on payments to subcontractors are typically set at relatively low levels, reflecting the fact that they are levied on a gross basis. In many circumstances, regional, multilateral or bilateral income tax, trade, and investment treaties may reduce withholding tax rates and may also take precedence over other general provisions of tax laws, dispute resolution procedures, or other statutory provisions.

1.3.4.10   Numerous other fees and taxes can become part of an overall fiscal package, including items such as customs duties, excise taxes, pipeline fees, export fees, property taxes, personal income taxes of employees, payroll taxes and environmental taxes. Source countries should be conscious of the overall fiscal package applicable to investors. The optimal design of any tax system governing the extractive industries, including the application of bilateral tax or investment treaties, will often be a blend of the fiscal instruments described above. As mentioned, fiscal policy will need to be designed to further a country's development plan, which is tasked with balancing various needs.

1.3.4.11   Tax provisions applicable to the natural resource sector may be the same as for all other industries and encompassed in a more general tax law. In other cases, there may be a desire for special tax legislation applicable just to the natural resource sector. A third option is to tax extractive industries according to the corporate income tax laws, but with additional provisions applicable specifically to their industry. Application of tax, trade or investment treaties may also be general or industry specific. The most effective overall design should provide a country with adequate resources and ensure administrative ease while being responsive to the needs of investors.

1.4   TRANSPARENCY AND DEVELOPMENT ISSUES FOR THE EXTRACTIVE SECTOR

1.4.1   Transparency

1.4.1.1   The extractive industries are the subject of a number of transparency initiatives, and the extractives sector is often in the forefront of a growing movement for greater transparency for all businesses.[24]

---

[24] In addition to EITI, a number of other important transparency initiatives exist that are specific to the extractive industries, including certain requirements under the Dodd-Frank provisions of US law, the European Union Accounting Directive, plus UK and Norwegian government payments rules, and the Extractives Sector Transparency Measurement Act (ESTM) in Canada. In addition, a major project within the IMF to update its general fiscal transparency code and to formalize the update as a new Natural Resources Fiscal Transparency Code is in

1.4.1.2   The Extractive Industries Transparency Initiative (EITI) resulted from the Extractive Industries Transparency Initiative London Conference, held in June 2003. This began by requiring (i) all investors doing business in the country to report all payments made to governments or their agencies; (ii) governments to publicly report on the payments as having been received; and (iii) an independent audit and reconciliation to be done. On its website, the EITI describes how "… it has evolved from its beginnings as a narrow set of rules focused on revenue collection into an international standard covering the wider governance of extractive resources. It now encompasses beneficial ownership disclosure, contract transparency, the integration of the EITI into government systems and transparency in commodity trading. The focus of EITI Reports has moved from compiling data to building systems for open data and making recommendations for reforms to improve the extractive sector governance more generally."[25]

1.4.1.3   Public access to extractive industries contracts between investors and countries is a growing element in promoting overall transparency. In some cases, governments are now requiring such publication, and in most cases more general transparency initiatives (like the EITI) either recommend or require extractive industries finalized contracts to be made publicly available.[26] A number of multinationals in the extractives sector voluntarily publish information on their taxes paid in countries where they operate, and some publish Country by Country Reporting information.

1.4.1.4   A properly designed and cost-effective reporting mechanism can help to create a climate of trust between investors and governments, and with the public, with respect to natural resource development.

1.4.1.5   Investments in natural resources in developing countries can play an important role in providing governments with the resources needed to reduce poverty while meeting the world's energy and economic needs. However, natural resource development must be done safely, efficiently, and in an environmentally sound way. Investors, working together with developing country governments and local communities, must earn trust and support. Likewise, governments must gain the trust and support of investors. And both governments and investors, given the high impact (both physically and financially) of natural resource development, must also gain the trust and support of the public at large. Transparency in reporting is a key element contributing to the development of trust.

---

its final stages. See http://www.imf.org/external/np/exr/consult/2016/ftc/. See also, Transparency Mechanisms and Movements: Tools to Foster Openness and Accountability, Natural Resources Governance Institute (2015). Available at http://www.resourcegovernance.org/sites/default/files/documents/nrgi_primer_transparency-mechanisms.pdf.

[25] See https://eiti.org/history.

[26] In addition to EITI (https://eiti.org/) other sources include the EI SourceBook available at http://www.eisourcebook.org, Open Oil, available at openoil.net and Resource Contracts, available at http://www.resourcecontracts.org/. Sample mining agreements and models/examples of mining contract provisions are available under the Model Mining Development Agreement Project, available at http://www.mmdaproject.org/.

1.4.2   Issues for developing countries; the role of the United Nations Tax Committee

1.4.2.1   As evident from this Overview, designing appropriate tax regimes in resource-rich countries is far from easy. Developing countries are faced with additional difficulties given the often-prevalent lack of resources in tax administrations. As mentioned above, the need for revenue should be balanced with the need to attract foreign investment. At the same time, governments have to ensure that investments adequately contribute to economic growth and employment creation, while adhering to social and environmental standards.[27]

1.4.2.2   In addition to this slightly updated overview and the Handbook on Selected Issues for Taxation of the Extractive Industries has been enriched with five new chapters including (i) Tax Incentives; (ii) Tax Treatment of Subcontractors and Service Providers; (iii) Production Sharing Contracts; (iv) Tax Treatment of Financial Transactions in the Extractive Industries; and (v) Audit. Further, two existing chapters, Transfer Pricing and Decommissioning, were updated in part to align with the new chapters. A summary of the chapters in the first edition and of topics discussed in this second edition follows, in the order of chapters presented.

The government's fiscal take

1.4.2.3   This chapter describes the various forms of payments and other compensation that governments can receive from the development of natural resources, their timing and responsiveness to differing economic environments, implications of each together with their cumulative impact on investors, and the sensitivities associated with their interaction with other statutory tax rules.

Tax aspects of negotiation and renegotiation of contracts

1.4.2.4   How countries attract outside investment while balancing their economic, environmental, and social needs is a major challenge, requiring careful upfront planning and priority setting. In some countries, laws are independently enacted governing the framework for investments in resources, and investors must determine whether they will invest based upon those prescribed rules. In many developing countries, however, where resource development is beginning, no overall framework exists, and often a negotiated framework for development between an investor or investors and the government governs natural resource development. This chapter reviews various issues that arise in connection with the negotiation of such contracts, and the options regarding their renegotiation as circumstances or the parties involved change.

---

[27] See Africa Progress Panel, *Equity in Extractives. Africa Progress Report* (2013), p. 63. Available at https://static1.squarespace.com/static/5728c7b18 259b5e0087689a6/t/57ab295 19de4bb90f53f9fff/1470835029000/2013_African+Progress+Panel+APR_Equity_in_Extractives_25062013_ENG_HR.pdf

Production sharing contracts

1.4.2.5   The chapter examines the concept and some of the mechanisms of Production Sharing Contracts or Agreements (PSC or PSA) in detail. PSCs are among the most common types of contractual arrangements for petroleum Exploration and Production (E&P).

1.4.2.6   PSCs typically relate to the petroleum industry and are rarely seen in the mining industry. This is largely related to the fact that direct participation of government bodies in mining is not as common as in the oil and gas industry. However, some countries have recently explored the possibility of PSCs in the mining sector. PSCs are used worldwide, and most common in African and Asian countries, as well as in certain countries of South America.

1.4.2.7   This chapter intends to improve understanding as to what PSCs are, including relevant terminology, what the tax mechanisms of the contracts are and what areas need attention in a PSC. It intends to discuss aspects of interest to tax administration, investors and other stakeholders.

Tax incentives

1.4.2.8   This chapter provides a general framework on the design and use of tax incentives with a specific analysis of their use in the extractives sector in developing countries. The chapter attempts to define what qualifies as "tax incentive." At the simplest level, a tax incentive could be considered a difference between the default regime, and the one that is being examined that results in a reduction in the tax burden (whether in the quantum or timing of the tax liability of the taxpayer).

1.4.2.9   In its subsequent sections the chapter describes the legal framework for an effective tax incentive policy before delving into its concrete application in general and within the extractive industries. The application is described in two different concepts, namely profit-based incentives and cost-based incentives. Before concluding, the chapter examines the interaction with investor and other tax regimes and how incentives in one country influence the beneficiary company and its tax planning for other activities in different jurisdictions.

1.4.2.10   The effectiveness of certain tax incentives may be impacted by the OECD's global minimum tax proposals, known as "Pillar 2."

Tax treaty issues

1.4.2.11   Bilateral tax treaties play an important role in coordinating tax rules for cross-border activities and eliminating obstacles to cross-border trade and investment. Extractive activities usually include numerous cross-border elements. They are undertaken by investors, licence holders, service providers and suppliers who are often not resident in the source country. Natural resources produced are typically exported. These elements raise several tax treaty issues for the extractive industries that are discussed in this chapter.

1.4.2.12   In particular, the chapter includes commentary on which taxes are covered by a treaty, when activities of investors, contractors and subcontractors are taxable, how tax jurisdiction may vary throughout the life cycle of a natural resource project, how the term "royalties" as used in tax treaties differs from mineral/oil and gas royalties, whether a tax or other levy is creditable in the resident state of the investor, aspects of non-discrimination, and the territorial scope of the treaties.

1.4.2.13   The chapter also introduces the concept of permanent establishment (PE) and issues that arise in its application, considering the perspectives embodied in the United Nations Model Convention and its Commentary, as well as references to the Organization for Economic Cooperation and Development Model Convention and other specific bilateral treaties.

Permanent establishment issues

1.4.2.14   This chapter focuses on Article 5 of the United Nations Model Convention and how this article influences the taxation of the extractive industries. Whereas the permanent establishment issue is addressed more generally in Chapter 2 on tax treaty issues, this chapter elaborates in-depth on the significance and existence of PEs of the investor and its subcontractors as a result of different activities performed by the extractive industries in the source country.

1.4.2.15   In the extractive industries, costs often arise before a permanent establishment is set up or after a permanent establishment has ceased to exist. Preparatory costs can include planning or exploration costs. Subsequent costs can arise due to decommissioning or activities associated with other liabilities. In addition, issues with respect to companies that rent drilling rigs, perform their activities on-board such rigs, and activities that take place at different wells or contract areas are also covered.

Tax treatment of subcontractors and service providers

1.4.2.16   This chapter considers the taxation issues that arise from the use of subcontractors in the extractive sector. The increased complexity of extractive activities led to specialist businesses that are subcontracted by resource companies. Subcontractors open the market to more competitors, including local companies in developing countries. More competitors increase the number of bidders on projects and allow for new partnerships and operating models.

1.4.2.17   The use of subcontractors also gives rise to complex tax issues and some countries' tax administrations may have limited experience in administering these challenges. This chapter is focussed on a limited range of key tax issues specific to subcontractors engaged directly by resource companies and that are not otherwise covered in the general discussions in this Handbook.

Tax treatment of financial transactions in the extractive industries

1.4.2.18   The chapter elaborates on different financing approaches commonly used in the mining, oil and gas sectors and provides guidance on tax-related issues.

1.4.2.19   There are a lot of crosscutting issues between financial transactions in extractive industries and intragroup transfer pricing within the same MNE. This chapter focuses on tax treatments of financial transactions that are not discussed in the United Nations Practical Manual on Transfer Pricing. The transfer pricing considerations related to the intra-group financial transactions along the value chain are not addressed as such in the United Nations Practical Manual on Transfer Pricing. In addition, because of the importance of intra-group financing in the extractive industries, beyond the market price compliance issues, thin-capitalisation and important financial expenses may constitute a risk of base erosion for local companies. Such issues are discussed here.

1.4.2.20   This chapter elaborates on the thin capitalization rule in the extractive industries, reviews current debate on interest limitation issues and provides concrete application examples in developing countries as part of financing mechanisms. Other topics developed include hedging instruments, performance guarantees, and farm-in/farm-out agreements.

Indirect transfer of assets

1.4.2.21   Indirect transfer of assets broadly refers to the transfer of shares in a company, where the underlying assets of the company relate to extractive assets in a developing country. This chapter first discusses the issue of whether and how a capital gains tax could be implemented. Domestic legislation could tax gains on sales of capital assets as general ordinary income, as capital gains taxable under the corporate income tax law, or under a stand-alone capital gains tax law. In cases where there is a capital gains tax on sales occurring within a country, there is a question of whether and how gains from indirect sales should be taxed. Instead of transferring an asset (e.g., a mine itself (direct transfer)), the owner of an entity holding the asset may transfer its interest in that entity (thus "indirectly" transferring the underlying asset).

1.4.2.22   In the case of a direct transfer of a mining or petroleum right, even by a non-resident, the source country can levy a tax under its domestic law on the gain from the sale of such property. The chapter reviews issues and considerations a country may face in taxing or, in some circumstances, not taxing such direct transfers. Next, the chapter considers indirect sales of mining or petroleum assets.

1.4.2.23   For example, in order to protect the tax base of the source country in those cases, an indirect transfer tax rule could be implemented to tax gains from indirect sales. The chapter reviews issues involved in making, implementing, and administering such a decision. An indirect transfer tax rule may involve both domestic law and applicable tax treaty issues, and the interrelationship of these is outlined in depth.

Transfer pricing issues

1.4.2.24   This chapter considers and analyses several examples of transfer pricing issues that arise in the extractive industries. It focuses on issues relating to the major stages in the extractive industries value chain; and suggests methods and approaches that might be considered in addressing the particular issues identified. Thereafter, the chapter provides several case examples that apply to both mining and O&G followed by more specific examples focused first on mining, and then on oil and gas, reflecting that mining and petroleum, while similar, also have certain important differences.

1.4.2.25   The chapter provides background information and a useful summary and checklist for developing countries in addressing some of the issues that commonly arise in the extractive industries. It should be used in conjunction with the recently updated United Nations Practical Manual on Transfer Pricing for Developing Countries (2021).

Value added tax

1.4.2.26   The chapter on value added taxes (VATs) covers the key issues raised in applying VAT on the extractive industries, including policy and administration issues over the life cycle of natural resource projects. In particular, since many developing countries export most of their natural resource production, a VAT intended to tax domestic consumption should not provide a large source of lasting revenue, but timing and refund issues can be significant. The chapter covers these issues and addresses the effect a VAT may have as a barrier to direct investments. Implications on local content sourcing and other local economy spill over effects are described.

Issues and generally acceptable practices in auditing oil, gas and mining activities

1.4.2.27   The audit chapter looks at the relevance of site visits and considers the planning and risk analysis; field audit recommendations; and post-audit reporting. The chapter looks at audit tools and capacity building possibilities; and examines the detection and auditing of trade mispricing.

The tax treatment of decommissioning/rehabilitation[28]

1.4.2.28   At the end of its life cycle, the decommissioning of an extractive facility in a way that avoids environmental damage and adverse effects on local populations must be addressed. For onshore operations this extends to restoring the site to its former state and considering the economic and social impacts on the local community once extractive operations cease.

---

[28] Hereafter referred to as "decommissioning" for ease of reference.

1.4.2.29   A key element in achieving comprehensive closure/dismantling of extractive facilities is ensuring adequate financial resources are available on closure. Properly taking into account decommissioning at the outset of projects and when designing fiscal rules governing the extractive industries is particularly important in developing countries where, quite often, there may be a lack of general legal framework addressing these issues.

1.4.2.30   Further, the financial and budget consequences must be planned for in advance of and throughout natural resource projects. For example, where a government directly participates via an equity share in a project, or through involvement of its national oil company, it will have to plan for funding the share of decommissioning costs associated with its participating interest. In addition, even without direct participation, project-related net income, and thus income taxes paid to the government, will be reduced by the costs incurred in performing the decommissioning work. Where decommissioning cost deductions are not permitted until their actual expenditure (generally at the end of the project) tax losses may be incurred. How these are treated for income tax purposes will have an impact on when decommissioning is conducted and can significantly affect government budgets and even the overall value obtained by a country from the development of its natural resources. Governments must carefully plan for this impact.

1.4.2.31   This chapter describes these issues and examines the tax treatment and considerations involved in dealing with them. Examples from countries that have specific rules on decommissioning are reviewed and options for decommissioning, and their implications, are presented for consideration by countries in formulating their national policies and legislation.

ANNEX I

Africa Progress Panel, *Equity in Extractives, Africa Progress Report* (2013). Available at https://static1.squarespace.com/static/5728c7b18259b5e00 87689a6/t/57ab 29519de4bb90f53f9fff/1470835029000/2013_African+Progress+Panel+APR_ Equity_in_Extractives_25062013_ENG_HR.pdf.

L. Burns, *Income Taxation through the Life Cycle of an Extractive Industries Project*, Asia-Pacific Tax Fiscal Regimes for Extractive Industries Bulletin, vol. 20, no. 6 (18 November 2014), p. 401.

Economic Commission for Africa and The African Union, *Minerals and Africa's Development: The International Study Group Report on Africa's Mineral Regimes.* Available at http://www.africaminingvision.org/amv_resources/AMV/ISG%20 Report_eng.pdf.

EI SourceBook. Available at http://www.eisourcebook.org/.

International Monetary Fund, *Fiscal Regimes for Extractive Industries: Design and Implementation* (2012). Available at https://www.imf.org/external/np/pp/ eng/2012/081512.pdf.

International Monetary Fund, *Guide on Resource Revenue Transparency* (2007). Available at http://www.imf.org/external/np/pp/2007/eng/ 051507g.pdf.

Philip Daniel, Michael Keen and Charles McPherson (Eds.), *The Taxation of Petroleum and Minerals: Principles, Problems and Practice* (Routledge: New York, 2010). See particularly Chapter 4: Carole Nakhle, Petroleum fiscal regimes: evolution and challenges, p. 89, and Chapter 5, Lindsay Hogan and Brenton Goldsworthy, International Mineral Taxation: experience and issues, p. 122.

Silvana Tordo, *Fiscal Systems for Hydrocarbons: Design Issues,* World Bank Working Paper No. 123 (World Bank: Washington, D.C., 2007).

Extractives Industry Transparency Initiative, *2016 Progress Report.* Available at https://eiti.org/eiti and https://eiti.org/files/progressreport.pdf.

Chapter 2

The Government's Fiscal Take

2.1   INTRODUCTION

2.1.1   Executive summary

2.1.1.1   A government's share from the development of the country's natural resources can include many components whose nature and scope can be wide ranging. This is likely to include income taxes and royalties normally associated with the extractive industries. However, the government's share can also include other taxes and fees, as well as non-fiscal benefits through obligations placed upon investors, such as making infrastructure investment, employing and/or training residents, purchasing services and supplies from local businesses, and contributions to decommissioning and environmental costs. It is this total contribution to a developing country's economy that should be considered in evaluating fiscal take.

2.1.1.2   Both government and investor or company objectives should be clear—and clearly communicated—in order to create a framework to design and apply a sustainable fiscal regime. The government should form an idea of its potential resource revenues, how it wants to receive its resource value as well as the timing of the expected return, and how it wants to manage and use the funds generated by its resources. The private sector should provide a clear description of the risks they perceive as investors, and the measures required to achieve successful development of the natural resources at issue. Key elements in this assessment for both the government and potential investors are the fiscal instruments a government ultimately applies.

2.1.1.3   There is great variation in the types and design of fiscal instruments and each one has different implications for both governments and investors. Fiscal policy for the extractive industries often consists of a combination of such instruments, and given the long-term nature and scope of these projects, long-term government objectives should be taken into account in the choice of instruments.

2.1.1.4   Implementation issues for any particular fiscal regime (including monitoring, auditing and revenue collection) should also be considered at an early stage. Fiscal policy, no matter how well designed, will fail to achieve its objectives if implemented poorly. It is therefore crucial to have upfront and ongoing coordination between the various governmental departments relevant to the government take, such as the Ministry responsible for mining, the tax administration and the customs authorities. Consideration should be given upfront to allocation of tax revenues between parts of the national government and between various sub-national entities such as provinces or municipal authorities, in order to ensure that long-term investments in natural resources are sustainable for all the parties involved in the administration and execution of the project.

2.1.2   Purpose

2.1.2.1   The purpose of this chapter is to provide context on the different fiscal regimes and tools available to share benefits from the development of a country's natural resources between the government and investors. The chapter looks at how various fiscal instruments can influence investment as well as the interaction of the regime with both domestic and international tax systems.

2.1.2.2   This chapter is intended to assist governments of developing countries in participating effectively in extractive industries tax policy development and tax implementation as well as to provide information to other stakeholders. It should allow policymakers and tax administrators to understand implications of the choices they make when formulating tax policy and when applying existing legislation. Since fiscal policy and decisions around government take are at times made outside the Ministry of Finance (e.g., by a Ministry of Mines and Energy) the chapter underscores the importance of tax authorities' participation with their counterparts in other departments in ensuring that tax policy decisions can be applied consistently and in alignment with the existing constitutional and fiscal framework.

2.1.2.3   This chapter provides a broader context for viewing the overall issue of natural resource taxation and relates to other chapters that give more detail on these issues.

2.1.3   Background

2.1.3.1   Developing a country's natural resources can provide a significant boost to economic development for a country. Planned well, and implemented accurately, natural resource development can provide revenues and other economic benefits to a country and its citizens. Special considerations are required when a country decides to develop its natural resources since such resources are finite; the country would thus generally focus on obtaining the maximum benefit from the "one-time" extraction of such natural resources. From an investor standpoint, extractive industries investment has unique considerations as compared to regular investments. While the resources are finite, their extraction and development are risky and capital intensive, with large investment required at the early stages of the project life and a long lead time until profitability is achieved. The sector also requires highly specific expertise for extraction and development.

2.1.3.2   Countries embarking on natural resource development will seek to find a balance between achieving a maximum benefit for the country in a sustainable way, while providing investors with a return on their investments commensurate with the risks taken. Governments should set up clear rules on appropriate fiscal regimes to secure an appropriate government share from these finite resources. While it is difficult to provide guidance that applies equally in all circumstances, there are general considerations that are relevant when designing and implementing extractive fiscal systems around the world.

2.1.4   Scope

2.1.4.1   To assist policy makers and tax authorities in developing countries to contribute to the design of extractive industries fiscal systems and to administer such systems in an effective manner, this chapter:

- Elaborates on framework considerations both the resource holder and the investor may have when developing and evaluating the fiscal terms;

- Describes the most typical fiscal instruments used in the extractives industries;

- Lists potential consequences of the interaction between the various instruments as well as with the general tax regime; and

- Considers some specific issues regarding tax administration and their impact on the effectiveness of a fiscal system.

2.1.4.2   This chapter does not deal with the determination of what an appropriate risk/return and fiscal share allocation should be. This will vary from country to country and even from project to project within a country. More importantly, the share of natural resource value that a resource holder receives from resource development is larger than the pure fiscal take. Therefore, the mandate to determine the appropriate return as well as the expertise to determine it will generally be beyond the tax administration's mandate and jurisdiction. The content of this chapter should, however, allow the relevant tax authorities to challenge assumptions made regarding fiscal take determinations and contribute to the design of fiscal terms to ensure policymakers include tax-specific considerations and interactions when defining the contractual arrangement for exploration of resources and negotiations of terms for an agreement.[1]

---

[1] Economic modelling is very relevant and tax experts should be involved in the economic modelling done by a country on the fiscal take from extractive industries. They should be in a position to challenge what tax assumptions have been made for the modelling and whether the pre-existing fiscal rules have been considered in the overall economic modelling. Modelling support is available with the International Monetary Fund (IMF) (e.g., its FARI model) and various other institutions (e.g., Columbia University Centre on Sustainable Investment's economic modelling on gas, available at http://ccsi.columbia.edu/work/projects/open-fiscal-models/).

2.2 FISCAL TAKE AND THE RISK/RETURN EQUATION

2.2.1 Allocation of risk

2.2.1.1   One of the most important considerations is how various risks involved in natural resource development are allocated between the resource holder and the investor. Risks include many items—geological, political and development risks—that influence the ongoing operating costs and the inherent and high risk in the pricing (or value) of the revenue stream over long periods of time.

2.2.1.2   Activities related to the extractive industries typically carry higher levels of risk than for other business sectors. For example, the typical success rates for an oil and gas greenfield[2] exploration activity globally vary from one in three, to one in four. This is fundamentally a risky, capital-intensive business that can take decades to provide an economic return to an investor. The presence of fiscal stability affects the risk/return balance. Some of the risks can be influenced by the resource holder or the investor, while some risks will be beyond the control of either party.

2.2.1.3   Investors generally bear the risks of providing the funding and technical expertise for the exploration and development of a natural resource project. Overall, they are willing to bear the risks associated with the geology, development, overall project costs and commodity prices. They are more averse to—and seek ways to reduce or minimize—political risks, including changes in fiscal terms. But they evaluate the investment on the basis of the full level of risks involved at the time they make their investments compared to the level of economic return that they can expect. The fiscal terms and overall government take will be a very important part of this evaluation.

2.2.1.4   The risk/return ratio can change over the life cycle of the development of resources. The return required to induce initial investors that were prepared to take on the "higher risk/higher return" activity may be quite different from what may be required at later stages in the development of a country's natural resources. It can be influenced by the accuracy of the seismic information or sampling of the underground and its analysis, but also by the price at which the resource is being traded internationally, the scarcity of the resource, the existing technology used to extract the resource and other factors. Countries should, as a policy, consider whether they would be willing to provide a better treatment for investors who were, from the start, ready to undertake a "high risk/high return activity" as a way to attract that form of investment. These considerations will be influenced by the type of natural resource the country has within its territory, the historic risk associated in removing that resource from the soil, the location of the resources as well as other factors.

---

[2] Greenfield exploration implies no previous exploration and production activities have taken place in an area. Only theoretical information is available about the underground and quality of the resources to be extracted. In case of pre-existing drilling, the term used is "brown field."

2.2.2   Interaction of costs and fiscal terms

2.2.2.1   The interaction between costs and fiscal terms is critical in the design of the fiscal system. Terms that are sensitive to the cost intensity of the resource being developed will be the most effective. For example, in the oil and gas industry, the adage "cheap oil and tough terms come together" has been well demonstrated by resource-holding countries around the world that typically command a high level of government take for low cost/low risk developments onshore. The opposite is also true; high cost/high-risk exploration (e.g., in frontier deep water areas) typically requires higher levels of investor return potential to incentivize companies to take on these higher risks.

2.2.2.2   Different perspectives on the geological attractiveness of the area, the long-term commodity price outlook, risk appetite, and internal profitability screening criteria often lead to a range of bids from interested companies. These risks and criteria are not assessed in the same way by all actors. Host countries may be more risk averse than potential investors. In the oil and gas industry, for example, national oil companies will very often have drivers and internal criteria that are different from international oil companies' standards for determining economic return.

2.2.2.3   Throughout the life cycle of a project, the host government may want to increase employment or develop domestic capacity. Developing countries may consider local content or other infrastructure requirements placed on investors to meet these objectives, and that approach may be given priority over an increased fiscal take. The specific requirements for investors will generally change the overall cost and risk profile of the venture for an investor, and as a result, will impact the fiscal terms.

2.2.2.4   Finally, with declining reserves of oil and gas, investors and resource rich countries are now pursuing unconventional opportunities, such as shale gas and oil sands development. These are difficult and more expensive to extract. Unconventional oil and gas projects may require an adjustment of existing terms on offer: for example, the risk/return ratio may be different from conventional oil and gas opportunities; the cost structure, impact on environment and even the timing required to generate profit may be different.

2.2.3   Predictability

2.2.3.1   In contrast to geological risks or commodity price uncertainties, for example, investors that are averse to shouldering fiscal uncertainty. Risks associated with an unstable tax environment impact an investor's overall risk profile and subsequently the return levels required. Investors view fiscal uncertainty as a risk but host countries can control or guarantee fiscal certainty; by doing so, host countries create a win-win outcome. The more a government can reduce investor risks, the higher the amount the investor will be willing to pay in terms of government take.

2.2.3.2   All things being equal, stability and predictability of a fiscal regime positively influence the risk/return ratio by creating certainty, which is more likely to attract and sustain investment. Often fiscal regimes are stabilized in the contract to ensure predictability.

2.2.3.3   The ideal tax policy should anticipate as many scenarios as possible (e.g., high and low prices, drilling and other development cost changes and recoverable reserve levels) and develop flexible fiscal terms to deal with such possibilities from the start. These can ideally address a variety of technical risks and different types of opportunities as well (e.g., onshore, deep water and unconventional oil and gas developments). To illustrate, Russia considered a tax system that proposes different terms depending on the type of opportunity (onshore, shallow offshore, deep water, arctic). This reduces with uncertainty by providing flexibility in a predictable manner. If this flexibility cannot be established at the onset, investors will value (and see less risk in) changes introduced by modifying the terms of the successive licencing rounds, if available, or via a mutual renegotiation process rather than through unilateral modification of the fiscal terms.

2.2.3.4   While there may be merit in competitively tendering exploration areas, there may be other situations where it is not in the best interest of the government to follow this approach. This includes, e.g., where licences are due to expire and it is mutually advantageous to enter into negotiations to extend the licence. See also Chapter 14, Tax Treatment of Decommissioning.

2.2.3.5   Predictability is also enhanced through simplicity of terms. Terms should be clear and simple enough to be administered with the human and financial resources and capacity at hand, especially when considering administrative implementation.

2.2.4   Long-term perspective

2.2.4.1   Many oil and gas fields have a life cycle from exploration to abandonment of 30 to 40 years or more. The life cycle of mining activities can be even longer. Fiscal certainty over a long time-span is critical in investment decision-making.

2.2.4.2   In the taxation of extractive industries, it is important to look at profitability over the life cycle of projects, which underscores the benefit of developing a fiscal terms structure that is flexible and responds to periods of both high and low prices and costs. The focus should be on the overall government take, rather than comparing individual elements of a fiscal regime. Especially in developing countries, government take almost always includes indirect benefits such as investments based on infrastructure, employment and training.

2.2.4.3   Integrating environmental considerations in fiscal regime design is also important and is often not effectively addressed since environmental considerations may be dealt with by another part of government. Policymakers should consider including a framework to manage those issues and obligations upfront, even if environmental requirements such as decommissioning are expected to come in only at the end of the project's life cycle. See also Chapter 14, Tax Treatment of Decommissioning.

2.3   STRUCTURE AND DESIGN OF THE REGIME

2.3.1   Simplicity and clarity

2.3.1.1   There are a number of ways to structure and design the administration of the regime. Favouring simplicity in design and ensuring flexibility in the system while avoiding multi-tiered and complex "creaming mechanisms" (which allow for the proportion of government revenue to increase if certain aspects of the extraction or relevant financials improve) are two of those features. "Simplicity" should be the guiding principle, not in the least to ensure effective and efficient enforcement.

2.3.1.2   Predictable and stable fiscal regimes that are simple enough to be applied effectively and consistently, can encourage long-term investment as well as reduce disputes. Developing a predictable and risk-based approach to deal with potential disputes and deal with compliance could help increase certainty while using government resources as efficiently as possible.

2.3.2   Stakeholder considerations

2.3.2.1   The overall framework determining government take will do more than allocate extractive industry revenues between the resource holder and the investor. The choice of specific extractive industries-related instruments, or combinations thereof, is likely to have an impact on the business a country seeks to both attract as an investor and tax, beyond that of creating a revenue-raising capability. This is more the case for extractive industry taxation than for general profit taxation, as general profit taxation is primarily set up to raise government revenue whereas an extractive industries fiscal regime allocates risks and returns of a venture.

2.3.2.2   There are extractive industries specific drivers that need to be considered in order to fully understand a fiscal regime and its potential consequences on government and investor behaviour. The more clarity various stakeholders have with respect to each other's objectives, the more they can be aligned, which in itself will improve the sustainability of the project.

2.3.3   Resource holder considerations

2.3.3.1   **Overall government take.** A country's natural resources should contribute to the general development of an economy. The way the government take is designed and applied will directly affect the ability of a country to achieve those objectives and determine if, and how, investors engage in natural resource development projects. When assessing the level of government take that will come from developing the country's resources, the government should consider the total contribution this development could and should make and what the economic and social developments are that they wish to achieve with and through this contribution. This may include the development of new infrastructure, eventual transfer of infrastructure and assets, the fulfilment of local content requirements and contribution to training funds and community projects, as well as tax, royalty and other revenues that arise as a result of the fiscal terms. Local content development is often very important for developing countries and can be achieved through regulations or contract requirements as well as through monetary contributions to the state.

2.3.3.2   **Timing.** Government is often faced with managing expectations from its citizens with respect to ongoing exploration activities, especially as they become successful. Owing to the long-term nature of extractive projects, the timing of revenue generation needs to be carefully planned and managed. Governments can make use of different fiscal tools in order to obtain the government share and many have different timing effects: some are more "front-loaded" than others, having an earlier "realization" date. Front-loading provides government with early revenues but negatively impacts the investors' cash flow. Since front-loading generally negatively impacts the risk/return assessment by investors, the balance in addressing a country's expectations on timing and the competitiveness of its regime is critical to a successful outcome.

2.3.3.3   **Funding concerns.** Fiscal terms can often include the government owning an equity stake in a project. If a government considers taking on an equity stake, how it will fund its obligations for exploration, production and decommissioning costs is a key question. Where high-risk exploration is involved, such as in areas without existing fields or mines, a country's willingness to accept this risk, in whole or in part, can introduce new challenges for governments. This decision will be influenced by their ability to bear risks and costs; for example, drilling exploration wells is very costly, and how to deal with public concerns and expectations in the case of unsuccessful results must be considered. Not all governments will have the funds or technical expertise to undertake such projects. The funding requirements for the host government will be even larger if a national oil company (NOC) or national mining company participates in the venture. The NOC will have to finance its stake, often with revenues only coming in much later in the life of the project. Even governments that do have the funds available may decide to rely on investors for funding such higher-risk projects and reserve their own funds for other important country objectives. Funding concerns will also come up at the end of the project, when funds need to be available to deal with decommissioning and/or restoration costs—a time when the revenues from the ventures are, at very least, in decline.

2.3.3.4   **Government objectives.** Resource-rich countries may seek to achieve different objectives, and thus tailor fiscal terms quite differently, depending on the level of political, economic and natural resource development:

- In the early years of exploration, a government may want to focus on encouraging high-risk exploration activity (e.g., to "prove" that the acreage has oil and gas resources or to assess the grade of the minerals). Terms can be tailored accordingly to achieve this objective.

- Once the acreage has been "de-risked" and the geological play has been "proven," the focus may switch to maximizing early revenues to the government (e.g., to fund social development programmes). Terms can be tailored to achieve this objective.

- In mature hydrocarbon fields, governments may shift their focus to maximizing ultimate economic recovery from a basin, particularly if there are limited windows of opportunity from an infrastructure or resource perspective. For example, the reservoir pressure for oil and gas reserves tends to diminish towards the end of life in a basin. Effective production may require artificially increasing pressure, the costs of which may make a venture economically unattractive at a certain point. Again, terms can be tailored to meet this objective.

2.3.3.5   **Environmental impact.** Host countries are increasingly concerned about the potential impact of extractive industries on the environment and specific ecosystems. With extraction becoming technically possible in more remote areas—and in situations such as extreme deep water or unconventional resources requiring hydraulic fracturing technology—consideration will be given to how the risk of extraction to the environment will be managed and allocated. Applicable environmental taxes will be considered in determining the overall fiscal take, as will required contributions or reserves for decommissioning and/or restoration. Environmental conservation is often dealt with by different government departments and governmental organizations to those involved in fiscal take, however. In any case, environmental issues need to be considered upfront, to ensure appropriate decommissioning regulation and tax treatment.

2.3.3.6   **Competitiveness.** Upfront clarity on both the overall objectives as well as the future use of expected revenues is very relevant to assessing whether the resource holder can, should or wants to provide incentives to attract foreign direct investment in, or related to, the development of its extractives sector. Overall, countries that are perceived to have lower levels of risk (technical, political or economic) will be able to command higher levels of government take–that is, higher taxes or other fees and obligations. Countries perceived to have higher levels of risk will need to design their fiscal regimes to be more attractive to incentivize companies to put capital at risk. There are ways related to contract negotiation and renegotiation that can address the competitiveness issues.

2.3.3.7   **Internal allocation:** funding subnational entities. Projects and investments tend to be more sustainable if the overall sharing of risks and benefits within a country (among subnational entities) is clear; this is especially the case in larger countries or in cases where the extractives are centralized in certain areas of the country. Involving local communities at the negotiation stage and through the project lifecycle should be considered, to ensure their buy in. Such clarity is important for policymakers as well as investors. If the allocation of funds is not clear, this could have a negative impact on the stability of the terms agreed.

2.3.3.8   **Interaction with pre-existing legislation.** The specific fiscal instruments for extractive industries will interact both among themselves and with the corporate and other tax systems that may be applicable in the national or subnational sphere of the country. This interaction is not always addressed in a timely or appropriate manner, due largely to the fact that the upstream fiscal instruments are often regulated by a government department (e.g., a Ministry of Mines and Energy) other than the one dealing with the general tax system (generally the Ministry of Finance or the Treasury Department). It will be important for a country to ensure close coordination among the affected government departments to ensure that whatever is negotiated or regulated by one Ministry is not inconsistent with laws and regulations that have to be administered by other government departments or governmental agencies.

2.3.4   Investor considerations

2.3.4.1   **Risk/return.** In the global competition for limited capital and human resources, investing companies will seek investment opportunities which offer the best risk/return balance. Attempts to introduce higher resource taxes after investment has been made can also lead to capital flight, which in turn may require counteracting measures (such as the introduction of incentives) to try to bring capital back.

2.3.4.2   **Free-market fundamentals.** They can be achieved through competitive bid rounds and through direct negotiations when the technical scope or economics of an area are difficult or require expertise that is limited. Considering extractive industries' life cycles, terms required to promote investment in the early stages of exploration of a frontier resource may evolve for future licencing rounds, when activities become less risky. While governments may desire to improve their revenue collections on such future activities, making changes retroactively to projects undertaken under higher risk conditions is likely to be viewed negatively by investors and could well affect future investments in other higher risk areas within the country.

2.3.4.3   **Stability.** If companies need to manage the risk around an unstable tax and operating environment, this will impact the overall risk profile, and therefore, the underlying return. Investment decisions are impacted by the risk of adverse fiscal change, meaning the return required by an investor will increase if faced with an uncertain fiscal environment. That will result in much less attractive bids for governments as investors factor in potential future changes. Fiscal uncertainty can also adversely affect the transfer of properties and licences among different companies, which in turn can lead to less than optimal development of the resources.

2.3.4.4   **Competitiveness.** Many types of fiscal regimes can work if they are competitive and predictable for investors. However, it is important to understand the allocation of risks and returns under the fiscal regime ultimately adopted by the country. While any fiscal system can be designed to give a level of economic return at a specific commodity price, the interest levels from investing companies will depend on the underlying risk and return profile changes under different cost/revenue scenarios. Progressive systems are often considered more competitive by investors as they move the timing of government share closer to the economic break-even point. Front-loaded systems (such as systems including signature bonuses or introducing ring-fencing per field) are generally considered less competitive by investors.

2.3.4.5 **Predictability.** Changes to the tax law in general will impact the return to investors. As noted above, investors place a high value on stability, and stability includes the consistent application and administration of tax rules and regulations. It is important that countries' treasury and tax officials be aware of these considerations and engage with their counterparts in other government departments before making general changes to tax law. Attempts to introduce higher government take, such as increased rent taxes, after investment has been made can also lead to reduced investment, which in turn may require the introduction of incentives to try to encourage new investment.

2.3.4.6 **Benefit.** Similarly, investors see a benefit when other government agencies engage with the treasury and tax authorities before finalizing fiscal take. Often, the interaction between fiscal terms and general taxation is only considered when actually applying the fiscal regulations. This can be, e.g., at the moment of filing returns, tax assessment or tax collection, which can be too late if there is any ambiguity or misunderstanding between government agencies regarding the interpretation and application of fiscal terms. Resolving such ambiguities or misunderstandings at the negotiation stage (or at the time fiscal terms are developed and statutorily approved) reduces investor risk and benefits both the investor and the country. Also, for the country itself, a specific fiscal policy will not yield the desired government revenue if ambiguities and inconsistencies exist and the responsible government department is not in a position to consistently and predictably assess and collect revenues.

2.3.4.7 **Ownership of underlying reserves.** One of the performance metrics relevant to international oil and gas companies is the Reserves Replacement Ratio (RRR). The RRR indicates to what extent companies are able to find and "book" hydrocarbon reserves to replace the amounts produced each year. A company would have an RRR of 100 per cent if for every barrel of hydrocarbon produced another barrel is found/discovered and booked. The required ownership interests in the reserves needed to "book" such reserves will be determined by the contractual arrangements. Generally, concessionary systems and contract systems contribute to RRR, but acreage covered by service contracts will not.

2.3.5   Fiscal tools for government share

2.3.5.1   A whole range of extractive industries-specific instruments are available to allow resource-rich countries to collect the revenue from their natural resource wealth and to tax the extractives industries sector.[3]

---

[3] Sources that describe extractive industry fiscal instruments are included in the "For more information" section at the end of this Chapter. Specifically, a number of basic works

2.3.5.2   The share a government will receive or retain regarding development
and production of a country's natural resources can take many shapes and forms.
As noted, overall government take is certainly not limited to the taxation of the
revenues generated by the extractive industries, but can also include the following:

- Signature bonuses, to be paid, often in cash, at the moment the
  contract is granted to a specific area;

- Part of the production, which can be obtained directly by the host
  country in various ways:

  • Through state participation in the venture in which case the
  host country will obtain a certain part of the production in accordance
  with its participation; the country will generally have to contribute its
  share of the costs as well;

  ➤ In cases where the host country is not required to fund its part
  of the costs, it can be "carried" by the investors, who then may
  receive an additional share of the production until repaid; the host
  country does however participate in sharing remaining revenue,
  and may use that for future costs;

  • Through a production sharing contract, where a fixed share of
  production is reserved for the government;

- Production-based contributions like royalties, often determined based
  on volume or price of the commodity;

- Various forms of taxation on the corporate result, taxing either the
  profit or the cash flow generated, such as corporate taxation, hydrocarbon taxation, resource rent taxation;

- Indirect taxation such as value added tax (VAT) as well as customs,
  other import or export related taxation, environmental taxation;

- Required investment in training, infrastructure (such as production
  or transport facilities) and local social or educational facilities; stipu-
  lations are often included that transfer ownership of these facilities to

are recommended for further reading on this subject: Philip Daniel and Michael Keen (Eds.),
International Taxation and the Extractive Industries (New York: Routledge, 2016); International
Monetary Fund, *Fiscal Regimes for Extractive Industries: Design and Implementation,* (2012)
available from https://www.imf.org/external/np/pp/eng/2012/081512.pdf; Silvana Tordo, *Fiscal Systems for Hydrocarbons: Design Issues,* World Bank Working Paper No. 123, (Washington,
D.C.: World Bank, 2007); Carol Nakhle, "Petroleum fiscal regimes: evolution and challenges,"
in *The Taxation of Petroleum and Minerals: Principles, Problems and Practice,* ed. Philip Daniel, Michael Keen and Charles McPherson (Routledge: New York, 2010) p. 89; Lindsay Hogan
and Brenton Goldsworthy, "International Mineral Taxation: experience and issues," also in *The
Taxation of Petroleum and Minerals: Principles, Problems and Practice,* p. 122.

the national or local government at some point; and

- Other contributions.

2.3.5.3   There are various aspects to determining a government's share: Who owns the resources throughout the development? Who is responsible for the costs? Who is entitled to the revenue? Who makes the decisions? The eventual tax take will be influenced by different allocations of risks and revenues and by the resulting rules that are not always drafted for and by tax officials.

2.3.5.4   Determining who owns the resources and the revenues is largely governed by the local legal framework, statutory rules, or contractual arrangements between the resource owner and the entity exploring and developing the resources. Therefore, understanding these arrangements is critically important to understanding a government's fiscal take risk/return.

2.4   OVERALL OBJECTIVES

2.4.1   Clarifying the objectives of fiscal instruments

2.4.1.1   To evaluate whether fiscal instruments achieve overall governmental objectives, it is important for the host country to ensure clarity and transparency on its objectives. Various fiscal instruments in the extractive industries give rise to specific consequences besides the generation of revenue.[4]

2.4.2   Progressivity versus regressivity

2.4.2.1   A potential proxy for assessing the risk/return balance is the progressive versus regressive nature of a fiscal instrument.

2.4.2.2   Profit taxation is progressive to the extent the tax burden increases if the taxable base increases—that is, it both encourages incremental investment in small opportunities (which may be marginally economic) and provides a proportionally higher share of the economic rent to the government at higher commodity prices or if large discoveries are made. Progressivity is particularly important in the later stages of the basin life where the size of discoveries becomes smaller and smaller. It helps to manage the risk that discovered resources might be left in the ground. Progressive systems can also be designed to cater for different conditions, such as water depths, remoteness of locations, production levels and discovery size.

2.4.2.3   Progressive fiscal attributes often make it easier to ensure that the

---

[4] International Monetary Fund, *Fiscal Regimes for Extractive Industries: Design and Implementation*, (2012), p. 19, available at https://www.imf.org/external/np/pp/eng/2012/081512. pdf. See also Chapter 1 (Overview), including its discussion of principles for extractive industry investment in developing countries.

interests of all parties remain aligned over the life of the venture, and under a wide range of macroeconomic conditions. R factors[5] or internal rate of return (IRR) creaming mechanisms[6] are examples of fiscal attributes that are progressive in nature. Value-based creaming mechanisms, for example, can be tuned to ensure that the government keeps an appropriate share of the economic rent from the natural resource development interests regardless of the commodity prices. This avoids the need for arbitrary/unilateral increases in levels of taxation, which may not always be reduced when prices fall (i.e., the "ratchet" effect). Taxation levels should respond automatically to changes in both cost and revenues.

2.4.2.4   Windfall profit taxes are not always progressive, due to the cyclical nature of the extractive industries and commodity pricing. It can be difficult to determine what constitutes a windfall for such industries. For example, should the determination of whether or not extraordinary or windfall profits have been realized be made on a one-year comparison basis or should the long-term and cyclical nature of an extractive industries investment be considered?

2.4.2.5   Ring-fencing is not progressive; ring-fencing occurs when a portion of a company's assets or profits are taxed separately even though they are not part of a separate entity. Ring-fencing in the context of oil and gas generally accelerates the timing of taxation—often before profitability of a venture—and it influences the risk/return balance. In the context of oil and gas, where assets are ring-fenced on a well basis or on a field or licence basis, the revenue generated by one field or licence will not be offset against the losses generated by another field or licence of the same investor, thus giving rise to tax payments irrespective of the fact that the investor may not be profitable overall. In the mining context, ring-fencing applies with respect to surface mining.

2.4.2.6   While royalties can be very attractive to host governments (by providing early revenue) they are by nature regressive. In some cases, they may result in resources being left in the ground, either by (i) early termination of economic cash flows (i.e., early abandonment); or (ii) making small discoveries uneconomical to develop, since they can result in governments taking a proportionally larger economic share of small discoveries and a smaller share of large discoveries).[7]

---

[5] R factor is a ratio of revenues to expenses. R factors deal with various revenues versus expense variables that affect project economics depending on how they are defined; for example, some are defined considering gross revenues instead of net earnings. R factors can be determined on accrued total expenditures or on a field-by-field basis. In general, the use of R factors reduces an investor's potential upside from price increases, but also protects the downside.

[6] Creaming mechanisms are any aspects of a fiscal regime that increase government take in the event of an increase in revenue. Some are more balanced than others. For example, an increase in royalty rates related to price increases is considered less balanced by investors than a sliding royalty rate based on internal rate of return (IRR). An increase in commodity price will generally induce an increase in cost, something not considered in a change in royalty rate based on price alone.

[7] For example, assume Projects A and B each produce 100 units, but Project A earns net income of $100 and Project B, because of higher costs, earns net income of $50. A 20 cent/unit of production flat rate royalty will take 20 per cent of the income from Project A, but 40 per cent of the income from Project B. Costs for smaller developments tend to be proportionately higher

2.4.2.7   For example, over the life of oil and gas basins, many royalty systems have had to be changed frequently by governments wishing to remain competitive and to continue ensuring that investments in improvements are made. Effectively, the changes have been made to give a royalty system features of a profit-based system, thereby making it more progressive.

2.4.2.8   While some governments have chosen to abolish royalties (e.g., Norway and the United Kingdom) for the reasons outlined above, they remain a popular choice for governments that seek to guarantee early cash flow in the life of an oil or gas field development. However, absolute royalty levels need to be carefully considered so as not to lead to the regressive and counter-productive attributes described above.

2.4.2.9   The desire to tax revenue rather than profit is generally disfavoured by investors because in times of low commodity prices, companies are likely to be in a financial loss position for a considerable period of time. In spite of that, companies will still be required to make royalty payments. Thus, taxes on profit rather than on revenue generally remain the preferred fiscal model of investing companies. Policymakers therefore need to be aware of the potential regressive nature of fiscal instruments—or certain aspects of regressivity that exist—so that they can strive to achieve and maintain a satisfactory balance between various concerns for resource holders (e.g., timing of the income) and investors.

2.4.3   Issues of interaction

2.4.3.1   Fiscal systems for the extractive industries have continued to pro-liferate and increase in complexity over time. Governments should assess the economic impact from the utilization of several different fiscal instruments. They should analyse how the fiscal instruments relate to each other and how they interact with the general tax legislation. See further 2.6.

2.4.4   Risks of interaction between various fiscal instruments

2.4.4.1   Each of the various instruments serves specific objectives and can promote certain intended behaviours.[8] However, once various instruments are combined, the intended objective can be counteracted by other considerations. For example, subjecting the extractive industries to a royalty system can more quickly provide governments with revenue. It is, however, a regressive system, and when combined with other regressive instruments, such as a signing bonus

---

than costs for larger developments (e.g., the cost of casing a well for a small development will cost the same for a well producing more or a well relating to a larger oil and gas deposit). There-fore, a flat rate government take on a small development will be relatively more onerous than on a larger production. This disproportionality, in comparison to profitability, can be addressed by applying a sliding royalty rate—related to R factors, for example.

8 See International Monetary Fund, *Fiscal Regimes for Extractive Industries: Design and Implementation* (2012), p. 19, for a summary of various instruments and the key objectives they serve.

or a ring-fenced system, a tax system can become so front-loaded that it becomes uncompetitive. This may delay exploration or production, leading to reduced or no revenue.

2.4.5 Delineation issues

2.4.5.1   Where various types of taxation or rates are combined, the delineation of costs and revenue will require special attention in the legislative process and/or in the contract design and negotiation.

2.4.5.2   The rules need to be clear and precise as to which costs and which revenue belong in which instrument. If not, the overall fiscal and tax regime becomes unclear in its results. For example, in cases where activities are ring-fenced, the legislator should determine against which revenues the costs are to be deducted. It is not always clear which activities are covered within each ring-fenced instrument and a specific separation or allocation of costs is not always possible. When costs are incurred that do not relate uniquely to one well or pit, allocation keys may need to be agreed. Since the costs associated with the extractive industries tend to be quite high, the risk of not being able to deduct appropriately is highly problematic.

2.4.5.3   Enforcement equally poses additional concerns and may become cost prohibitive. Countries may want to consider including examples of tax base calculations into legislation and/or commentaries to the legislation, or implement agreed upon principles and their application in regulations that have the effect of legislation. Delineation issues are especially relevant in profit-based taxation as well as in capital gains taxation.[9]

2.5   CONTRACTUAL ARRANGEMENTS

2.5.1   Types of contractual arrangement

2.5.1.1   The resource holder sets the legal framework within which to work or agree with the investor. Sometimes the details of the legal arrangements are set by law or even by the country's Constitution; sometimes only the framework is set. In certain countries, the terms are negotiated and set contractually.

2.5.1.2   Regardless of the legal instrument involved, there are basically three different types of natural resource arrangements: concessionary systems, production sharing contracts and service contracts.

2.5.1.3   The different systems tend to differ in the level of risk and ownership that is granted to the investor, with the concessionary systems generally transferring most away from the resource holder and service contracts transferring least.

---

9 See Chapter 10 (Indirect Transfer of Assets).

2.5.1.4   As noted, any fiscal system can be designed to give a level of economic return at a specific commodity price, but how the underlying risk and reward profile changes under different cost/revenue scenarios will determine the government share as well as the interest levels from investing companies.

2.5.2   Concessionary systems

2.5.2.1   A concession is an agreement regarding a fixed area where government grants a company the exclusive right to explore for, develop and produce resources at its own risk and expense, generally for a specific period of time. The company is entitled to ownership of the resources it produces from the concession when extracted at the wellhead (or at another agreed point of transfer of title).

2.5.2.2   A concession is sometimes called an exploration licence or production lease. These systems apply to both the oil and gas, and the mining sectors. In the mining sector, such concessionary systems are generally implemented by way of leases that cover a specific area for underground or surface mining.

2.5.2.3   Unlike contractual systems, where the production allocation under the contract itself is part of the fiscal take, the concession agreement itself contains few specific fiscal features. The production of natural resources under a concession system is itself generally subject to a variety of fiscal instruments. Commonly, the concession holder will be taxed on the profits generated, often under the general corporate income tax regime. In addition, the concession holder is likely to be required to compensate the resource holder (country) for the resources extracted in the form of an oil and gas or mineral royalty. Concession systems are therefore often referred to as tax/royalty systems. It is not uncommon for resource holders to add elements of government take on top of the regular corporate income tax and royalty. For example, many countries impose an additional profits tax on top of, or separate from, the general income tax.

2.5.3   Production sharing contracts

2.5.3.1   Various types of contract systems are possible. Under the more typical ones, a company is designated as a contractor in a certain area. The title to the resources (in this case, generally oil and gas) will remain with the State and the resources produced will belong to the government until and to the extent it is explicitly shared under the contract terms. The company operates in accordance with the terms of the contract, at its own risk and expense under the control of government. The government agrees with the company that the company contract partner meets and finances the exploration and development costs in return for a share of production in kind or in cash.

2.5.3.2   Contract arrangements are generally called production sharing agreements (PSA) or, most commonly, production sharing contracts (PSCs). Besides specifying the terms and conditions under which production will occur, a PSC specifies the percentage of production each party will receive after the participating parties have recovered a specified amount of costs and expenses. They tend to principally be used in the oil and gas sector, but may be used in mining projects. Often various international oil companies and national oil companies are partners under the same PSC, with one of the partners designated as the operator. Depending on the circumstances, it can be the party with the highest participation, or the party with the longest history or largest presence in the host country. The choice can also be determined by the specific expertise or technology one of the parties has and it can be a different party for the various stages of the contract. The operator is not considered a subcontractor and is entitled only to reimbursement of its costs (without any markup). PSCs are discussed in detail in Chapter 4.

2.5.3.3   In the oil and gas industry, PSCs are used in cases where the parties agree to share the production and related costs of the oil and gas produced. A PSC will be specific about how the contract partners share the production and uses specific terminology to describe how they "split the barrel" of oil. The split can be done in cash or in kind. To understand the fiscal take under a PSC, it is important to understand certain terminology:

- The barrel will first and foremost contain cost oil. Costs that can be recovered can be exhaustively listed or generally indicated in the PSC and typically include exploration costs like seismic tests, drilling of wells, or sample analysis, production costs of production facilities and infrastructure investments, plus other technical and administrative services. The costs that are allowed to be recovered as "cost oil" under the PSC are often similar but may be different from costs acceptable for accounting purposes or corporate income tax.

- The amount of costs recoverable is sometimes limited to an amount called the "cost stop." The company is entitled to recover only the amount of costs up to the limit of the cost stop. If the costs exceed the cost stop the contract is defined as saturated and the excess costs will not be recoverable (at least during that period of operations). The cost stop guarantees a part of the production to the government (as long as the value of the crude produced is higher than the cost stop) and can be especially important during the first (and potentially last) years of production when the costs are higher. The cost stop can be a fixed amount but, in most cases, it is a percentage of the costs of the crude oil. If a cost stop is in place, it is often important to specify what that will mean to the determination of the taxable result under the applicable income tax. There is often disagreement as to whether the cost stop also means some costs are non-deductible or can be carried forward or back for income tax purposes, making certain costs potentially non-recoverable under both the production sharing formula and the corporate income tax.

- When the costs incurred are less than the cost stop, the difference between the costs and the cost stop is called excess oil. Usually, but not necessarily, the excess oil is shared between the government and the company according to the same rules applied to the profit oil (see below). Again, it is important to specify what this means for the determination of the taxable base.

- Profit oil after allocation is generally the portion of production that will constitute the basis on which to apply profit taxes under the PSA. It is important to determine how much of the costs will be deducted from the profit oil and how the countries' tax rules will apply to the taxable profit oil allocation.

- Certain contracts refer to "tax oil." In case the contract is a "tax paid PSC," the government partner, generally a national oil company, pays the income tax for and on behalf of the investors. In this case, there is no explicit tax oil as the tax would be paid out of the host government's share of the profit oil. In effect, a tax paid PSC provides greater stability to the investor on its income tax as any changes in the tax rules would affect only the allocation of the government's share into profit and tax oil. Tax paid PSCs act like stability clauses. They can be set up on a simple basis, where the income tax is calculated normally on the profit oil. Alternatively, they can be set up on a gross-up basis.

2.5.3.4   Unlike the concessionary systems, various aspects of a PSC give rise to government take or impact the eventual tax burden. Part of the government take will come from the production sharing, with the cost reimbursement—as defined in the cost oil terms under the PSC—also being an important part of the calculation. Any ring-fencing, cost stop or other restrictions on cost compensation will increase the government take and influence the risk/return balance. The profit oil—which generally is represented by the profit but is increased by any restrictions on cost compensation—will then be subject to income tax rules. Any income tax due constitutes an additional part of the government take. The determination of the taxable profit may, however, be different under general tax rules compared to the PSC determination of costs and profit oil. Clarity needs to be provided on how the various rules interact and it is highly recommended to include these clarifications in the PSC, the income tax code or both.

2.5.3.5   In the mining sector, agreements on production sharing tend to include:

- Lease rental payments; and

- Hard minerals distributed in kind in lieu of royalty payments or dividends.

2.5.4   Service contracts

2.5.4.1   Service contracts are sometimes referred to as "technical assistance contracts" or "technical service agreements" because they are generally contracted regarding existing fields. Service contracts tend to be typical for countries where the country only seeks to attract additional expertise. The contractor tends to hold less risk in these situations and provides its services for a fee. In some cases, the contractor may be exposed to cost overruns as compared to approved budgets, and thus sometimes these arrangements are referred to as risk service contracts. As the marginal costs are more relevant in these types of contracts, cost and timing estimates as well as fiscal terms are critical. Very often it is a State company or NOC that manages the actual resources and contracts with the service provider. The service provider has no right to the underlying resources.

2.5.4.2   In the mining sector, the lease holders may choose to mine the leased area themselves (known as owner mining) or subcontract the mining operations to a subcontractor based on clear production and cost criteria (known as contract mining). In addition, service providers (generally known as mine support service companies) may be awarded contracts to perform specific services (such as drilling, blasting or hiring of a mining fleet).

2.5.4.3   The service provider is generally subject to the general corporate income tax system, potentially at an increased tax rate. In addition, certain fiscal instruments will be added.

2.6   FISCAL INSTRUMENTS

2.6.1   Types of fiscal instrument

2.6.1.1   A multitude of fiscal instruments[10] exist that can generate revenue for the resource-holding country.

Table VII.1
Revenue-generating instruments for resource-holding countries

Mechanism	Description	Prevalence Mining	Number of countries Petroleum
Signature bonus	Up-front payment for acquiring exploration rights	1	16
	Commonly used as a bid parameter (notably for petroleum in the US offshore continental shelf)		

---

10 International Monetary Fund, *Fiscal Regimes for Extractive Industries: Design and Implementation* (2012). Available from https://www.imf.org/external/np/pp/eng/2012/081512.pdf, p 22.

Table VII.1 (cont'd)

Mechanism	Description	Prevalence Mining	Number of countries Petroleum
Production bonus	Fixed payment on achieving certain cumulative production or production rate	None	10
Royalties	Specific (amount per unit of volume produced)	2	1
	Ad-valorem (percentage of product value)	17	31
	Ad-valorem progressive with price	1	9
	Ad-valorem progressive with production		8
	Ad-valorem progressive with operating ratio/profit	3	1
	Royalty applied to operating margin (net profits royalty)	2	0
State, provincial, and/or local CIT	Rate of corporate income tax at the state, provincial, or local level in addition to federal level	2	5
	Common in Canada and the U.S. as a province/state resource charge in addition to federally imposed CIT		
Variable income tax	CIT where the tax rates increase with the ratio of taxable income to revenue, between an upper and lower bound	3	None
Resource rent taxes	Cash flow with accumulation rate/uplift. Can be assessed before or after CIT	5	5
	Cash flow with limited uplift on losses (UK) (surcharge tax on cash flow)	None	2
	Allowance for Corporate Capital	None	1
	Allowance for Corporate Equity	None	1

Table VII.1 (cont'd)

Mechanism	Description	Prevalence Mining	Number of countries Petroleum
Other additional income taxes	Other profit taxation mechanisms that do not fall under any of the categories above	1	3
Production sharing	Fixed production share	None	5
	Cumulative production	None	None
	R-Factor: ratio of cumulative revenues to cumulative costs	None	13
	Rate of return, pre- or post-tax	None	3
	Production level	None	13
State participation	Free equity: government receives percentage of dividends without payment of any costs	2	None
	Carried equity: government contributions met by investor and recovered from dividends with interest	3	8
	Paid equity: government pays its share of costs	None	19
Social investments/ infrastructure	Resource companies build infrastructure or make other social investments (hospitals, schools, etc.)	1	6

2.6.1.2   Some of the revenue sources are profit related, others volume related, and they can be specifically applied to the extractive industries or to certain types of extractives. Alternatively, the extractive industries can be subject to the general taxation rules of the country. There is an increasing variety of fiscal instruments and they are often used in combination. The indirect taxation of the extractive industries also forms part of the fiscal take.[11]

2.6.2   Profit-based fiscal instruments

2.6.2.1   Profit-based fiscal instruments include:

___

11 Specific value added tax (VAT) issues are elaborated in Chapter 12 (Value Added Tax). Oil and gas tend to be excisable products, therefore customs and excises are relevant. As explained in Chapter 12, it is important to point that where a country largely exports its natural resource production, VAT should not be viewed as a viable source of country revenues and fiscal take, since VAT is rebated on exports.

- **Corporate profits tax**, which applies to mining as well as oil and gas activities, can be a flat tax rate on profit or a variable rate to capture more revenue when profits are above a given threshold (generally called an R factor). The corporate tax applied can be the corporate profit tax generally applicable to all businesses, either at the same rate or a special rate. For example, Italy and the United Kingdom apply a supplementary tax for oil and gas; the corporate tax base of oil and gas companies is subject to an additional percentage of profits tax. It can also be a specific corporate profits tax applicable only to extractive industries;

- **Special petroleum/hydrocarbon tax**, which is strictly for oil and gas, is often based on a country's corporate profit tax but with special features that can significantly deviate from the general regime. Whereas the general corporate profit tax on extractive industries is generally covered under double tax treaties, special petroleum taxation is sometimes not covered. This can impact investors differently, depending on their home country tax regimes and is important for a developing country to consider (see Chapter 6 on Tax Treaty Issues);

- **Resource rent taxation**, which can be applied to mining as well as oil and gas, is generally a profit-related tax, but is not calculated on the basis of normal corporate profits. It is usually based on gross revenue from the resource development, and allows for certain allowances or deductions. Often, interest costs are not considered deductible and restrictions are in place for cost deductions regarding overhead services. It shares similar features with hydrocarbon taxation;

- **Windfall profits tax**, also referred to as excess profits tax or a cash flow tax, can be profit related. A windfall profits tax imposes a higher tax rate on profits or gains realized from a sudden windfall of a particular company or industry. Often the windfall or the increase in rate to deal with the windfall is not directly profit related but is linked to commodity price hikes, which are generally viewed as triggering disproportionate increases in profits;

- **Tax on mining revenue**, which is a tax triggered once the project has reached a predefined rate of return and beyond which it generates an extraordinary profit or revenue. The revenue is a kind of "abnormal" profit linked with the scarcity of the resource. In practice, the revenue is calculated as the total cash receipts in excess of the cumulative costs that are increased by a rate of return required by the investor. The mining revenue—or economic revenue—is the difference between the gains generated by the mining activity and the expenses; these gains include a "regular" return on capital. In theory, the surplus can be taxed at 100 per cent without affecting the exploitation of the resource. That is, mining (or economic) revenue is a source of revenue collection of particular interest to governments without affecting the choice of the investor and without economic distortions. The return level on the capital invested, however, needs to take into account the full level of risks of the investor at the time the investments are made. The calculation is done by increasing the annual losses by the rate of return required by the investor ("uplift") and by adding them up to a level at which the losses are recovered. (In accordance with what has been developed initially in the economic literature, the uplift is fixed in a way to give the investor a minimum required rate of return, but this choice is now disputed.) Everything that goes beyond these plus costs is the revenue that can be taxed at a rate to be determined. Australia uses this mechanism for mining activities of coal and iron. It is also planned to be implemented in Sierra Leone with a deduction of the corporate tax paid from the taxable base. It is generally applied with a tax barrier (ring-fence) by licence.

- **An additional tax on cash flow** is available as a revenue source. The taxable base is the positive cash flow of the project, once the investment is recovered and by including the costs of the corporate tax. The profit is adjusted annually by adding the depreciation and the interest, by deducting any expense on capital. This can also be the base of a plus tax. Instead of allowing a supplementary provision in respect of losses carried forward, as is done in the case of the tax on mining revenue, a simple provision (or uplift) can be added for the investor to recover the expenses on capital at the beginning of the wproject. This is done in the United Kingdom through an additional allowance of losses limited in time.

2.6.2.2   Special features of profit-based taxation:

- **Depreciation rates.** These are rates for capital expenditure deduction that provide an optimal level for both tax revenue and investment. For instance, assets that require high capital expenditure may have a high depreciation rate to encourage investment. In both mining and oil and gas taxation, accelerated depreciation is often available, sometimes limited or focused on the early years of production. Increased depreciation rates generally support asset investment.

- **Uplift.** Unlike accelerated depreciation, where depreciation rates are increased but the amount of depreciation in total is limited to the investment costs (i.e., the depreciation base) an uplift actually increases the depreciation base. To illustrate, one approach is: for every dollar of investment, an uplift of 25 per cent is permitted, such that depreciation on $1.25 is allowed. For example, both Denmark and Norway apply an uplift in their hydrocarbon taxation. Uplifts have been used effectively by both countries to keep the asset investment pipeline filled despite being mature oil and gas provinces.

- **Ring-fencing.** This occurs when certain costs or revenues are considered separate from other costs and revenues, creating separate bases for taxation within a single taxable entity. The ring-fencing can occur per type of activity. For example, in the United Kingdom, the upstream taxable base is ring-fenced and subjected to a higher rate compared to other business activities. The ring-fence can go into further detail (e.g., requiring a taxable base to be determined per mine or per field). Ring-fencing will accelerate the timing of realization of government take for the government. It may give rise to tax payments before an overall venture is profitable. In case certain mines or fields never become profitable, ring-fencing will actually create sunk costs— costs that will never be recovered by the investor in the host country, although the investor may be making tax payments on other mines or fields in the country. Such systems can delay capital investments and improvements.

2.6.3   Production-related taxation

2.6.3.1   The main example of production-related taxation or government take is the royalty. Royalties are paid by the holder of the right to extract natural resources to the resource holder to compensate for natural resources that are extracted. Royalties are generally determined: (i) on gross production; (ii) based on either volume or value of the extracted commodities; and (iii) at a certain rate, which can be fixed or at a sliding scale.

2.6.3.2   A second form of taxation comes in the form of severance taxes. In jurisdictions where most extraction occurs on privately owned land or where sub-surface minerals are privately owned (for example, the United States of America) the main production-related taxes are called severance taxes.[12] Severance taxes are defined as volume or value-related payments due when non-renewable natural resources are extracted (or severed) within a taxing jurisdiction. Resources that typically incur severance taxes when extracted are oil, natural gas, coal, uranium and timber. Some jurisdictions use other terms such as a "gross production tax." Where the resources are publicly owned to begin with (for example, in most Commonwealth and European Union countries) a resource royalty is paid instead of a tax.

2.6.4   Specific arrangements

2.6.4.1   Other arrangements often used to tax extractive industries or to provide resource holders with additional revenues or other economic value include:

- State participation (mainly for oil and gas);

---

12 Since royalties are generally paid to the resource owner, in the case of private ownership they are paid to the private owner(s). Severance taxes are imposed in addition to any private royalty payment obligations, and are paid to governmental bodies.

- Bonus payments (often related to the signature of the contract or the transfer of the lease);

- Carry (mainly for oil and gas and generally involving PSCs);

- Land rentals (mainly for mining); and

- Other non-revenue/cash-based systems, such as:

  ➢ Infrastructure requirements, including building roads, hospitals, schools, water projects, housing communities (e.g., in Ghana, one investor has committed to building a 15km road, taking this responsibility over from Government);

  ➢ Infrastructure transfer/intellectual property transfers;

  ➢ Training levy/support for study costs; and

  ➢ Sponsorship of specialist courses at universities.

2.6.4.2   State participation can be another effective route to ensuring governments secure an appropriate share of the upside in times of high prices or lower costs, while maintaining progressivity. Government equity ownership essentially places the government, or a government-owned entity, in the position of a partner in the joint venture, along with the operator and any other investor partners involved. This participation can align investor and government interests, providing project advantages such as risk sharing, development ownership, and ensured support for development. Participating partners are, however, expected to share equally in the costs of the venture; thus, the government will have to consider how to fund this. State participation is far less common in mining than it is in oil and gas.

2.6.4.3   Bonus payments provide early, upfront revenue to countries, and thus have a timing appeal to governments, but are least favoured by investors, as they are upfront payments unrelated to actual production, and thus, are most regressive. Where bonus payments are involved, it will be important to consider which part of government receives the payment, how transparent the payment is and whether it goes to the national budget or to the budget of the administrative entity where actual exploration and extraction will take place. Bonus payments occur both in mining and in oil and gas.

2.6.4.4   A "carry" is a situation whereby a party pays for an agreed part of another party's share of the cost in proportion to the participating interest in a jointly owned exploration licence/venture in the expectation of recovering those costs from a share of future production. As it generally relates to situations covered by PSCs, it is more often applicable in oil and gas ventures and it generally only applies during the exploration phase. The carry can apply towards another IOC as well as towards the government or NOC. To the extent that a carry is in place for state participation or involvement by the NOC, a carry can be part of the government take. In any case, it is important to be clear on the general tax treatment of costs paid under a carry for profit and potential capital gains taxation in case of subsequent alienation.

2.6.4.5   Some special extractive taxation consists of one-off levies targeting specific sectors. An example of one such special tax is the National reconstruction levy/National Fiscal Stabilization Levy (NFSL) in Ghana, where the levy was earmarked to finance a specific sector of the economy. In 2013, the Government of Ghana announced a number of tax initiatives passed by Parliament. The initiatives included reinstatement of the National Fiscal Stabilization Levy Act. Under the Act, a 5 per cent national fiscal stabilization levy was applied on profits before tax for specific companies and institutions operating in the country. The list included companies providing mining support services.

2.6.5   Indirect tax

2.6.5.1   Indirect taxation is the taxation not of profits, but of certain transactions. Often, an indirect tax exists that can be specified for certain products or transactions. It is generally considered as part of the fiscal take, at least by the investor. Some examples are:

- VAT, with a focus on extractive industry-related issues and impact on government take/fiscal terms;[13]

- Import/export-related taxes, duties, or fees;

- Excise taxes for certain related products, such as mining imports of certain fuel or pre-curser chemicals, which are key components in mining processes.

2.6.5.2   Special issues regarding indirect taxation for extractive industries are covered in Chapter 12 (VAT).

2.6.6   How to evaluate fiscal instruments

2.6.6.1   To make an investment sustainable and guarantee the revenue flow to the resource holder, all stakeholders' interests should be balanced when managing the fiscal instruments applicable to the extractive venture. To do so, it is important to understand the effects of each of the typical instruments, including their impact on the timing of the revenue, on a country's overall policy objectives, and on the risk/return balance.

2.6.7   Timing of revenue

2.6.7.1   Certain fiscal instruments focus on achieving government take from ventures early on, often regardless of whether the venture is generating profits

---

13 See Chapter 12 (Value Added Tax).

or even revenue. These instruments accelerate taxation or government take to a date before the venture achieves profitability. In these cases, the taxation of the venture is said to be "front-loaded."

2.6.7.2　　From a government point of view, some front-loading may be required to manage the expectations of the country or to ensure government funding can be achieved to ensure participation in the venture. Generally, front-loaded systems are more "regressive"—that is, they are less related to profit and effectively tax lower return ventures/production relatively more heavily than high return ventures—whereas progressive systems tend to be more profit related, taxing more profitable projects more than less profitable ones and generally delaying the timing of taxation until profits are realized. (See below for further discussion of progressivity and regressivity in fiscal terms.)

2.6.7.3　　From an investor point of view, front-loading negatively affects the risk/return balance which, depending on degree, can affect the project's competitiveness. Investors generally evaluate and compare projects on a discounted cash flow basis, thus the timing of investments or payments has a direct impact on the investor's estimated return from a project. From the investor's point of view, terms that defer cash pay-outs or accelerate the tax deductibility of costs are favoured.

2.6.7.4　　Signature bonuses generate revenue very early in the venture. They provide government take before any revenue or even production is generated from the venture. If equity elements (i.e., state participation rights) are reserved, depending on their size and funding, they also can impact the risk/return balance significantly. Equity rights generally do not require cash payments from investors (unlike, especially, the signature bonus), except when the equity rights of the government include a carry arrangement.

2.6.7.5　　Royalty systems come into play once production starts but do not require the venture to be profitable. As they are production related, their make-up may have an impact on the production profile. They are less regressive than bonus payments since they at least require production and thus some revenue generation, but they are less progressive than income or profit-related payments.

2.6.7.6　　Profit-related fiscal instruments give rise to government share around the time the venture becomes profitable. However, there are aspects of profit-related instruments that may front-load through ring-fencing or other types of limitations of cost recovery, which accelerate the moment of taxation and impose taxes before the investor, on an overall basis, is profitable.

2.6.7.7　　Uplifts and accelerated depreciation, on the other hand, delay the time when government revenue is achieved through profit-related fiscal instruments. Depending on how the depreciation regime is set up, these instruments generally have a positive impact on the level of asset investment.

Figure 2.F.1: Life cycle of an extractive industry project

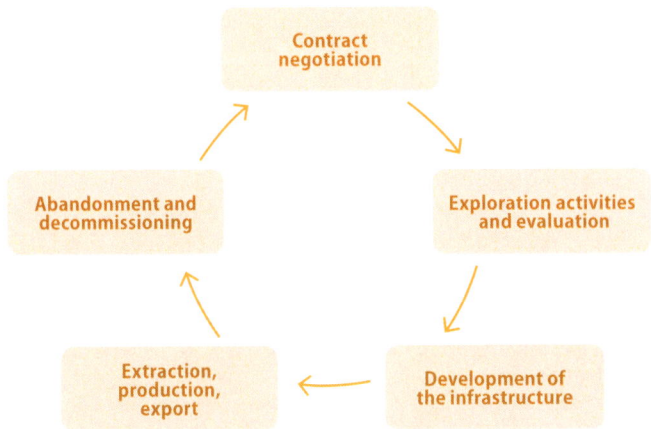

Source: UN/DESA.

2.7   IMPLEMENTATION OF FISCAL TAKE POLICY

2.7.1   Using multiple taxation instruments

2.7.1.1   When using multiple taxation instruments, it is important to determine how the various taxes relate to each other. Some taxes are deductible costs in computing other taxes. For example, pipeline fees or royalties are often considered tax deductible costs for profit-based taxes. In other cases, the various taxes may be credited against each other.

2.7.1.2   If the various instruments provide revenues to various government institutions (e.g., with some revenues going to the Ministry of Minerals and others to the Ministry of Finance), it is important to ensure a full understanding and agreement on the matter by all of the different government entities to ensure a sustainable enforcement.

2.7.1.3   The interdependency with subnational taxation also needs to be addressed and clarified. It is important to know whether the taxation at various levels can be credited or deducted.

2.7.1.4   Each of these issues, if not clarified, will increase uncertainties and risks, adversely affecting the risk profile of the country from an investor standpoint, and consuming resources of the government in their ultimate resolution. Avoiding an inefficient use of such resources and providing clarity from the outset benefits both the country and the investor. Again, agreeing on numerical examples of how the taxes and levies are to be computed and detailing these in contracts or regulations upfront can avoid uncertainty upon assessment.

2.7.2 Interaction between extractive industries taxation and general taxation

2.7.2.1   It is not always clear how to deal with the production that is allocated under a PSC in conjunction with the general corporate income tax system. Production can be shared in cash or in kind. There are various aspects that can have interactions with general corporate income taxation. It is important to understand how production sharing is done, and how and where the volume of the production and the sharing is determined.

2.7.2.2   Timing, responsibility of measurement, reporting and verification requirements are important, as is the allocation of risks. It is important to understand who will bear the commodity price risk in case production is shared in kind and who bears the exchange rate risk, and for how long, in case of sharing in cash. If the PSC and the corporate income tax are mute on these points, or if the arrangements under the PSC are not in line with the corporate income tax, it will be unclear as to how these issues will be dealt with under the general taxation regime.

2.7.2.3   When sharing production, the composition of the group of investors and their legal arrangements should also be considered from a tax point of view. Apart from the potential direct tax consequences, the indirect tax consequences should be considered. For example, under PSCs, the production tends to be transferred from the government to the operator and from the operator to the joint venture or the joint venture partners. Especially in the case of transfers in kind, each of these transfers could be subject to indirect tax at a federal or subnational level. It may not be economically intended to levy tax at each of these transfers, but arrangements need to be made to ensure the applicable laws are complied with and expectations are managed. Again, resolution and clarity of these types of interactions are "common ground" for both countries and investors to benefit.

2.7.3 International tax aspects

2.7.3.1   It is important to ensure the alignment of provisions in domestic law and tax treaties in relation to the fiscal take. A key element of this is whether and which part of the fiscal take is considered eligible for foreign tax credit purposes. This is influenced by the provisions of the relevant double tax agreement as well as by the characterization of the tax or levy in the relevant law or contract and by the taxation rules of the home country of a particular investor. Even if the tax or levy is clearly profit related, attention needs to be given to the description and features, especially if agreed in a PSA.

2.7.3.2   The existence, as well as the wording of a double tax treaty and of national tax law in the home country of the investor, are relevant for the eventual tax burden on a project. The interaction between the tax system of the home country of the investor and that of the host country of the investment influences the eventual economics of a project. In other words, clarity in these rules, and often the existence of a negotiated tax treaty, can allow an investor to enter a higher bid.

2.7.4   Allocation of revenue and relevance of subnational taxation

2.7.4.1   It is important to consider how the revenue from the extractive industries is to be allocated among the subnational levels of government of the host country. The imposition of taxes and their allocation depend on the country's constitutional, legal and administrative structure.

2.7.4.2   In certain countries, subnational levels of government have a mandate to introduce their own fiscal instruments. In other countries, only the federal government imposes taxes and subsequently appropriates the revenue.

2.7.4.3   Without clarity on allocation, the fiscal terms may not be stable as local entities may become dissatisfied with the revenue they are receiving.

2.7.5   Best practices in administration and enforcement

2.7.5.1   To ensure effective enforcement, best practices should be considered when designing, negotiating and applying the applicable fiscal systems.

Best practices should ensure the following:

(i)   A tax administrator must be part of the team to test administrative ease and feasibility of execution;

(ii)   Examples should be included on how to calculate the taxable base as well as taxes due in the relevant legislation or contracts. This should provide clarity to tax administrators and taxpayers on how to implement extractive industries taxation; and

(iii)   Alignment must exist in definitions and enforcement between various taxes, both federal as well as subnational.

2.7.5.2   The administrative capability of the government can be a limiting factor in the options for fiscal regimes. Using multiple systems can cover multiple policy objectives in revenue raising but often puts additional strain on limited resources. Coordination and exchange of information between departments and parts of government can assist in improving efficiency and reducing costs related to information gathering and audits.

2.7.5.3   Improving administrative capability could be addressed by creating a dedicated office/unit within the tax administration that focuses on the extractive industries. See also Chapter 13 (Audit). Sustainable and appropriate resourcing should be ensured when setting up such administration. This would include:

•   Appropriate training of staff: audit routines, understanding of the extractive industries (e.g., the mining cycle and risk areas that can impact revenue);

- Appropriate audit tools and equipment;

- Framework to access third party information on production (e.g., from the Ministry of Mines, energy or customs); and

- Sharing of experiences and knowledge with other countries addressing similar extractive industries issues.

2.7.5.4   For resourcing and capacity-building initiatives, it is important to include other government departments from the start. Capacity-building is offered by various international organizations and through exchanges with other country tax authorities. Multi-stakeholder capacity-building—involving not only other government officials but also academics and expert business representatives—is not always readily available but can provide valuable information and perspectives. Exchanges with taxpayers that increase capacity can include work on cooperative compliance and other forms of dispute avoidance.[14]

ANNEX I

For more information

Jack Calder, *Administering Fiscal Regimes for Extractive Industries: A Handbook* (Washington, D.C: International Monetary Fund, 2014).

Philip Daniel, Michael Keen and Charles McPherson (Eds.) *The Taxation of Petroleum and Minerals: Principles, Problems and Practice* (New York: Routledge, 2010).

Philip Daniel and Michael Keen (Eds.) *International Taxation and the Extractive Industries* (New York: Routledge, 2016).

Lindsay Hogan and Brenton Goldsworthy, "International Mineral Taxation: experience and issues," in *The Taxation of Petroleum and Minerals: Principles, Problems and Practice*, ed. Philip Daniel, Michael Keen and Charles McPherson (New York: Routledge, 2010), p. 122.

International Monetary Fund, *Fiscal Regimes for Extractive Industries: Design and Implementation* (2012) available at https://www.imf.org/external/np/pp/eng/2012/081512.pdf.

Daniel Johnston, *International Petroleum Fiscal System and Production Sharing Contracts* (Tulsa: PennWell Books, 1994).

Honore Le Leuch, "Recent Trends in Upstream Petroleum Agreements: Policy, Contractual, Fiscal, and Legal Issues," in *The Handbook of Global Energy Policy*, ed. Andreas Goldthau (New York: Wiley, 2013).

---

14 For example, participation in advance pricing agreements and processes involving third-party expertise can support capacity development.

Carol Nakhle, "Petroleum fiscal regimes: evolution and challenges," in *The Taxation of Petroleum and Minerals: Principles, Problems and Practice*, ed. Philip Daniel, Michael Keen and Charles McPherson (New York: Routledge, 2010) p. 89.

Open Oil, *Oil Contracts--how to read and understand them*. Available at http://openoil.net/understanding-oil-contracts/.

Silvana Tordo, *Fiscal Systems for Hydrocarbons: Design Issues*, World Bank Working Paper No. 123, (Washington, D.C.: World Bank, 2007).

Chapter 3

Tax Aspects of Negotiation and Renegotiation of Contracts

3.1   INTRODUCTION

3.1.1   Executive summary

3.1.1.1   The purpose of this chapter is to provide an overview of some of the tax and fiscal-related issues developing countries face in the negotiation and possible renegotiation of long-term natural resource contracts. It will also provide some additional perspective on the negotiation and renegotiation process.

3.1.1.2   The content is intended to help developing country policymakers and administrators, and to provide information to other stakeholders, on both substantive and procedural approaches to agreements between such countries and the investors they seek to attract in the development of their potential oil, gas, and mineral resources. The background contained in this chapter is intended to provide a broader context for options and approaches available in negotiating long-term contracts.

3.1.2   Background

3.1.2.1   Developing countries offer prospects for major extractive industry investments over the next several decades. The impact of the COVID-19 pandemic means there is a need for significant levels of investment in the energy sector to sustain and boost employment, and boost economic growth.[1] The International Energy Association estimates that reaching the climate goals of the Paris Agreement would mean a quadrupling of mineral requirements for clean energy technologies by 2040.[2] This will require significant investment in energy transition minerals such as copper, lithium, nickel and cobalt with the bulk of that being in developing countries. Such countries must undertake careful upfront planning and priority setting to attract outside investment while balancing their economic, environmental, and social needs.

3.1.2.2   In some countries, laws are independently enacted governing the

---

[1] International Energy Agency, *World Energy Investment Outlook 2014*, p. 22, available at https://www.iea.org/publications/freepublications/publication/WEIO2014.pdf.

[2] International Energy Agency, *The Role of Critical Minerals In Clean Energy Transition. World Energy Outlook Special Report*, May 2021, p.8

framework for investments in resources, and investors must determine whether they will invest based upon those prescribed rules.[3] In many developing countries, however, where resource development is beginning, a fully developed, detailed sector-specific framework may not exist, and thus, many of the fiscal elements governing a natural resource development project may be established by negotiations between an investor and the government.

3.1.2.3   It is generally beneficial to define as many of the natural resource development rules as possible, including fiscal terms, in legislation, leaving only limited matters to negotiation. This ensures consistency and transparency while allowing for flexibility to address some project-specific considerations. However, in the early stages of resource development, where the rules are evolving, countries may in practice rely on project-specific contract negotiations for many items governing natural resource development, including key fiscal terms.

3.1.2.4   This chapter will review various considerations and concerns of governments and investors involved in a natural resource contract negotiation, or possible renegotiation, as the circumstances or parties change. Particular attention will be paid to tax and fiscal issues. While the most common tax issues will relate to the provisions directly affecting government take—such as royalties, income and additional profit taxes, withholding taxes, VAT, and export taxes—other contractual terms (e.g., decommissioning or requirements to fund infrastructure) and even the procedures in negotiations can have tax implications. Some of those more important concerns are also addressed in this chapter.

3.1.2.5   The ultimate objective for both the government and the investor in a natural resource development project is success over a very long-term period. The nature of the original agreement terms should provide a structure that maximizes chances to achieve results beneficial to governments and investors alike. It should also promote an arrangement where, as differences of view arise over the course of the 20–30+ year relationship, the parties agree to work together to resolve those differences in a mutually satisfactory way.[4]

---

[3] Some countries might also have prescribed rules for the mining sector, but which may not be entirely appropriate for the oil and gas (O&G) sector, and vice versa.

[4] Two very helpful resources covering a wide range of issues in natural resource contracts are "Mining Contracts—how to read and understand them" (hereafter "Mining Contracts") and "Oil Contracts—how to read and understand them" (hereafter "Oil Contracts"). These sources contain a wealth of information, examples and considerations related to understanding and negotiating long-term natural resource contracts, as well as basic information about the mining and O&G industries. They each also contain extensive and helpful glossaries of mining and oil terms, and are available for free download from https://s3.amazonaws.com/s3.documentcloud.org/documents/1279596/mining-contracts-how-to-read-and-understand-them.pdf (for mining contracts) and http://openoil.net/wp/wp-content/uploads/2016/12/oil-contracts-v1.2-dec-13.pdf (for oil (and gas) contracts). In addition, the International Institute for Sustainable Development has published the IISD Handbook on Mining Contract Negotiations for Developing Countries, Volume One: Preparing for Success (April 2015) (hereafter "IISD Handbook") available from http://www.iisd.org/sites/default/files/publications/iisd-handbook-mining-contract-negotiations-for-developing-countries-volume-1.pdf with legal background in contract negotiations as well as negotiating preparation and implementation procedures and practices.

3.1.3 Relationship with other chapters of the Handbook

3.1.3.1   Where other chapters of this Handbook cover particular issues more directly, they will be referenced in this chapter. To avoid duplication, the reader is invited to review the more specific text in those chapters. In particular, Chapter 1 (Overview) provides a context for understanding the nature of the oil and gas (O&G) and mining industries, including the various phases in the lifespan of natural resource projects (i.e., exploration, development, production, processing and decommissioning).

3.1.3.2   Chapter 1 (Overview) also summarizes the types of fiscal regimes that generally apply in these industries, while Chapter 2 (The Government's Fiscal Take) provides additional important details on the elements of such regimes. Chapter 4 covers Production Sharing Contracts, a form of natural resource contract that is common in the oil and gas industry. Together, those chapters provide additional context for the issues reviewed in this chapter.

3.2   NEGOTIATION BACKGROUND: COUNTRY PERSPECTIVES

3.2.1 Balancing investment attractiveness with obtaining resource value

3.2.1.1   In designing a fiscal plan for developing resources, one key objective is maximizing the present value of government revenues. Other important objectives also exist, such as employment creation, training, local content, infrastructure requirements and environmental concerns.[5] When seeking an investor to bear some or all of these costs along with the other risks associated with developing resources, a country will also need to consider what terms are required to provide investors an adequate return for the risks they take.

3.2.1.2   A country may address these issues in its statutory provisions related to resource activities, or it may address them on a project-by-project basis via contractual negotiations. These may be based upon a model contract, but in practice, such a model tends to be a guideline, or a country's "opening position" in what becomes a more specific negotiation, taking into account the specific characteristics of the particular resource to be developed.

3.2.1.3   Ideally, whether in a statutory or contractual mechanism, the terms and conditions for natural resource projects should be flexible to meet government and investor objectives over an extended period of time, and under different and changing price and cost environments. This can be advanced via a choice of various fiscal tools but, in many cases—in more extreme circumstances— the agreement of the parties to re-open or renegotiate certain provisions is included in contracts. The

---

[5] See International Monetary Fund, *Fiscal Regimes for Extractive Industries: Design and Implementation* (2012), p. 13.

renegotiation could be at a specific point in the future; triggered by certain criteria; or at regular intervals determined at the time of the original agreement.

3.2.2   Priority setting

3.2.2.1   As suggested in the Overview, a key starting point in establishing a fiscal regime, via a general statutory approach or in a particular contract negotiation is for the country (and the investor) to identify its principles, priorities, and objectives to be achieved.[6] This can take time, and involve input from multiple stakeholders in the planning process.[7] Once a set of objectives is determined, the ongoing design of the fiscal regime and other key statutory or contractual conditions should be tested against their impacts on achieving the base objectives.

3.2.2.2   One of the benefits of relying on a statutory approach for fiscal regimes is that it can embody the agreed upon objectives and ensure consistency among projects.[8] Where more of the terms are left to negotiations, the risks increase that the ultimate contract will not be as fully consistent with the country's agreed upon priorities.

3.2.2.3   Experts increasingly suggest that the model with more detailed laws and regulations "…creates a stronger foundation upon which a country can manage its extractive industries according to national priorities. In addition to helping investors feel like they are being treated equally across deals, consistent terms across projects can streamline monitoring for government institutions. A robust legislative framework may also result in greater public input and transparency because the public can more easily participate in the legislative process than in individual contract negotiations."[9]

---

[6] See the Background section of Chapter 1 (Overview) of this Handbook.

[7] See, for example, the extensive work done in developing the Mozambique Natural Gas Development Plan, available at http://documents.worldbank.org/curated/en/324191468054279630/pdf/806830WP0Mozam0Box0379812B00PUBLIC0.pdf ; Uganda's Vision 2040 covering overall country development, but noting the importance of contributions to be made by the O&G and mining sectors, available at http://npa.ug/wp-content/themes/npatheme/documents/vision2040.pdf, pp. 47–51; specifically for mining, see the African Mining Vision and "Building a sustainable future for Africa's extractive industry: From vision to action," particularly the key tenets of the Vision and programme clusters, available at https://au.int/sites/default/files/documents/30995-doc-africa_mining_vision_english_1.pdf, p. 9. Also see the Natural Resources Charter, Precept 1, which states "[e]ffective and sustainable resource management requires an inclusive and comprehensive national strategy. To achieve this, the government must make a series of key decisions that will affect different groups and set choices extending far into the future. To avoid making decisions in a piecemeal fashion and to build a shared sense of direction, governments should, in dialogue with stakeholders, use a national strategy process to guide extractive resource management decisions." Available at https://resourcegovernance.org/sites/default/files/NRCJ1193_natural_resource_charter_19.6.14.pdf, and IISD Handbook, section 4.5.1, pp. 49–50.

[8] Consistency among investors and projects can be important from a non-discrimination and anti-corruption perspective. A further benefit to consistency in terms and terminology that a statutory approach provides is the facilitation of administration and compliance enforcement.

[9] Natural Resources Governance Institute, *Legal Framework: Navigating the Web of Laws*

3.2.2.4   Some of the fiscal regime provisions are included in statutes while others are negotiated, and the negotiations present the very real risk that conflicts may arise between statutory rules and the contract provisions. This is addressed more fully below in the context of having tax and customs representatives involved in fiscal terms negotiations to ensure enforceability of the contract terms and their conformity with the statutory provisions in place.[10]

3.3   PARTIES INVOLVED FROM THE COUNTRY STANDPOINT (internal and external stakeholders)

3.3.1   Local government

3.3.1.1   A key factor that distinguishes natural resource development from many other investments is that they involve "exhaustible" resources—considered to be country assets, the benefit of which should belong to the people of the country. In addition, considerations of how those benefits are shared between current and future generations are also involved.

3.3.1.2   Finally, while the benefits are often viewed as benefitting the entire country, the disruptions that naturally occur in development activities can disproportionately be borne by the region or locations where most of the activities are conducted. Thus, special consideration for such localities must be taken into account.

3.3.2   National government representatives[11]

3.3.2.1   The establishment of a country's taxation and fiscal regime is a complex exercise, given the many issues involved and, in terms of governmental

---

and Contracts Governing Extractive Industries, NRGI Reader (March 2015) p. 6. Available from http://www.resourcegovernance.org/analysis-tools/publications/primer-legal-framework .

[10] Where a statutory rule is no longer realistic or is not sufficiently flexible to accommodate projects that country negotiators wish to have developed, it is arguably better to adjust the statutory rules themselves than to seek to override or modify them via a contract. An attempted "override" may simply be unenforceable, and lead to conflicts and ambiguities that only increase risk and uncertainty.

[11] While this chapter addresses taxation issues, and thus, the following subsections focus on Finance and Resources (petroleum and mining) ministries, there are of course many other national level ministries (or organizations) that need to be included, such as ministries overseeing health, safety and environment, labour and employment, and of course any national mining or oil company. Even when the focus is on taxation and other more purely fiscal terms, involvement of these other representatives is often important since they will provide valuable input into the underlying objectives in their areas. Similarly, even when non-tax or fiscal terms are discussed, inclusion of tax representatives is important since decisions in those areas will no doubt have tax impacts that should be understood and carefully considered. See, for example, Mining Contracts, pp. 22–24. Generally, the parties involved should be largely symmetric, as between the government and the investor.

responsibilities, the numerous agencies or departments involved or affected. Thus, broad collaboration is essential. Benefits of establishing a regime under a statutory approach, in addition to those already noted, include the likelihood of this broad range of input being obtained, and a higher degree of transparency being achieved. When a country determines its regime under a contractual, project-by-project approach to resource development, the challenges of appropriate and full participation are greater. Even in this case, however, establishing a "model contract" can be a productive exercise and a means of obtaining input from as wide a group within government as possible.[12]

3.3.2.2   Further, in light of the long lead times in generating production (and, following that, net revenues after cost recoveries), clear descriptions of project results, and their timing, should be communicated. This will help to anchor expectations, particularly with respect to the timing of anticipated benefits, in a realistic context.

3.3.3   Finance ministry/planning ministry

3.3.3.1   Given the key importance of taxation (including all forms of government take) in contract negotiation, it is essential that the Ministry of Finance be included in the development of objectives, in statutory regime structuring, and in specific contract negotiations, as the case may be. In collaboration with the Ministry of Finance, the further involvement of the tax administration, as well as the Customs Administration is essential.

3.3.3.2   Ministry of Finance and tax administration representatives bring skills to the negotiating team that are particularly important, including the likelihood of being able to conduct economic and financial modelling of the impact of various negotiation proposals and a knowledge of tax policy and practice to assist in determining and evaluating the composition and approach regarding which fiscal tools to use.

3.3.3.3   Further, the involvement of tax administration representatives in the negotiation process creates a better understanding of how the provisions are intended to operate in practice and ensures that they can in fact be implemented as intended. Many examples exist where without involvement of the tax (and customs) administrations, a negotiation will result in provisions that are contrary to the existing tax laws (including tax treaties) or may use terms that have different definitions under such tax provisions than the negotiators may intend, creating immediate ambiguities, if not outright conflicts, in the interpretation of the agreement and its enforceability under the other statutory requirements in place.[13]

---

[12] See, for example, Liberia Model Production Sharing Contract, available at Liberian Production Sharing Contract | Extractives Hub; Tanzania Model Production Sharing Contract, available at: TPDC | Welcome... Mexico's National Hydrocarbons Commission documents, available at http://www.gob.mx/cnh/#documentos; and Timor Leste Model Production Sharing Contract, available at: https://www.laohamutuk.org/Oil/PetRegime/PSC%20model%20270805.pdf.

[13] See, for example, a Parliamentary Briefing issued by the Natural Resource Governance Institute noting, "Through their oversight role, parliamentarians should (···) [e]nsure that all legislation affecting the fiscal elements of oil, gas and mining projects are coherent. Some countries have wrestled with inconsistencies between pieces of legislation." Getting a Good

In one African Tax Administration Forum (ATAF) meeting, one country representative noted that its tax administration, which had not been involved in a negotiated contract, found itself unable to implement the terms of a negotiated contract, since they were in conflict with the specific tax laws of the country. This forced a renegotiation of a contract that the investor and the government negotiators had signed (and thought was finalized). This result can be largely eliminated by including tax and customs administrations in the negotiation process.[14]

3.3.3.4   Such inclusion can be achieved by having representatives of the affected agencies on the negotiating team or, at a minimum, available to and regularly consulted by the team throughout the process. It is equally important that investors work with the negotiating parties to clarify that such involvement and consultation is undertaken.

3.3.3.5   Uncertainties that may exist in the implementation of any aspect of the agreement will simply increase the risks for the investor, and will therefore affect the terms of the negotiations. Reducing these types of risks is beneficial to all.

3.3.3.6   Full inclusion in the negotiating process may sometimes be harder to achieve in very limited negotiations, and is one reason to avoid those processes. Where that is not possible, it is again in both the country's and the investor's interest to minimize risk through consultations with tax and customs representatives.

3.3.4   Resource (petroleum and mining) ministries

3.3.4.1   The petroleum or mining ministries will clearly be involved in contract negotiation and in some, if not all, of the fiscal (government take) structuring. They are most likely to know the asset characteristics (e.g., the geology, market and necessary infrastructure) that are key elements in understanding and estimating the value of the resource itself. Again, however, given the clear overlap with numerous tax issues, the resource ministries should coordinate closely with the finance ministry (and tax and customs administrations) to ensure full

---

Deal from Oil, Gas and Mining Parliamentary Briefing January 2015 Fiscal Regimes for Oil, Gas And Minerals, in http://resourcegovernance.org/sites/default/files/documents/nrgi_fiscal-regime_20150311.pdf. p. 4. While ambiguities in statutory interpretations can occur, generally providing for as many of the fiscal terms as possible in statutes, and minimizing the terms that are agreed to via separate contracts, will help to reduce ambiguities. Ghana presents an interesting dichotomy here given that it has traditionally provided the fiscal terms in the mining sector on a negotiated contract basis, while it is generally standardizing terms in the oil and gas sector by means of statutory requirements. Further, the language differences of negotiators, and differences between the language in which the negotiations are conducted and the ultimate contract language, can affect how agreements are understood by the parties, and is another area that can generate ambiguities.

[14] Another example of conflicts between contracts and statutes involved a country where separate contracts negotiated with a number of mining companies specified different periods for the carry-forward of losses for tax purposes. In some cases, the contracted period was longer than the country's statutory one, while in other cases it was shorter. Each of these presented issues of interaction between the contract and the existing tax law, and provided outcomes that could be very different from what the negotiators intended.

enforceability of the arrangements and complete understanding of their economic effects.

3.3.4.2 In the fiscal regime planning stage, it is important to have robust economic (including tax) modelling tools to evaluate the impacts of the various options and fiscal tools that ultimately will form the overall fiscal regime. Similarly, where some or a large portion of that regime is developed under a project negotiation, having project-based economic modelling tools is essential. Those with knowledge of the specific resource need to combine efforts with those with the financial and economic evaluation skills to understand the predicted outcomes under numerous scenarios, such that they are fully prepared for how the negotiations will transpire and can provide key information to the ultimate decision makers.

3.3.4.3 Before finalizing an agreement, an important "best practice" is again to work through all of the proposed fiscal terms under several development and production scenarios, doing so with input and computations developed or reviewed by the agencies responsible for each particular item of significance (i.e., customs agencies on duties, tax administrations on various taxes involved, natural resource and finance ministries for royalties and other financial payments, etc.). Doing this in as much detail as possible can ensure alignment and understanding within the government, and between the government and investor(s), of how the terms are intended to operate in practice and can provide the opportunity to revise or clarify provisions where ambiguities are found.

3.3.4.4 To achieve full benefit from the concession contracts it negotiates, the Government will have to effectively monitor, and ensure compliance with, the terms of its negotiated agreements.[15]

3.3.4.5 Thus, having a complete and agreed understanding of what the negotiators intended the agreement terms to mean is a clear prerequisite to ongoing successful implementation, monitoring and enforcement. Finally, public disclosure of the agreement provides transparency of the terms agreed. For example, the Extractives Industry Transparency Initiative requires public disclosure of contracts with governments. Refer to section 3.9.2.4 further below.

3.3.5 Regional and local counterparts

3.3.5.1 In addition to ensuring that all relevant governmental concerns at a federal level are addressed, it is also very important to involve regional and local governments—those where the operations will take place—in the planning stages (i.e., before an area is opened up for exploration or for bidding, and before activities commence) and in the negotiation process. While this is a clear issue in terms of how the project will actually be physically implemented (with roads, port expansions and other infrastructure directly impacting local and regional

---

[15] Raja Kaul and Antoine Heuty with Alvina Norman, *Getting a Better Deal from the Extractive Sector—Concession Negotiation in Liberia, 2006–2008*: A report to the Liberian Reconstruction and Development Committee Office of the President (hereafter Liberian Renegotiation Report) Republic of Liberia, Revenue Watch Institute, 2009, p. 77.

areas) the mechanism by which a fair sharing of government revenues occurs is a critical issue that should be covered by statute or a negotiated contract. Failure to address this issue adequately—both at the planning stage and during the negotiations—can lead to project delays and inefficiencies as well as disruptions due to local discontent.

3.3.6   Negotiation team participation

3.3.6.1   The makeup of the country's negotiating team is a key issue. While the team conducting the actual negotiations with potential investors cannot practically include all interested and important members, a mechanism to ensure their input is critical to the success of the negotiation.

3.3.6.2   There is no one structure for government negotiating teams. Practice is diverse across the globe. Composition of the government negotiation team is key. The team should be cross-functional with the proper expertise. Negotiation teams that are more than 5-6 people rarely achieve an outcome. It is important to highlight that an attempt to involve all interested parties directly within the actual negotiation will result in the process being slow and cumbersome. In such case, it will also be difficult to align different interests and positions among the government bodies. Most importantly, the relevant team will need to be mandated to reach an agreement. Ideally the "negotiation mandate" sets up a "framework," which provides some room for flexibility depending on how the negotiations progress, rather than very specific outcomes that must be achieved. Confusion, distraction, and divide-and-conquer techniques can occur with large negotiating teams.[16]

3.3.6.3   One framework to consider is having a relatively small core negotiating group that conducts the formal negotiations, with a larger team of negotiation advisers who provide relevant input before and throughout the negotiation process on issues consistent with their expertise. In addition, when particular negotiating sessions focus on certain specific issues, it may be appropriate to include in the session the subject matter expert. For example, if there are specific taxation issues that are to be negotiated, a government tax administration representative could be included in that session, even if financial issues are otherwise handled by the Ministry of Finance. However, tax issues may be part of a wider fiscal framework, for example if the government is also a shareholder as well as a contracting party. Communication between different expert groups will therefore be necessary.

3.3.6.4   How the political dimension of a negotiation is handled, including interaction with the negotiating team, is a critical issue. The Liberian renegotiation study noted the benefit of strong and engaged leadership:

---

[16] Mining Contracts, pp. 22–24. See also "Truth 45: Building the winning negotiating team," in *Leigh Thompson, The Truth About Negotiations* (Upper Saddle River, N.J.: FT Press, 2008), pp. 169–171.

- President Sirleaf's leadership in the ArcelorMittal and Firestone negotiations was key to the success Liberia achieved. From the beginning of the process, the President managed the negotiating process and allowed a direct reporting line from the Chairman of the negotiating team to herself. Among other things, President Sirleaf [...]"...clearly communicated a vision of national priorities to the nation and investors"[...].

- The President's leadership [...]"... displayed her consistency, integrity (the negotiation team knew they could count on her backing if needed) and involvement. She sought updates, listened to the negotiating team and its advisors, was accessible, was a consensus builder, held people accountable, had substantive knowledge of the issues being negotiated, and was decisive."[17]

3.3.7   Communication protocols

3.3.7.1   A mechanism to ensure robust communication among the negotiating team and advisers is important to achieving a successful outcome and an agreement that can be implemented as intended. For example, almost all issues have a tax implication—whether it is income, VAT, excise, customs, withholding or individual taxation matters—including, where applicable, tax treaty issues. It is therefore always helpful to ensure tax issues are understood by the negotiators.

3.3.7.2   To illustrate this point, the termination provisions of a contract will likely provide some requirement to reclaim and restore the mining or oil and gas (O&G) production sites. The issue of who will bear this cost and how those costs are addressed under the country's tax law (or if the negotiators wish to provide tax treatment under the contract) are key to the economics of the deal. Negotiators who are not experts in tax matters may not immediately appreciate the tax implications of various options for addressing this issue. Having an effective communication procedure in place with advisers will ensure the negotiators understand and account for the tax effects of various proposals. See Chapter 14 (The Tax Treatment of Decommissioning) for additional detail on this topic.

3.3.7.3   When negotiations are at certain critical stages, there may be concerns about information sharing outside a relatively small group. Again, however, that group should ensure that it has a full understanding of the tax implications of the decisions being considered. The best way to ensure this is to include a tax representative within that group; failing to do that, the next best approach is to have a consultation with the tax representative and fully explain what is being proposed. In this context, the tax representative needs to be entrusted to understand the full context of the issue—in some cases, country tax representatives

---

[17] See the Liberian Renegotiation Report, p. 9. See also the IISD Handbook, Section 4.4.5, p. 45: "The role of the Minister or President in any negotiation is critical. It can be extremely constructive when Ministers are fully onside with the negotiating strategy, and very destructive to longer-term national goals when short-term personal or political goals are at the forefront of their individual objectives."

have noted that they have been asked "hypothetical" or "piecemeal" questions, and this can lead to responses that are different from what would apply if the full context of the facts involved were known.

3.3.8 Model issue notes

3.3.8.1   One way to provide input where individual involvement may not be practical is via written issue notes on items of importance. For example, a tax administration note outlining some of the basic rules in the tax law applicable to resource investments could further highlight that if the negotiators desire to deviate from statutory rules, they will need to obtain legislative amendments or the tax administration will be unable to implement them.

3.3.8.2   In addition to model issue notes that may be provided as background within a negotiating team, explanatory notes may also be helpful, and exchanged, with the opposite negotiating team. This can help negotiators from both sides to have the same understanding of how tax provisions important to each side operate in practice. When creating issue notes—meant either for one's own team members or to be exchanged—making a record of the note, including the legislative provisions which form the basis of the note, and its transmission details is a best practice. It is also best practice to formulate community support related provisions of the relevant agreements. Inclusion of communities in the process early on can help ensure that the terms of the agreement are crafted to address their concerns and needs.

3.3.9 Other stakeholders and constituents

3.3.9.1   Consultation with non-governmental stakeholders in the planning and implementation of awarding resource contracts, or in structuring a statutory regime covering resource development should be considered. Such engagement is important for generating trust in both the process and the outcome of such activities. Community engagement prior to any negotiations and during the process itself and formulating community-support related provisions of the relevant agreements can be a key factor in gaining community support. Such consultations and ongoing input also need to be appropriately managed in terms of time frame and subject matter. Inclusion of communities in the process early on can help ensure that the terms of the agreement are crafted to address their concerns and needs.

3.3.9.2   As noted in the context of the Liberian contract renegotiations, "…[a] majority of government officials including the President are favourable to consultations with non-governmental stakeholders as long as they are time bound and focused." Consultations with non-governmental stakeholders should take place early in the concession award process as part of the bid tender, evaluation, or award process. If there have been no consultations as part of the process to select the concessionaire, then a time-bound and focused consultation at the outset of the contract review phase is advisable.

3.3.9.3   Public sector representatives have pointed out that soliciting third-parties' input during the concession negotiation phase runs the risk of breaching the confidentiality required during negotiations. The development of a non-governmental stakeholder consultation mechanism should be done. "...Prior to finalizing such a mechanism, input should be sought from non-governmental groups such as community representatives and labour unions."

3.3.9.4   Consultations with stakeholders should occur as part of the concession bid tender, evaluation and award process. If this is not possible, then consultation with non-governmental stakeholders should occur as part of the contract review process. In adopting rules for consultations with stakeholders, the Government should require that such consultations occur early in the negotiation process (i.e., during the contract review process and prior to the development of a draft term sheet); as part of a formal public process; and in a time-bound and focused manner.[18]

3.3.9.5   Some outside groups push for inclusion on the negotiating team but this is usually not accommodated. The more common practice appears to be consultation prior to and at appropriate times during the negotiations, plus review of the draft final contract. Each country will have to determine the best-balanced approach to this issue.

3.3.9.6   There are often times during the negotiations when confidentiality is important. There may be proposals and counterproposals on important negotiating points, including proposed trade-offs among various terms. Negotiations conducted "publicly" on these positions are far less likely to be successful.[19] Nevertheless, the final product, including explanations of the various trade-offs embodied within it, should be available for review and comment. Negotiators should also be prepared to explain their final positions taken in concluding the overall agreement.

3.4   EXTERNAL RESOURCES

3.4.1   Outside adviser resources

3.4.1.1   Investors negotiating natural resource development agreements may possess asymmetric information and skills, given their technical expertise and

---

[18] Liberian Renegotiation Report, p. 61.

[19] The substantive renegotiation by Liberia of the ArcelorMittal iron ore and associated minerals concession contract began in New York for several reasons, including the consideration that "(···) [h]aving the discussions in New York also increased the Government's chances of maintaining confidentiality around the negotiations. The Government and its technical advisors felt that strict confidentiality at this stage of the process was absolutely necessary if Liberia was to succeed in its bid to renegotiate the MDA [Mineral Development Agreement]. Everyone acknowledged that negotiations conducted through the press would make it harder if not impossible for the Government to reach agreement with ArcelorMittal." Liberian Renegotiation Report, pp. 33–4.

greater experience in such matters. There are several ways to address this issue, depending on time and resources available.

3.4.1.2   It is first necessary to identify the information and skills the government needs. This can include: valuation of the resource or project, overall market analysis, legal or other negotiation skills, environmental expertise and economic modelling and tax expertise.

3.4.1.3   The next step is to then identify which of these can be adequately covered from within the government itself. In many cases, countries do in fact have the knowledge and skills required and should take full advantage of these resources. Where it is determined that gaps exist, or where additional augmentation is desirable, identifying options and putting together a plan for dealing with these is the next step. A number of possible approaches exist.

3.4.1.4   One option is to hire outside advisers as needed to meet the country's needs. There are a number of organizations available to provide natural resource project support—some on a pro bono basis and others on a partial or full funding approach. However, when a country is preparing to embark on serious, substantive negotiations, there is no substitute for hiring technical, legal and financial advisers from the private sector for pre-negotiation planning and negotiation support. In some cases, funding support for this may be available, but even where that is not the case, given the overall size and significance of natural resource projects, and the amount of potential revenues involved, the immediate and consistent availability of dedicated service support is worth the cost. Even with all of the expertise that investors have, they often also hire outside assistance. To equalize negotiating strength, it is strongly recommended that where dedicated, longer-term, project-negotiating support is required, countries should seriously consider hiring such high-level, private sector support.[20]

3.4.1.5   Many organizations are available to provide overall background to a country beginning or enhancing its education on important natural resource development issues. These include well known international and regional financial and development organizations, assistance organizations supported by one or a small number of countries or other organizations, and numerous non-governmental organizations dedicated to providing support with respect to natural resource matters. These can be quite helpful in providing basic information that is more general in nature, rather than specific technical support for a particular project or contract.

---

[20] See, for example, the German government publication: *Federal Ministry for Economic Cooperation and Development, Natural Resource Contracts as a Tool for Managing the Mining Sector,* 2015, pp. 54–56, in support of this point and for a general discussion of the role of outside advisers and the "Question of External Assistance," available at https://www.bmz. de/g7/includes/Downloadarchiv/Natural_Resource_Contracts.pdf. See also IISD Handbook, section 4.4.4, "Outside Expertise: Capacity provision and capacity building," pp. 47–49. In addition, when a country does decide to hire outside support, a robust and transparent process for identifying and hiring advisers is essential. It would be doubly harmful to incur the costs for an outside adviser that fails to provide the level of technical, financial or legal assistance needed.

3.4.1.6   In addition to more generalized information and support, specific project-related negotiation support is also provided by several organizations. An excellent window into the array of advisers, technical assistance programmes, and other advisory and support tools for negotiations is the Negotiations Portal for Host Country Governments.[21] The Portal, operated by the Columbia Center on Sustainable Investment (CCSI) is part of the G7 2014 CONNEX Initiative to "provide developing country partners with extended and concrete expertise for negotiating complex commercial contracts."[22]

3.4.1.7   The   Code   of   Conduct   for   the   CONNEX   initiative   states: (...) the objective of the initiative is to strengthen advisory support to low-income country governments in negotiation of complex commercial contracts – to make the support that is available more comprehensive and more responsive to government's needs and to contribute to fairer, more sustainable investment deals. This includes not only the provision of information and capacity building, but also the improvement of advisory services involved directly in contract negotiations.[23]

The CONNEX initiative is especially directed to natural resources.[24]

The CCSI has compiled a helpful database of significant negotiation support organizations, with background and contact information for each of the organizations listed.[25]

3.4.1.8   A country utilizing pro bono support—or even fee-based support when the fees are paid by others—needs to assure itself as to the quality of the expertise being provided, including that the donor organization's technical support provider is sufficiently experienced in the particular area where advice is being sought. For example, one would not expect to obtain top-level tax law advice from anyone other than a tax specialist, and thus a securities or contract lawyer should not be utilized to provide the level of technical tax support that might be sought. In addition, a country considering reliance on outside organizations for support should assure itself that the support needed will be timely, and sustained, throughout the negotiation process.[26]

---

[21] See http://negotiationsupport.org/.

[22] The Brussels G7 Summit Declaration, June 5, 2014. Available from http://europa.eu/rapid/press-release_MEMO-14-402_en.htm.

[23] See http://www.bmz.de/g7/includes/Downloadarchiv/150505_CONNEX_Code_of_Conduct_final.pdf.

[24] See http://www.bmz.de/g7/en/Entwicklungspolitische_Schwerpunkte/Connex/index.html.

[25] See http://negotiationsupport.org/providers for a list of specific organizations that provide support, together with the nature of such support, during the planning, preparation, negotiation, monitoring and implementation stages of natural resource projects.

[26] For a discussion of some of the issues countries should consider when relying on outside support organizations, see Federal Ministry for Economic Cooperation and Development, Natural Resource Contracts as a Tool for Managing the Mining Sector, 2015, pp. 54–56. Available at https://www.bmz.de/g7/includes/Downloadarchiv/Natural_Resource_Contracts.pdf.

3.4.2   Outside legal advisors

3.4.2.1   In addition to resources available through organizations such as the International Senior Lawyers Project,[27] and others included in the Negotiations Portal for Host Country Governments list of support organizations, some major law firms make their partners available from time to time to assist countries in negotiating activities. See the Liberia Renegotiation Report summary noting that certain law firms provided valuable assistance to the Liberian negotiating team.

3.4.3   Project forecast models

3.4.3.1   The International Monetary Fund (IMF) has developed and issued a Fiscal Analysis of Resource Industries (FARI) tool[28] which can model project level cash flows for both petroleum and mining projects. A technical explanation of the model is also available.[29] The FARI model has been successfully utilized in a number of Asian and African countries, and the IMF is available to consult and assist in the implementation in appropriate circumstances by longer-term FARI training for government officials, hands-on modelling workshops and remote assistance from Washington, D.C.

3.4.3.2   Other investment advisors with modelling capability can be accessed, and the Negotiations Portal for Host Country Governments' list of support organizations referenced above can be consulted for some of these additional providers.

3.4.3.3   As previously noted, economic modelling capability is crucial for governments. The benefits of contract/project-based economic models are summarized as follows:

Governments can use models to experiment with various policy options and measure their impact. They can use them to assess the impact of modification of fiscal terms proposed in contract negotiations in a range of alternative price, cost, and production level scenarios. Companies generally use economic models to assess natural resource tax regimes and for contract negotiation, and governments are at a serious disadvantage if they do not have the same tools at their disposal.[30]

3.4.4   Sample contracts

3.4.4.1   A number of sample contracts are available from various sources,

---

27 See http://islp.org/.

28 See http://www.imf.org/external/np/fad/fari/index.htm#2.

29 See http://www.imf.org/external/pubs/ft/tnm/2016/tnm1601.pdf.

30 Jack Calder, *Administering Fiscal Regimes for Extractive Industries: A Handbook* (Washington, D.C.: International Monetary Fund, 2014), p. 95: https://www.elibrary.imf.org/view/books/071/20884-9781475575170-en/20884-9781475575170-en-book.xml.

31 See http://www.eisourcebook.org/676_58ContractNegotiationsandDisputeSettlement.html.

including the Extractive Industries Source Book,[31] Open Oil,[32] and Resource Contracts.[33] As of 2013, Open Oil had suggested that either model or actual signed contracts were publicly available for Afghanistan, Angola, Azerbaijan, Bangladesh, Brazil, Burkina Faso, Cambodia, Colombia, Congo, Cyprus, the Democratic Republic of the Congo, Ecuador, Equatorial Guinea, Ethiopia, Ghana, India, Iraq, Jordan, Kenya, Liberia, Libya, Mauritania, Mexico, Mongolia, Mozambique, Nicaragua, Peru, Senegal, Sierra Leone, Timor-Leste, Trinidad and Tobago, Turkmenistan, Uganda and the United Republic of Tanzania.[34]

3.4.4.2   Sample mining agreements and models/examples of mining contract provisions are available under the Model Mining Development Agreement Project.[35]

3.4.4.3   In its directory of Petroleum and Mineral Contracts, Resource Contracts has at least one contract (model or actual) for 89 countries.[36]

3.5   NEGOTIATION BACKGROUND: INVESTOR PERSPECTIVES

3.5.1   Understanding country priorities

3.5.1.1   Just as it is important for a country to critically evaluate its priorities and key objectives in developing its resources, it is basic to a successful negotiation that the investor engages in ongoing dialogue with the country to ensure a full understanding of the country's goals. Ideally, the initial discussions can be at a high level where basic principles, objectives and obligations are articulated and debated. Seeking to understand the underlying interests that the parties have can often lead to solutions to problems that might otherwise appear to be intractable.[37]

---

[32] See http://repository.openoil.net/wiki/Downloads.

[33] See http://www.resourcecontracts.org/. In addition, over 40 Production Sharing Contracts entered into by the Kurdistan Regional Government are available from http://cabinet.gov.krd/p/p.aspx?l=12&p=1.

[34] See http://openoil.net/2013/10/07/openoil-is-looking-for-partners-to-analyse-oil-contracts-around-the-world/.

[35] See http://www.mmdaproject.org/.

[36] See http://www.resourcecontracts.org/.

[37] "Negotiators too often state their positions as opposed to their underlying interests. For example, an IMC [International Mining Company] will state that it will not pay income tax above a certain rate and it will not agree to a cap of deductible costs. Meanwhile the government will state that a large front-end payment is mandatory and that taxes are payable on the date of a commercial discovery. If they were talking about their respective interests, the IMC would explain that it needs a minimum Internal Rate of Return (IRR) on its capital to get approval from its Board of Directors, failing which its investment committee will not approve the project. The government would state that it needs income as fast as possible, or it could face mounting political pressures. When interests are clearly expressed, it is easier to see where the parties can compromise." Mining Contracts, pp. 184-185. See also chapter 3, "Focus on Interests, Not Positions," in Fisher and Ury, *Getting to Yes* (New York: Penguin books, 1983) pp. 41-57.

3.5.2   Look for long-term relationships

3.5.2.1   Investors will explain that one of their basic objectives is to develop a long-term, mutually beneficial relationship with the country. Agreements that are overly favourable to one side are not likely to be lasting ones and certainly will not operate to maximize the value of the resources to be developed. If overly favourable to the investor, the country will press to renegotiate or simply impose new terms. If overly favourable to the country, the investor will likely terminate the contract at the first opportunity, and development of the resource itself may be jeopardized. Agreements that provide a balance of interests, and which provide some degree of flexibility in case of material and substantial changes in circumstances, can create an underlying contractual structure most supportive of a successful long-term partnership.

3.5.3   Articulation of investor needs and investor risks[38]

3.5.3.1   The extractives industries are unique in many ways. The sector is shaped by high sunk costs in the form of substantial investments that often cannot be recouped if a project is unsuccessful; long lead times from initial investment to project start-up; fluctuating costs and prices that in turn influence the profitability of exploration, development and extraction; volatile demand; very long production/project lives; and substantially greater environmental and social impacts to address, including ultimately decommissioning or reclamation responsibilities.[39]

3.5.3.2   An investor committing to the substantial outlays required for these investments will look for a satisfactory return, taking into account all of the risks

---

[38] For a more complete list of the risk factors investors face, see Table 1.4, "Categories of risk facing an energy investment project," International Energy Agency, World Energy Investment Outlook 2014, p. 32. Available at https://www.iea.org/publications/freepublications/publication/WEIO2014.pdf.

[39] It is important to assess the risks at the time they are undertaken. A simple example illustrates this point. Assume A offers to sell to B a right to receive $1000 if B can toss a coin and get heads 5 times in a row. The odds of this occurring are 1 in 32 (i.e., 0.55). The risk-weighted value of this is 1/32 x $1000 or just over $31. This is therefore what A can expect B to pay for this contract right. Suppose after B has obtained 4 heads in a row, it wishes to "cash out" and offers to sell its rights to C. The odds at this point of realizing the $1000 payment have increased from 1/32 to one in two, and the value of the "contract" has increased from $31 to $500. To say that B is being "overcompensated" since he paid only $31 for the contract rights, which now have a $500 value, is simply not correct since it ignores all of the risks taken by B up to that point. A was fairly compensated for its sale and B is now fairly compensated as well. One can change this example to add a feature to the original contract such that, in the event B does obtain 5 heads in a row, in addition to the $1000 it will receive, it will have a chance to receive an additional $10,000 by rolling a dice and it coming up as a 6. The odds of getting the additional $10,000 at the outset are 1/192 (1/32 x 1/6). The additional price B would pay A for this significant "upside," at the outset, would be $52. But after B had achieved four heads in a row, the odds of the significant upside became 1/12, with an expected value of $833. This latter example could be viewed as similar to a case where an unexpected, or low probability but sustained upside in resource prices occurs well after the original contract date. The underlying economics of the contract would have built this into the original expected value (as well as offsetting unexpected downsides).

the investor bears. This is one reason why it is difficult to compare fiscal regimes and general return levels across countries, since the degree of geologic, political and economic risks varies from country to country and even project to project.

3.5.3.3   One key consideration that can benefit a country in its negotiations is that the more a country can reduce investor risks, the lower the return the investor will need, and hence the more it will be willing to pay. Investors themselves further seek to reduce risks given the large and usually upfront amounts they make, and hence generally see benefits in stability and predictability of laws and fiscal arrangements.

3.5.3.4   It is important to recognize the balance between t risk and reward. If a resource state can help reduce the investor's perception of risk they should be prepared to give a bigger share of the reward. Offering a stable, consistent and predictable tax environment, with a fair, transparent, timely and reliable appeals process is very valuable to investors. Public sector negotiators who can convince the investor that such a regime is available will be able to achieve a higher government take.[40]

3.5.4   Stability or fiscal stabilization clauses[41]

3.5.4.1   Investors frequently seek provisions in contracts that operate to limit the changes that can be made over time, most especially to the fiscal terms. This is because the projects generally involve substantial upfront capital and the project lives are expected to last for long periods. As noted, investors seek to reduce risks as much as possible, and given that government policies and officials will almost certainly change over time, a way to provide some degree of stability against such changes is often sought. "Stability" or "stabilization" provisions are common in natural resource contracts and are one of the mechanisms used to reduce political and legislative risks.

3.5.4.2   Stabilization clauses have themselves evolved over time. Most of

---

[40] Bill Page, *Petroleum Tax Administration in EAC Countries: A Private Sector Perspective.* Paper presented at Fiscal Management of Oil and Natural Gas in East Africa—East African Community and International Monetary Fund Workshop, 15–17 January 2014, Arusha, Tanzania.
    Workshop materials available at https://www.imf.org/external/np/seminars/eng/2014/eac/pdf/031514.pdf, pp. 132, 137.

[41] A number of helpful articles and sources deal with stability clauses and related issues. For example, see Michael Polkinghorn, *Stabilization Clauses And Periodic Review Outline,* available at http://www.energycharter.org/fileadmin/DocumentsMedia/Events/CCNG_2015_Michael_Polkinghorne.pdf; Carole Nahkle, *Fiscal Stabilization in Oil and Gas Contracts – Evidence and Implications,* available at https://www.oxfordenergy.org/publications/fiscal-stabilization-in-oil-and-gas-contracts-evidence-and-implications/; Oyewunmi, Tade, *Stabilisation and Renegotiation Clauses in Production Sharing Contracts: Examining the Problems and Key Issues* (2011). Oil, Gas & Energy Law Intelligence Journal (OGEL) 2011, Vol. 9 - issue 6 pg. 1–25. Available at SSRN: https://ssrn.com/abstract=2776677; and Philip Daniel and Emil M. Sunley, "Contractual assurances of fiscal stability," in *The Taxation of Petroleum and Minerals: Principles, Problems and Practice,* eds. Philip Daniel, Michael Keen and Charles McPherson (New York: Routledge, 2010) p.405.

the early clauses generally froze the important aspects of the fiscal and legal regime applicable to the particular project to what was, in effect, the contract that was agreed upon at the time. This provided investors with a higher degree of confidence that the important fiscal and other legal provisions upon which their economics were based would last throughout the project. A criticism of such "freezing" clauses is that they infringed on a country's sovereignty to change its laws over time. However, stabilization provisions simply provide that any changes in law with respect to stabilized clauses will not be applicable to the relevant Project. Other provisions provided a contractual right to the investors that, should such changes be made, a contractual payment for "damages" would be due.

3.5.4.3   Nevertheless, clauses have generally evolved from the "freezing" type of provisions to ones with more of an economic equivalence approach. Accordingly, many clauses now provide that should certain governmental changes occur (e.g., an increase in the tax rate) the parties agree to negotiate changes to the contract to place the investor back in the general economic position it would have experienced had the particular change in law not occurred. If the parties cannot successfully negotiate a change in the overall contract, in certain circumstances an investor may nevertheless be able to seek compensation based on the economic equivalence provision. See also Chapter 5 which discusses stabilization clauses in the context of tax incentives.

3.5.4.4   In some cases, the law itself can actually contain stability related provisions. For example, in South Africa fiscal stability is viewed as an important tool in facilitating future oil and gas investment. Current income tax law grants the Minister of Finance the power to enter into binding fiscal stability agreements with oil and gas companies. The predetermined terms were developed in a legislative process which allowed all interested parties to provide input and comments. This included presentations to the Parliamentary Committee on Finance which required written responses by the National Treasury.

3.5.4.5   A fiscal stability agreement concluded between the South African Minister of Finance and an oil and gas company in respect of an oil and gas right guarantees that the provisions of the Tenth Schedule to the Income Tax Act of 1962,[42] on the date of conclusion of the agreement, will continue to apply to the

---

[42] The fiscal stability provisions set out in paragraph 8 of the Tenth Schedule to the South African Income Tax Act of 1962 are as follows:
FISCAL STABILITY
    8. (1) (a) The Minister may enter into a binding agreement with any oil and gas company in respect of an oil and gas right held by that company, and that agreement so entered into must guarantee that the provisions of this Schedule (as at the date on which the agreement was concluded) apply in respect of that right as long as the right is held by the oil and gas company.
    (2) (a) In the case of a disposal of an exploration right (···) an oil and gas company that has concluded an agreement as contemplated in subparagraph (1) in respect of that right may (···) assign all of its fiscal stability rights in terms of that agreement relating to the exploration right disposed of to any other oil and gas company.
        (b) In the case of a disposal of a production right (···) an oil and gas company that has concluded an agreement as contemplated in subparagraph (1) in respect of that right disposed

oil and gas right as long as the right is held by the oil and gas company. However, an oil and gas company may unilaterally terminate the agreement if so desired. The reason for termination could be that subsequent tax changes are more tax-payer favourable than the tax rates, deductions and rules applying to the disposal of oil and gas rights, provided for in the Tenth Schedule on the date of conclusion of the agreement.

3.5.4.6   It is likely that an investor will seek some form of a stabilization agreement, and each country must decide whether, and the degree to which, it is willing to provide such stability. South Africa and the Netherlands[43] provide some aspects of stability by means of statutory provisions. When implemented on a negotiated contract basis, the trend appears to be towards using economic equivalence types of provisions requiring a good faith negotiation between the parties.

3.5.4.7   One other important technique that provides stability with respect to income- or profits-based taxes is a "pay-on-behalf" approach. Egypt provides a clear example of this since, under its production sharing contract (PSC) provisions, the governmental entity that is a party to the PSC makes income tax payments to the Government on behalf of the contractor.[44] The contractor, however, is still subject to Egyptian income tax and continues to file its own tax return. Under the "pay-on-behalf" approach, the Government effectively withholds amounts due to the contractor equal to the contractor's tax liability and remits such amounts to the Government, since these amounts are treated as additional taxable income to the contractor that must be reported on its Egyptian income tax return. Nevertheless, this contractual approach effectively insulates the investor from changes in the income tax laws with respect to the project.[45] Further infor-

---

of may (···) assign all its fiscal stability rights in terms of that agreement relating to the production right disposed of to another company if that other company is a company within the same group of companies as the oil and gas company transferring the fiscal stability right at the time the agreement is concluded.

(3) An oil and gas company that has concluded an agreement contemplated in subparagraph (1) in respect of an oil and gas right may at any time unilaterally terminate the agreement in respect of that oil and gas right so held with effect from the commencement of the year of assessment immediately following the notification date of the termination.

(4) If the State fails to comply with the terms of the agreement contemplated in subparagraph (1) and that failure has a material adverse economic impact on the taxation of income or profits of the oil and gas company that is party to that agreement, that oil and gas company is entitled to compensation for the loss of market value caused by that failure (and interest at the prescribed rate calculated on the compensation from the date of non-compliance) or to an alternative remedy that otherwise eliminates the full impact of that failure.

[43] See article 55 of the Netherlands Mining Act.

[44] Egypt enacts into law each production sharing agreement, and thus the entire contract has the force of law and cannot be changed except with the approval of the Minister of Petroleum and the Parliament. See "Production Sharing Agreements: An Overview," on the Egypt Oil and Gas Web Portal (March 2015) available from http://www.egyptoil-gas.com/publications/production-sharing-agreements-overview/.

[45] Ernst and Young, *Global Oil and Gas Tax Guide*, (2015). Available at http://www.ey.com/Publication/vwLUAssets/EY-2015-Global-oil-and-gas-tax-guide/$FILE/EY-2015-Global-oil-and-gas-tax-guide.pdf. See also *Understanding Egypt: Production Sharing Contracts and Tax Barrels,*

mation on PSCs is set out in Chapter 4.

3.5.4.8   As noted, contractual stabilization provisions have to be evaluated in terms of their relationship with general statutory rules in existence or enacted later. The effect of such stabilization provisions may generally be more effective and more supportable as they apply to fiscal terms, versus human rights or other social issues, since they do not have to override the law (i.e., payments to the government can be made consistent with new rules followed by a contractual "reimbursement").

3.5.4.9   Stabilization rules that apply to other conduct may not be as easily addressed, although in theory a monetary cost of the new rules or standards compared with those in effect at the date of the contract could be calculated, and thus compliance with the new standards would be achieved, but monetary offsets would be contractually provided, just as in the fiscal term example above. Nevertheless, many countries restrict the scope of stabilization provisions to fiscal matters, to avoid any concerns about their ability to change non-fiscal-related rules, and/or limit their duration.

3.5.4.10   In administering stabilization provisions, it will be necessary to clearly understand how the parties view their operation in practice. For example, if the negotiators view the tax rules in effect at the time of the contract to be the ones that will govern actual payments to the government over the life of the project, this can place the tax administration in a clear conflict position. The legal standing of stability agreements is critical. If the contract does not have the force of law in the country (sufficient to override other conflicting tax laws) tax administrators will naturally seek to impose the tax law rather than the tax rules under the stability agreement.

3.5.4.11   The negotiators—on both sides—need to understand that they may not be able to "compel" this result, unless stabilization is specifically allowed e.g., under the constitution or other governing laws; and in such cases, should mutually agree that they will address the financial impact of the changes by means of a contractual adjustment.[46] It is also important to clarify within the stabilization provisions what exactly is being stabilized. Any ambiguity around the scope of stabilization (e.g., whether only the rate of a certain category of tax is being stabilized, or the whole regime) will lead to difficulties in the operation of such clauses in practice. In some cases, there could be a need for a clear process to be put in place to transparently address issues, if for instance the tax law and regulations were silent on a specific point at the time the agreement was approved and ratified.

3.5.4.12   Finally, if the stabilization provision operates to actually change or fix

---

Apache Corporation (2014), available at http://files.shareholder.com/downloads/APA/0x0x728759/af4015b8-478d-4506-a57c-7558d74b1a0a/Apache_Understanding_Egypt_20140226.pdf.

46 Complicating this even further, of course, is the tax treatment of such an adjustment. If taxable itself under the country laws, the amount of the adjustment should be clarified as to whether it is to be "before" or "after" any country tax due.

the law with respect to the project, the country will need to understand whether this may trigger "non-discrimination" provisions elsewhere in the country's laws or treaties.

3.5.5   Parties involved from an investor standpoint

3.5.5.1   In the mining industry, typically one investor is involved, while in the oil and gas industry it is common to have joint ventures, where several companies participate. Where multiple investors are involved, they will usually nominate one as the lead negotiator, but all major participants are generally present, and even with those not present, or with other members of their teams, there is frequent and detailed consultation and communication. Whether one or multiple investors, the investor team will typically be led by their exploration and/or project development personnel, and will be supported by geologists, engineers, and other technical personnel. Other key participants will include financial (including tax) and legal representatives of the investor(s) both in-house and, often, outside advisors. Other support personnel (e.g., government and public affairs, health, safety, and environmental, or marketing groups) may be either included on the teams or consulted with on a regular basis.

3.5.5.2   Prior to and during negotiations, project planning (reserves, mining/ drilling plans, infrastructure needs, etc.) and financial (costs, prices, markets, etc.) assumptions will be modelled and project economics will be developed on the basis of a number of scenarios. As negotiations proceed, investors generally rerun models as new information becomes available or assumptions change. These economic evaluations, along with overall strategic and business judgment, are used to assist in the negotiations and in the ultimate determination of whether the investor will agree to undertake a particular project. Typically, investors have multiple investment opportunities and must evaluate each one on its own risk and return levels as well as in comparison with the other competing projects being considered.

3.5.5.3   Given the usually large commitments that are at stake, it is not uncommon for companies to use outside consultants to assist on a number of issues prior to and during the negotiations. This can be viewed as placing the country negotiators at a "knowledge" disadvantage, and approaches to dealing with this are suggested above, in the section on negotiation background.

3.6   INVESTMENT PHASES

3.6.1   Exploration

3.6.1.1   In the exploration phase, minerals or oil and gas will generally be sought out by reconnaissance and seismic surveys. Contracts covering exploration will generally provide for a certain workplan, over a certain time frame and geographic area. The contractor will generally have the right to exploit the resource, if found in commercial quantities, subject to submission and approval of a development plan.

3.6.2   Development

3.6.2.1   After a feasibility study following exploration efforts, a development plan will generally be proposed and relevant government approvals will be required. In a contractual arrangement, the actual terms (including fiscal terms) may be negotiated in a context where the investor sets forth what it believes will be necessary for a commercial project to be viable, and the government will seek to maximize its benefits, consistent with a project going forward.

3.6.2.2   If there is the opportunity to negotiate a lower tax or royalty rate or any other payment to government, any rational company would take it. If there is an argument that the proposed arrangements in the model agreement are uneconomic, then a company would not be irrational to negotiate terms that made the mine or hydrocarbon field economic under even the worst scenarios. However, a forward-looking investor might be cautious about signing a deal that is "too good to be true," anticipating government dissatisfaction and potential conflict down the road. The company will want to make sure its operation is still sufficiently profitable to compete with other similar projects worldwide on an after tax basis.

3.6.2.3   The government will, in turn, want to be sure of some things as well. Its job is to maximize the total net benefit to the country. This needs to take into account the costs as well as the benefits of mining, and sustainability of the economy and community, for the long term.[47]

3.6.3   Production/operations

3.6.3.1   Once the facilities have been constructed or developed, including production, processing, and other infrastructure requirements, production operations will begin and production levels will be ramped up until production amounts set forth in the development plan are achieved (or levels are readjusted based on further agreement). The contract may call for some levels of minimum production to be required.

3.6.4   Expansions

3.6.4.1   Project expansions may be either envisioned in the contract itself, such as development in prescribed phases, or may be acknowledged as possibilities in the contract, and subject to approvals and possible expansion plan negotiations. Even where expansions have been envisioned, and where the expansion development plans have been set forth, it is possible that terms may need to be renegotiated to take into account new circumstances. These may include situations which either make a possible expansion uneconomic—such that it will not occur without modification—or make the terms to government unacceptable,

---

[47] Mining Contracts, p. 50.

given changes in assumptions upon which the original terms were set.

3.6.5 End of project obligations

3.6.5.1   The contract will also need to address the obligations of the contracting parties upon termination of the project. It is standard practice for contracts to require contractors—once mining or petroleum operations are no longer economic—to restore the affected properties to a suitable condition.

3.6.5.2   Such obligations could include removing production and processing structures and equipment and restoring the production site to an environmentally and ecologically stable and acceptable state. The general requirements for this "decommissioning" are typically covered in the contract (or licensing) terms. See further Chapter 14 (the Tax Treatment of Decommissioning).

3.7   SOME PRACTICAL ASPECTS OF SUCCESSFUL NEGOTIATION [48]

3.7.1   Practical considerations

3.7.1.1   Preparing for negotiations is a time-consuming process. Getting the negotiating process right is also time consuming. Both are essential, however, if the result is to be constructive.[49]

3.7.1.2   The following is a brief summary of some major practical considerations that can help achieve success:

- Prepare and develop policy objectives before negotiations commence;

- Consider the long-term relationship and seek a result that is positive for the government, the community and the investor;

- Prepare by understanding the value of the resource and the economic development goals, including revenues, employment, infrastructure, downstream opportunities, local content, environmental stewardship, education and training;

- Build a negotiating team with interdepartmental representation and strong communication and decision-making protocols and experience in the relevant region;

- Carefully design mechanisms to ensure public outreach and involvement;

---

[48] For additional background on this section, see the IISD Handbook, Parts 3 and 4, pp. 19–56.

[49] Ibid, p. 56.

- Understand investor needs and objectives in order to identify and negotiate upon common interests;

- Obtain agreement on how to negotiate (place, language, timing, duration);

- Obtain agreement on what to negotiate (overall and in each session);

- Stay focused on objectives and avoid distractions;

- Develop strong team leadership and team discipline;

- Have political support for the negotiating team, including the ability to discontinue negotiations;

- Provide for public information and for community development agreement; and

- Assume transparency of the ultimate contract as a means of ensuring community support and a long-term relationship focus.

3.8   OTHER CONTRACT NEGOTIATION ISSUES

3.8.1   Due diligence in pre-negotiation research

3.8.1.1   Before any negotiations begin, both the investor and the government will do research on one another, with the investor seeking to understand the goals and backgrounds of the governmental negotiators and information about the country, and countries equally seeking to understand the nature of the potential investor and its negotiators.

3.8.1.2   The term "due diligence" generally refers to an investigation carried out by a party to learn and verify the full background, history and current situation of the other party(ies) with which it may contract. Due diligence takes time and is expensive, but thorough due diligence will prevent and/or mitigate unwelcome surprises down the road. It is an essential tool in the decision-making process of any investor, financial institution or government.

3.8.1.3   Potential investors will do due diligence on governments, to ascertain the stability of the government, and its political institutions, to determine the political and economic risk of doing business in the country. Investors will also look at the stability and independence of the judicial system, the economic (debt) situation, the electoral situation, the human rights situation, and any other issues that could affect the profitability of an investment and the reputation of the investor.

3.8.1.4   Governments should do similar due diligence of potential investors to ascertain financial stability, expertise, experience, track record on environmental and human rights practices, history of disputes and the like. Not all investors are equal. A government may do much less due diligence on a well-known international company with public financial statements and a long track record than it would on a privately held company that is less established.

3.8.1.5   The manual *Mining Contracts: how to read and understand* them notes that "…investigators will look for potential risks which could affect the company's ability to perform its obligations, such as the company's financial capacity to fund the mining project, its level of expertise and experience and its capacity to reimburse financing. Red flag items could be large unfunded reserves for potential losses, outstanding mass litigation such as asbestos or other product liability issues, ongoing criminal investigations concerning corruption, money laundering or other alleged crimes, allegations of human rights abuses or environmental neglect, and other reputational, financial or legal issues. If a red flag issue is identified, permission will often be requested to interview the company management, auditors and lawyers."[50]

3.8.1.6   The fiscal system of the country where the investor is located can have an impact on its negotiation positions. For example, companies resident in a country where relief from double taxation is granted by means of a foreign tax credit may have requirements, e.g., fiscal periods for which relief is available that are different from those of companies resident in a country operating an exemption system. The investor's head office country of residence also determines whether such a company is able to claim the benefits of a treaty concluded between the country of source of income and the country of residence.

3.8.1.7   Different tax treaty applicability can affect the relative positions of various investors. Tax treaties will also impact the government's fiscal take, for example from withholding tax rates on dividends, interest and royalties. This should be taken into account in the value assessment from the government's perspective. Finally, even greater differences may apply in the case of a state-owned investor competing against a private investor. Thus, based on these and other considerations, the economics of a transaction may look quite different as between potential investors.

3.8.1.8   A final aspect of due diligence is understanding the nature of the contracting parties. The contracting party on the investor side may be a subsidiary of an investor incorporated in the host country, or of a company incorporated elsewhere and doing business in the host country via a branch. The country should seek to understand the nature of the investor, and the entire ownership chain leading to the ultimate owner(s). This is particularly important when some type of performance guarantee may be required by the country from a company higher up in the chain of ownership. Investors will want to understand who the contracting party will be on behalf of the country, i.e., is it a Ministry of the country, a

---

[50] Mining Contracts, pp. 179–80; see Footnote 4 above.

government-owned natural resources company, or a combination of both?

3.8.2   Transparency

3.8.2.1   In countries that specify their natural resource rules by statute (e.g., the United States of America with respect to federal lands) the terms governing natural resource exploration and development are specified in law and regulations available to all, and successful bids are public. In these regimes, transparency regarding contract terms is complete, and applicable to all investors.

3.8.2.2   In countries that licence resources via private negotiations, the rules vary. In some countries, the law requires negotiated contracts to be approved by a legislative body, and hence the contract is generally, though not always, publicly available. In other countries, the law requires that contracts (even if not subject to legislative approval) need to be made public as well.

3.8.2.3   However, some countries do not have requirements to make contracts available to the public, and while some may be, or become, public, this outcome cannot be relied upon. In some cases, the contracts are explicitly confidential and terms are not generally available to the public.

3.8.2.4   Increasingly there is a movement to publicize contracts. Organizations such as the IMF, World Bank, Organisation for Economic Co-operation and Development and the Extractive Industries Transparency Initiative generally agree that a best practice in promoting overall transparency, is that final contracts relating to the extractive industries should be made publicly available.[51] This is in addition to publishing financial information and payments made under the relevant contracts.

3.8.2.5   As noted earlier, a country will generally want to involve, via consultation at a minimum, outside groups at various stages of the negotiation process. This is an important element in obtaining support for the process and the ultimate contract award, and ultimately can be viewed as increasing the overall "stability" of the contract itself.

3.8.2.6   Contracts negotiated by the Government often have a tremendous impact on the lives of communities affected by the operation of these agreements. In many developing countries, concession agreements also have nation-wide economic and social implications and can even affect state security. The Liberian Renegotiation Report notes that: "...Recognizing the impact of these concession agreements on Liberia, the Government committed to transparency by making the ArcelorMittal and Firestone agreements public documents. Contract transparency is in the best interest of the government, private investors and citizens. The disclosure of contracts expresses the public ownership of the exploited natural resources. Transparency also ensures that expectations from communities

---

[51]   See http://www.resourcegovernance.org/blog/takeaways-eiti-2016-contract-transparency-becoming-norm.

affected by the contracts are managed and realistic. Public disclosure of the terms of concession agreements provides a safeguard for private investors to ensure contract stability and avoid abuse in contract implementation."[52]

3.8.2.7   Investors may prefer confidentiality to protect proprietary and competitive information and it is likely to streamline the process of finalizing an agreement, but their main objective appears to be that the rules be applied uniformly. Thus, rules that may apply only to certain types of investors (e.g., publicly traded companies) and thus treat competitors differently, can inappropriately provide a competitive advantage to some at the expense of others.

3.8.3   Dispute resolution under a specific contract[53]

3.8.3.1   Given the number of issues that can arise under natural resource contracts, and the long timeframes of the projects governed by such contracts, it is almost certain that disagreements on both the meaning of the contract terms and the compliance with the contract obligations (by either party) will arise. The contract itself generally provides mechanisms for resolving such disputes, with the ultimate resolution mechanism usually being litigation. However, there are often several steps that may be followed in resolving disputes other than by going to court:

(i)   Seeking to settle the dispute among the parties themselves;

(ii)   Referring to the issue to a technical expert, whose conclusion may be binding or simply advisory;

(iii)   Referring to the issue for mediation (usually non-binding) - ideally, contracts should provide a strong incentive for governments and investors to act promptly to resolve disputes bearing in mind that all parties are working together to lay the foundation for a stable agreement that is beneficial to all parties; and

(iv)   Referring to the issue for arbitration (which may be binding or non-binding).

3.8.3.2   In the context of reducing risks, investors often seek, as the ultimate dispute resolution mechanism, a binding arbitration approach under international arbitration rules.[54] A number of different international arbitration rules exist,

---

[52] Liberian Renegotiation Report, p. 62.

[53] Generally, a country will have established resolution procedures for tax disputes under its laws. However, a negotiated contract may provide mechanisms to resolve other disputes that may arise in the interpretation of that contract. Where such contractual dispute resolution procedures cover items that are otherwise covered in a country's statutes, they raise the same issues as discussed earlier with respect to possible conflicts which need to be clearly understood and addressed.

[54] "Whilst host country citizens may find the suggestion that their courts are not impartial or fair somewhat insulting, the reality is that in many jurisdictions the court process may not be

under the auspices of various international arbitration organizations, such as the United Nations Commission on International Trade Law (UNCITRAL), the London Court of International Arbitration, the International Chamber of Commerce, and the International Centre for Settlement of Investment Disputes.

3.8.3.3   It is important to note that even where international arbitration is invoked, and even if it is conducted outside the resource country, the governing substantive law under which the contract is to be interpreted, and which the arbitrators must apply, is most often the law of the resource country.

3.8.3.4   Where arbitration is not binding, the ultimate step for dispute resolution remains litigation, and generally under the courts of the resource country or a country agreed upon by the parties which otherwise may have jurisdictional rights.

3.8.3.5   Dispute resolution that extends beyond the parties themselves tends to be expensive and time consuming. Each party takes the "dispute resolution risk" regarding the ultimate outcome. Hence, by far the preferred dispute resolution mechanism is for the parties to settle the issue or issues via mutual agreement.

3.8.4   Applicable law—domestic and international agreements

3.8.4.1   Whether in arbitration or litigation, the law to be applied in resolving a particular conflict is most often the law of the resource country.[55] But the laws of the resource country, may also include a provision to apply bilateral or multilateral tax and/or investment treaties. How such treaties interact with the other laws of the country can be very important, since they can in effect limit or even override what otherwise is the domestic law. There may be other considerations in addition to specific laws, including any constitutional provisions and other statutory or similar laws applicable to the investor(s) and project operations.

3.8.4.2   Further, in the negotiation of such tax or investment treaties, just as in the negotiation of resource contracts, again all affected departments within the government should be involved to avoid overriding domestic law without full consideration of the consequences. In some cases, it has been noted that those negotiating investment treaties have sought to use that mechanism to alter tax laws (including tax treaties) and practices, contrary to the policies and positions of the tax administrations. One example of this is where tax disputes are to be resolved by administrative review, and ultimately litigation, under domestic law,

---

independent, or may be slow, and international investors generally···prefer not to take that risk." Oil Contracts, p. 183.

[55] In purely contractual arrangements, it may be possible for the contract rights to be adjudicated based on laws other than those of the resource country, assuming all parties agree. Further, it would be possible, in an agreement with the country and ratified or passed by the body that has legal authority to make law within the country, to adopt laws governing the particular contract arrangement based on laws of other countries.

but an international investment treaty changes this to an arbitration approach.

3.8.4.3   An excerpt from a relevant Parliamentary Briefing from the Natural Resource Governance Institute is extracted below.

3.9   ACHIEVING A GOOD DEAL: FISCAL REGIMES FOR OIL, GAS AND MINING[56]

3.9.1   Goals in designing a fiscal regime

3.9.1.1   When designing or assessing fiscal regimes for oil, gas, and mining, government officials should take into account the following goals:

- **Fiscal regimes need to create sufficient incentives for private companies to invest.** Extractive projects have large upfront exploration and development costs and long production timelines. The fiscal regime must assure companies that the rules will not be unduly changed once investments are made. Stable fiscal regimes that provide a fair return to both investors and the state[57] under a variety of circumstances will be less likely to attract pressure for renegotiation.

- **Fiscal regimes should divide risk appropriately between the investor and the state.** Uncertainty is inherent in the extractive sector. The fiscal regime should ensure that the state does not end up bearing a share of risk disproportionate to its expected return.

- **The state should be compensated for the loss of resources, regardless of the profitability of a given operation.** This is because oil, gas and mineral resources are finite. Fiscal instruments such as baseline royalties provide a guaranteed return for the state even if a project runs losses.

- **Fiscal regimes should be progressive.** Extractive projects can generate substantial rents. Rents (sometimes called "windfalls") are the financial returns above those a company requires to make the investment profitable. Mechanisms to measure and tax a share of windfalls can enhance state returns in times of high profits and adjust to allow for adequate company returns during times of low profits.

---

[56] Natural Resource Governance Institute, Parliamentary Briefing. Available at: http://www.resourcegovernance.org/sites/default/files/nrgi_FiscalRegime_20150311.pdf, 2015.

[57] For clarity purposes, note that references in this document to "state" are to the overall country involved rather than to any regional or local subdivision.

- **Countries should set fiscal instruments through laws rather than individual contracts.** Negotiated rather than standardized fiscal regimes are prevalent in the extractive sector. Setting fiscal regimes through laws increases transparency and accountability, because contracts are more likely to be kept secret. Also, negotiations bring additional opportunities for corruption or manipulation. Additionally, if the applicable fiscal regime varies from contract to contract, it can make monitoring onerous and frustrate the efforts of policymakers to carry out policy reforms.

- **Transparency and consistency can help strengthen the state's position.** The extractive industries are characterized by significant asymmetries between states and private actors. Companies often have more information about the specific parameters of extractive projects and are more sophisticated in tax planning, which can give them the upper hand in negotiations.

3.10   CONTRACT RENEGOTIATION ISSUES

3.10.1   Background

3.10.1.1   Ideally, contract or licensing rules applicable to long-term natural resource projects will be flexible enough to "self-adjust" as circumstances change.[58] For example, in times of increased prices, fiscal terms that automatically adjust the amount of government take per a prescribed formula can ensure that a fair revenue sharing occurs, even as total revenues increase. Conversely, in times of very low prices or increased costs, ideally the terms will adjust to promote continued operation of the project rather than making it even less economical. Thinking through items (or assumptions) that may change significantly over time and providing flexibility in the design of contract terms (such that potential changes may automatically be accounted for in the contract) can obviate the need for a "renegotiation" to occur.

3.10.1.2   Prior sections noted the use of stability clauses to address law or government policy changes. The more modern stability clauses call for the parties to enter into good faith negotiations to place the investor in a similar economic position as if the rules had not changed. This can be viewed as a means of acknowledging the right of the government to change its laws over time, while still protecting the economic interests of the investor and reducing its risks. This also, however, provides an obligation in effect to renegotiate terms in good faith.

3.10.1.3   In addition to renegotiations that may be implicated as a result of

---

[58] As noted, in addition to those providing for self-adjustment mechanisms, agreements that from the outset also reflect a fair balance of interests are less likely to generate a need for renegotiation.

stability clauses, contracts also may have particular renegotiation clauses that can be invoked under circumstances specifically or more generally described in the clause. For example, an exploration and development agreement that covers oil may sometimes not cover natural gas, and thus may explicitly require that in the event that commercial quantities of natural gas are found, a new negotiation will take place regarding the terms of its development. More generally, some contracts may provide for "re-opening" certain provisions in the event of exceptional, unforeseeable or profound changes in circumstances.

3.10.1.4 To illustrate the above, an oil contract from Liberia provides:

"The State and the Contractor shall meet if the State or the Contractor gives at least forty-five (45) days' Notice to the other that it reasonably considers a Profound Change in Circumstances to have occurred. At the meeting, the State and the Contractor shall review the relevant facts and circumstances and determine whether or not a Profound Change in Circumstances has occurred. To the extent that a Profound Change in Circumstances has occurred, the State and the Contractor shall enter into good faith discussions to consider and shall make such modifications to this Contract as they may through good faith discussions propose as necessary or appropriate to restore the economic, fiscal and financial balance of the Contract."[59]

3.10.1.5   Increasingly, clauses explicitly recognizing the right to renegotiate contracts have become more common. Given the long-term nature and complexity of issues involved in these contracts, it is highly likely that significant changes in circumstances will occur sometime during their existence. Assuming adjustments have not been built into the contract to cover these particular changes, the parties can address these in a number of ways:

(i)   The investor or the government can argue that a contract must be complied with, and the other party (the one seeking a modification) has no recourse but to abide by the original contract terms;

(ii)   The government (but not the investor) can impose changes on a take-it-or-leave-it basis, which, in the worst-case scenario, can lead to an expropriation if the investor does not agree; or

(iii)   The parties can come together, recognize that under certain circumstances some modifications to the original contract may be appropriate, and negotiate in good faith to achieve an agreed solution.

3.10.1.6   Obviously, the third scenario is best in terms of achieving an ongoing, mutually beneficial relationship. But political changes, public perception

---

[59] Jacky Mandelbaum, Salli Anne Swartz and John Hauert, *Periodic review in natural resource contracts*, Columbia Center for Sustainable Investment Briefing Note 1, June 2014, p.10. Available at http://ccsi.columbia.edu/files/2014/08/Periodic-review-in-natural-resource-contracts-Briefing-Note-FINAL-8.11.pdf.

pressures, or even prior history can force an outcome under the first and second scenarios above. Special circumstances calling for renegotiation of contracts can occur in post-conflict situations, where of course the nature and level of risks accepted at the time of the original agreement have changed substantially.[60]

3.10.1.7   The consequences of the first scenario are obviously not helpful to a long-term, sustained relationship. What may be an advantage taken by one party (e.g., where the investor fails to work with the government in times of unexpectedly favourable conditions) can later become a disadvantage (e.g., where costs rise or prices drop for a prolonged period) and there will be little "sympathy" given the prior position taken.

3.10.1.8   Where the government has the upper hand, choosing either the first or second scenario can lead to an outcome where the resource becomes unproductive, with the result that the project is either mothballed or terminated prematurely. For example, where conditions change to the detriment of the investor, such as a long-term decrease in prices or highly escalating costs of meeting commitments, it may seek some relief from the government.[61] Where relief is not provided, the investor will nevertheless be obligated to fulfil its contract terms. However, if the project is in its early stages, one could expect the investor to do the minimum required under the project terms, or even exercise a contract right to terminate. This may not be in the best interests of either party, and hence it is usually better to find some way to make adjustments—as long as they are reasonable and balanced. An investor requesting a delay in meeting drilling commitments (to mitigate a spike in drilling costs) could perhaps be granted that by the government in return for a small delay payment. Thus, a true negotiation, with each side giving and getting something, takes place.

3.10.1.9   On the other hand, when the government approaches an investor to renegotiate contract terms, the investor who is likewise interested in promoting and growing a long-term relationship, should be open to a negotiation where each side gives and receives something. For example, an investor might agree on the renegotiation of a particular fiscal term sought by the government in return for a modification to the duration of the contract.

3.10.2   Case studies[62]

Case A.

---

[60] Phillippe Le Billon, "Contract renegotiation and asset recovery in post-conflict settings," in *High-Value Natural Resources and Peacebuilding*, eds. P. Lujala and S. A. Rustad (London: Earthscan, 2012). Available at https://environmentalpeacebuilding.org/assets/Documents/Library-Item_000_Doc_087.pdf.

[61] It is not only countries that desire to renegotiate contracts; investors sometimes also seek modifications.

[62] Case A is based upon Liberia's post-conflict contract renegotiations. Cases B, C, and D are not country specific, but reflect factual elements in each case that were present in several countries.

3.10.2.1   As referenced earlier in this note, extensive analysis has been done of Liberia's renegotiation of a number of resource contracts following the end of the civil war in 2003. Following her government coming to power in 2006, President Ellen Johnson Sirleaf ordered a review of all concession agreements, with priority given to the two largest, one with ArcelorMittal and the other with Firestone.[63]

3.10.2.2   When approached pragmatically, contract reviews and concession negotiation can benefit both government and industry. The amended Liberian contracts offer significant gains for the state and for the communities where Firestone and ArcelorMittal operate. The new agreements also pose no threat to the companies' profitability, and pave the way for a more stable partnership between the companies and the Liberian government. ArcelorMittal's decision to increase investment in Liberia by half a billion dollars shows plainly that better contractual terms and heightened investor interest can, in fact, go hand in hand.

3.10.2.3   The ArcelorMittal amended agreement had some 30 improvements over the original contract; the Firestone amendment had nearly 40 improvements. "The Government has widely cited the re-negotiations of the ArcelorMittal and Firestone contracts as proof of investor confidence that Liberia is "re-opened for business." Liberia's successful negotiations with ArcelorMittal and Firestone have caught the attention of other African governments seeking to maximize value from concession agreements covering their natural resources."[64]

3.10.2.4   The report provides extensive background on how the negotiations were conducted, and the give and take that ensued, ultimately arriving at agreements accepted by the parties. It shows how a principled approach to renegotiations, coupled with a sound justification underpinning them, with strong preparation, technical assistance, and political support, led to a successful result.

Case B.

3.10.2.5   In several countries, major natural resource discoveries have been made but development agreements and terms have yet to be finalized. Oil-related contracts previously in place were renegotiated when natural gas was discovered to reflect the different economic and infrastructure requirements for that resource. Disputes have arisen as to whether the country negotiated sound revised contracts. Even where independent evaluations of the revisions supported the contract terms, public opposition continued because of the higher costs and

---

[63] For an extensive report on the negotiations process and results, see Raja Kaul and Antoine Heuty with Alvina Norman, "Getting a Better Deal from the Extractive Sector—Concession Negotiation," in Liberia, 2006–2008; *A report to the Liberian Reconstruction and Development Committee Office of the President, Republic of Liberia* (New York: Revenue Watch Institute, 2009). It is worth emphasizing this case as a post-conflict transition to a democratic regime and that given the history involved and the vast changes in circumstances both inside the country and in the overall markets, the likelihood for a successful renegotiation was increased. Further, renegotiation in a transitional context may receive greater support from a country's "international partners" which can have a significant impact.

[64] Liberian Renegotiation Report, pp. 1–2.

risks associated with new production.

3.10.2.6   Given the uncertainties with respect to the renegotiated arrangements, as well as additional negotiations for new projects, finalization of terms continues to be delayed. An additional delay in the finalization of all contracts has been caused by the fact that several of the contracts have different terms, and there is now a desire to conform them all. In the meantime, investments that could have been started are on hold.

3.10.2.7   This case illustrates two important issues. First is the need to address public expectations and for the negotiators to explain the contracts they negotiate and defend their provisions.[65] With that, there will no doubt still be some opposition, but without that, the opposition can be based on inaccuracies and speculation.

3.10.2.8   The second issue is that negotiating separate terms for separate contracts can become a problem. In this case, the country has determined—after the fact in some instances—to try to combine parts of the projects and is now seeking to conform the terms. This effectively creates a renegotiation of several contracts, further delaying progress.

Case C.

3.10.2.9   A country's reaction to dissatisfaction with the amount and pace of revenues coming into the Government during years of large price increases led to new taxes being imposed on the industry, and the obligation of existing contract holders either to sign new contracts or face expropriation.

3.10.2.10   A key element of the Government's approach was, despite the threat of expropriation, to offer attractive terms even after its new rules were imposed. In the end, most investors did, in fact, sign new agreements. Showing its flexibility, in light of a subsequent downturn in prices and the need for additional investment, the Government relaxed some rules and announced some new investment incentives for domestic and foreign investors.

3.10.2.11   This case illustrates that even in a rather extreme case, involving the threat of expropriation, negotiating by still providing investors with what they needed (i.e., an attractive return based on the risks they had taken) resulted in most of them staying and even re-investing in the country. One factor that assisted in this outcome was that both parties benefitted from higher commodity prices following the renegotiations. But when prices dropped, the country understood future investment would be hampered by the changed circumstances and reacted accordingly.

---

[65] This underscores the importance of involving the public via consultations and dialogue throughout the process and providing for appropriate regional and local support in the agreement or in separate agreements (such as community development agreements).

Case D.

3.10.2.12   In some cases, the results of expropriation threats or actions do not end as well as in Case C, and more companies decide not to renegotiate. In this case, while some important investors did renegotiate, other significant investors did not, and the amount of new investment decreased. Further nationalizations were undertaken. Finally, after a number of years and in order to stem the investment declines, more favourable terms were provided, and some new investment began to be committed.

3.10.2.13   This case illustrates that, where a government appears to "overshoot" the balance and imposes terms that may be too onerous, there is an increased risk that it could be counterproductive to its long-term goals. In the end, promoting policies and an atmosphere that suggest the desire for, and support the possibility of, a long-term relationship between investors and the country creates a higher chance of attracting, and sustaining, the investments that are critical to natural resource development.

Conclusions from cases

3.10.2.14   Each of the cases above, except for Case B, which is still in essence a work in progress, involved a degree of unilateralism on the part of the government. But in Case A, a true renegotiation took place and the basis for the renegotiation was a substantial change in circumstances compared with those underlying the original contracts.

3.10.2.15   In Case C, fair compensation and a desire for an ongoing relationship (coupled with the fortuitous timing of the events which allowed both parties to gain from the significant price increases following the changes) provided confidence that ongoing investments were still justified. In Case D, the terms of the renegotiations, coupled with additional nationalizations in other industries, resulted in a real aversion to continued investments.

3.10.2.16   It might be concluded that renegotiations can be successful and can avoid or at least reduce collateral downside effects. This applies even in the context of a partial ownership level change, if based upon real changes in circumstances and in an environment where the government makes it clear it still desires a positive although changed ongoing relationship, But where done in a less constructive manner, they can stifle ongoing investment and ultimately be counterproductive.

3.10.3   Consequences on specific projects—unilateral or negotiated adjustments

3.10.3.1   If all or a part of a particular project is "expropriated" or nationalized, there can be obvious implications on continuing project investments and operations. Where the private investors are completely removed, the government must be comfortable that it can take over the management and operations, and provide the funding necessary for capital and operating needs. Owing to the negative impact expropriation may have on the willingness of other investors to proceed with their investments, expropriation should only be a last resort.

3.10.3.2   If the government feels there are benefits to continuing outside inves-tor participation, e.g., to provide funding or technical expertise, it will need to consider this in how it effects its changes. If changes are unilaterally imposed, it is likely that investors (whether the original or replacements) will be more cau-tious, or seek additional new protections, before investing, since they will per-ceive the risks as having increased. This can lead to significant delays in project development.

3.10.3.3   In addition, there are potential direct financial implications for the government, such as where an investor invokes an arbitration provision. Where changes are negotiated, and some "give and take" is provided, even where on an overall basis the terms become more favourable to the government, there is a strong likelihood that the relationship will not be unduly harmed, and that a posi-tive and mutually reinforcing partnership may result from it.

3.10.3.4   Similarly, an investor who is faced with a unilateral, or negotiated, contract change to a project needs to determine the project's long-term goals and act accordingly. If it also seeks a positive, long-term relationship, it needs to nego-tiate (or, in the case of a unilateral change, react) in a positive and constructive manner. If it concludes that the best it can achieve is an exit, with compensation, then it needs to be prepared for a prolonged dispute over valuation, likely in a highly adversarial context.

3.10.4   Consequences on other investments—unilateral or negotiated adjustments

3.10.4.1   The actions of a government with respect to one project can have spillover effects on other existing, or proposed, projects and investments. Thus, other current and prospective investors will closely follow how any particular contract renegotiation (or nationalization) proceeds. Just as with respect to the project itself, the ability to achieve long-term private sector investment will be impacted by how the government approaches any specific project renegotiation.

3.10.4.2   Where changes are unilaterally imposed, without consultation or ongoing discussion, other investors will view this with apprehension, which could reduce or delay additional investments in the natural resources sector or more broadly within the country. Further, the costs of future projects may increase due to a perception of an overall increase in country-related risks. Conversely, where the renegotiation is principle-based and proceeds fairly, such factors can greatly mitigate the otherwise negative collateral effects of a project renegotiation.

3.10.5   Changes in overall tax law in licence or contract countries

3.10.5.1   Finally, while this chapter has focused on negotiations and renegotia-tions of natural resource contracts, many countries' rules are set forth in law and in licensing procedures, rather than being individually negotiated. In this context, unilateral changes are equally possible, by a mere change in the laws themselves. For example, countries such as Norway and the United Kingdom put new excess profit taxes in place back in the 1970s in light of increased crude oil prices.

3.10.5.2   While there is almost always some degree of consultation with affected taxpayers at the time new legislation is proposed, the ultimate decision is a unilateral one. Just as in contract situations, investors take note of these changes and react accordingly. In some cases, there may be effective-date relief or legislated "stability" clause provisions that may be helpful. But more frequently, the law changes are imposed and investors change their behaviour by adjusting their operations and future investments, given that their economics have been altered. Maximizing consultation, and perhaps providing some offsetting relief to the investors, can help to build or maintain an environment of mutual trust.

3.10.5.3   Ideally, as with contract situations, statutory provisions that will govern the large investments of the natural resources sector should be developed by anticipating and reflecting as many conditions as can reasonably be envisioned. If, for example, an excess profit tax is envisioned in high price environments, having one in place, even if current conditions do not trigger it, is by far a better course than imposing it later, after the fact.

3.11   CONCLUSIONS

3.11.1   Involvement of tax authorities in designing rules

3.11.1.1   Some countries govern the development of their natural resources via published laws and licensing rules. The licensing provisions will cover the terms of making resources available for exploration and development, and will normally also provide for full life cycle obligations that a licensee accepts, including decommissioning at the termination of the project life. Tax rules may be covered under the general tax laws, or specific laws or provisions applicable to natural resources.

3.11.1.2   Other countries govern the development of their natural resources with negotiations done on a project-by-project basis. Where this occurs, there may be published model agreements covering the host of issues and obligations in a natural resource project. However, the final negotiations on a particular project may deviate from the model in a number of areas, including the fiscal terms and possibly some stability provisions.

3.11.1.3   Irrespective of whether a country uses a statutory or negotiated contract approach in structuring long-term natural resource investments, it is key that there be up-front and continuous involvement of the tax authorities. In designing statutory rules, tax policy and administration experts are essential participants in ensuring the tax rules ultimately adopted are consistent with sound tax policy and the priorities of the country, and are enforceable. Similarly, when fiscal rules are set in a negotiated contract approach, tax experts should also be involved to ensure that provisions of the contract do not conflict with existing laws or regulations, that the provisions are clearly understood by all, and that they can be implemented as intended.

3.11.1.4   Given their long-term nature, economic and political conditions are bound to change over the course of natural resource projects. A best practice is to address, in some form or another, as many of these possibilities as can be envisioned at the beginning of the investment relationship; some can be handled by designing laws and licensing rules, or specific negotiated contracts, with as much flexibility and as many self-executing adjustments as can be developed to minimize disputes.

3.11.1.5   Nevertheless, it is not likely that all of the possible scenarios that may arise can be anticipated, and thus mechanisms to deal with such circumstances will need to be developed. Appropriately structured stability clauses may be one way to deal with changes in circumstances, but they tend to cover only some of the possible events. Re-opener or renegotiation clauses can be useful, and they can at least provide some general conditions that serve as trigger events for either party to seek contract adjustments. Since these may provide at most an agreement to negotiate in good faith, they do not in themselves compel or guarantee a result, but they can provide an expectation and a framework supportive of a mutually beneficial, long-term relationship.

3.11.2   A final note on confidentiality and transparency

3.11.2.1   It is clear that openness and engagement of the entire community can help achieve buy-in and support for the ultimate contract negotiated. But this must be managed with care. At times, particularly when contract negotiations are proceeding and proposals (and counter proposals) are being reviewed, confidentiality is crucial to the integrity and effectiveness of the process.

3.11.2.2   When the negotiations are complete, however, it is incumbent on the negotiators to explain and defend the bases for their results. This is clearly the case when such agreements are subject to final review by outside groups or other governmental bodies before becoming effective. But even when that is not the case, presentations explaining the agreement terms and answering questions about them are equally important in order to gain public confidence and longer-term support, which benefit both governments and investors interested in positive, long-term relationships.

ANNEX I

Mining Contracts—how to read and understand them. Available at https://3. amazonaws.com/s3.documentcloud.org/documents/1279596/mining-contracts-how-to-read-and-understand-them.pdf.

Oil Contracts—how to read and understand them. Available at http://openoil.net/understanding-oil-contracts/.

International Institute for Sustainable Development, *Handbook on Mining Contract Negotiations for Developing Countries, Volume One: Preparing for Success* (International Institute for Sustainable Development: Winnipeg, Manitoba, April 2015). Available at http://www.iisd.org/sites/default/files/publications/iisd-handbook-mining-contract-negotiations-for-developing-countries-volume-1.pdf.

Natural Resources Governance Institute. "Legal Framework: Navigating the Web of Laws and Contracts Governing Extractive Industries." *NRGI Reader* (March 2015). Available at http://www.resourcegovernance.org/analysis-tools/publications/primer-legal-framework.

George Kahale, III, "The Uproar Surrounding Petroleum Contract Renegotiations." *Oxford Energy Forum* (August 2010). Available at http://www.curtis.com/siteFiles/AttorneyFiles/Oxford_Energy_Forum.pdf.

EI SourceBook. Available at http://www.eisourcebook.org/. See in particular http://www.eisourcebook.org/642_5PolicyLegalandContractualFramework.html.

International Monetary Fund, *Fiscal Regimes for Extractive Industries: Design and Implementation* (2012). Available at https://www.imf.org/external/np/pp/eng/2012/081512.pdf.

Environmental Law Alliance Worldwide, *Natural Resource Contracts: A Practical Guide* (2013). Available at https://elaw.org/sites/default/files/images_content/general_page_images/publications/Natural_Resource_Contracts_Guide.pdf.

David Kienzler with the collaboration of Perrine Toledano, Sophie Thomashausen and Sam Szoke-Burke, *Natural Resource Contracts as a Tool for Managing the Mining Sector.* Federal Ministry for Economic Cooperation and Development (2015) Available at https://www.bmz.de/g7/includes/Downloadarchiv/Natural_Resource_Contracts.pdf.

Lisa E. Sachs, Perrine Toledano and Jacky Mandelbaum, with James Otto, *Impacts of Fiscal Reforms on Country Attractiveness: Learning from the Facts.* Available at: http://ccsi.columbia.edu/files/2013/11/Impacts_of_Fiscal_ Reforms_on_country_attractivness-_Website1.pdf.

OECD, *Guiding Principles for Durable Extractive Contracts*, available at: https://www.oecd.org/development/guiding-principles-for-durable-extractive-contracts-55c19888-en.htm

Chapter 4

Production Sharing Contracts

4.1 INTRODUCTION

4.1.1 Executive summary

4.1.1.1   The aim of this chapter is to describe the main tax and tax-related issues arising from upstream production sharing contracts.

4.1.1.2   The chapter examines the concept and some of the mechanisms of Production Sharing Contracts or Agreements (PSCs or PSAs) in detail. PSCs are among the most common types of contractual arrangements for petroleum exploration and production (E&P). Under a PSC the state, as the owner of mineral resources, contracts an oil company or a group of oil companies to invest their technical and financial capabilities to explore and develop the country's hydrocarbon resources. The state is traditionally represented by the host government or one of its entities such as the national oil company (NOC).

4.1.1.3   A PSC is, therefore, a type of contract signed between a government entity or entities and a company or companies involved in natural resource exploration and production, intended to establish the rights and obligations of the parties, including how the costs incurred and revenue generated by the project will be allocated among the parties. PSCs are widely used worldwide, and most common in African and Asian countries, as well as in certain countries of South America.

4.1.1.4   PSCs typically relate to the petroleum industry and are rarely seen in the mining industry, where there is often less direct participation of government bodies. Nevertheless, there is great interest in the implementation of PSCs in the mining sector among developing countries, for example in Senegal, Gabon, Uganda, or Papua New Guinea.

4.1.1.5   There is no uniform approach or standard model to a PSC. Features from other petroleum fiscal regimes like the concessionary system[1] (also known as tax-royalty) can generally be found in PSCs. PSCs may also cater to how the contract terms interact with general tax or other legislation. It is common for different versions of a PSC to be used for different areas of production within the same jurisdiction.

---

[1] See Chapter 2: The Government's Fiscal Take.

4.1.1.6   To provide a general overview of PSCs, the chapter starts by considering how a PSC differs from other types of fiscal regimes; it explores some of the reasons why a country would choose a PSC and provides an overview of the general terms and common tax clauses. When discussing terms, the chapter goes into practical tax problems that are often encountered in PSCs and finally describes a few current PSC systems around the world.

4.1.1.7   This chapter intends to improve understanding of PSCs, including relevant terminology, the tax mechanisms of the contracts and what areas need attention in a PSC. The chapter discusses aspects of interest to tax administrations, investors and other stakeholders.

4.1.2   Overview: production sharing contracts

4.1.2.1   Chapter 2 - The Government's Fiscal Take - provides a general overview of fiscal instruments, including PSCs, their features and characteristics. While Chapter 2 covers fundamentals of PSCs, this Chapter provides a more in-depth review of PSC related features and issues.

4.1.2.2   Fiscal arrangements between governments and Oil & Gas (O&G) companies normally fall into one of two main categories: concessionary and contractual. The major difference between them generally lies in their approach towards ownership of the resources[2] and how the revenues generated by the project are shared.

4.1.2.3   Prior to the development of production sharing contracts, exploration and production of oil and gas was typically granted to investors by way of concessions, which are still widely used in many countries. Nowadays, PSCs are a very common means by which developing countries award investors the right to participate in the hydrocarbon industry within their jurisdictions.

4.1.2.4   According to most countries' Constitutions, natural resources belong to the government, on behalf of the people. They generally remain so at least until resources are extracted. In general, under the concessionary system, the investor has title to the hydrocarbon produced while in the contractual system, the government retains title to the resources,[3] however mixed systems (systems that share features of both systems) may apply.[4]

---

[2] Daniel Johnston, International Exploration Economics, Risk, and Contract Analysis, PennWell , 2003, pp. 12-13.

[3] Another aspect regarding ownership relates to equipment, as typically under contractual systems, once production equipment or facilities are landed in the host country, title to the equipment passes to the host government. Nevertheless, this does not apply to leased equipment or equipment brought in by service companies. Daniel Johnston, International Exploration Economics, Risk, and Contract Analysis, PennWell , 2003, pp. 12-13.

[4] For example, in Brazil, under both systems the ownership of natural resources belongs to the government until some time after production begins.

4.1.2.5   Contractual arrangements are divided into service contracts and PSCs. Under service contracts, the investor(s) typically receive a fixed financial compensation from the government, while under PSCs they receive a share of production.[5] Therefore, PSCs usually allocate more risk (and a higher reward in case of success) to the investing parties, whereas service agreements allocate less risk (and a lower reward) to the investing parties.

Fig. 4.F.1:
Petroleum Fiscal Regimes

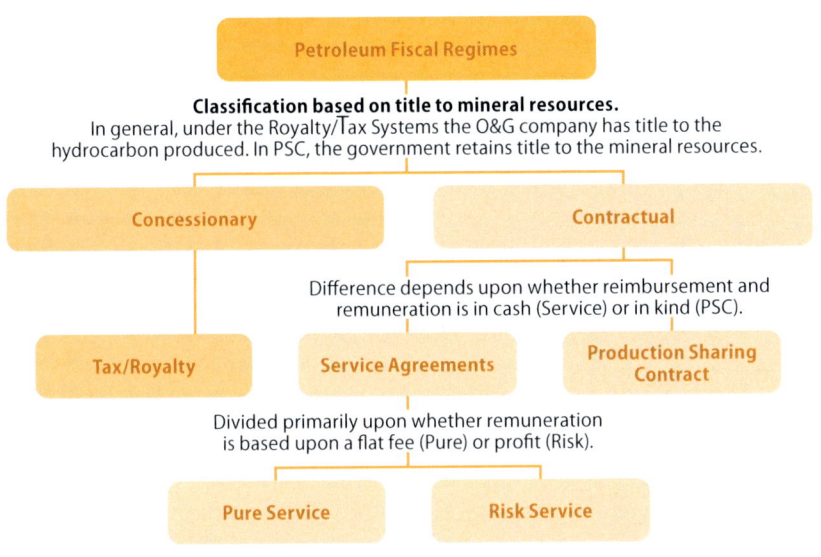

4.1.2.6   In some jurisdictions that still adopt a concessionary regime investors may sign contracts, also called concession agreements. These agreements in general are less detailed and less flexible than pure contractual arrangements like PSCs and service contracts, at least in the oil and gas sector.

4.1.2.7   PSC enables the government to maintain formal ownership of the natural resources, while permitting a private or public company to exploit them. Under a PSC, a State contracts with an investor or a group of investors to invest their financial and technical capabilities to explore, develop and produce oil and gas within the PSC's contract area. The investor bears the entire risk of the project and will be entitled to a portion of production to cover its costs and, from the

---

[5] Ib. P. 13. See also Carole Nakhle, *Mining and Petroleum Taxation: Principles and Practices*, Revenue mobilization and Development IMF, DC, 2011

remainder, a share of production to enable a return on its investments. The State will usually be represented by the Ministry in charge of hydrocarbons or the NOC, and the extent to which the NOC is involved with the investment and operations varies from country to country.

4.1.2.8   PSCs were introduced in Indonesia in 1966. The first PSC ever signed was by IIAPCO and Permina, the Indonesian National Oil Company at the time (now Pertamina).[6]

Basic features of the first PSC contract:

• Title to the hydrocarbons remained with the state.
• The National Oil Company maintained management control, and the contractor was responsible for the execution of petroleum operations in accordance with the terms of the contract.
• The contractor was required to submit annual work programs and budgets for scrutiny and approval by the NOC.
• The contract was based on production sharing and not a profit-sharing basis.
• The contractor provided all financing and technology required for the operations and bore the risks.
• During the term of the contract, after allowance for up to a maximum percentage of annual oil production for recovery of costs, the remaining production was shared on a percentage basis with the National Oil Company [NOC]. The contractor's taxes were paid out of the NOC's share of profit oil.
• A notable simplification feature was that tax was calculated using audited Profit Oil as taxable income, with only minor adjustments; the ordinary rules for calculating taxable income did not apply.
• All equipment purchased and imported into the country by the contractor became the property of NOC. Service company equipment and leased equipment were exempt.
• There was no royalty payment.

4.2   PSCS: DESIGN CONSIDERATIONS

4.2.1   Overview

---

[6] Daniel Johnston, *International Petroleum Fiscal Systems and Production Sharing Contracts*, (PennWell Books, Tulsa, Oklahoma,1994). Page 40.

4.2.1.1   In theory, governments can achieve similar profiles of revenue through the different types of O&G regimes, with different instruments, because the fiscal terms of a tax/royalty regime can be replicated in a PSC regime, and vice versa. Therefore, there is no intrinsic tax reason to prefer a concessionary or tax/royalty regime over a PSC regime.

4.2.1.2   However, many governments favor PSC regimes because the State retains ownership of reserves, the government can consume or sell its share of production, and the State retains ownership of oil and gas infrastructure upon expiration of the contract. PSCs are also typically comprehensive contracts that provide a degree of flexibility not found in concessionary regimes, even when they include concession agreements. Governments need, however, to consider how to optimize this level of flexibility, and decide to invest resources in designing and negotiating PSC terms.

4.2.2   Contract and license allocation

4.2.2.1   Governments sign PSCs following either a competitive allocation system, through bidding rounds, or based on bilateral negotiations with investors interested in a particular area.

4.2.2.2   If there is sufficient competition from investors to develop a particular area, it is always in the government's interest to allocate contractual rights through a transparent, competitive bidding round. This ensures the government allocates its resources to the most capable companies. When there is insufficient competition, in particular when governments lack geological data on the areas to be allocated, it may be necessary to enter into PSCs through bilateral negotiations.

4.2.2.3   PSCs can be signed under different levels of geological information. In some cases, contractors are responsible for undertaking exploration in an area with no prior evidence of commercially viable deposits. If no discovery is made, funds invested in exploration are not recoverable. The historical economic success rate in frontier areas is approximately 5%. In other cases, sufficient information exists to limit the exploration risks taken by investors. PSC fiscal terms typically account for such different situations, providing more generous terms to governments when there is more certainty on the commercial viability of hydrocarbons in PSC contract areas.

4.2.2.4   Regardless of the allocation process, it is good practice for governments to provide a model PSC, which improves the predictability and legal certainty of the allocation process. A model PSC contains the basic provisions that the government expects to be followed by any contractors and leave certain provisions that are more specific to the development of a particular geological field blank. The more prior information the government has on a particular area, the more specific the model PSC can be. For instance, Tanzania's 2013 model PSC applies to any area to be allocated to a contractor,[7] whereas in Mexico, for

---

[7] http://www.wgei.org/wp-content/uploads/2015/10/Tanzania-Model-Production-Sharing-

each area allocated in the bidding rounds organized between 2015 and 2018, the regulatory agency provided tailored model contracts, many of them PSCs.[8] The blank areas in a model PSC are then finalized based on either the proposal of the winning company in a bidding round, or bilateral negotiations between the government and the company. In some cases, minimal bilateral negotiations are necessary to finalize a PSC following a successful bidding round.

4.2.3   The status of PSCs in the legal framework

4.2.3.1   Agreeing on detailed contractual terms can be helpful in situations where the local legal and fiscal framework for oil and gas development is absent, insufficient, or inappropriate. Countries where no oil and gas development has taken place may have no or limited legislation or regulations for hydrocarbons, and the tax law may not be well adapted for the oil and gas sector. This has been an important factor in many countries for adopting a PSC regime. Countries where the legislative system is well established often prefer to set hydrocarbon taxation through general legislation or adjust the existing fiscal system through a concessionary system.

4.2.3.2   A PSC system can be clearer on how differences in accessibility, nature, quality and/or extent of resources will be considered in a particular area. For example, countries with mining legislation but no oil and gas legislation may want to allow prospecting for oil and gas. In the long run, governments should develop a detailed legal and regulatory framework for hydrocarbons, including model PCS. While adapting mining legislation or introducing new comprehensive oil and gas legislation, parties can still achieve agreement on their rights and obligations for specific prospective areas in a contractual form, such as a PSC.

4.2.3.3   Some countries enact PSCs into law to provide a stronger legal standing, while others do not. If they do, such contracts may need to be passed or confirmed by the Parliament to be enacted into law. It is often easier to confirm contracts containing specific conditions for specific areas and activities than to pass general legislation that could impact the whole oil and gas sector.

4.2.4   Flexibility advantages in PSCs

4.2.4.1   A PSC can be easily adapted for different types of geological sites or other circumstances. They allow contracting parties to fine-tune the risk-reward allocation, adapting it to geological or other geographical conditions of an area, over a long period of time.

4.2.4.2   This may be used by certain countries to attract investments by providing more favorable fiscal terms to less developed areas (i.e., frontier areas) where there is a low chance of a successful O&G discovery and risks are high, or providing less favorable fiscal terms where the chance of a successful discovery is higher. In

---

Agreement-2013.pdf

[8] https://rondasmexico.gob.mx/esp/rondas/ronda-1/cnh-r01-l022015/documentos-de-la-licitaci%C3%B3n/contratos/

this respect, countries with both on-shore and offshore O&G developments commonly have PSCs with different fiscal and contractual terms between the on-shore and offshore regimes, to reflect the different levels of costs and risks involved.

4.2.5   Transparency

4.2.5.1   In the past, many petroleum agreements were kept confidential. Governments around the world have chosen to respond to public demands for transparency by publishing or requiring the publication of petroleum agreements. Governments, companies and civil society organizations have agreed to adopt contract transparency as a requirement of the Extractive Industries Transparency Initiative (EITI).[9] [10] Allocation processes, government regulation and oversight of PSCs are all improved by the adoption of an open contracting principle.[11]

4.2.5.2   Transparency can be achieved through publishing all individual resource contracts, which many countries do.[12] It can also be achieved by designing detailed model PSCs linked to the generally applicable legal framework, where overarching legislation sets the general conditions and terms within which individual PSCs should be adopted. For countries that require Parliament to ratify PSCs, this also tends to imply a process with a certain level of transparency.

4.2.6   Tax administration

4.2.6.1   PSCs are often implemented and administered by Ministries, other than the Ministry of Finance, that are responsible for energy and mining. Tax authorities in charge of collecting corporate taxation may not be equipped to assess, implement and review the fiscal implications of a PSC, and may consider them complex and difficult to administer. It is therefore important to:

i.   Achieve a government consensus on how hydrocarbons should be taxed;

ii.   Build the capacity of the tax administration to understand PSC terms;

iii.   Give authority to the Ministry of Finance and its internal tax experts to review and validate the fiscal terms in all PSC design and allocation;

iv.   Foster a strong interagency collaboration to ensure a smooth implementation of PSC tax provisions such as the pay-on-behalf system.

---

[9] https://eiti.org/contract-transparency/

[10] Oxfam. Contract disclosure survey 2018. A review of the contract disclosure policies of 40 oil, gas and mining companies: https://oxfamilibrary.openrepository.com/bitstream/handle/10546/620465/bp-contract-disclosure-extractives-2018-030518-en.pdf;jsessionid=85E D532E904F3E7780333E8BD76EF700?sequence=4

[11] https://resourcegovernance.org/analysis-tools/publications/open-contracting-oil-gas-and-mineral-rights

[12] https://resourcecontracts.org/countries

4.2.6.2   At the extraction phase, oil and gas tend to be subject to a variety of fiscal terms that can include bonuses, royalties, production sharing and various taxes, including corporate income tax. Tax administration is easier when there is a high degree of standardization across PSCs in a given country, and when model contracts include tax provisions. This helps to facilitate consistency, fairness and transparency and to reduce tax administration costs.

4.2.6.3   It is important to regulate the interaction between the tax clauses in PSCs and the domestic general tax system, specifying, if necessary, in the contract or in the domestic law, the relation between both systems. Using a PSC may require more alignment and more rules to provide clarity and certainty of the oil and gas tax regime with regular corporate and other taxes.

4.2.6.4   An example can be seen in Article 17.1 of the Liberia Model contract "*Unless otherwise provided for in this Contract the Contractor shall, in respect of its Petroleum Operations, be subject to the laws generally applicable and the regulations in force in Liberia concerning taxes which are or may be levied on incomes, or determined thereto.*"

4.2.6.5   It is crucial (and advisable) that the law regulates all tax issues, especially when exemptions are involved, and that the tax law includes a specific chapter for the O&G sector.

Fig. 4.F.2:
Flowchart of tax regimes applicable to extractive industries

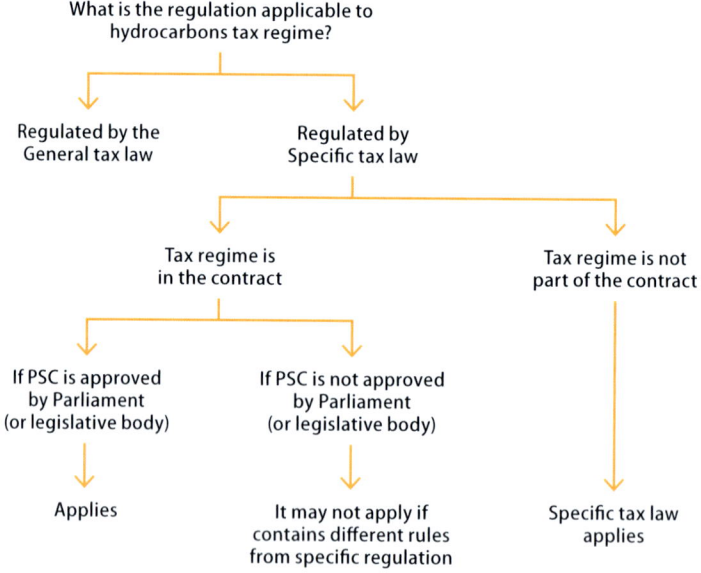

4.3   ROLES OF PRIVATE AND PUBLIC ACTORS IN PSCS

4.3.1   Overview

4.3.1.1   The parties to a PSC contract will often be the NOC, or relevant ministries on behalf of the government (e.g., the ministry in charge of petroleum), and one or more O&G companies or investors (it is common to be a consortium of investors).

4.3.1.2   PSCs describe and regulate various aspects of the future relationship the O&G company will have with the government or government company entrusted with the oversight of the contract and operations and allocate the risks and rewards related to potential hydrocarbon resources to be explored and developed. Below are common features usually found in PSCs.

4.3.2   Transfer of resource ownership

4.3.2.1   Under concessionary systems, transfer of title of the O&G to an extracting company will occur upon production (at the well head). Under contractual systems the government still retains full ownership of resources and O&G companies have the right to receive a share of production to recover their costs and make a profit at the delivery point to be mutually agreed upon by the parties (e.g., the point at which petroleum reaches the outlet flange of the tanker in the oil export facility). Under a service contract, the contractor is normally paid a fixed remuneration and does not acquire the title to the resource.

4.3.2.2   An example of the definition of a delivery point can be seen in the PSC from Iraq (Kurdistan Regional Government): "*Delivery Point means the place after extraction, specified in the approved Development Plan for a Petroleum Field, at which the Crude Oil, Associated Natural Gas and/or Non-Associated Natural Gas is metered for the purposes of Article __, valued for the purposes of Article __ and ready to be taken and disposed of, consistent with international practice, and at which a Party may acquire title to its share of Petroleum under this Contract or such other point which may be agreed by the Parties.*"

4.3.3   Government participation

4.3.3.1   A PSC does not require government participation. Even without any direct participation in the project, the government is entitled to a share of production, after cost recovery.[13] This was a key reason for Nigeria's decision to adopt PSCs.

4.3.3.2   Nigeria factored in the following considerations regarding the distinction between Concessionary and Contractual Systems which led them to move to one system:

---

[13] Daniel Johnston, *International Exploration Economics, Risk, and Contract Analysis,* (PennWell Books, Tulsa, Oklahoma, 2003). Page 197.

a.　Funding: Under the Concessionary system, all parties to the Joint Venture (JV) fund the operations of the JV in proportion to its equity ownership or economic interest. Whereas, under the Contractual system, the Contractor bears the funding obligation 100%.

b.　Funding is the major reason why the Nigerian government moved from the JV Concessionary arrangement to Production Sharing Contracts as the government is unable to meet its cash call obligations under the Numerous JVs owned by the Nigerian National Petroleum Corporation (NNPC).

c.　Risk: Under the Concessionary System, risk is shared among the parties to the JV in proportion to their equity ownership, whereas under the contractual system, based on the terms of the contract, the risk is borne 100% by the contractor.

d.　In addition, under the contractual system, there is no compensation if exploration is unsuccessful or a dry hole is drilled. For this reason, other mechanisms, such as exemptions during the exploration phase, are set up.

4.3.3.3　However, it is common for governments to take a direct participating interest in the investments under a PSC, thereby sharing in the associated risks and rewards. Many governments have opted for state participation in petroleum joint ventures (JVs) via an option for the NOC to participate in development projects. The State would then be required to contribute to the costs of the project in proportion to its participation, and would be entitled to a share of the profits as a participant, in addition to other revenues it would receive from the project as a regulator (e.g., bonuses, royalties, taxes, etc.).

4.3.3.4　The government's contribution to exploration costs is often paid out of subsequent production. Such structures effectively allow a government to reduce or eliminate the need to allocate cash from other sources until a discovery has been made. However, such a structure will affect the risk/reward balance for investors, and the terms of such a "carried" participation, or other elements of the fiscal regime, would have to compensate other investors.

4.3.3.5　Equity or direct participation in the project for governments can take several forms, including:

- A full working interest, which places the government on a par with a private investor. In this case, the government is an equal partner in the PSC from the start, taking up its full obligations and rights relating to its participation in the venture in the same way as other partners;

- Paid-up equity on concessional terms (i.e., government back-in), where the government acquires its equity share, sometimes at below market price, especially when being able to buy into the project after a commercial discovery has been made but at a price set in advance;

- A carried interest, where government does not contribute to the investment obligations in line with its share, up to an agreed project milestone, typically discovery. Government may pay for its carried equity share out of its own share of production proceeds, including an interest charge.

4.3.4   The joint operating agreement (JOA)

4.3.4.1   JOAs can be relevant in any petroleum agreement, including PSCs, where multiple parties own a working interest. These parties may include the host government (directly or, more commonly, through a government-owned oil company).[14] The JOA is a private agreement entered into between the investors that constitute the investor group, to govern the relation of those parties as it relates to the petroleum operations under the petroleum agreement. Where an O&G company participates in more than one PSC in a country, a different JOA will be signed for each of the PSCs in which it has a working interest. Where there is more than one investor with a participating interest, each PSC is independently managed through a consortium governed by the investors under the corresponding JOA.[15]

4.3.4.2   The legal framework for joint ventures can have indirect taxation consequences, for instance in case the ownership of resources passes upon production or subsequently from joint ventures to eventual participants.

4.3.4.3   An example may be seen in Article 2 of the Liberia PSC Model (Scope of the Contract)

1   The Contract is a Production Sharing Contract and includes all the provisions of the agreement between NOCAL and the Contractor.

2   NOCAL authorizes the Contractor to be the Operator pursuant to the terms set forth herein and to carry out the useful and necessary Petroleum Operations in the Delimited Area, on an exclusive basis.

3   The Contractor undertakes, for all the work necessary for carrying out the Petroleum Operations provided for hereunder, to comply with good international petroleum industry practice and to be subject to the laws and regulations in force in Liberia unless otherwise provided under this Contract.

4   The Contractor shall supply all financial and technical means necessary for the proper performance of the Petroleum Operations.

5   The Contractor alone shall bear the financial risk associated with the performance of the Petroleum Operations. The Petroleum Costs

---

[14] JOA has no relevance if the O&G company is the 100% owner of the working interest.

[15] See Chapter 7 (Permanent Establishments) for the treatment and consideration of PSCs as a separate permanent establishment from other PSCs.

related thereto shall be recoverable by the Contractor in accordance with the provisions of Article ... __

6 *During the term hereof, in the event of production, the Total Production arising from the Petroleum Operations shall be shared between the Parties according to the terms set forth in Articles ... and ...*

4.3.5 The JOA accounting procedure

4.3.5.1 JOAs include an accounting procedure, which is a critical part of the governance when multiple investors are party to the petroleum contract. However, the JOA accounting procedure does not determine the proper treatment of cost before the State. The latter is provided for in a distinct accounting procedure provided for in the PSC itself, not the JOA.

4.3.5.2 Under the JOA, the costs incurred by the operator for the benefit of the joint operation and associated with a specific joint operation are recorded in a joint account. The operator must estimate, every month, the cash that will be required to pay invoices and meet obligations for the upcoming month and will require the collection of cash from the other partners by means of cash calls (estimation of costs in advance) or billing and payment (utilization of own funds by the operator which bills non-operators afterwards). For these purposes, the operator is commonly required to maintain an office where, amongst others, all such accounting records, receipts, invoices, etc. are kept.[16] Normal practice in the petroleum industry is for the US dollar to be used as the functional currency for cost accounting and budget records, with the US dollar also being used for international commodity pricing and income.

4.3.5.3 In this respect, the operator is obliged to keep the accounts and provide the other partners with the data that will allow them to prepare their tax returns. Furthermore, each partner in the investor group is responsible for including the relevant data in its tax return.

4.3.5.4 Typically, non-operators, including the government-owned oil company, are entitled to conduct audits at their own costs and raise any objection, but generally it is not acceptable for them to deduct the disputed charge from cash-calls or payments. Most JOAs contain time-limits for audits, which would supplement any prescription periods that have effect under the applicable law or the PSC itself.

4.3.6 The PSC operating committee

4.3.6.1 A common feature of most PSCs is the formation of an operating committee, normally composed of representatives from the contractor and the entity with responsibility for oversight of the PSC. The role of the operating committee

---

[16] See Chapter 3 (Permanent Establishments) for the treatment and consideration of the office as a separate permanent establishment.

is to permit the government and the rest of participants to get involved in the operations of the block. The operator usually prepares an annual work program and budget for review by the operating committee. The role of the operating committee is often of an advisory nature with State approval by the Ministry, whereas in some countries the operating committee can have an approval authority, e.g., for the most relevant decisions (approval of major expenditures, evaluation of results, determination of the commerciality of discoveries).

4.3.6.2   The appraisal activities attempt to determine if a discovery can be a commercial success. If the investor determines the discovery to be economically viable, the investor will typically submit a declaration of commerciality to the operating committee or the relevant Ministry for their review. The investor will subsequently develop a field development plan (FDP) which will typically need to be submitted to the suitable approval authority, e.g., a Ministry or operating committee. The government approval of the FDP typically signifies the formal authorization for the investor. If no further exploration or development is intended by the investor, the investor may take the decision to relinquish parts or the entire area or transfer its participation (upon government approval) to a third party by notifying its decision to the relevant authority.[17]

4.3.7   No profit-No loss principle

4.3.7.1   One of the foundations of all JOAs, and also the usual practice of the activity of the E&P, is that the operator will perform functions at cost, without adding any margin to the operation. Nevertheless, the operator has the right to charge an overhead, to reflect the costs resulting from the work carried out by the operator function. The overhead/indirect charges are normally set up according to the investments and vary from the stage of exploration and development to production.

4.3.7.2   The operator will normally be part of an international cost-sharing arrangement under which it will have access to technology and services developed or provided by its foreign affiliates. Normal practice, established more than fifty years ago, in the E&P sector of the petroleum industry is that the operator is charged for its contribution to such an arrangement at cost, with no mark-up. A more detailed description of cost-sharing arrangements and documentation requirements can be found in Chapter VIII of the Guidelines on Transfer Pricing for Multinational Enterprises and Tax Administrations (OECD 2017).

4.3.7.3   The no profit – no loss principle is also found in farm-in/out transactions where the farmor seeks to share the risks of the operation rather than obtaining a gain. The farmee is typically unwilling to pay more than past costs when recoverable reserves are yet to be discovered, or discoveries are still uncertain, in particular at the exploration stage. A more detailed description of farm-in and farm-out transactions can be found in Chapter 9 on Financial Transactions.

---

[17] See Chapter 7 (Permanent Establishments) for the moment when discontinuation or transfer to a third party of an E&P related PE determines the cessation of existence of the PE.

4.3.8   Economic stability

4.3.8.1   Economic or fiscal stability is often granted to investors in the extractive industries through stabilization provisions, discussed in detail in Chapter 3 (Tax aspects of negotiation and renegotiation of contracts) and Chapter 5 (Tax Incentives). In jurisdictions that offer fiscal stability to investors, such provisions are included in PSCs.

4.3.8.2   An example of an economic stability clause in a PSC can be seen from the Qatar Economic Stabilization clause: *"Economic Stabilization: In the event CONTRACTOR is subjected by GOVERNMENT or QP, to any additional liabilities, fees, taxes, imposts or costs of any sort or kind, other than de minimis ones, during the term of this Agreement, then CONTRACTOR shall have the right to request from QP a modification to the terms and conditions of this Agreement that will restore CONTRACTOR to the economic position it was in prior to the imposition of such liabilities, fees, taxes, imposts, or costs."*

4.3.8.3   The more recent best practice on economic stability clauses in contracts can be found in the Guiding Principles for Durable Extractive Contracts, a set of principles developed by multiple stakeholders as part of the OECD policy dialogue on natural resource-based development. The 7th principle states that:

"Durable extractive contracts are consistent with applicable laws, applicable international and regional treaties, and anticipate that host governments may introduce bona fide, non-arbitrary, and non-discriminatory changes in law and applicable regulations, covering non-fiscal regulatory areas to pursue legitimate public interest objectives. The costs attributable to compliance with such changes in law and regulations, and wholly, necessarily and exclusively related to project specific operations, should be treated as any other project costs for purposes of tax deductibility, and cost recovery in production sharing contracts.

If such changes in law and/or applicable regulations result in the investor's inability to perform its material obligations under the contract or if they lead to a material adverse change that undermines the economic viability of the project, durable extractive contracts require the parties to engage in good faith discussions which might eventually lead the parties to agree to renegotiate the terms of the contract." [18]

4.3.8.4   In some PSCs taxes are paid for and on behalf of the contractor out of the NOC share of profit (also known as "taxes in lieu"). This type of PSC provides an additional measure of economic stability, because if the tax law is amended, it would not affect the financial position of the IOC.

---

[18] OECD Policy Dialogue on Natural Resource-based Development, Guiding Principles for Durable Extractive Contracts, 2020   http://www.oecd.org/dev/Guiding_Principles_for_durable_extractive_contracts.pdf

4.4   PRODUCTION SHARING FRAMEWORK

4.4.1   General framework

4.4.1.1   Determining the production, how it is lifted and shared, is a main feature of the PSC. It will form a major part of the fiscal take, and the contract clauses regarding production and production sharing will influence other fiscal considerations.

4.4.1.2   PSCs include a fiscal instrument that defines some of the production as "Cost Oil/Gas," and the rest as "Profit Oil/Gas" which is shared between the State and the Contractor.

Fig. 4.F.3:
Example: Framework of a simple PSC

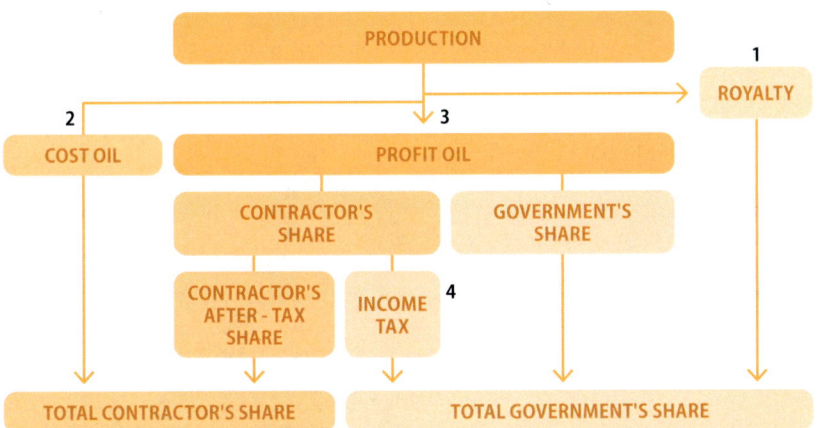

2. Cost Oil: share of total production, which can be retained by the contractor to recover costs incurred, normally subject to a maximum amount (cost oil limit).

3. Profit Oil: share of remaining oil after cost recovery. Profit oil is divided between the government and the contractor accordin to some formula set out in the PSC.

4.4.2   Cost oil

4.4.2.1   Most PSCs contain a cost recovery provision, which determines the procedure by which the contractor will recover its costs. The share of production that goes to the working interest partners to allow them to recover their costs is referred to as "cost oil" or "cost gas."

4.4.2.2   Therefore, "cost oil" is the oil retained by the contractor to recover the costs of exploration, development and production. Most PSCs limit the amount of cost oil that can be retained in a given accounting period, so that the State receives a share of production as profit oil as soon as production commences, whether or not the contractor's project is profitable. The amount of hydrocarbons to be recovered through the "cost oil" is limited to a percentage of the production. Costs that are not recovered are carried forward and recovered later. Most PSCs allow virtually unlimited carry forward, with some exceptions, and if production is sufficient during the life of the contract, the working interest owners will eventually recover all their recoverable expenditures.

4.4.2.3   An example can be seen from the Angola Deep Water Model Contract, 1999. This states *"Contractor Group shall recover all exploration, development, production and administration and services expenditures incurred under this agreement by taking and freely disposing of up to a maximum amount of 50% per year of all crude oil produced and saved from development areas and not used in petroleum operations."*

4.4.2.4   PSCs normally specify which costs are eligible for cost recovery. Usually, these include unrecovered costs carried forward from previous years, operating expenditures (OPEX), capital expenditures (CAPEX) and abandonment costs. They may also specify the limitations on recoverability. For example, some contracts limit recoverability by depreciating development costs, which means that only a fraction of such costs is recovered each year.

4.4.2.5   In addition, most contracts specify the order in which costs are to be recovered. This is important to contractors when they finance the whole exploration activity but share the operating and development activities with the government. A common order of cost recovery would be: (i) current year operating costs, (ii) unrecovered exploration and appraisal expenditures, (iii) unrecovered development expenditures, (iv) capitalized interest, if allowed, (v) any investment credit or uplift and (vi) future abandonment cost fund.[19]

4.4.2.6   Expenses not eligible for cost recovery may include (depending on government policy) bonuses, royalties, interest or other financing related payments and overheads beyond specified limits; and costs outside the budget (unless approved by government).

4.4.3   Profit oil

4.4.3.1   Profit oil is the share of production remaining after royalty (and other production taxes, if any) is paid and cost oil has been delivered to the contractor, paid in cash or in kind.[20]

4.4.3.2   Profit oil is shared between the parties, allocating a specified percentage of the profit oil directly to the government, with the members of the contractor group, which may include the government-owned company, sharing the remaining oil in proportion to their participation under a formula established in the PSC.

---

[19] Charlotte J. Wright and Rebecca A. Gallun, Fundamentals of Oil & Gas Accounting (Pen-Well Books, Tulsa, Oklahoma, 2008).

[20] Please Note: The Indonesian Government released a new O&G gross split regime in 2017, which coexists with the current cost recovery regime.

4.4.3.3   For example, if a company is a party to a contract that specifies a royalty of 10% and a cost recovery oil equal to a maximum of 50% of gross production, until all development costs are recovered, profit oil would be 40% (100% - 10% -50%).

Fig. 4.F.4:
Example of government share of revenue

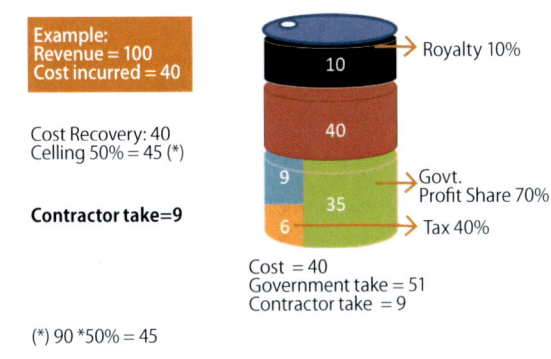

Example:
Revenue = 100
Cost incurred = 40

Cost Recovery: 40
Celling 50% = 45 (*)

Contractor take=9

Royalty 10%

Govt.
Profit Share 70%

Tax 40%

Cost = 40
Government take = 51
Contractor take = 9

(*) 90 *50% = 45

	Gross Revenue	
Contractor share	**100**	**Government share TOTAL**
	Royalty (10%)	
	90	10
	Cost Recovery	
40	50% limit: 45	
(Assumed cost)	**50**	
	Profit Oil Split	
Profit Sharing Revenue: 15	30% / 70%	35
Tax (40%) -6		6
(After-tax) **9**		**51** **60**

Government share is Royalty + ProfitShare + Tax = 10+35+6=51
Government share (%) = 51/60 = **85%**

4.4.3.4   In most countries, the contractual terms of distribution of the production of liquid and gaseous hydrocarbons are different, with the terms for gas usually more beneficial for the contractor due to higher development costs, longer schedules, a need for gas market development and/or a lower sale price for natural gas.

4.4.3.5   The profit-sharing formula is generally specified in the contract (and oftentimes in the government's legislation). There are many ways to distribute the Profit Oil. The most common are:

- Fixed percentages: The portion allocated to the government can vary between 40% and 85%.

- Variable scales: The percentages of distribution can vary depending on one or several variables. There are four main categories of production sharing formula developed by host governments.[21]

4.4.3.6   An example of the contractual production sharing formula is shown below.

Table 4.T.1

Production Sharing formulas	
Daily Rate of Production (DROP)	Government share of profit petroleum increases with the daily rate of production from the field. Its strength is simplicity. Its main weaknesses are that field size is often a poor proxy for project profitability and the mechanism is not progressive with respect to oil prices or costs. Attempts have been made to blend this with a scale of prices.
Cumulative production from project	Government share of profit petroleum increases as total cumulative production increases. This is also an inaccurate proxy for project profitability, and such schemes are becoming less common.
'R-Factor'	Government's profit share increases with the ratio of contractor's cumulative revenues to contractor's cumulative costs (the 'R factor'). This improves production based formula in being a more direct measure of profitability, and is commonly used. Its weaknesses are that it does not take into account the time value of money, that current project profitability has no/low impact on the R-factor value, because it is cumulative, which can make some recurring investment more challenging especially later in the life of the project.
Rate of Return (ROR)	The government's share is set by reference to the cumulative contractor rate of return, with single or multiple tiers. It can take into account the time value of money by using discounted cash flows. Like the R-factor, this is traditionally a cumulative indicator, and will make ongoing investment more challenging unless its calculation is designed to be dynamic, e.g., to reflect the current project profitability.

---

[21] IMF, Fiscal Regimes for Extractive Industries: Design and Implementation (15 August 2012).

Example Daily Rate of Production:

Daily Production Rate (thousands bbls/day)	Government Profit Share (%)
0-25	30%
>25-50	35%
>50-75	40%
>75-100	55%
>100	60%

If average daily production for the agreed time period was 45,000 bbls per day
Government Profit Share = [(30%*25,000) + 35% (20,000)]/45,000
Government Profit Share = 32.2%

4.4.3.7   Finally, in a PSC regime, the IOC is generally required to file a tax return showing the value of its share of production (both profit oil and cost oil) as income, less deductions permitted by the tax law. The tax due is then payable either directly by the IOC or, as mentioned above, by the NOC on behalf of the IOC.

4.5   PRINCIPAL FISCAL RELATED CLAUSES IN PSCS

4.5.1   Overview

4.5.1.1   Besides sharing production, other instruments allocate production, revenues or profit. Some of these instruments include more direct allocation of production whilst others cover the revenue that governments indirectly receive as part of the overall fiscal take.

4.5.1.2   PSCs include fiscal clauses that determine the fiscal treatment of the production shared. The primary fiscal components of a PSC may include: (i) bonuses, (ii) royalty, (iii) cost recovery, (iv) profit oil and (v) taxes.

4.5.2   Bonuses

4.5.2.1   Contractors often pay signature bonuses for acquiring the right to explore, develop and produce. Signature bonuses are a pre-payment of government take of future cash flows. Bonuses can be negotiated, set by the host government or biddable for each contract and may be different depending on the stage of the O&G project:

Type of Bonus	Description
Signature Bonus	Payment made by the contractor to the government at the time that the petroleum contract is granted. It may be determined through a bidding process, negotiation, or set by legislation.
Development Bonus	A relatively smaller sum of money paid at the signing of the contract with another payment being due if and when the decision is made to develop a field within the contract area.
Discovery Bonus	Payment made at the time that a commercial discovery is declared.
Production Bonus	Payment made at a certain point in time during the life of the petroleum contract, typically at the time that petroleum production begins, at a defined production rate or at a defined quantity of cumulative production.

4.5.2.2   In choosing to require bonus payments at discovery or production, the government is assuming some risk since if O&G not discovered no additional bonus would be received. However, bonuses are typically a regressive fiscal instrument that are more commonly charged for highly prospective areas, or as part of a competitive bidding round.

4.5.2.3   An example can be seen from the Libya Model PSA: *Signature bonus: as a signature bonus, a lump sum amount of .... US Dollars (US$ ....);*

Production bonus: (a) an amount of XX US Dollars (US XX) to be paid in respect of each Commercial Discovery within thirty (30) days after Commercial Production Start Date of such Commercial Discovery; and (b) an amount of XX US Dollars (US XX) upon achieving cumulative production of XX (XX) Barrels of oil equivalent from each Commercial Discovery and thereafter, an amount of XX US Dollars (US XXX) upon achieving each additional thirty million (XX) barrels of oil equivalent.

4.5.2.4   Typically, bonuses are not recoverable through cost recovery, but they could be deductible against income and withholding taxes. However, countries may adopt different approaches depending on their domestic policy, as shown in the examples below:

Country	Bonus Treatment
Malaysia	Signature bonuses to be paid are cost recoverable, and for tax purposes are qualifying exploration expenditure and tax deductible under Initial Allowance of 10% and Annual Allowance of 15% or calculation based on a formula, whichever is the greater.
Vietnam	Non recoverable/tax deductible.
Indonesia	Non recoverable/non tax deductible.

4.5.3   Rentals (land, surface fees)

4.5.3.1   These are generally paid annually on the basis of the size of the acreage under lease, normally at the beginning of the calendar year or contract year. They may take on different forms: the rental could be a fixed amount for the contract or per square km. of operations land, the "object value" or a negotiated amount.

4.5.3.2   The basis for charging may vary between the exploration/exploitation phase or onshore and offshore and may be payable depending on the territorial zone in which operations are carried out. Normally they are considered as a recoverable or deductible cost.

4.5.3.3   The rentals provide the government with regular income and encourage voluntary relinquishment of acreage. However, they may raise issues regarding the delimitation of the "area."

4.5.3.4   One example is the Indonesia Land and Building Tax (PBB) which is charged at a rate of 0.5% of a "deemed" tax base (ranging from 20% up to 100% of the "object value," being a statutory value). It was changed in 2013 to provide for post GR 79 PSCs to pay a self-remit tax and claim it as cost recovery. This change became a concern as most post GR 79 PSCs were still in the exploration phase (uncertainty of cost recovery). The Directorate of General Taxes (DGT) issued a clarification for the "offshore" component of objects to specify that it only applies to the area "utilized" (the term "utilized" was not defined). Later, the DGT issued new compliance and calculation procedures for PSCs, where the definition of "offshore area" did not refer to "utilization," giving rise to uncertainty, and a "zone" concept was introduced, which could include areas outside the PSC contract area. However, clarification by tax authorities is still required in relation to the distinction between the surface working area and the subsurface reservoir area.

4.5.3.5   Nigeria's Signature Bonuses and Lease Rental provisions provide another example. IOCs pay a signature bonus to the government for the right to an Oil Mining Lease (OML) after which a PSC contract is signed with the government or holder. The signature bonus is not recoverable. The OML is a license granted to an IOC to extract crude oil and/or gas in commercial quantities from a defined area for sale or export. The money paid to government upon the award of this license is known as "Signature Bonus," and this is a one-off payment.

4.5.3.6   In addition to the Signature Bonus, the IOC in Nigeria will pay lease rental or concession rental to government on an annual basis. The lease rental is likened to rent of the land/area where the OML is granted. The difference between the Signature Bonus and Lease Rental is that: (i) Signature Bonus is a one-off payment upon award of an OML. It is capitalized and not allowed for Cost recovery. (ii) Lease Rental is an annual payment for the duration of the OML which allows for tax deduction and cost recovery. In a PSC an OML is granted for a duration of 30 years whereas in a JV the duration is 20 years. At the expiry of the license, the government may renew it or award the license to another company. The Signature Bonus is paid upon the award of an OML irrespective of whether the IOC is renewing such license.

4.5.4   Royalties

General

4.5.4.1   Most PSCs contain provisions whereby a royalty is paid to the government out of production, although royalties are not an essential feature of PSCs. The combination of a cost oil limitation and a minimum share of profit oil to the state actually replicates the economic features of a royalty: it guarantees that the government collects a share of the value of production, as soon as production starts.

4.5.4.2   Royalties are based on the volume or value of petroleum extracted and can be paid either in cash or in kind. Payment in kind involves delivery of physical quantities of oil and gas to the government (normally in some cases by the government-owned company).

4.5.4.3   Royalties based upon gross revenues can be determined at different points of valuation: e.g., wellhead, block boundary, export terminal or point of sale. The point of sale, however, may be different from the point of valuation. The statutory royalty may allow transportation costs from the point of valuation to the point of sale to be deducted (netback transportation cost).

4.5.4.4   Royalties may become obstacles to new investments in marginal fields, or lead to the early abandonment of marginal producing fields, due to their regressive effect. To prevent these situations, contracts may include royalties paid on a sliding scale, so that the royalty rate varies based on selected variables such as price, hydrocarbon type, etc. The rate can be lower with lower production or price and increase as production or price increases.

TYPE OF ROYALTIES		
Fixed Percentage	Of Production (e.g., 10% of oil extracted).	Easy to administer, but does not take into account the profitability of the project (regressive).
Sliding Scales	• Level of field Production, • Level of well Production, • Level of well Production and Price, • Cumulative Production, • Based on payout, • Based on R-factor • Based on Internal Rate of Return, • Based on gravity of oil, • Based on elapsed time • Etc.	More progressive than fixed royalties, depending on the mechanism adopted. Variable royalties can be more burdensome to administer.

4.5.4.5   Some exclusions from royalty payment apply with respect to e.g., oil and gas vented or flared (with approval), reinjected or used in field operations, or in the case of acceptable losses.

Sliding Scale Royalties

4.5.4.6   Sliding scale royalties are used to escalate the royalty based on a factor or factors agreed in the contract that tend to predict the profitability of a project. Normally production levels are a poor proxy for profitability, but there are other factors that can be used (e.g., prices, costs and timing, production, IRR). Instead, price is a more reliable indicator for profitability.

4.5.4.7   An example can be seen from Algeria. The rate is determined in each contract. However, the law has fixed a minimum rate per area.[1]

EXAMPLE:

Production (BOE)/Area	A	B	C	D
0-20,00 BOE/day	5.5%	8.0%	11.0%	12.5%
20,001-50,000 BOE/day	10.5%	13.0%	16.0%	20.0%
50,001-100,000 BOE/day	11.5%	18.0%	20.0%	23.0%
>100,000 BOE/day	12.0%	14.5%	17.0%	20.0%

R-factor

4.5.4.8   Some countries have designed the royalty rate to depend on the "R factor" ("R" stands for "ratio"), similar to the one used to split profit oil. The R-factor model varies depending on the profitability of the project from different aspects, e.g., oil prices, project costs, production profile and reserves. A common "R-factor" is the ratio of cumulative receipts from the sale of petroleum to cumulative expenditures.

$$R = \text{Cumulative Revenue} (^1)/\text{Cumulative expenditure} (^2)$$

(1)   Cumulative net revenue actually received by the contractor for all tax years less taxes paid.

(2)   Cumulative expenditure, exploration and appraisal expenses, development and operating costs actually incurred by the contractor from the date the contract is signed. Therefore, cumulative expenditure is defined as the accumulated capital expenditure (Capex) and operating expenditures (Opex).

4.5.4.9   The factor R is calculated in each accounting period; and once the threshold is crossed, then the new tax rate will apply in the next accounting period.

4.5.4.10   The ratio is initially zero during exploration as there is no sale of petroleum while there may be considerable expenses, and the sales gradually grow over time. An R-factor less than 1 would mean that costs have not been fully recovered yet (total expenditures exceed total receipts). At payout, the R-factor will be equal to 1 and the larger the R-factor, the more profitable the operation. The royalty rate or the government's share of production may increase with increasing R-factors.

4.5.4.11   When the threshold is reached, the R-factor can be applied as follows:

- Increasing the royalties;

- Increasing the Profit Oil;

- Increasing the corporate income tax.

4.5.4.12   Some advantages of applying the PSC sliding scale system using the R-factor are as follows:

- Provide a progressive fiscal system that can balance interests between the government and the investors;

- Create incentives for the investor company to maintain the level of project profitability;

- Minimize the need for changes or renegotiation of contract terms.

4.5.4.13   However, there are some challenges of implementing a PSC sliding scale with the R-factor:

- Creating the wrong incentives: The contractor may incur relatively unnecessary costs to keep a lower R-factor that maintains a higher company share (*"gold plating"*);

- Determining the R-factor band: The band should be adapted to each field, target a reasonable rate of return for investors and a fair share of profit oil to the host country.

4.5.4.14   If designed well, PSC sliding scale systems may offer a progressive system that can be attractive for marginal projects, balancing the risks in facing price surges, e.g., oil price volatility, during the field lifetime, i.e., exploration, development and production.[22]

Corporate income tax

4.5.4.15   Most PSC-based systems include a corporate income tax which may have different forms of calculation:

- Corporate income tax is calculated separately, but with the same

---

[22] Trian Hendro Asmoro. PSC Sliding Scale as A Fiscal Model For Marginal Fields In Indonesia. IPA16-25-BC. 2016.

calculation as that used for Cost Oil. In these cases, the corporate income tax is simply a percentage of Profit Oil;

- Corporate income tax is calculated separately, in accordance with the corporate income tax law which are different from the bases used to calculate Cost Oil and Profit Oil;

- Corporate income tax is included in Profit Oil/Gas paid by the state company "on behalf of" the contractor (Gross Up/Tax Paid PSC/Taxes "in lieu") and the basis for its calculation is provided in the tax law and/ or the PSC.

4.5.4.16   Direct payment by the contractor: An example of a PSC with payment of direct taxes by the contractor is the Indonesia model where the contractor must satisfy a corporate income tax at an effective rate of 45%:

- Corporate tax, at a rate of 25%; and

- Tax on the remittance of funds ("final tax on profits after tax deduction") at the rate of 20%, payable regardless of whether a dividend is distributed or there is a remittance of funds from the branch to the central house and an international CDI between the country of residence of the operator and Indonesia.

4.5.4.17   The alternative is government (including National Oil Companies) payments on behalf of the contractor. The contractor's profit share is taxable. Some host countries pay such taxes on behalf of the contractor from their own share of the production (also known as "taxes paid on behalf" or "in lieu").

4.5.4.18   Examples of PSCs with payment of tax by the NOC are found in Egypt, Libya, Guyana and Iraq (Kurdistan). In these countries the profit oil of the State includes a volume of hydrocarbons sufficient to satisfy the corporate income tax of the contractor (in some cases, also other additional taxes), so that in order for the contractor to calculate the tax base of the corporate income tax, it is necessary to use the gross-up formula and apply the local corporate income tax rate to calculate the tax payment.

4.5.4.19   The fact that the government satisfies the tax in the name and on behalf of the contractor, does not exempt the latter from presenting a corporate income tax declaration and fulfilling the rest of the formal obligations in the country, since the contractor remains the corporate income tax taxpayer, regardless of whether the government is responsible for payment of the tax.

4.5.4.20   For double taxation relief purposes in the contractor's resident country, it is relevant that the contract establishes the necessary documentary requirements showing that obligations derived from PSCs are equivalent to the payment of income tax (e.g., a tax paying certificate).[23]

---

[23] In 1976, the Internal Revenue Service of the USA ruled that oil companies would not

4.5.4.21   The following example illustrates the application of the gross-up: in Guyana, in addition to the corporate income tax, the Government undertakes to satisfy, with its share of profit oil and on behalf of the contractor, not only the corporate income tax, but also the royalties and any other similar tax that may arise.

4.5.4.22   In Iraq (Kurdistan) the model provides that *"The share of the Profit Petroleum to which the GOVERNMENT is entitled in any Calendar Year in accordance with Article __ of this Contract shall be deemed to include a portion representing the corporate income tax imposed upon and due by each CONTRACTOR entity, and which will be paid directly by the GOVERNMENT on behalf of each such entity representing the CONTRACTOR to the appropriate tax authorities in accordance with Article __ of this Contract. The GOVERNMENT shall provide the CONTRACTOR with all written documentation and evidence reasonably required by the CONTRACTOR to confirm that such corporate income tax has been paid by the GOVERNMENT."*

"Each CONTRACTOR entity shall be subject to corporate income tax as provided in Article __ below, which shall be deemed to be inclusive and in full and total discharge of any corporate income tax of each such entity. Payment of the said corporate income tax shall be made for the entire duration of this Contract directly to the appropriate Kurdistan Region tax authorities by the GOVERNMENT, for the account of each CONTRACTOR entity, from the GOVERNMENT's share of the Profit Petroleum received pursuant to…"

4.6   NON-FISCAL CLAUSES GENERATING TAX ISSUES

4.6.1   General

4.6.1.1   To understand the full potential of the interaction between PSCs and corporate and other taxation, it is necessary to be aware of some of the other features of PSCs.

4.6.1.2   PSCs may contain **non-fiscal clauses** related to the duration of exploration and exploitation, bonuses, duties, the state participation in the operations, domestic market obligations, work program, local content (e.g., training programs), etc. It is important to be aware that non-fiscal clauses may have an impact on the ultimate fiscal take.

4.6.1.3   One type of non-fiscal clauses concern the corporate investment structure in the country of operation. Some countries require the IOCs to form an "office," branch or company. This may happen during the exploratory stage, and it is possible to invest through a branch, but for the presentation of the FDP it is

---

enjoy a tax credit on foreign income derived from PSCs as it was characterized as a royalty and concluded that this obligation did not constitute an "income tax."

necessary to invest through a local company. The main issues in this regard are covered in Chapter 7 (Permanent Establishments), including the fact that more than one PE may actually exist within one country. This is often the case as the common construct is to have one JOA for each underlying petroleum agreement. Further, other non-fiscal clauses that clearly affect tax matters are described under the following headings.

4.6.2   Contract period

4.6.2.1   Considerable time may elapse between investment in the extractives industry and the realization of profits. PSCs are therefore long-term in nature. Typically, they provide for a term of 20 or 25 years or longer from the commercialization of the asset and usually provide for extensions of the contract duration if continued commercial exploitation is expected. One of the differences between oil and gas due to market constraints is timing of production (typically gas discoveries take longer).

4.6.2.2   The following framework can be found in some PSCs regarding the contract period:

Exploratory phase: First phase X years (minimum commitments XX M USD with/without exploratory drilling) and second phase Y years (minimum commitment YYY M USD - YY exploratory drilling). Maximum extension of Z years.

Development and production phase: (i) Crude: X years, with potential extension period(s): X + X + X. If an extension is requested, the fiscal terms can be maintained or renegotiated depending on the terms of the PSC. (ii) Gas: X years, divided with potential extension periods: X + X + X.

4.6.3   Ring fence vs. consolidation

4.6.3.1   Ring-fencing is a rule that prevents costs or losses in one activity (e.g., oil and gas) or area being offset against income in another activity or area. For example, all costs associated with a given area must be recovered from revenues generated within that area, which can have an impact on the recovery of exploration costs and end up in final sunk costs (i.e., if the country of residence does not allow for deduction).

4.6.3.2   Some countries allow only certain classes of costs associated with an area to be recovered from revenues from another field (e.g., only exploration, but not development costs) or allow deduction of exploration costs incurred on an abandoned area with revenues from a producing area.

4.6.3.3   Where ring-fencing applies, investors having signed more than one PSC within a country will be compelled to independently manage each area through the corresponding joint venture, consortium or association (accounting and business, legal and tax obligations).

4.6.3.4   In imposing ring-fencing, governments make a trade-off between investment incentives and revenue collection. Ring-fencing prevents the postponement of tax revenue. Without ring-fencing, a company undertaking a series of projects would be able to deduct exploration or development expenditures from each new project against the income of projects that were already generating taxable income, which would be an incentive to invest in new fields.

4.7   Domestic market operation (DMO)

4.7.1.1   Many PSCs require the contractor to sell a portion of its share of production to the host government to help meet the local market demand. This requirement is referred to as the domestic market obligation (DMO) and is based on some governments' policy to supply and satisfy domestic demand ahead of export requirements. In some PSCs, such obligation applies only if the government's and the NOC's share of production are not sufficient to meet local demand. Usually, this contractor obligation is proportional to its share of production relative to the total production of the host country, and in some cases subject to a cap defined in each PSC.

4.7.1.2   In some PSCs, the price the contractor can charge for the DMO oil or gas is at a discount to world market prices; occasionally, the contract establishes a maximum price. This comes at a cost for the investor and will be typically incorporated in the contractor's project economics. In some PSCs, the government may also pay for the domestic crude in local currency at a predetermined exchange rate. Such DMO terms may expose the investors to lower price realization and foreign exchange risks, with a negative impact on the investment terms, and investors may require a higher share of the profits as a result. Both aspects need to be carefully and clearly established in the PSC for the sake of certainty.

4.7.1.3   Example of a DMO clause follows:

After commercial production commences, to fulfill its obligation towards the supply of the domestic market, CONTRACTOR agrees to sell and deliver to the Government of __ a portion of the share of Crude Oil, (...), calculated for each year as follows:

   (a)   *Compute [X] per cent of CONTRACTOR's entitlement (...) multiplied by total quantity of Oil produced from the Contract Area;*

   (b)   *The price at which such Oil can be [or "is"] delivered and sold (...) shall be [X] per cent of the price determined under Sub-section (...), and CONTRACTOR shall not be obligated to transport such Oil beyond the Point of Export, but upon request CONTRACTOR shall assist in arranging transportation and such assistance shall be without cost or risk to CONTRACTOR.*

4.8 Work commitments program

4.8.1.1 A key issue in PSC negotiation is the work program that outlines the contractor's commitments regarding e.g., seismic, drilling, information disseminations, financial obligations, and employment of the local workforce.

4.8.1.2 Examples of minimum work obligations in the Exploration phase:

- Specified in terms of kilometers of seismic data and number of wells to be drilled. Seismic work may constitute the only work in least explored (frontier) areas, and may consist of seismic data acquisition with an option to drill exploration wells;

- Acquire and interpret certain seismic data required to decide whether to drill a well.

4.8.1.3 Sometimes a minimum expenditure level is required in the work commitment. The terms of the work commitment outline indemnities for non-performance (e.g., failure to drill a well) as established in the petroleum contract. It is a sensitive aspect for exploration activity (as this embodies most of the risk).

4.8.1.4 An example is an excerpt from the from the Equatorial Guinea Model PSA:

(a) *obtain...all existing 2D and 3D seismic data and Well data at a purchase price of [__] Dollars ($[__]) ...and the Contractor shall undertake to interpret such information;*

(b) *reprocess [__] km. of existing 2D seismic data and [__] km. of 3D seismic data; and*

(c) *acquire [__] kilometers of new 3D seismic data. During the Second Exploration Sub-Period, the Contractor must drill a minimum of [__] Exploration Well[s] to a minimum depth of [__] meters below the seabed. The minimum expenditure for this period shall be [__] Dollars ($[__]).*

4.8.1.5 A further example is an excerpt from the India Model PSA 20051:

During the currency of the first Exploration Phase···, the Contractor shall complete the following Work Programme:

(a) *a seismic program consisting of the acquisition, processing and interpretation of [__] line kilometres of 2D and/or [__] sq. kms. of 3D seismic data in relation to the exploration objectives; and (b) [__] Exploration Wells shall be drilled to at least one of the following depths: i) [__] metres and [__] (geological objective); ii) to Basement; and iii) that point below which further drilling becomes impracticable due to geological conditions encountered and drilling would be abandoned by a reasonable prudent operator in the same or similar circumstances. Abandonment of drilling under this provision by the Contractor, would require unanimous approval by the Management Committee.*

4.9 Responsibility for decommissioning

4.9.1.1   The resource ownership may lead to the subject of decommissioning under a PSC. Under a concessionary system, the investor is typically responsible for decommissioning,[24] whereas under PSCs, unless specific provisions have been included in the contract the government is typically legally responsible for decommissioning . Properly structured, the abandonment cost can be estimated and anticipated through cost recovery during the producing years.[25]

4.9.1.2   Example of abandonment responsibility of contractor: PSC Kenya.

> *"If the Government does not elect to continue using such facilities, assets or wells, **the Contractor shall be responsible for their abandonment and decommissioning** upon termination of this Contract or of the Development Area within the corresponding Development area, if earlier. Contractor may in consultation with Government defer the abandonment and decommissioning operations for a reasonable length of time if this would result in operational efficiencies, which minimize the cost for all parties."*

ANNEX I: Country example - Brazil

1.4.8   Brazilian geological area subject to production share contracts

The Brazilian Production Share regime is limited to a particular geological formation, known as pre-salt. This is defined by the Law number 12.351, enacted on 22 December 2010, in the Annex.

The pre-salt polygon, which has approximately 800 km in length and 200 km in width, is located in Brazil, offshore, from the Santa Catarina state coast to Espírito Santo state coast, with an area of around 149 thousand km².

The pre-salt is a geological formation where a thick salt layer holds a massive amount of oil and gas below it. Located in offshore ultra-deep waters, the pre-salt layer has up to 2,000 meters of thickness.

The region also has other oil and gas fields above the pre-salt layer, which are called post-salt deposits, and these deposits are the conventional oil and gas ruled

---

[24] Silvana Tordo, *Fiscal Systems for Hydrocarbons. Design Issues*, World Bank working paper no. 123 (2007). Page 8.

[25] See Chapter 14: "The tax treatment of decommissioning."

by concession regimes. The production share regime governs the exploration and production of the pre-salt deposits.

The reason to have a different regime to the pre-salt deposits is that these geological formations have a very low exploratory risk and they are likely to have a high production level.

The Brazilian Fiscal Regime for the oil and gas industry is a mixed regime with concession and production sharing schemes. Brazil charges royalties and special participations (windfall tax) over production. The special participation is charged over fields with large production, and it is a kind of profit tax. These government interests are managed by the National Agency of Petroleum, Natural Gas and Biofuel (ANP – Agência Nacional do Petróleo, Gás Natural e Biocombustíveis).

The other part of government fiscal take directly involves the Federal Tax Administration and Tax Administrations of the subnational States. Brazil charges income tax at a 34% nominal rate, and this is a federal tax. For income tax purposes the signature bonuses, royalties and special participation are deductible.

1.4.9 PSC consortiums Brazilian government representatives

The Brazilian State is represented in all PSCs by a wholly state-owned company called Empresa Brasileira de Administração de Petróleo e Gás Natural S.A. – known as Pré-Sal S.A., or simply PPSA. This company was incorporated by Decree number 8,063, enacted on 1 August 2013.

Who is the consortium operator?

All PSCs in Brazil will be conducted by a consortium because, irrespective of the bid outcome, the winner is obliged to associate with PPSA which will indicate the Operational Committee president and half of its members.

With this in mind, there will be two different situations: the first is when Petrobras chooses to participate in the exploration and production, in which case, Petrobras will be the operator with nothing less than 30% of the equity participation; the second situation is when Petrobras does not use its right, and the operator will be a free choice of the contracted companies.

1.4.10 Tax issues in PSC regimes

The Brazilian oil and gas regulatory regime is independent of the Brazilian income tax legislation, irrespective of whether it is a concession or a PSC regime. The regulatory regime deals with Brazilian government interests which are: royalties and special participation (windfall tax) in a concession regime; or royalties and State profit oil in a PSC; and a signature bonus in both cases.

These government interests are charged on a ring fence base considering the field as a production unit, split from the other enterprises of a company for determining the profits or the amount of royalties, and in the case of PSC, the oil and gas volume in regard to the State profit oil share.

The Brazilian oil and gas income tax legislation follows the general taxation rules. There are many laws, decrees, and instructions that rule the Corporate Income Tax, but only two norms deal with the oil and gas industry income tax in particular. These are Law number 13.586, enacted on 28 December 2017, and normative instruction number 1.778, enacted on 29 December 2017.

The same law, combined with other normative instructions, (in particular number 1,781 enacted on 29 December 2017) and Decree number 9,537 enacted on 24 October 2018, deals with the Customs regime for the oil and gas industry, called REPETRO.

The establishment of cost oil and profit oil, and therefore the State share of production, has a close connection with the accounting rules and principles, as well as with the taxation rules and principles; however, they are ruled by the contract provisions.

Many different expenses are non-deductible for cost oil determination, for instance: royalties and signature bonus, interest and financial expenditures and income tax, although these expenses are deductible for corporate income tax.

The cost oil in a Brazilian PSC allows the expenses with decommissioning provisions, and annually the balance amount shall be adjusted by a contractual finance index.

None of these PSC provisions are allowable in the accounting/tax standards.

It is important to note that transactions between related companies are subject to transfer pricing rules, usually the same as those in the tax legislation, regarding cost oil ascertainment.

All the expenses which are allowable to be recovered as cost oil are registered in a proper account, mixing investments and operational costs, referred to as the Cost Oil account. The rate which the company is allowed to use for the cost oil amount in each year varies from 50% to 100% of the gross production value.

The value which exceeds the cost oil recovery limits can be carried forward to the next fiscal year.

For taxation matters, the investment expenditure and the operational costs are subject to different treatment. The investments may qualify for a capital allowance which consists of a rate of amortization of 2.5 times the unit product method rate, and the operational costs are deductible on an accrual basis.

1.4.11   Non-produced resource ownership

The non-produced oil and gas belongs to the Brazilian State. The company's production ownership arises at the production share point, after the PPSA has audited the cost oil and profit oil.

There is a clause which restricts the export of production in emergency cases, and establishes in this case that the production must be sold in the Brazilian market.

1.4.12   Risks and equity

All expenditures, in all project phases, including the entire risk of project failure, or loss, and the environmental restoration in the case of an accident, or compensation for third parties, are the company's liabilities.

However, there is a legal provision that allows the Brazilian Government to establish a fund that would invest in selected projects, assuming part of the risks as an enterprise partner, but this has not yet been set up.

1.4.13   Ownership of assets

The assets belong to the consortia; however, they can revert at the end of the contract or at the relinquishment of the contract area's plots to the Brazilian State. The conditions for the application of this provision are determined by the need for these assets to continue the operations in the contract area.

There is a difference between this provision and the property reversion to the Brazilian Government in concession contracts, since the latter is only applied when the asset acquisition cost is deductible for the calculation of the windfall government interest (special participation), and the National Oil Agency must consider that the asset is required to continue the operations in the decommissioning area.

1.4.14   Government interests

The government interests charged in the Brazilian Production Share Agreements are royalties at a 15% rate and signature bonuses only. The Brazilian revenue arising from the Union oil share in 2018 was around USD 353.9 million.[26]

1.4.15   Local content

There are local content requirements established in the contract. They vary from a global percentage of local equipment and service purchases, as well as a percentage of local content per phase, with different rates for different fields.

---

[26] Available in https://www.presalpetroleo.gov.br/ppsa/conteudo/147_326_relatorio_anual_administracao_2018.pdf

1.4.16   Work program

There is a work program, and the companies must present financial guarantees for the estimated value of seismic research and drilled wells in the contract.

1.4.17   Tax clauses

There are no tax clauses.

1.4.18   Tax stability clauses

There are no tax stability clauses.

1.4.19   Economic stability clauses

There are no economic stability clauses.

1.4.20   Brazilian government fixed percentages of the profit oil share

Round	Field	Government % Share
First	Libra	41,65
Second	South of Gato do Mato	11,53
	Around Sapinhoá	80
	North of Carcará	67,12
Third	Peroba	76,96
	High Cabo Frio West	22,87
	High Cabo Frio Central	75,8
Fourth	Três Marias	49,95
	Uirapuru	75,49
	Dois Irmãos	16,43
Fifth	Saturno	70,2
	Titã	23,49
	Pau-brasil	63,79
	South West of Tartaruga Verde	10,01

ANNEX II: Country example - Nigeria

1.4.21 Overview

Three categories of PSCs were executed in Nigeria;

- The 1991/1993 PSCs.

- The 1998 PSCs.

- The 2005 PSCs.

Some of the major fiscal terms of each of these classes of PSC were:

1.4.22 The 1991/1993 PSCs

- OPL Obligation – 50% of contract area to be relinquished after 10 yrs.

- OML/Production Period – for a renewable minimum period of 20 yrs.

- Production Bonus – 0.2% for Cumulative Production up to 50 million barrels, 0.1% for Cumulative Production up to 100 million barrels (this is calculated on current price at the time of attainment of target). Bonus is fiscally deductible but not recoverable from cost oil.

- Royalty rate is a graduated percentage of production volume ranging from 12% to 0% for the Deep Offshore, and 10% for the Inland Basin (Benue Block).

- Tax Rate – the Deep Offshore and Inland Basin Act (DOIBA) provides for the determination of the petroleum profit tax (PPT) payable in accordance with the provision of the Petroleum Profit Tax Act (PPTA) with a provision that the tax shall be at the flat rate of 50% of chargeable profit for all PSCs.

- Investment Tax Credit (ITC) – an amount equal to 50% of qualifying capital expenditure (QCE) incurred in the year to be set-off against assessable tax to arrive at chargeable tax.

- No cost recovery limits.

- Profit Oil = Production – Royalty Oil – Cost Oil – Tax Oil.

1.4.23 The 1998 PSCs

The same terms of the 1993 PSCs were maintained except for:

- Introduction of the Investment Tax Allowance (ITA) which replaced the Investment Tax Credit (ITC). ITA is an amount equal to 50% of QCE incurred to be claimed as part of capital allowances.

- Introduction of cost recovery limits.

1.4.24   2005 PSCs

Same fiscal terms as the 1998 PSCs with the introduction of:

- Increased Signature Bonus.

- Royalty rate 0% until water depth exceeds 1000m. 1% royalty rate for water depth beyond 1000m.

ANNEX III: Sources of information

A directory of Petroleum and Mineral Contracts.

Daniel Johnston, *International Petroleum Fiscal Systems and Production Sharing Contracts,* (PennWell Books, Tulsa, Oklahoma,1994).

Daniel Johnston, *International Exploration Economics, Risk, and Contract Analysis*, (PennWell Books, Tulsa, Oklahoma, 2003).

Charlotte J. Wright, Rebecca A. Gallun, I*nternational Petroleum Accounting* (PenWell Books, Tulsa, Oklahoma, 2005).

Charlotte J. Wright and Rebecca A. Gallun, *Fundamentals of Oil & Gas Accounting* (PenWell Books, Tulsa, Oklahoma, 2008).

E. Sunley et al., *Revenue from the Oil and Gas Sector: Issues and Country Experience* (Washington, DC: IMF, 2002), http://siteresources.worldbank.org/INTTPA/Resources/SunleyPaper.pdf

Emil M. Sunley, Thomas Baunsgaard and Dominique Simard, *Revenue from the Oil and Gas Sector: Issues and Country Experience*

Examining the Crude Details: Government Audits of Oil & Gas Project Costs to Maximize Revenue Collection (Oxfam November 2018). https://www.oxfam.org/en/research/examining-crude-details

IMF, *Fiscal Regimes for Extractive Industries: Design and Implementation,* 15 August 2012: https://www.imf.org/external/np/pp/eng/2012/081512.pdf

John Abrahamson, *International Taxation of Energy Production and Distribution,* Series of International Taxation 65. Wolters Kluwer (2018).

Jones Day, *Indonesia's New Gross Split Production Sharing Contracts for the Oil & Gas Industry.*

Kirsten Bindemann, *Production-Sharing Agreements: An Economic Analysis*, Oxford Institute for Energy Studies, 1999.

Silvana Tordo, *Fiscal Systems for Hydrocarbons: Design Issues*, World Bank working paper no. 123 (2007).

WoodMackenzie,PinsentMasons,*Indonesia'snewGrossSplitPSC*,https://www.pinsentmasons.com/PDF/2017/Asia%20Pacific/Indonesias-new-Gross-Split-PSC.pdf

Chapter 5

Tax Incentives

5.1 INTRODUCTION

5.1.1 Executive summary

5.1.1.1. This chapter provides a general framework on the design and use of tax incentives (in Section 5.1-2 and 5.3) as well as specific analysis of their use in the extractives sector in developing countries (in Sections 5.3 to 5.5). It has been written as a reference document and is not intended to replicate the work undertaken by others. A bibliography of reference documents is included for further research.

5.1.1.2. Section 5.5. looks at typical types of tax incentive available in the extractives sector, including incentives within export processing zones.

5.1.1.3. Section 5.6. looks at cost based incentives available in relation to direct taxation, customs duties and VAT. The section also examines production royalty-based incentives and looks at the potential issues arising from their use.

5.1.2 What is a tax incentive?

5.1.2.1 The first challenge for this chapter is the definition of a tax incentive. At the simplest level, a tax incentive could be considered as the difference between the default regime (generally applicable regime), and the one that is being examined, that results in a reduction in the tax burden (whether in the quantum or timing of the tax liability). These special provisions would clearly be captured by this definition. However, this definition may be too wide as it captures differences to the default regime that are structural in nature and intended to reflect the particular features of an industry.

5.1.2.2 Consider, as is common in the extractives industry, a tax that imposes a charge on the taxpayer on a cash basis, rather than on an accruals basis as may be the normal (default) approach. This is a structural choice of the government, which may create more progressivity in the fiscal regime and encourage investment. This objective may be achieved by providing immediate offsetting of capital expenditure against income (otherwise known as 100% tax depreciation or capital allowances) and then denying tax relief for the cost of funding (i.e., denying tax relief for interest incurred on debt which would normally be allowed under the default regime). Under the above definition, the 100% tax depreciation would be seen as a tax incentive despite the fact that it is a normal feature of a tax based on cash flow and may be partly offset by the denial of relief for funding costs. Therefore, it is important to consider the context of the whole tax regime and identify any related (and offsetting) elements of the tax regime.

5.1.2.3　　　Drawing on Norway's experience, Box 5.B.1 demonstrates the importance of considering incentives in the context of the fiscal regime as a whole.

BOX 5.B.1:

In Norway, under the special petroleum tax regime relating to extraction and transportation by pipeline of oil and gas on the Norwegian Continental Shelf (NCS), costs incurred to acquire relevant fixed assets for production, processing and transportation on the NCS may be depreciated at an annual rate of 16 2/3 per cent starting in the year of investment. Such straight-line depreciation over six years deviates from the general rules of the General Tax Act in that it will normally represent earlier depreciation and 'pay back' to the investor, rather than following the trajectory of the economic life of the asset which is the principle underlying the depreciation rules of the General Tax Act.

The depreciation profile in the petroleum tax regime is one element among others intended to achieve a balanced distribution of risks and rewards between the investors and the State. Front loading of recovery of investment costs is beneficial to the investor and contributes to the reduction of investment risks. However, the design of the petroleum tax system as a whole, including the timing aspects of the special tax base, should be understood in the context of a combined tax rate of 78 per cent (compared to the general corporation tax rate of 22 per cent). The special petroleum tax regime is designed to capture as much as possible of the resource rent for the State and establishes a much higher level of taxation. The special rules on capital allowances should not be seen as a net tax incentive.

5.1.2.4　　　A potential definition for an incentive could therefore rest on the overall impact of the tax burden on the taxpayer for undertaking the activity. This would involve comparing the investment as a whole and identifying the total payments to government under the default regime and under the regime that is operating in practice. Such an approach will necessarily look beyond the tax system to all financial contributions. As noted in Chapter 2 (on the government's fiscal take), the extractives industry can be subject to commitments to make investments (such as in infrastructure) that go beyond what they would need to operate.

5.1.2.5   Based on careful consideration and the above caveats, this chapter uses the following more restricted definition of a tax incentive: "the net difference between the burden imposed under the generally applicable regime   and the burden that is predicted to be borne by the taxpayer under the incentive regime, across the lifetime of the project."

5.1.3   What might be the role of tax incentives?

5.1.3.1   Tax incentives are generally used to attract investment or otherwise change the behaviour of potential investors. They represent a deviation from the generally applicable regime; incentives are generally justified by policymakers on the basis that the targeted investment or behaviour would not have occurred under general regime.

5.1.3.2   However, the effectiveness of tax incentives at attracting investment is not clear-cut. The *United Nations Handbook on Selected Issues in Protecting the Tax Base of Developing Countries* states that the rise of the multinational enterprise and capital mobility have made tax incentives more important. However, while tax incentives may make an investment more attractive, in developing countries in particular, they   generally will not compensate for deficiencies such as a lack of infrastructure, reliable power, or weak rule of law.[1] Moreover, where incentives have been found to have a positive impact on inducing investment, there has been no knock-on effect on increasing fixed assets such as machinery and buildings, which are more likely to generate structural economic growth than other forms of investment.[2] The conclusion is that tax incentives alone will not attract investment.

5.1.3.3   The effectiveness of tax incentives is examined further in relation to the extractives industry in Section 5.2.3. However, at this stage, it is sufficient to note that the empirical evidence of the effect of tax incentives is mixed. While there can be valid reasons for providing incentives, there are some instances where tax incentives have gone beyond what is necessary to deliver the intended outcomes. It is therefore important to have a clear critical framework for considering the merits of tax incentives.

5.1.4   International initiatives on harmful tax incentives

5.1.4.1   Given that tax incentives deviate from the default regime, they can raise concerns from other countries that the resulting tax environment could be deemed to be harmful to their tax revenue base. Thus, in addition to weighing

---

[1] Zolt, E. Tax Treaties and Developing Countries, UCLA School of Law, Law-Econ Research Paper No 18-12 (12 September 2018) p. 527 to 528. Other relevant studies include Van Parys, S. and James, S., Investment Climate and the Effectiveness of Tax Incentives, World Bank Group (2009); and Rolfe, R.J. & White, R.A. *Investors' assessment of the importance of tax incentives in locating foreign export-oriented investment: An exploratory study*, in The Journal of the American Taxation Association, 14(1), 39, 1992

[2] Klemm and Parys 2011

the advantages and disadvantages of tax incentives from a domestic standpoint, countries should consider the international initiatives listed in Box 5.B.2.

BOX 5.B.2:

Harmful Tax Practices

The recent work on tackling Base Erosion and Profit Shifting ("BEPS") by the G20 and the OECD has focused attention on the potential for "harmful tax practices," which can include the use of incentives that are targeted purely at inbound investors. The Forum on Harmful Tax Practices ("FHTP") has refocused its attention to identify those tax practices, following the publication of the BEPS Action Plan, Action 5 (on countering harmful tax practices more effectively). Members of the OECD's Inclusive Framework on BEPS have committed to ensuring that all new incentive regimes comply with the Action 5 requirements, and all regimes are actively peer reviewed.

EU list of non-cooperative jurisdictions

The European Union has issued a list of non-cooperative tax jurisdictions.[3] The review criteria include transparency and exchange of information; the existence of preferential tax regimes; and no corporate income tax or a zero corporate tax rate. Jurisdictions are selected for review based on the strength of their economic ties with the EU; level of financial activity; and whether they would be considered a safe place where tax avoiders could move their money.[4]

State Aid

'State aid' is defined as an advantage in any form whatsoever conferred on a selective basis to undertakings by national public authorities. The EU has agreed not to allow state aid that distorts competition and is likely to affect trade between member states. If an EU country granted a lower than normal tax rate for extractives, thus gaining an advantage with respect to attracting extractive industry investment compared to other EU countries, this could be considered state aid and may be disallowed unless it is subject to a specific exception or within certain specified limits.[5]

---

[3] The African Tax Administration Forum (ATAF) has raised serious concerns about the EU approach, particularly with respect to the requirement to implement the OECD BEPS minimum standards.

[4] https://ec.europa.eu/taxation_customs/sites/taxation/files/2016-09-15_scoreboard-indicators.pdf

[5] The EU allows some level of state aid, for example regional state aid as a percentage of investment.

Exceptions to state aid rules may be granted where there is a clear need. For example, to enable Liquified Natural Gas (LNG)-related investments in the northernmost part of Norway, the government introduced an accelerated depreciation rate of 33 $^{1/3}$ per cent, which was twice as fast as the standard depreciation rate for other petroleum investments. The measure was approved by state aid rules in 2002. It was a deliberate incentive to facilitate the development of the Snøhvit gas field in the Arctic, and the transportation system to bring the natural gas onshore and to the LNG plant at Melkøya.

5.2   A CRITICAL FRAMEWORK FOR CONSIDERING TAX INCENTIVES

5.2.1   Introduction

5.2.1.1   As noted above, it is important to consider the role of tax incentives with a clear conceptual framework in mind. Tax incentives have been analysed by economists, academics, governments, NGOs, and industry, and the consensus conclusions in relation to governance, efficiency, effectiveness and ease of administration are considered in this section.

5.2.2   Governance

5.2.2.1   It is important that any deviations from the default tax regime are subject to an impact analysis so that the government has a clear understanding of the costs and benefits before it decides to grant an incentive. Incentives should also be governed transparently, so that taxpayers understand the taxes they will pay, and the public can hold governments accountable.

5.2.2.2   The following are considered best practices:

- **Prescribed in law.** Tax reliefs and incentives should be set out in the law with clear criteria for claiming them. Defining a range of possible incentives in law will limit the extent of any negotiation. Incentives should be based on clear, measurable policy objectives in order to enable monitoring and accountability. Should government choose to give decision-makers discretion with respect to granting incentives, these powers should be limited, transparent, and subject to checks and balances, to prevent the risk of corruption. Ideally, tax incentives should be approved by parliament. Box 5.B.3 sets out the legislative system for granting tax incentives in South Africa.

- **Transparent.** Where incentives and reliefs are negotiated for individual projects as part of the investment agreement they should be disclosed. The best practice, according to the IMF transparency code, is when: "the revenue loss from tax expenditures is estimated by sector or policy area and is published at least annually. There is control on, or budgetary objectives for, the size of tax expenditures."[6] In addition, the B Team[7] Responsible Tax Principles developed by a group of businesses state: "Ideally, tax exemptions and reliefs should be specified by law and generally available to all market participants. Where there are exceptions, we will work with relevant authorities to encourage publication of those incentives and contracts."

- **Monitored.** The value of tax incentives and reliefs should be reported annually by government as part of tax expenditure reports. The IMF and other international organisations provide detailed methodology and support to develop tax expenditure assessments.[8] There should be clear parameters for review, as well as sunset clauses to reduce the potential costs of badly designed tax incentive programmes. The revenue authority should also monitor the use of the incentives in its risk and audit programmes. Extractive companies should also report publicly on the incentives utilized in order to further strengthen transparency on both sides.

BOX 5.B.3:

In South Africa, tax incentives are only granted through national legislation. According to section 77 of the Constitution, a money bill imposes national taxes, or reduces or grants exemptions from any national taxes. Furthermore, section 73(2) of the Constitution stipulates that only the Cabinet member responsible for national financial matters may introduce a money bill in the National Assembly; i.e., only the Minister of Finance may introduce a bill dealing with tax exemptions in Parliament, to be considered via the legislative process.

5.2.3   Effectiveness

5.2.3.1   Tax incentives are introduced for a purpose, namely, to influence a decision by the taxpayer which may otherwise be less optimal than the alternative that the government wishes to encourage. This provides a natural framework for examining the effectiveness of the incentive – i.e., will the incentive change

---

[6] https://blog-pfm.imf.org/files/ft-code.pdf

[7] A-New-Bar-for-Responsible-Tax.pdf (bteam.org)

[8] https://www.imf.org/en/Publications/Fiscal-Affairs-Department-How-To-Notes/Issues/2019/03/27/Tax-Expenditure-Reporting-and-Its-Use-in-Fiscal-Management-A-Guide-for-Developing-Economies-46676

behaviour in the way intended by the government.

5.2.3.2　This evaluation needs to go beyond the question of whether the desired behaviour was achieved and question whether the desired behaviour has been stimulated by the incentive. If the behaviour would have happened in the absence of the incentive, then the incentive would be ineffective and a dead-weight cost to the budget.

5.2.3.3　The UN Handbook on Protecting the Tax Base[9] notes that most surveys of business executives conclude that taxes were rarely a major consideration in deciding whether and where to invest. However, the predictability of the fiscal regime is likely to be a factor as noted below. The primary question for the business is the probability of recoverable mineral reserves and the factors in Box 5.B.4 that impact the ability to produce and market the reserves, after which the effective tax rate becomes relevant. Box 4 is a list of non-tax factors that influence investment decisions (source: UN Handbook on Protecting the Tax Base).

Box 5.B.4:
Non-tax factors influencing investment decisions

1. Consistent and stable macroeconomic and fiscal policy.
2. Political stability.
3. Adequate physical, financial, legal and institutional infrastructure.
4. Effective, transparent and accountable public administration.
5. Skilled labour force and flexible labour code.
6. Availability of adequate dispute resolution mechanisms.
7. Foreign exchange rules and the ability to repatriate profits.
8. Language and cultural conditions.
9. Factor and product markets—size and efficiency.

5.2.3.4　Hence, there is no 'one-size-fits-all' framework to determine whether and which tax incentives will be effective. Tax incentives can be effective stimulants to long term investment and economic growth if used as part of a well-conceived and well-implemented strategy to achieve certain development objectives, in addition to a predictable, and efficient tax regime.

5.2.3.5　It is best practice for tax incentives to be developed as part of clear, established objectives. The objective of a tax incentive and the decision to use it should be based on a broad economic assessment by the relevant country, including, for example, its financial, social or environmental requirements. The objective may be broad (e.g., to attract new investment) or narrow and examples include:

---

[9] *United Nations Handbook on Selected Issues in Protecting the Tax Base of Developing Countries:* Second Edition, 2017.

- The creation of a set number of new jobs;

- Expansion of a facility;

- The development of local skills, including those required for future jobs, or;

- Investment in schools and hospitals.

5.2.3.6   These activities may also be tied to a particular region or locality in order to promote broader welfare benefits in that area. Irrespective of the contents, clearly defining the objective up-front is essential if effectiveness is to be assessed.

5.2.3.7   The application of this principle to the extractive industry is discussed further below (see Section 5.5), but, in general, studies to date have shown that although tax rates are a consideration for whether a project goes forward, they are less of a priority for locational decisions (security is usually first, and predictability second).[10]

5.2.4   Efficiency

5.2.4.1   A tax incentive is efficient when it achieves the policy objective at minimum social cost. Such costs include net revenue losses for government, the cost of administering the incentive, as well as social costs such as the displacement of other investments.

5.2.4.2   Like effectiveness, efficiency is also a relative concept. The lower the cost of the incentive in meeting the policy objective, the more efficient it is, and vice versa. In this way, a tax incentive can be evaluated against alternative ways that the investment could be induced (e.g., a government grant for infrastructure costs). The option that best meets the policy goal at the lowest cost is considered the most efficient option. This requires a "joined up government" approach to avoid decisions that are optimal when considered in isolation resulting in an outcome that is sub-optimal when considered together.

5.2.4.3   The potential loss of tax revenue through the use of tax incentives should be considered on the basis of the full project, including other risk compensation, economic benefits to the broader economy, and negative externalities (e.g., environmental degradation, negative health impacts). For example, tax incentives that enable first entrants of foreign direct investment into a sector may increase economic growth and development through the broader development of the sector and associated skills and technology. The risk of these developments not occurring needs to be considered in the analysis. Any revenue impacts (positive and

---

[10] The Fraser Institute's survey of mining and exploration companies (2017) lists the following factors in order of priority: (1) quality of the resource; (2) economic factors such as location of the resource, price outlook for target minerals and technology; and (3) policy climate such as enforcement of existing rules, taxation, security of tenure, infrastructure, and political stability etc.

negative) should be considered over the life of the investment and this should be in the context of the overall fiscal package, not a standalone incentive. It is important to note, however, that governments may face annual budget cycles and hence may need to explain business cases for investments with a longer payback period.

Box 5.B.5:
Analyzing and monitoring the cost of incentives

Cost-benefit analysis is an assessment of the social costs and benefits of a proposed incentive, or package of incentives within an overall fiscal package. This should be done in advance of the granting of an incentive and then used in monitoring the incentive's impact over its duration. It requires estimating the benefits generated by the investment, and the net costs in terms of lost revenues.

Given likely volatility in commodity prices throughout the life of an investment, as well as other uncertainties such as delays and cost increases, governments should model the value of an incentive at various price scenarios.

Tax expenditure analysis is also used to monitor the nominal value of incentives as they are used over time. Under 'Tax expenditure' analysis an amount of tax not collected is considered in the same way as an amount of revenue spent. This is important for transparency, and to periodically reassess the cost-benefit analysis of granted incentives. However, as the up-front cost benefit analysis highlights, the nominal cost of the tax relief in accounting terms is not the same as the net cost or benefit to public revenues, or the net cost or benefit overall.

Apparent tax expenditures may not be net incentives but structural features, where there is an offsetting tax collected. As noted above, the immediate expensing of capital investment within a cash flow tax that denies relief for funding cost (i.e., interest) can be seen to be structural rather than an incentive.

5.2.5   Ease of administration

5.2.5.1   Incentives complicate tax administration, especially where they are granted on a discretionary basis, creating competing fiscal regimes.

5.2.5.2   Incentives should be carefully defined with clear rules about what type of activity or expenditure qualifies for the incentive. Poorly designed incentives may further expose governments to the risk of profit shifting and tax avoidance, and thus increase the administrative burden. Incentives that create parallel fiscal regimes, may give rise to concerns over the veracity of transfer prices.

5.2.5.3   The abrupt ending of a tax incentive may also create an incentive to accelerate profits to avoid paying taxes when the incentive ends.

5.3   Application to the extractive industry in developing countries

5.3.1.1   The extractive industry is different from other sectors. Mineral and petroleum resources are finite, and generally owned by the state (or region) for the benefit of its citizens. There is also the prospect of substantial revenues, which, if managed well, have the potential to create lasting development outcomes. Thus, any use of tax incentives should be considered carefully, to avoid forgoing government revenues unnecessarily.

5.3.1.2   If governments choose to offer tax incentives, these incentives should be carefully designed to align with the special features of the extractive industries:

- Capital-intensive, with significant investment in exploration and development mostly sourced from the private sector;

- Long periods of pre-production during which no revenue is earned;

- High risk because it depends on exploration being successful, and its profit is sensitive to commodity prices and exchange rates, which can be volatile.

5.3.1.3   These features may require a special fiscal regime, which diverges from the general tax regime, such as incentives that mitigate environmental and social impacts by encouraging companies to procure supplies locally or restore mine sites, for example.

5.3.1.4   Designing resource tax policy may require certain trade-offs. In some cases, it may be worth forgoing some government revenue in order to attract productive investment. However, the benefits of the investment must outweigh the amount of revenue forgone, as well as other costs. Incentives that are too generous risk being politically unsustainable and may lead to a less stable and predictable fiscal regime.

5.4   APPLYING THE EVALUATIVE FRAMEWORK

5.4.1   Governance

5.4.1.1   It is common for countries to have numerous laws that set out the extractive industry fiscal regime. Each of those laws may contain tax incentives.

5.4.1.2   The general income tax code may include special provisions for mining, oil and gas either in a separate schedule or chapter, or in the main part of the code. These could, for example, provide for a different rate of corporate income tax for these sectors.

5.4.1.3   The mining or petroleum law may contain more details on the sector-specific fiscal regime, for example, a reduced rate of tax or duty collected on imported goods for mining.

5.4.1.4   The production sharing contract could provide for the payment of corporate taxes from the government share of profits on behalf of the extractive company.

5.4.1.5   Taxes paid by foreign investors are also often influenced by Double Taxation Agreements (DTAs), and national investment laws. DTAs are bilateral or multilateral agreements between countries that set out which country has the right to collect tax on different types of income (see Chapter 6). DTAs are another aspect of the legal framework that interacts with tax incentives in the primary law, and project contracts.

5.4.1.6   As in all sectors, tax incentives granted to extractive companies should be publicly disclosed. This implies that governments should publish not only all the laws and international agreements mentioned above, but also any contractual agreement with oil, gas and mining companies. This is in line with the contract disclosure requirement under the Extractive Industry Transparency Initiative ("EITI") standard as of 2021.[11] By publishing all extractive industry contracts, any incentive granted to a specific project is disclosed to all relevant parties: government agencies, the legislature, audit institutions, other companies, and taxpayers in general. Such contract disclosure should also apply to tax incentives granted in addenda or appendices.

5.4.2   Effectiveness

5.4.2.1   Investment decisions are based on the net present value of cash flows (after tax) that the investor expects to generate from the investment over the life of the project. The investment decision is impacted primarily by the quality of the resources, the price outlook for target minerals, and the cost of constructing and operating the project. The upfront cost to develop the project is impacted by the location of the resource, the degree of technical risk related to extraction, and the availability of existing transport infrastructure. The policy climate, including regulatory stability, security of tenure and the rule of law, also generally tends to play a key role. Once these key investment hurdles have been satisfied, the tax regime will be relevant to the decision to invest. In this regard, incentives may be a less important factor in attracting investment than in other sectors, such as those that are more mobile, and thus, more responsive to preferential tax treatment.

---

[11] https://eiti.org/news/eiti-launches-2019-eiti-standard

5.4.2.2   Should governments choose to offer tax incentives, those incentives should be effective – i.e., they should make a difference to the investor's behaviour. This means that incentives will necessarily be targeted to marginal investors, such as those who would not have invested otherwise. There is no one-size-fits-all approach to determining when an incentive is necessary to attract investment; however, as in the case of the tax holiday given in Box 5.B.6, financial modelling can assist.

Box 5.B.6:
Assessing the cost of a tax incentive – Yaoure gold mine

Cote D'Ivoire sought to attract international investment to its gold mining sector, which is relatively undeveloped compared to established regional producers. As part of its new mining code developed in 2014, it gave a five-year tax holiday to new mining projects.

The government of Cote d'Ivoire developed a basic financial model of the Yaoure gold mine, to assess the potential cost of this incentive. The analysis, using information published by Amara Mining, estimated that the investor could achieve an internal rate of return without the tax incentive of between 15% to 34% for a gold price between $1,000-$1,500/oz.[12] The tax incentive was estimated to increase companies' IRR in its base scenario by around five percentage points. However, the government also noted that there is a three-percentage point difference between the IRR in their model and that given by the company, possibly due to different cost estimates, and other fiscal costs. The rate of return would also need to be adjusted for country risk.

The government concluded that the tax holiday in the case of the Yaoure mine was not necessary to provide an attractive enough investment prospect. The government has since removed the tax holiday from the mining code.

5.4.2.3   A core element for delivering an effective incentive is a predictable and stable tax system. Tax incentives are more likely to be sustainable if they do not overreach in terms of time, and value. There should be clear parameters for review, as well as sunset clauses to reduce the potential costs of badly designed or inefficient tax incentives programmes. For example, a government could specify that an investment tax credit be carried forward for the first three "profitable" years. This would prevent the deferral of tax payments for long periods. Moreover, tax incentives should not exceed the time it takes to recover the investment (i.e., the pay-back period), unless there is a good reason according to the cost-benefit analysis.

---

[12] N'Guessan, Ernest Koudajo, and Esse, Bienvenu, (2017) *Yaoure Gold Mine Project Financial Model*, Open Oil, https://openoil.net/portfolio/yaoure-model-and-narrative-report/

Box 5.B.7:
When a tax holiday starts: Rio Tinto Simfer – Guinea

One of the key elements of a tax holiday is its duration, which determines the total cost in lost revenue. Depending on how the tax holiday provision is drafted, it may start at the date when a mine enters into its production phase or from the year in which 'first taxable profits' are generated. In this example from Guinea, in relation to the iron ore SIMFER project, Rio Tinto and the government of Guinea agreed in article 29.1 of the 2014 mining agreement that the eight-year tax holiday starts at the date of "first taxable profits."[13] This represented a departure from the applicable mining law at the time the contract was signed, according to which income tax holidays started in the year of the first production.[14]

From the investor's perspective, the start date of the tax holiday meant it could recover the carried forward tax losses, before getting the benefit from the tax holiday. However, from the government's perspective, the first taxable profits may arise a number of years after first production, depending on the pace of production, mineral prices and amortisation rules; thus extending the tax holiday further into the future, and deferring government revenues for a considerable time.

5.4.2.4   Incentives that depend on the achievement of certain goals (see Box 5.B.8, and 5.B.9) or adapt with changing economic circumstances (Box 5.B.10) are also more likely to be sustainable, although potentially harder to administer. If governments offer tax incentives and subsequent changes in circumstances make it uneconomic, or politically unfeasible to uphold these commitments, they may feel pressure to unilaterally change the terms, adversely affecting the predictability of the investment environment. If, however, they design incentives to automatically adapt to profitability, for example, to reduce the incentive when commodity prices rise, the result may be more acceptable to government and hence less susceptible to change.

[13] https://www.contratsminiersguinee.org/contract/ocds-591adf-0925073922/view#/pdf

[14] http://www.droit-afrique.com/upload/doc/guinee/Guinee-Code-1995-minier_Abroge.pdf

Box 5.B.8:
'Pioneering status' in Singapore

The Government of Singapore offers a concessionary tax rate or complete exemption to "pioneering" investors for 5 to 15 years, provided they fulfil certain conditions on an annual basis, including total business expenditure, the creation of jobs, payments to local suppliers, and knowledge and technology transfer. The incentive in the law is available to all investors that fall into the category of "pioneering." If the conditions are not met, the tax rate steps up. Until the end of the incentive period, the investors may have their profits taxed at a concessional rate if certain conditions are met.

The incentive is monitored by the Economic Development Board (EDB). Investors that are granted the incentive must submit regular progress reports to the EDB for the evaluation of performance. If there is any breach of conditions, the incentive may be revoked, and associated benefits recovered.

Box 5.B.9:
Tax incentive calculation for gold production in South Africa

Companies earning taxable income from mining for gold in South Africa are not taxed at the general corporate tax rate of 28 per cent, but are taxed (since 1936) at a rate determined by applying a formula. The formula is to be determined separately for each gold mine and is progressive in nature. It was designed to encourage the mining of marginal ore and mining of ore at great depth.

In 2019, the formula that applied to all gold mines was: $y = 34 - (170 \div x)$, where y is the rate to be determined and x is the ratio, expressed as a percentage, of taxable income to income. The ratio is effectively profit over revenue. The effect of applying the formula is that the tax rate applying to gold mines can vary from 0 per cent to 32.3 per cent. An important feature of the formula is that the rate of 0 per cent is available for gold mines that are not profitable or have taxable income of not more than 5 per cent of gold mining income.

> **Box 5.B.10:**
> **Oil recovery tax credit linked to reference price**
>
> The United States provides an incentive to encourage enhanced oil recovery projects in the United States. This incentive allows a tax credit, enhanced oil recovery credit ("EOR credit"), of (generally) 15% of costs identified as qualified enhanced oil recovery costs. The credit percentage is reduced to the extent the reference price of oil is in excess of the base value (adjusted for inflation) of 28 USD. This credit is provided for in the U.S. Internal Revenue Code and as such, is available to any investor involved in a qualified enhanced oil recovery project that has qualified enhanced oil recovery costs for the year.
>
> The credit can be viewed as a very effective targeted incentive, achieving the goals of the investor, the government and the public. The incentive is transparent, has certainty of application and can be viewed as equitable to both the investor and the government.
>
> The credit is designed to encourage investors to invest in projects to produce oil that might otherwise be less profitable to produce and thereby increase the supply of oil for the country. From the perspective of the government, the cost of the incentive is reduced or eliminated to the extent the value of the oil produced increases beyond a designated level, which might otherwise provide an unintended benefit to the investor.

5.4.3   Efficiency

5.4.3.1   Tax incentives should be evaluated against alternative ways that the mining investment could be induced (e.g., government paying for infrastructure to reduce mine costs). The option that best meets the policy goal at the lowest cost is considered the most efficient option. In extractives, as in other sectors, redundancy is more likely to be avoided if incentives are targeted to marginal investors who would not have invested otherwise. Project-specific financial modelling is critical to such a determination.

5.4.3.2   Cost-benefit analysis is another way to assess the efficiency of potential tax incentives. The objective is to compare the costs and benefits of offering tax incentives to extractive industry investors. The latter must outweigh the former for the incentive to be efficient. The analysis should focus on direct impacts that are more easily measured, for example, jobs, and taxes; versus secondary impacts such as household consumption by mine employees.

5.4.3.3   Detailed consideration of the net benefits of a project is needed in order to make an informed decision. Table 5.T.1 sets out the main costs and benefits of tax incentives in the extractives sector.

Table 5.T.1. Costs and benefits

Costs	Benefits
• The amount of revenue foregone from the incentive, assuming the investment would have occurred without it;	• The amount of economic value the extractive operation brings to the economy (including through the multiplier effect);
• Environmental, economic and social costs;	• Employment: the number of jobs created by the extractive industry operation;
• Administrative costs of implementing and monitoring incentives;	• Skills development;
• Economic distortions introduced due to differential treatment of certain investments;	• Government revenues: the amount of revenue generated for the host government by the extractive industry operation.
• Potential for corruption or abuse in the granting and administration of tax incentives. Whilst this risk may be difficult to measure, it can be minimised through good governance practices (see paragraph 5.2.2).	

5.4.3.4   A cost-benefit analysis should be considered as part of the broader framework of the economic impact of investment. As such, it may factor the development of infrastructure, including ports, roads, airports, hospitals, schools, health and community centres, as well as social and environmental impacts, including displacement of communities, pollution of water resources, and potential conflict. These costs and benefits relate to evaluating extractive industry investment generally, not tax incentives specifically. Incentives may also be used to motivate companies to invest in practices that contribute to sustainable development, and, in this way, create additional benefits that could also feature in a cost-benefit analysis.

5.4.3.5   Governments should use financial models to quantify the revenue impact of tax incentives both in terms of the cost (i.e., revenue forgone, non-fiscal costs of extraction), and the benefit (i.e., the amount of revenue and other economic benefits generated by the extractive industry operation).

> **Box 5.B.11:**
> **Excessive tax breaks: Rusal Compagnie**
> **des Bauxites de Kindia – Guinea**
>
> In many cases, tax incentives are granted on the basis of contributions made by an extractive company to the economy of the host country, which can be assessed and debated (see section on governance). In rarer cases, governments have granted large tax breaks without substantial evidence of their benefit to the host country.
>
> For example, Guinea granted a mining concession for the producing Kindia bauxite mine to Rusal in 2000. In the accompanying mining agreement, the company was granted a complete exemption of most of the taxes normally applicable to the sector, including corporate income tax and withholding taxes on dividends. The agreement also replaced the ad valorem royalty on bauxite from the mining code with a fixed royalty of 1 USD per ton of bauxite, in effect lowering the royalty payable by the company. Without time limitation on these tax breaks, the company has enjoyed a very generous fiscal regime (compared to the default) for almost twenty years, resisting several government initiatives to review mining contracts.[15]

5.4.4   Ease of administration

5.4.4.1   Ease of administration relates to the cost and difficulty of tax enforcement and compliance. Incentives may complicate extractive tax administration, especially where they are granted on a discretionary basis, as they create numerous regimes to be administered. Moreover, specific types of tax incentives may increase the administrative burden. Customs duty relief, for example, whilst easier to administer, provides greater relief for higher priced plant and machinery, which may need to be countered with closer scrutiny of such deductions in the source country. Specifically, countries may need to rigorously apply additional base protection rules, particularly those relating to transfer pricing.

5.4.4.2   Poorly designed incentives may further expose governments to compliance risk, such as profit shifting, (see Box 5.B.12 for a list of the top ten abuses), and thus increase the need for administrative measures and compliance obligations. These concerns are not unique to the extractives sector. Administrative issues to consider include:

---

[15] https://www.itiedoc-guinee.org/document-archive/rapport-du-comite-technique-de-revue-des-titres-et-conventions-miniers-ctrtcm-19-avril-2016/
https://www.contratsminiersguinee.org/contract/ocds-591adf-9112931197/view#/pdf/page/24/annotation/2769

- Incentives that create parallel fiscal regimes may exacerbate transfer pricing risks. One such example would be if incentives apply to one segment of the value chain such as processing, but not the extractive activity.

- The abrupt ending of a tax incentive may also create an incentive to accelerate profits to avoid paying taxes when the incentive ends. For example, in the case of a time-limited income tax holiday, investors may increase the rate of extraction or preferentially extract high-grade ore compared to what they would otherwise do in the absence of tax considerations.

- Cost-based incentives should be carefully defined to prevent cost overstatement. For example, in the case of an investment allowance, it is necessary to clarify what type of expenditure is included; wheth er losses can be carried forward to be offset against income in future years, and if they can be added to deductible expenditure in the current tax year.

Box 5.B.12:
Top ten abuses of tax incentive regimes

1. Existing firms transforming to new entities to qualify for incentives.
2. Domestic firms restructuring as foreign investors.
3. Transfer pricing schemes with related entities (sales, services, loans, royalties, management contracts).
4. Churning or fictitious investments (lack of recapture rules).
5. Schemes to accelerate income (or defer deductions) at the end of a tax holiday period.
6. Overvaluation of assets for depreciation, tax credit, or other purposes.
7. Employment and training credit (fictitious employees and phony training programmes).
8. Export zones (leakages into the domestic economy).
9. Diverting activities outside of regional and enterprise zones.
10. Disguising or burying of non-qualifying activities into qualifying activities.

Source: Handbook on Selected Issues in Protecting the Tax Base of Developing Countries (United Nations, New York, 2015) p476

5.5 TYPICAL TAX INCENTIVES IN THE EXTRACTIVE SECTOR

5.5.1 Introduction

5.5.1.1   The multitude of factors and risks that exist underscore the "no one-size-fits-all" approach to tax incentives. Tax incentives that work in one country may not be effective in another. The next section sets out the different types of tax incentives commonly used in the resource sector, and the advantages and disadvantages of each.

5.5.1.2   In general, tax incentives may be classified into two categories:

- Profit-based incentives, and;

- Cost-based incentives.

5.5.2   Profit-based incentives

5.5.2.1   Profit-based incentives generally reduce the tax payable once the project is profitable, such as through tax holidays, tax sparing,[16] or preferential tax rates. These types of incentives will be less effective in encouraging investment compared to incentives that reduce the capital cost if profitability is low. When profits are earned due to location-specific factors such as natural resources, profit-based incentives tend to be associated with high redundancy rates and are ineffective at attracting investment.[17] Notwithstanding, in other cases, the incentive can improve the project economics, thereby strengthening the justification for the investment.

5.5.2.2   Moreover, marginal mines are likely to benefit less than profitable mines from this type of incentive, whereas a pro-investment incentive should aim to encourage investment in marginal mines. For example, if a mine's gross income is $200, its operating costs are $50 and the tax rate that normally applies is 50%, a tax holiday means the taxpayer earns a profit of $150. Whereas for a mine that has the same gross income, but costs of $100, and pays tax at 50%, it earns a profit of $50. Whereas it is the marginal mine that is more likely to require an incentive to encourage the investment, government is effectively incurring higher tax losses on the mine that needs the least financial support.

5.5.3   Income tax holiday

5.5.3.1   A tax holiday applies during a specified tax-free period. The duration may vary from one year to the full term of the project. It may take the form of a complete exemption from profits tax, or a reduced rate, or a combination of the two.[18]

5.5.3.2   For the reasons highlighted above, income tax holidays may be a less

---

[16] Tax sparing is a provision, usually in a tax treaty, where one state allows a credit for taxes "spared" (removed because of an incentive) in another country. The provision prevents the shifting of the benefit of an incentive from the taxpayer to whom it was intended, to another country in which the taxpayer is subject to tax.

[17] Platform for Collaboration on Tax, *Options for Low Income Countries' Effective and Efficient Use of Tax Incentives for investment*, (2015) pg. 20

[18] Zolt, Eric: *Tax Incentives: Protecting the tax base*, UN, 2015

efficient and effective incentive for the extractive industries.[19]

5.5.3.3   Income tax holidays for extractive projects tend to incentivise commercial behaviour which moves profitable activity into the time period covered by the incentive. Resource companies may increase the rate of extraction, or preferentially extract high-grade ore during tax free periods. Governments report the problem of high-grading as a potential response by mining companies to tax holidays. "High-grading" refers to companies increasing the rate of extraction, or preferentially extracting high-grade ore, compared to what they would otherwise do absent tax considerations. Of course, tax may not be the only factor – companies will generally want to mine high value, easy to access ore first, to improve their cash flow. Nonetheless in estimating what the overall cost of a tax holiday will be, governments should anticipate behavioural responses that the tax incentive will generate.

5.5.3.4   From an investor point of view, a tax holiday which begins at the start of the project's development will be of uncertain value (and hence less effective as an incentive), since project delays will reduce the tax-free period. This is why investors may prefer tax holidays that commence from the first taxable year. However, in a project that requires massive amounts of investments, the first taxable profits could be years after the date of the first production, depending on the pace of production, mineral prices and amortization rules. Thus, from government's perspective, aligning a tax holiday to the first taxable profits could extend the tax holiday further into the future than the government may expect.

5.5.3.5   If a government chooses to offer a tax holiday, it should limit the incentive to the time anticipated for a specified tonnage to be extracted. Once the agreed tonnage has been extracted, the tax holiday expires; thus limiting the risk of high-grading. In addition, government should require that companies deduct depreciation allowances during the tax holiday (as if there were no incentive), so they cannot be offset after the holiday expires, reducing future revenue collection.

5.5.4   Withholding taxes on income remitted abroad

5.5.4.1   Many developing countries favour withholding taxes on outbound services, interest and royalties. This is because withholding taxes are easier to collect than other taxes, and thus, a reliable source of revenue, as well as discouraging base erosion and profit shifting. By lowering or exempting withholding tax, developing countries become more vulnerable to cross-border tax planning by multinational companies.[20]

---

[19] Tax holidays are widely regarded as a particularly ill-designed form of investment incentive, and one that poses considerable dangers to the wider tax system." Keen et al., *Revenue Mobilisation in Sub-Saharan Africa: Challenges from Globalisation*, (2009) pg.14

[20] OECD, *Measuring and Monitoring BEPS, Action 11—2015 Final Report*, supra note 23, 157, recognizes that withholding taxes "can influence cross-border tax planning opportunities" and can "discourage profit shifting via strategic allocation of debt and intangible assets."

5.5.4.2   In the case of loans from foreign related parties, governments may end up with interest as a deductible expense, and no tax[21] on the interest income received by the related party, unless they charge withholding tax. Moreover, subject to thin capitalisation and transfer pricing rules, the MNE will have an added incentive to highly leverage its subsidiary in order to strip profits out via interest expense. The same risks arise for management service payments; although the risk is lower in the context of Joint Venture arrangements, where shared costs (e.g., management fees) are reviewed by non-operating partners.[22] Additionally, it may be difficult for governments to determine the extent to which the services are performed offshore and are exempt from withholding tax versus services performed onshore (Article 12A of the UN Model imposes withholding tax on payments to non-residents for services performed irrespective of where the services were performed).[23] Incentives relating to dividend withholding tax are less problematic because, unlike interest and management fees, dividends are not tax deductible. However, governments may wish to tax dividends for other reasons, including encouraging reinvestment or putting resident and non-resident investors on a level playing field.

5.5.4.3   Despite the strong justification for retaining withholding taxes, developing countries should consider the potential impact on investment. For example, during the development and production stages of an extractives project, internal debt may be a major, or the only, source of funding, in which case withholding tax will increase the overall cost of the project. This cost may be passed on to the resident company in the form of a higher interest rate, thereby reducing its taxable income. Similarly, with any large-scale project there may be significant project management and technical service expertise required from outside the country and the imposition of a withholding tax will increase the cost of such services to the project. Government should also consider that charging withholding tax on any dividends it receives from a project may increase the overall share of distributed dividends it collects, beyond what was negotiated with the investor.

5.5.4.4   These trade-offs are important considerations. However, the administrative constraints, base erosion, and profit shifting risks suggest that developing countries may find withholding taxes a necessary feature of the resource tax system.

5.5.5   Export processing zone (EPZ)

5.5.5.1   A common characteristic of EPZs is the provision of special incentives to attract investment, mostly foreign, for export production. Incentives may include tax holidays, duty free export and import, and free repatriation of profits. In the mining sector, EPZ status is usually granted to a company's mineral

---

[21] For more guidance on the level of withholding tax, see the UN Model commentary on Article 12A, paragraph 2, points 44 and 45.

[22] The risk of management fees being inflated should be reduced in the context of a Joint Venture arrangement where the operator is subject to the no-profit rule.

[23] See Chapter 2 of the UN Handbook on Protecting the Tax Base for a detailed discussion of taxation of income from services.

processing operations. On the one hand, EPZ status may be an important factor in encouraging value addition in the host country, in which case governments should have clear criteria about what "processing" means. Notwithstanding, governments should be mindful that any tax differentiation between the mine and the processing facility may lead to domestic transfer pricing issues. Specifically, if the mine is subject to a higher tax rate, there may be an incentive to shift profits to the processing facility by under-pricing the intermediate mineral product transferred to the processing facility.[24] Tax authorities should ensure that audits also cover transactions with EPZs.[25]

5.6   COST-BASED INCENTIVES

5.6.1   Introduction

5.6.1.1   Cost-based incentives include investment allowances, investment tax credits, accelerated depreciation and loss carry-forwards, all of which decrease the capital cost, and so make a greater number of investment projects more profitable at the margin—that is, generate investments that would not otherwise have been made.

5.6.1.2   The capital-intensive nature of resource investments makes cost-based incentives better suited than profit-based incentives. This is because they allow taxpayers to recoup their investment through appropriate deductions from their taxable income or directly from their tax bill, deferring tax to later stages in a project's life and therefore not reducing cash flows in the initial critical years when capital is most needed. From an administrative perspective, it is also easier to anticipate the revenue cost of cost-based incentives because it is based on the amount of investment.

5.6.2   Investment allowances and credits

5.6.2.1   Investment allowance: An investment allowance gives the taxpayer the right to offset a percentage of its capital expenditure against its taxable income in the year the expenditure is made, rather than spread over time through regular depreciation. E.g., if the taxpayer spends $200 and the allowance is 50 per cent, it can deduct $100 from its taxable income in the first year. Applying a 20 per cent corporate income tax rate means the taxpayer's tax liability is reduced by $20. This enables even quicker cost recovery than accelerated depreciation, depending

---

[24] Countries should also be mindful that export related tax incentives may contravene the OECD initiative on Harmful Tax Competition launched in 1998 and, more recently, BEPS Action 5, as well as World Trade Organisation (WTO) rules.

[25] For further reading on the international tax and trade policy issues reference is made to the book "Special Tax Zones in the Era of International Tax Coordination" published by IBFD in 2019 covering not only tax and trade policy aspects of special tax zones (including also export processing zones), but also their constitutional and tax treaty application aspects and effectiveness, as well as the special tax zones in 19 countries.

on the rate, although standard depreciation would still apply for the remainder of the investment.

5.6.2.2   Investment tax credits: An investment tax credit enables a taxpayer to reduce the amount of tax payable by a portion of its investment expenditure in the first year, rather than reduce its taxable income, as with investment allowances. For example, if the investment is $200 and the investment credit is 50 per cent, the taxpayer can reduce its tax liability in that year by $100. If the tax payable is $40, the taxpayer can apply this $100 investment credit to reduce its tax liability to minus $60. This balance could be carried forward to offset tax liabilities in future years, or expire. Depending on the tax rate, the investment credit can be up to four times more generous than the investment allowance.

5.6.2.3   Investment allowances and tax credits will only be relevant once the taxpayer is in a taxpaying position, unless loss carry forward is allowed.

5.6.3   Customs duty reductions or exemptions

5.6.3.1   Import tax is usually based on the value of the good. For example, if import duty is 10 per cent on mining inputs, a company that brings in drilling equipment valued at $500,000 will have to pay $50,000 in duties.

5.6.3.2   Customs duty relief is often provided to enable the company investor to import specific plant and equipment duty free and to obtain refunds of excise paid in relation to fuel used to power machinery or in off-road vehicles. These incentives are common in developing countries, where mining investments are very reliant on imported equipment, fuel and construction materials.

5.6.3.3   The main tax risk from customs duty relief is the incentive for companies to pay more for imported equipment and materials from related parties. This would reduce taxable income in the host country and duty relief removes a financial cost of such a strategy (i.e., importing goods at higher prices). For example, the depreciation/valuation policy on older equipment and machinery that has been used by an affiliate company elsewhere should be reviewed to ensure that items are not purchased at the retail price but at a lower price that reflects the reduction in the value of the asset, particularly due to wear and tear.

5.6.3.4   Moreover, by exempting customs duties, there is less incentive for customs authorities to verify the cost of mining imports, which would otherwise be helpful to tax authorities when they come to compute corporate income tax in later years. Another option for government, should it choose to provide duty relief, would be to offer a lower, or graduated import duty rate, providing greater information to government but with an increase in administration costs.

Box 5.B.13:
Import duty exemptions target exploration and development phases

The Petroleum Code of Senegal from 1998 provides an exemption from Customs Duties and VAT during the exploration and development phase of an oil and gas project. Although the Petroleum Code from 1998 has been replaced by the Petroleum Code enacted in 2019, the 1998 Petroleum Code continues to apply to license holders granted prior to 2019. This incentive is provided in Articles 48 and 49 of the Petroleum Code and applies during the exploration and development stage of all oil and gas projects in Senegal. This incentive allows the import of materials during the relevant phases of the project free of customs duties and VAT. In addition, exports of petroleum products are not subject to export duties. After completion of the specified phases of the project the general rates of customs duties and VAT apply.

This type of incentive can be viewed from the perspective of the government as an enticement to investors to assume the risk of proving the existence and economic production of oil or gas in a new or unproven resource prospect. This position is reflected in the "Explanatory Statement" to the Draft Bill 98-05 establishing the Petroleum Code, which provides the following: "In order to be competitive, Senegal must not only take into account the evolution of the worldwide energy data, but also offer to prospective investors of the petroleum industry, conditions which are attractive and susceptible of promoting the development of petroleum investments in the exploration or production of our national territory."

This draft Petroleum Code takes into account the specific characteristics of the exploration and exploitation of hydrocarbons in our onshore and offshore sedimentary basin, the existing conditions, and the expected growth of the petroleum industry.

From an investor's perspective, an incentive that provides a reduction of cost, especially during the exploration and development stages of a project before there is certainty of future income from the project, can be viewed as particularly beneficial to the project economics.

5.6.4   VAT exemptions on imports

5.6.4.1   As described in Chapter 12 of this handbook, many resource-rich countries have difficulties with large VAT credits owed to export-oriented extractive industries. These industries pay VAT on inputs but do not collect VAT on exports. They are therefore owed large VAT refunds by the tax authorities. Delays in VAT refunds may become an impediment to investors. As the greatest proportion of input values subject to VAT tend to arise from imports into extractive operations, it is possible to simply exempt imported inputs used in oil and gas operations from VAT. This approach eliminates (or reduces) the churning created by imposing VAT with immediate refund, but creates two additional problems:

- First, VAT on domestic supplies is not exempt under this scheme and so an artificial import bias is created by exempting imports only. In effect, domestic suppliers are placed at a competitive disadvantage because of the import exemption. Such negative protection may hamper efforts to use the extractive industries to create downstream linkages to the rest of the economy.

- Second, an exemption for imports can be a source of leakage and fraud. Extractive companies and their employees may import consumer and other goods not used in production and such imports should be subject to full VAT. In addition, if there is an exemption, there is an incentive to use the exemption to import goods that are resold into the domestic market free of VAT. Thus, the administrative requirements for monitoring an exemption system are largely the same as those required for monitoring the VAT in general.

Box 5.B.14:
REPETRO – BRAZIL

The Petroleum Code of Senegal from 1998 provides an exemption from REPETRO was a tax exemption scheme relating to upstream oil and gas imports in Brazil. It used to be the most important tax instrument in Brazilian oil legislation. It was a temporary admission regime with a tax holiday for rental or freight contracts until 2020, or until the end of these contracts. All equipment, parts, and tools were eligible for REPETRO.

On the one hand, REPETRO played a role in increasing Brazil's oil and gas reserves and production. When REPETRO was introduced in 1997, the oil price was not above US$ 20/bbl, and the Brazilian industry only had one oil company, Petrobras. REPETRO was a way for the Brazilian government to enable the oil companies to use the global market to supply their projects in Brazil, in an economical way. Brazilian oil proven reserves increased by 80% from 1997 to 2017. Oil production increased by 211% and gas production by 306% from 1997 to 2017.

Notwithstanding, there were some side effects. The way the regime was designed created a large accumulation of assets abroad, creating many transfer pricing risks, as well as capital gains tax issues in farm out operations and in services supplied by related parties, especially on specialized vessels freights, such as Floating Production Storage and Offloading (FSPOs) and drill ships. The REPETRO fiscal waiver was an average of US$ 3.2 billion a year. This represented the amount of tax exempted for the importation of goods, which amounts to an average of US$ 13.7 billion per year in value (CIF values).

Another issue about REPETRO was the presence of different lists of products eligible for the tax incentives, for the Federal Tax Administration and subnational State Tax Administrations (Customs duties and VAT), which created a problem of transparency in tax legislation.

Brazil's new tax legislation, enacted at the end of 2017, establishes that the ownership of production equipment and vessels (subsea and top side) must be accounted as assets of Brazilian oil and gas companies. It recognizes the risk distribution between taxpayers and government and deals with it through import tax exemptions and a capital allowance, which includes a higher amortization rate, based on the fact that the technical and financial feasibility studies consider that the cash flow of enterprises, and the timing to charge the corporate tax, have a key role in the decision-making process of the investors.

The new oil and gas federal tax legislation is aligned with the subnational States' indirect taxation including VAT, since both the Union and the States now share the same list of goods exempted from Customs duties and subnational States' VAT (ICMS), making the legislation more transparent. Some VAT distortions were addressed by extending the exemption for two more layers of the domestic supply chain in order to avoid the credit refund problem for export companies in the extractive industry. The new scheme also gives Brazilian suppliers the same conditions as the foreign suppliers.

5.6.5   Production royalty-based incentives

5.6.5.1   Royalty-based incentives may be agreed to reduce the burden on the project during the first phase until recovery of sunk costs. They are sometimes offered in developed countries to incentivise new entrants and to prevent early termination of mineral production as the natural resource approaches exhaustion. These may be reasonable trade-offs, depending on the circumstances. Nevertheless, governments should be mindful that royalties are a payment for the right to extract a finite, non-renewable resource, and, as such, incentives should not be given lightly. Again, there is a risk that investors may speed up the rate of production, and extract the highest value ore, to maximise sales revenue during the royalty-free period.

5.6.5.2   Countries that choose to provide production royalty-based incentives to extractive industry investors should establish clear and objective criteria, and procedures to waive or exempt royalty payments.

5.6.5.3   Criteria may include:

- Cash flows are negative in the short term;

- The cash flow difficulties are temporary and can be overcome (i.e., waiver or exemption should be for a short period such as a few months);

- The mine may have to close with job losses if royalties were demanded.[26]

5.6.6   Fiscal stabilization

5.6.6.1   Fiscal stabilization is intended to preserve the taxation, production-sharing, pricing, or state participation rules that govern the division of proceeds from a resource project at the time of contract. The primary justification for this is to ensure the feasibility of projects in countries with higher levels of political risk. Therefore, fiscal stabilisation assists investors in reducing the relative risks of projects. There are generally three approaches to stabilization:

- The fiscal collection procedures (or contract terms) in force on the date of agreement are frozen;

- Any future tax policy changes that would increase the tax burden on the project will not apply, although the project can benefit from tax decreases;

- Changes in the tax regime will apply but the government is required to negotiate. There is an agreement with the company to negotiate to maintain the preceding economic equilibrium if there are any adverse changes[27]).

5.6.6.2   For most businesses, stable rules are necessary to achieve the economic results that were anticipated when the investment was made, e.g., in order to maintain the necessary level of production, projected profit levels or to obtain the necessary maintenance and expansion of funds. The risk of instability will be factored into the overall cost of the investment. The bigger and more immovable the investment, the more relevant it will be. Consequently, from the investor's viewpoint a well-designed stability agreement can remove a significant amount of tax and related profit risk and allow for more accurate forecasting of the future fiscal collection impact on project cash flows.

---

[26] World Bank, *How to Improve Mining Tax Administration*, 2013, pg.44

[27] Daniel, P. and Sunley, E.M. *Contractual Assurances of Fiscal Stability*, IMF Conference on Taxing Natural Resources, 2008.

5.6.6.3   However, where fiscal stabilisation is used, and depending on how the provisions are drafted, they may extend beyond standard fiscal terms, and also apply to tax incentives provided for in domestic law, or at the contract level, as of the date the investment agreement is signed, or ratified by parliament when this is required by law (as in many developing countries). If there is a significant change in circumstances, for example, commodity prices rise making it easier to attract investment, or a tax incentive is used in a way that the government did not anticipate, unintended benefits to the company may result. The risk is that fiscal stabilization also locks in all the aforementioned behavioural responses linked to incentives.

5.6.6.4   If governments choose to offer fiscal stabilisation, such clauses can be designed to minimise the general tax policy impact, by limiting their scope to specific key fiscal terms (not all fiscal terms) for a specific period of time (not indefinitely), and possibly by applying a stability premium on tax rates.[28] Tax authorities should also be involved in negotiations with investors about possible stability clauses. Any agreement must be sustainable such that it does not lead to the host country being unable to address unintended outcomes or implement global reforms such as those championed by the OECD Base Erosion and Profit Shifting tax programme. In practice, long term stabilisation agreements that lock in unstainable benefits for investors, that do not allow for regular review by host country/company investors, and are not publicly available for scrutiny, often lead to dissatisfaction and dispute.

5.7   INTERACTION WITH INVESTOR AND OTHER TAX REGIMES

5.7.1.1   The tax regime of the investor will impact on the attractiveness of the incentives. For example, an investor which operates a worldwide tax regime, such that foreign income taxed below a minimum rate will result in additional tax (up to the minimum rate) in the investor location, is unlikely to be attracted by the incentive. Instead it is likely to represent a shift in taxation from the investee country to the investor country.

5.7.1.2   At the time of writing, governments of the more than 130 jurisdictions that are members of the OECD/G20 Inclusive Framework (IF) on Base Erosion and Profit Shifting (BEPS) are deliberating over possible actions to address the tax challenges arising from the digitalization of the economy. This process could have a significant impact on the effectiveness of incentives in all countries, regardless of the importance of digital businesses in their economies. Some of the proposals being considered would cover all sectors of the economy, including extractives. All of the proposals could eventually be adopted globally.

5.7.1.3   A minimum tax on multinational profits has the potential to impact

---

[28] Section 53, OECD, *Guiding Principles for Durable Extractive Contracts*, 2018, available at http://www.oecd.org/dev/Guiding_Principles_for_durable_extractive_contracts.pdf

the effectiveness of profit-based incentives. Should such a change be adopted in investor jurisdictions, governments should factor this in and explicitly consider how their incentives interact with global changes, particularly in relation to minimum tax rates.

5.8   CONCLUSIONS

5.8.1.1   Tax incentives can be used to encourage certain behaviours and, if properly designed, managed and reviewed, may be a useful tool of social and economic policy. Experience in tax incentives has been varied and they should be used with care.

5.8.1.2   This chapter recommends the adoption of an evaluative framework that covers:

- Governance;

- Effectiveness;

- Efficiency; and

- Ease of Administration.

5.8.1.3   It has then considered the most common incentives within the extractives sector, categorising them between profit-based and cost-based incentives.

ANNEX 1

IMF, OECD, World Bank, UN (2015), Options for Low Income Countries' Effective and Efficient Use of Tax Incentives for Investment, a paper for the G20' Development Working Group, October. https://www.imf.org/external/np/g20/pdf/101515.pdf

James, Sebastian, 2013, "Investment Incentives in Other Geographies," mimeo, World Bank.

James, Sebastian, 2014, "Tax and non-tax incentives and investments: Evidence and Policy Implications," Investment Climate Advisory Services. World Bank Group, June 2014.

James, Sebastian, and Stefan Van Parys, 2009, "Investment Climate and the Effectiveness of Tax Incentives," World Bank Group.

Laukanen, Antti; Pistone, Pasquale; de Goede, Jan; 2019, Special Tax Zones in the Era of International Tax Coordination, IBFD.

Otto, James (2018) Extractive Industries: The Management of Resources as a Driver of Sustainable Development. (chapter 14) Published to Oxford Scholarship

Online: November 2018 https://www.oxfordscholarship.com/view/10.1093/oso/9780198817369.001.0001/oso-9780198817369-chapter-14 .

United Nations, 2017, United Nations Handbook on Selected Issues in Protecting the Tax Base of Developing Countries: Second Edition.

Zolt, Eric, 2018. Tax Treaties and Developing Countries. UCLA School of Law, Law-Econ Research Paper No. 18-10. 12 Sep 2018

Chapter 6

Tax Treaty Issues

6.1 INTRODUCTION

6.1.1 Executive summary

6.1.1.1   The extractive industries play an important role in the process of sourcing natural resources, which are critical for the development of many economies. Both developing and developed countries are actors in the process of natural resource extraction, both as host countries to the extractive activities and also as countries where the extractive industry companies have their head offices, raise capital and make strategic decisions. A number of international tax issues arise from extractive activities, which often include a cross-border element due to global business models and integrated value chains. Investors, licence holders, service providers and suppliers involved in a project are often not residents of the source country.

6.1.1.2   This chapter reviews tax treaty articles which are potentially relevant to extractive industries. It highlights issues that countries, especially developing countries, may wish to take into consideration in designing their tax treaty policy, negotiating (or re-negotiating) tax treaties and applying such tax treaties. While this chapter deals with tax treaty issues, especially from the perspective of the United Nations Model Tax Convention (UN Model Convention), reference is also made to the Organisation for Economic Co-operation and Development Model Tax Convention (OECD Model Convention) where appropriate. In addition, some tax treaty concepts are presented that depart from both the United Nations and the OECD Model Conventions and address specific problems related to extractive industries.

6.1.1.3   The issues raised in this chapter affect both the tax revenue of the jurisdictions involved and the tax position of companies involved in the extractive activities.

6.1.2 Background

6.1.2.1   Bilateral double tax agreements (DTAs) play an important role in coordinating the rules of cross-border tax treatment. They help avoid double taxation and facilitate cross-border trade and investment by reducing the risk of excessive tax costs from cross-border transactions. Tax treaties allocate taxing rights to one of the Contracting States, and limit the other Contracting State in exercising its domestic tax laws to the extent provided for in the treaty. The restriction may either be of an absolute nature—i.e., the tax treaty allocates an exclusive taxing right to the residence State or to the source State—or of a relative nature in that the tax treaty limits the source State to tax certain income only at a maximum applicable rate of tax and requires the residence State to either exempt the income or to grant a tax credit. Moreover, a tax treaty may also allocate non-exclusive unlimited taxing rights at source— e.g., for income from immovable property. Tax treaties limit the taxing rights of both the source and the residence States and may thus limit the ability of the source State to collect tax on income earned/sourced within the jurisdiction, and of the residence State to tax its residents on their worldwide income.

6.1.2.2   It should be stressed that tax treaties always operate in conjunction with domestic law. Tax treaties play an important coordination role between the tax systems of two[1] Contracting States. Domestic law establishes and determines the issues relevant to the existence of the tax liability, while a tax treaty may suppress (fully or partially) or confirm this tax liability. The general view is that tax treaties do not create tax liability.[2] Therefore, where the domestic law fails to establish such liability, the tax treaty will not remedy this situation.

6.1.2.3   Tax treaties also provide for measures to assure administrative cooperation. Article 25 of the United Nations Model Convention[3] provides for a mutual agreement procedure to eliminate double taxation in situations where the "competent authorities" of two Contracting States have different interpretations of the tax treaty. Article 25 of both the United Nations and OECD Model Conventions gives an important role to the competent authorities of the two states in avoiding or resolving disputes. If the taxation of one of the Contracting States is not in line with the tax treaty, the taxpayer may, under that article, initiate a mutual agreement procedure to resolve the situation. Article 26 contains rules regarding the exchange of information. Article 27 (when it exists in a treaty) provides for assistance in the collection of taxes.

6.1.2.4   The United Nations and the OECD Model Conventions are used by many States as the basis for their tax treaty negotiations and therefore have considerable influence on international tax law. Currently, both the United Nations Model Convention (2021) and the OECD Model Convention (2017) contain only very

---

[1] In rare instances, tax treaties may have a multilateral character (e.g., the Nordic Tax Treaty concluded between Denmark, Finland, Iceland, Norway, Sweden and the Faroe Islands).

[2] Some countries—Australia and France, for example—follow the practice that tax treaties may establish a tax liability.

[3] Unless otherwise noted, Articles referenced, due to publication deadlines, are those in the 2017 United Nations Model Double Taxation Convention between Developed and Developing Countries (2017). The 2017 version of the Model is available at http://www.un.org/esa/ffd/ffd-follow-up/tax-committee.html. The 2021 update of the UN Model will be available on the website of the UN Committee of Experts on International Cooperation in Tax Matters at https://www.un.org/development/desa/financing/what-we-do/ECOSOC/tax-committee/tax-committee-home.

few provisions specifically addressing issues arising in the extractive industries. The general rules contained in the tax treaty are also applied to specific issues and situations arising in the extractive industries. Due to the special nature of the extraction of natural resources, several countries have however included specific provisions regarding extractive industries in their tax treaties. One common example is a specific "Offshore Activities Article" in the Nordic Convention.[4] Some European States[5] have declared reservations to the OECD Model Convention and inserted such articles in their tax treaties.

6.1.2.5   Countries that neglect to pay special attention to the specific issues arising in the extractive industries when designing their domestic tax law and negotiating their tax treaties may potentially lose taxing rights in respect of income and capital raised by extractive activities taking place within their jurisdiction. They therefore may fail to obtain tax revenue which could otherwise be available for development activities. Furthermore, countries should be aware of possible situations where double taxation may arise along with the economic consequences thereof.

BOX 6.B.1:
Example: Article 21 of the Denmark – Latvia Income and Capital Tax Treaty (1993)

Activities in connection with preliminary surveys, exploration or extraction of hydrocarbons.

Notwithstanding the provisions of Article 5 and Article 14, a person who is a resident of one of the Contracting States and carries on activities in connection with preliminary surveys, exploration or extraction of hydrocarbons situated in the other Contracting State shall be deemed to be carrying on in respect of those activities a business in that other Contracting State through a permanent establishment or fixed base situated therein.

Notwithstanding the provisions of paragraph 1, drilling rig activities carried on offshore shall constitute a permanent establishment only if the activities are carried on for a period or periods exceeding 365 days in aggregate in any 18-month period. However, for the purpose of this paragraph, activities carried on by an enterprise associated with another

---

[4] See, for example, Article 21 of the Nordic Convention; and Article 21 of the tax treaty between Denmark and Latvia (1993). A special Article for the exploration and extraction of hydrocarbons can be found in the treaties of Argentina, Australia, Denmark, Greece, Ireland, Latvia, Lithuania, Malta, the Netherlands, Norway, Sweden, the United Arab Emirates, the United Kingdom of Great Britain and Northern Ireland, and the United States of America.

[5] See reservations to the OECD Model of Denmark, Greece, Ireland, Latvia, Lithuania, Norway and the United Kingdom.

enterprise within the meaning of Article 9 shall be regarded as carried on by the enterprise to which it is associated if the activities in question are substantially the same as those carried on by the last-mentioned enterprise.

Notwithstanding the provisions of paragraph 1, profits derived by a resident of a Contracting State from the transportation by ship or aircraft of supplies or personnel to a location where offshore activities in connection with preliminary surveys, exploration or extraction of hydrocarbons are being carried on in the other Contracting State or from the operation of tugboats and similar vessels in connection with such activities, shall be taxable only in the first-mentioned State.

Salaries, wages and other similar remuneration derived by an individual who is a resident of a Contracting State in respect of labour or personal services rendered aboard a ship or aircraft covered by paragraph 3 shall be taxed in accordance with paragraph 3 of Article 15.

Notwithstanding the provisions of Article 13, a capital gain on drilling rigs used for activities mentioned in paragraph 2 which is deemed to be derived by a resident of a Contracting State when the rig activities cease to be subject to tax in the other Contracting State shall be exempt from tax in that other State. For the purpose of this paragraph, the term "capital gain" means the amount by which the market value at the moment of transfer exceeds the residual value at that moment, as increased by any depreciation taken.

6.2   OVERVIEW OF THE EXTRACTIVE INDUSTRIES LIFE CYCLE IN RELATION TO CROSS-BORDER TAX ISSUES

6.2.1.1   Extractive industries activities often take place over a long period of time. The different critical activities can be divided into five main stages: (i) contract negotiation; (ii) exploration activities and evaluation; (iii) development of the infrastructure; (iv) extraction, production and export; and (v) abandonment and decommissioning. These stages could be further separated, for example, the abandonment and decommissioning can be considered as two separate stages. Furthermore, the stages can overlap. While the exploration may be still ongoing, the development and even extraction can occur at the same time. This life cycle is illustrated in the next figure; see further Chapter 1, Overview.

6.2.1.2   Different international tax issues arise in each of the stages of the life cycle (see further Chapter 1) of an extractive industry project. The following figure and table summarizes the key activities by the life cycle issues alongside the key domestic and international tax considerations.

Figure 6.F.1: Life cycle of an extractive industry project

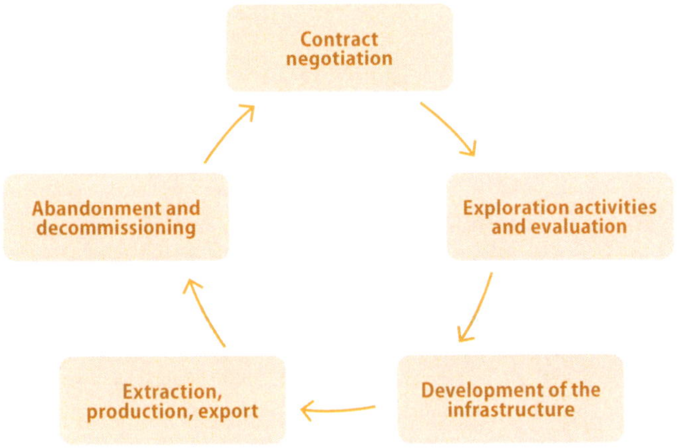

Source: UN/DESA

Table 6.T.1: Stages, activities, actors, domestic tax issues and potential international tax issues

Stages	Key activities	Actors	Domestic tax issues	International tax issues
Contract negotiation and signature	Extractive companies (investors may engage in competitive bidding or contract negotiation with the assistance of advisers and lawyers.	Extractive company (operator or licence holder); consortium members; advisers, lawyers, financiers.	Obligatory (tax) payments, such as signature bonus; payments to advisers and withholding tax consideration.	Applicability of a DTA; DTA coverage of signature bonus payments; taxation of income to advisers.
Exploration activities and evaluation	Exploration activities take place in various forms: geological studies, drilling and seismic tests, sample-taking and analyses; evaluation of potential for further extraction.	Extractive company; subcontractors specializing in the exploration activities (onshore or offshore); analysts.	Obligatory (tax) payments, such as discovery bonus, payments to subcontractors and the relevant tax considerations (including withholding tax); country's exercising of taxing rights over the territorial waters and exclusive economic zone.	DTA coverage of discovery bonus payments; taxation of income to subcontractors; existence of permanent establishment (PE); tax treaty coverage of relevant offshore area.
Development of the infrastructure	Development of extractive facility (mining pits, extraction wells) and supportive infra-structure including transportation (roads, railway, pipelines) accommodation and office units as well as ancillary infrastructure; activities related to environmental and resettlement issues.	Extractive company; subcontractors for construction, installation and drilling companies.	Obligatory (tax) payments, such as development bonus (unusual); payments to subcontractors and the relevant tax considerations (including withholding tax).	DTA coverage of development bonus payments; subcontractor's PE (or absence thereof).
Extraction, production and export	Extractive activities take place on a commercial scale; resources are processed and/or sold/ transported/ exported.	Extraction company; subcontractors for processing, transportation, and other services.	Extraction taxes (royalties, share from production sharing agreement, hydrocarbon taxes, corporate income tax);	DTA coverage of extraction-related taxes; subcontractor's PE (or absence thereof); treatment of transfer pricing adjustments of prices for natural resources;

Table 6.T.1 (cont'd)

Stages	Key activities	Actors	Domestic tax issues	International tax issues
Extraction, production and export			export-related taxes (excise, export customs duty, export rent taxes, and other); payments to subcontractors and the relevant tax considerations (including withholding tax); adjustments to prices for natural resources (transfer pricing); tax implications of profit repatriation and payments to capital providers (rent and debt).	tax treaty implications of profit repatriation and payments to capital providers.
Abandonment and decommissioning	Extractive activities are finalized and are replaced by decommissioning activities, clean-up of pollution and removal of infrastructure	Extraction company; subcontractors specializing in decommissioning and environmental clean-up activities.	Special decommissioning/ rehabilitation allowance or reserve created during the life of the project; considerations of deductibility and subsequent taxation of excess reserve; payments to subcontractors and the relevant tax considerations (including withholding tax).	DTA provision for taxation of the excess decommissioning/ rehabilitation allowance/ reserve; subcontractor's PE (or absence thereof).

6.3   SCOPE OF TAX TREATIES

6.3.1   Personal scope of tax treaties

6.3.1.1   The general principle of Article 1 is that tax treaties should apply only in respect of the persons (natural persons as well as legal persons, such as companies) that are residents of one or both of the Contracting States. Article 4 subsequently provides a definition of who is a resident of a Contracting State for treaty purposes and, in doing so, the Article refers back to the domestic law of the Contracting States.

6.3.1.2   Many extractive projects may be organized in the form of incorporated or non-incorporated joint ventures (also known as consortia). Incorporated joint-venture projects would, in most cases, be carried out through a separate legal entity, which is usually subject to tax in its country of residence. This should not cause special issues in respect of the tax treaty application, with the exception of treaty shopping, which is addressed below.

6.3.1.3 Non-incorporated joint ventures may, in particular, raise questions on the application of tax treaties. Non-incorporated joint ventures will operate not as a single legal entity, but as a contractual venture between several investors, where they jointly carry on the extractive activities and co-own both the assets and income arising thereon. They are thus jointly liable for the costs related to the extraction project and potential liabilities. In such arrangements, one of the partners may be appointed as operator of the project, who will then be responsible for the accounting as well as operational aspects of the project. The tax liabilities are, however, individually borne by each member of the consortium.

6.3.1.4 Such arrangements give rise to issues under domestic tax law and tax treaties. At the level of domestic law, issues of tax liability will be critical (i.e., are the partners of the consortium liable to taxation in both the source State and the residence State?). The consortium as such is generally not liable to tax. Under a tax treaty, one question will be whether the consortium will be entitled to benefits arising from the tax treaty (e.g., reduced rate of branch profit tax). Since non-incorporated joint ventures are contractual arrangements with several investors, they can be regarded as a "body of persons" for treaty purposes.[6] The investors may also come from different jurisdictions, which can further complicate these challenges. A particular tax treaty may only apply to those partners of the joint venture who qualify as residents of the Contracting States. In such a situation there may only be a proportional entitlement to benefits arising from the tax treaty.

6.3.1.5 Another potential issue in the extractive industries is the "improper use" of tax treaties that include treaty shopping practices. In this respect, neither the United Nations Model Convention nor the OECD Model Convention provide specific provisions, although the Commentary to Article 1 explains how improper use of treaties may be combatted.[7]

6.3.1.6 In light of the OECD/Group of Twenty (G20) Base Erosion and Profit Shifting (BEPS) project,[8] it is likely that based on recommendations under Action 6, the Limitation of Benefits clause and/or a general anti-abuse rule based on the principal purposes of transactions or arrangements (the principal purposes test) will become more widely used to counter treaty shopping. It is

---

[6] As stipulated in the United Nations Commentary to Article 3, citing the OECD Commentary, the term "person" should be interpreted very broadly.

[7] Addressed in the Commentary on Article 1 of both the United Nations and the OECD Model Conventions.

[8] The Base Erosion and Profit Shifting (BEPS) project was undertaken by the OECD on behalf of the Group of Twenty (G20) and proposed 15 Actions that are intended to provide countries with domestic and international instruments that will better align taxing rights with economic activity.

also advisable that developing countries consider domestic law anti-avoidance measures, which, as established in both the United Nations and OECD Model Convention Commentaries, are acceptable and can be applied alongside treaty-based anti-avoidance measures, at least when they meet certain criteria.

6.3.1.7   Further, it is recommended that countries establish measures of an administrative nature to enable the tax authorities to pre-screen transactions prior to the application of tax treaties. While such measures may on the one hand work as a natural deterrent to some of the most frequent treaty abuse practices; on the other hand, such measures may also create compliance and administrative costs.

6.3.2   Substantive scope of tax treaties

6.3.2.1   As noted earlier, with respect to most types of income relevant for the extractive industries, tax treaties aim to eliminate double taxation by limiting or eliminating source State taxation. Where the source State retains the taxing right and levies tax on the income, treaties oblige the State of residence to eliminate double taxation through the granting of a credit or an exemption.

6.3.2.2   Many countries have developed special tax regimes regulating the tax and compliance obligations of companies engaged in extractive activities. As different special taxes can be found in the extractive industries, the question arises as to which of these special taxes are covered by the scope of tax treaties. These special tax systems can be designed in different ways and can use different instruments, the characteristics of which may determine whether the particular type of tax may be covered by the scope of the tax treaty.

6.3.3   Profit taxes

6.3.3.1   Some countries design their extractive taxation system using a profit tax as the main instrument, just as in other sectors. Some countries apply a higher-than-standard tax rate while others have separate income tax regimes addressing sector-specific issues. Alternatively, some countries may have a special progressive tax rate scale for highly profitable operations (excess profit tax or windfall tax).

BOX 6.B.2:
Example: Norwegian special petroleum tax

A special petroleum tax is levied on profits from petroleum production and pipeline transportation on the Norwegian Continental Shelf. The special petroleum tax is currently levied at a rate of 51 per cent. The special tax is applied to relevant income in addition to the standard 27 per cent income tax, resulting in a 78 per cent marginal tax rate on income subject to petroleum tax. The basis for computing the special

---

> petroleum tax is the same as for income subject to ordinary corporate income tax, except that onshore losses are not deductible from the special petroleum tax and a tax-free allowance, or "uplift," is granted at a rate of 5.5 per cent per year. The uplift is computed on the basis of the original capitalized cost of offshore production installations. The uplift may be deducted from taxable income for a period of four years, starting in the year in which the capital expenditure is incurred. Unused uplift may be carried forward indefinitely.

6.3.3.2   Those taxes levied on profits—such as corporate income tax, special surcharges on extractive companies and excess profit taxes—are usually covered by the scope of Article 2 (Taxes Covered). In order to avoid diverging interpretations by the competent authorities, countries may seek to include special taxes applying to the extractive industries in the list of examples in Article 2, paragraph 3.

BOX 6.B.3:
Example: Article 1 of the United States-Norway Income and Property Tax Convention
(as amended through 1980)

The taxes that are the subject of this Convention are:
…in the case of Norway, the national and municipal taxes on income (including contributions to the tax equalization fund) and the special tax administered under section 5 of the Act of 13 June 1975, No. 35, relating to the taxation of submarine petroleum resources, as in effect on the date of signature of the Protocol to this Convention, and taxes substantially similar thereto enacted after such date.[a]

---

[a] United States-Norway Income and Property Tax Convention, Article I, para. 2(a (ii). Available at https://www.irs.gov/pub/irs-trty/norway.pdf.

6.3.4   Bonuses

6.3.4.1   Bonus payments have to be paid for obtaining the right to explore or extract the natural resources. Bonuses are one-off (or sometimes staged) payments that may be fixed, the result of a bid, or negotiated, and are generally linked to particular early project events such as licence awards or signature. They provide early revenue to the government and are easy to administer, and as such, can be attractive from a government or resource-owner standpoint. From the investors' side, bonuses are often made in advance, potentially before knowledge of commerciality, and are unrelated to production and thus generally less attractive to investors. The bonuses are not levied with reference to profit; rather, they are payments for obtaining the exploration and extraction rights, and they would therefore not normally be considered to constitute a tax on income or capital, which could be covered by the scope of the tax treaty.

6.3.5   Royalties

6.3.5.1   Royalties are the equivalent to the purchase price of the natural resource and entitle the extractive company to the ownership and subsequent sale of the natural resource. They are generally calculated as a percentage of the gross volume or value of the production and are due once production commences. In most countries,[9] royalties are not levied with reference to profit and they would therefore not be considered to constitute a tax on income or capital, which could be covered by the scope of the tax treaty.

6.3.6   Production sharing contracts

6.3.6.1   Production sharing contracts (PSCs) generally provide a formula for sharing the production between the investor and the government. They are used in the oil and gas industry especially, but mining PSCs also exist. A certain percentage of production is allocated to cover the actual investment and production costs borne by the investor (called "cost oil" in that industry) and the remaining amount is shared between the investors and the government (called "profit oil"). Profit oil may be the only payment to the government and it can be made in cash or in kind, i.e., in oil. Alternatively, the investor's portion of the profit oil may also be subject to profit taxes imposed. Profit taxes imposed on the profit oil will usually fall within the scope of the tax treaty. However, especially where the source State obtains a larger in-kind allocation in lieu of taxes on the investor's income, the treaty should clarify that this falls within the scope of the tax treaty.

6.3.6.2   In addition to the different types of special tax payments made by participants in the extractive industries, there are the standard types of taxes that may relate to payments made to resident and non-resident employees, service providers or taxes applicable to profit distribution and other types of passive income. The type and nature of these traditional types of taxes rarely raises issues regarding the substantive scope of the tax treaty. Table 6.T.2 below lists the different types of taxes and obligatory payments to governments levied during the different stages of extractive industries activities, and indicates whether or not these types of taxes are to be covered by the scope of tax treaties.

6.3.6.3   If these special types of taxes are not covered by tax treaties (i.e., are outside of their scope) the host States can still levy these taxes, but conversely, the other Contracting States will have no treaty obligation to eliminate the potential

---

[9] For example, South Africa determines the applicable royalty rate with reference to "earnings before interest."

double taxation by granting a credit or exemption. As no treaty limitations and obligations arise, this may lead to higher overall tax costs related to the particular investment and commercial activities. Therefore, many countries hosting extractive activities seek to design their tax systems in such a way as to assure two objectives:

1) The country establishes and retains the taxing rights in respect of extractives and related activities;

2) The taxes levied on the extractive activities can be credited in the investor's residence State.

6.3.6.4   In addition, the scope of the tax treaty provided for by Article 2 is also relevant for Article 25 (mutual agreement procedure) unless the scope of this article is extended to include additional taxes not covered by Article 2. Articles 26 and 27 under the United Nations Model Convention apply to taxes of every description, not only taxes covered under Article 2. Therefore, the key question may often be whether the special levy is properly regarded as tax for the purposes of the treaty.

6.3.6.5   Tax treaties usually cover taxes on income and on capital. Neither the United Nations nor the OECD Model Convention contains special provisions to address which special taxes applicable to the extractive industries are covered by a tax treaty. However, country practices indicate that some countries seek to include taxes levied on extractive activities in the scope of their tax treaties as long as these taxes meet the character of taxes on income or capital. To assure this outcome, countries may consider designing the relevant taxes to assure the nature of these taxes meet the character of taxes on income or capital. It is also appropriate to address the issue during negotiations, and to specifically state in the tax treaty that a special tax (or taxes) levied in the extractive industries is to be covered by the treaty. This will ensure a credit or exemption for such taxes.

6.3.6.6   In cases where special taxes in the extractive industries levied by the source State are covered by a tax treaty, the residence State has the obligation to apply Article 23 to eliminate double taxation. Some treaties specifically provide special rules for the calculation of the maximum tax credit that the residence State must provide.[10]

---

[10] See, for example, Article 23 in the United States-Norway DTA.

Table 6.T.2: Types of taxes levied at different stages of extractive project and the applicability of tax treaty

Stages	Type of taxes and obligatory payments to governments	Typical characteristics	Covered by scope of the DTA?
Contract negotiation and signature	Signature bonus	A payment in the form of a percentage (e.g., 1% of expected value of natural resources) or a fixed amount	Usually not (unless the payment is designed in a way that it can be considered a tax on income credited against the corporate income tax)
Exploration activities and evaluation	Exploration bonus	Similar to signature bonus	Usually not
	Rent payments	Payments for the use of land	Usually not
	Tax levied on employees	Income taxes	Yes (individual)
	Tax levied on service providers	Income taxes	Yes (service providers - subcontractors)
Development of the infrastructure	Bonuses and rentals	Same as bonuses and rental payments above	Same as bonuses and rent payments above
	Taxes on employees and subcontractors	Same as taxes levied on employees and subcontractors above	Same as taxes levied on employees and service providers – subcontractors, above
	Import duties and levies, VAT	Indirect taxes and levies	No
Extraction, production, export	Royalties	Payment on the volume or value of the extracted resource	Usually not
	Bonuses and rentals	Same as bonuses and rentals above	Same as bonuses and rentals above
	Production sharing payments	Percentage of production paid to State	Usually not, unless designed as a tax on income/percentage of profit
	Profit taxes and excess profit tax	Tax on income/profit	Yes
	Export duties and export levies	Tax on value of exported resource	No
Abandonment and decommissioning	Environmental fees or penalties	Fines or penalties for pollution	No
	Taxes on employees and subcontractors	Same as taxes levied on employees and subcontractors above	Same as taxes levied on employees and subcontractors above

191

6.3.7   Territorial scope of tax treaties

6.3.7.1   Neither the United Nations nor the OECD Model Convention contains terms/definitions that would specifically address issues of the extractive industries. However, since many countries, in their practices, include the definition of "Contracting States" in Article 3, this definition determines the geographic scope of the application of the tax treaty. Such a definition may include notions of territory and territorial waters, which are usually automatically included in the notions of state territory, but may also be expressly extended to include the continental shelf and the exclusive economic zone within which the States may exercise taxing rights in accordance with international law.

6.3.7.2   The issue of whether or not to include specific reference to particular geographical areas in a tax treaty, as well as any potential consequences of such inclusion or non-inclusion, should be discussed during the treaty negotiations, and if necessary, can be specifically addressed in the text.

6.4   BUSINESS PROFITS AND PERMANENT ESTABLISHMENT ISSUES

6.4.1.1   Profits from commercial activities will usually be covered by Article 7 (Business Profits) unless other articles apply to the specific type of income. Article 7 allocates exclusive taxing rights to the State of residence of the recipient of the income, unless the enterprise carries on business in the source State and such activities are conducted through a permanent establishment (PE). In such a case, profits from such activities that are attributable to the PE may be taxed in the country of source. If economic activities do not fall within the definition of a PE, the profits from such activities may only be taxed in the country of residence. This general rule and principle may not be considered appropriate by a country that hosts extractive activities. Such a country may include specific provisions in its bilateral tax treaties that further alter the default rules of Article 7 and Article 5 to address its priorities.

6.4.1.2   The provisions of Articles 7 and 5 will be relevant for different actors in the extractive sector. Investors and operators in the sector that operate in a host country without having established an incorporated entity rely on these Articles to provide guidance on their tax status.[11] The existence of a PE will determine whether the country may levy tax on profits made by the investor, but these provisions will be also relevant for various non-resident service providers and suppliers in the sector.

6.4.1.3   The term "permanent establishment" is an important threshold that is central to Article 7 and is defined in Article 5. However, it is also critical for the operation of other articles regulating the taxation of income such as dividends, interest, royalties, capital gains, income from employment as well as other income and capital. While this chapter addresses issues relevant for tax treaty

---

[11] Some countries (Brazil and Nigeria, for example) may require the investor to be incorporated within the country to obtain a license to explore or extract resources.

negotiations generally, Chapter 3 (Permanent Establishment Issues) addresses more specifically the practical aspects of the permanent establishment concept in relation to the extractive industries.

6.4.1.4   "The term 'permanent establishment' means a fixed place of business through which the business of the enterprise is wholly or partly carried on" (Article 5(1) of the United Nations Model Convention). The condition that the place of business, or the use of it, has to be "permanent" is explained in the OECD Commentary (cited in paragraph 3 of the United Nations Commentary on Article 5(1)) in the sense that a PE can be deemed to exist only if the place of business has a certain degree of permanency (i.e., if it is not of a purely temporary nature). A place of business may, however, constitute a PE even though it exists, in practice, only for a very short period of time because the nature of the business is such that it will only be carried out for that short period of time. It is sometimes difficult to determine whether this is the case.[12]

6.4.1.5   In addition, Article 5(2) lists specific operations that *prima facie* constitute a PE. It especially includes "a place of management, a branch, an office, a factory, a workshop, and a mine, an oil or gas well, a quarry or any other place of extraction of natural resources." The OECD Commentary to this paragraph (also cited in the United Nations Commentary at paragraph 5) states that "the term 'any other place of extraction of natural resources' should be interpreted broadly" to include all places of extraction of hydrocarbons, whether onshore or offshore. This is the only provision specifically addressing extractive industries activities and the illustrative example indicates that extractive activities carried out by non-resident investors and subcontractors will usually constitute a PE in the source country. Thus, the income derived and capital owned in respect of operating a mine, oil or gas well, as well as any other place of extraction of natural resources by the non-resident enterprise, may be subject to tax in the country of source (the location of the natural resource).

6.4.1.6   Article 5 of the UN Model, however, addresses only extraction activities and does not address the issue of exploration activities. The OECD Commentary, which is also quoted in the United Nations Commentary on Article 5 at paragraph 5, offers in this regard several policy options to be addressed in bilateral negotiation:

The Contracting States may agree, for instance, that an enterprise of a Contracting State, as regards its activities of exploration of natural resources in a place or area in the other Contracting State:

a)   Shall be deemed not to have a permanent establishment in that other State; or

b)   Shall be deemed to carry on such activities through a permanent establishment in that other State; or

c)   Shall be deemed to carry on such activities through a permanent

---

[12] See 2017 United Nations Model, Commentary on Article 5, paragraph 3.

establishment in that other State if such activities last longer than a specified period of time.

The Contracting States may moreover agree to submit the income from such activities to any other rule.[13]

6.4.1.7   Accordingly, some countries exercise this policy option and include exploration activities in Article 5(2) of their tax treaties.[14] Without providing any further rules, the general provisions of the permanent establishment definition (Article 5(1)) will apply to such exploration activities.

6.4.1.8   Alternatively, a treaty could provide for exploration to be a PE in a separate provision.[15] Such a provision may either provide that the exploration activities (onshore or offshore) are deemed to constitute a PE irrespective of the duration of activities. Other countries will include provisions with a specific time threshold[16]— for example, the 30-day rule, based on which the exploration activities are deemed to constitute a PE if they continue for more than 30 days.

6.4.1.9   Both the United Nations and the OECD Model Conventions also have a provision dealing with construction sites. In this respect, however, the two models differ from each other: whereas Article 5(3) of the OECD Model states that "a building site or construction or installation project constitutes a permanent establishment if it lasts more than twelve months," the UN Model gives the host country broader taxing rights by providing for a six-month duration test for building and construction PEs and expressly includes supervisory activities. This may be especially relevant in the extractive industries, since significant construction and installation of infrastructure takes place in the development stage. In the oil and gas industry, it is commonly understood that the well is being constructed, since it requires significant other construction activities beyond the mere drilling activity, including concrete works, welding, cementing, etc.

6.4.1.10   Furthermore, some countries in their DTAs also deem a PE where "substantial equipment" is used "by, for or under contract" with the taxpayer.[17] Where countries introduce such provisions, interpretation issues may arise in respect to the term "substantial" equipment.[18]

---

[13] Such an extraction provision can be found, for example, in Article 5(8) of the Canada-Papua New Guinea tax treaty, where activities in connection with exploration or exploitation of natural resources that last more than 30 days in total during a 12-month period will be deemed to constitute a permanent establishment.

[14] See for example, Article 5(2)(f) of the Canada-Kazakhstan tax treaty of 25 September 1996.

[15] See for example, Article 5(3)(c) of the Australia-China tax treaty of 17 November 1988.

[16] See for example, Article 21 of the Nordic Convention.

[17] See for example, the DTAs of Australia, Ghana and other mining countries; Article 4(3)b of the Australia-Singapore DTA; Article 5(3)c of the Australia-Switzerland DTA.

[18] See Australian Taxation Office, ATO Interpretative Decision 2006/306, available at: https://www.ato.gov.au/law/view/document?src=hs&pit=99991231235958&arc=false&start=1&pageSize=10&total=1&num=0&docid=AID%2FAID2006306%2F00001&dc=false&stype=find&

6.5   TAXATION OF SERVICES

6.5.1.1   As noted above, a significant part of the activities related to explo-ration, development of deposits, and extraction activities are performed by various service providers and suppliers. The services carried out may encompass the drilling of wells (directional drilling, tubular running, cementing, etc.); logis-tics (communication, helicopter, logistic base, etc.); construction work, including maintenance and repair work, preventive maintenance, engineering and consul-tancy services, catering, supply and hotel services. This naturally leads to ques-tions, such as to what extent can the profits earned by the service providers and subcontractors be taxed by the source State, where these activities take place.

6.5.1.2   The host country is usually only allowed to tax a service fee paid to a subcontractor under the applicable tax treaty if (i) the non-resident subcontractor has a PE in the host country; and (ii) the service fee is attributable to the PE.

6.5.1.3   In this respect, the UN Model contains special provisions, which are designed to provide the country of source extended taxing rights as compared to the OECD Model. Specifically, under the UN Model, a PE also encompasses a situa-tion where services are furnished in the country, including consultancy services, by enterprises through employees or others for more than 183 days within any 12-month period (Article 5(3) of the United Nations Model Convention). This pro-vision (often called the "services PE provision") thus permits the country of source to levy taxes on business profits of enterprises without a fixed place of business in the source country, in case their activities in the source country exceed the 183 days threshold. As this threshold may still be high for certain activities, especially in the extractive sector, a number of countries have introduced a lower threshold for exploration activities as mentioned above. This also means that those activi-ties, which would escape the "services PE," would be considered to constitute a PE if such a special provision is included.

6.5.1.4   "Independent" agents may also constitute a PE when the activities of such an agent are devoted wholly or almost wholly on behalf of the enterprise, and the agent is not dealing on an arm's-length basis with the enterprise (Article 5(7) of the UN Model).

6.5.1.5   By including these UN Model provisions, countries significantly increase their right to levy tax on services provided in their territory.

6.5.1.6   Since there may be also significant amounts of profits earned by non-residents who do not have a significant presence in the country, have a high degree of mobility, or provide part or all of the services from outside the host juris-diction, some host countries are increasingly applying a final withholding tax to service fees paid to non-residents without a taxable presence in the jurisdiction. The withholding tax may apply to independent services in general or be limited to the provision of "technical services." On the one hand, final withholding tax on ser-vice fees offers some protection to the host country revenue against base erosion

tm=phrase-basic-2006%2F306.

that may otherwise arise when service fees are paid to non-residents.[19]   On the other hand, the gross income taxation may mean that the tax costs may exceed the net profit (where the profit margin is lower than the rate of the withholding tax) and thus can increase costs for the investors, because many of the service providers may insist that the cost of services should be increased to reflect these tax costs. Further, no double tax relief may be granted in the State of residence for most of the withholding tax, since the tax liability exceeds the tax liability on the net income. However, some countries may provide the tax relief in any event.[20]

6.5.1.7   A host country wishing to maintain a withholding tax on fees for technical services may want to preserve its taxing right in its tax treaties. In cases where the host country wants to prevent treaty shopping by the subcontractor, an effective way would be to include a rule in the income tax legislation that generally confines the benefits of a tax treaty to genuine residents of the other Contracting State.

6.5.1.8   Further, in order to retain the taxing right in non-abusive situations, the host country may negotiate specific provisions in its tax treaties. For the treatment of services under tax treaties, it is important that the UN Model maintains Article 14 dealing with independent personal services. Accordingly, the UN Model allocates taxing rights to the source state over such income when a fixed base is available, or if the stay is for a period or periods amounting to or exceeding, in the aggregate, 183 days in any 12-month period. This applies in addition to the taxation of business profits in case there is a PE in the host country. This threshold criterion thus raises similar issues like the threshold criterion for a PE. Countries may wish to consider whether similar considerations with respect to specific types of PE, including the reduced time periods relevant for exploration/extraction activities, need to be introduced and applicable under Article 14.

6.5.1.9   Some countries include in their tax treaties special provisions covering income from "Technical Services," which permit the country of source to levy tax on income derived by non-residents even if the time/location threshold is not exceeded (i.e., even when the PE/fixed base test is not met). Moreover, the United Nations Tax Committee decided to add a new Article to the UN Model dealing with "fees for technical services."[21] Article 12A allows the host country to tax "technical services" up to a certain percentage of the gross amount even if the non-resident subcontractor does not have a PE in the host State. This provision significantly extends the taxing rights of the source state as compared to other model treaties. It permits the country to levy tax on income from services derived by contractors and subcontractors in respect of services that may be provided

---

[19] See L. Burns, *"Income Taxation through the Life Cycle of an Extractive Industries Project,"* Asia-Pacific Tax Bulletin, vol. 20, no. 6 (18 November 2014), p. 401.

[20] Many countries also grant a credit for taxes paid on gross income. See, for example, Section 903 Internal Revenue Code for the United States and Section 34c Income Tax Act for Germany.

[21] United Nations Tax Committee of Experts on International Cooperation in Tax Matters, Report on the Tenth Session (27–31 October 2014). E/2014/45-E/C.18/2014/6, para. 74ff. It is Article 12A of the 2017 Model.

as part of the process of exploration activities, consulting or other specialized services. See further Chapter 8 for a detailed discussion of tax issues applicable to subcontractors and service providers.

6.5.1.10   On 20 April 2021, the UN Committee approved the final draft of Article 12B of the UN Model, relating to income from automated digital services. The article would give the contracting states the right to tax the income from automated digital services where it arises, at a maximum rate to be determined by negotiation between the contracting states. However, under paragraph 3 of the article, the beneficial owner of the income would have the right to be taxed on qualified net profits from automated digital services at the domestic rate of tax in the source state. The qualified profits for this purpose are 30 per cent of the amount resulting from applying the taxpayer's profitability ratio (or the profitability ratio of its automated digital business segment, if available) to the gross annual revenue from automated digital services in the source state. Where the taxpayer belongs to a group, the relevant profitability ratio of the group is to be used. The article would cover services provided through the internet or electronic networks where there is minimal human involvement by the provider of the service, but not including payments qualifying as fees for technical services under Article 12A.[22]

6.6   OTHER TREATY PROVISIONS

6.6.1   Article 6: Income from immovable property

6.6.1.1   Article 6 allocates the right to tax income from immovable property to the State where the property is situated. Both the United Nations and the OECD Models state in Article 6(2) that the term "immovable property" shall have the meaning that it has under the domestic law of the State where the property is situated. "Rights to variable or fixed payments as consideration for the working of, or the right to work, mineral deposits, sources and other natural resources" should be considered as "immovable property." "Working a resource" means removing the natural resources from the landed property.[23] Income from exploitation of natural resources is therefore, in general, taxable in the State where they are extracted.

6.6.1.2   In some treaties, a specific provision is included, often in a Protocol, clarifying that exploration and exploitation licences relating to natural resources should be regarded as immovable property situated in the State to which they appertain (sometimes also deeming such licences to pertain to a PE situated in that State).[24] This means that the income derived by a non-resident from the

---

[22] United Nations Model Tax Convention (2021).

[23] Ekkehart Reimer and Alexander Rust (Eds.). Klaus Vogel on Double Taxation Conventions (New York: Wolters Kluwer 2015) Chap. III. Article 6.

[24] This can for example be found in the Protocol to the Croatia-Netherlands tax treaty of 23 May 2000.

operations related to immovable property (including extractive activities) is subject to taxation in the country of source (location of the extractive activities) irrespective of whether the activities may constitute a PE or not.[25] This also has relevance for the ability of the host country to tax the capital gains from the sale of such licences.

6.6.2   Article 8: International shipping and air transport

6.6.2.1   While Article 8 takes away the taxing rights from the country of source, some treaties have addressed the operation of tugboats and similar transport vehicles in the territorial waters and continental shelf by providing to exclude them from the possible scope of this article.

6.6.2.2   It should be borne in mind that if the scope of the State has been extended to the continental shelf, any movements of boats, etc., between the onshore/harbour and a point on the continental shelf of the same State automatically falls outside the scope of Article 8 and the rules related to international traffic do not apply in respect of such activities.

BOX 6.B.4:
Example: Article 6, paragraph 2 of the Singapore-UK Tax Treaty of 12 February 1997

The term "international traffic" means all movements by a ship or aircraft operated by an enterprise of one of the Contracting States, **other than movements solely between places in the other Contracting State or solely between such places and one or more structures used for the exploration or extraction of natural resources situated in waters adjacent to the territorial waters of that other Contracting State.**

6.6.2.3   Countries may also want to ensure that they are not accidentally including other means of transport in the scope of this Article, as they may lose the taxing rights over different transport operators involved in the transport of natural resources, possibly giving up the right to tax significant profits that may arise from transporting natural resources.

6.6.3   Article 9: Associated enterprises

6.6.3.1   While Article 9 foresees primary and corresponding adjustments in situations where transfer prices depart from the arm's length price, consideration could be given to situations where the countries operate regulations requiring

---

[25] Article 6, paragraph 3 establishes that the provisions of Article 6 apply irrespective of the provisions of Article 7.

that the transfer price should not depart from a certain price set by regulatory bodies.

6.6.3.2   Such benchmark or reference prices are used by different countries in respect of hydrocarbons and minerals, and since discussion may arise as to whether these benchmark prices are an arm's-length price, one could consider whether this specific aspect should be mentioned in the wording of Article 9 or should be provided as a clarification to Article 9 in the Protocol to the treaty.

6.6.3.3   Chapter 5 of this Handbook addresses some of the specifics of transfer pricing in the extractive industries.

6.6.4   Articles 10, 11, 12: Dividends, interest, royalties

6.6.4.1   These articles may not raise specific issues related to extractive activities; nevertheless, they may still raise issues relevant to developing countries and tax base erosion.

6.6.4.2   There is a specific difference between the UN and OECD Model Conventions in Article 12 (Royalties), where the OECD Model Convention allocates the exclusive taxing right to the country of residence, while the UN Model Convention allocates the right to tax royalty to the country of source with a limited tax rate. In addition, the definition of Royalty in Article 12, paragraph 3 of the UN Model Convention extends the definition to include payments for the use of scientific, commercial and industrial equipment, thus permitting the country of source to levy tax on both payments for the use of intangible property and payments for the use of tangible property (including rental payment for the specific equipment used in exploration, drilling, mining and other activities).

6.6.5   Article 13: Capital gains

6.6.5.1   Capital gains from the sale of licence or similar rights to extract natural resources, as well as the sale of shares of companies who possess such rights, may present significant tax revenue potential on the one hand, as well as challenges for the extractive companies, since significant tax costs can be involved. Since this topic deserves detailed policy analyses, this chapter limits itself to some general observations. Chapter 4 of this Handbook (Indirect Transfer of Assets) addresses this topic in more detail.

6.6.5.2   Article 13 generally mirrors the principles for allocation of taxing rights for particular types of income and allocates the right to tax gains from the alienation of assets to the country that had the right to tax income generated by those assets. Gains from the sale of mineral/hydrocarbon resources extracted from or exploited in one Contracting State are therefore generally taxable in that State. Some countries have extended the taxation right for the source State to also include maritime mineral deposits and assets in connection with the exploration and/or exploitation of such mineral resources and hydrocarbons such as oil and gas offshore. Often, such provisions are found in a separate article for the exploration and exploitation of hydrocarbon resources. For example, Article 21(9) of the Nordic Convention allocates the right to tax gains from the alienation of the right to survey and explore or exploit hydrocarbon deposits, including a right to a share in or profits from such deposits to the source State.

6.6.5.3   In most cases of a direct transfer of a mining or petroleum right the source State would be allowed to tax the income from sale as gains from immovable property under the applicable tax treaty (assuming the licence is considered immovable property). It is, however, a common form of tax planning for non-residents to invest through a multi-tier non-resident corporate structure so as to facilitate a possible tax-free exit from the investment. Instead of directly selling a mine, a non-resident could avoid capital gains taxation by an offshore sale several companies up the line; see Chapter 10 for a detailed discussion of tax issues around the indirect transfer of assets. Some countries (France, for example) therefore extend the definition of immovable property in Article 6 to include shares in companies deriving their value from immovable property. Consequently, Article 13(1) allows them to tax both the direct transfer of extraction/exploration rights and the indirect transfer of such rights via the sale of shares of companies which possess such rights, if the natural resources are located in their country.

6.6.5.4   In this regard, it is also appropriate to highlight the existence of Article 13(5) of the UN Model Convention, which permits the country of source to tax the income from capital gains also where shares derive more than a specified percentage of their value from immovable property. However, the provision applies only in direct transfers of shares and comparable interests, so it may not be as effective in indirect transfer situations.

6.6.5.5   In case Article 6 does not include shares in companies deriving their value from immovable property, the same result can be achieved by Article 13(4) of the UN Model Convention. It allocates the right to tax indirect transfers of immovable property to the source country where the immovable property is located. This rule applies, however, only when the value of the entity is derived "principally" from interests in immovable property in the jurisdiction. If the 50 per cent threshold is satisfied, then the whole gain is taxable. If a company is sold that holds interests in mining or petroleum rights in different countries, the arrangement could be structured in a way that the threshold is not satisfied in relation to any country. Even if in such a case the gains of alienation of shares consist only of mining rights, none of the source countries might be allowed to impose a tax because the 50 per cent threshold must be fulfilled in respect of one single country. The impact of such tax planning can be limited by implementing a lower threshold.

6.6.5.6   Where the taxation of capital gains takes place from such indirect transfers of shares, it is appropriate to ensure that the potential double taxation is relieved. This can take place through cost recovery methods or through measures in the country of residence of the seller.

6.6.5.7   In this respect, it is important to point out the limitation in the wording of the 2011 version of the UN Model Convention, which limits the right of the country of source to levy tax on such transfers, where the company is carrying on active business. In particular, Article 13(4) states that:

"[n]othing contained in this paragraph shall apply to a company, partnership, trust or estate, other than a company, partnership, trust or estate engaged in the business of management of immovable properties, the property of which consists directly or indirectly principally of immovable property used by such company, partnership, trust or estate in its business activities."

6.6.5.8   This limitation may prevent the source State from levying a tax on capital gains from the transfers of shares of extractive companies. It was removed in the 2017 Model Convention. The issue of the operation of Article 13(4) is considered in more detail in Chapter 10 of this Handbook (Indirect Transfer of Assets).

6.6.6   Article 15: Dependent personal services

6.6.6.1   The provisions of Article 15 provide an exclusive taxing right to the country of residence of the employee, with exceptions when the employee exercises the employment in the country of source and some of the conditions in Article 15, paragraph 2 are not met (the employee is present for more than 183 days in the country of source, or the salary is paid by an employer who is resident in the country of source, or the salary is borne by the PE of the employer in the country of source). This also means that where the shorter time threshold (e.g., 30 days) applies to certain activities (such as exploration) the salaries of staff carrying out these activities (connected to the PE) become taxable in the source State.

6.6.6.2   Assuming the PE definition in Article 5 takes into consideration the specifics of extractive industries (such as the short-term activities of various service providers), the provisions of Article 15 will automatically reflect the adjustments made by the definitions in Article 5 - especially where the PE is deemed to exist immediately or after a short period of time (e.g., after 30 days) and thus no further changes are required to the tax treaty provisions. Where the activities constitute a PE, including where there is a deemed PE, as a result of specific activities related to the extractive industries, the host country will be able to tax the salaries of the personnel engaged in providing the services and activities.

6.6.7   Articles 16 and 19: Director's fees and government service

6.6.7.1   In respect of Article 16 (Director's Fees) it is advisable to follow the United Nations Model Convention, which extends the application of this article to the remuneration of the top management of companies.

6.6.7.2   One specific issue that may arise in respect of Article 19 (Government Service) is the establishment of a national oil and gas or mining company by a Contracting State. In this case, the activities of the Contracting State should be considered as those mentioned in Article 19, paragraph 3, and the provisions of Article 19, paragraphs 1 and 2 should thus not apply in respect of the remuneration received by the employees of these state companies.

6.6.8   Article 21: Other income

6.6.8.1   The UN and OECD Model Conventions differ in respect of the allocation of taxing rights of other income. The type of income that is not covered specifically in other provisions of the tax treaty should be subject to tax in the country of residence (according to the OECD Model Convention)[26] and also in the treaty party that is the country of source (according to the United Nations Model Convention) when the income is paid from that country to a resident of the other country.

6.6.8.2   Many countries prefer to follow the UN Model version of Article 21, as situations may arise in which certain payments related to the extractive industries may fall into the category of Article 21 "other income" (e.g., various compensation payments, payments from insurance compensation, arbitration awards, etc., assuming a tax on these payments would fall under Article 21).

6.6.9   Article 22: Taxation of capital

6.6.9.1   While Articles 6 to 21 of the UN and the OECD Model Conventions deal with the taxation of cross-border income of a recurrent nature, Article 22 of both models governs the taxation of capital in cross-border cases. In substance, Article 22 mirrors the treatment and definitions in the allocation rules related to corresponding items of income. It thus refers to the definition of immovable property in Article 6, the permanent establishment in Article 5 and the scope of Article 8 (Shipping and Air Transport). The meaning of such terms used in Article 22 is identical to the meaning of the same terms in the other treaty articles.

6.6.10   Article 23: Elimination of double taxation

6.6.10.1   As was noted earlier, the elimination of double taxation through the methods of credit and exemption play an important role in the extractive industries.

6.6.10.2   The specific issue related to the extractive industries would be the obligation of the country of residence to eliminate double taxation, where the country of source was entitled to levy tax on income or capital. Specifically, the question will arise as to whether the specific types of taxes levied on the extractive activities fall within the scope of the tax treaty, in accordance with Article 2, and whether the country of residence has to provide credit in respect of the particular type of tax. Countries of residence may seek to limit the maximum credit available as can be demonstrated from the example below.

---

[26] Except when this other income is attributable to the permanent establishment (Article 21(2)).

BOX 6.B.5:
Article 23 of the United States-Norway Income and
Property Tax Convention

The appropriate amount allowed as a credit by the United States shall be based upon the amount of income taxes paid or accrued to Norway.

However, the credit shall not exceed the limitations (for the purpose of limiting the credit to the United States tax on income from sources outside of the United States) provided by United States law for the taxable year. In addition, in the case of income taxes paid or accrued to Norway by persons subject to the special tax referred to in subparagraph 2(a)(ii) of Article 1 (Taxes Covered) or to a substantially similar tax, the appropriate amount allowed as a credit by the United States shall be limited to the amount of income taxes paid or accrued to Norway attributable to Norwegian source taxable income in the following way:

i) With respect to income taxes paid or accrued to Norway on oil and gas extraction income from oil or gas wells in Norway, the amount to be allowed as a credit for a taxable year shall not exceed the product of:

> (a) The maximum statutory United States tax rate applicable to a corporation for such taxable year; and

> (b) The amount of such income;

(ii) Further, the lesser of:

> (a) The amount of taxes paid or accrued to Norway on oil and gas extraction income from oil or gas wells in Norway that is not allowable as a credit under subparagraph (i); or

> (b) Two per cent of such income for the taxable year;

shall be deemed to be income taxes paid or accrued in the two preceding or five succeeding taxable years, to the extent not deemed paid or accrued in a prior taxable year, and shall be allowable as a credit in the year in which it is deemed paid or accrued subject to the limitation in subparagraph (i);

(iii) The provisions of subparagraphs (i) and (ii) shall apply separately, in the same way (but with the deletion, in the case of subparagraph (ii) of the words "the lesser of (a)" and "or (b) two percent of such income for the taxable year") to the amount of income taxes paid or accrued to Norway on:

> (a) Norwegian source oil related income not described in sub graph (i); and

> (b) Other Norwegian source income.

6.6.11   Article 24: Non-discrimination

6.6.11.1   Tax treaties contain the principle of non-discrimination, a principle that is also relevant for the extractive industries, since it prohibits different and less favourable treatment in respect of taxation of permanent establishments (Article 24(3)) and discriminatory treatment in deductibility of certain expenses (Article 24(4)). Situations that may give rise to discrimination considerations include those cases in which the host country levies a higher tax rate on operators of the extractive industries. However, if this higher tax rate applies irrespective of the residence of the investor or the head office of the extractive company, they are not to be considered as discriminatory.

6.6.11.2   Similarly, where the host country levies a special branch profits tax, the issue may arise as to whether this branch profits tax is in accordance with a tax treaty. Country practices indicate that many countries have chosen to clarify these issues in Article 24(3) through a special provision inserted in Article 10 (Dividends) or in the protocols to the tax treaties.

6.6.11.3   Situations where the host country opts for indirectly taxing the non-resident subcontractor by denying a deduction for the payment of the fee at the level of the payer may be also considered discriminatory if similar payments made to residents are deductible.

ANNEX 1

Catherine Brown, "Permanent Establishments and the Mining Industry–A Roadmap to the Taxation of Resource-Based Activities under Tax Treaties," *Asia-Pacific Tax Bulletin*, vol. 18, no. 1 (16 January 2012), p. 5.

L. Burns, "Income Taxation through the Life Cycle of an Extractive Industries Project," *Asia-Pacific Tax Bulletin*, vol. 20, no. 6 (18 November 2014), p. 410.

Philip Daniel, Michael Keen and Charles McPherson (Eds.), Philip Daniel, Michael Keen and Charles McPherson (Eds.), *The Taxation of Petroleum and Minerals: Principles, Problems and Practice* (New York: Routledge, 2010).

Ekkehart Reimer and Alexander Rust (Eds.), *Klaus Vogel on Double Taxation Conventions* (New York: Wolters Kluwer 2015), pp. 310–311.

Chapter 7

Permanent Establishment Issues

7.1 INTRODUCTION

7.1.1 Executive summary

7.1.1.1   This chapter examines the concept of permanent establishment (PE) in the extractive industries in detail. In this respect, it focuses on the main PE taxation issues relating to the extractive industries taking into consideration the relevant articles and Commentaries in the United Nations Model Convention (2021),[1] the Organization for Economic Cooperation and Development (OECD) Model Convention (2017) and the United States Model Convention (2016).[2]

7.1.1.2   While reference is made to the mining sector as relevant, the chapter mainly deals with the PE concept in the oil and gas (O&G) sector, where a wide array of taxation issues arise. This paper elaborates on the implications of recognizing the presence of a PE, distinguishing the tax consequences for the contractor and subcontractors as a result of the particular business features and different activities performed in a country.

7.1.1.3   The PE concept is one of the central elements of international taxation, particularly the law of tax treaties, and is primarily used for the purpose of the allocation of taxing rights when an enterprise of one State derives business profits from another State. The concept of PE is used in tax treaties to determine the right of a State to tax the profits of an enterprise of the other State. Specifically, the profits of an enterprise of one State are taxable in the other State only if the enterprise maintains a PE in the latter State and only to the extent that the profits are attributable to the PE. See further 6.4 et seq.

7.1.1.4   While the PE concept has a long history, its practical application still raises a number of issues as reflected by the numerous articles, case law and disputes between taxpayers and tax authorities on what constitutes a PE. Questions

---

[1] The 2017 version of the UN Model is available at http://www.un.org/esa/ffd/publications/model-double-taxation-update-2017.html. An update has been prepared for 2021, see Update of the UN Model Double Taxation Convention between Developed and Developing Countries – Technical changes proposed for the 2021 Update of the UN Model | Financing for Sustainable Development Office. https://financing.desa.un.org/document/update-un-model-double-taxation-convention-between-developed-and-developing-countries-20

[2] The relevant permanent establishment provisions of the OECD Model Convention are broadly included in the United Nations Model, with certain exceptions highlighted in this chapter.

have been posed about whether the current wording of PE provisions in the Model Conventions (in their articles and relevant Commentary) remain sufficient to establish the proper allocation of taxing rights between the source State (State of the PE) and the residence State (State of the head office of the company itself). For example, the OECD has proposed updates to the PE concept and proposed changes to the Commentary under the Base Erosion and Profit Shifting (BEPS) Project, to prevent the artificial avoidance of PE status. The OECD and UN Models have accordingly been updated.[3]

7.1.1.5   Notwithstanding its strong physical presence in the source country—which leads to the existence of a PE—the extractive sector, and oil and gas activities in particular, comprise different phases and quasi-unique features and activities[4] that need to be examined on a case-by-case basis to determine the existence of a PE, based on the facts and circumstances involved.

7.1.1.6   In general, States enter into negotiations with oil and gas companies (contractors) regarding the primary economic aspects of the contract that specifies the extractive operations to be performed, also referred to as the "work commitment," which includes, for example, signature bonus, seismic acquisition and number of wells to be drilled).[5] Very frequently, these negotiations also address the fiscal regime that governs the allocation of revenues resulting from oil and gas activities (e.g., royalties, cost recovery, taxes, and government participation)[6] that are applicable to such operations.[7] These contracts generally grant legal rights for exploration and production in a given delimited acreage (hereinafter referred to as contract or contractual area) which is normally managed by several oil and gas companies (consortium or association) under a Joint Operating Agreement (JOA) with normally one company appointed as the operator.

7.1.1.7   Another important aspect of the oil and gas sector is that a great number of subcontractors are normally hired by the company appointed as the operator in the JOA. The need for and use of numerous subcontractors is driven by the specialized and diverse types of work required on site where exploration and production activities take place (e.g., seismic work, drilling, casing, catering, logistics and health, safety and environment (HSE)). PE issues with respect to drilling rigs deserve particular attention. This aspect is discussed in detail in Chapter 8, Subcontractors.

---

[3] OECD (2015). *Preventing the Artificial Avoidance of Permanent Establishment Status, Action 7–2015 Final Report.* Available at http://www.oecd.org/tax/preventing-the-artificial-avoidance-of-permanent-establishment-status-action-7-2015-final-report-9789264241220-en. htm. The 2017 OECD Model has made such changes and the 2017 and 2021 United Nations Models in many respects followed such updates.

[4] Exploration and production of hydrocarbons is characterized as highly intensive in capital investment with a low level of success in locating raw materials and, therefore, having a high level of risk.

[5] See also Chapter 3 (Tax Aspects of Negotiation and Renegotiation of Contracts).

[6] Many systems provide an option for national oil companies to participate in development projects.

[7] See also Chapter 2 (The Government's Fiscal Take).

7.1.1.8   This chapter also makes reference to other aspects of PEs in the extractive industries that might be relevant for determining whether a PE exists and should be taxed. One example is the "services PE," where a PE exists when an enterprise provides services under certain conditions within a source country through its employees or other personnel.

7.1.1.9   Accordingly, this chapter is structured in three main parts. The first part discusses the different sections of the United Nations Model Convention applicable to the oil and gas industry and how those provisions impact the different phases of the oil and gas production chain. The second part focuses on the construction work clause and how this clause applies to different relevant services performed by subcontractors. The final part, structured to address several issues, identifies other elements of the United Nations Model Convention or activities in the sector that need to be taken into consideration when drafting a regulatory framework for the oil and gas industry.

7.1.1.10   The purpose of this chapter is to provide an overview of some of the most prominent aspects of PE taxation as applied to the oil and gas sector in particular. The PE concept is a very complex subject and this chapter only attempts to assist policymakers and administrators in developing countries in evaluating the different tax options available to them, with respect to some of the PE issues that they may face in dealing with the oil and gas sector.

7.1.2   Background

7.1.2.1   When entering a country, oil and gas companies often structure their investment using a PE rather than incorporating a subsidiary. The main reason is generally non-fiscal, as PEs provide more flexible commercial features than subsidiaries. As a general rule, a PE can be easier to set up and close down, making this structure more convenient for oil and gas companies that frequently enter into new countries without full knowledge of and experience in those countries' markets. If the investment turns out to be unsuccessful (e.g., there is no commercial discovery during the exploration phase), the company can smoothly withdraw from the block or contract area, sometimes leading to de-registration of the branch.

7.1.2.2   Article 7(1) of the UN Model Convention provides that the business profits of a foreign enterprise are taxable in a State only if the enterprise has a PE to which the profits are attributable in that State. According to the Commentary to the UN Model Convention, this Article allocates taxing rights with respect to the business profits of an enterprise of a Contracting State if these profits are not subject to different rules under other Articles of the Convention.[8] It incorporates the basic principle that unless an enterprise of a Contracting State has a PE situated in the other State, the business profits of that enterprise may not be taxed by that other State unless these profits fall into special categories of income for

---

[8] United Nations, Department of Economic and Social Affairs (2017), *United Nations Model Convention*, Commentary on Article 7, para. 1.

which other Articles of the Convention specifically allocate taxing rights to that other State.

7.1.2.3   Article 5 of the UN Model Convention, which includes the definition of a PE, is therefore critical to the determination of whether the business profits of an enterprise of a Contracting State may be taxed in the other State. If economic activities do not fall within the definition of what constitutes a PE, the profits from such activities may only be taxed in the country of residence.

7.1.2.4   The UN Model Convention contains few specific provisions or commentary paragraphs dealing with issues related to the tax treatment of PEs in the extractive industries. The general rules contained in various articles of tax treaties have, however, been applied by countries to specific situations in the oil and gas industry, giving rise to different interpretations about the existence of a PE in some cases. Further, due to its special nature and a frequent desire to preserve taxation on oil and gas activity performed within their jurisdictions, several resource-rich countries have opted to include specific provisions regarding extractive industries in their tax treaties.[9]

7.1.2.5   Before the OECD released its final reports regarding base erosion and profit shifting (BEPS) on 5 October 2015,[10] the definition of PE had not been subject to major changes since its adoption by the League of Nations in the 1920s.[11] OECD Commentaries on the articles of the OECD Model Convention, mainly reproduced in the UN Model Convention Commentaries, have been changed on different occasions with respect to PE in order to, for example, create specific rules for a characterization of a services PE by countries wishing to have such a provision, or due to the progressive evolution of e-commerce.[12]

7.1.2.6   Notwithstanding the unchanged definition of PE in the OECD Model articles, divergent interpretations of the meaning of this term can be found for similar situations in different countries. This could be due not only to their different fiscal interest or their capacity to develop the natural resources with companies established within the country (e.g., countries without the technology and know-how necessary to explore and exploit their resources versus those having such expertise and skills) but also to the fact that, in general, the concept of PE can give rise to different interpretations because of the language used in tax treaty models.

---

[9] See, for example, Article 21 of the Nordic Convention. A special article for the exploration and extraction of hydrocarbons can be found in the treaties of Argentina, Australia, Denmark, Greece, Malta, the Netherlands, the United Kingdom of Great Britain and Northern Ireland, Ireland, Latvia, Norway, the United Arab Emirates and the United States of America.

[10] In particular, BEPS Action 7: *Preventing the artificial avoidance of PE status.*

[11] *Double Taxation and Tax Evasion Report.* League of Nations Doc. C.216.M.85 1927 II (1927).

[12] For example, the OECD 2008 Model Convention made changes which reflected the outcome of the OECD Technical Advisory Group created in 1999.

7.1.2.7   Exploration and production (E&P)[13] activities are usually carried out by oil and gas companies. Such entities are granted a licence either to explore and develop oil and gas in a delimited area within a country or to enter into agreements with the government of a country to explore and exploit resources in a designated area in that country.[14]

7.1.2.8   The numerous kinds of contracts or fiscal arrangements (hereinafter referred to as petroleum contracts) can generally be divided into the following categories: concession or licence contracts, pursuant to which the hydrocarbon belongs to the oil and gas company; Production Sharing Contracts (PSCs), in which the State shares in the results of the oil or gas operation through obtaining a government take (see further Chapter 4); or services agreements by which the State is the owner of the results of the operation but pays a fee to the oil and gas company for the services provided.[15]

7.1.2.9   The ownership of the hydrocarbon is the fundamental distinction between a concessionary and contractual system. However, most petroleum contracts grant oil and gas companies the right to explore, develop, produce and market natural resources for a given delimited area and duration. The contractual area comprises a geographical area identified and delineated in the petroleum contract (i.e., the block or field).

7.1.2.10   As far as the extraction (production) of oil and gas is concerned, there is no doubt that the fixed character of this activity constitutes a PE. The problem generally concerns various other activities carried out in connection with exploration and exploitation of the natural resources. In this respect, among others, the following issues and their PE implications will be further developed in this chapter (not in the order specified):

- Illustrative list of PEs ("positive list");[16]

- Studies or reconnaissance permits;

- Exploration activities;

---

[13] Exploration and Production is the process that includes searching for and extracting oil and gas underwater or underground. It is generally known as the "upstream" process.

[14] Governments and O&G companies normally negotiate their interests in one of two basic systems: concessionary and contractual, with ownership (of the hydrocarbon) being the fundamental distinction. Under the concessionary system, the O&G company has title to the hydrocarbon produced. Under the contractual system, the government retains title to the resources. However, both systems may coexist in one jurisdiction (for the mining and the O&G sector or, even, for the O&G sector) or mixed systems (a system that shares features of both systems) may apply.

[15] For a more detailed information about contractual arrangements, please refer to Chapter 7 (The Government's Fiscal Take) and Chapter 8 (Tax Aspects of Negotiation and Renegotiation of Contracts).

[16] United Nations, Department of Economic and Social Affairs (2021). United Nations Model Convention, Article 5(2): "A mine, an oil or gas well, a quarry or any other place of extraction of natural resources."

- Existence of more than one PE;

- Registration of a branch;

- Representation office used for market research;

- Office used for supporting activities; and

- Consideration of non-operators as a PE.

7.1.2.11   Investors generally share the high investments and high risks involved in these projects by signing a JOA with other partners to carry on activities in the contract area. Under the JOA, one of the partners is designated the operator of the block and assumes responsibility for contracting the resources and subcontractors necessary to carry out the activities committed with the State under the petroleum contract. The other partners in most cases make cash contributions in proportion to their interest in the joint venture.

7.1.2.12   A very important aspect of a PE relates to subcontractors hired to perform a wide range of activities in the source country. These subcontracting companies are characterized by their high degree of mobility and how quickly they complete activities related to seismic issues, drilling, testing, maintenance, catering, engineering and/or consultancy services, among others. In principle, if not already established, their presence in a country will be temporary with no aim or need for it to continue once they have finished their work. The construction or installation PE clause[17] and its relevance in respect of, for example, drilling rigs, support vessels and other related services will be the subject of analysis.

7.1.2.13   Long distance pipelines are used to transport oil and gas, sometimes crossing other countries and territories. The product is moved by pump stations along the pipeline. The PE tax treatment of this service of transport is also described in this chapter.

7.1.2.14   Certain countries have included specific provisions ("offshore clauses") in their tax treaties that allow source-state taxation to a greater extent than the ordinary PE provision does. In this context, it should be noted that several member States of the OECD have recorded reservations to offshore hydrocarbon exploration and exploitation and related activities, and have thereby reserved the right to insert provisions related to such activities in a special article of their treaties.[18]

7.1.2.15   Finally, mention will be made of the technical services provision, included in the 2017 version of the United Nations Model Convention as Article 12A (Fees for Technical Services).

---

[17] United Nations, Department of Economic and Social Affairs (2021), United Nations Model Convention, Article 5(3): "The term 'permanent establishment' also encompasses: (a) A building site, a construction, assembly or installation project or supervisory activities in connection therewith, but only if such site, project or activities last more than six months."

[18] OECD, Model Tax Convention on Income and Capital, 2014, para. 47 of the Commentary on Article 5.

7.1.2.16   Countries should balance the pros and cons of all the above-mentioned provisions, their adoption and application, according to their tax and economic policy and taking into consideration the country's overall fiscal system. For example, if developing countries consider that introducing an "offshore clause" in their tax treaties is favourable as it extends the scope of PE taxation, they should also assess the cost-benefit balance of managing a greater number of PEs because of the increased number of subcontractors that would fall under the conditions established in this clause.

7.1.2.17   Other means of achieving taxation on income obtained from activities that have reached a certain level of performance in the source country could be examined by developing countries. For example, a withholding tax could be imposed on cross-border payments (gross) that are deductible by the payer in determining tax on income. This system—which is part of a simpler and easier means of enforcement—reduces tax compliance costs for both the subcontractor and the source jurisdiction, but still requires a definition of a level of business required to trigger such withholding and the rate of withholding tax applicable to the payment. Other issues may be the fact that such payments could not be immediately deductible, not be deductible at any point (cost-oil) and that the payer may be required to be responsible for collecting and remitting the withholding tax.

7.1.2.18   It should be noted that to apply the appropriate taxation rules, income must first be characterized in the appropriate category. As mentioned above, several articles of the applicable tax treaty might become relevant and disputes may arise between the taxpayer and the tax authorities over which would be the applicable treaty provision. For example, in a case related to the income tax treaty between India and the Netherlands, it was questioned whether the consideration paid by the Indian company to the Dutch company for the performance of an airborne geophysical survey fell within the definition of "fees for technical services" under Article 12 of such tax treaty.[19]

7.1.2.19   In summary, the UN Model Convention contains a number of provisions that allow States to design a competitive tax system aimed at the extractive industries, taking into account that several factors determine such competitiveness: structure and rate of taxes, cost recovery of business investment, tax rules for foreign earnings, the administrative cost for tax administrations and businesses (e.g., registration and de-registration procedures for tax purposes, filing tax returns on time, reporting tax liabilities, payment of taxes on time, auditing of returns, and effective and timely resolution of disputes), among others.

7.2   THE BASIC RULE OF PERMANENT ESTABLISHMENTS

7.2.1   General principle

7.2.1.1   Article 7(1) of the UN Model Convention establishes that "the profits of

---

[19] De Beers India Minerals Pvt. Ltd. v. ITO. (2008) 113 TTJ (BANG) 101.

an enterprise of a Contracting State shall be taxable only in that State unless the enterprise carries on business in the other Contracting State through a permanent establishment situated therein." It is noted that paragraph 6 of Article 7 lays down a rule of interpretation in order to clarify the scope of application of this Article in relation to the other Articles dealing with a specific category of income. It follows from the rule that this Article will be applicable to business profits that do not belong to categories of income covered by the special articles on dividends (Article 10), interest (Article 11), royalties (Article 12) and other income (Article 21). It is understood that the items of income covered by the special articles may, subject to the provisions of the convention, be taxed either separately or as business profits, in conformity with the tax laws of the Contracting States.

7.2.1.2   The requirement for a PE or fixed base is, therefore, a threshold that needs to be satisfied before a source country can tax residents of other treaty countries on business profits. Unlike e-commerce, the extractive industries cannot be carried out remotely. Extractive activities require a fixed place of business or the physical presence of the contractor (e.g., the oil and gas company) and require most subcontractors to be in the source country.

7.2.1.3   Under the UN Model Convention, the examples of PE based on physical presence commonly include: a place of management, branch, office, factory, workshop, mining site, farm or forest, or a long-term building site. The examples of PE based on activity in the jurisdiction include the use of substantial equipment over an extended period, supervisory activities carried on over an extended period, and the presence in the jurisdiction of an employee for an extended period.

7.2.1.4   However, the PE concept does not have a harmonized application in practice and countries have applied and interpreted the PE thresholds differently with respect to taxing the extractive industries depending, in general, on the fiscal interests of the country[20] and the means available to collect the tax effectively.[21]

7.2.1.5   Under the definition included in Article 5(1) of the UN Model Convention (basic general rule) which is the same as Article 5(1) of the OECD Model Convention: "(…) the term 'permanent establishment' means a fixed place of business through which the business of the enterprise is wholly or partly carried on."

7.2.1.6   Article 5(2) of the UN Model Convention, as in the OECD Model Convention, sets forth a non-exhaustive list of concepts which often constitute a PE in the State in which they are located: "The term 'permanent establishment' includes especially: (a) a place of management, (b) a branch, (c) an office, (d) a factory, (e) a workshop, (f) a mine, an oil or gas well, a quarry or any other place of extraction of natural resources." However, according to the Commentary to the

[20] Arvid A. Skaar, *Permanent Establishment. Erosion of a Tax Treaty Principle*, Series on International Taxation (Wolters Kluwer: Boston, 1991) p. 3.

[21] Brian J. Arnold, "*Threshold requirements for taxing business profits*" in: The taxation of business profits under tax treaties (Canadian Tax Foundation, 2003) p. 56.

UN Model Convention, it is assumed that States interpret the terms listed "in such a way that such places of business constitute permanent establishments only if they meet the requirements of paragraph 1."[22]

7.2.1.7   Accordingly, the following sections list conditions that a priori must be fulfilled to determine the existence of a PE.

7.2.2   The "place of business" test

7.2.2.1   A distinguishing feature of the PE for source-taxation based on the enterprise's trade or business is the requirement of a "fixed place of business." Article 5(1) of the UN Model Convention defines the term PE emphasizing its essential nature as a "fixed place of business" with a specific "situs." Although there is no definition of "fixed place of business" as such in the UN Model Convention, the test is composed of three elements:

(i)   Determining the existence of a "place of business," i.e., a facility such as premises or, in certain instances, machinery or equipment;

(ii)   This place of business must be "fixed," i.e., it must be established at a distinct place with a certain degree of permanence; and

(iii) The carrying on of the business of the enterprise through this fixed place of business. This means usually that persons (personnel) not "independent" of the enterprise conduct business in the State in which the fixed place is situated.

7.2.2.2   The mere fact that an enterprise has a certain amount of space at its disposal used for business activities is sufficient to constitute a place of business.[23] The place of business, however, has to be a fixed one. Thus, following the Commentary to the UN Model Convention, there has to be a link between the place of business and a specific geographical point. However, no physical attachment to the soil is necessary, something that may be pertinent for assets that can be regarded as connected to a certain site, as may be the case for drilling rigs.[24]

7.2.2.3   It is widely accepted that a PE is constituted only if the place of business remains at a "distinct" place, or a particular site. An extractive industry example referred to in the Commentary states that: "[a] mine clearly constitutes a single place of business even though business activities may move from one location to another in what may be a very large mine as it constitutes a single geographical and commercial unit as concerns the mining business."[25]

[22] United Nations, Department of Economic and Social Affairs (2017). United Nations Model Convention, Commentary on Article 5, para. 4

[23] Ibid., para. 3 of Commentary on Article 5 reproducing para. 4 of the OECD Model Convention.

[24] Ibid., para. 3 of Commentary on Article 5 reproducing para. 5 of the OECD Model Convention.

[25] Ibid.

Companies involved in the extractive industries often span a large geographical area. However, mining over a delimited area should constitute a single place of business, and the work done in that area should be considered to be taking place in a particular geographical location.

7.2.2.4 According to the Commentary on Article 5 of the UN Model Convention,[26] in order to have a single "place of business," both geographical and commercial coherence is required. In this respect, the geographical and commercial coherence is normally defined by each of the contractual areas where oil and gas companies perform their activities through different joint ventures within a country. For a more comprehensive explanation of the geographical and commercial coherence test, please see the geographical and commercial coherence test section of this chapter.

7.2.2.5 It should be noted that E&P activities in a country are normally established by oil and gas companies signing a single contract per geographical area with the corresponding governmental authority. Each geographical area subject to the exploitation: (i) is usually separated and isolated from all others; (ii) may contain a different type of hydrocarbon (e.g., oil or gas); (iii) is participated in by different partners associated in a joint venture or association which is governed by a JOA; and (iv) often has different legal and tax regimes applicable to each petroleum contract depending on the date signed, as certain tax stability clauses may apply. Further, some countries establish a "ring-fence" rule by which profits in one area may not be offset against losses in another area.

7.2.2.6 The joint venture's partners appoint one member as the operator of the area to carry out the E&P activities and execute the commonly agreed decisions. Every joint venture (i) performs the activity within the area in a self-standing manner; (ii) has its own accounting, independent from other contract areas; and (iii) has its own employees, equipment, work procedures and techniques. The head office registers its assets, liabilities, income, and losses attributable to the joint venture participants in accordance with their percentage of the participation.

7.2.2.7 In this respect, it is anticipated that every contractual area can be considered an independent PE, and, if ring-fencing applies under local law on the same basis, the investor would not be able to offset profits and losses from different contractual areas (e.g., where one area is incurring losses because it is under exploration and another area is obtaining profits because it is already in production). Some countries permit the consolidation of profits and losses from different contract areas (i.e., from different PEs) to make their regime more attractive for investments.

7.2.3 "Permanence" test

7.2.3.1 In order for a place of business to be "fixed," it is also necessary

---

[26] Ibid., para. 3 of Commentary on Article 5 reproducing para. 3 to 11 of the OECD Model Convention.

that the presence of the business is not of a temporary nature. According to the Commentary on Article 5 of the UN Model Convention,[27] while a six-month time limit is normally long enough for a business to be considered fixed, it is recognized that a PE may exist for a shorter period of time under certain circumstances.[28] However, States and domestic courts diverge when it comes to determining the minimum period of time needed to establish a PE.

7.2.3.2   In any event, oil and gas companies normally comply with the "fixed place" definition in Article 5(1) as most countries require a local presence for performing E&P activities. Given the expected timeline for E&P operations, that presence normally exceeds a year.[29] This test becomes more relevant with respect to subcontractors due to the shorter period they usually spend in the source country.

7.2.4   The "right of use/at the disposal" test

7.2.4.1   Paragraph 3 of the UN Commentary on Article 5 (citing paragraphs 4 to 4.2 of the OECD Commentary on Article 5) explains that a place of business may constitute a PE of an enterprise if that place is "at the disposal of" the enterprise. Following the UN Commentary, "no formal legal right to use that place is (...) required." The Commentary further clarifies that "[w]hilst no formal legal right to use a particular place is required for that place to constitute a permanent establishment, the mere presence of an enterprise at a particular location does not necessarily mean that that location is at the disposal of that enterprise."[30]

7.2.4.2   It is, therefore, generally accepted that no legal title is required to use a particular place of business. The Commentary on Article 5 of the UN Model Convention notes, in particular, that "[i]t is immaterial whether the premises, facilities or installations are owned or rented by or are otherwise at the disposal of the enterprise."

7.2.4.3   Although not formally implemented in the 2014 or 2017 OECD Model Conventions, it is interesting to note that in 2012 the OECD proposed changes in the Commentary to the term "at the disposal"[31] to emphasize the fact that where an enterprise has an exclusive right to use a particular location, which is used for carrying on the business of the enterprise, that location is clearly at the disposal of the enterprise, and therefore leads to a PE:

---

[27] Ibid., para. 3 of Commentary on Article 5 reproducing para. 6 of the OECD Model Convention.

[28] Supra.

[29] A typical schedule would provide 6 to 8 years for exploration in 3 exploration periods. Duration for production should be a minimum of 25 years for oil.

[30] United Nations, Department of Economic and Social Affairs, op.cit., para. 3 of Commentary on Article 5.

[31] Discussion draft of 19 October 2012 on *Revised proposals concerning the interpretation and application of Article 5 (Permanent Establishment)*.

BOX 7.B.1: 2012 OECD-discussed changes in Commentary to the term "at the disposal"

"4.2 [···] Whether a location may be considered to be at the disposal of an enterprise in such a way that it may constitute a "place of business through which the business of [that] enterprise is wholly or partly carried on" will depend on that enterprise having the effective power to use that location as well as the extent of the presence of the enterprise at that location and the activities that it performs there. This is illustrated by the following example. Where an enterprise has an exclusive legal right to use a particular location which is used only for carrying on that enterprise's own business activities (e.g., where it has legal possession of that location) that location is clearly at the disposal of the enterprise."

7.2.4.4   As mentioned above, the signing of a petroleum contract between the oil and gas company and the government is, in general, the starting point that leads to physical presence in a country. Such a contract entitles the oil and gas company to carry out E&P activities within a delineated geographical area. Notwithstanding the proposed changes in 2012 addressing legal rights as an element that satisfies the "at the disposal" test in the OECD Model, certain tax treaties had already considered that the conferral of legal rights towards the exploration or extraction of natural resources gives rise to the existence of a PE.

7.2.5   The "business connection" test

7.2.5.1   An enterprise performing a "business activity" and maintaining a fixed place of business in another country may still not have a PE in such country. The

---

BOX 7.B.2: Examples of tax treaties referring to legal rights related to the extractive industries as a PE

Protocol to tax treaty between the Netherlands and Oman of 5 October 2009
"VI. Ad Articles 5, 6, 7 and 13. It is understood that, for the purposes of this Agreement, **the rights** to the exploration, exploitation or extraction of natural resources granted by a Contracting State according to the laws of that State shall also be deemed to be a permanent establishment in that State, without prejudice to the laws of the Contracting

---

States relating to the natural resources or the exploration, exploitation or extraction of those resources."

Protocol to tax treaty between the Netherlands and United Arab Emirates of 8 May 2007
"V. Ad Articles 5, 6, 7 and 13
It is understood that exploration and exploitation **rights** of natural resources, including rights to interests in, or to the benefits of, assets to be produced by such exploration or exploitation, shall be regarded as immovable property situated in the Contracting State the sea bed and sub-soil of which they are related to, and that these rights shall be deemed to pertain to the property of a permanent establishment in that State and the profits attributable to the permanent establishment shall be taxable in accordance with the national tax laws and regulations of that State."

PE definition establishes that the business activities must be carried on "through" a fixed place of business.

7.2.5.2   According to the UN Commentary on Article 5, "the words 'through which' must be given a wide meaning so as to apply to any situation where business activities are carried on at a particular location that is at the disposal of the enterprise for that purpose. Thus, for instance, an enterprise engaged in paving a road will be considered to be carrying on its business 'through' the location where this activity takes place."[32]

7.2.5.3   To apply the "business connection" test "it is important to identify the party whose business is served by the place of business. In the extractives sector, the activity performed through the place of business may not be the business of the contractor, but of the subcontractors. This may give rise to one or more overlapping PEs in the same situs—one from the contractor (each contractual area is independently managed through the corresponding JOA) and, subject to its own tests, a PE of the subcontractor or subcontractors performing activities in the contractual area. For example, the subcontractor itself would have a PE at the site if its activities there last more than six months.

7.2.5.4   Even though the JOA appoints one of the oil and gas partners as the operator of the block, non-operator partners would also be deemed to have a PE in the source country because the business activity carried out at the contractual area is regarded to be a joint business activity. It is important to note that typically all partners have signed the petroleum contract with the corresponding authority, generally being jointly responsible (according to their participating interest) and having their corresponding legal rights regarding the

---

[32] United Nations, Department of Economic and Social Affairs, op.cit., para. 3 of the Commentary on Article 5 reproducing para. 4.6 of the OECD Model Convention.

delimited acreage established in such contract. Therefore, non-operators will be regarded as having a PE and generally will pay their income taxes based on the financial information provided by the operator.

7.3   Exceptions to the notion of PE

7.3.1.1   Article 5(4) of the United Nations Model Convention lists a number of business activities which are treated as exceptions to the general definition of PE laid down in paragraph 1 and which are not PEs ("negative list") even if the activities are carried on through a fixed place of business. The common feature of these activities is that they are, in general, preparatory or auxiliary activities and the reason for their exclusion could be found in the difficulties connected with the attribution of profits to such marginal business activities (which in most cases are cost centres).

7.3.1.2   The OECD Model Convention classifies as preparatory or auxiliary, inter alia, the activity of keeping a stock of goods and merchandise for storage, display, delivery or processing by another enterprise, as well as purchase of goods or merchandise and collecting of information for the use of the headquarters abroad.

7.3.1.3   In this respect, Article 5(4) of the UN Model Convention reproduces Article 5(4) of the OECD Model Convention with one substantive amendment: the deletion of "delivery" in subparagraphs (a) and (b).[33] The deletion of the word "delivery" reflects the view of the UN Tax Committee that a "warehouse" used for that purpose should, if the requirements of paragraph 1 are met, be a PE. Where an exclusion does apply, it is required that the activities be limited to the excluded activities. If an excluded activity is combined with a core business activity performed through the same place of business, a PE is created.

7.3.1.4   It is often difficult to distinguish between activities that have a preparatory or auxiliary character and those that do not. The decisive criterion is whether the activity of the business in itself forms "an essential and significant part of the activity of the enterprise as a whole."[34] Each individual case has to be examined on its own merits.[35]

---

[33] Article 5(4) of the United Nations Model Convention: "Notwithstanding the preceding provisions of this Article, the term 'permanent establishment' shall be deemed not to include (a) the use of facilities solely for the purpose of storage or display of goods or merchandise belonging to the enterprise; (b) the maintenance of a stock of goods or merchandise belonging to the enterprise solely for the purpose of storage or display; (c) the maintenance of a stock of goods or merchandise belonging to the enterprise solely for the purpose of processing by another enterprise; (d) the maintenance of a fixed place of business solely for the purpose of purchasing goods or merchandise or of collecting information, for the enterprise; (e) the maintenance of a fixed place of business solely for the purpose of carrying on, for the enterprise, any other activity of a preparatory or auxiliary character; (f) the maintenance of a fixed place of business solely for any combination of activities mentioned in subparagraphs (a) to (e) provided that the overall activity of the fixed place of business resulting from this combination is of a preparatory or auxiliary character."

[34] United Nations, Department of Economic and Social Affairs, op.cit., para. 24 of the Commentary on Article 5, which reproduces the same paragraph of the Commentary to Article 5 of the OECD Model.

[35] In this regard, the Report on BEPS Action 7 proposed to add to the Commentary that

7.3.1.5   Typical PE issues that may arise concerning the application of Article 5(4) of the UN Model Convention in the extractive sector are those related to representative offices, warehousing and pipelines, which are discussed below.

7.4   APPLICATION OF THE PE CONCEPT

7.4.1   Application to phases of extractive industries project life cycles

7.4.1.1   The stages of a typical extractive industry project can be divided into the following phases: (i) licensing; (ii) exploration and appraisal; (iii) development; (iv) production; (v) abandonment; and (vi) activities to be performed after abandonment (primarily decommissioning). Each of these phases has a particular level of uncertainty (e.g., geological, financial and political) associated with it.

7.F.1: Phases of extractive industry project

- • Licensing
- • Exploration
- • Development
- • Production
- • Abandonment
- • Decommissioning

7.4.2   Licensing activities

Representative office

7.4.2.1   It is quite common for oil and gas companies initially to establish a representative office instead of, or prior to, registering a branch. The representative office performs market research, coordination or other limited non-income generating activities. In this regard, many representative offices are established to look for oil and gas opportunities (i.e., information gathering) in the country of establishment or in other countries within the region.

"[a]s a general rule, an activity that has a preparatory character is one that is carried on in contemplation of the carrying on of what constitutes the essential and significant part of the activity of the enterprise as a whole. […] An activity that has an auxiliary character, on the other hand, generally corresponds to an activity that is carried on to support, without being part of, the essential and significant part of the activity of the enterprise as a whole." This is now included as paragraph 60 of the 2017 OECD Model's Commentary on Article 5 and is repeated in the UN Model.

7.4.2.2   Jurisdictions may adopt different views with regard to the nature of the activities performed by representative offices. To the extent that representative offices do not sell goods or services generating income, many countries do not regard them as PEs and, accordingly, they are not subject to corporate income tax due to the presumed non-income nature of their activities. However, under their own domestic law, other countries consider that a representative office does constitute a PE and, therefore, is subject to tax.

7.4.2.3   It should be noted that the representative office may operate over a protracted period of time and representative offices might become branches (in the countries which do not automatically regard them to be PEs) if the activities ultimately go beyond those of a mere preparatory or auxiliary nature.

7.4.3   Joint studies/reconnaissance contracts

7.4.3.1   Market surveys and the collection of other information about a foreign country normally constitute the first step towards a more substantial engagement. Many countries sign certain types of contracts (joint studies, reconnaissance contracts, etc.) with oil and gas companies, allowing for geological surveys in a delimited area. These contracts are precursors to a government offering petroleum contracts, with study participants having certain priority rights (e.g., the right to match the highest bid for any resultant petroleum contract in an area wholly or partly overlapping the area of the survey).

7.4.3.2   According to the Commentary to Article 5[36] of the UN Model Convention, should preparatory activities lead to core business activities, a PE could be constituted retrospectively from the date it started the first activities. A PE begins to exist as soon as the enterprise commences to carry on its business through a fixed place of business. This is the case once the enterprise prepares, at the place of business, the activity for which the place of business is to serve permanently. The period of time during which the fixed place of business itself is being set up by the enterprise should not be counted, provided that the preparatory activities differ substantially from the activity for which the place of business is to serve permanently.

7.4.3.3   Certain countries have considered that geological surveys that lead to signing a petroleum contract by the same participants would be a PE from the start of the survey. Other countries have considered that each type of contract (the geological survey and the petroleum contract) has a different scope and that it cannot be inferred that the survey contract directly led to the award of the petroleum contract. This is because the survey contract only grants a priority right and the contractual area does not always completely overlap the whole survey area. In the latter case, in those countries the PE only begins to exist when the petroleum contract is signed, and expenses incurred during the survey normally cannot be set off against future profits derived by the PE.

---

[36] United Nations, Department of Economic and Social Affairs, op.cit., para. 3 of the Commentary to Article 5 reproducing para. 11 of the OECD Model Convention.

7.4.4 Place of management, branch and office

7.4.4.1   The "positive list" in Article 5(2)(a) 5(2)(b) and 5(2)(c) of the UN Model Convention gives examples of PEs with a characterization of the enterprise's use of the place. This is the case for branches, offices and places of management.

7.4.4.2   Once an oil and gas company has been awarded a petroleum contract, and sometimes even before, as required by domestic legislation, a branch is registered. The registration does not create presence by itself, but the oil and gas company usually sets up an office in a main city of the country in order to represent the company before the corresponding authorities as well as to provide certain support to the E&P activities carried out within each particular area. The activities provided by the office are typically those carried out by a coordination centre, which includes corporate functions (i.e., accounting, administration, finance, human resources, treasury, information and communication, technical support, and supervision activities).[37]

7.4.4.3   In general, domestic legislation requires the registration of branches, but the relevant element for determining the existence of a PE is whether the branch has an office. This office is usually registered as a branch and, therefore, the office is designated as a branch office in the country. The same applies in certain countries to contractual areas that likewise are registered as branches.

7.4.4.4   The place of management is a place where the business of the whole or part of the enterprise is conducted. When the business is conducted from various places, each place may constitute a place of management. It usually presupposes the existence of an office or other facilities, following the Commentary to the UN Model Convention,[38] but must not be confused with the term "place of effective management," which is the absolute centre of management of the enterprise. Therefore, a place of management can be identified as the part of the enterprise where certain key decisions are made, but not to the extent that all important decisions for the business are made through such an establishment.

7.4.5 Exploration activities

7.4.5.1   Article 5(2)(f) of the UN Model also lists the following as examples of places that will often constitute a PE: a mine, an oil or gas well, a quarry, or any other place of extraction of natural resources.

7.4.5.2   In discussing this subparagraph (f) the Commentary states that "the term 'any other place of extraction of natural resources' should be interpreted broadly" to include, for example, all places of extraction of hydrocarbons whether on or offshore.

---

[37] Jan de Goede and Ruxandra Vlasceanu, *Permanent Establishment Implications for Coordination Centres in the Oil and Gas Industry*, IBFD Bulletin for International Taxation, (September 2013), p. 466.

[38] United Nations, Department of Economic and Social Affairs, op.cit., para. 24 of the Commentary to Article 5: "(...) a permanent establishment will normally be deemed to exist, because the management office may be regarded as an office within the meaning of paragraph 2."

7.4.5.3   Oil and gas companies ordinarily operate within delimited areas geographically identified in the petroleum contract signed with the State's government; the Commentary example only refers to oil or gas wells. These commitments could vary from drilling no wells (e.g., just seismic works) to drilling one or more exploration wells during the exploration phase. The Commentary suggests that a broad interpretation should be given of the term "place of extraction of natural resources." Accordingly, in the oil and gas sector, the PE will normally be the contractual area where activities are performed through a joint venture or association which is governed by a JOA, rather than each of the wells drilled within the contractual area.

7.4.5.4   While "exploitation" activities would always be taxable in the source country under Article 5 of the UN Model Convention, exploration activities are not mentioned in subparagraph (f). Article 5(1) of the UN Model Convention will govern whether exploration activities are carried on through a PE.

7.4.5.5   The UN Model Convention reproduces the OECD Commentary[39] which states that Contracting States: "may agree, for instance, that an enterprise of a Contracting State, as regards its activities of exploration of natural resources in a place or area in the other Contracting State: a) shall be deemed not to have a permanent establishment in that other State; or b) shall be deemed to carry on such activities through a permanent establishment in that other State; or c) shall be deemed to carry on such activities through a permanent establishment in that other State if such activities last longer than a specified period of time. The Contracting States may moreover agree to submit the income from such activities to any other rule."

7.4.5.6   In this respect, many treaties merely reproduce Article 5(2) of the UN Model Convention without specifying whether "exploration" activities are considered as constituting a PE. In such cases, as mentioned above, the basic rules contained in paragraph 1 of Article 5 of the UN Model Convention shall govern whether exploration activities are carried out through a PE.

7.4.5.7   Examples with respect to items of the above-mentioned Commentary that expressly include exploration activities in Article 5 of the treaty are widely found in bilateral tax treaties:

BOX 7.B.3: Examples of treaties that expressly include "exploration" in the definition of PE

Article 5(1)(f) of the tax treaty between Gabon and Canada of 14 November 2002:
"…a mine, an oil or gas well, a quarry or any other place relating to the exploration for or the exploitation of natural resources."

---

[39] United Nations, Department of Economic and Social Affairs, op. cit., para. 5 of the Commentary to Article 5 reproducing para. 15 of the OECD Model Convention.

Article 5(1)(f) of the tax treaty between Iran and the Slovak Republic of 19 January 2016:
"...a mine, an oil or gas well, a quarry or any other place of exploration, exploitation and/or extraction of natural resources."

7.4.5.8   Other countries have preferred to include the alternative proposed under item (c) above, which considers a PE to exist if exploration activities last longer than a specified period of time:

BOX 7.B.4: Example of a treaty that considers "exploration" activities as a PE if such activities last longer than a specified period of time

Article 5(3) of the tax treaty between Spain and Kuwait of 26 May 2008:
"The term permanent establishment also encompasses any place relating to the exploration of natural resources, provided such activities exists for a period or periods aggregating more than six months within any twelve-month period."

7.4.5.9   A particular case is Article 5(3) of the United States Model Income Tax Convention, which departs from the United Nations and the OECD Model Conventions and includes an express rule for drilling rigs and ships used for the exploration of natural resources for a period longer than 12 months.

7.4.5.10   Under an E&P project (new ventures and business development, exploration, development and production), the exploration does not always result in a hydrocarbon discovery that is followed by a development and production phase. As a result, the activity is frequently discontinued with no income having been generated. The associations, joint ventures or consortiums set up by the companies that participate in each contractual area, after a technical and economic analysis, take the decision to terminate the exploration of the contractual area or let the contract expire. Discontinuation or transfer to a third party of an E&P related PE will be considered to cease the existence of the E&P for the oil and gas company at the time the decision on the termination of the exploration was taken and notified to the relevant authorities.[40] The notification to the authorities is also the moment the E&P company's right of disposal of the contractual area ends, since following that notification the government could offer such area to new investors.

---

[40] For example, binding tax ruling of 9 December 2015 of the Spanish General Directorate of Taxes (number V3926-15), under which the discontinuation of a PE of an O&G company occurred at the time the decision on the termination of the exploration was taken, and such decision was notified to the relevant authorities.

> ## BOX 7.B.5: Example under the United States Model Income Tax Convention
>
> *Article 5(3) of the tax treaty between the United States of America and Malta of 8 August 2008:*
> "A building site or construction or installation project, or an installation or drilling rig or ship used for the exploration of natural resources, constitutes a permanent establishment only if it lasts, or the exploration activity continues for more than twelve months."

7.4.6   Development

7.4.6.1   The development phase starts when an exploration prospect results in a commercial discovery. Unlike the exploration phase, the value of the project increases once a commercial discovery is realized. In the former, other companies may join the project (farm-in/farm-out agreements) by paying a prorated share of exploration costs or providing a carry of certain future exploration costs[41] to the initial exploration company. While farm-in/farm-out agreements are still possible in the development phase, such agreements, and especially outright sales of interests in the licence, may give rise to capital gains attributable to a disposition of immovable property and business assets used in a PE and situated in the source country depending on that country's tax laws. See further Chapter 10 on the Indirect Transfer of Assets. The same treatment would follow under the production phase as a PE then clearly exists.

7.4.7   Production

7.4.7.1   Production activities begin after development is completed, during which hydrocarbons are extracted from the reservoir, refined and sent to market by pipeline or ship. The productive life can last decades and the reservoirs are continuously monitored to optimize production. The extraction of hydrocarbons could take place onshore or offshore, as onshore production is more economically viable and is less elaborate and more cost-effective. A whole range of different structures is used offshore, depending on size and water depth.

7.4.7.2   There is no doubt that the oil and gas company will have a PE during the production stage, whereas the different subcontractors that perform activities at the site would have a PE depending on their specific facts and circumstances.

---

[40] Those conducting the exploration are able to get reimbursement on a portion of past costs, typically geological and geophysical (G&G) work.

7.4.8   Abandonment

7.4.8.1   In general, a site continues to exist until the work is completed or permanently abandoned.[42] Therefore, the PE will continue to exist for the oil and gas company during the development and production phases until completion of production (COP) has been declared and the "well plug and abandon" operations have been performed. However, the oil and gas company may continue to have a PE during the decommissioning phase as explained in the following paragraphs. It should be noted that no income will arise during the decommissioning phase but, depending on the tax regime, it could be relevant for the oil and gas company or the source country to maintain the existence of a PE.

7.4.9   Decommissioning

7.4.9.1   As the oil and gas reservoirs become depleted, however, the facilities require decommissioning and remediation (see Chapter 14 on the Tax Treatment of Decommissioning). During this phase, even if the oil and gas company may have returned the block to the government, it is normally responsible for the decommissioning and remediation work.

7.4.9.2   With respect to subcontractors hired to perform the decommissioning work, it seems clear that they will have PEs at the site if their activities there last more than six months, as established in the construction work clause (see the construction work clause section below).

7.4.9.3   This has been the approach adopted, for example, by the Income Tax Rulings Directorate of Canada in response to a letter dated 27 June 2016, in which the taxpayer asked whether a "building site or construction or installation project" exists at a location where a structure is being dismantled or decommissioned regarding a number of offshore oil and gas platforms.

7.4.9.4   As a technical explanation, the Canadian Tax Directorate response of 16 January 2017 noted that Article 5(3) has nothing that would suggest that dismantling or commissioning activities (referred to as "demolition") would not fall under the construction PE provision. It quoted the work of Professor Klaus Vogel to indicate that "[t]he term 'building site or construction project' also covers demolition and clearing operations" and concludes that the decommissioning work would likely be considered to fall under the scope of the construction PE provision.[43]

7.4.9.5   With respect to the oil and gas company, the existence of a PE could derive from the situation described in paragraph 54 of the Commentary on Article

---

[42] United Nations, Department of Economic and Social Affairs, op. cit., para. 11 of the Commentary on Article 5, which reproduces paragraph 19 of the OECD Model Convention.

[43] 16 January 2017 External T.I. 2016-0655701E5—Article 5(3)—Demolition, citing *Klaus Vogel on Double Taxation Conventions*, 3rd ed. (Cambridge, MA: Kluwer Law International), at 306; available at https://taxinterpretations.com/node/453050

5 of the United Nations Model Convention, which states that "[i]f an enterprise (general contractor) which has undertaken the performance of a comprehensive project subcontracts parts of such a project to other enterprises (subcontractors) the period spent by a subcontractor working on the building site must be considered as being time spent by the general contractor on the building project." It is relevant to note that due to its complexity and size, the contractor normally performs "supervisory activities," which are expressly included in the PE concept under Article 5(3)(a) of the United Nations Model Convention: "[a] building site, a construction, assembly or installation project or supervisory activities in connection therewith, but only if such site, project or activities last more than six months."

7.5 THE CONSTRUCTION WORK CLAUSE

7.5.1 General concept

7.5.1.1   Following Article 5(3)(a) of the UN Model Convention, the term PE also encompasses "a building site, a construction, assembly or installation project or supervisory activities in connection therewith, but only if such site, project or activities last more than six months."

7.5.1.2   Article 5(3) of the UN Model Convention covers a broader range of activities than Article 5(3) of the OECD Model Convention, which states: "[a] building site or construction or installation project constitutes a permanent establishment only if it lasts more than twelve months." In addition to the term "installation project" used in the OECD Model Convention, subparagraph (a) of Article 5(3) of the UN Model Convention includes an "assembly project" as well as "supervisory activities" in connection with "a building site, a construction, assembly or installation project." However, while the OECD Model Convention uses a time limit of 12 months and the UN Model Convention reduces the minimum duration to six months, these periods could be reduced in bilateral negotiations, generally to no less than three months.

7.5.1.3   The period of time under the construction PE provision may, accordingly,

---

BOX 7.B.6: Examples of tax treaties specifying a different time period under the construction clause

Article 5(3) of the treaty between Morocco and the United Arab Emirates of 9 February 1999:
"The term 'permanent establishment' also encompasses:

(a) a building site, assembly or installation project or supervisory activities in connection therewith, but only if such site, project or activities last more than <u>eight months</u>."

> **Article 5(1)(g) of the treaty between Jordan and Romania of 10 October 1983:**
> "…a building site or construction or assembly project which exists for more than <u>seven months</u>."
>
> **Article 5(3) of the treaty between Austria and South Africa of 4 March 1996:**
> "A building site or construction or installation project constitutes a permanent establishment only if it lasts more than <u>twelve months</u>."

be agreed by the Contracting States and may vary from one treaty to another:

7.5.1.4   The Commentary on Article 5(3) of the OECD Model Convention, reproduced in the UN Model Convention, extends the scope of the definition of construction to "the laying of pipe-lines and excavating and dredging."[44] Likewise, as mentioned above, drilling activities are treated as construction work with a similar "duration test" in many treaties which adopt rules similar to that in the UN Model Convention.

7.5.1.5   The difference between the basic rule in Article 5(1) and Article 5(3) of the UN Model Convention is that the latter provides an explicit definition of the duration, turning the "permanence test" of the basic rule into a "duration test," as a construction site is by its very nature temporary.

7.5.1.6   The purpose of this provision is to allow taxation of PE activities that do not last for an indefinite period of time. In this respect, a construction site is by definition not intended to be permanent. In addition, while construction tasks usually have an undisputable location, certain works will not be performed at one specific place, because the site will be moved as the work proceeds (e.g., road construction or pipeline laying). However, as mentioned by the Commentary on Article 5(1) of the UN Model Convention,[45] the words "through which" must be given a wide meaning so as to apply to any situation where business activities are carried on at a particular location that is at the disposal of the enterprise for that purpose.

7.5.1.7   As previously noted, it is not generally significant for oil and gas companies whether Article 5(1) or the construction work clause established in Article 5(3) of the UN Model Convention applies. E&P activities of oil and gas companies by definition have local presence that constitutes a PE or more than one PE within the source country and, in any case, would exceed the time thresholds of most construction clauses.

---

[44] United Nations Model Convention Commentary on Article 5, paragraph 15.

[45] United Nations, Department of Economic and Social Affairs, op. cit., para. 3 of the Commentary on Article 5 reproducing para. 4.6 of the OECD Model Convention

7.5.1.8   But, as noted, numerous subcontractors perform various activities in the contractual area. The type of services and supplies rendered are of a very different nature and, generally, separate contracts are signed with each of the subcontractors, the most important being the drilling activity.

7.5.1.9   Identification of construction works has been a concern for many countries in order to protect the taxable base. Such identification can be justified if different works form a commercially and geographically coherent whole. Both the commercial and geographical aspects of this "coherent whole" test need to be met as, under the Commentary to the UN Model Convention,[46] "where there is no commercial coherence, the fact that activities may be carried on within a limited geographic area should not result in that area being considered as a single place of business" and what constitutes a "coherent commercial whole may lack the necessary geographic coherence to be considered as a single place of business."

7.5.1.10   As further explained below, the UN Model Convention includes a sub-paragraph (b) in Article 5(3) providing a specific provision in relation to the furnishing of services by an enterprise through employees or personnel engaged for that purpose.[47] According to the Article 5 Commentary, the reason for including the rationale of this subparagraph is that "[m]any developing countries believe that management and consultancy services should be covered because the provision of those services in developing countries by enterprises of industrialized countries can generate large profits."[48]

7.5.1.11   The Commentary on Article 5 of the UN Model Convention, at paragraphs 11 and 12, deals with those situations where: "taxpayers may be tempted to circumvent the application of that provision by splitting a single project between associated enterprises or by dividing a single contract into different ones so as to argue that these contracts cover different projects."

7.5.1.12   It should be mentioned that certain countries have included in their tax treaties' special provisions stating that the oil and gas offshore activity constitutes a PE if it lasts for more than 30 days, notwithstanding the other provisions of the treaty. This specific "offshore clause" does not require the usual geographical test, as any activity performed within the offshore area could lead to the existence of a PE.

7.5.2   Drilling activity

7.5.2.1   Many types of platforms exist depending on the circumstances. In

---

[46] United Nations Model Convention Commentary on Article 5, paragraph 3.

[47] United Nations, Department of Economic and Social Affairs, op. cit., para. 3(b): "The furnishing of services, including consultancy services, by an enterprise through employees or other personnel engaged by the enterprise for such purpose, but only if activities of that nature continue (for the same or a connected project) within a Contracting State for a period or periods aggregating more than 183 days in any 12-month period commencing or ending in the fiscal year concerned."

[48] United Nations Model Convention Commentary on Article 5, paragraph 9.

general, platforms may be fixed to the ocean floor or may float. Fixed platforms are fixed to the same geographical area for long periods of time and, therefore, satisfy the "fixed" test. Whether mobile drilling rigs are considered to comply with the "fixed" test should be considered on a case-by-case basis. Drilling rigs can remain in the same spot for a long period of time or just a couple of months. It could also happen that more than one well is drilled in the same contractual area of the oil and gas company, either on a back-to-back basis or in different time periods.

7.5.2.2   Following the criteria that each contractual area (field or block) constitutes a PE of the oil and gas company and complies with the geographical and commercial coherence test, a drilling rig moving around in the same oil field would, therefore, satisfy the conditions of a PE if the activity lasted more than six months under the UN Model Convention definition. The actual duration, not the intended one, should be the relevant standard and, therefore, if a drilling activity is intended to last four months but ultimately lasts for more than six months, the activity should be considered to meet the PE timing criteria.

7.5.2.3   A general point of clarification is given by the Commentary on Article 5 of the UN Model Convention reproducing the OECD Commentary:[49] "(...) no account should be taken of the time previously spent by the contractor concerned on other sites or projects which are totally unconnected with it."

7.5.2.4   It can normally be assumed that works conducted under the same contract will be considered a coherent whole, but to address any possible abuse derived from signing several contracts with different durations, the UN Model Convention reproduces what the OECD Commentary observes, with changes noted in parentheses to take account of the different time periods in the two Models: "The [six]-month threshold has given rise to abuses; it has sometimes been found that enterprises (mainly contractors or subcontractors working on the continental shelf or engaged in activities connected with the exploration and exploitation of the continental shelf) divided their contracts up into several parts, each covering a period of less than [six] months and attributed to a different company, which was, however, owned by the same group. Apart from the fact that such abuses may, depending on the circumstances, fall under the application of legislative or judicial anti-avoidance rules, countries concerned with this issue can adopt solutions in the framework of bilateral negotiations."[50]

7.5.2.5   The start of the duration test is relevant in this short-term works context where a single day's difference could lead to the establishment of a PE. The issue is to decide when a construction or installation actually starts and terminates. With respect to drilling rigs, relevant work normally commences on "spud day"—when the process of beginning to drill a well starts—and ends when the well has been completed.

---

[49] United Nations, Department of Economic and Social Affairs (2017) op. cit., Commentary on Article 5, para. 11.

[50] Ibid.

7.5.2.6   Owners of rigs may provide drilling services by way of a time charter, whereby the owner provides the rig with a full crew to operate the rig, or on a "bareboat" basis, just renting the rig itself, often to a related company. If rent for equipment is classified as a royalty under a treaty definition (the UN Model Convention defines royalties to include payments for the rental of industrial, commercial or scientific equipment[51]) the royalty provisions apply unless the rent is beneficially owned by a resident of the other contracting state that carries on business in the source State through a PE in that State and the rent is effectively connected to that PE.

BOX 7.B.7: Article 12 (Royalties) of the tax treaty between Canada and Denmark of 17 September 1997

"4. The term "royalties" as used in this Article means payments of any kind received as a consideration for the use of, or the right to use, any copyright, patent, trade mark, design or model, plan, secret formula or process or for the **use of, or the right to use, industrial, commercial or scientific equipment**, or for information concerning industrial, commercial or scientific experience, and includes payments of any kind in respect of motion picture films and works on film or videotape or other means of reproduction for use in connection with television."

7.5.2.7   In a Norwegian case dealing with leasing out of equipment in the offshore industry,[52] the Supreme Court held that the rental of a drilling rig on bareboat terms was insufficient to cause the rig owner to be taxable in Norway as the rig owner did not take part in the risk of operating the rig. The case refers to two foreign companies, Tric and Trag, that were controlled by the same owners. Tric (resident in Liberia) was the owner of a drilling rig that was hired out on a bareboat charter to Trag, and Trag (resident in Switzerland) operated the rig on the Norwegian Continental Shelf and was liable to tax in Norway for that activity. The tax authorities argued that Tric and Trag carried out joint activities in Norway and that Tric took part in the business activity that was taxable in Norway. For its part, Tric argued that it merely hired out the rig to Trag and that hiring out equipment to a Norwegian entity did not constitute taking part in joint business activities in Norway.

7.5.2.8   It was not disputed that Trag engaged in a business activity that was taxable in Norway as a PE under the offshore clause. However, as Norway does not have a tax treaty with Liberia, the dispute in respect of Tric was decided only on the basis of Norwegian domestic law. In this case, the Supreme Court ruled in

---

[51]In 1992, the OECD Model Convention was revised to remove equipment rentals from the definition of royalties. However, some OECD member countries entered reservations to Article 12 of the Model to maintain a limited right to tax royalties at source, including rents paid for the use of equipment.

[52] NO: HR, 1997, Tric/Trag, Rt 1997, at 1646.

Tric's favour as it considered that the mere lease of a rig on a bareboat charter for use in Norwegian waters did not constitute participating in an activity in Norway and the activity was not performed for the joint account and under the joint liability of the parties, irrespective of the close cooperation between both companies. Consequently, Tric was not considered to have a PE in Norway.[53]

7.5.2.9   In another case, the Canadian Income Tax Rulings Directorate, Legislative Policy and Regulatory Affairs Branch of Canada concluded in an advance income tax ruling[54] that entering into a bareboat agreement for a ship to be used in Canadian waters could not be regarded as constituting a PE.

7.5.2.10   In some tax treaties, the use of "substantial equipment" in the source country has been included in the definition of a PE. In these cases, bareboat agreements could lead to the existence of a PE. Examples of treaties that have included "use of substantial equipment" in the definition of a PE follow:

BOX 7.B.8: Article 5(4) of the tax treaty between Australia and South Africa of 1 July 1999 (as amended in 2008):

"…where an enterprise of a Contracting State:

(b) carries on activities (including the operation of substantial equipment) in the other State in the exploration for or exploitation of natural resources situated in that other State for a period or periods exceeding in the aggregate 90 days in any 12-month period; or

(c) operates substantial equipment in the other State (including as provided in subparagraph (b)) for a period or periods exceeding 183 days in any 12-month period, such activities shall be deemed to be performed through a permanent establishment that the enterprise has in that other State, unless the activities are limited to those mentioned in paragraph 6 and are, in relation to the enterprise, of a preparatory or auxiliary character."

7.5.2.11   As mentioned, in the UN Model Convention, drilling rigs and ships are expressly included in the construction PE definition, insofar as these are used in exploration for natural resources for a period of longer than 12 months. Recall, however, that the construction clause can be applied to offshore exploration and drilling even if the tax treaty does not contain an express reference.

7.5.2.12   It should also be noted that the definition of royalties in Article 12

---

[53] Eirik Jensen, "Permanent Establishments and Allocation Questions Pertaining to Them—Judgements of the Norway Supreme Court," *IBFD Bulletin for International Taxation* (August/September 2002), pp. 394–395.

[54] CA: ITRD, Advance Income Tax Ruling, 2006-0211991.

of the UN Model Convention includes "(...) payments of any kind received as a consideration for the use of, or the right to use (...) industrial, commercial or scientific equipment."[55] Many countries include these payments in the definition of royalties in their tax treaties:

BOX 7.B.9: Article 12(3)(c) of the tax treaty between Australia and Chile of 10 March 2010:

"3. The term "royalties" in this Article means payments or credits, whether periodical or not, and however described or computed, to the extent to which they are made as consideration for: (...) the use of, or the right to use, industrial, commercial or scientific equipment;"

7.5.2.13   This means that a bareboat lease of equipment, i.e., drilling rigs, vessels or other equipment, may result in the imposition of withholding tax under Article 12 of these tax treaties if domestic legislation imposes withholding tax on such payments, as long as the activity does not constitute a PE.

7.5.3   Service and supply ships

7.5.3.1   A number of service and supply ships operate by supporting oil and gas companies during drilling campaigns. The most prevalent are platform supply vessels (PSVs) used for transporting supplies to the rig from port facilities. Other vessels are used for towing and anchor handling, construction support, multi-purpose support, and specialized health safety and environment services, their common character being their mobility.

7.5.3.2   The issue in question is to what extent personnel and supply transportation vessels, and other auxiliary vessels, fall under the PE concept, taking into consideration that they are not geographically fixed to a place. Notwithstanding the general understanding that a moving ship would typically not constitute a fixed place, the OECD proposed in a 2012 discussion draft the addition of a new paragraph 5.5 to the Commentary on Article 5, which considers ships to be a PE:

- If a vessel operates in areas that are considered to be geographically and commercially coherent, the fixed test may be satisfied. The commercial coherence test is very ambiguous and could be interpreted in different ways. In considering this question, several factual issues—such as whether the services are done under the same contract, for identical or different clients, and invoiced under the same or different work orders or invoices—should be taken into account.

---

[55] Up to 1992, the definition of royalties in Article 12 of the OECD Model Convention also included the right "to use industrial, commercial or scientific equipment"; however, some countries have made reservations to maintain such taxation right.

> **BOX 7.B.10: A possible new paragraph 5.5 in the OECD Model Convention (as per 2012 discussion draft)**
>
> "5.5 Similarly, a ship or boat that navigates within territorial waters or in inland waterways is not fixed and does not, therefore, constitute a fixed place of business (unless the operation of the ship or boat is restricted to a particular area that has commercial and geographic coherence). Business activities carried on aboard such a ship or boat, such as a shop or restaurant, must be treated the same way."

7.5.3.3   Please note that certain tax features of these services have been covered in section 7.5.2 above.

7.5.4   Pipelines

7.5.4.1   The Commentary on Article 5 of the UN Model Convention[56] states, when referring to cables or pipelines, that "(...) income derived by the owner or operator of such facilities from their use by other enterprises is covered by Article 6 where they constitute immovable property under paragraph 2 of Article 6."

7.5.4.2   . Apart from the fact that income derived by the owner or operator of cables or pipelines is covered by Article 6 if considered as immovable property by the domestic law of the source State, the issue is whether any exception listed in Article 5(4) related to activities of a preparatory or auxiliary nature applies and, therefore, the facilities are not considered a PE. In this respect, each case is to be considered in light of its particular circumstances. If these facilities are used to transport goods owned by third parties, then they are considered to be a PE with respect to the owner/operator of the pipeline, and neither Article 5(4)(a)[57] (which is restricted to delivery of goods or merchandise belonging to the enterprise that uses the facility) nor Article 5(4)(e)[58] (since the cable or pipeline is not used solely for the enterprise and given the nature of the business) applies. If these facilities transport goods owned by the owner/operator of the pipeline, Article 5(4)(a) would be applicable if such transport is merely incidental to the business of the enterprise, as in the case of an enterprise that is in the business of refining oil and that owns and operates a pipeline that crosses the territory of the country solely to transport its own oil to its refinery located in another country.

---

56 United Nations, Department of Economic and Social Affairs, op. cit., paragraph 18 reproducing paragraph 26.1 of the OECD Model Convention.

57 (a) The use of facilities solely for the purpose of storage or display of goods or merchandise belonging to the enterprise.

58 (e) The maintenance of a fixed place of business solely for the purpose of carrying on, for the enterprise, any other activity of a preparatory or auxiliary character.

7.5.4.3   As mentioned above, cables or pipelines that cross the country would be considered to be a PE if these facilities are used to transport property belonging to other enterprises. For the customer of the operator of the cable or pipeline (the enterprise whose product is transported from one place to another) who does not have the cable or pipeline at its disposal, the cable or pipeline cannot be considered a PE.

7.5.4.4   In a decision of the German Bundesfinanzhof (Federal Tax Court),[59] a Dutch company owned an underground pipeline for transporting third-party customers' crude oil and petroleum products. That pipeline was situated in the Netherlands and Germany. The Dutch company operated the pipeline remotely from the Netherlands, without having any personnel in Germany. The Court concluded that since transportation of crude oil and petroleum products was the core business of the Dutch company, the transportation activity could not be regarded as a preparatory or auxiliary activity for the purposes of determining the Dutch company's PE in Germany. As a consequence, the Dutch company was considered to have a PE in Germany in respect of the portion of the pipeline crossing German territory. In the Court's view, for a PE to exist, it was not necessary that the pipeline had to be operated by personnel belonging to the Dutch company in Germany. Even a fully automated installation could be regarded as a PE.

7.5.4.5   The German decision is relevant as it confirms that a pipeline can be considered a PE of a company whose business is to transport oil and petroleum products, even if the company has no personnel in the jurisdiction where the pipeline is located.

7.6   TERRITORIAL SCOPE OF TAX TREATIES

7.6.1   Extent of territory

7.6.1.1   Article 29[60] of the United Nations Vienna Convention on the Law of Treaties of 23 May 1969 establishes that "[u]nless a different intention appears from the treaty or is otherwise established, a treaty is binding upon each party in respect of its entire territory." Since many countries include the definition of "Contracting States" in Article 3 on tax treaties,[61] this definition determines the geographic scope of the application of the tax treaty. Such definition may include the notions of territory and territorial waters, which would be automatically included in the notions of State territory.

---

[59] Pipeline Case (No. IIR 12/92 dated 30 October 1996).

[60] On the territorial scope of treaties.

[61] Article 3 of the United Nations Model Convention is the same as Article 3 of the OECD Model Convention, except that Article 3 of the OECD Model Convention defines the terms "enterprise" and "business" in subparagraphs c) and h) of paragraph 1 while Article 3 of the United Nations Model Convention does not. This is because the OECD Model Convention has deleted Article 14 (Independent Personal Services) while the United Nations Model Convention still maintains it.

7.6.1.2   On the other hand, according to Article 77 of the United Nations Convention on the Law of the Sea (UNCLOS), coastal States may exercise "sovereign rights" for the purposes of exploration and exploitation of some of their natural resources over the continental shelf.[62] These rights are exclusive in the sense that if the coastal State does not explore the continental shelf or exploit its natural resources, no one may undertake these activities without the express consent of the coastal State.

7.6.1.3   Therefore, the taxing jurisdiction of a State may be extended to include exclusive economic zones or the outer continental shelf if the activities are connected to exploration or exploitation of natural resources, within which the States may exercise taxing rights in accordance with international law.

7.6.1.4   In this respect, many States have extended the operation of the tax treaties into the same area outside their territory in which such States purport to extend their taxing power. Accordingly, the terms "a Contracting State" and "the other Contracting State" normally include a reference to the continental shelf, as follows:

Box 7.B.11:

Section 5 of Canada's Income Tax Conventions Interpretation Act, RSC 1985, c. I-4, as amended:

"Canada means the territory of Canada, and includes every area **beyond the territorial seas of Canada** that, in accordance with international law and the laws of Canada, is an area in respect of which Canada may exercise rights with respect to the seabed and subsoil and their natural resources, and the seas and airspace above every area described in paragraph (a)."

Article 3 (b) of the tax treaty between the United Kingdom of Great Britain and Northern Ireland and Russia of 15 February 1994:

"b) The term 'the Russian Federation', when used in the geographical sense, means its territory, including its territorial waters as well as economic zone and **Continental Shelf** where this State exercises sovereign rights or rights and jurisdiction in conformity with international law and where its tax laws are effective."

---

62 Article 76 of the United Nations Convention on the Law of the Sea (UNCLOS) defines the continental shelf as "the seabed and subsoil of the submarine areas that extend beyond its territorial sea throughout the natural prolongation of its land territory to the outer edge of the continental margin, or to a distance of 200 nautical miles [370.4 Km] from the baselines from which the breadth of the territorial sea is measured where the outer edge of the continental margin does not extend up to that distance."

7.6.1.5   However, some treaties—such as old treaties signed when the development of natural resources on the continental shelf was not technologically feasible—do not expressly cover the continental shelf. Different interpretations about the application of a tax treaty can arise in such a case. It could be argued that the tax treaty applies in the same area as the domestic tax legislation of the two contracting States; the continental shelf would be covered if domestic legislation also encompasses the natural resources in the seabed. Another interpretation would be that the tax treaty only applies within the territorial area specifically referred to in the tax treaty, regardless of the domestic tax legislation.[63]

7.6.1.6   A case arose in Norway under the Norway-Switzerland tax treaty of 7 December 1956, which did not expressly extend to Norway's continental shelf area. The decision of the Supreme Court of Norway[64] held that the tax treaty did not apply to the Norwegian continental shelf area, as was also agreed between the competent authorities of the two countries in 1982.[65] As a consequence, tax liability in Norway with respect to business activities carried out in the continental shelf area could be decided on the basis of Norwegian law.

7.6.1.7   Therefore, it is advisable that the issue of whether or not to include specific reference to particular geographical areas in a tax treaty should be discussed during the treaty negotiations, and if necessary addressed in the text.

7.6.2   Source-state taxation: the offshore clause of other resource-rich states with a coast line

7.6.2.1   The economic importance of the offshore petroleum industry in some coastal States resulted in a special clause in their bilateral negotiations—a clause assuming the existence of a PE if a hydrocarbon-related business activity is performed on their continental shelf. This is the case, for example, with Norway or the United Kingdom. An example from the treaty practice of the former follows:

Box 7.B.12: Article 21 (Offshore activities) of the tax treaty between Norway and South Africa of 1996:

"The provisions of this Article shall apply notwithstanding any other provision of this Convention.

A person who is a resident of a Contracting State and carries on activities offshore in the other Contracting State in connection with the exploration or exploitation of the seabed and subsoil and their natural resources

---

[63] Maja Stubbe Gelineck, *"Permanent Establishment and the Offshore Oil and Gas Industry-Part 1,"* IBFD Bulletin for International Taxation (April 2016), p. 209.

[64] Heerema Marine Contractors SA v. Ministry of Finance, of 9 November 1992, 122/1992.

[65] In an exchange of letters of 29 November and 14 December 1982.

situated in that other State shall, subject to paragraphs 3 and 4 of this Article, be deemed in relation to those activities to be carrying on business in that other State through a permanent establishment or fixed base situated therein.

The provisions of paragraph 2 shall not apply where the activities are carried on for a period not exceeding 30 days in the aggregate in any period of twelve months commencing or ending in the fiscal year concerned. However, for the purposes of this paragraph, activities carried on by an enterprise associated with another enterprise, within the meaning of Article 9, shall be regarded as carried on by the enterprise with which it is associated if the activities in question are substantially the same as those carried on by the last-mentioned enterprise, except to the extent that those activities are carried on at the same time.

Profits derived by a resident of a Contracting State from the transportation of supplies or personnel to a location, or between locations, where activities in connection with the exploration or exploitation of the seabed and subsoil and their natural resources are being carried on in a Contracting State, or from the operation of tugboats and other vessels auxiliary to such activities, shall be taxable only in the Contracting State of which the enterprise is a resident."

7.6.2.2   This alternative implies that several of the traditional features of a basic PE are removed. In particular, under the offshore clause neither a "fixed place of business" nor a "right of use test" or a "business connection test" seem necessary to constitute a PE. In this respect, the offshore clause does not require a specific geographical location within this area, the test being whether or not the activities are to be performed within the overall offshore area.

7.7   THE "GEOGRAPHICAL AND COMMERCIAL COHERENCE" TEST

7.7.1   More than one PE

7.7.1.1   As previously noted, the "geographical and commercial coherence test" provides that, in principle, any geographical area that commercially or economically constitutes a unit may be considered as a fixed place of business for PE purposes.

7.7.1.2   From the perspective of an oil and gas company, legal title by means of a petroleum contract in the form of a concession or a Production Sharing Contract is granted over a contractual area (geographic element). This is normally governed by several partners under a JOA, one of them being designated the operator. Therefore, from a factual point of view, each contractual area (geographical element) is independently managed through a consortium (commercial element). Accordingly, when an oil and gas company has entitlement to more than one contractual area in a country, it would normally be considered that it has more than one PE within that country.

7.7.1.3   This result is supported by many factors involving the oil and gas structure. As mentioned above, E&P activities in a country are normally established by signing a single contract per geographical area with the corresponding governmental authority. Each geographical area is subject to exploitation, usually separated and isolated from each other. Sometimes they contain different kinds of hydrocarbons (oil or gas) or involve different partners associated in different joint ventures or associations which are governed by different JOAs. Frequently, separate petroleum contracts have different legal and tax regimes, depending on the date signed, as certain tax stability clauses may apply.

7.7.1.4   It should also be noted that each joint venture, consortium or association has its own financial accounts, independent from those formed in other areas. Therefore, each contractual area is managed independently from one another, each having its own operating management. Each joint venture, consortium or association normally files income tax returns on behalf of its participants to whom they then attribute the revenue and the taxes paid.

7.7.1.5   In addition, many countries have established "ring-fence" regulations, which disallow offsetting losses from one field against profits of another. Even in countries that permit consolidation of losses between contract areas, as long as the separate contract areas are distinct in the other ways noted above, each contractual area will nevertheless usually be considered a separate PE.

7.7.1.6   While the E&P blocks are located in specific areas, being defined by the concession or petroleum contract signed for each of them, the office is normally established in the main city of the country, which could be far away from the mentioned blocks. Following the example provided in the Commentary on Article 5 of the UN Model Convention[66] regarding a consultant performing similar activities as part of the same project to distinct branches, it may also be argued that the office constitutes a separate PE from the blocks due to lack of geographical coherence.

7.7.1.7   Commercial coherence takes several indicators into consideration, such as the contract, the client, the time factor, the functions performed and the participants in the project. All of these factors should be analysed on a case-by-case basis. A decisive factor for treating different operations as one project is when one contract has been concluded. In the case of oil and gas companies, since blocks are generally managed through different JOAs, each block is normally considered as an independent commercial unit.

---

[66] United Nations Model Convention Commentary on Article 5, paragraph 3, reproducing paragraph 5(4) of the OECD Model Convention Commentary.

7.7.1.8   The Commentary on Article 5 of the OECD Model Convention[67] (the UN Model Convention does not adopt this aspect of the OECD Commentary) contains some additional criteria for establishing the commercial coherence of "connected projects" within the alternative services PE rule, which could also be considered to be relevant in addressing the commercial coherence or fixed place of business under Article 5(1). This Commentary states that the reference to "connected projects" is intended to cover cases where the services are provided in the context of separate projects carried on by an enterprise but these projects have a commercial coherence. The determination of whether projects are connected will depend on the facts and circumstances of each case, but factors that would generally be relevant for that purpose include:

- Whether the projects are covered by a single master contract;

- Where the projects are covered by different contracts, whether these different contracts were concluded with the same person or with related persons and whether the conclusion of the additional contracts would reasonably have been expected when concluding the first contract;

- Whether the nature of the work involved under the different projects is the same; and

- Whether the same individuals are performing the services under the different projects.

7.7.2   Splitting up of contracts

7.7.2.1   The six-month test established under Article 5(3) of the UN Model Convention applies to each individual site or project. In determining how long the site or project has existed, no account should be taken of the time previously spent by the contractor concerned on other sites or projects which are totally unconnected with it. A building site should be regarded as a single unit, even if it is based on several contracts, provided that it forms a coherent whole commercially and geographically.[68]

7.7.2.2   However, as mentioned above under the Drilling activity section, the six-month threshold has given rise to abuses as it has been found that enterprises (mainly contractors or subcontractors working on the continental shelf or engaged in activities connected with the exploration and exploitation of the continental shelf) divided their contracts up into several parts, each covering a period of less than six months and attributed to a different company, which was, however, owned by the same group.

---

[67] OECD, op. cit., para. 42.41 of the Commentary on Article 5.

[68] United Nations Model Convention Commentary on Article 5, paragraph 11, reproducing paragraph 18 of the OECD Model Convention Commentary.

7.7.2.3   In this respect, the Commentary to the UN Model Convention observes that: "[a]part from the fact that such abuses may, depending on the circumstances, fall under the application of legislative or judicial anti-avoidance rules, countries concerned with this issue can adopt solutions in the framework of bilateral negotiations."

7.7.2.4   In a similar way, OECD BEPS Action 7 specifically addresses the splitting up of construction contracts between group companies into shorter periods of time in order to benefit from the "construction site" exemption. The OECD sets out that the splitting should be prevented by applying the principal purposes test, proposed as part of Action 6 on the prevention of treaty abuse, or by a specific provision which aggregates the activities of closely related enterprises on the same site during different periods of time (each exceeding 30 days) for the purpose of determining the 12-month period. The proposed provisions read as follows:

Box 7.B.13: Paragraphs 52-53 of the OECD Commentary on paragraph 3 of Article 5 replaced by BEPS Action 7

"For the sole purpose of determining whether the twelve-month period referred to in paragraph 3 has been exceeded,

a) where an enterprise of a Contracting State carries on activities in the other Contracting State at a place that constitutes a building site or construction or installation project and these activities are carried on during periods of time that do not last more than twelve months, and

b) connected activities are carried on at the same building site or construction or installation project during different periods of time, each exceeding 30 days, by one or more enterprises closely related to the first-mentioned enterprise,

these different periods of time shall be added to the period of time during which the first-mentioned enterprise has carried out activities at that building site or construction or installation project.

The concept of "closely related enterprises" that is used in the above provision is defined in subparagraph b) of paragraph 6 of the Article (see paragraphs 119 to 121 below).

53. For the purposes of the alternative provision found in paragraph 52, the determination of whether activities are connected will depend on the facts and circumstances of each case. Factors that may especially be relevant for that purpose include:

> whether the contracts covering the different activities were

---

> concluded with the same person or related persons;
>
> › whether the conclusion of additional contracts with a person is a logical consequence of a previous contract concluded with that person or related persons;
>
> › whether the activities would have been covered by a single contract absent tax planning considerations;
>
> › whether the nature of the work involved under the different contracts is the same or similar; or
>
> › whether the same employees are performing the activities under the different contracts."

7.7.2.5   The E&P blocks are where the actual E&P activities are performed, and each block is generally governed under distinct petroleum contracts assigned to joint ventures with different partners governed under a JOA, while the office as a coordination centre provides administrative and technical support, and supervisory activities to each of the blocks in which the company has a participation. Therefore, the E&P blocks and the office are considered to carry on different activities, which cannot be regarded as a single project.

7.7.2.6   With respect to subcontractors, the individual circumstances of each case have to be considered, since having signed different contracts with different clients—as long as no abusive elements are found—should not lead to an aggregation of the projects into a single project with regard to the calculation of the timing threshold established in the tax treaty.

7.8   The attribution of profits to a PE

7.8.1.1   Once a PE is deemed to exist in the source country, its mere existence does not, by itself, mean that additional taxes are owed to the country where the PE is located. The 2008 OECD Report on the Attribution of Income to Permanent Establishments adopts a "functionally separate entity" approach, where the PE is treated as an entity distinct from its overseas parent for several purposes.

7.8.1.2   However, the United Nations Tax Committee decided at its annual session in 2009 not to adopt the OECD approach to Article 7 arising from the OECD 2008 report. The 2008 OECD Report envisions dealings between different parts of an enterprise (such as a PE and its head office) to a greater extent than is recognized by the UN Model Convention. The United Nations Tax Committee decided not to adopt this OECD approach because it was in direct conflict with paragraph 3 of Article 7 of the UN Model Convention, which generally disallows deductions for amounts "paid" (other than towards reimbursement of actual expenses) by a PE to its head office. That rule is seen as continuing to be appropriate in the context of the UN Model Convention, whatever changes have been made to the OECD Model Convention and Commentary. It should also be noted that only a few countries have implemented the "functionally separate entity" approach and many others have made their outright reservation and will not apply the rule.

7.9   Services PE

7.9.1.1   In the 2008 proposal for amendments of the UN Model Convention, the United Nations Tax Committee already recognized the difficulties in combining Article 14 and Articles 5 and 7[69] and decided to retain Article 14, although an alternative provision was introduced in the Commentary for States that wished to remove Article 14:

Box 7.B.14: UN Model Convention alternative text for countries deleting Article 14

"15.5 Article 14 would be deleted. Subparagraph (b) of paragraph 3 of Article 5 would read as follows:

(b) the furnishing of services by an enterprise through employees or other personnel engaged by the enterprise for such purpose, but only if activities of that nature continue (for the same or a connected project) within a Contracting State for a period or periods aggregating more than 183 days within any twelve-month period commencing or ending in the fiscal year concerned;

15.6 The changes to the version of this subparagraph in the 1999 UN Model Convention are minor, comprising (i) the deletion of the words "including consultancy services," after the words "the furnishing of services," on the basis that the wording was unnecessary and confusing, such services being clearly covered; (ii) the replacement of the six-month test with the 183 days test, (...); and (iii) the use of a semicolon rather than a period at the end of the subparagraph, with the introduction of

---

[69] United Nations Economic and Social Council Committee of Experts on International Cooperation in Tax Matters, E/C.18/2008/CRP.4. See http://www.un.org/esa/ffd/tax/thirdsession/EC18_2007_CRP4.pdf After considering the arguments for and against deletion of Article 14, the subcommittee concluded that retaining the combination of Article 14 and Articles 5 and 7 would continue to cause difficulties, ambiguities and uncertainty in the application that benefit neither administrations nor taxpayers. These difficulties include the uncertainties over the personal scope of Article 14, the scope of activities that fall under Article 14, the possible interpretation of a difference between the concepts of PE and fixed base, difficulties over the taxation of partnerships under Article 14 (especially when of a mixed individual/company character) and in relation to the taxation of large worldwide partnerships of lawyers.

subparagraph (c). In relation to the wording of subparagraph (b) some members of the Committee consider, however, that the words "(for the same or a connected project)" should be eliminated as no such requirement exists in Article 14.

15.7 A new subparagraph (c) of paragraph 3 would also be inserted, as follows:

(c) for an individual, the performing of services in a Contracting State by that individual, but only if the individual's stay in that State is for a period or periods aggregating more than 183 days within any twelve-month period commencing or ending in the fiscal year concerned.

Subparagraph (c) is intended to ensure that any situation previously covered by Article 14 would now be addressed by Articles 5 and 7. The wording reflects the fact that deletion of Article 14 of the UN Model Convention would involve deletion of the "days of physical presence" test found in subparagraph (b) of paragraph 1 of Article 14 of that Model, which had no counterpart in the OECD Model Convention when the deletion of Article 14 was agreed for that Model."

7.9.1.2   In accordance with paragraph 3(b) of Article 5 of the UN Model Convention, the furnishing of services, including consultancy services, through employees or other personnel of an enterprise of one Contracting State, constitutes a PE in the State where such services are performed if the activities for the same and connected projects continue there for a period or periods aggregating more than 183 days within any 12-month period. The UN Model Convention goes beyond the fixed base concept, since under the rule, the mere furnishing of services as such already leads to the taxation of the enterprise by the source State, even if the enterprise has no fixed base in that State. This extension of taxation by the source State is of particular significance in connection with making personnel available and with providing technical assistance; under the UN Model Convention, and contrary to the situation under the OECD Model Convention, both activities would result in taxation by the State benefiting from the services.[70]

7.9.1.3   In this case, the requirements of Article 5(1) of the UN Model Convention, described above in the section on the basic rule of permanent establishments, do not have to be fulfilled. This provision is of particular significance in connection with making personnel available in respect of certain services or activities not covered by Article 5(3)(a) of the UN Model Convention (e.g., technical assistance or repair services) explained above in the construction work clause section.

---

[70] Ekkehart Reimer and Alexander Rust (Eds.), *Klaus Vogel on Double Taxation Conventions* (New York: Wolters Kluwer 2015), pp. 310–311.

7.9.1.4   In addition, it should also be noted that Contracting States may characterise fees for technical services as royalties under Article 12 of the UN Model Convention or under the "fees for technical services" provision, described below in section 7.10, rather than assuming the existence of a PE. In such a case, the source State will apply a withholding tax irrespective of the duration of the services.

7.9.1.5   In 2000, Article 14, related to "Independent Personal Services," was deleted from the OECD Model Convention as it was concluded that there was no practical difference between Articles 7 and 14 or, where such differences existed, there did not appear to be any valid policy justification for them.[71]

7.9.1.6   However, in 2008, the OECD included a service PE alternative provision to Article 5 in the Commentary for States that believe that additional source taxation rights should be allocated under a treaty with respect to services performed in their territory.[72] The OECD included the provision in the Commentary and not in the Model Convention articles because the Committee identified a number of compliance and double-taxation issues associated with the provision, which are explained in the Commentary.[73]

7.10   Fees for technical services

7.10.1.1   Owing to the difficulties in dealing with the concept of PE in relation to technical services, and the issue of base erosion in developing countries, Article 12A was added to the 2017 UN Model Convention. This allows a Contracting State to tax fees for certain technical and other services made to a resident of the other Contracting State on a gross basis at a rate to be negotiated by the Contracting States.

7.10.1.2   Until the addition of Article 12A, income from any service of a managerial, technical or consultancy nature derived by an enterprise of a Contracting State was taxable exclusively by the State in which the enterprise was a resident. However, if the enterprise carried on business through a PE in the other State (the source State) or provided professional or independent personal services through a fixed base in the source State, the source State was entitled to tax the income attributable to the PE or fixed base under Article 7 or 14 respectively. In the absence of a PE or fixed base in the source State, it was thought that an enterprise resident in a Contracting State was not sufficiently involved in the economy of the source State to justify that State taxing the income. However, with the rapid changes in modern economies, particularly with respect to cross-border services, it is now considered possible for an enterprise resident in one State to be substantially involved in another State's economy without a PE or fixed base in that State and without any substantial physical presence in that State.

---

[71] OECD, Issues Related to Article 14 of the OECD Model Convention. 1 April 2000.

[72] OECD Model Convention Commentary on Article 5, op. cit., paragraph 42.43 (Alternative service provision).

[73] OECD, Model Convention Commentary on Article 5, op. cit., paragraph 42.12.

Box 7.B.15: Article 12A of the United Nations Model Convention

"Fees for Technical Services"

Fees for technical services arising in a Contracting State and paid to a resident of the other Contracting State may be taxed in that other State.

However, notwithstanding the provisions of Article 14 and subject to the provisions of

Articles 8, 16 and 17, fees for technical services arising in a Contracting State may also be taxed in the Contracting State in which they arise and according to the laws of that State, but if the beneficial owner of the fees is a resident of the other Contracting State, the tax so charged shall not exceed __ per cent of the gross amount of the fees [the percentage to be established through bilateral negotiations].

3. The term "fees for technical services" as used in this Article means any payment in consideration for any service of a managerial, technical or consultancy nature, unless the payment is made

> to an employee of the person making the payment;

> for teaching in an educational institution or for teaching by an educational institution; or

> by an individual for services for the personal use of an individual.

4.   The provisions of paragraphs 1 and 2 shall not apply if the beneficial owner of fees for technical services, being a resident of a Contracting State, carries on business in the other Contracting State in which the fees for technical services arise through a permanent establishment situated in that other State, or performs in the other Contracting State independent personal services from a fixed base situated in that other State, and the fees for technical services are effectively connected with

> such permanent establishment or fixed base, or

> business activities referred to in (c) of paragraph 1 of Article 7.

In such cases the provisions of Article 7 or Article 14, as the case may be, shall apply.

5. For the purposes of this Article, subject to paragraph 6, fees for technical services shall be deemed to arise in a Contracting State if the payer is a resident of that State or if the person paying the fees—whether that person is a resident of a Contracting State or not—has in a Contracting State a permanent establishment or a fixed base in connection with which the obligation to pay the fees was incurred, and such fees are borne by the permanent establishment or fixed base.

6. For the purposes of this Article, fees for technical services shall be deemed not to arise in a Contracting State if the payer is a resident of that State and carries on business in the other Contracting State through a permanent establishment situated in that other State or the third State, or performs independent personal services through a fixed base situated in that other State and such fees are borne by that permanent establishment or fixed base.

7. Where, by reason of a special relationship between the payer and the beneficial owner of the fees for technical services or between both of them and some other person, the amount of the fees, having regard to the services for which they are paid, exceeds the amount which would have been agreed upon by the payer and the beneficial owner in the absence of such relationship, the provisions of this Article shall apply only to the last-mentioned amount. In such case, the excess part of the fees shall remain taxable according to the laws of each Contracting State, due regard being had to the other provisions of this Convention."

7.10.1.3   Article 12A allows fees for technical services to be taxed by a Contracting State on a gross basis. Many developing countries have limited administrative capacity and need a simple, reliable and efficient method to enforce tax imposed on income from services derived by non-residents. A withholding tax imposed on the gross amount of payments made by residents of a country, or non-residents with a permanent establishment or fixed base in the country, is well established as an effective method of collecting tax imposed on non-residents. Such a method of taxation may also simplify compliance for enterprises providing services in another State since they would not be required to compute their net profits or file tax returns.[74] In this respect, the Commentary observes that:

"A precise level of withholding tax on fees for technical services should take into account several factors, including the following:

- the possibility that a high rate of withholding tax imposed by a country might cause non-resident service providers to pass on the cost of the tax to customers in the country, which would mean that

---

[74] United Nations Model Convention Commentary on Article 12A, paragraph 28.

the country would increase its revenue at the expense of its own residents rather than the non-resident service providers;

- the possibility that a tax rate higher than the foreign tax credit limit in the residence country might deter investment;

- the possibility that some non-resident service providers may incur high costs in providing technical services, so that a high rate of withholding tax on the gross fees may result in an excessive effective tax rate on the net income derived from the services;

- the potential benefit of applying the same rate of withholding tax to both royalties under Article 12 and fees for technical services under Article 12A(...).

- the fact that a reduction of the withholding rate has revenue and foreign-exchange consequences for the country imposing withholding tax; and

- the relative flows of fees for technical services (e.g., from developing to developed countries)."

7.10.2   Alternatively, countries wishing to obtain additional taxing rights on fees for technical services that may be concerned with the broad scope of Article 12A, may consider agreeing to amend Article 12 (Royalties) to permit taxation of certain "fees for included services." This is an approach that is found in a number of bilateral tax treaties between developing and developed countries.

ANNEX 1

For more information

Arvid A. Skaar. "Permanent Establishment. Erosion of a Tax Treaty Principle" in *Series on International Taxation*. (Wolters Kluwer Law and Taxation Publishers, Deventer, Boston, 1991).

Brian J. Arnold. "Threshold requirements for taxing business profits" in *The taxation of business profits under tax treaties*. (Canadian Tax Foundation, 2003).

Jan de Goede and Ruxandra Vlasceanu. *Permanent Establishment Implications for Coordination Centres in the Oil and Gas Industry*. (IBFD Bulletin for International Taxation, September 2013).

Eirik Jensen, Supreme Court Barrister, *Permanent Establishments and Allocation Questions Pertaining to Them—Judgements of the Norway Supreme Court*. (IBFD Bulletin for International Taxation, August/September 2002).

Maja Stubbe Gelineck. *Permanent Establishment and the Offshore Oil and Gas Industry* — Part 1 and 2. (IBFD Bulletin for International Taxation, 2016).

Arvid A. Skaar, Jacques Sasseville (Eds.), *Is There a Permanent Establishment?*, (IFA Cahiers de Droit Fiscal International, 2009).

Bart Kosters and Roberto Bernales: *Oil and Gas Operational Structure Based on Joint Operation Agreements Gives Rise to Multiple Permanent Establishments within a Single Country.* European Taxation, September 2015 (Volume 55) No. 10.

United Nations, Department of Economic and Social Affairs (2011). 2011 *United Nations Model Taxation Convention between Developed and Developing Countries.* Available at http://www.un.org/esa/ffd/documents/UN_Model_2011_Update.pdf.

United Nations, Department of Economic and Social Affairs (2018). 2017 *United Nations Model Taxation Convention between Developed and Developing Countries.* Available at http://www.un.org/esa/ffd/ffd-follow-up/tax-committee.html

Chapter 8

Tax Treatment of Subcontractors and Service Providers

8.1   INTRODUCTION

8.1.1   Executive summary

8.1.1.1   This chapter addresses the tax issues that arise from the use of subcontractors in extractive industries. It provides a background of the growth of the use of such businesses and their typical roles at various stages of an extractive project. It then discusses the various tax issues that arise in dealing with such subcontractors.

8.1.1.2   The discussion of the typical tax issues outlines specific issues that present complex tax questions. An analysis is provided of each area to help frame the pertinent issues for users of the Handbook.

8.1.1.3   The chapter then addresses the key tax areas which give rise to complexities – PE issues specific to subcontractors; characterization of income and withholding tax questions; indirect tax matters including those related to customs duties; and the application of payroll taxes. A separate section also addresses issues regarding independent service providers and raises questions of whether the service provided is under an employment contract (contract of service) or in the capacity of an independent contractor (contract for services).

8.1.1.4   The last section of the chapter then presents a number of examples to illustrate the analysis provided in earlier sections. They provide a summary of other associated tax issues that arise from transactions involving subcontractors and service providers.

8.1.2   Scope of chapter

8.1.2.1   The chapter considers the taxation issues arising from the use of subcontractors in the extractive sector. The increased complexity of extractive activities is leading to specialist subcontractors being subcontracted by resource companies. Subcontractors open the market to more competitors, including local companies in developing countries. More competitors increase the number of bidders on projects and allow for new partnerships and operating models. Additional challenges arise due to the often short duration of subcontracts that may last from a few days to a few months, which generally creates challenges for taxation in the state where the natural resources are located. Further, large scale long term contracts can be complex in nature, requiring a mix of services performed in the resource state as well as those performed overseas. Some tax administrations may have limited experience in administering the different challenges arising from the use of subcontractors.

8.1.2.2   The common features of subcontracting arrangements include:

- Subcontractors generally provide specialised services at a specific stage of the project. Unlike resource companies, they generally do not invest to derive a return on the resources extracted (rather they earn a fee for services performed);

- Subcontractors supply services to multiple companies, located on different extractive sites;

- Subcontractors and the resource company they provide services to are often tax resident in different jurisdictions. Subcontractors may also not be resident in the country where the extractive site is located; and

- Subcontractors' services may be entirely performed remotely in a different jurisdiction from the resource company and/or the extractive site.

8.1.2.3   This chapter is focussed on a limited range of key tax issues specific to subcontractors engaged directly by resource companies and that are not otherwise covered in the general discussions in this Handbook. General issues applicable to subcontractors but also relevant to other industry participants are not discussed.

8.2   THE ROLE OF SUBCONTRACTORS IN THE EXTRACTIVE SECTOR

8.2.1   Subcontractors in the stages of resource extraction

8.2.1.1   In the extractive industries, subcontractors perform certain activities that resource companies have chosen to outsource. In other instances, subcontractors perform technologically advanced activities or have developed specialist technologies or expertise. Resource companies choose to outsource for a variety of commercial reasons such as to improve cost efficiencies, to get access to technical expertise and experience and resources etc. The type of activities depends on the stage of resource extraction (as set out in Chapter 1 of the Handbook). It should be kept in mind that for oil and gas projects, the typical life cycle is between 15 to 30 years and mining projects can exceed 50 years. Subcontractors can, therefore, be long-term partners in a project.

8.2.1.2   The development of these expert service providers has had an overall positive impact, for three reasons:

- The availability of specialist service providers with specific expertise has improved the efficiency of execution of extractive projects;

- It may provide developing countries with the opportunity to develop their own resource sector through national oil companies (NOCs) or private sector extractive companies based in developing countries which then utilize specialist subcontractors to fill gaps in their areas of expertise;

- Finally, the development of these specialist providers has increased the pool of companies which can pursue extractive sector projects. Developing countries gain by having that larger pool of potential bidders for projects beyond the "majors/supermajors" and major mining companies. It is however important to ensure that developing countries have appropriate transfer pricing regimes; see further 8.2.3 in case transactions take place between associated enterprises.[1] Further, developing countries are also seeking to ensure that there is more local content in the provision of services, and are creating the conditions for the development of a service sector in the extractives area.

8.2.1.3   At the resource contract or license negotiation stage, subcontractors can be professional firms (e.g., law firms) that advise resource companies on negotiations or firms that provide technical support to help acquire the concession. Subcontractors can also be business development partners who provide services in facilitating and maintaining the concession.

8.2.1.4   At the exploration and evaluation stage, resource companies often rely on the specialized technical skills of subcontractors to evaluate the project. These skills involve technical and economic analysis, mine planning, platform design services, and geological, geophysical, and geochemical analysis using sophisticated software and technologies. Subcontractors often conduct geological mapping and surveys, seismic capture and sampling, analysis, drilling of exploratory wells or excavation services. With technological developments, many of these services can be provided remotely, without substantial need for physical presence in the resource state. Remote engagement with the resource state and the tax treatment of remote services is an evolving area and should be analyzed in line with the approach and guidance being developed in the UN Model Convention and its Commentary, especially the UN Model Art. 12A[2]. The resource company may also outsource local staffing, logistics support, and other ancillary services.

8.2.1.5   At the development and implementation stage subcontractors often provide procurement, engineering, construction, drilling and processing services

---

[1] See also the UN Practical Manual on Transfer Pricing at: TP_2021_final_web (1).pdf (un.org)
[2] Art. 12

to resource companies. The goods produced may relate to upstream or downstream activities and be located onshore or offshore.

8.2.1.6   At the extraction, production and exportation stage subcontractors assist oil and gas companies in production support, pipelines, transportation, by-product processing, secondary oil recovery, and production management services. In the hydrocarbons sector, technological developments allow resource companies to increasingly manage, monitor and operate production of resources using remote sites, which may be located outside the resource state. The services to mining companies generally relate to the operation of the mine, expansion of the existing operations, and transportation. There are also ancillary services provided to resource companies at this stage, such as aviation, logistics, catering, health and safety, road construction, and habitat relocation services.

8.2.1.7   At the abandonment and decommissioning stage, subcontractors are used to remove structures and rehabilitate the extraction site. These subcontractors are generally specialised in these activities and not involved in the earlier stages of the project.

8.2.2   Location of services provided

8.2.2.1   The different locations where subcontractors can perform their services result in tax challenges, for instance, residency status and place of supply/provision of services issues. Some of these subcontractors are small, private companies that predominantly perform their services from outside the resource state in the early stages of extraction and from inside the resource state in the latter stages. Remote supplies from outside the resource state are also possible with the introduction of new technologies. The tax challenges that arise can be further magnified since subcontractors may operate in multiple jurisdictions and provide services from multiple jurisdictions.

8.2.2.2   Using non-resident subcontractors in extractive projects is currently unavoidable in most developing countries. Although the institutional framework of developing countries may inhibit or encourage the use of resident subcontractors, the local economy often does not offer the expertise required for some activities needed for the project. For instance, the large-scale development of an underground mining project will require sub-contractors with appropriate technology and expertise. These technologies and expertise may not be available in the local market. Extractive industry contracts often include provisions for skill development and technology transfer by the resource company; developing countries may consider similar approaches for services delivered by subcontractors with appropriate tax treatment of any transfers of intangibles that may take place.

8.2.3   Subcontractors related to resource companies

8.2.3.1   The operating models of subcontractors give rise to tax challenges. The subcontracting arrangement can either be with associated enterprises under the control of a resource company (partially or wholly) or with a subcontractor wholly independent of the resource company. If under the control of the resource company, issues relating to affiliates may arise. Affiliated enterprises include those in a direct ownership relationship but also those that are related through a third enterprise and/or a chain of direct investment relationships. This section is relevant for subcontractors under the control of a resource company, but essential guidance on these transactions should be sought on the application of the arm's length principle (Chapter 5) and Arts. 12(6) and 12A(7) of the UN Model and its Commentary.

8.2.3.2   Subcontractors who are not under the control of the resource company may nevertheless be involved in the functions, assets, and risks of a project. Under such hybrid operating models, subcontractors realise returns over a longer-term; a "life-of-field or mine" basis. It is also possible under such models that subcontractors and resource companies jointly own intellectual property that each party exploits in a different manner. Since most subcontracting entities are multinational companies, international taxation issues relating to residency, transfer pricing and withholding taxes may also arise.

8.2.3.3   These complex operating models result in circumstances where developing countries need greater disclosure of information regarding transactions between subcontractors and resource companies. Tax administrations in developing countries may, for instance, request mandatory or voluntary disclosure of such transactions from resource companies operating in their jurisdiction, e.g., where there are specific concerns about rates being offered to the resource company at a global or regional level, to enable accurate tax treatment of these transactions (see Chapter 11 of this Manual and see also the UN Transfer Pricing Manual). (See further Chapter 11 of this Manual for a list of transfer pricing issues that impact subcontractors in the extractive sector).

8.3   SPECIFIC TAX ISSUES RELATING TO SUBCONTRACTORS

8.3.1   Main tax issues

8.3.1.1   As mentioned above, subcontractors could be professional firms advising resource companies on negotiations or providing technical support in acquiring a concession, or they could be business development partners providing services in maintaining a concession. It should be noted that compensation for such services is generally on a fixed fee basis; such compensation can however sometimes be on a "carried interest" basis that can, depending on the contract, result in non-cash returns. An example of this can be "end of life" projects where a specialized subcontractor with expertise in recovering resources from a depleted field can be brought in under a contract that rewards them with a set fee and bonuses based on recovery beyond what the resource company would expect the well to produce at that stage of the project. Another example in the mining sector is where a subcontractor is engaged to operate the mine ('contract mining') with a performance based component in their compensation.

8.3.1.2   The gross revenues earned by subcontractors in a developing country that is the resource state may be substantial and would be a large proportion of the capital investment made by a resource company. The tax treatment of
these revenues is, therefore, important towards domestic resource mobilisation
in developing countries. In principle, such non-resident subcontractors with a
presence meeting or exceeding a specific threshold (e.g., a PE threshold) should
only be taxed on their profits which can be allocated to such presence in the
resource state, and (for VAT purposes) on goods and services supplied and consumed in the resource state. In practice, however, it is difficult for many countries
to track and identify income flows or where the presence threshold is not met;
they often rely on withholding taxes on gross income.

8.3.1.3   The main tax issues are:

- Identification of income that should be subject to tax in the resource
  state, generally based on source rules;

- Characterisation of income to be taxed under income tax,
  withholding tax, or another instrument;

- Determining the nature and location of the services performed;

- Determining the arm's length consideration for goods, services and
  financing where intra-group transactions are involved in the provision of subcontracting arrangements;

- Applying PE rules to subcontractors;

- Determining the place of supply and consumption for VAT purposes;

- Establishing the customs treatment of imported equipment and
  inputs; and

- Establishing whether payroll withholding taxes apply.

8.3.1.4   These issues are discussed in this Chapter and followed by relevant
case studies. The challenges relate not only to tax policy issues but also to tax
administration. The general principles of good tax administration are, therefore, also applicable to subcontractors, although not discussed in-depth in this
Chapter. This Chapter also does not consider the general tax policy approach of
developing countries regarding subcontractors. The preferred policy approach
of each country would depend on its administrative capacity, institutional framework and economic environment, which differ between countries.

8.3.1.5   General design principles of tax instruments apply to subcontractors -
for instance, balancing revenue with investment objectives - and useful guidance,
specifically in regard to withholding taxes can be found in Article 12A of the 2017
UN Model Convention. Where Article 12A applies, it should be borne in mind
that the responsibility of withholding taxes may be passed through to domestic

consumers. Further, a withholding tax rate higher than the foreign tax credit limit may increase the cost of investment and a high withholding tax rate on gross fees may result in an excessive effective tax rate on net income. There is also a benefit in applying the same rate to royalties and technical services to avoid tax arbitrage and classification disputes. Finally, a reduction in the withholding tax rate, or a choice to apply Article 12A in treaty policy will impact tax revenues.[3] These factors need to be balanced when setting withholding tax rates. An example of the impact of a chosen withholding tax rate is provided in 8.9.4.

8.3.1.6   Apart from the main issues identified, there are other technical tax issues that arise due to the use of subcontractors. This section briefly discusses issues that arise due to the use of certain complex contracts. These complex contracts require expert knowledge in tax administrations to determine their legal and commercial nature and consequent tax implications. Since these are high-value contracts, they will impact cost recovery in a production sharing contract (see Chapter 4) and the value and timing of other taxes. Double tax treaty (hereafter referred to as DTA) and transfer pricing issues also arise due to the use of proprietary technologies and intangibles, deduction of depreciation, costs of equipment not in use, and payment for services rendered by affiliates of subcontractors. Resolution of these issues should be guided by the Commentary to the UN Model and the UN Practical Manual on Transfer Pricing. This chapter only outlines the nature of some key transactions and raises the tax points to be considered in light of the above guidance.

8.3.2   Split contracts

8.3.2.1   A key area is the need to address mismatches and challenges around-split contracts. These are more likely to be encountered in the initial stages of the life cycle of extractives projects, as described at 8.2.1 above. Split contracts are often used for services partly provided within the jurisdiction of the resource state and partly outside of this jurisdiction. Contracts for services to be provided might be split up into an onshore (i.e., within the resource state) component and an offshore (outside the resource state) component. An example of this can be where the construction part of a project is carried out in the resource state but where the engineering design part is carried out at the foreign office of the non-resident subcontractor. There can be good reasons for the above, e.g., the skills and expertise may simply not be present in the resource state and it is neither cost-effective nor practicable to bring them to the resource state.

8.3.2.2   Two possible allocation approaches can be taken to address this issue:

- Consider the entire contract while it is being performed, and determine what is carried out in the resource state, possibly by the financial year or other assessment period under the domestic law of the resource state; or

---

[3] See in particular, Para 32, of the Commentary to Article 12A of the UN Model Convention, guidance on application of Article 12A

- Split contracts up-front and allocate a separate contract for the resource state activities. While the actual contracts are entered into by the resource company and the subcontractor, a tax administration may provide guidance on its preferred allocation approach.

8.3.2.3   A typical example would be the attribution to income in the resource state for "in country handling services" related to the delivery of the products to a client warehouse and "in country performance testing services" carried out by personnel of the subcontractor in a resource state on the drilling equipment. There would be a need to correctly identify the transactions, and address the appropriate PE and transfer pricing challenges, where associated entities were involved in the delivery of the onshore service. It is thus necessary to establish the facts and circumstances of the transaction and determine the best tax treatment in line with guidance in the Commentary to the UN Model Convention and the UN Transfer Pricing Manual. Each country should decide its own allocation approach, based on its administrative capacity and risk analysis. Splitting the contract upfront can provide certainty but can be inefficient administratively, because not all the facts are known, and the activities performed when services take place may not be aligned with the original allocation.

8.3.2.4   Tax authorities in the resource state may raise queries regarding the relative pricing of the services being provided offshore and onshore, and the timing thereof, for tax reasons such as managing PE thresholds. Challenges can also arise at different levels – at the level of the main subcontractor, or at the lower tiers of subcontractors. A concern for developing countries is that the resource company and its subcontractors, having more insight and control over project operations, as well as longstanding relationships distinct from a specific project, may be able to modify contract operations in split contracts including presence at operation sites. These changes limit predictability, negatively impacting the tax authority and favouring the private sector. It is also felt that the private sector, having access to financing options which cushion it from the effects of the changes in the contracts is at an advantage as opposed to the revenue authorities who are tasked with maintaining a predictable and sustainable tax system.

8.3.2.5   However, such practices may be difficult to identify for tax authorities in developing countries. To the extent that the resource state relies on the approach outlined in the UN Model including its Commentaries, the payments made arise in the resource state, and the treaty partner accepts that approach, the entire consideration for the split contract would be deemed to be sourced in the resource state. The full amount of subcontractor remuneration may be allocated to the resource state as the starting point and subsequently the actual taxation would be limited to income which in accordance with an applicable DTA can be allocated to the resource state. It should also be noted that many developing countries have a small treaty network; developing countries with significant resource endowments could perhaps consider providing administrative guidance on how domestic tax law would treat split contracts.

8.3.2.6   However, where the treaty partner does not apply the same approach, split contracts may become a transfer pricing issue to the extent that the service provider or its related parties (within the meaning of the domestic transfer pricing legislation) are providing the services themselves. The application of the arm's length standard should satisfy those concerns, but it may be necessary to have detailed descriptions of the services as comparable prices for these services might not be publicly available. Where, on the other hand, the services are provided by genuine third parties, there should not be a concern as both the service provider and its client (the resource company), would have an incentive to ensure that the price was appropriate. Development of good internal guidance on timing of revenues will be an important part of the solution to these issues. Chapter 11 of this Handbook provides further guidance on transfer pricing; see 8.4.4. for additional discussion on PE issues in split contracts.

8.3.2.7   Key concerns regarding split contracts in the extractive sector can be summarized as follows:

- Whether artificially splitting one project into separate projects or artificially splitting time periods results in the avoidance of time based PE rules;

- The allocation of pricing between provision of IP vs. services may result in different tax treatment, e.g., for royalties; and

- Challenges in relation to identifying onshore and offshore services where the contract contains a combination of both, and where the tax law applies to them differently.

8.3.3   Construction contracts

8.3.3.1   The second challenge is around consideration for larger, long term Engineering Procurement and Construction ('EPC') contracts and Engineering, Procurement and Construction Management Contracts ('EPCM'). Contracts are often used for delivery of large-scale projects in the resource sector, typically at the development/construction phase or for major expansions and in the abandonment stages of a project. The remuneration, i.e., the contract price, is awarded on an estimated lump sum basis, but the entire project contract is broken down into several sequential contracts. The project is managed by the resource company which bears the entire cost risk.

8.3.3.2   However, the contract stages are awarded to the contractor in sequence, and after completion of every stage or milestone, the contract price for the next stage is renegotiated, so that the overall contract price for the project is progressively adjusted for variations and changes in scope. This is done to ensure flexibility for project development and to ensure that contracted values reflect market conditions as actual costs are incurred. E.g., the price of steel, which is prone to significant fluctuations, is a large component in an offshore hydrocarbon platform; contracts must be flexible to reflect that reality and ensure that the project gets completed on time. The contract price is thus progressively converted from a target price into an actual contractual liability. Developing countries have expressed concerns that this type of change limits predictability, and that the private sector has an information advantage compared to the revenue authorities. Where these concerns arise, they can be addressed through clear administrative guidance with disclosure requirements on the contract and the allocation of risks therein.

8.3.3.3   While the precise nature of the contracts varies, in general, they can be explained as follows:

- **EPC contracts:** Under an EPC contract, the contractor provides a single point of responsibility for all activities from design to procurement and construction and will deliver a fully constructed project to the end user or owner. Unlike an EPCM contractor, an EPC contractor will perform the physical construction work. Also, under an EPC contract there will be very limited ability for the end user or owner to be involved once the contract is signed.

- **EPCM contracts:** Under an EPCM contract, the contractor generally provides detailed design, procurement, construction management and project coordination necessary to deliver a project. EPCM contracts are typically used for higher risk, complex projects where the contractor does not wish to be exposed to project risk and the resource company wishes to have greater control over not just what is constructed, but how it is constructed. Typically an EPCM contractor will coordinate and manage the construction performed by other contractors engaged by the resource company. In addition, while the EPCM contractor may provide 'procurement' services, the actual purchase of equipment and materials for a construction project may be undertaken directly by the resource company.

- Another contracting model is 'Build, Own, and Operate' ('BOO'). These contracts are more common for infrastructure projects such as power stations (which supply electricity to a mining project), especially where there are multiple investors and/or external finance is required to develop the infrastructure. Under these contracts, the resource company is generally not the owner of the infrastructure, but rather pays for the goods or services supplied by the owner of the infrastructure. The operator of the infrastructure (often different from the resource company) will build, own and operate the infrastructure and will charge a fee to the resource company for its operations or sell the output (e.g., electricity) to the resource company.

8.3.3.4   It is important for tax administrations to understand the legal and commercial nature of the different contracting models, in order to assess their tax implications. Each contract needs to be considered on a case-by-case basis. However, a tax administration might be unfamiliar with this type of complex contracting vehicle, and there may be legitimate concerns regarding the transparency about contract values between the resource company and the service provider. As these are often significant sums, the consideration paid will also impact the cost recovery mechanisms in a PSC structure (see Chapter 4) and contract variations will impact withholding taxes paid to subcontractors and other service providers, as well as the payments from the resource company to the main service provider. Tax administrations should therefore develop some expertise in monitoring such longer term contracts and familiarize themselves with the timing points to ensure that the right amount of tax (WHT, VAT/GST) is paid at the right time. Development of administrative guidelines on long term and milestone-based contract vehicles would help tax officials in the field address these issues. Such guidance would necessarily extend beyond service providers in the extractive sector and could cover construction and project management businesses. The case study on EPCM contracts in 8.9.3 highlights the issues faced.

8.3.4   Use of proprietary technology and intangibles/transfer pricing

8.3.4.1   There are also potential challenges from new technological developments including the increased use of intangibles in the provision of services. E.g., it is now possible to manage some offshore platforms on a purely unmanned basis, using remote management centres and by use of information and communication technologies (ICT). It is conceivable that a resource company may operate such an offshore concession through a completely outsourced operational model, using proprietary technology owned by the service provider, or jointly owned intellectual property. In the mining sector, it is not uncommon to have contract mining operations carried out by a third party contractor or managed services contracts by mining engineering companies that are compensated at least partially based on the profitability of a project; see 8.2.1 for some examples of oil/gas and mining projects of this nature. This point was considered during the deliberations on the commentary to Art. 12A UN Model Convention, where the majority view was to resolve the issue by application of source taxation to the entire consideration; however, the minority view seems inclined to take a more "classical" approach of seeking to attach liability based on services actually performed in the resource state.

8.3.4.2   There are wider interpretative issues in dealing with questions that these new technological developments pose. Tax administrations could seek to develop a general approach in dealing with these outsourced models, informed by the requirements of domestic law and possible interpretive guidance from the UN Practical Manual on Transfer Pricing. Such administrative guidance should be broad and provide some distinct approaches without being prescriptive, as each project will have unique features arising from the contractual issues related to the project.

8.3.4.3   In general, transactions between subcontractors and their clients, i.e., resource companies for transfer pricing purposes, are at arm's length as they are usually between unrelated companies. Where resource companies do use related companies to provide services, or there are transactions between related companies which are both engaged in the provision of services[4] (e.g., between subsidiaries

---

[4] Many subcontractors themselves are part of global MNE groups and have intra-group transactions.

of the same MNE subcontractor where the drilling company is the contracting entity and accesses technology legally owned by a separate group entity), the guidance in the UN Practical Manual on Transfer Pricing should be consulted. It should be noted that resource companies may form a contractor group/joint venture for a given venture, and in such cases the Joint Operating Agreement (JOA) usually provides each member company with audit rights. The industry view is that this is an effective mechanism to ensure arm's length transactions. The case studies utilized in this chapter do raise some transfer pricing issues, and the possible solutions are outlined in the Case Studies section, 9.9. (See further Chapter 11).

8.3.5   Tax treatment of depreciation

8.3.5.1   A separate issue relates to deductions for depreciation in the case of a service provider that contends that it has been non-resident, but has been deemed to have a PE and is subject to taxation on a net basis rather than a withholding tax on gross income. In such cases, the equipment in question is owned by the service provider and is temporarily deployed in the resource state. Use of such equipment can be highly intensive, and use in adverse conditions in remote or offshore locations can result in depreciation beyond normal rates allowed for in domestic tax legislation. Since the equipment is typically high in value, any allowable depreciation under domestic law can be material. Domestic rules may however not actually allow deductibility of depreciation, especially where specific equipment is only used for a limited period within the resource state. This is an important issue, as typically the accounting depreciation cost of equipment will be built into the consideration due for the services provided; in the absence of tax relief, this will affect cost recovery and may influence investment choices.

8.3.5.2   In a different situation, equipment reaches the end of its useful life during a particular deployment in a resource state, and it is not worthwhile to pay for it to be transported to the head office location. The question is then whether the difference between the depreciated value at the date of entry into the resource state and the realized scrap or sale value can be deductible in the resource state, when it is likely that much of the actual depreciation has occurred in other jurisdictions.

8.3.5.3   The general guidance from the UN is to base the tax considerations of transfers of such goods starting from book value;[5][6] but this may not cover the specific circumstances outlined above, and more detailed guidance may be necessary. Developing countries may wish to specially consider depreciation treatment in designing administrative principles for taxation of subcontractors and service

---

[5] Para 18 of the Commentary to Art. 7(3), UNMC reproduces Paras 27-44 of the Commentary to the OECD Model, includes Para 33 of the latter commentary, which recommends the use of book depreciation to deal with cases of partial or temporary use (p. 232, Commentary to UNMC 2017).

[6] E.g., tax treatment of "revaluations resulting from the adjustment of the book-value to the intrinsic value of a capital asset" in UN Model Convention 2017, the Commentary on Art.13, para 8 is to be guided by Art. 2.

providers. Key factors in establishing accurate depreciation rules are:

- Reasonably accurate valuation for tax purposes of movable assets that are transferred into and out of a taxing jurisdiction;

- Treatment of Customs Duty and VAT/GST on import, especially where equipment is scrapped or sold;

- Appropriate taxation rules for import duties and taxes for *temporary importation* of high value equipment into the resource state;

- Establishing approximately accurate depreciation schedules for specialised equipment used in extractive exploration and production, which might not be included in the standard depreciation schedules contained in the income tax law;

- Tax issues in the acquisition and disposal of capital assets, bearing in mind the guidance of the Commentary to the UN Model, to ensure that only depreciation related to the use of the asset in the resource state is allowable under depreciation rules and any non-allowable element is treated as a capital item.[7]

8.4 PE ISSUES IN DOMESTIC LAW AND TREATIES

8.4.1 General PE issues regarding subcontractors

8.4.1.1 Chapter 7 of this Handbook provides detailed discussion on the application of PE issues in the extractive sector, including activities of subcontractors; see further 7.5. for a detailed discussion. This section focuses on specific points of detail in PE issues applicable to subcontractors.

8.4.1.2 If a non-resident subcontractor has a PE in a resource state it will be liable to pay corporate income taxes in that country. Subcontractors are less likely than resource companies to establish an office or other establishments in a resource state, which results in a PE. The general mobility and shorter period of operation of subcontractors, therefore, give rise to different PE issues than for resource companies. The period of operation of a subcontractor in a resource state may determine whether it is regarded as having a PE in that country. Specifically, the timing thresholds in the treaty, or domestic rules if no treaty applies, are relevant. This is particularly important where treaties provide for "construction PEs" and "services PEs" and the relevant activities of the subcontractor are performed in the resource state for a period in excess of the timing threshold. The

---

[7] On the other hand, the Commentary on Art. 7, para 33, says that "where goods are[…] for temporary use in the trade so that it may be appropriate for the parts of the enterprise which share the use of the material to bear only their share of the cost of such material e.g., in the case of machinery, the depreciation costs that relate to its use by each of these parts."

timing threshold may be much lower where the resource state has an "offshore clause" in the case of activities carried out offshore in its treaty.

8.4.2   Service PE issues

8.4.2.1   Article 5(3)(b) of the 2017 UN Model Convention deals with the furnishing of services, including consultancy services, through employees or personnel where "activities of that nature continue within a Contracting State for a period or periods aggregating more than 183 days in any twelve-month period commencing or ending in the fiscal year concerned." The 2011 UN Model included "for the same or a connected project" in this article and many bilateral treaties based on the UN model contain this provision; if the time threshold is met, a PE is considered to be present. The broader scope of the 2017 UN Model means subparagraph 3(b) will apply in certain circumstances instead of new Art 12A in relation to technical service fees.

8.4.2.2   The amendments to Article 5(3)(b) in the 2017 UN Model are relevant to subcontractors performing activities through employees or personnel in the resource state. Although certain services may be performed remotely, subcontractors generally perform activities in the resource state. They can enter into several contracts in a jurisdiction with one or more resource companies. Where the treaty relies on the 2011 UN Model, the extent to which projects are connected needs to be considered. If connected, the number of aggregate calendar days of all connected projects determines whether a PE exists. In a case in India[8], the court concluded that a PE existed where a company engaged in carrying out a series of activities for three different but connected clients. One of these contracts was conducted on board an Indian vessel belonging to one particular client, while for another client, the subcontractor mobilized its own vessel.

8.4.2.3   It is also possible that a seismic survey vessel is regarded as a "fixed place permanent establishment" as, for instance, by the Indian Authority for Advance Rulings in the case of SeaBird Exploration FZ LLC.[9] If this is the case and depending on the applicable treaty, the period of activities may be irrelevant. It should be noted, however, that this is an interpretation developed on the basis of Indian domestic law, and may not be consistent with the domestic law principles of other resource states.

8.4.3   Construction PE issues

8.4.3.1   Article 5(3) of the UN Model Convention provides for a six-month threshold for a construction site to be regarded as a PE. The issues that arise with respect to subcontractors in relation to this clause are similar to those for resource companies and are set out in Chapter 6.

---

[8] Fugro Engineering B.V. v. ACIT [2008] 122 TTJ 655 (Del)

[9] A.A.R. No 1295 of 2012 of 28 March 2018. Available at http://aarrulings.in/it-rulings/uploads/pdf/1522930483_1295-seabird-exploration.pdf

8.4.4 PE identification challenges from related or split contracts

8.4.4.1   Contracts may be artificially split to avoid the relevant timing thresholds that determine whether a PE exists, as, for instance, contained in Article 5(3) of the UN Model. This has been discussed above, and may trigger anti-abuse approaches by the tax authorities of the resource state. However, subcontractors may also split and sign different contracts for bona fide commercial reasons. For instance, the contracts may relate to distinct projects (either with the same resource company or with different resource companies), or the contract may be split to limit local currency exchange risks. Contracts may also be split to cover services performed in the resource state as opposed to outside of the resource state.

8.4.4.2   Since PE, withholding tax and VAT/GST rules can differ depending on where services are performed, resource companies and subcontractors may consider it simpler to administer their tax compliance obligations by splitting contracts. Contracts that involve the supply of services along with intellectual property might be split to ensure the correct tax treatment of payments which are 'royalties' and payments that are for services. Developing country tax administrations have valid concerns on whether contracts have been split to avoid or reduce taxation, or exposure to PE thresholds. Developing country tax administrations should seek to create a transparent, predictable system for dealing with PE issues arising from split contracts which is easy for them to operate.

8.4.4.3   Action 7 of the OECD/G20 BEPS Action Plan addresses the splitting up of construction contracts. It recommends that artificial splitting should be prevented by applying a principal purpose test or by a provision that goes further and aggregates the activities of closely related enterprises on the same site during different periods of time. As an example of such a provision, Article 5(4) of the Australia – United Kingdom DTA (2003) states that the duration of activities "will be determined by aggregating the periods during which activities are carried on in a Contracting State by associated enterprises provided that the activities of the enterprise in that State are connected with the activities carried on in that State by its associate." A similar example is contained within Article 27(a) of the Canada - United Kingdom DTA (1978).

8.4.4.4   The 2017 Commentary to Article 5(3) of the UN Model at para 11 also recognizes the risk of abuse of PE rules through artificial splitting of contracts between related companies, as outlined in the OECD Model Commentary, with appropriate changes. It recommends the use of an anti-abuse rule under Article 29(9) of the 2014 OECD Model Convention, and recommends a provision, with model language, to deter such artificial splitting where the anti-abuse rule at Art 29(9) is not implemented. It further notes that several countries have implemented anti-abuse rules on this point in their domestic law.

263

8.4.5 Subcontractors contracted by subcontractors

8.4.5.1 There may be situations where a subcontractor provides only supervisory activities from a different jurisdiction than the resource state, e.g., by contracting other subcontractors to perform the actual physical activities in the resource state. In such a case, sub-subcontractors may be the ones actually performing the service in the resource state and the main subcontractor may just be performing supervisory activities, even remotely. Since the UN Model, especially its commentary on Article 5(3)(a), includes supervisory activities under the definition of a PE, a supervising subcontractor with no physical presence may still be regarded as having a PE in the resource state if it meets the domestic law and applicable treaty tests for a PE.[10]

8.5 CHARACTERIZATION OF INCOME AND WITHHOLDING TAX ISSUES

8.5.1 Charge to withholding taxes

8.5.1.1 Payments to subcontractors are often subject to withholding taxes as determined under domestic laws and treaties. Only the domestic law will apply for operations in non-treaty jurisdictions and for subcontractors operating in the resource state. In other cases a treaty will apply, and the withholding tax will be influenced by whether the treaty is based on the UN Model or OECD model and the specifics of the treaty.

8.5.1.2 Articles 12(5)/12A(5) of the UN Model deem royalties and technical service fees "to arise in a Contracting State when the payer is a resident of that State or if it is borne by a permanent establishment in that State." For detailed guidance on the scope of this rule, refer to the Commentary to the UN Model, particularly Para 13 and 16 of Article 12A's Commentary.[11]

8.5.1.3 It should also be noted that Art 7 takes preference over Article 12A where an enterprise of one Contracting State provides technical services through a PE and receives fees for those technical services within the scope of Article 12A(4). These fees could, therefore, be taxed through a profit tax, rather than a withholding tax.

8.5.2 Characterization of income to charge withholding taxes

8.5.2.1 The meaning of royalties and technical services fees in a treaty (where a treaty exists) determines the extent to which withholding taxes will apply. As

---

[10] See further Para 7, Commentary to Art. 5(3), p.156, Commentary to UN Model Convention 2017. The para includes the sentence "(T)he Committee notes that there are differing views about whether subparagraph (a) of paragraph 3 is a 'self-standing' provision."

[11] The issue of characterization of the payments of the use of such databases could give rise to questions of the application of the relevant tax treaties; this point is however not addressed here.

noted above, the UN Model provides for Article 12 and 12A to cover allocation rights for both royalties and technical service fees. The key phrase in this regard is whether the payments are covered by the phrase "for information concerning industrial, commercial or scientific experience" in the definition of royalties at Article 12(3) of the UN Model. A concern raised by developing countries is the characterisation of database access fees for remote access to technologies and know-how. If such fees could be characterised as information concerning industrial, commercial or scientific experience, they would be considered a royalty (subject to domestic law on such transactions and the language of any applicable treaty) and subject to WHT.

8.5.2.2   Where the treaty is based on the UN Model, the broader definition of these terms in the UN Model compared to the OECD model will benefit the resource state. Prior to the introduction of Article 12A UN Model, it was important to characterize payments as royalties or fees for services, owing to the different tax treatment thereof; see further para 99-103 of the Commentary to the UN Model. In general, this is now less important; however, the specific treaty needs to be referred to in determining whether payments constitute royalties or technical service fees.[12] Paras 12, 24, 60 and 85 of the UN Model, Commentary to Article 12A are of particular importance in interpreting the meaning of these terms in relation to subcontractors. Para 12 distinguishes between know-how and services, as elaborated in Para 60. Para 24 provides a narrower interpretation of technical service fees and Para 85 comments on distinguishing between technical service fees and royalties.

8.5.3   Tax treatment of leased assets and of lease payments

8.5.3.1   Services are often provided under different types of contracts using leased assets. The subcontractor can lease the equipment in the terms of a finance lease and use the equipment in the resource state, which may give rise to withholding tax on the lease payments made from the resource state. The subcontractor can also lease the equipment by an operating lease to the resource company from another jurisdiction and this may also give rise to withholding taxes. Article 12 of the UN Model includes payments for the "use of industrial, commercial or scientific equipment" within the scope of royalties; a treaty that uses the same language would allow a charge to withholding tax if imposed by domestic law, although Para 13.2 of the Commentary should be referred to. Guidance on whether finance lease payments are indeed made for the use of equipment falling under Article 12 or are to be characterized as sales proceeds falling under the other articles of the treaty is provided at Para 13.3 of the UN Model Commentary on Article 12.

8.5.4   Computation issues and split contracts

8.5.4.1   Subcontractors may require contracts to be inclusive of the withholding tax and this carries risks of double taxation by taxing the withholding tax. This risk

---

[12] Especially since many existing treaties at the time of writing this chapter do not have an Article based on the UN Model Art. 12A

is reduced by domestic laws that exclude the withholding tax on this higher contract price for other tax purposes. Further issues arise where contracts include clauses that regard the subcontractor as liable for amounts of withholding tax not withheld as enforced by tax authorities. To finance this risk, subcontractors may increase their contract price. Under a PSC, this may reduce the profit share of the resource state, especially in PSC regimes where this would be part of the recoverable cost structure. On the other hand, developing countries may take the view that the amount withheld is an easy to administer part of the fiscal take of the resource state, and is more transparent and certain.

8.5.4.2   All parties involved in the extractive activities may benefit from clear guidance on computational issues by tax authorities and provisions in the domestic law that reduce the risks of double taxation. To this end, Paras 14 and 15 of the Commentary to Article 12A are particularly useful. See also 8.3.2.

Use of ships and aircraft to provide services

8.5.4.3   Subcontractors may use specialised ships or aircraft to provide their services. Article 12A ("fees for technical services") or Article 8 ("the operation of ships or aircraft in international traffic, or the operation of boats in inland waterways") of the UN Model may apply to these payments. Article 8 takes preference if both articles apply and the Commentary to this article provides further guidance. If neither Article 8 nor Article 12A applies, domestic law and Articles 5 and 7 of an applicable treaty will need to be considered, especially whether a ship constitutes a PE (as discussed in 8.4).

8.5.5   Relief for withholding tax in the residence state

8.5.5.1   Relief for withholding taxes paid in the source state would need to be obtained from the residence state of the subcontractor. The rules governing this relief may be based on the relevant articles on withholding tax and/or Article 23A/23B in the treaty; reference can also be made to unilateral relief rules of the residence state. It is important that tax administrations provide clear guidance on documentary and other requirements to obtain withholding certificates. Improved efficiency by tax administrations in issuing withholding certificates may increase the investment attractiveness of developing countries' extractive sectors.

8.5.6   Relief for withholding tax in the resource state

8.5.6.1   Many resource states require provisional withholding of tax on any payment made to a non-resident for services rendered. Such withholding tax is usually considered, under domestic law, as a withholding on account of potential tax liabilities, and not the final tax of the non-resident. However, it should be noted many developing countries implement a flat withholding tax and see this as an effective tool for domestic revenue mobilization. Where such a flat tax is imposed, there would be no further relief due in the resource state and the withholding is effectively the final tax.

8.5.6.2   Where, however, a withholding tax is considered as a withholding on account of potential tax liabilities, resource states may consider two possible solutions to provide relief:

- **Solution 1:** Domestic tax rules in many countries may already have measures to provide such relief. This applies where the subcontractor can show that the withholding is more than its potential tax liability, either due to treaty benefits or based on a net income calculation after deduction of allowable expenses under domestic law. The withholding tax can be either reduced on the basis of a net income calculation agreed with the tax administration or refunded after provision of information as required by regulations to implement the relief regime. Further, such a regime should also consider the overall cost of compliance for withholding tax relief, which usually requires the filing of a tax return. Subcontractors have to balance the benefit from withholding tax relief with the costs of tax compliance, especially in resource states where tax authorities do not provide clear guidance or have complicated documentation requirements.

- **Solution 2:** As an alternative, a simpler solution might be to provide subcontractors resident in treaty partner states with administrative relief. Where domestic administrative rules do not already have provision for a reduced withholding certificate where the recipient of income is eligible for tax treaty benefits, the relief mechanism could be implemented by allowing such a reduction or exemption certificate to the subcontractor subject to the provision of a tax residence certificate from the residence state.

8.5.7   Withholding tax procedures

8.5.7.1   The Commentary to Arts. 12 and 12A of the UN Model clarify that each country can apply its own procedures in administering withholding taxes. See further 8.5.6 for a possible approach to make administrative procedures simpler for subcontractors and to reduce costs of compliance.

8.6   INDIRECT TAXATION ISSUES

8.6.1   Primary VAT issues

8.6.1.1   In principle, VAT should not be a component of the profit and loss account of subcontractors; input VAT paid on purchases should either be offset against output VAT received from purchasers or be refunded by governments. Complexities in the sector do, however, provide challenges in applying, complying with, and administering the VAT.

8.6.1.2   The primary VAT issues regarding subcontractors are:

- Territorial scope of the VAT: when is a supply imported or exported?

- Cross-border supplies of services and intangibles: where is a service or good supplied and consumed?

- Refunds: how can they be avoided and paid when are they due?

- VAT registration: why should suppliers be allowed to voluntarily register?

These issues are not specific to subcontractors but arise throughout the extractive sector. Chapter 9 of this Handbook addresses these questions in depth. This chapter discusses secondary issues that are applicable to subcontractors, but less applicable to resource companies.

8.6.2   Secondary VAT issues

8.6.2.1   The mobility of subcontractors may give rise to VAT challenges. One challenge is when subcontractors temporarily enter a country for a short-term assignment. When this happens, sub-contractors would prefer to voluntarily register for VAT to be able to deduct input VAT. Registration may, however, be delayed by the revenue authority to verify that the subcontractor is a legitimate business and to combat fraud.

8.6.2.2   The voluntary registration rules relating to subcontractors are, therefore, important. These rules should balance the risk of fraud by businesses with the economic costs of businesses being unable to register. Preliminary approval of VAT registration may also be a useful practice to reduce investor uncertainty. Related to this, VAT laws should allow for the deduction of input VAT on the first tax return after registration on capital equipment incurred before registration. Disallowing these deductions may decrease economic activity by increasing the cost of capital.

8.6.2.3   Another VAT challenge relates to the valuation of capital goods that are temporarily imported and then, after being used, re-exported by subcontractors. When importing capital goods, subcontractors will generally pay import VAT. After importation, a full input tax deduction of this import VAT will be made in most cases. As a result, the net amount of VAT paid on imports will be nil in most cases and the value assigned by customs on these imported goods is irrelevant for VAT. This result, however, requires that VAT refunds are promptly paid if they are claimed by subcontractors.

8.6.2.4   One way to avoid these refund claims without changing the VAT consequences is to allow subcontractors to defer import VAT to their first VAT return following importation. This implies that subcontractors declare import VAT in this return and deduct an equal amount of input VAT, the net effect being nil. See Chapter 9 (VAT) for more information on deferral. Where, however, the full amount of input VAT cannot be relieved, and/or the country in question does not offer VAT refunds and only allows a carry forward of VAT credit, there will be a challenge of unrelieved VAT. A further issue is the valuation of the goods for customs purposes on temporary importation (see 8.6.4. below) and the proper application of the "order of charge" for VAT purposes.

8.6.2.5   After using the imported capital goods, subcontractors can either export the goods or supply them to a domestic recipient. If capital goods are exported, the value of these goods is irrelevant since the supply will be zero-rated. If the capital goods are supplied to a domestic recipient, VAT should be charged on the value of the supply. If the recipient is not a connected person or a related party to the subcontractor (in terms of the VAT law), the value of the supply will be the amount charged on the sale. If such a person is a connected person or a related party, the value of the supply will generally be the market value of the goods. Determining this value is only important if the recipient of the goods will not only make taxable supplies but also may make exempt supplies. For large capital equipment, as generally supplied by subcontractors, it seems unlikely that the recipient will use the equipment for a purpose other than making taxable supplies and the value should, therefore, be irrelevant. It should also be borne in mind that the recipient may be non-resident and not a vendor, and the supply may be zero-rated. If, however, exempt supplies will be made by the recipient of the equipment, the tax administration would have to assess whether the value determined by the subcontractor is market-related.

8.6.2.6   VAT challenges also arise where subcontractors move capital equipment between states in a federal country. Where VAT is administered at state-level or at the state and federal-level, together with the open borders between states, challenges in administering the VAT arise:

- How to ensure that only the state of final consumption receives VAT, which often requires transfers to the federal administration on inter-state supplies; and

- Different tax rates may apply for supplies in and between different states.

8.6.2.7   That said, the movement of capital equipment by a subcontractor between states should not be considered a supply for VAT purposes; there should not be any VAT consequences. Only if such capital goods are sold to another person (as defined by the VAT law) will there be a supply. In such cases, the supply will generally be charged at the VAT/GST rate of the state of the recipient of the goods.

8.6.2.8   A separate VAT/GST challenge arises where the supply may have taken place in exclusive economic zones outside the territorial waters of the resource states, and the question is whether the resource state has the right to levy VAT in that area. A related issue may arise in Joint Development Areas (JDAs) where more than one sovereign state shares a development area and the charge to VAT/GST is not clarified in the JDA agreement.

8.6.2.9   Some countries also have an administrative procedure under which subcontractors are not required to pay VAT on output services, which is instead paid by the resource companies. This breaks the chain and it would be worthwhile to consider an administrative mechanism to deal with accumulated input credits permitted under the VAT law of the resource state; measures such as a deemed credit could reduce costs for the project and/or cost of capital.

8.6.3   Services to a head office or from staffing companies and accounting firms

8.6.3.1   In the short-term contract market, it is industry practice to share the procurement of services between Head Office and the local PE, as well as for centralization of certain work at Head Office/Regional Office level. For VAT purposes, a single supply of a service cannot be made to more than one recipient. If it appears that there is more than one recipient, this means there is more than one supply or one recipient is acting as an agent (and the supply is only to the principal). It will, therefore, be necessary to identify and value the separate supplies made to the different recipients of the supplies. An invoice needs to be generated for each supply and VAT charged at the applicable rate, including zero-rate for an exported service. If the supply is to an agent, the purchase is generally deemed to be made by the principal and not the agent. The ultimate consumer of the service is the recipient of the service, even if transacted by another party.

8.6.3.2   Subcontractors may also make use of staffing companies to provide personnel. In most instances, these companies will act as the agent of the subcontractor. This means that the salaries paid by the staffing company should not be subject to VAT. A similar issue may arise where subcontractors make use of accounting firms to manage their payrolls. It is required to distinguish between the service component that is charged with VAT and the salary component for which the staffing company or accounting firm act as an agent. The principle is that a supply to or from agents retains its nature, in this case, a supply of employment that falls outside the scope of VAT in all jurisdictions.

8.6.4   Customs duty issues

8.6.4.1   Subcontractors can face unique challenges regarding customs duties. A frequent issue is whether a country has taxing rights on imports into areas such as the exclusive economic zone or the JDA. The domestic customs duty law would determine the tax consequences in this regard. Temporary admissions of high-value exploration equipment are another challenge. Many countries refund customs duty based on the depreciated value of the temporarily admitted equipment at the time of export. Clear rules governing such temporary exports by tax administrations would assist subcontractors in the industry. These rules can focus on valuation of equipment, ring-fencing of equipment, equipment sold into the domestic economy subsequent to temporary import, and related party transactions.

8.6.4.2   An example of a solution for Customs classification issues through advance rulings is the practice in South Africa. The Commissioner for the South African Revenue Service may in writing issue a "non-binding ruling" determining the tariff headings, tariff sub-headings or tariff items or other items of any Schedule to the Customs and Excise Act, 1964, under which inter alia any imported goods shall be classified. An importer may make an application to the Commissioner to make such a determination in respect of a specific consignment of goods imported or to be imported.

8.7   PAYROLL TAXES[13]

8.7.1   Application of payroll tax: Characterization of income received by personnel

8.7.1.1   Subcontractors regularly deploy in resource states personnel who are essential to the delivery of services. Such personnel can be part of the service contract, e.g., they operate the equipment or deliver tasks within the contractual framework for services, etc. Alternatively, the provision of staff is itself a service, a staffing service, where the provider is essentially deploying staff who work on the resource company's site and with their equipment. The specialized nature of the work involved means that many essential skills are provided by individuals, who for a variety of reasons prefer to remain self-employed, and hire themselves out on a daily rate basis. The characterization of income received by personnel to identify whether there is a "contract of service" (i.e., an employer-employee relationship) or a contract for services (i.e., the person receiving payment does so in their capacity as an independent subcontractor) is thus an important issue to be determined.

8.7.1.2   The first issue to consider is to determine whether an individual is an employee, either of a staffing company or of a subcontractor, or alternatively whether that person is an independent subcontractor (see 8.8). An associated issue is whether, instead of either of those alternatives, the resource company itself can/should be considered the employer. This can arise e.g., when an employment agency is hiring out labour to a customer and the employment agency is the formal employer; however, in substance, the client/user of the labour (the resource company) is the economic or substantive employer. The key consideration is therefore to determine whether an individual is a person who has a contract of service or has a contract for services.

8.7.1.3   An employee is a person who, under domestic law, has a contract *of service*, while a person with a contract *for services* is an independent contractor. The treatment of independent subcontractors is considered separately at 8.8.1,

---

[13] The term "payroll taxes" is used in this section to cover all taxes and levies on employment income. Typically, domestic laws require an employee to file a tax return, or an employer to withhold tax from the employee, or a combination of these approaches. Domestic laws may also include charges and levies payable by employers.

which also covers the treatment of personal service companies; and 8.8.2. deals with the treaty aspects including relief from double taxation. This section of the chapter focuses on individuals treated as an employee. That employer-employee relationship may exist between a subcontractor or staffing company and its employee. It may also exist in the case of formal employees of a service provider who are considered, in substance, to be the employees of a resource company.

8.7.2   Application of payroll tax: Identifying the employer

8.7.2.1   The second issue to consider in the application of payroll tax is which entity will be considered to be the employer under domestic law in the resource state. Depending on the rules regarding tax characterization of employment income under domestic law, there may be a determination that a resource company that utilizes the services of a staffing services provider is the actual economic employer of the personnel deployed, irrespective of the fact that the legal employer is the staffing company. The consequences of this interpretation might be quite significant in cases where the resource company has operated on the assumption that it has no liability as an employer; beyond the immediate issues of liability for payroll tax and withholding obligations, this may also give rise to complications in settling cost sharing arrangements on the investor side.

8.7.2.2   Accordingly, where there is no doubt about employee status, there can still be an issue on the entity that could or should be considered the employer:

- Where the subcontractor is actually providing a service to a client via its own employee. In this case, the subcontractor is the employer in both a formal and substantive sense;

- Where the subcontractor is an employment agency hiring out labour to a resource company or another subcontractor. The agency is the formal employer but in substance, the client/user of the labour is the economic or substantive employer.

8.7.2.3   It is therefore useful to bear in mind that there can be three possible parties in identifying the employer in a transaction, i.e., a subcontractor, a service or staffing company which then hires out staff to the subcontractor, and finally the resource company. See further 8.7.4. for the tax issues that arise.

8.7.3   Consequences of characterization and treaty application

8.7.3.1   Personnel considered to be employees can be part of the service contract, i.e., they operate the equipment, deliver tasks within the contractual framework for services, etc. Alternatively, the subcontractor can only provide a staffing service where they deploy staff (often called hire-out of labour) who work on the resource company's site and with the resource company's equipment. Many of these services are specialised and the charge out for personnel can often be a daily rate. Issues arise in determining whether personnel provided should be regarded as employees of the subcontractor, the resource company or an independent subcontractor (the latter case being dealt with at 8.8). As mentioned above, while a formal employment contract may exist with a staffing company or subcontractor, the personnel concerned could be considered as employees of the company making use of the services under a substantive and economic approach. This can be contrasted with staff hired out by a subcontractor (where the staff are considered employees of the subcontractor) who carry out services for a resource company client.

8.7.3.2   The domestic law of the resource state often contains tests to distinguish between "contracts of service" and "contracts for services." Assuming that the domestic law requirements for identifying a contract for services are not satisfied, a resource state's tax administration, relying on its own rules for contracts of service vs. contract for services, may insist on treating subcontractors as the employees of the resource company or the service provider. This could be done on the basis that the individual in question is purely providing labour and is using the site, equipment and materials provided by the resource company/service provider to do so.

8.7.3.3   Detailed examination of the facts and circumstances of the arrangements are appropriate in cases where there is some question about whether an individual concluding a contract with a "client/employer" to provide certain services is doing so as an employee. The analysis must include a consideration of whether Article 15 would be applicable or whether treatment as an independent service provider covered by Article 14 of the UN Model is appropriate. If the parties think it is a contract of service they assume no withholding obligations, but if the tax administration takes the view that the individual is an employee the client/employer may be subject to withholding obligations and Article 15 would apply to the salary.

8.7.3.4   Allocation of taxing rights for employees is made under Articles 15(1) and 15(2) of the UN Model. Para 8.4 of the Commentary to these Articles states that it is for the source state to characterise contracts of service versus contracts for services on the basis of its domestic law. Paras 8.5-8.9 clarify that such recharacterization may, in abusive cases, take place even where domestic law in the source state does not have a provision for questioning a formal contractual relationship between an employer and employee. Paras[14] 8.13 and 8.14 outline a number of tests for determining the employer-employee relationship. This examination may also include whether accurate characterization as the economic employer in substance would have consequences for the application of Article 15.

8.7.3.5   A further consideration is a case where an individual is to be treated as an employee, but questions arise on who can be considered the employer. This can come up where an individual has what he or she believes to be a contract for services with a subcontractor, but where the substance leads the tax administration to conclude that the resource company is the employer. This may lead to

---

[14] 8.13 provides the first criterion; 8.14 refers to "additional" criteria if, after the first test, it seems possible that there is, in substance, an employer which is not the formal employer of record.

a different interpretation of Article 15(2) because if the formal employer (service provider or employment agency) is not considered as the economic or substantive employer but the person ("hiring the labour") then the exception in Article 15(2)(b) does not apply.

8.7.3.6   The consequences of accurate characterization can thus result in the following situations:

- A person who has a formal contract of employment with a staffing company or a subcontractor could be considered an employee of a resource company.

- Persons who consider themselves to have self-employed status, and to have a contract in that form with a subcontractor or with a resource company, could be considered to be employees of either the subcontractor or of the resource company, depending on the actual substance of the activity.

8.7.3.7   If personnel were, based on these rules, treated as employees instead of independent contractors, or employees of a different employer for tax purposes, large compliance costs arise. The employer of record would then be liable for compliance with rules regarding payroll taxation of employees, including withholding tax, labour fund and social security contributions, as well as sanctions and interest arising from delays in meeting obligations of an employer. On the other hand, where a staffing company is involved, it may have already deducted the relevant withholding tax and other levies, and paid them over. The resource company would then be faced with a long and complex process to recover such misapplied withholding tax and levies, assuming such a procedure is allowed by law, resulting in significant costs that would potentially be partially borne by the resource state under cost sharing mechanisms. These costs may also partly have to be carried by the resource state under the cost recovery provisions of a PSC.

8.7.3.8   The result of such a determination of the relevant employer, especially in retrospective situations, can result in further challenges. A subcontractor may also have left the resource state at the time of the recharacterization. The establishment of an advance ruling system, on whether personnel should be regarded as employees or independent contractors as part of the administrative arrangements for extractive sector taxation, would reduce these challenges. Guidance provided by tax administrations as to when a person is an employee, including the impact of paying day rates, can also reduce uncertainties in this regard.

8.7.4   Employer tax issues

8.7.4.1   If personnel are regarded as employees, it is required to establish the entity that is their employer. This employer will have the responsibility to withhold payroll taxes. The employer is determined in terms of the domestic law of the resource state. It should be noted that some countries only recognize a formal employer – employee relationship, in which case only the person having concluded the formal labour contract with the employee is considered an employer. On the other hand, in other countries (as outlined in 8.7.2. above) the economic or substantive employer relationship can take precedence, where a person who is not the formal employer is responsible for all relevant responsibilities and duties of an employer.

8.7.4.2   Subcontractors may retain a local payroll company to handle payroll as they themselves may not have the size and scale to do so efficiently. Further, such a payroll company can also be a service provider to the resource company. However, there can be risks for the application of VAT/GST and potentially withholding taxes from the client companies to the service provider. A country might have language in its taxing statutes regarding a withholding tax on gross income; it is thus possible that the tax administration considers the entire transaction as subject to withholding tax and VAT/GST, including the salaries which would be paid to the employees. It is therefore worthwhile for governments to issue clear guidance on this area to clarify that only the service element of payroll management would be subject to withholding tax and VAT/GST.

8.7.4.3   Depending on these rules, it may be determined that a resource company using the services of a staffing company is the employer of personnel of the staffing company. There may be some challenges in identifying which is the subcontractor and which is the staffing company. It is possible to have three parties in an assignment, i.e., a subcontractor, a service or staffing company, and finally the resource company. The staffing company hires out staff to the subcontractor who then hires out staff onwards to the resource company. The transaction could thus have two parties or may have a third one. If otherwise interpreted by the resource company, this determination may also give rise to significant compliance costs. If it is determined that the staffing company is the employer and that company is a non-resident, compliance challenges may arise since the domestic rules are designed with domestic employers in mind. Issues also arise where a subcontractor is deemed to be an employer after leaving a resource state but tax on wages was not withheld by such a subcontractor. In such cases, the resource state may be unable to collect the outstanding tax from the subcontractor.

8.7.4.4   An associated issue is the contribution to be made to any worker's compensation scheme or other industrial labour welfare funds in the resource state. The employee, typically a non-resident, is unlikely to access the fund but on the other hand such contributions are usually mandatory. The employer would be liable for contributions to such funds if they meet the criteria, and typically most large service providers would probably qualify. And where the responsibility to withhold payroll taxes shifts as a result of an interpretation by the resource state that the true economic employer is as described in 8.7.2, the resource company or service provider may be liable for significant sums of money over the life of the project, which were not within the cost analysis done for the investment. Further, in the absence of social security totalization agreements, there may be little opportunity for the employee, normally a tax resident in another state, to benefit from contributions made in his/her name.

8.7.4.5   An advance ruling system with additional guidance can reduce these compliance costs. Awareness that non-resident staffing companies often require domestic accounting firms to manage their payroll and that many employees are compensated at a day rate in the industry may be reflected in this guidance.

8.7.5   Employee tax residence

8.7.5.1   Where a person is regarded as an employee in terms of the domestic law, the tax residence status of the employee should be determined to establish the state that has taxing rights to the income derived. This depends on the residence rules (e.g., based on Art.4 of the UN Model) in the two jurisdictions and on the terms of any relevant DTA. Art 15(1) of the UN Model provides for income from employment derived by a resident of a treaty state to be taxable in that state only, unless the employee carries out the employment in the other state; in the latter case the income derived from the other state will be taxable in the state where the employee is present and performing the work. This principle applies to salaries, wages, and benefits in kind and should apply without any regard to where the income is paid to the employee.

8.7.5.2   The three exceptions from this general rule at Article 15(2) UNMC are where:

- The employee is present in the other state for not more than 183 days in a tax year;

- The salary is paid by an employer who is not resident in the state where the employee is working; and

- The remuneration is not borne by a PE of the employer in that other state.

8.7.5.3   Staff resident in one state and working abroad for short periods could, therefore, remain exempt from tax in the destination country. This exemption allows employers to send employees to work for short periods in other states without the employees becoming liable to tax in those other jurisdictions. This may not however be applicable, in most cases, in practical terms. Since most successful extractive projects are long term undertakings, it is possible that employees who may consider themselves non-residents may be considered residents under domestic law due to their frequent travel and presence in the country over a period of time.

8.7.5.4   In many cases where an individual works in a foreign country for longer terms or works for a foreign employer, the treaty provisions will not prevent them from becoming resident in that foreign state. The following cases might apply:

- If the individual stays longer in another country, the person may become a resident of the other state and in case a treaty applies, the residence article of that treaty could determine that a dual residence situation exists;

- Where the person does not become a resident of the other state, or works for an employer (formal or substantive, see above) in the other country or a PE, in which cases the exception no longer applies.

8.7.5.5   Accordingly, the exemption will not apply and the state where the work is performed will have taxing rights to the income derived. Some additional factors also need to be taken into account in determining residence and taxability. E.g., in one country, individuals with a presence of 182 days or more in an income year or a presence of 90 days or more in an income year and of 365 days or more during the preceding 4 income years are deemed residents for tax purposes.

8.7.5.6   The Commentary to Art. 15 of the UN Model, which essentially repeats the guidance in the Commentary to the OECD Model, provides detailed guidance on these issues. It should be further noted that there are special rules regarding deemed PEs on the continental shelf in the Commentary to Article 15 of the UN Model which impacts the usual application of Article 15;[15] there are special rules not requiring the normal 183-day presence for taxing the salaries of personnel deployed in such a deemed PE.[16]

8.7.5.7   There may be a need to consider the tax formalities associated with the shift of residence, where appropriate. Either the employee or the employer would need to notify the tax administration of the date on which the employee is leaving their state of tax residence, and any relevant form or tax return should be completed and sent to the tax administration. The employee may need to request a tax return to declare the income earned in that tax year up to the date of departure from the country if that is required by the national tax rules in the home country. It would also be appropriate to consider special rules regarding expatriate employees, and possibly special occupations such as development work, work on ships or work on oil and gas platforms.

8.7.5.8   The difference in tax treatment between residents and non-residents can be significant. A non-resident may be taxable on a gross basis through a withholding tax, while a resident will usually be able to benefit from allowances, rebates, credits and exemptions available under domestic law. These challenges could be significantly mitigated by guidance on available thresholds for establishing tax residence, declaration procedures to show actual total compensation paid and what duties such compensation is intended to compensate and treatment of short term employment contracts.

8.7.6   Computation of taxable income and other payroll tax issues

8.7.6.1   The amount of taxable income should be determined where a

---

[15] As then the employee may work for a PE of his employer as meant under para 2 (letter c) of that Article.

[16] Employee related payroll tax issues may also have interplay with the visa requirements of that country.

jurisdiction has taxing rights to income derived from employment. Determining taxable income is complicated by contracts of employment that allocate different values for work in the resource state and work in another country by the employee. Issues relating to split contracts may also arise and these include tax evasion risks. Guidance regarding thresholds to establish tax residency, procedures to show how different duties performed by employees are compensated, and guidance on the treatment of short-term employment contracts, can assist tax administrations and taxpayers in this regard.

8.7.6.2   An associated issue around payroll tax is the issuance of work permits. This is because some countries require the statement of gross salaries and their payment mode on the work permit. The tax aspect arises from the calculation of gross income, as this can depend on the payment mode mentioned in the work permit. A work permit might specifically mention the monthly gross salary; the complexity arises where the employee deployments are for specific periods shorter than a full month. The tax administration may then still assess the stated total monthly gross salary.

8.8   INDEPENDENT SUBCONTRACTORS

8.8.1   Tax issues related to independent subcontractors

8.8.1.1   Staff working on an extractive project may be regarded as independent subcontractors and not employees. Such an independent contractor will be liable to pay tax in the resource state on the profits earned in that state. This tax will be payable either in his or her personal capacity or in the capacity of his or her own personal service company. The administrative challenge for tax administrations is to detect disguised self-employment, especially in countries where the laws allow lower effective tax rates for independent contractors or personal service companies[17] than for employees; see 7.1/7.2. above. Anti-avoidance rules that equate these tax burdens may, therefore, assist to combat this form of tax avoidance. Such rules could include the application of a "look-through" of the personal service company and assessing the person (owner of the service company) directly on the compensation received under the appropriate qualification of income.

8.8.1.2   Developing countries may also have concerns that independent contractor treatment could allow some private sector players to receive unintended tax benefits. Where these differences are material, a specific tax regime could be set up for independent contractors and such tax treatment notified to independent contractors on the issuance of work permits. Tax administrations in developing

---

[17] Where individuals work for a period on an extractive project in a foreign country, they may structure the contract differently, working for an umbrella company or for their own service company, rather than as an employe subject to payroll taxation rules, as above. An individual using a service company would of course be liable to tax in the resource state on the profits earned there.

countries should, where the amounts at issue seem material, set up mechanisms to detect situations where actual employment is presented as self-employment. The impact of this is to receive only part of the total payment by the service company[18] as salary whereas the remaining amount may not be taxable if there is no PE in the source state. By doing so, appropriate taxation of employment income under domestic law as modified by any applicable tax treaties will be possible, and the use of personal service companies (often located in low tax jurisdictions) will be discouraged.

8.8.1.3   Where the individual is an independent subcontractor or working for a personal service company, the rules as set out in 8.4 and 8.5 of this Chapter apply. If the relevant treaty includes provisions similar to Art 14 of the UN Model, the income from the services performed may be allocated between two states. Where application of the PE rules is difficult, the rules of the resource state to look through the corporate structure to the individual owners of the personal service company are relevant. If these rules exist and an equivalent of Art 14 is in the relevant tax treaty the resource state may tax the owners of the personal service company as if they are employees (see 8.7). Only income derived from activities in the resource state may be taxed. Similarly, countries can tax the incomes from "the independent activities of physicians, lawyers, engineers, architects..." as mentioned in Art 14. Many of these independent activities apply to the extractive industries.

8.8.1.4   Developing countries could consider establishing an advance rulings system to address these specific tax characterization issues for employers and employees as part of the administrative arrangements for extractive sector taxation. This function could be located in the large taxpayer unit (LTU) if there is one, or a tax administration office that deals with extractive sector taxation.

8.8.2   Tax treaty issues

8.8.2.1   Para 8.10 of the Commentary to the UN Model clarifies that where a resource state recharacterizes a contract *for* services as a contract *of* services under Art 15, relief from double taxation by the resident state should still apply. Para 8.12 clarifies that any disagreements between the resource state and the residence state of the subcontractor should be resolved through a mutual agreement procedure or following the examples provided by the Commentary. The examples at Paras 8.22 and 8.24 are particularly relevant in this regard.

8.9   CASE STUDIES[19]

---

[18] The personal service company enters into a "contract for services" in form, but on examination of the substance, this may be considered to be a "contract of service."

[19] The case studies in this section apply the principles discussed in the previous sections to specific situations. Members of tax administrations and companies in the services sector were engaged in formulating the cases. The cases are based on three contracts and different scenarios are explored within each contract.

8.9.1   Contract I – Seismic data capture and analysis

Domestic supplies

Oil Company (OC), a special purpose entity formed in Julfar (resource state), contracts with Seismic Company (SC), a specialist oilfield service firm that is a tax resident in Julfar, to provide all necessary seismic data capture and analysis in an offshore block. The offshore block is located in Julfar and OC is the concessionaire. SC has the required expertise, combined with the ability to contract additional service firms in Julfar to perform the services in accordance with current standards and practices of the industry as set out in the contract. The contract requires that SC shall at its own cost and expense furnish supervision, personnel, equipment, materials, and supplies necessary to perform the service in a diligent manner.

In terms of the contract, OC will pay SC for the service at the time(s) and in the manner prescribed by the contract. All contract rates and other prices agreed on include any charges and provisions necessary for the completion of the contracted services. It is deemed to cover all expenses and dues, including taxes born by SC. The case is illustrated below.

In this domestic scenario there is no treaty applicable and, assuming Julfar does not administer a withholding tax on domestic supplies, SC and Domestic Seismic Vessel Company (DSV) will remit income tax to the revenue service of Julfar. This is illustrated below.

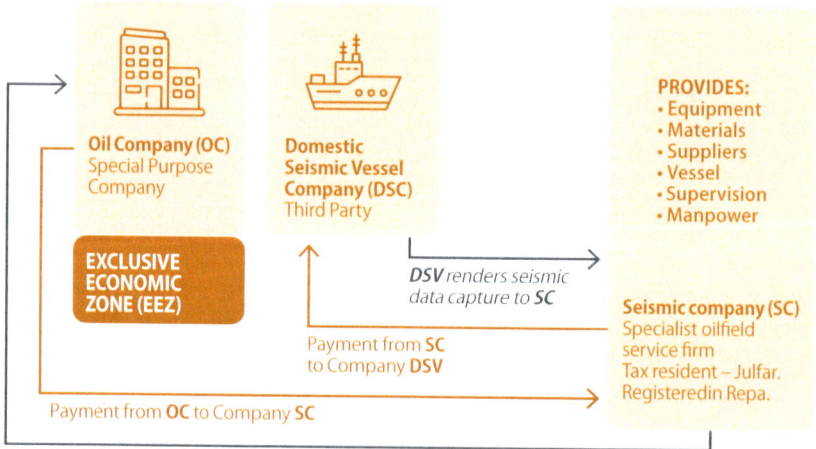

SC renders Final Services to OC including some seismic data capture from DSV

Services delivered through a PE

Oil Company (OC), a special purpose entity formed in Julfar (resource state), contracts with Seismic Company (SC), a specialist oilfield service firm with a PE in Julfar, on the basis of a PE, to provide all necessary seismic data capture and analysis in an offshore block. The offshore block is located in Julfar and OC is the concessionaire. SC has the required expertise, combined with the ability to contract additional service firms in Julfar to perform the services in accordance with current standards and practices of the industry as set out in the contract. The contract requires that SC shall at its own cost and expense furnish supervision, personnel, equipment, materials, and supplies necessary to perform the service in a diligent manner.

JULFAR (Resource country)

Oil Company (OC)
Special Purpose Company

EXCLUSIVE ECONOMIC ZONE (EEZ)

Domestic Seismic Vessel Company (DSC)
Third Party

PROVIDES:
• Equipment
• Materials
• Suppliers
• Vessel
• Supervision
• Manpower

TAX DEPARTMENT

Seismic Company (SC)
Specialist oilfield service firm
Tax resident – Julfar.
Registered in Repa.

DSV renders seismic data capture to *SC*

Payment from **SC** to Company **DSV**

Payment from **OC** to Company **SC**

——— Services Performed
——— Payment Made
——— Tax Payments

In these circumstances, the outcome is the same as the example at 8.9.1.1

Triangular services

For purposes of the following discussion, all the facts of the contract as discussed above still apply. It is, however, assumed that SC is not a tax resident in Julfar, but in another country named Repa.

The services in terms of the contract between OC and SC are extended and it is agreed that SC will also explore the Exclusive Economic Zone (EEZ) in Julfar. SC decides to outsource some of the seismic data capture and contracts with three additional companies. The first company is Domestic Seismic Vessel (DSV) which operates in Julfar and is unaffiliated to SC. The second company is Overseas Seismic Vessel (OSV), which is based *outside* of Julfar and a related party to SC.

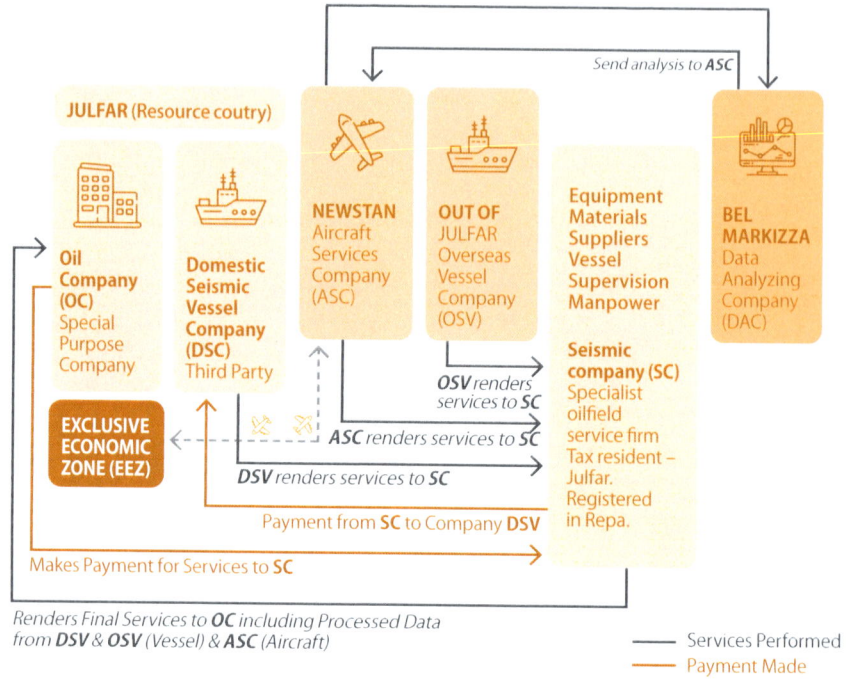

Renders Final Services to **OC** including Processed Data
from **DSV** & **OSV** (Vessel) & **ASC** (Aircraft)

—— Services Performed
—— Payment Made

The third is Aircraft Services Company (ASC), which is based in Newstan and unaffiliated to SC. ASC uses the latest aerial surveying technology by conducting the seismic data capture process by aircraft. The aircraft departs from Newstan, flies over the EEZ in Julfar and returns to Newstan. The data captured by ASC is sent to Data Analysing Company (DAC), a tax resident in Bel Markizza. Repa and Bel Markizza have a DTA with Julfar. This case is illustrated below.

Triangular services – no PE

If SC has a PE in Julfar, its income will be subject to corporate income tax. The solution if this is the case is provided in the next subsection. Here it is considered that SC does not have a PE in Julfar, and its income will be subject to withholding tax under the domestic law of Julfar. The facts as presented here also assume that the other non-resident contractors do not have a PE in Julfar. The withholding tax rates are set out in the domestic tax law but are modified by the tax treaty between Julfar and Repa. The treaty places a maximum percentage on the amount of tax that can be withheld by Julfar on royalties and technical service fees; its technical service income is mainly from supervision and manpower services. The

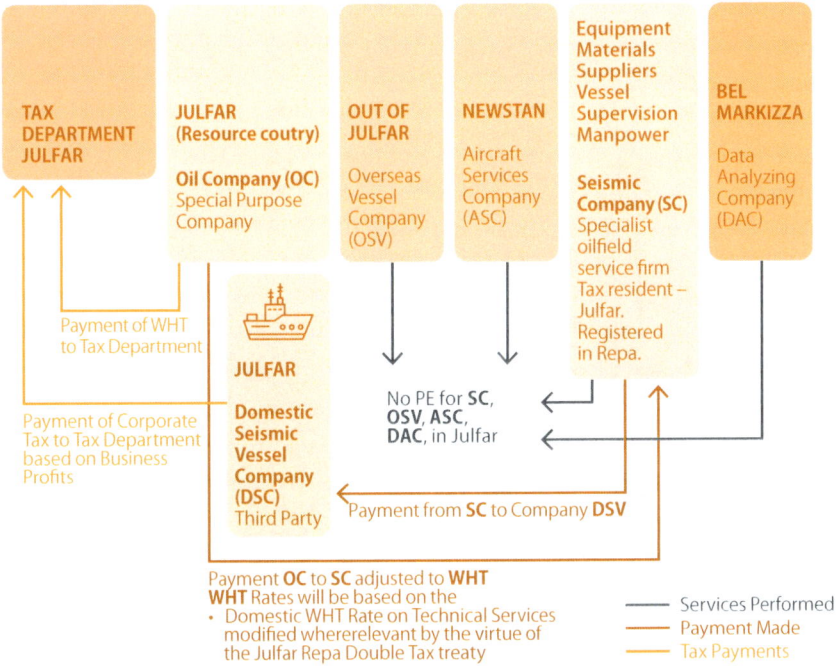

withholding tax rates are set out in the domestic tax law but are modified by the treaty between Julfar and Repa. The treaty places a maximum percentage on the amount of tax that can be withheld by Julfar on royalties and technical service fees. Assuming that the definition of technical service fees in the tax treaty is in line with the UN Model and Repa accepts the broader approach than pure source-based, withholding tax by Julfar will apply to the entire services of the contract. This is illustrated below.

Triangular services – PE

We now consider the case where SC has a PE in Julfar; SC will be liable to corporate income tax on payments from OC. A PE may normally be created if the foreign enterprise has a fixed place of business in the host country, or if it concludes contracts through a dependent agent in the host country. Some countries have a provision for a "service PE" in their national tax law, under which a PE is created if a foreign enterprise has employees or other staff working in the host jurisdiction for a specified length of time.

The definition of a PE will be modified by the treaty between Julfar and Repa. The treaty may also contain provisions for a "service PE" specifying that a PE will be created if services are performed in the host country for a specified length of time. If the length of time the personnel will be required to work in the host country is

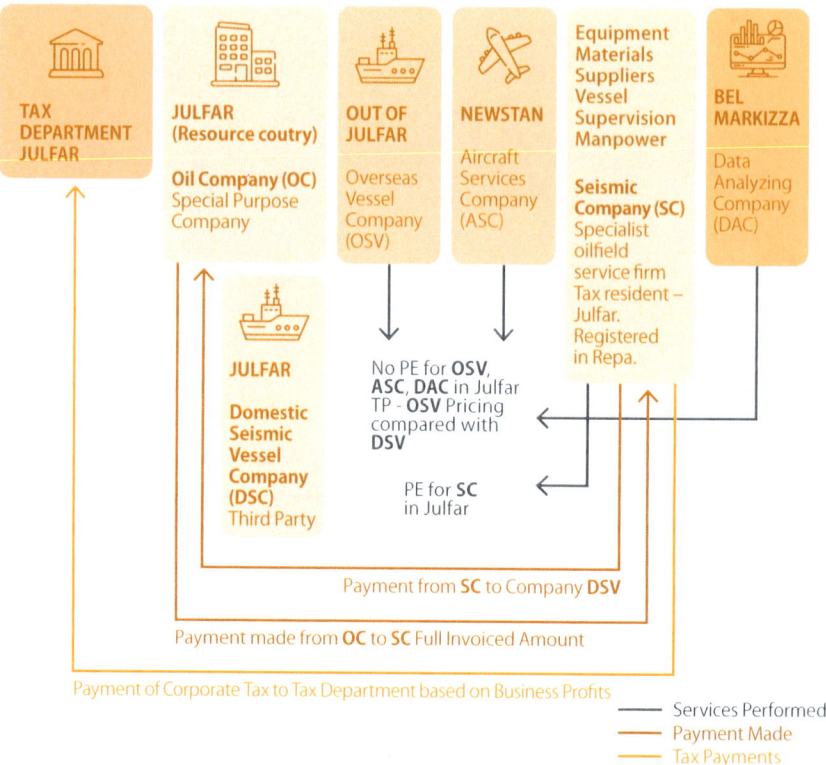

sufficiently long (for example 90 days in any twelve-month period) this could give rise to a service PE in Julfar. If SC requires an office or other establishments to perform the services in Julfar, SC will likely have a PE in Julfar. Also, if the performance of the seismic survey involves the presence of employees or other staff in Julfar for a period of time this could give rise to a "service PE." This is illustrated below.

Transfer pricing

The transfer pricing discussion pertains to the triangular supply case where SC is a tax resident of Repa.

The transfer price charged by DSV (a domestic third party) and OSV (a related entity) to SC should be compared. SC must ensure that the intercompany price charged by OSV to SC for similar services is in line with the arm's length principles or fully justify and substantiate any difference in price. The Julfar tax authorities would have an interest in ensuring that the pricing is at arm's length. This is illustrated below.

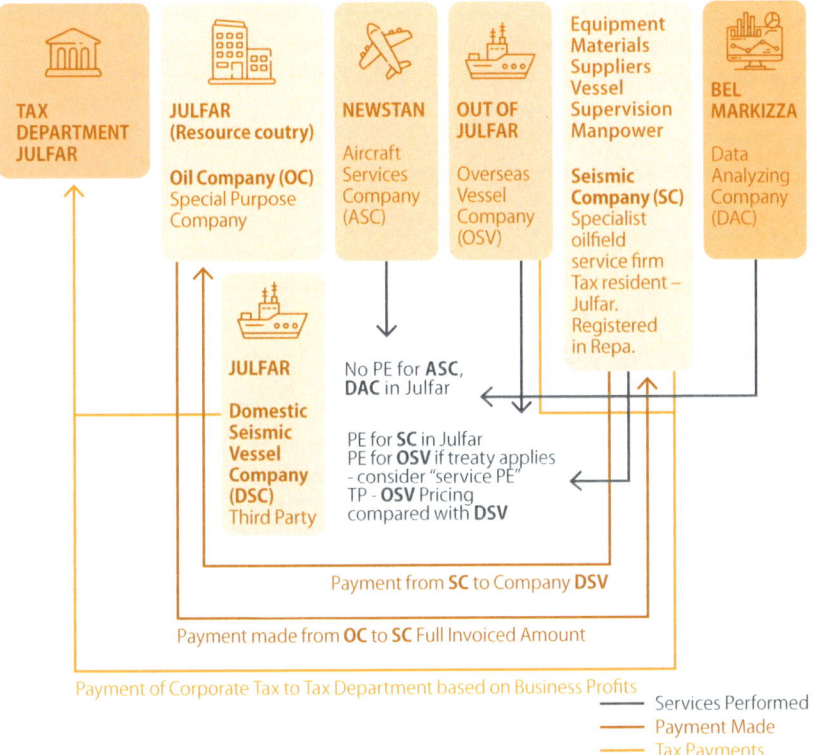

VAT [20]

It needs to be considered whether SC, which provides services to OC, is registered or required to be registered for VAT in Julfar. If SC is not registered for VAT in Julfar, it may be required to do so depending on the domestic VAT law of Julfar. Registration will also depend on whether the services supplied are regarded as imported services, or services supplied from within Julfar. Alternatively stated, whether the place of supply is in Repa (imported services to Julfar) or Julfar (domestic services in Julfar). It is unlikely that registration is required if services are deemed to be imported, but the applicable law should be consulted to confirm this.

SC will be able to deduct all "Repa input VAT" paid in their tax return to the revenue service of Repa. SC will only be allowed to deduct "Julfar input VAT" paid in their tax return to the revenue service in Julfar if they are VAT registered in

---

[20] The VAT consequences discussed pertains to the triangular supply case where SC is a tax resident of Repa. It is assumed that the value of the supplies of any company exceeds the VAT registration threshold in any country.

Julfar. VAT paid in one jurisdiction, for instance, Julfar, cannot be deducted in another jurisdiction, for instance, Repa.[21]

Whether SC should charge "Julfar output VAT" on the supply to OC will depend on where the service is deemed to be supplied and consumed. If the service is deemed to be supplied from outside of Julfar and not consumed in Julfar – the EEZ is deemed to be outside the VAT jurisdiction of Julfar - "Julfar VAT" will not be applicable.

If the service is deemed to be supplied from outside Julfar, but consumed in Julfar, SC will not charge "Julfar or Repa output VAT," but the service will be an imported service. This means that OC will have to both pay "Julfar output VAT" and deduct this VAT paid in a future tax return, or ideally, Julfar applies the reverse-charge principle; so OC does not pay the VAT. It should be noted that the net VAT received by government is nil under both alternatives.

If the service is deemed to be supplied from within Julfar and consumed in Julfar, SC will likely have to register for VAT and charge "Julfar output VAT" on the supply of the service. If Julfar's legislation does not require VAT registration, then no VAT is charged on the supply of the service. SC will pay import VAT on all goods imported into Julfar and deduct this VAT in its next tax return (unless specific provisions apply that result in the imported goods not being charged with VAT).

The VAT implications for the other companies follow a similar argument to that of SC. If the place of supply of these companies' services is deemed to be within Julfar or Repa, they would likely have to register and charge "Julfar output VAT" or "Repa output VAT" on their supplies to SC. The place of supply and consumption of their services will determine whether their supplies are regarded as domestically supplied or imported services. For instance, the services by DSV will be charged with "Julfar output VAT" if the EEZ is deemed to be within Julfar. If the EEZ is deemed to be outside of Julfar, no "Julfar output VAT" or any other VAT will apply. No other VAT applies since the services are not imported into another jurisdiction.

Many jurisdictions have specific place of supply rules to assist in determining the VAT consequences of inter-jurisdictional transactions. The OECD also provides useful guidelines[22] where such rules do not exist. The VAT consequences for the transaction between SC and OC are illustrated below.

---

[21] It should be noted, however, that there are mechanisms to recover such VAT (EU, the Gulf countries) even if this is not always a simple process.

[22] https://www.oecd.org/ctp/international-vat-gst-guidelines-9789264271401-en.htm

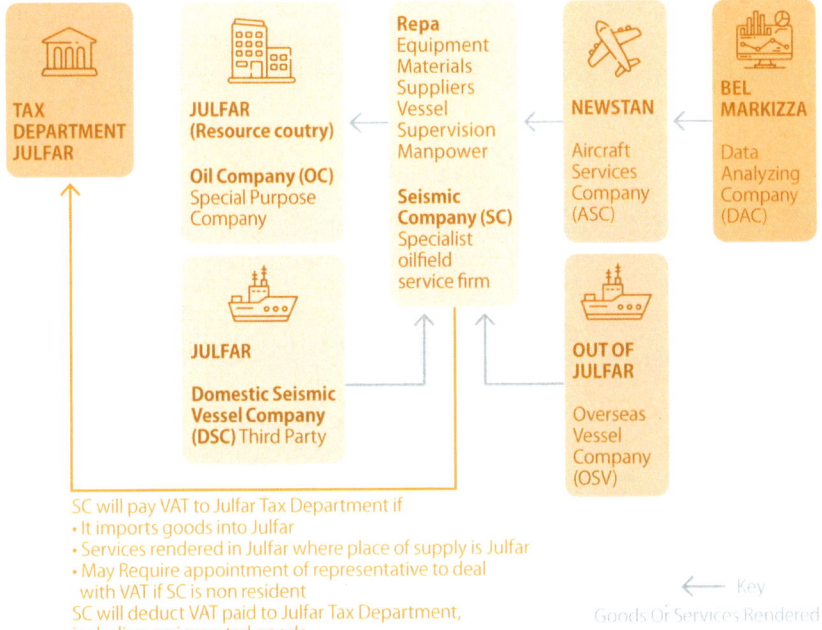

SC will pay VAT to Julfar Tax Department if
• It imports goods into Julfar
• Services rendered in Julfar where place of supply is Julfar
• May Require appointment of representative to deal
  with VAT if SC is non resident
SC will deduct VAT paid to Julfar Tax Department,
including on imported goods

← Key
Goods Or Services Rendered

8.9.2   Contract II - Single point coordinated contracts

Transaction details

The national oil company of Julfar (resource state), Julfar Oil Company (JOC) has a policy that limits the number of contracts that may be signed with any supplier. Only a single contract may be signed with suppliers on projects carried out in Block C (Nemr Basin) in Julfar. So as not to lose the single point of responsibility for a contract, JOC prefers to take a 'turnkey' position with its suppliers. Both onshore and offshore suppliers are required to enter into an overarching umbrella agreement with JOC ensuring the turnkey principle is judiciously followed.

JOC decides to contract with a third-party named Services Company (SC), a foreign entity resident in Repa, for work on Block C. SC should supply JOC with fishing equipment, and fishing[23] and side-tracking services and is responsible for all aspects of engineering, procurement, construction, installation, and com-

---

[23] Fishing services are used at the Exploration, Appraisal, Development and Production stages of the field lifecycle. Fishing in this sense refers to the act of retrieving fallen items (fish) from a well or a borehole. Fishing costs may account for 25% of the total drilling costs and are a necessary part of the drilling process as well as during the life of the well through to its abandonment. See further William Lyons and Gary Plisga, *Standard Handbook of Petroleum and Natural Gas Engineering* Elsevier, 2005

missioning. SC possesses all the necessary expertise to perform the services in accordance with current standards and practices of the industry, subject to the provisions in the contract.

SC is unable to supply the fishing equipment and with the consent of JOC contracts Domestic Product Sale Entity (DPSE), a third-party located in Julfar, to supply the equipment. To abide by the JOC single contract policy, a tri-partite agreement is signed between JOC, SC, and DPSE for the supply of the equipment. In order to ensure consistent service quality and delivery of services in line with JOC standards, the supply of goods and services is at the JOC site in Block C. The delivery requires all costs to be borne by the supplier (whether domestic or foreign) to the JOC warehouse and covers the entire value of products, applicable customs duty, port handling charges, inland transportation and insurance charges up to the delivery at the JOC warehouse ("in-country handling services").[24]

As the project progresses, JOC requires drilling equipment and contracts with SC for the supply of this equipment. SC contracts with Overseas Product Sales Entity (OPSE), a related party of SC located in Newstan, to supply the equipment. The terms are the same as the previous contract and the umbrella agreement is extended to include SC, DPSE, and OPSE.

Since OPSE does not have a PE in Julfar, it prefers to sell drilling tools from Newstan to JOC through a direct sales agreement. JOC requires the delivery of drilling tools to be made to its warehouse in line with product delivery conditions. In addition to supplying the tools, OPSE must carry out performance tests locally on the drilling equipment. These performance tests can only be undertaken by OPSE personnel in Julfar. The tests will not require the OPSE personnel to remain in Julfar for a cumulative period of more than a week every year. An initial question, therefore, is consideration of the PE issues on the additional supply of customized drilling equipment through the extension of the tri-partite agreement between OPSE and JOC, and impact of PE characterization for recurrent activities.

OPSE insists that the contractual terms allow that ownership of the equipment is passed to JOC prior to the equipment entering Julfar. This would be achieved by OPSE supplying the drilling tools to JOC using the Incoterm Delivered at Place Unloaded (previously called Delivery at Terminal or DAT)[25] and will qualify as an offshore sale of products under the current Julfar legislation. The relevant "in-country handling services" required by the delivery conditions will be performed by SC in Julfar.

---

[24] It should be noted as a general principle that the so called "Incoterms" just govern the split of costs from a commercial perspective. They can support the ownership transferred outside the country, but the mere reference to the Incoterms is not sufficient to establish where the sale happened. However, the reference is made only for the purposes of this particular example, and it is not meant to cover all scenarios. As a general principle, the risks and title transfer would be in the contract in addition to the Incoterms.

[25] https://www.incotermsexplained.com/the-incoterms-rules/the-eleven-rules-in-brief/delivered-at-place-unloaded/

The price covering the offshore supply of equipment itemizes two components: the sale price for the offshore supply of equipment and the "in-country handling services" rendered in Julfar. Included in the first component, the sales price for the offshore supply is the consideration for the performance testing services on the drilling equipment.

There is a tax treaty between Julfar and Repa, but no treaty between Julfar and Newstan.

Fishing equipment, and fishing and side-tracking services supplied

The supply of services is made by a tri-partite agreement between DPSE, SC, and JOC in Julfar. SC (a foreign-registered entity) through its registered PE in Julfar will pay all relevant taxes in terms of the domestic legislation of Julfar. This includes the supply of the fishing and side-tracking services and "in-country handling services."[26] The results are the same for DPSE through its registered PE in Julfar. [27]

Withholding tax on the additional supply of customized drilling equipment

The supply of such equipment is through the extension of the agreement between OPSE and JOC. Since the drilling tools are supplied from Newstan and there is no DTA between Newstan and Julfar, the domestic withholding tax provisions would apply. The tools are contractually an offshore sale (see further notes on PE below) so withholding tax should not be applied on payments from Julfar to OPSE in Newstan.

Permanent establishment considerations

The supply of goods and services by locally registered entities has been discussed under 8.9.2.2. However, where there is an additional supply of customized drilling equipment PE issues may arise when this is done through the extension of the tri-partite agreement between OPSE and JOC. For the offshore supply of drilling equipment by OPSE to JOC, the price components consist of the offshore supply of equipment, and "in-country handling services." The consequences are that the delivery and sale of the offshore equipment were made prior to the tools entering

---

[26] The status of SC as a foreign registered entity could also be considered; a tax treaty may apply, and the application of rules would need to take this into account. However, this is not analyzed further here. The focus of the example is on a Domestic Product Sale entity and the supply under this agreement in Julfar. This comes under the heading Contract II- Single Point Coordinated Contracts. The section is not intended to extend to all DPSE worldwide revenue streams and tax consequences.

[27] The tax implications around the supply of fishing equipment can be complex, including Customs (where such supply requires importation from outside the jurisdiction of the wells), withholding taxes (where the individual 'fishermen' being nationals of a different jurisdiction, and where the individual permanent residence tests do not apply, receive payment for their services and VAT (where the equipment in question is subject to VAT and not exempted).

Julfar. Subsequently, payment was made by JOC to OPSE, which is in Newstan. Furthermore, the contractual terms support the conclusion that the delivery of goods was outside Julfar. Consequently, the DAT portion of the transaction should not be taxable in Julfar as the supplier is a non-resident and there is no territorial nexus of this income in Julfar.

The income of which the source is Julfar will include the "in-country handling services" and the performance testing services carried out by OPSE personnel. The relevant "in-country handling services" required by the delivery conditions will be performed by SC in Julfar and will therefore be included. The price covering the offshore supply of equipment itemizes two components: the sale price for the offshore supply of equipment and the "in-country handling services" rendered in Julfar. Included in the first component, the sales price for the offshore supply is the consideration for the performance testing services on the drilling equipment. These services are performed in Julfar, and the tax treatment in alternative circumstances is discussed below:

- Regarding the "in-country handling services," these will be taxable in Julfar based on the profits sourced in Julfar. JOC and OPSE have contractually agreed to separate this portion of the services and assign it to SC. If there is an association drawn between OPSE and SC, the tax administrations could conclude that this part of the sale transaction has been concluded in Julfar and should be taxed in Julfar. In this case, the profits from the transaction must be attributed to SC on a reasonable basis. This can be a subjective attribution. An alternative would be for OPSE to contract with a third-party agent in Julfar to deliver the drilling tools to the JOC warehouse. The agent could be remunerated on a cost-plus basis and this portion of the supply will then be subject to tax in Julfar.

- Regarding the performance testing services, their consideration is not separately identified but included in the offshore sale price. A portion of the offshore sales price, therefore, has to be attributed to activities performed in Julfar and taxed in Julfar; see further 8.3.2. above.[28] The number of days that OPSE personnel visits Julfar would also have to be counted to determine whether a PE is created, based on the domestic legislation (no treaty applies). This will influence the portion of the supply liable to tax in Julfar.[29] The testing services could be taxed via corporate tax on Julfar's locally sourced revenue. Alternatively, the Julfar tax administration could withhold tax on any payments made locally.

---

[28] See discussion at 8.3.2. above regarding split contracts.

[29] The number of days of presence in the country plays a role on determining whether a PE is created or not, but the degree to which it influences the amount attributable to the PE has to be considered with other factors.

Transfer pricing considerations

Transfer pricing considerations can arise on the additional supply of customized drilling equipment through the extension of the tri-partite agreement between OPSE and JOC. The pricing of the "in-country handling services" is negotiated between SC/OPSE and a third party, JOCA. This is, therefore, an arm's length transaction and requires no further transfer pricing verification. However, if OPSE decides to use an affiliated third party agent to perform these services (to avoid the association of the offshore supply with SC), the cost-plus price that it pays the agent would require benchmarking. This benchmarking should be based on the profit margins of companies engaged in similar activities under similar circumstances.

8.9.3   Contract III - EPCM

8.9.3.1   Mining Company (MC), a subsidiary of a multinational mining company group, holds a mining licence in Julfar (the resource state). MC has approval to develop and operate an open cut mine and processing plant on the mining licence area. MC has engaged Engineering, Procurement and Construction Managers (EM), a specialist EPCM service provider resident in Repa, to design and project manage the construction of the mine and processing plant.

8.9.3.2   Under the EPCM contract, EM will perform the following services:

- Engineering designs for the open cut mine and processing plant, which will be prepared at MC's headquarters in Repa (services outside of Julfar);

- Project management of the end-to-end construction of the plant to be undertaken in Julfar (services in Julfar); and

- Procurement, on behalf of MC of all equipment for construction to be undertaken in Julfar (services in Julfar).

8.9.3.3   The project will take three years (one year of design and two years of construction) and during the construction phase, EM will establish a project management office (PMO) near the site. EM's overseas employees will be based at the site during this time. EM will also employ local personnel. Throughout the construction period, engineers from EM's overseas headquarters will make several short trips to the mine site in order to inspect the construction progress.

Summary of the potential tax consequences

8.9.3.4   A summary of the potential tax consequences is set out in the table below. In practice, the consequences will depend on the relevant domestic tax law and applicable DTA.

Activity of EM	Corporate Income Tax	WHT	VAT
Services in Julfar	There will be a PE in Julfar under Julfar's domestic law and if a treaty applies, it is likely Julfar would have the right to tax the profits of the PE – net profits subject to tax in Julfar.	If a treaty applies, there is no WHT since there is a local PE. If a treaty does not apply, there may be no WHT if PE is registered with the local tax administration. If not, WHT on gross income applies. This should be refunded against income tax paid on PE profits.	EM may be required to register for VAT in Julfar. VAT is charged on supplies and deducted on inputs in Julfar. VAT is refunded if required.
Services outside of Julfar	The net profits are only taxed in Repa.	If a treaty applies, there is likely to be WHT on gross income (e.g., for 'technical services') – possibly at a reduced rate from the domestic rate. If no treaty applies, there is likely to be a WHT on gross income	VAT applicable but subject to reverse charge mechanism (no net VAT collected).
Short term visits by EM's employees	The net profits are taxed in Julfar, irrespective of whether a treaty applies.	If a treaty applies, there is no WHT since there is a local PE and the visits are connected to this PE. If a treaty does not apply, there will be no WHT if PE is registered with the local tax administration. If not, WHT on gross income applies. This should be refunded against income tax paid on PE profits.	EM may be required to register for VAT in Julfar. VAT charged on supplies and deducted on inputs in Julfar. VAT refunded if required.

WHT issues – services in Julfar

8.9.3.5   If there is a tax treaty between Julfar and Repa, there will generally not be WHT for services in Julfar on the basis that EM has a PE in Julfar. It is not essential to apply withholding tax to services in Julfar provided by non-residents, as the PE rules require EM to pay tax on net profits; this is on the basis that some countries do not impose withholding tax on payments to PEs, in cases where the PE is registered with the local tax authority.

8.9.3.6   Developing countries will, however, often apply withholding tax to payments, due to the challenge of ensuring compliance by non-residents even where a PE exists. In these cases, the withholding tax would generally be creditable against tax payable on the net profit (and refundable if the withholding tax exceeded the tax on net profit). These challenges should be less for large EPCM service providers due to the extent of their presence in the country. Ensuring that the PE is registered, or that a local company is incorporated should also assist in ensuring compliance.

WHT issues – services outside of Julfar

8.9.3.7   The payment for engineering services undertaken outside of Julfar may be subject to withholding tax. If EM is not resident in a country that has a tax treaty with Julfar, then the domestic rate of withholding tax will apply. If EM is resident in a tax treaty country (residency will be determined by the treaty) and is entitled to benefit from the tax treaty, then the rate of withholding tax will depend on the relevant treaty. The ability to apply the treaty may also be subject to anti-treaty abuse rules in domestic law or in the treaty, for example, Art 29(9) of the UN Model. The withholding tax rates will depend on whether a treaty exists and withholding tax rates vary widely among treaties – some treaties reduce the rate to 5% or even nil. Tax administrations may implement compliance procedures to ensure that EM is entitled to apply the treaty – e.g., they may request EM to provide a certificate of tax residence from the Repa tax authority in order to allow application of the treaty rate of withholding tax.

8.9.3.8   Given the different withholding tax positions for services in Julfar and services outside of Julfar, MC and EM may enter into separate contracts for these services to effectively manage tax compliance and to appropriately split the fees. The tax administration in Julfar should consider how to review the allocation between these services. This would require sufficient expertise and experience in relation to assessing the activities undertaken.

Possible variation: a local subsidiary of EM established

8.9.3.9   In some cases, MC may request that EM establish a company that is tax resident in Julfar so that all payments are to a resident company and not subject to withholding tax. In this case, the risk of managing withholding tax is transferred to the local subsidiary of EM, which will be required to pay its parent headquarters for services outside of Julfar net of local withholding tax. All of the same issues as above arise. However, they are managed by the EM and its subsidiary.

8.9.3.10   Establishment of local resident companies, rather than operating through a PE may also be administratively simpler for the tax administration. It may reduce the complexity of attributing a share of EM's 'profit' to the local PE. The charges between the local subsidiary of EM and MC's headquarters will, however, be subject to transfer pricing rules. If a local resident company is established, its profits would ultimately be returned as dividends to Repa and may also be subject to withholding tax.

PE issues – services in Julfar

8.9.3.11   EM may have a PE in Julfar based on their activities as a construction site, a fixed place of business, or an office. This would be determined in terms of the domestic law of Julfar. Under Article 5(2)(a) of the UN Model a PE specifically includes an office, and Article 5(2)(b) includes a place of management. Article 5(3) specifically includes a "building site, or construction or installation project or supervisory activities in connection herewith, but only if such site, project or activities lasts more than 6 months." EPCM will, therefore, have a PE and be required to pay income tax on profits attributable to its services in Julfar.

8.9.3.12   If a PE arises and there is a relevant treaty, the profits of the PE should not be subject to tax in Repa. If a treaty does not apply, double taxation should be relieved assuming that Repa's domestic tax law has a foreign branch exemption regime, or provides credit for foreign tax payable. Relief from double taxation is an important consideration for an EPCM contractor.

PE issues – services outside of Julfar

8.9.3.13   Profits from engineering services performed outside of Julfar will not be subject to a profits-based tax in Julfar. Rather, those profits will be taxed in Repa. EM and MC may, therefore, establish separate contracts for services outside of Julfar and services in Julfar. This will simplify their tax compliance obligations. Separate contracts will ensure appropriate splitting of contract prices between these services where withholding tax and VAT outcomes may vary. If EM established a local subsidiary in Julfar, the profits of the local subsidiary would be subject to tax in Julfar.

Short-term visits by EM's employees

8.9.3.14   Short-term visits by EM's employees would generally be treated as connected to the local PE and profit from this activity should be included in the PE's net profit. If short-term visits were occurring in isolation of the construction project, a PE will generally not be created unless the time spent in Julfar exceeded a specified threshold. However, assuming that EM is not resident in Julfar, and if these services are compensated from the Julfar source, there could be withholding tax on such services.

VAT issues – services in Julfar

8.9.3.15   Due to the extensive activities in Julfar, EM will be required to register for VAT purposes in Julfar (assuming the registration threshold is exceeded). If registration is delayed, MC should be allowed to input VAT deductions for expenses incurred prior to registration that included "Julfar VAT." Delaying registration will increase the extent of VAT refunds payable to EM upon registration. It is, therefore, important that registration is not unnecessarily delayed. When the refunds arise, this should be paid promptly, or be offset against other tax liabilities.

8.9.3.16   EM will, subsequent to registration, charge "Julfar output VAT" on its supplies to MC. MC will be entitled to an input VAT deduction of the amount of VAT paid to MC. Refunds will arise if MC is unable to offset all "Julfar input VAT" against "Julfar output VAT." Not paying these refunds promptly may result in a large disincentive in using subcontractors in the extractive sector; resource companies may rather perform the services themselves, avoiding the VAT paid to subcontractors and not (promptly) refunded by revenue services (called vertical integration). Vertical integration may lead to efficiency losses in the sector, and resource companies not using the services of local contractors, weakening the economy. Even where vertical integration does not take place, the VAT refund practice of the resource state will be factored into investment decisions. Not paying VAT refunds promptly may result in investors disregarding an investment opportunity in a specific resource state.

VAT issues – services outside of Julfar

8.9.3.17   The place of supply of the offshore engineering services is in Repa. The place of consumption of these services is, however, in Julfar. These services will, therefore, constitute exported services in Repa and imported services in Julfar. EM will deduct "Repa input VAT" for the exported services that will be zero-rated in Repa. MC will apply the reverse charge principle (if available) in Repa, meaning no VAT becomes payable on the imported service. It is, however, important that the imported services be indicated as a separate supply on the invoice from EM to MC. Not doing so may unnecessarily complicate the VAT treatment of the engineering services.

8.9.4   The impact of the WHT rate on the cost of offshore subcontractor services

8.9.4.1   The technical expertise required on complex, large scale projects may necessarily be obtained from outside the resource state and developing country tax administrations will have legitimate concerns in relation to ensuring appropriate tax compliance, especially withholding tax compliance on fees for technical services. As noted above the rates of withholding tax on technical services vary widely and the precise level of withholding tax on fees for tax on technical services should take into account a number of factors including from a tax authority perspective that withholding tax on gross amounts of income is administratively easy to handle, and the effect that the reduction of the withholding tax rates has on revenue. It has been argued from the investor's perspective that high withholding tax rates may increase the cost of engaging sub-contractors, and therefore increase the cost of investment, as illustrated below:

For illustrative purposes, it is assumed that a subcontractor typically earns a 15% gross profit margin; for every $100 of income the subcontractor has $85 expenses and generates a $15 profit. Further, we assume that the profit tax rate is 25%. The impact of the chosen WHT rate on offshore services is illustrated below.

	WHT of 0%	WHT of 5%	WHT of 20% (no gross up)	WHT of 20% ($20 gross up)
Gross income	$100	$100	$100	$120
Costs	$85	$85	$85	$85
Net pre-tax profit (a)	$15	$15	$15	$35
Profit tax in residence country @ 25% (b)	$3.75	$3.75	$3.75	$8.75
WHT in resource state (c)	0	$5	$20	$24
Foreign tax credit (limited to profit tax) (d)	0	$3.75	$3.75	$8.75
Total tax in residence country (b) – (d) = (e)	$3.75	$0.00	$0.00	$0.00
Total tax (c) + (e) = (f)	$3.75	$5.00	$20.00	$24.00
After tax profit (a) – (f)	**$11.25**	**$10.00**	**($5.00)**	**$11.00**
Effective tax rate (f)/(a)	25%	33.3%	133.3%	68.6%

8.9.4.2   The example demonstrates that a high rate of withholding tax can result in a high effective tax rate that may result in a subcontractor making an after-tax loss. The subcontractor may attempt to shift the cost of this loss onto the domestic recipient of the supply. The overall cost of investment can, therefore, be significantly increased by high rates of withholding taxes.

8.10   Other tax issues relevant to subcontractors

8.10.1   A range of additional issues arise in dealing with the international tax treatment of subcontractors in the extractive sector. Given the complexity of these issues, and the possible tax treatment of these matters subject to the issue of further guidance that is being developed at the global level, these are summarized below for reference purposes only.

Risk assessment and emerging challenges	Tax treatment of transactions by and with subcontractors will be affected by growing use of intangibles, such as proprietary technologies by such businesses, and by complications from fragmentation of physical operations and business functions in the digitalized economy. This will possibly modify current business models away from fees from services to more risk-based models. The reduced need for physical presence for the provision of services, and increasing divergence on characterisation of transactions as fees for technical services by some countries are likely to increase complexity in determining agreed tax treatment. Issues such as the attribution of services by non-residents to PEs of group companies, splitting of services between related parties, and connected and associated services attributed to different companies are possible areas of continuing challenges. Developing countries may wish to consider developing a risk assessment format to understand possible risks to revenue from these current and emerging challenges and determine a cost-effective approach for tax policy and administration in this regard.

Treatment of service companies within incentive regimes for the extractives sector	The grant of incentives for the extractive sector is covered in Chapter 5 of this Handbook. Many of these issues apply equally to subcontractors. Where developing countries determine that it is appropriate to grant incentives to the extractive sector, the approach to subcontractors needs to be addressed. Some key issues in this regard are: • Application of incentives, if any to subcontractors; • The need to state the scope of any incentives – e.g., where a project is granted specific exemptions or relaxations, such as customs duty exemptions on imported equipment, it is important to also provide for the limitation of use, disposal of used equipment, etc.; and • For the mining sector, project area limitations for incentives are an important consideration to prevent abuse.
Contractor treatment in Production Sharing Contracts	There may be provisions affecting subcontractor tax in PSCs and in some cases a specific rate of withholding tax on the subcontractor or specific treatment for VAT, especially temporary admission goods, may be set out in the agreement. However, some PSC regimes are not clear on whether the subcontractor is covered under the general tax regime or under the specific PSC tax regime. The appropriate tax treatment of subcontractors should be considered in the design and drafting of PSCs, as they affect both the tax take of the resource state at the exploration and development stage, but also affect cost recovery over the life of the project. Challenges in rules regarding the taxation of subcontractors can also translate into high development costs which may affect investment decisions.
Role of NOCs in "tax paid" PSC structures	Certain PSCs have a "tax paid" clause where the NOC undertakes responsibility for the resource state domestic corporate income tax/VAT and other applicable taxes of the resource company. This is typically then recognized in the commercial terms between the resource company and the NOC/other authority of the resource state. However, withholding tax application to subcontractors, and responsibility for payment of such taxes, can cause administrative challenges and distort returns for the resource state.
Application of fiscal stability clauses to subcontractors	Fiscal stability clauses are quite common in extractive sector contracts; see the Fiscal Take chapter (Chapter 2). The position of subcontractors in such clauses, especially in application of withholding tax could raise challenges in the future, especially where subcontractors are involved in the production stage with their compensation tied in whole or part to the profitability of the project.
Services delivered in special economic zones or special areas	Resource companies may be entitled to specific tax treatment in a Special Economic Zone or in special exploration areas with particular characteristics. However, these measures rarely address the treatment of subcontractors; in so doing, these measures may not achieve the goals of drawing investment into that area.

Chapter 9

Tax Treatment of Financial Transactions in the Extractives Industry

9.1   INTRODUCTION

9.1.1   Executive summary

9.1.1.1.   Natural resources play a key social, economic and political role in 81 countries which, globally, account for a quarter of GDP and half of the population. Africa alone accounts for about 30% of the world's mineral reserves, 10% of oil and 8% of natural gas.[1] Financial transactions are an important component of the business in the extractive industries as funding requirements and financial risks are significant.

9.1.1.2.   This chapter elaborates on different financial transactions relevant to the extractives sector and provides guidance on tax issues. The chapter also covers joint venture arrangements which are common in the industry, and farm-in and farm-out arrangements which can be used to fund early- stage project expenditures such as exploration. There are a lot of crosscutting issues between financial transactions in extractive industries and transfer pricing as financial transactions may involve related parties. This chapter will focus on the tax treatment of financial transactions that are not discussed in the United Nations Practical Manual on Transfer Pricing.

9.1.1.3   The transfer pricing considerations related to the intra-group financial transactions along the value chain are not addressed in Chapter 9 of the Manual. In addition, because of the importance of intra-group financing in the extractive industries, beyond the market price compliance issues, thin-capitalisation and financial expenses may constitute a risk of tax base erosion for local jurisdictions. Chapter 9 of the UN Transfer Pricing Handbook does not deal with these issues.

9.1.1.4.   Considering the importance of this issue for the extractive industries in developing countries, and in view of the difficulties encountered in applying the arm's length principle to financial transactions, particularly with regard to the comparability analysis, this chapter elaborates on the thin capitalization rule in the extractive industries, reviews current debate on interest limitation issues

---

[1] https://www.worldbank.org/en/topic/extractiveindustries/overview

and provides concrete application examples in developing countries. Useful guidance is also provided in the United Nations Practical Portfolio, *Protecting the Tax Base of Developing Countries against Base-eroding Payments: Interest and Other Financing Expenses.*

9.1.1.5   This chapter addresses five important topics concerning financial transactions: financing mechanisms, hedging instruments, financial and performance guarantees and farm-in/farm-out agreements.

9.2   MAIN RISKS AND FINANCING MECHANISMS IN THE EXTRACTIVE INDUSTRIES

9.2.1   Overview

9.2.1.1   In view of the capital intensive nature of extractive projects and their exposure to varying degrees of risk depending on the stage of development, investors typically require different sources of financing over the life of the project. This chapter takes into consideration the typical features of extractive industry financing, including the large scale of projects, with long-term time periods and subject to high uncertainty at their inception, and numerous risks of various types. Some of these risks are described below.

9.2.1.2   Some of the risks faced by the extractive industries are common to all types of industry, for example, market risk triggered by a disrupting factor such as geopolitical tension or a pandemic event, which could generate global recessionary conditions and lead to an economic downturn. Others, however, are inherent to the sector and deserve special attention.

9.2.2   Geopolitical risk

9.2.2.1   Geopolitical risk is the risk an investment could suffer as a result of political changes or instability in a country. It involves political revolutions, coups, elections, ethnic conflicts, disputes in the national or international policy arena, property rights, the route of pipelines, navigation, etc.

9.2.2.2   Extractive industry activities are sometimes carried out in countries that present or may present scenarios of social, political or economic instability that could lead to situations such as the increase of taxes and royalties, the establishment of production limits and volumes for exports, mandatory renegotiation or annulment of contracts, regulation of product prices, and (in rare circumstances) nationalization, expropriation or confiscation of assets, loss of licences, changes in government policies, changes in commercial customs and practices or delayed payments.

9.2.3   Commodity price risks

9.2.3.1   Fluctuations in benchmark prices of natural resources are probably one of the main risks faced by companies involved in the extractive industry. Commodity prices are subject to exogenous factors (geopolitical environment, influence by international players or relevant countries, technological changes or natural disasters) and therefore to volatility, as a consequence of fluctuations in international supply and demand.

9.2.4   Interest rate risks

9.2.4.1   The rate of interest on financial transactions is determined by market rates and the creditworthiness of the borrower. Where such transactions include a reference rate (e.g., Euribor[2] or borrowing costs), the interest rate risk refers to the chance that such borrowings will become more expensive as a result of unexpected interest rate changes. This risk is common to all industries however the risk can be important for long life projects which are carried out in the extractives industry. The extractive company's policy will determine whether there is a preference for exposure to floating rates, fixed rates or a combination of both.

9.2.4.2   Companies may seek to manage interest rate risk by hedging their debt with interest rate swaps and other instruments.

9.2.5   Currency risks

9.2.5.1   Currency risk, commonly referred to as exchange-rate risk, arises from the change in price of one currency in relation to another. Investors or companies that have assets or liabilities denominated in foreign currency or business operations across national borders are exposed to currency risk that may create unpredictable profits, losses and cash flows. The extractive industry operates with the United States dollar in international markets, this being the currency normally used in trading.

9.2.5.2   Currency risk and the resulting volatility can be managed by hedging.

9.2.6   Geological risks

9.2.6.1   The extractives sector is exposed to geological risk, which includes the risk of not discovering a resource through exploration. However, it is not enough to find hydrocarbons or mineral resources, but the discovery should be economically profitable during the expected life term of the project. Significant investment is required to determine whether a resource can be viably extracted and sold in the market. Geological risk also exists throughout the construction and operation phases of extractive projects. For example, when the permeability of a hydrocarbon deposit is overestimated, the ore is more variable than expected or ground conditions are less favourable than estimated.

9.2.6.2   Unlike other types of risks, uncertainty from geological risks cannot

---

[2] Euribor, the Euro Interbank Offer Rate, is a reference rate representing the average interest rate offered by eurozone banks for unsecured short-term lending in the inter-bank market.

be minimized through hedging or other derivatives, but by sharing or minimizing such geological risks through joint-ventures or exchanging an interest in the project in consideration for work performed (farm-in and farm-out agreements).

9.2.7   Safety and operational risks

9.2.7.1   For completeness, it is noted that safety and operational risk is another very material risk in the extractives sector. To some degree the financial impacts of operational risk are managed by extractive companies through an insurance company which may be part of the corporate group (a 'captive' insurer). Essentially this is a form of self-insurance of relatively small events that happen often.

9.2.7.2   It is more challenging to fully mitigate the financial risks related to a once off catastrophic event resulting from major operational failures such as, for a mining operation: tailings and water storage, underground event or geotechnical event resulting in multiple fatalities, operations cessation and significant financial impact. This chapter does not cover this topic further.

9.3   EXTRACTIVE INDUSTRIES VALUE CHAIN AND FINANCING DECISIONS

9.3.1   Value chain

9.3.1.1   This section presents the peculiarities of the value chain of the oil and gas and mining industries. The activities in the oil and gas industry are grouped into three main segments: upstream, midstream and downstream.

9.3.1.2   Upstream encompasses exploration, development and production, and decommissioning. In the upstream sector, oil can be either unconventional or conventional depending on the method of extraction, although there is no consensus on what methods or processes are unconventional. Unconventional sources may become conventional over time, as the unconventional technologies become better understood and more widely adopted.

9.3.1.3   The midstream sector is composed of assets and services that provide a link between the supply side and demand side of the value chain, and include the activities of storage and transportation of oil, natural gas and processed products, from production sites to refineries via pipelines, trains, tankers, and trucks.

9.3.1.4   Downstream comprises refining and marketing refined petroleum products. In the downstream sector, refineries convert crude oil into a variety of products that are consumed by residential and commercial users, industrial users, and electric utilities. Petroleum products, like crude oil, are traded globally.

9.3.1.5   All segments of the value chain are capital intensive. Some companies specialize in just one component of the value chain, while others, called integrated companies, participate in all of them.

9.3.1.6   Mining industry structure has similarities with hydrocarbon structure. The main activities in the mining process can be classified into extractive related, which involves exploration, development and mining; processing related, which encompass processing or beneficiation, smelting and refining and other added value activities; and transport and storage.

9.3.1.7   In the mining industry different value chain stages are undertaken depending on the type of mineral product sold. The figure below displays the typical stages in the mining value-adding chain from initial exploration to marketing of refined metals on terminal markets.

Figure 9.F.1: Mining life cycle and financing requirements

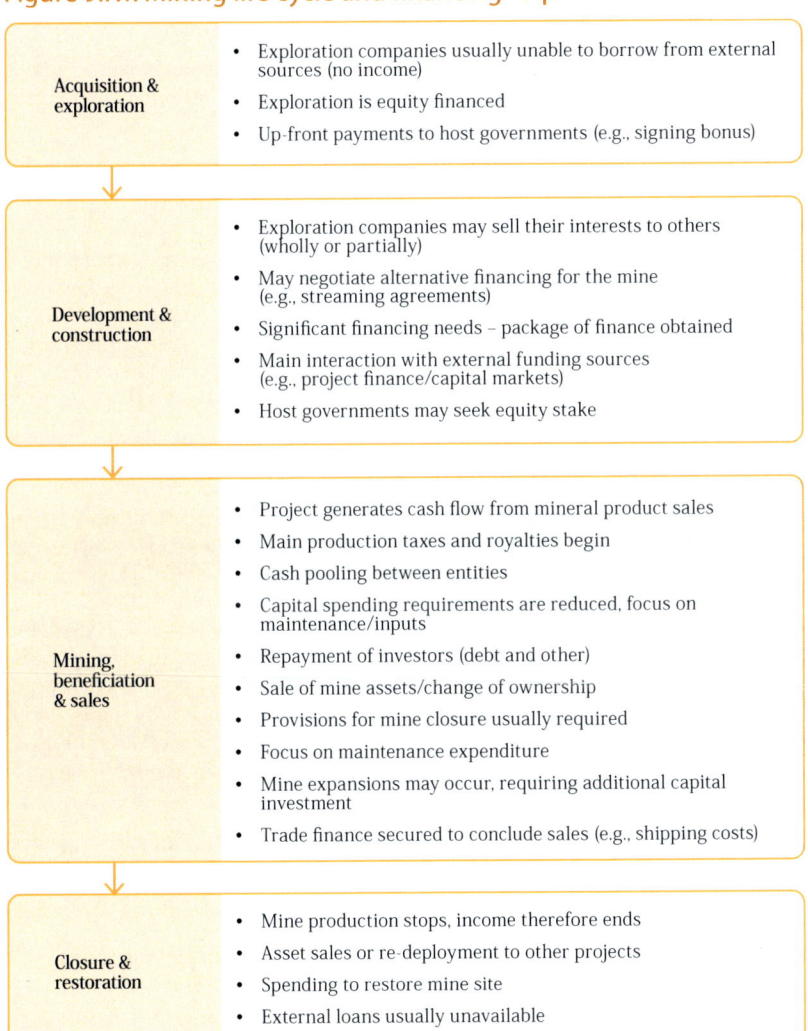

Acquisition & exploration
- Exploration companies usually unable to borrow from external sources (no income)
- Exploration is equity financed
- Up-front payments to host governments (e.g., signing bonus)

Development & construction
- Exploration companies may sell their interests to others (wholly or partially)
- May negotiate alternative financing for the mine (e.g., streaming agreements)
- Significant financing needs – package of finance obtained
- Main interaction with external funding sources (e.g., project finance/capital markets)
- Host governments may seek equity stake

Mining, beneficiation & sales
- Project generates cash flow from mineral product sales
- Main production taxes and royalties begin
- Cash pooling between entities
- Capital spending requirements are reduced, focus on maintenance/inputs
- Repayment of investors (debt and other)
- Sale of mine assets/change of ownership
- Provisions for mine closure usually required
- Focus on maintenance expenditure
- Mine expansions may occur, requiring additional capital investment
- Trade finance secured to conclude sales (e.g., shipping costs)

Closure & restoration
- Mine production stops, income therefore ends
- Asset sales or re-deployment to other projects
- Spending to restore mine site
- External loans usually unavailable

Source: IGF and OECD (2018).

9.3.1.8   Financing needs and instruments in the extractive industries will vary at each stage of the value chain.

9.3.2   Financing decision and the value chain

9.3.2.1   The financing decision in the extractive industries broadly follows the same reasoning as in other industries. In the course of doing business, companies seek funding from two sources: equity and debt. However, in extractive industries, the financing needs, and therefore the type of financial instruments, depend on the business requirements along the value chain. During development and production, companies will generally use a combination of debt and equity.

9.3.3   Financing at the exploration stage of a project

9.3.3.1   The exploration phase of an extractive industry project is characterized by its capital intensity, high risk, and uncertainty involved in finding a commercial discovery of natural resources.

9.3.3.2   In general, during the exploration phase, companies are unable to borrow to fund exploration due to the high risk during this phase. Financing of exploration is therefore mainly through equity. For stand-alone exploration companies without other producing operations, equity issuance would more clearly be the first or only option as these companies generally have low debt capacity due to a lack of proven reserves and cash flow. Companies and MNE groups with other operating projects and cash flow may be able to raise additional debt to fund exploration. However, in general, MNE groups use equity or equity like instruments to fund subsidiaries undertaking exploration.

9.3.4   Financing at the development and production stages

9.3.4.1   The evaluation and appraisal phase involves confirming and evaluating the presence and extent of reserves shown by the works (i.e., testing and exploratory drilling) performed during the exploration stage. The information provided from testing and exploratory drilling as well as other geological and available information allows the company to move forward with development. In addition to information obtained from exploration drilling, extensive work is required to determine the viability of the extractive project and this is covered by a feasibility study covering, for example, technical extraction methods, early design works, assessing infrastructure requirements such as access to utilities, pipelines, roads, rail and ports, processing methods, and impacts on the environment and local communities.

9.3.4.2   Where the existence of proven resources (considered commercially producible) starts to become clearer or, more evidently, construction or production begins, companies may seek external funding, including structuring finance.

9.3.4.3   In the extractive industries, host government partners in extractive projects are common and this is a key factor influencing the choice of financing arrangements. For example, when equity funding is provided it may dilute the interest of Government shareholders, which do not contribute to their share of funding, in which case debt may be the preferred method of funding.

9.4   TRADITIONAL SOURCES OF FUNDING

9.4.1   Overview

9.4.1.1   The extractive industry business traditionally has been financed directly from the partners in a joint venture by equity in the more risky stages of the project. However, more complex financing schemes can be developed depending on financing needs, certainty of future cash flows, company size, and risks.

9.4.1.2   Traditional sources of financing include a wide range of financial instruments: debt, equity, joint venture agreements, project finance, flow-through shares (FTS), etc.

9.4.2   Debt financing

9.4.2.1   When companies raise capital by issuing debt, they have several potential sources from which to seek funds. Types of corporate debt issued by companies include: bank debt, notes, debentures, mortgage bonds, and asset-backed bonds. Bank debt is the most common instrument, especially for small and medium sized businesses. It is often secured by company assets or other types of collateral that may be required by the bank.

9.4.2.2   Debentures and notes are unsecured debt, which means that in the event of a bankruptcy, bondholders have a claim to only the assets of the firm that are not already pledged as collateral on other debt. Typically, notes have shorter maturities (less than 10 years) than debentures. Asset-backed bonds and mortgage bonds are secured debt: specific assets are pledged as collateral that bondholders have a direct claim to in the event of bankruptcy. Mortgage bonds are secured by real property, whereas asset-backed bonds can be secured by any kind of asset.

9.4.3   Equity financing

9.4.3.1   Equity financing generally involves the issue of shares in a company and giving a portion of the ownership of the company to investors in exchange for cash. In the case of extractive industries, particularly mining and oil and gas given the high level of risk during the exploration stage, the financial capital is obtained primarily by way of equity and the return to investors may be by way of a capital gain should the project be disposed of, or through future dividends if exploration leads to a profitable mining operation.

9.4.3.2   The principal advantage of equity financing is that it carries no repayment obligation and provides extra working capital that can be used to grow a business. Since equity financing is a greater risk to the investor than debt financing is to the lender, the cost of equity is often higher than the cost of debt.

9.4.4   Joint venture agreements

9.4.4.1   Normally, single companies may not wish to assume full exposure to an investment where there are no proven reserves. To gain access to larger, high-value projects that they could not access alone, companies enter into joint ventures with other companies as a mechanism to access resources and share the risks that exist at different stages of the life cycle of the project. Some joint ventures do not involve creation of a separate entity (i.e., they are 'unincorporated joint ventures'). In other cases, companies may opt to set up a separate legal entity such as a jointly owned company (incorporated joint ventures).

9.4.4.2   Under an unincorporated joint venture each participant holds an undivided interest in the project, as well as a direct interest in the assets and production from the project in proportion to its specified working interest. Where more than one working interest owner exists, normally a joint operating agreement contractually establishes how the project will be operated and how the costs will be shared.

9.4.4.3   Under an incorporated joint venture the project and assets and productions are held by a company, with each participant holding shares in the company proportionate to its interest. In this case, shareholder agreements, establish how the project is operated and how costs are shared. Where a host country government holds a partial equity stake in a project, this is the typical structure i.e., the host country government (or government-owned entity) is a shareholder in the company which owns the extractive project.

9.4.4.4   The typical joint venture in the extractive industry is where one of the participants manages and runs the entire operation (operator), with the others contributing only funding and, potentially, input on strategic-level decisions. The joint venture agreement or shareholder agreement requires all participants to pay their share of expenses upon a cash call by the operator. In some cases, the operator or a related party to the operator receives a management fee for providing management services in relation to the project.

9.4.4.5   For unincorporated joint ventures, financing of the project is made through cash-calls or advances, which are requests for payment sent by the operator to non-operating partners for anticipated future capital and operating expenditures. Under this approach, the operator first estimates how much cash will be required for the operations during a certain period of time, normally a month, and then makes the cash-call to the rest of the non-operator partners. Since it is based on estimations, it is unlikely that the cash-calls equal the actual cash expenditure. Once the actual cost has been determined, the operator issues a billing stating the correct amount. The difference, over or under, is generally adjusted in the next cash-call.

9.4.4.6   An alternative approach for the operator to collect cash would be to directly use a billing and payment approach, where the operator uses its own funds throughout a period, normally on a monthly basis, to pay suppliers and sub-contractors, and afterwards sends the non-operators a billing statement requesting them to pay their proportionate share of the billing.

9.4.4.7   All these forms of funding are made through transitory accounts in the balance sheet of the operator and no interest is derived from debt financing. In the petroleum industry, goods or services charged into the joint venture by the operator are generally required under industry practice to be at cost (no mark-up) and subject to audit by the co-venturers.

9.4.4.8   For incorporated joint ventures, a similar process is followed, however 'cash calls' are generally provided by shareholders by way of equity contributions in relation to existing shares, or by shareholder loans.

9.4.4.9   Funding some specific projects under an unincorporated joint-venture regime where a National Oil Company (NOC) is a party can however be quite challenging when it fails to meet its cash call equity obligations upon demand. In Nigeria, the cash call gaps between the national oil company and its joint-venture partners were funded initially through Alternative Funding Agreements (AFA) or Carry Agreements (CA) model and were subsequently improved upon as Modified Carry Agreements (MCA).

9.4.4.10   Example of Modified Carry Arrangement (MCA) in Nigeria, upon full recovery by the Carry Party.

A Modified Carry Agreement is a financing agreement whereby the International Oil Companies (IOCs) in a Joint Venture will advance a loan to the Nigerian National Petroleum Corporation (NNPC) for the purpose of investing in upstream projects. The MCA introduces a greater level of transparency and accountability with repayment and compensation being on a cash basis, not oil. The NNPC lifts and markets the Carry Oil and Share Oil, due to the Carrying party, and pays cash to the operator for the cash financing provided. The Carrying party recovers the Carry Capital Cost (CCC) in Dollars. An Escrow Account is opened, and the sale proceeds with respect to the Carry oil and Share oil are paid into the Escrow Account. NNPC's Portion of the Agreed Capital Cost approved by the Joint venture partners is financed by the JV Operator through monthly cash call payments into a dedicated account for the project.

The NNPC would allow the other JV partners to take capital allowances as allowed by the Petroleum Profit Tax (PPT) to recover 85 per cent of the principal loan. By taking the allowance, the IOCs are reducing their taxable profit. The remaining 15 per cent plus eight per cent interest would be paid in cash from the increased production from which the investment was made. If for any reason, the oil field where the invest-ment was made could not produce, then payment of the 15 per cent plus the eight per cent interest would be stopped.

9.4.5   Project finance

9.4.5.1   Project financing involves the financing of projects based on the projected cash flows of a particular project rather than the balance sheet or cash flows of its owners.   For large scale mining projects in developing countries, project finance can be used as a risk- sharing tool for investors.

9.4.5.2   Project finance is generally issued on a 'limited' or 'non-recourse basis', as in the event of default lenders only have recourse to the specific project assets and cash flow rather than other assets of investors. This may mitigate financial risk for project owners, including host governments which may hold an equity stake in the project. During the construction phase, a guarantee may be required from one of the investors but once construction is finished and the project generates cash flow, the guarantee will generally be removed. It is common for project finance to be provided by a consortium of lenders including institutions such as the World Bank.

9.4.5.3   For oil and gas, project financing is more prevalent in the downstream sector than in the more capital-intensive and high-risk upstream sector. The fact that the latter is long-term in nature implies that future revenue streams are less stable and less predictable than in other large-scale projects that are not exposed to, amongst others, commodity price risk. In some cases project finance lenders may require borrowers to undertake foreign exchange or commodity price hedging to remove volatility and ensure there are sufficient cash flows to service project finance debt.

9.4.6   Flow-through shares

9.4.6.1   A flow-through share (FTS) is a tax-based financing incentive that is available to, among others, the mining sector. An FTS is a type of share issued by a corporation to a taxpayer, pursuant to an agreement with the corporation under which the issuing corporation agrees to incur eligible exploration expenses in an amount up to the consideration paid by the taxpayer for the shares.

9.4.6.2   The corporation "renounces" to the taxpayer an amount in respect of the expenditure so that the exploration and development expenses are considered to be the taxpayer's expenses for tax purposes. As a result of the corporation renouncing the expenses, the shareholder can deduct the expenses as if incurred directly.

9.4.6.3   An example of a flow through share in Canada is provided below:

Flow-through share (FTS) in Canada

In Canada, the FTS regime allows public companies to issue a unique type of equity that allows individual and corporate investors to deduct the purchase cost from their personal income for tax purposes, provided that the company issuing the shares spends the funds on prescribed exploration and development expenses for Canadian projects.

According to the Canada Revenue Agency (CRA): "Certain corporations in the mining, oil and gas, and renewable energy and energy conservation sectors may issue FTSs to help finance their exploration and project development activities. The FTSs must be newly issued shares that have the attributes generally attached to common shares. Junior resource corporations often have difficulty raising capital to finance their exploration and development activities. Moreover, many are in a non-taxable position and cannot deduct expenditures against taxable income which they do not yet generate in that phase. The FTS mechanism allows the issuer corporation to transfer the resource expenses to the investor. A junior resource corporation, in particular, benefits greatly from FTS financing. The FTS program provides tax incentives to investors who acquire FTSs by allowing:

> Deductions for resource expenses renounced by eligible corporations; and

> Investment tax credits for individuals (excluding trusts) on resource expenses in the mining sector that qualify as flow-through mining expenditures.

9.4.6.4   In addition to traditional instruments, some promoters of extractive projects are increasingly resorting to sector-specific innovative financing and hybrid instruments which combine the characteristics of equity and debt.

9.5   ALTERNATIVE SOURCES OF FUNDING

9.5.1   Overview

9.5.1.1   In a context where access to traditional financing is becoming complicated, mining companies are increasingly turning to alternative financing and creative deal structures for growth and funding. These have included hybrid instruments and streaming agreements.

9.5.2   Hybrid financial instruments

9.5.2.1   **Hybrid financing** instruments are sources of finance which possess characteristics of both equity and debt. Some well-known hybrid financing instruments are preference shares, convertible bonds, warrants and options.

9.5.2.2   **Preference shares** are special types of share capital having fixed rates of dividend and carrying preferential rights over ordinary equity shares in sharing of profits and also claims over assets of the firm. They are ranked between equity and debt as far as priority of repayment of capital is concerned. Similarly to debt that carries a fixed interest rate, preference shares have fixed dividends attached to them. But the obligation of paying a dividend is not as rigid as in the case of paying interest on debt. Non-payment of a dividend would not amount to bankruptcy in the case of preference shares.

9.5.2.3   A **convertible bond** is a bond that gives the holder the option to convert or exchange it for a predetermined number of shares in the issuing company. Because convertibles can be changed into stock and, thus, benefit from a rise in the price of the underlying stock, companies offer lower yields on convertibles. If the stock performs poorly, there is no conversion and an investor is stuck with the bond's sub-par return—below what a non-convertible corporate bond would get. As always, there is a trade-off between risk and return.

9.5.2.4   Companies issue convertible bonds for two main reasons. The first is to lower the coupon rate on debt. Investors will generally accept a lower coupon rate on a convertible bond, compared with the coupon rate on a regular bond, because of its conversion feature. This enables the issuer to save on interest expenses, which can be substantial in the case of a large bond issue. The second reason is to delay dilution. Raising capital through issuing convertible bonds rather than equity allows the issuer to delay dilution of the interests of its equity holders. A company may be in a situation wherein it prefers to issue a debt security in the medium-term—partly since interest expense is tax-deductible—but is comfortable with dilution of shareholder interests over the longer term because it expects its profits and share price to grow substantially over this time frame.

9.5.3   Streaming agreements

9.5.3.1   Streaming arrangements can vary in their precise form. Typically they are contracts for ongoing supply of mineral production under which, upon advance payment of a premium, the buyer agrees to purchase, at a fixed, discounted and predetermined price, all or part of the mineral production to be extracted by a mining company during a certain period or even throughout the life of the mine.

9.5.3.2   This arrangement provides the funding necessary for a mining company to develop, construct and operate or expand the mine. This arrangement also allows the mining company to capitalize on the basis of proven but still unexplored mineral reserves as an alternative to loans or more equity. Streaming arrangements are typically entered into by extractive companies which are not able to access liquidity *via* conventional debt markets.

9.5.3.3   Contrary to capital investment financing, streaming arrangements enable mining companies to minimize the risk of dilution of the interests of shareholders and avoid debt financing costs, particularly at times when credit access conditions are unfavourable. Streaming transactions may also benefit the purchaser in a scenario of increasing commodity prices, as it will be able to freeze the price of a mineral whose price tends to increase, and resell such product at market price.

9.5.3.4   Streaming transactions involve certain risks. One of them is the possibility of the production being none or insufficient, preventing the seller from delivering the mineral as agreed. Purchasers reduce their exposure by demanding guarantees traditionally offered to financial agents in financing transactions. Another risk is market volatility, as price fluctuations may affect the profit margins originally envisaged by the purchaser and ultimately render production and, consequently, streaming itself, impossible.

9.5.4   Asset-backed finance

9.5.4.1   Asset-backed finance is a method of providing companies with working capital and term loans that use accounts receivable, inventory, machinery, equipment, or real estate as collateral. It is essentially any loan to a company that is secured by the company's assets.

9.5.4.2   Asset-backed finance lenders tend to prefer liquid collateral that can be easily turned into cash if a default on the loan occurs. Physical assets, like machinery, property, or even inventory, may be less desirable for lenders. When it comes to providing an asset-backed loan, lenders prefer companies with not only high quality assets but also well-balanced accounts.

9.5.4.3   For less liquid assets, companies are moving towards securitization mechanisms. Securitizations involve a credit-enhancing financial structure in which an owner of cash flow-producing assets pools some of those assets and transfers them to a newly-formed, special purpose entity, or SPE. The SPE then issues notes in a private placement or public offering. The notes are secured by the SPE's assets, but are non-recourse to the sponsor. The proceeds received by the SPE from the notes' issuance are then transferred to its parent sponsor company in exchange for the transferred assets.

9.5.4.4   In the extractive industries, mineral interests, non-operating and operating working interests, royalty interests, overriding royalty interests and volumetric production payments can be transferred to an SPE and can serve as the source of funds to service the notes issued by the SPE. Transfer pricing issues may arise, since these transactions are often carried out as intra-group transactions.

9.6 TAX ISSUES FOR FINANCING INSTRUMENTS

9.6.1 Equity tax issues

9.6.1.1   Returns on equity are generally in the form of dividends. The tax treatment of dividends depends on specific tax rules in the paying jurisdiction and the recipient's jurisdiction. Most tax regimes would not provide tax deductions for dividends paid, and shareholders would typically be corporate entities located in offshore jurisdictions where dividends are unlikely to be subject to tax due to an exemption regime. In other words, there could be symmetry of tax treatment for the payer and the recipient in that dividends paid are not deductible, and dividends received are not assessable.

9.6.1.2   Dividends may be subject to withholding tax in the paying jurisdiction depending on domestic law and the applicable tax treaty. Other shareholders may be the host country government which would typically invest through a domestic corporation (in which case the normal tax rules for distribution of dividends between domestic corporations would apply).

9.6.2 Debt financing tax issues

9.6.2.1   Debt financing comes from bank loans, intragroup borrowings or the issuance of securities such as bonds or treasury bills issued to private investors. The advantages of debt financing are numerous. The lender has no control over the company, and therefore debt financing avoids capital dilution. This is particularly relevant in joint ventures where there may be a partner (including host country governments) that is unable to contribute to its share of funding or participate in additional equity rights issues. In this case, debt is likely to be preferred over equity otherwise the partner's interest would be diluted. Finally, it is easy for the company to forecast expenses because loan repayments are generally non-contingent obligations, and do not fluctuate, unlike dividends which are generally discretionary. This allows the company to retain any additional profits due to the fixed nature of the repayment.

9.6.2.2   Finally, interest on debt is generally tax deductible and therefore reduces the borrower's cost of funding, compared with equity. Interest will typically be subject to tax for the recipient (unless a specific exemption regime exists), however, as lenders for developing country projects are typically non-resident, debt financing has an impact on the tax base for developing countries through the deductibility of interest expenses[3] if the recipient is not taxed in the same country. This impact can be more severe if the level of debt is excessive compared to the level of equity or if interest rates on intra-group loans are not in accordance with transfer pricing regulations. However, it is noted that it is quite common for large mining projects to be in a tax loss position in the early stages of their life

---

[3] This is generally the case under general corporate income tax rules but e.g., in production sharing agreements, deductions for interest is often excluded. Reference is made to Chapter 4 on Production Sharing Agreements.

cycle, due to the larger up-front capital investments involved. Where the use of loss carry forward is restricted, then the tax advantage from interest deductions may be lost in which case tax base erosion may not arise.

9.6.2.3   Interest payments will typically be subject to withholding tax depending on domestic law, the relevant tax treaty and the nature of the lender. However, in the commercial context of the extractive sector, the choice of financing, and therefore interest deductibility, depends on the location in the value chain.

9.6.2.4   As mentioned above, during the exploration phase, equity is dominant and debt financing is rarely available as a financing choice for non-revenue generating exploration activities. Indeed many production sharing contracts (PSC) or the domestic law expressly determine that interest payments from loans are a non-recoverable or non-deductible expense when related to the extractive industry.

9.6.2.5   As an example of interest deductibility in Indonesia under production sharing contracts, the following is specifically provided at Article 13 of the government regulation of the Republic of Indonesia number 27 of 2017.

"Categories of non-recoverable operating costs in production sharing and income tax calculation comprise:

- (...) Costs for interest on loans;"

9.6.2.6   If exploration is successful, significant amounts of up-front capital are required for the construction of the mine, the production platform or construction of wells. Capital continues to be required during the productive life of a mine to maintain operating capacity and to fund possible expansion. For new projects, the process of raising equity through the stock market is complex and expensive and initiators of a project try to avoid excessive dilution of their ownership in the project by relying on additional equity. Mature extractive companies finance projects *via* internally generated funding and/or a mixture of short term commercial paper programs and medium to long term debt.

9.6.2.7   Companies in developing countries may face difficulties in mobilizing debt directly from third parties. As a result, multinational companies set up treasury centres, or internal banks, centralizing capital raising and liquidity mobilization at the MNE group level. Centralized financial management is a necessary instrument to meet the significant financing needs in the extractive sector. It is therefore common for developing country projects to be funded by equity and debt from related parties. The provision of debt from related parties, including centralized financial centres, may give rise to profit shifting and transfer mispricing issues in developing countries. Firstly, a high level of intra-group debt can lead to thin capitalization, consequently, a high amount of interest is paid to affiliated companies, reducing the taxable profit of a local mining company.

9.6.2.8   Secondly, the significant size of financing for a mining business means that even minor mispricing of related party debt can have a material impact on taxable profits. Thirdly, hybrid financial instruments (convertible bonds, redeemable preference shares, subordinated loans) can create tax arbitrage opportunities by taking advantage of mismatches in tax treatment between the tax systems prevailing in different countries. The hybrid nature of certain financial instruments makes it difficult to distinguish between what constitutes debt and what constitutes equity, and therefore complicates the task of the tax authorities to firstly appropriately characterize the instrument to determine the appropriate tax treatment, and secondly, if it is determined to be debt, to establish the arm's length interest rate. Finally, although hybrid arrangements such as mandatory redeemable preference shares are rare in capital markets, the relative complexity of hybrid instruments and their associated risks would normally be associated with a higher charge, which makes it relatively easy to manipulate the related spread to shift profits.[4]

9.6.3   Interest expenses limitation

9.6.3.1   Where interest rates and debt are in line with market practices, and within the limits prescribed by each country's own legislation, interest charges are tax deductible. However, as noted above, the deduction of interest may create the possibility of profit shifting, while the different taxation systems (due to different tax rates or different tax base definitions among countries) create the incentive to use a debt tax planning strategy. Debt tax planning as defined by the OECD (2016) includes:

- Groups placing high levels of third-party debt in high tax countries;

- Groups using intra-group loans to generate interest deductions in excess of the group's actual third-party interest expense; and

- Groups using third-party or intra-group financing to fund the generation of tax-exempt income.

9.6.3.2   To cope with these risks of profit shifting using debt, the international institutions and tax authorities favour rules limiting interest deductions and thin-capitalization. In this framework, the approach recommended by OECD (BEPS Action 4) can be described as follows: the deduction of interest and payments economically equivalent to interest is limited to 10-30% of the entity's/group's taxable earnings before interest, taxes, depreciation and amortization (EBITDA).

9.6.3.3   Following BEPS Action 4, *"the best practice approach is based around a fixed ratio rule which limits an entity's net interest deductions to a fixed percentage of its profit, measured using EBITDA based on tax numbers. This is a*

---

[4] Several anti-hybrid mechanisms have been introduced to limit abuse: in the US and Australia, anti-hybrid legislation will deny deductions for interest where there is a payment, and the recipient is not subject to tax. EU Anti-Hybrid Legislation (ATAD 2) rules and OECD Pillar 2 discussed below address profit shifting.

straightforward rule to apply and ensures that an entity's interest deductions are directly linked to its economic activity. It also directly links these deductions to an entity's taxable income, which makes the rule reasonably robust against planning" (BEPS Action 4, para 23).

9.6.3.4   The limitation of the deductibility should include all deductible net financing costs. This includes intra group interest as well as third party interest, to ensure the total level of debt is within the acceptable limits.

9.6.3.5   At the European Union level, the Anti-Tax Avoidance Directive (ATAD) obliges the EU Member States to introduce an EBITDA rule. Following ATAD (article 4) *"exceeding borrowing costs shall be deductible in the tax period in which they are incurred only up to 30 percent of the taxpayer's earnings before interest, tax, depreciation and amortisation (EBITDA)."* EBITDA is calculated by adding back to the income subject to corporate tax in the EU Member State of the taxpayer the tax-adjusted amounts for exceeding borrowing costs as well as the tax-adjusted amounts for depreciation and amortisation. Tax exempt income is to be excluded from the EBITDA of a taxpayer.

9.6.3.6   ATAD 2[5] introduces new rules addressing hybrid mismatches (article 9):

1) **To the extent that a hybrid mismatch results in a double deduction: (a) the deduction shall be denied in the Member State that is the investor jurisdiction; and (b) where the deduction is not denied in the investor jurisdiction, the deduction shall be denied in the Member State that is the payer jurisdiction.**

2) **To the extent that a hybrid mismatch results in a deduction without inclusion: (a) the deduction shall be denied in the Member State that is the payer jurisdiction; and (b) where the deduction is not denied in the payer jurisdiction, the amount of the payment that would otherwise give rise to a mismatch outcome shall be included in income in the Member State that is the payee jurisdiction.**

9.6.3.7   In a number of developing countries, the following measures are used to address thin-capitalization:

- Capitalization rules setting a limit on the ratio of debt to equity;

- Interest capping rules that limit the amount of interest that can be deducted by an entity for tax purposes in any one year as a proportion of their gross income or EBIT; and

- Group-wide rules that allocate interest expense as a function of the subsidiaries' individual contributions to the MNE's consolidated revenue or earnings.

---

[5] COUNCIL DIRECTIVE (EU) 2017/952 of 29 May 2017 amending Directive (EU) 2016/1164 as regards hybrid mismatches involving third countries.

9.6.3.8   In **Rwanda,**[6] the interest paid on loans and advances from related entities is not tax deductible to the extent that the total amount of loans/advances exceeds four times the amount of equity during the tax period. This provision does not apply to commercial banks, financial institutions, and insurance companies.

9.6.3.9   In **Senegal,**[7] the deduction of interest by local companies is limited by Senegalese tax legislation. This limitation is attached to the rate and the amount:

- RATE

  > The rate of interest paid to shareholders, partners or other persons with whom the company has a non-arm's length relationship, on the basis of the amounts they directly leave or make available, or through intermediaries, to the company in addition to their share of capital, whatever the form of the company, cannot exceed the rate for advances of the issuing institution (BCEAO) plus three points.

- AMOUNT

  > Interest paid to legal persons is not allowed as a deduction in the case of:

- Remunerated amounts made available that exceed one-and-a-half times the share capital; and

  > If, at the same time, it exceeds 15% of profit from ordinary activities plus interest, depreciation and provisions.

9.6.3.10   Interest is only deductible if the capital is fully paid up. Also, the deduction of interest paid to persons is limited to the interest on the sums made available by those persons that do not exceed one and a half times the amount of the share capital; this limitation does not apply to interest paid by companies not subject to corporation tax to their associates who are subject to a tax on income in Senegal because of this interest.

9.6.3.11   The total amount of deductible net interest owed annually on all debts incurred by an enterprise that is a member of a group of companies does not exceed 15% of ordinary activity income plus interest, and depreciation and provisions allowable. But this limitation does not apply if the company provides evidence that the net interest expense ratio of the group of companies is greater than or equal to its own net interest charge ratio.

9.6.3.12   Certain adjustments are made in relation to the limitation of interest paid or owed by financial institutions or by insurance companies covered by the CIMA[8] code and companies that are members of a group of companies composed

---

[6] EY, Worldwide Corporate Tax Guide, 2019

[7] Chambers and Partners: Doing Business In.. 2020 - Senegal | Global Practice Guides | Chambers and Partners

[8] Conférence interafricaine des marchés d'assurance (CIMA)

solely of those resident in Senegal.

9.6.3.13   In **Gabon,**[9] thin capitalisation rules have been introduced by the Finance Act, 2018. A company is deemed thinly capitalised when the amount of interest paid on inter-company loans exceeds, simultaneously, the three following limits during the same fiscal year: (i) the product of interest payments on inter-company loans x ((1.5 x equity)/loans granted to group affiliates); (ii) interest received by the company from affiliates; (iii) 25% of the profit before tax + interest paid + depreciation taken into consideration to be deducted from the tax profit + share of the rents of leasing taken into account for determining the transfer price of the property at the end of the contract. When the company paying the interest is deemed to be thinly capitalised, only a portion of that interest may be deductible from the taxable result.

9.6.3.14   In **Brazil,**[10] under thin-capitalization rules, interest expense arising from a financial arrangement with a related party is deductible only if the related Brazilian borrower does not exceed a debt-to-net equity ratio of 2:1. In addition, interest expense arising from a financing arrangement executed with a party established in a low-tax jurisdiction (LTJ) or benefiting from a privileged tax regime (PTR) is deductible only if the Brazilian borrower does not have a debt-to-net equity ratio of greater than 0.3:1.

9.6.3.15   In **Mongolia**, from 1 January 2020, interest deductions for related party interest are limited to 30% of EBITDA.

9.6.3.16   In **Vietnam,** a new decree effective from 1 May 2017 introduces interest restrictions based on a fixed-ratio rule limiting tax relief for a company's total interest costs to 20% of its EBITDA.

9.6.4   Tax issues of streaming arrangements

9.6.4.1   Tax outcomes are fact specific and can depend on the terms of the arrangement as well as the accounting treatment of the arrangement. Tax issues include:

- Tax treatment of the up-front payment as well as tax treatment of the ongoing payments and receipts from the counter-party. For example, revenue may be recognised over the term of the arrangement as the product is delivered, or taxed up-front upon receipt of cash, or it may be treated as a financial arrangement, akin to a loan (with no tax up-front, but interest payments may be deductible and subject to WHT).

- Whether the streaming arrangement (any interest component) attracts WHT, and whether it is treated as debt for the purposes of interest restriction/thin capitalization rules. If it is considered to be a financing arrangement that has an interest component, whether interest is deductible may be relevant – some countries do not give tax

---

[9] Code Général des Impôts, Art.11-II-2-a.(LF2018).

[10] EY, Worldwide Corporate Tax Guide, 2019

deductions for 'conditional' interest payments.

- If the arrangement is with a related party, transfer pricing would be relevant.

Streaming arrangements tax issues: Chilean case

Under Chilean law, a non-resident Buyer will not be levied with taxes for deliveries of metal, whereas the resident Operator will be levied with general income taxes upon receipt of the consideration or purchase price. However, considering that the Operator may be required to repay the uncredited amount of the upfront payment under certain circumstances, such initial upfront payment may be structured as a security or as a payment subject to a condition so that the corresponding taxes are only accrued and paid once the streamed metal is delivered and actually credited against the received funds. Also, if the deposit's repayment obligation bears interest, the interest is subject to a withholding tax at a rate of 35 per cent of the amount paid.

Conversely, purchase of streamed metal by a local Buyer from a non-resident Operator is also subject to a withholding tax at a rate of 35 per cent of the amount paid.

Finally, if both parties are residents, payments made under the streaming agreement are subject to general income taxes as well as value added tax at a rate of 19 per cent of the amount paid.

9.7   HEDGING INSTRUMENTS IN EXTRACTIVE INDUSTRIES

9.7.1   Introduction

9.7.1.1   A company's business may be affected by different types of business and financial risk that can have a significant impact on its profits and cash flows. These risks arise as a consequence of volatility in exchange rates, interest rates and commodity prices. Many risks are common across industries. However, more than in other sectors, the extractive industries are more exposed to some of these risks. For example, a large proportion of the transactions in the extractive sector are exposed to foreign currency risks – the importation of equipment, the export of extractive material and operational costs can all be in different currencies. Many extractive operations are carried out in developing countries and due to the narrowness of local financial markets, exposure to interest rate risk on international markets through debt funding can be more pronounced and subsequently affect profitability. Finally, mineral products, oil, gas and other extracted natural resources can be subject to price volatility, which again has the potential for a material impact on profitability.

9.7.1.2   Hedging is a form of insurance to reduce the risk of adverse price movements in an asset or product. Hedging is used by parties who seek to manage existing risks by entering into a derivative transaction which reduces their risk or exposure to a potential future event. It attempts to eliminate the volatility associated with the price of an asset or product by taking offsetting positions contrary to what the investor currently has. Used effectively, hedging is a good strategy for securing profits in an uncertain world, particularly protecting earnings against currency fluctuations arising from timing differences between costs and revenues. A true hedging pattern will mean that derivatives are generally bought more when a price curve is approaching a top or in a falling price trend than in rising price trends, thus achieving the goal that the hedging is specific to each underlying transaction.

9.7.1.3   In a hedging transaction a mining company enters into the futures or options market taking an opposite position to the position they have outside the futures or options market (for example, a contract to sell commodities at a particular price). A hedge results in a gain or loss in the futures or options market, offsetting the gain or loss in the physical commodity. Thus, this type of futures or options strategy is entered into for the purpose of price insurance (hedging).

9.7.1.4   In contrast to hedging to manage risk as described above, companies may also use derivatives for speculative purposes. The main purpose of speculation is to profit from betting on the direction in which the price of an asset will be moving. Speculators trade based on their analysis of where they believe the market is headed. For example, if a speculator believes that a commodity is overpriced, they may short sell the respective commodity futures and wait for the price to decline, at which point the speculator will buy the commodity at a lower price for delivery and realise a profit. Unlike ordinary hedging transactions, there may be no opposite position outside of the futures market (for example, no underlying commodity sale agreement that matches the hedge).

9.7.1.5   Speculators are exposed to both the downside and upside of the market; therefore, speculation can be extremely risky. In a hedging pattern where there is a component of speculation, the derivative buyer will try to lock in as low a cost or as high a revenue as possible, limiting the removal of the upside potential as much as possible. A speculative strategy consists of entering into futures or options market transactions with the motive of making money on the rise or fall of the market price.

9.7.1.6   Many countries have specific tax rules that apply to derivatives. For example, Zambia ring-fences hedging income from business income, thereby removing any incentive for companies to engage in abusive hedging.[11] Some countries have specific rules that deal separately with speculative hedging (e.g.,

---

[11] https://taxsummaries.pwc.com/zambia/corporate/income-determination

the United States). Certain gains and losses from speculative hedging are treated as capital gains and losses, whereas gains and losses from hedging that is undertaken for the purpose of risk management are taxable or deductible as ordinary income or expenses.

9.7.1.7   The analysis of hedging via derivatives is technically complex and this can further complicate a tax administration's analysis of the actual conditions of the transaction, as the counterparties may not be known, and this type of transaction may trigger events that may be within the control of the MNE. In addition, hedging transactions with related parties that are not matched by an external hedge by the MNE may constitute aggressive tax planning.[12] Following Pietro Guj and al[13] "where the risk has not in fact been transferred out of the MNE, it is problematic as to whether a charge for its transfer should stand and be deductible."

9.7.1.8   As with other types of services provided by a MNE through a low tax jurisdiction, there is a need to closely examine and verify that the arrangements are at arm's length, that is to say, that the terms and conditions are such that an independent party would have entered into the arrangement. As with captive insurance arrangements, the risk needs sufficient nexus to the mining activities to be a real rather than a theoretical risk. The host country tax administration should also verify that the services allegedly provided are for a real activity that is not duplicated.

9.7.1.9   For the management of the risk associated with extractive operations, independent companies analyze the most appropriate strategy for hedging. The extent to which extractive companies undertake speculative hedging will be governed by an entity's policy and risk appetite.

9.7.2   Diversification

9.7.2.1   Another way in which risk can be managed to some extent is through diversification. Diversification, that is investing in a variety of unrelated businesses, often in different locations, can be an effective way of reducing a firm's dependence on the performance of a particular industry or project. In theory, it is possible to "diversify away" all the risks of a particular project. In business practice, companies differentiate between company-specific risks that are diversifiable, such as the bankruptcy of a customer, and risks that concern the market as a whole that are not diversifiable. Financial theory holds that investors should not be remunerated for diversifiable risks, only non-diversifiable risks, also called market risks, are remunerated. In practice, however, diversification could be expensive or fail because of the complexity of managing diverse businesses. In any case, companies mainly use hedging instruments for non-diversifiable risks.

---

[12] OECD (2013) Aggressive Tax Planning Based on After-Tax Hedging https://www.oecd.org/tax/aggressive/after_tax_hedging_report.pdf

[13] Pietro Guj, Stephanie Martin, Bryan Maybee, Frederick Cawood, Boubacar Bocoum, Nishana Gosai and Steef Huibregtse: Transfer Pricing in Mining with a Focus on Africa. A Reference Guide for Practitioners. N° 1036.

9.7.2.2   For an independent company, given the sometimes high cost of hedging, it is a cost-benefit analysis that should determine whether or not to use hedging instruments. For group members of a MNE, however, there may be a group hedging strategy that involves, for group members, the use of instruments to hedge risks which, for an independent company, could be mitigated by diversification. In these circumstances, this practice could be considered as not at arm's length and subject to a thorough transfer pricing analysis. For more details on this aspect, reference is made to the UN Transfer Pricing Manual.

9.7.2.3   For most multinational groups, including extractive industries, there are different approaches in terms of how the strategy and policy in relation to the acceptable level of exposures to risks, and the approach to hedging them. In some cases, the policy is driven by a centralized treasury function which would assess the required external derivatives depending on the group's overall position and policy objectives. This policy is then applied to subsidiary operations in various jurisdictions. However, in practice policies of multinational groups will be different.

9.7.3   Derivative instruments

General

9.7.3.1   Derivatives are financial instruments (contracts) that do not represent ownership rights in any asset but, rather, derive their value from the value of some other underlying commodity or other asset. Usually, the underlying variables are the prices of traded assets: stocks, equity indices (S&P500, Nikkei225, CAC40), bonds (government, corporate), commodities (gold, platinum, oil) or interest rates (Libor, Eonia[14]). When used prudently, derivatives are efficient and effective tools for isolating financial risk and "hedging" to reduce exposure to risk.

9.7.3.2   Derivative contracts transfer risk, especially price risk, to those who are able and willing to bear it. Derivatives can be traded on organized markets, or alternatively agreed upon, between two counterparties ("over-the-counter" or "OTC" transactions).

Exchange traded derivative

9.7.3.3   An exchange traded derivative (ETD) is a standardized financial instrument that is traded on an organized exchange market. When traded on an organized market, a derivative has a market observable price. When dealing in exchange traded financial instruments the terminology is standardized and the clearinghouse guarantees that the other side of any transaction performs its obligations. That is, it assumes all contingent default risk so both sides do not need to know about each other's credit quality. Since the contracts are standardized, accurate pricing models are often available.

---

[14] Eonia is a reference rate based on the weighted average of unsecured overnight interbank lending in the EU and the European Free Trade Association (EFTA).

9.7.3.4   Standardization makes it easy for the investor to determine how many contracts can be bought or sold. Each individual contract is also of a size that is not daunting for the small investor.

9.7.3.5   Exchange traded derivatives can be used to hedge exposure or speculate on a wide range of assets like commodities, equities, currencies, and even interest rates.

Over the counter (OTC) derivatives

9.7.3.6   An over the counter (OTC) derivative is a financial instrument traded off an exchange, the price of which is directly dependent upon the value of one or more underlying securities, equity indices, debt instruments, commodities or any agreed upon pricing index or arrangement. If the derivative is an OTC derivative, its value can be calculated using a model, but the price is not observable on a market.

9.7.3.7   OTC markets are less transparent and operate with fewer rules than exchanges. All of the securities and derivatives involved in the financial turmoil that began with a 2007 breakdown in the U.S. mortgage market were traded in OTC markets. This market still accounts for the bulk of derivatives trade today. The notional value of outstanding OTC derivatives increased from $532 trillion at end-2017 to $595 trillion at end-June 2018 (BIS, 2018).

9.7.3.8   In the extractive industries, given the variety of operators' needs and profiles, OTC derivatives dominate the market. The most common strategies include foreign exchange risk hedging, interest rate swaps and commodity price risk.

9.7.4   Foreign exchange risk hedging

9.7.4.1   Movements in foreign exchange rates can result in gains and losses. Exposure to this volatility generally arises when a company enters into transactions that are in a different currency from their accounting or tax currencies (often referred to as 'functional currency'). Many resource groups' accounting functional currency is US dollars, given that commodity sales transactions are in US dollars. However, local operations of multinational groups may be required to adopt local currency for accounting and tax purposes, depending on specific accounting and tax rules, as well as company policy. Many countries allow resource companies to calculate taxable profits in US dollars rather than local currency. Accounting standards set accounting rules.

9.7.4.2   Company policy and risk management strategy will inform acceptable exchange rate risk and determine which risks should be actively managed through hedging.

9.7.4.3   Foreign exchange risk (FX risk) hedging is a method used by companies to eliminate or "hedge" their foreign exchange risk resulting from transactions in foreign currencies. An FX risk hedge transfers the foreign exchange risk from the trading or investing company to a business that carries the risk, such as a bank. There is cost to the company for setting up a hedge. By setting up a hedge, the company also forgoes any profit if the movement in the exchange rate would be favourable to it.

9.7.4.4   Companies in extractive industries are involved in international trade and are more exposed to FX risk due to the nature of their business. FX risk makes the economic planning process for businesses difficult and financial outcomes uncertain. These companies are mainly exporters. They pay for goods in the local currency while their revenue is denominated in a foreign currency. The appreciation of the local currency means receiving less revenue in local currency for an exporter that sells products abroad and conversely, increased revenue in local currency, if the national currency depreciates.

9.7.4.5   Importers pay for imported goods in a foreign currency and generally generate revenue in the domestic currency. Unlike exporters, the depreciation of the local currency is unfavourable for importers as they will have to pay more local currency to suppliers for the same amount in a foreign currency. If the national currency appreciates, an importer will have to pay fewer amounts in local currency.

9.7.4.6   FX volatility can also arise for debt funding arrangements: either with third parties or between related parties, e.g., where the currency of the debt is in a different currency from the currency of the lender's or borrower's country.

9.7.4.7   FX risk makes financial outcomes uncertain for exporters and importers as they cannot incorporate this risk in their price setting process and this also makes the business planning process difficult.

9.7.4.8   FX hedging is a way to reduce the FX risk. FX hedging enables importers and exporters to:

- Project cash flows in different currencies;

- Determine the prices that were foreseen in business plans;

- Maintain operational stability.

9.7.4.9   One of the hedging instruments used by companies in extractive industries to mitigate FX risk is the currency forward contract. A currency forward contract is a binding contract in the foreign exchange market that locks in the exchange rate for the purchase or sale of a currency on a future date.

Example - Foreign Exchange (FX) Hedging

Assume a Belgian export company (BelCo) is selling USD 1 million worth of goods to a U.S. company and expects to receive the export proceeds a year from now. BelCo is concerned that the Euro may have strengthened from its current rate of USD1 = €1.09 (1€ = USD 0.91) a year from now, which means that it would receive fewer Euros per US dollar. BelCo, therefore, enters into a forward contract to sell USD 1 million a year from now at the forward rate of USD 1 = €0.90 (€1 = USD 1.11).

If a year later the spot rate is USD 1 = €0.87 (€1 = USD 1.15)—which means that the Euro has strengthened as the exporter had anticipated – by locking in the forward rate, the exporter has benefited to the tune of €30,000 (by selling the USD 1 million at €0.90, rather than at the spot rate of €0.87). BelCo has received €870,000 for the sale of goods in addition to the gain from the forward contract of €30,000. On a net basis they receive a total of €900,000.

On the other hand, if the spot rate a year later is €0.92 (i.e., Euro weakened contrary to the exporter's expectations), BelCo will receive €920,000 for the sale of goods and will have a loss from the forward contract of €20,000. As above, on a net basis BelCo receives a total of €900,000.

In both cases, the effect of the forward contract hedge is that BelCo has ensured that it receives €900,000 by locking in the exchange rate of USD 1 = €0.90.

Without undertaking the hedge, BelCo would have been exposed to unpredictable exchange rate volatility. Had the currency weakened the company will have received only €870,000. Had the currency appreciated the company would have received €920,000.

The sale of goods will be taxable and the exchange gain or loss on the forward contract will be taxable or deductible, so on a net basis, BelCo would be appropriately taxed on the net receipt of €900,000.

9.7.5   Interest rate swaps (IRS)

9.7.5.1   The interest rate risk refers to the exposure to movements in interest rates. Debt such as bonds can be issued at either fixed or floating interest rates. For resource companies, treasury policy and risk management strategy will determine whether there is a preference for exposure to fixed interest rates, floating rates, or some combination of the two. For resource companies, this interest rate risk can be managed by using interest rate swaps which can swap fixed interest rates for floating rates, or vice versa. A typical example would be where a resource company has issued fixed rate bonds in order to raise finance from third party investors, and the company chooses to swap the exposure to fixed rate so that it is instead exposed to a floating interest rate. The resource company will enter into an interest rate swap with another third party (typically a bank) or a centralized treasury company capable of undertaking hedging activities.

9.7.5.2   An interest rate swap (IRS) is an agreement between two counterparties to exchange interest rate cash flows at specified intervals. Interest rate swaps usually involve the exchange of a fixed interest rate payment based on a particular notional amount for a floating rate payment on that same notional amount, or vice versa. If a counterparty holds a "payer swap," it pays a fixed rate and receives a floating rate from the other counterparty. The counterparty that pays a floating rate and receives a fixed rate is said to hold a "receiver swap."

9.7.5.3   At the time of the signing of an IRS agreement, the present value of the swap's expected fixed rate flows will be equal to the present value of the expected floating rate payments. As interest rates change, so will the value of the swap. IRS are typically quoted in terms of fixed rate, or alternatively the "swap spread," which is the difference between the fixed rate of the swap and the equivalent local government bond yield for the same maturity. The floating rate index is commonly an interbank offered rate (IBOR) of a specific tenor in the appropriate currency of the IRS. Normally, the parties do not swap payments directly, but rather each sets up a separate swap with a bank. In return for matching the two parties together, the bank takes a spread from the swap payments (example 0.30% overall, or 0.15% from each party).

Example 1 – Interest Rate Swap Contract

In 2018, companies A and B made an interest rate swap agreement with a nominal value of USD 100,000. Company A believes that interest rates are likely to rise over the next couple of years and aims to obtain exposure to potentially profit from a floating interest rate return that would increase if interest rates rise. Company B is currently receiving a floating interest rate return, but is more pessimistic about the outlook for interest rates, believing they will fall over the next two years, which would reduce their interest rate return. Company B is motivated by a desire to secure risk protection against possible declining rates, in the form of getting a fixed rate return locked in for the period.

The two companies enter into a two-year interest rate swap contract with the specified nominal value of USD 100,000. Company A offers Company B a fixed rate of 5% in exchange for receiving a floating rate of the LIBOR rate plus 1%. The current LIBOR rate at the beginning of the interest rate swap agreement is 4%. Therefore, to start out, the two companies are on equal ground, with both receiving 5%: Company A has the 5% fixed rate, and Company B is receiving the LIBOR rate of 4% plus 1% = 5%.

Now assume that interest rates do rise, with the LIBOR rate having increased to 5.25% by the end of the first year of the interest rate swap agreement. Also, assume that the swap agreement states that interest payments will be made annually, and that the floating rate for Company B will be calculated using the prevailing LIBOR rate at the time that interest payments are due.

Company A owes Company B the fixed rate return of USD 5,000 (5% of USD 100,000). However, since interest rates have risen, as indicated by the benchmark LIBOR rate having increased to 5.25%, Company B owes Company A USD 6,250 (5.25% plus 1% = 6.25% of USD 100,000). To avoid the trouble and expense of both parties paying the full amount due to each other, the swap agreement terms state that only the net difference in payments is to be paid to the appropriate party. In this instance, Company A would receive USD 1,250 from Company B. Company A has benefited from accepting the additional risk inherent with accepting a floating interest rate return. Company B has suffered a loss of USD 1,250, but has achieved protection against a possible interest rate decline.

What if at the end of the first year of their agreement, the LIBOR rate had fallen to 3.75%? With its fixed rate return, Company B would still be owed USD 5,000 by Company A. However, Company B would only owe Company A USD 4,750 (3.75% plus 1% = 4.75%; 4.75% of USD 100,000 = USD 4.750). This would be resolved by Company A paying USD 250 to Company B (USD 5,000 minus USD 4,750 = USD 250). In this scenario, Company A has incurred a small loss and Company B has benefited.

Example 2 – Mining Company IRS Arrangements

In this example, Mining Company raises debt in the external bond market with a fixed coupon and seeks to manage the exposure with an interest rate swap to convert the economic exposure to floating rates.

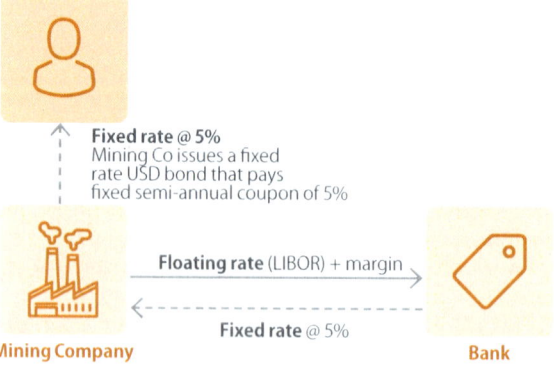

Bondholders

Fixed rate @ 5%
Mining Co issues a fixed rate USD bond that pays fixed semi-annual coupon of 5%

Floating rate (LIBOR) + margin

Fixed rate @ 5%

Mining Company　　　**Bank**

Key features of the above arrangement include:

> Mining Company issues a bond (in order to raise funds) that pays its investors based on a fixed interest rate of 5%.

> Under Mining Company treasury policy, there is a preference for floating rather than fixed interest rates.

> Mining Company executes an interest rate swap with an external counterparty, usually a financial institution (in this case the 'Bank'). In practice, the mining company will often execute multiple interest rate swaps of smaller notional amounts with different banks to manage its counterparty credit risk exposure to the banks.

> The interest rate swap is an agreement between the two parties to exchange interest payments based upon a specified notional principal amount for a specified term with all terms documented.

> Effectively the above arrangement transfers the interest rate risk in relation to the fixed rate bonds to the Bank in exchange for a floating rate. The Bank charges the Mining Company a small execution fee and a credit charge, which will be factored into the overall margin charged by the bank to the mining company. Except for the bank's margin, the swap contract is intended to have a zero net present value when executed. If it did not, an up-front payment on receipt would typically arise to make a gain or loss when entering into the contract. Either party could then make a gain or loss, depending on the change in market interest rates; this being the nature of the hedge.

> Mining Company continues to pay interest at the fixed rate to the bondholders.

> Swap payments will be made periodically between Mining Company and the bank on a net basis (if settlement is agreed on this basis). If the floating rates exceed the fixed rates, Mining Company will pay the bank the difference. If fixed rates exceed the floating rates, the bank will pay the mining company the difference. On a net basis, Mining Company will have incurred interest expense based on floating interest rates.

> The floating leg rate of the swap is re-set periodically on a quarterly basis by reference to the benchmark, conventionally 3m US Libor. [Note: Global benchmark reform will alter the way in which floating rate swaps will be priced as Libor is phased out and replaced with the Secured Overnight Floating Rate (SOFR).]

Tax issues

> Mining company will continue to pay interest to the external bondholders. This will typically be deductible for tax purposes. The timing of deductions depends on specific tax rules, for example where accounting standards require derivatives to be accounted for at fair value and some jurisdictions may impose tax on fair value movements in the financial accounts. Interest deductions could be limited under thin capitalisation EBITDA-based tests discussed in this Chapter.

> Swap payments made to the bank would be deductible for tax purposes, and swap payments received from the bank will be taxable. In certain jurisdictions, they could be subject to similar restrictions on finance cost deductibility.

> If the bond-holders are non-resident, then interest payments might be subject to interest withholding tax.

> Several countries would treat swap payments as 'interest' from the perspective of EBITDA-based interest restrictions, and some would impose withholding tax subject to specific relief (e.g., tax treaty relief). Others such as the UK have a specific exemption from withholding taxes, but have a separate rule disallowing deductions for net payments to tax havens.

Related party swaps:

It is common for multinational mining groups to centralise treasury functions including legal relationships with derivative counterparties. This can result in cost, certainty and time efficiencies. Therefore, it would be common for a centralised treasury entity to enter into the swap with the external bank. This may be a different entity from the entity with the underlying debt instrument. In these cases, it would be common for the treasury entity to enter an internal back-to-back swap on identical commercial terms with the Mining Company that has issued the external bonds. On a net basis, Mining Company therefore has the exposure to floating interest rates and the Treasury entity is net neutral. The Treasury entity would likely charge a fee to Mining Company for executing the swap.

9.7.6   Examples

9.7.6.1   A full list of examples that illustrate the transactions described in this section are set out below.

9.7.7   Commodity price risk hedging

How does commodity price hedging work?

9.7.7.1   Commodity price risk refers to the uncertainties of future market prices and of the size of the future income, caused by the fluctuation in the prices of commodities. These commodities may be gold, oil, grain, metals, gas, electricity, etc. Diversified multinational resource companies are exposed to commodity price risk. Company policy and strategy determine the level of commodity price hedging that is undertaken: ranging from limiting hedging only where there are fixed price commodity contracts (reflecting a preference for exposure to floating commodity prices), to sophisticated speculative hedging which carries a higher potential financial reward, but also a higher risk. Other resource investors may prefer a fixed income stream without volatility and would therefore hedge in order to replace floating prices with fixed commodity prices. Broadly, hedging involves entering into a derivative contract whose value moves in the opposite direction to its underlying position (e.g., the position of the physical sale of commodities), so the company neutralizes part or all of its potential risks.

9.7.7.2   Hedging can be performed by taking a long (buy) or short (sell) position against the asset or physical product. Long hedge position (buy) is a strategy generally taken by producers or manufacturers that need to acquire the commodity, to protect themselves from the prices of these commodities increasing in the future when they have to source the asset at a future price. A producer that buys a futures contract will, on contract expiry, receive delivery of the contracted quantity and quality of a commodity at the price determined when it purchased the futures contract.

9.7.7.3   A short hedge position (sell) is taken when a company is already selling the given commodity (or asset) and wishes for protection from the price reducing in the future (i.e., protection against a fall in revenue for the seller). A short position in the commodity market involves a company selling futures contracts. These contracts specify that the seller of the contract will deliver a stated amount of commodity (or asset) at a specified price, on the date specified on the contract. A company that has sold a futures contract will, on contract expiry, deliver the contracted quantity and quality of the commodity at the price determined when it sold the futures contract.

9.7.7.4   There are various financial instruments that can be used to hedge commodity price risk. These instruments consist of futures, forward contracts, options and swaps.

Commodity futures contracts

9.7.7.5   A commodity futures contract is an agreement to buy or sell a predetermined amount of a commodity at a specific price on a specific date in the future. Commodity futures can be used to hedge or protect an investment position or to bet on the directional move of the underlying asset. A futures contract executed on a commodity exchange can be physically settled upon contract maturity or cash settled. The pay-off structure is linear with respect to the market price at the time of settlement.

9.7.7.6   Commodity futures contracts are regulated and traded on exchanges and therefore standardized in terms of the quantity and characteristics of the underlying commodity. Although futures contracts are based on a future sale of a commodity, they are typically cash settled and rarely end in physical delivery. Therefore, market participants in the commodity futures trade are not necessarily commodity producers or buyers looking to hedge price risk, but often investors from outside the commodity space who aim at making a profit from transactions, taking advantage of commodity price movements. Commodity futures contracts can be used by speculators to make directional price bets on the underlying asset's price. Positions can be taken in either direction meaning investors can go long (or buy) or go short (or sell) the commodity.

Futures contract: Short Hedge Example

A coal mining firm has entered into a contract to sell 155,000 tons of coal, to be delivered in 3 months' time. The sale price is agreed by both parties to be based on the market price of coal on the day of delivery. At the time of signing the agreement, the spot price for coal is USD 74.45/ton while the price of coal futures for delivery in 3 months' time is USD 74.00/ton.

To lock in the selling price at USD 74.00/ton, the coal mining firm can enter a short position in an appropriate number of NYMEX[15] Coal futures contracts. With each NYMEX Coal futures contract covering 1,550 tons of coal, the coal mining firm will be required to short 100 futures contracts.

The effect of putting in place the hedge should guarantee that the coal mining firm will be able to sell the 155,000 tons of coal at USD 74.00/ton for a total amount of USD 11,470,000.

Scenario #1: Coal Spot Price Fell by 10% to USD 67.01/ton on Delivery Date

As per the sales contract, the coal mining firm will have to sell the coal at only USD 67.01/ton, resulting in net sale proceeds of USD 10,386,550.

By the delivery date, the coal futures price will have converged with the coal spot price and will be equal to USD 67.01/ton. As the short

---

[15] The New York Mercantile Exchange (NYMEX) is the world's largest physical commodity futures exchange.

futures position was entered at USD 74.00/ton, it will have gained USD 74.00 - USD 67.01 = USD 6.99 per ton. With 100 contracts covering a total of 155,000 tons, the total gain from the short futures position is USD 1,083,450.

Together, the gain in the coal futures market and the amount realised from the sales contract will total USD 1,083,450+ USD 10,386,550 = USD 11,470,000. This amount is equivalent to selling 155,000 tons of coal at USD 74.00/ton.

Scenario #2: Coal Spot Price Rose by 10% to USD 81.90/ton on Delivery Date

With the increase in the coal price to USD 81.90/ton, the coal producer will be able to sell the 155,000 tons of coal for sale proceeds of USD 12,694,500.

However, as the short futures position was entered at a lower price of USD 74.00/ton, it will have lost USD 81.90 - USD 74.00 = USD 7.90 per ton. With 100 contracts covering a total of 155,000 tons of coal, the total loss from the short futures position is USD 1,224,500.

In the end, the higher sale proceeds are offset by the loss in the coal futures market, resulting in net proceeds of USD 12,694,500- USD 1,224,500 = USD 11,470,000. Again, this is the same amount that would be received by selling 155,000 tons of coal at USD 74.00/ton (income of USD 11,470,000).

From a tax perspective, in each scenario, the gain or loss related to the coal futures contract is taxable or deductible, so that the net taxable income is the same i.e., USD 11,470,000. This hedge would be considered to be effective on an after tax basis.

Complexities can arise where the tax treatment of the coal futures contract is different from the sale of coal, or where the futures contract is with a related party.

The main concern for tax authorities would be related party transactions for which there is no external hedge available in the market (e.g., an internal hedge only). This is a transfer pricing issue so reference is made to the UN Transfer Pricing Manual.

Commodity forward contracts

9.7.7.7   Forward contracts are very common in extractive industries. A forward contract is an agreement between two parties – a buyer and a seller to purchase or sell a commodity at a later date at a price agreed upon when the agreement is concluded. The main features of a forward contract are:

- Forward contracts are bilateral contracts, and hence, they are exposed to counterparty risk.

- There is risk of non-performance of obligations by either of the parties, so these are riskier than futures contracts.

- Unlike futures contracts, which are always traded on an exchange, forward contracts always trade over-the-counter (OTC), or can simply be a signed contract between two parties. Each contract is custom designed and hence, is unique in terms of contract size, expiration date, the asset type and quality.

- The specified price in a forward contract is referred to as the delivery price. The forward price for a particular forward contract at a particular time is the delivery price that would apply if the contract were entered into at that time. Forward price and delivery price are equal at the time the contract is entered into. However, as time passes, the forward price is likely to change whereas the delivery price remains the same.

Example 1 - Aluminium Fixed Forward Contract

> Mining Co produces aluminium in Country X. Aluminium prices are generally based on prices referenced on the London Metal Exchange (LME). Pricing in contracts with customers is based on the prior months' monthly average LME price (i.e., the prices fluctuate based on the LME price).

> Mining Co's related entity 'Treasury Co' is resident in Country Y. Treasury policy has determined a preference to fix the price of aluminium sales for a period of 12 months. Treasury Co enters a fixed price forward contract with a bank, to fix the forward price of aluminium with the bank.

> Under the fixed forward contract, Treasury Co agrees to sell to the bank at the forward price and buy at the monthly average price (the same as the customer price). The ease with which this market price (the forward price) may be observed in the market may depend on the particular commodity being hedged; i.e., the depth and liquidity of the market in that commodity. And in some cases, a perfect hedge may well not be available – i.e., a widely available market price for a generic commodity may be used as a proxy.

> In practice, physical sales do not occur between Treasury Co and the bank, and the forward contract obligations are cash

settled on a net basis. If average monthly prices are higher than the forward price, Treasury Co will make a payment to the bank (the bank will make a gain). If average monthly prices are lower than the forward price, the bank will make a payment to Treasury Co (bank will make a loss).

> Treasury Co is a service provider to Mining Co, and therefore, it enters into a 'back to back' arrangement with Mining Co, so in effect, the gain or loss from the hedge is allocated to Mining Co, which is the company with the exposure. In all instances, the gains on aluminium selling prices will be offset by a derivative loss (and opposite for reduced aluminium selling prices).[16]

> The derivative allows both the buyer and seller to fulfil their commercial needs.

Tax issues

> Mining Co has in effect hedged its sales revenue so that it receives the agreed forward price. That is, they are receiving the prevailing (floating) price on the physical sale of aluminium, whilst paying or receiving the difference between the floating price and the forward derivative fixed price. The net revenue from the combination of the realisation of the physical sale and the derivative is taxable, less costs. There may be a timing difference in relation to cash flow and tax accounting of the gain or loss from the hedge compared to the underlying sale. Derivatives are accounted for and sometimes taxed on a fair value basis (i.e., based on a 'marked to market' valuation), whereas the underlying sale would be taxed on a receipt, accrual or accounting recognition basis.

> Where the hedge gain or loss is not taxed in the same way as the underlying sale, then the hedge will not be considered effective on an after tax basis.

> Treasury Co has facilitated the hedge on behalf of Mining Co, as it acts as an intermediary and is compensated as a service provider, based on its functions, assets and risks. Mispricing risks should not arise.

> In some cases a central Treasury entity may hedge on behalf of different producing companies in the group, in which case the back to back arrangements may not precisely mirror the single external hedge, but an appropriate allocation methodology should be used and the Mining Co should be required to demonstrate that the intra-group hedge pricing is

---

[16] As noted above, in reality it is unlikely that companies are able to obtain a perfect hedge due to market imperfections.

in accordance with arm's length terms.

> There are other trading models, which involve more complex transfer pricing considerations. These usually involve a group company, in this instance Treasury Co, taking positions (which may be speculative) in the market that result in greater risk and reward. In such instances, Treasury Co would require substantially more capital, undertake more functions (decision making) and bear significantly more risk, which would ultimately result in the potential for larger gains or losses.

> If the hedge is purely intra-group then transfer pricing risks may arise – Mining Co will need to demonstrate the pricing is in accordance with arm's length terms and should be prepared to explain the commercial basis for entering an intra-group

Example 2 – Speculative Commodity Forward Contracts in Mining

Some mining companies engage in more sophisticated trading and speculative hedging. They have the potential to profit if they believe the value of their commodity will move in an expected direction. For example, if a gold mining company (GoldCo) expects the gold price to fall and hence sell forward much more gold than GoldCo can produce in time for the forward sale - this is speculation as GoldCo will be required to buy gold from third parties at the spot price at the time to deliver into the forward contract.

This is particularly relevant in the mining industry as many miners are enticed by the potential substantial financial rewards if they can correctly predict the direction of their underlying commodity, e.g., if the prevailing market price for gold is USD 1300/oz, but GoldCo believes the market price will decrease to USD 1,000/oz, GoldCo can enter into a forward contract with a counterparty which would compel the counterparty to purchase a pre-agreed quantity of gold at the pre-agreed USD 1300/oz. When the contracted time for delivery arrives, GoldCo will then go to the market, buy the pre-agreed gold at the market prevailing price of USD 1,000/oz and sell to the counterparty at the pre-agreed USD 1,300/oz, hence locking in a profit from the trade.

However, this potential financial reward also carries a higher potential risk: if predictions of future prices are incorrect, large losses can arise. Resource company policies will generally determine the level of speculative hedging that can be undertaken.

Tax Issues

A taxable gain or loss would arise from the speculative hedge. Some countries' tax rules treat speculative hedging differently from other hedging (for example, India, as set out further below).

Another issue may be the appropriate entity in the resource company group where gains and losses from speculative trading should be recognized. This is governed by transfer pricing analysis.

Commodity swap contracts

9.7.7.8   A commodity swap is a type of derivative contract where two parties agree to exchange cash flows dependent on the price of an underlying commodity. A commodity swap is usually used to hedge against price swings in the market for a commodity, such as oil or livestock. Commodity swaps allow for the producers of a commodity and consumers to lock in a set price for a given commodity. No physical commodity is actually transferred between the buyer and seller. The commodity swap contracts are entered into between the two counterparties, outside any centralized trading facility or exchange and are therefore characterized as OTC derivatives.

9.7.7.9   In general, the purpose of commodity swaps is to limit the amount of risk for a given party within the swap. A party that wants to hedge its risk against the volatility of a particular commodity price will enter into a commodity swap and agree, based on the contract, to accept a particular price, one that will either be paid or received during the term of the agreement. Because swaps do not involve the actual transfer of any assets or principal amounts, a base must be established in order to determine the amounts that will periodically be swapped. This principal base is known as the "notional amount" of the contract.

Example – Commodity Swap Contracts in Oil

A refiner and an oil producer agree to enter into a 10-year crude oil swap with a monthly exchange of payments. The refiner (Party A) agrees to pay the producer (Party B) a fixed price of USD 25 per barrel, and the producer agrees to pay the refiner the settlement price of a futures contract for NYMEX[17] light, sweet crude oil on the final day of trading for the contract. The notional amount of the contract is 10,000 barrels.

---

[17] The New York Mercantile Exchange (NYMEX) is the world's largest physical commodity futures exchange. NYMEX is part of the Chicago Mercantile Exchange Group (CME Group). The CME Group is the world's leading and most diverse derivatives marketplace.

Under this contract the payments are netted, so that the party owing the larger payment for the month makes a net payment to the party owing the lesser amount. If the NYMEX settlement price on the final day of trading is USD 23 per barrel, Party A will make a payment of USD 2 per barrel times 10,000, or USD 20,000, to Party B. If the NYMEX price is USD 28 per barrel, Party B will make a payment of USD 30,000 to Party A. The 10-year swap effectively creates a package of 120 cash-settled forward contracts, one maturing each month for 10 years.

So long as both parties in the example are able to buy and sell crude oil at the variable NYMEX settlement price, the swap guarantees a fixed price of USD 25 per barrel, because the producer and the refiner can combine their financial swap with physical sales and purchases in the spot market in quantities that match the nominal contract size. The producer never actually delivers crude oil to the refiner, nor does the refiner directly buy crude oil from the producer. All their physical purchases and sales are in the spot market, at the NYMEX price.

9.7.7.10   The table below summarizes the characteristics, advantages and disadvantages of the main derivative instruments in commodities markets.

Product	Purpose	Advantages	Disadvantages
Forward contract	Can be used to facilitate planning and budgeting by locking in a future price and a fixed date for the transaction	• Can be tailored to specific delivery dates and quantities • Ensures physical delivery for both producer and consumer • Can be used to support feasibility of production, application for finance or pre-export finance	• Fixed contract that requires delivery • Credit or counterparty risk • Loss of profit where future price has had favourable movement at delivery • Pricing not transparent
Futures contract	Used to hedge price risk without needing physical settlement	• Contracts are standard with no need for negotiation • Minimal counterparty risk as futures are settled through clearing house • Initial position can be easily reversed	• Possible requirement to meet margin calls • Possible loss of profit where price at settlement is higher than futures price • Futures product may not match commodity being hedged

Product	Purpose	Advantages	Disadvantages
Commodity options	Used to protect against unfavourable movements in commodity price while providing some ability to participate in favourable movements in price before or at settlement date	• Ability to take advantage of favourable movement in commodity price • Can be tailored to suit organisation's requirements • Fewer cashflow issues than futures as often margin calls are not required • More effective hedging product where supply is uncertain	• Premiums can be expensive • Usually some loss of favourable movements of commodity price
Commodity swaps	Used to guarantee longer term income streams from commodity and to lock in longer term pricing	• Use of swaps can assist in obtaining finance for projects through locking in longer term pricing • Provides longer term hedge • Tailored to suit the organisation's needs • In some cases, no margin calls	• Counterparty risk • Possibility of taking advantage of favourable price movements may be lost • Difficult to close out

9.8   TAX ISSUES OF DERIVATIVES

9.8.1   Timing of recognizing gains and losses

9.8.1.1   Broadly, there are two main dimensions along which the tax treatment of hedging using derivatives can vary. The first is the timing of recognition of gains and losses for tax purposes. For some derivatives, gains or losses are not recognized until the underlying asset changes hands or the contract expires or is sold.

9.8.1.2   Other derivatives are taxed on a mark-to-market basis—that is, their gains and losses are calculated and taxed each year on the basis of the year-to-year change in the derivative's fair-market value. Some countries rely heavily on accounting treatment of hedges and some have specific tax timing rules.

9.8.2   The characterization of gains and losses

9.8.2.1   One of the tax issues is the recognition of gains and losses from hedging against movement in commodity price in calculating upstream taxes. There is variation in tax regimes among countries. Some countries may treat the gains and losses from commodity price hedging differently from the underlying sales. Some attempt to match the tax characterization of hedges to the underlying assets they are hedged against. For example, hedges in relation to sales contracts

337

would give rise to ordinary income and deductions whereas hedges related to capital assets may be taxed as capital gains and losses. Some have specific rules related to speculative hedging (for example, India, as discussed further below).

9.8.3   Transfer pricing issues

9.8.3.1   Hedging contracts sometimes involve affiliated parties, directly or indirectly, and transfer pricing issues should be addressed if hedging gains and losses have to be recognized. To challenge this issue, it is important to have a good understanding of commercial pricing of hedging instruments. Where the hedge is only with a related party and is not externally hedged by the MNE, this may raise further complexities. However, in some instances, there may be genuine commercial purposes for undertaking a hedge with a related party.

9.8.3.2   Tax authorities should seek to ensure the pricing is in accordance with arm's length terms and would expect to see documentation explaining the commercial basis for entering an intra-group hedge. The tax authorities' challenge may also be to ensure that the hedging relates to a "real" risk with a nexus with the mining activities and that this risk has actually been transferred out of the MNE. Further detail on risk can be found in section 3.4 of the UN Transfer Pricing Manual.

9.8.3.3   Tax authorities have concerns that hedging may be used for tax avoidance purposes. Many countries have specific anti-avoidance rules which may apply as well as rules requiring disclosure of derivative transactions so that they can be more readily identified.

9.8.3.4   Tax authorities' concerns may also relate to interest withholding tax, the currency of borrowing and rationale for hedging, pricing of swap payments, speculation using commodity futures or option contracts. Risk hedging via derivatives can further complicate a tax administration's analysis of the actual conditions as the counterparties may not be known, and this type of transaction may trigger events that may be within the control of the MNE.

Example - Taxation Issues of Derivatives in France

For the tax treatment of financial derivatives, the French Tax Code distinguishes the derivative products between over-the-counter transactions and transactions on organized markets.

Over-the-counter products:

The following instruments are considered as over-the-counter financial products:

> ›   Interest rate swaps;

>   Forward Rate Agreement;

>   Option-derived products (caps, floors, collars); and

>   Forward sale and purchase contracts.

The Tax Code provides that unrealized profits are taxable only at the outcome of the contract. The losses incurred may be deducted through a deductible reserve only to the extent that a global estimated budget of the operation involved has been prepared and reflects a global loss.

Organized market products:

The following products are considered as dealt in the organized market:

>   Contracts and options traded on the MATIF[17] and MONEP;[18] and

>   Foreign currency transactions (including currency swaps).

The Tax Code sets forth as a general principle the application of the mark-to-market rule to operations involving financial futures on organized markets. There is a special tax treatment for operations, when the sole purpose is the hedging of a transaction due to occur during the following financial year. In this case, the profit realized through the hedging instrument is not taxable at the end of the financial year but at the outcome of the contract. To qualify for the tax treatment of hedging transactions, an economic hedge must meet the following conditions:

>   The sole purpose of the use of a forward instrument must be hedging of a transaction due to happen in the following year and traded in another type of market;

>   The occurrence in the next year of the transaction must be highly likely; and

>   The correlation between the value of the hedging instrument and of the hedged element must be sufficient (however, a sufficient correlation is not defined).

In addition, a document indicating the main characteristics of the hedged element and of the hedging instrument must be transmitted to the tax authorities.

---

[18] Marché à terme international de France (MATIF)

[19] Marché des Options Négociables de Paris (MONEP)

Example - Taxation Issues of Derivatives in Nigeria

There are no specific rules for taxing derivative transactions in Nigeria. The general rules of taxation therefore become applicable. The first issue to deal with is a determination of whether there has been a gain, profit or loss that will be taxable under the Capital Gains Tax Act (CGTA) or Companies Income Tax Act (CITA). The general rule is that capital gains are ordinarily to be considered under the provisions of CGTA while trading profits or losses fall under the provisions of CITA.

Example - Taxation of Forward Contracts in India

Following the ICDS[19], a forward contract is defined as an agreement to exchange different currencies at a forward rate and includes a foreign currency option contract or another financial instrument of a similar nature. ICDS relating to the effects of changes in foreign exchange rates provides that forward contracts can be divided into the following types for the purpose of determining the tax treatment:

> Forward Contracts not intended for trading or speculation purposes and entered into for the purpose of settlement of a particular asset/liability on a future date;

> Forward Contracts intended for trading or speculation purposes and entered into for the purpose of gaining from such contract; and

> Forward Contracts entered into to hedge the foreign currency risk of a firm commitment or a highly probable forecast transaction.

(i) Forward Contracts not intended for trading or speculation purposes and entered into for the purpose of settlement of a particular asset/liability on a future date:

At the time of contract:

The difference between the spot exchange rate at the date of contract and the contracted forward rate is regarded as premium/discount on such forward contract. The exchange difference in relation to such contracts is required to be amortized as an income or expense within the period of contract.

---

[20] Income Computation and Disclosure Standards

On Contract renewal/cancellation:

Any profit or loss arising on the renewal/cancellation of a forward contract will be charged to profit or loss in the year of such cancellation/renewal.

On restatement of forward contract:

The restatement exchange gain/loss on forward contracts shall be allowed as deduction in the year of restatement (i.e., on the basis of its unrealized status).

On realization of forward contracts:

The realization exchange gain/loss on forward contracts shall be allowed as a deduction in the year of realization if the settlement has taken place within the same year.

(ii) Forward Contracts intended for trading or speculation purposes and entered into for the purpose to gain from such forward contract

ICDS provides that an exchange fluctuation loss/gain on foreign currency derivatives held for trading or speculation purposes is to be allowed only on actual settlement and not on mark to market ('MTM'). Hence, a gain/loss arising on a forward contract entered into for trading or speculation purposes is taxable or allowed as a deduction at the point of settlement.

(iii) Forward Contracts entered into to hedge the foreign currency risk of a firm commitment or a highly probable forecast transaction

The entire profit and loss impact, premium/discount and exchange difference on contracts that are entered into to hedge the foreign currency risk of a firm commitment or a highly probable forecast transaction shall be recognized at the time of settlement.

9.9   FINANCIAL AND PERFORMANCE GUARANTEES

9.9.1   Overview

9.9.1.1. In the extractive sector, as in most industries, guarantees are part of the business. Guarantees may be required for access to finance, to guarantee the proper execution of contracts or to ensure site rehabilitation when mining or oil operations are closed. In the extractive industries, broadly three types of guarantees can be distinguished: financial guarantees, performance guarantees and financial surety.

9.9.2 Financial guarantees

9.9.2.1   A financial guarantee is a contract by a third party (guarantor) to back the debt of a second party (the debtor) for its payments to the ultimate debtholder (investor or creditor). It provides for the guarantor to meet specified financial obligations in the event of a failure to do so by the guaranteed party. The ultimate aim of the financial guarantee is to enable the debtor to access credit on better terms than if it had borrowed solely on the basis of its creditworthiness.

9.9.2.2   Often, the guarantor is not a third party. In multinational enterprises (MNEs), financial guarantees may be granted by group members of the MNE. The guarantees may be formal, covered by a contract specifying the guarantor's commitments, or simply be implicit, resulting from the mere fact of being a member of the MNE.

9.9.2.3   Following the OECD[20] (2019), *"The accurate delineation of financial guarantees requires initial consideration of the economic benefit arising to the borrower beyond the one that derives from passive association" (D.1.1). (···) "The effect of potential group support on the credit rating of an entity and any effect on that entity's ability to borrow or the interest rate paid on those borrowings would not require any payment or comparability adjustment"* (C.1.3).

9.9.2.4   The analysis of financial guarantees related to financial transactions in extractive industries applies the same reasoning as for other sectors. Tax implications of intragroup financial guarantees are analyzed in the UN Manual on Transfer Pricing for Developing Countries (Section 9.13).

9.9.3 Performance guarantees

9.9.3.1   The aim of performance guarantees is to provide security for non-financial obligations issued to one party as a guarantee against the failure of the other party to meet obligations in the contract (other than obligations in respect of payments, indebtedness or other monetary obligations of any kind) as agreed between the parties. The performance guarantee may trigger the payment of an amount when the terms of the contract have not been fulfilled, and there is a resulting financial loss.

9.9.3.2   Traditionally, performance guarantees are used to hold suppliers accountable. Performance guarantees are commonly used in sectors where long-term and large contracts prevail, such as the natural resources or construction sectors. While financing guarantees assure repayment of money, a performance guarantee provides an assurance of compensation in the event of inadequate or delayed performance on a contract.

9.9.3.3   For example, in the Oil and Gas sector, engineering, procurement

---

[21] Transfer Pricing Guidance on Financial Transactions, BEPS Action 4, 8-10, February 2020

and construction (EPC) contracts contain performance guarantees backed by performance liquidated damages (PLDs) payable by the Contractor if it fails to meet the performance guarantees. Following the EPC contracts, in addition to delivering a complete facility, the Contractor must deliver that facility for a guaranteed price by a guaranteed date and it must perform to the specified level. Failure to comply with any requirements will usually result in the Contractor incurring monetary liabilities.

9.9.3.4   In the upstream industry governments usually secure projects by requiring local exploration and production (E&P) companies to provide additional guarantees aiming at ensuring compliance with the work commitments undertaken. Given the materiality of the investments needed and the high risk of the projects, as a general practice parent companies' guarantees are granted by the headquarters to the local E&P affiliates, for no consideration, since there is not a market for these guarantees (they are usually unlimited or disproportionately high considering the solvency of the affiliate and therefore no financial institution would be willing to grant such guarantees).

9.9.4   Financial surety

9.9.4.1   A financial surety instrument is an important tool in ensuring that funds are available to guarantee effective mine closure and rehabilitation. In the context of offshore oil and gas exploitation, it also includes dismantling of platforms and other installations.[21] It is the main financial tool used to insure that, for example, environmental liabilities are not passed on to the government after the mine closure or oilfield decommissioning. In general, financial surety is issued by financial institutions such as bonding companies, banks or insurance companies.

9.9.4.2   There are a number of different types of financial surety:[22] letter of credit, surety bond, trust fund, company guarantee, insurance scheme and pledge of assets.

Letter of credit

9.9.4.3   A letter of credit (LC) or bank guarantee is an unconditional agreement from a bank to provide funds to a third party on demand. An LC can be used for a variety of purposes. For example, extractive companies may obtain LCs to secure customer payments for commodities. They may also be used to secure funding for rehabilitation. In this case, the third party is the relevant government or other authorized body within the government. An LC includes the terms and conditions of the agreement between the extractive company and the government, with reference to the rehabilitation program and the agreed-upon costs. The LC is usually issued for a year and renewed annually following a review of rehabilitation requirements and costs. If an LC is not renewed and the extractive

---

[22] For more details on this issue, reference is made to Chapter 14 in this Handbook on Decommissioning.

[23] See European Commission (2007) Guidelines on Financial Guarantees and Inspections for Mining Waste Facilities

company fails to provide an acceptable alternative form of guarantee, then the government has the option of drawing the full amount prior to expiry. The funds held in an LC do not generate any interest.

Surety bond

9.9.4.4   A surety bond or a performance bond is an agreement between an insurance company and an extractive company to provide funds to a third party under certain circumstances. In this instance, the third party is the relevant government department. A surety bond includes the terms and conditions of the agreement between the extractive company and the government with reference to rehabilitation programs, agreed-upon costs, and conditions for the release of the bond.

9.9.4.5   A surety bond is issued by an insurance company, ideally one that is licensed under the relevant legislation. It is issued for a specific time period and can be renewed for further time periods based on a credit review of the extractive company. During this process, the amount of a surety bond can be increased or decreased depending on the amendments to the rehabilitation program. If a surety bond is not renewed and the extractive company fails to provide an acceptable alternative form of surety, then the government has the option of drawing the full amount. The extractive company should be responsible for all fees and charges associated with a surety bond.

9.9.4.6   The surety bonds are attractive to smaller companies as they do not involve tying up capital. However, as the cost of the surety depends on the rating of the extractive company, this cost could be substantially higher for small companies, especially those without proven track records.

Trust fund

9.9.4.7   A trust fund is a fund established pursuant to an agreement between a trust company and an extractive company for the sole purpose of funding the rehabilitation of a site. In addition to a trust fund, there should be a signed agreement between the extractive company and the government, administered by the trust company, that stipulates the extractive company's responsibility with regard to the trust. This agreement should identify who the ultimate beneficiary of the funds is, state that the trust fund exists to provide security for the rehabilitation costs of a particular site, specify the total amount required, and outline a schedule of payments.

9.9.4.8   A trust fund should be maintained by a trust company that may be required to be licensed under the relevant legislation. The types of investment available to the fund manager should be decided by the extractive company and the government and specified in the agreement. Contributions to a trust fund are usually structured as a series of payments over a specific time period. The management and performance of a trust fund should be subject to periodic review.[23]

---

[24] For more details on this issue, reference is made to Chapter 14 on Decommissioning.

9.9.4.9   Where a government-mandated mining rehabilitation fund is required, payments into the fund can be allowed as a deductible expense at the time they are made for purposes of income tax and mining taxes.

Company guarantee

9.9.4.10   A company guarantee or a self-guarantee is based on an evaluation of the assets and liabilities of the company and its ability to pay the total rehabilitation costs. A company guarantee requires a long history of financial stability, which can be evidenced by either audited financial statements prepared by an accredited accounting firm, or a favourable credit rating from a credit rating agency, or both.

9.9.4.11   Where the company is a member of a multinational group, it is the parent company or a financially robust affiliate that guarantees to provide the funds needed by the subsidiary to close and rehabilitate the mine site. The parent company consolidates the liabilities of its subsidiaries and the guarantees granted in the consolidated financial statements. If the parent is a large, financially healthy company, its guarantee is often more reassuring than that of the (usually smaller) local subsidiary. However, multi-nationals are not immune to financial difficulties either and may default on their guarantees, which could leave the government or civil society with the burden of clean-up and rehabilitation.

9.9.4.12   Many jurisdictions do not accept a company guarantee as a form of financial surety because of the public perception that a self-guarantee for a mining company is a contradiction in terms. Of those that do allow a company guarantee, some will accept this form of financial surety only for the first half of the life of the project or as part of the surety.

Insurance scheme

9.9.4.13   There is a wide range of insurance options. General forms of insurance schemes are, for instance, premium financing, commercial general liability and professional indemnity, which normally do not cover environmental liabilities or long term rehabilitation costs.

9.9.4.14   The difference between an insurance scheme compared with a surety bond is that the latter involves three parties: the person doing the work (principal or extractive company), the person requiring the work (obligee, or the government), and the surety company providing the bond (surety). The bond guarantees that the principal or extractive company will fulfill the terms of the contract and, if it does not, the obligee can file a claim against the bond to recover its losses from the surety. Insurance protects the extractive company. Surety bonds protect the obligee who contracted with the principal to perform specific work on a project, by reimbursing them when a claim occurs.

Queensland Mine Rehabilitation and Financial Assurance Regime

In order to manage environmental risk at mine sites, financial security, called a Financial Assurance (FA), is required to be provided by resource companies to the government prior to commencing mining activities. The amount of the FA is determined by the likely cost of rehabilitation for the area of disturbance, using the Queensland Government's FA calculator. The Mineral and Energy Resources (Financial Provisioning) Act 2018, in force from 1 April 2019, introduced revised financial insurance provisions and established the Financial Provisions Fund, otherwise known as the 'scheme fund.' The scheme fund will receive contributions made by the holders of environmental authorities. Other contributions will also be made to the scheme fund, including amounts earned as interest on cash surety held.

Pledge of assets

9.9.4.15   Pledge of assets takes the form of all surplus equipment and scrap metal that remains at the mining site after operations have ceased. The surplus equipment includes buildings and stationary equipment. The scrap metal includes all metal debris produced during site demolition and clean-up.

9.9.4.16   If a pledge of assets is being used as a financial surety, the government should make sure that, among other conditions, there is market demand for the assets. The value estimation should be carried out by a third party and should include the cost of retrieving and transporting the assets from the site to the marketplace. The estimate should also be recalculated periodically. This is generally viewed as a high risk form of financial surety and is not accepted in many countries.

9.9.5   Tax implications of financial surety

9.9.5.1   According to the World Bank (2009),[24] there are five separate issues related to tax and a financial surety fund.[25] These are:

- Whether money paid into the financial surety fund is counted as an operating cost or an expense, and is therefore tax deductible;

---

[25] World Bank (2009), « Financial Surety », Extractive Industries for Development Series #7, June 2009.

[26] For more details on this issue, reference is made to Chapter 14 on Decommissioning.

- Whether decommissioning and rehabilitation costs count as operating costs, and are, therefore, tax deductible;

- If any interest earned in the financial surety fund is taxable;

- If any capital gain made in the financial surety fund is taxable; and

- If the financial surety fund will be taxable when it is released back to the company.

9.9.5.2   If the funds paid into a financial surety fund are tax deductible, then the decommissioning and rehabilitation costs should not be and vice versa. Decommissioning and rehabilitation costs may not be tax deductible because those costs are incurred and paid after a mine has ceased operating, and there is no income against which the costs may be deducted. One way of getting around this problem is to allow a company to claim tax deductions for closure provisions based on a unit of production during the operating life of the project (World Bank, 2009).

9.9.5.3   The situation is more complex in the case of an intra-group guarantee where a parent company guarantees (ultimate parent or other suitable related entity) that it will perform the Contractor's obligations if, for whatever reason, the Contractor does not perform.

9.9.5.4   An intra-group performance guarantee involves three parties:

- The client – an unrelated entity seeking to buy goods or services from the group;

- The contractor – a group company that is primarily responsible for completing obligations towards the client; and

- The guarantor – a group company that promises to step in and take over if the contractor cannot fulfil its obligations.

9.9.5.5   Fees for performance guarantees are structured similarly to fees for financial guarantees. However, their valuation for transfer pricing purposes poses additional challenges.[26] The guarantee base represents the amount at risk and therefore depends on (i) events that trigger the contractor's failure to fulfil its obligations (contract default triggers), and (ii) the probability that they will occur. Activating an intra-group performance guarantee may result in the guarantor completing the task of the contractor, paying the client compensation or a combination of the above. As to financial guarantees, the criteria for deductibility depend on whether and to what degree the related arrangements actually shift risk from the MNE at the consolidated level to a third unrelated party.

---

[27] For the analysis of the transfer pricing aspects of performance guarantees, reference is made to the section 9.13 of the Transfer Pricing Manual on the application of the arm's length principle to intragroup financial guarantees.

9.9.5.6   According to the OECD (2017)[27], intra-group performance guarantees should be paid if:

- The guarantor should perform a deliberate concerted group action; just "being there" (passive association) is not enough. However, even when deliberate action is performed, it is not always clear that it involves the payment of a fee. For example, issuing a letter of comfort is a deliberate concerted action. Whether this is enough to warrant a fee remains unclear, since in many cases, a letter of comfort falls under passive association as it simply confirms certain facts.

- The contractor should benefit from this action: enhance its commercial or financial position. If the contractor has a strong track record and performance guarantees are routinely required then it could be argued that there may be little or no value in the performance guarantee.

9.9.5.7   Often, in addition to the intra-group guarantee, a guarantee is provided by a third party bank to secure the mining company's commitments to the host country. In such cases, the question is whether the guarantee provided by the third party bank does not cover all the commitments entered into by the mining company, in which case the intra-group guarantee is superfluous and should therefore not be remunerated. This scheme will require comparability analysis based on similar instruments provided by the related guarantor to the third party, if any, (internal comparable) or similar instruments provided by third parties in the market (external comparable).

9.10   FARM-IN/FARM-OUT AGREEMENTS

9.10.1   Purpose

9.10.1.1   The extractives industry is characterized by high risk in the exploration phase and high capital cost of development if the exploration results in a commercial discovery. For these reasons, it is not uncommon for the industry to spread risks and share costs by operating through joint ventures. Joint venture partners may also bring special expertise.

9.10.1.2   For example, some companies specialize in particular types of terrain, some may have knowledge of adjacent resource plays and others may have experience in managing large projects. Getting the right partners involved increases the prospect of a venture being a success and for that reason most governments support, or at least try not to discourage, efforts to bring new investors into an existing contract.

---

28 OECD (2017) Transfer Pricing Guidelines for Multinational Enterprises and Tax Administrations

9.10.2 Definitions

9.10.2.1   A farm-in/farm-out agreement is an agreement entered into by the holder of an extractive industry contract or licence (farmor) to assign an interest in the contract or licence to a new joint venture partner (farmee) in return for the farmee assuming responsibility for future obligations of the venture. The definition does not apply to a sale of assets or shares for immediate consideration. The holder of the existing contract or licence is called the "farmor" and is said to "farm out" part of its rights. The new investor is called "farmee" and is said to have "farmed in" to the contract or licence.

9.10.3 Types of assignment

9.10.3.1   There is no standard form of agreement or assignment as different types of farm-outs are available, depending on the resource to be extracted, the investment stage it has reached and the circumstances of the parties. However, the assignment will normally require the carrying out of a specified work obligation in respect of exploration or other commitments. It may also include an upfront cash amount payable when the agreement is signed.

9.10.3.2   Normally, whether the venture is successful or unsuccessful, the farmor has no obligation to reimburse the farmee for the expenses incurred. The farm-out agreement may relate to specified work commitments or work commitments up to a specified amount (so-called "capped"). If a commercial discovery has been made, the new partner may have to pay a premium over costs already incurred.

9.10.3.3   In consideration for the assumption of future obligations, the farmee will receive an agreed percentage of the farmor's participating interests in the contract. The transfer of the interest in the right may be immediate upon signing of the agreement or deferred to a later point in time, usually when the farmee has fulfilled its work commitments under the agreement, and may be subject to approval of the host government.

9.10.4 Farm-out before commercial discovery

9.10.4.1   In the case of a farm-out during the exploration phase, the farmee is taking a share of the risk of failure and would not normally have to pay a premium to come into the venture. In such a case, the farmor would transfer a percentage of any future revenues in return for the farmee bearing the same percentage of the cost of the agreed work commitment (what is called "at ground-floor"). However, there may also be an upfront cash payment from the farmee to reimburse the farmor for costs incurred prior to the farm-out ("promote agreement").

Tax treatment of farmor

9.10.4.2   The tax treatment of any upfront cash payment will depend on many facts but is typically treated as a reduction of past expenditures, the impact of which will depend on the tax treatment of the original expenditure, or typically, if in excess of prior expenditures, as an item of income. Thereafter, the farmor would claim tax relief on its own share of future expenditure and pay tax on its own share of future revenue.

Tax treatment of farmee

9.10.4.3   The tax impact to the farmee would normally follow the tax treatment realized by the farmor on the original expenditure. As in the case of the farmor, the farmee would claim tax relief on its own share of future expenditure and pay tax on its own share of future revenue.

9.10.5   Farm-out after commercial discovery

9.10.5.1   In the case of farm-out of a successful venture, the farmee is taking less risk and would be expected to pay a premium to secure a share of the future revenues. This premium could take the form of an upfront cash payment, or an agreement to undertake a percentage of future expenditure that is higher than the percentage of participating interests to be transferred, or payment of an overriding royalty or a combination of these.

Tax treatment of farmor

9.10.5.2   Any upfront cash payment would normally be taxed on the farmor as an item of income with respect to the premium received. Thereafter, the farmor would normally claim tax relief on its own share of future expenditure and pay tax on its own share of future revenue. In theory, this is similar to the tax treatment of a farm-out during the exploration phase but in practice, the farmor pays more tax in this case, because its share of future tax-deductible expenditure is less or its share of future taxable revenue is more. However, an alternative treatment would be to value the premium element implied by the difference in future expenditure and revenue sharing percentages and tax that element upfront. That would require a present value estimate to be made of future expenditure and revenue, a fairly complex exercise.

Tax treatment of farmee

9.10.5.3   The farmee would normally be allowed a tax deduction for any upfront cash payment to the extent that the farmor reported the same cash amount as taxable income. As in the case of the farmor, the farmee would claim tax relief on its own share of future expenditure and pay tax on its own share of future revenue. Again, in theory, this is similar to the tax treatment of a farm-out during the exploration phase but in practice, the farmee pays less tax in this case, because its share of future tax-deductible expenditure is more or its share of future taxable revenue is less. Under the alternative treatment described above, which involves valuing the premium and taxing it upfront, this means that the farmee is effectively able to claim a deduction equal to the amount of income reported by the farmor, but only later, as and when future expenditure is incurred and revenue earned.

9.10.6   Examples

9.10.6.1   In some countries, farm-out arrangements must be approved by the national authorities. In Chad, any farm-in/farm-out arrangement is subject to the prior written approval of the Chad Government (represented by the Minister of Petroleum). The request for approval is submitted by the farmer, after payment of a fixed fee depending on the petroleum operations stage. Upon approval and farming completion, the farmee is considered as holder or co-holder of concerned petroleum blocks from the beginning, in the proportion of the participating interest acquired.

9.10.6.2   The tax consequences of farm-in and farm-out arrangements must be considered on a case-by-case basis, depending on how the agreement is structured and whether the farm-out arrangement is before or after the commercial discovery.

Ghana

9.10.6.3   In Ghana, the farmee is entitled to a deduction for the cost it incurs over a period of five years from the date of commencement of commercial operations. Where there is a farm-in/farm-out agreement after the commencement of operations, the written-down value of the petroleum capital expenditure is apportioned between the farmor and farmee in proportion to their respective interests.

Kenya

9.10.6.4   In Kenya, the transferor in the farm-out transaction is taxed on the gain if the net gain forms part of the taxable income of the transferor and is taxed at the corporation tax rates. If an interest is transferred at the time of the agreement, the taxable income of the transfer shall not include the value of any work undertaken by the transferee on behalf of the contractor. If the transfer of an interest is deferred until some or all of the work undertaken by the transferee is completed, the amount payable to be included in the taxable income of the contractor as gains or profits from business excludes the value of the work undertaken by the transferee on behalf of the contractor.

Nigeria

9.10.6.5   According to the Nigerian Petroleum (Amendment) Decree 1996 (Decree No. 23) "farm-out" means "an agreement between the holder of an oil mining lease and a third party which permits the third party to explore, prospect, win, work and carry away any petroleum encountered in a specified area during the validity of the lease."

Scenario	Tax treatment of farmor	Tax treatment of farmee
Farm-out pre-discovery at cost: tax treatment of upfront cash payment	Upfront cash payment is used to reduce pre-production costs of the farmor.	Upfront cash payment forms part of the farmee's pre-production costs, to be amortized against future revenue when the block commences production.
Farm-out pre-discovery at cost: tax treatment of ongoing expenditure commitment	All pre-discovery costs are capitalized as part of the farmor's pre-production costs to be amortized against future revenues.	All pre-discovery costs are warehoused as part of the farmor's pre-production costs to be amortized against future revenues.
Farm-out post-discovery at a premium: tax treatment of upfront cash payment	Where it is discovered that the farmor has enjoyed a Capital Gain from the upfront payment at a premium, then Capital Gains Tax at 10% is applied on the difference between sales proceeds (upfront cash) and the cost of the portion farmed out. The farmor reports the overriding royalty received from the farmee as income and it is subject to tax.	Total upfront cash payment forms part of the farmee's costs in the joint venture and is deductible against revenue from the joint venture project. The farmee pays an overriding royalty to the farmor on production revenues.
Farm-out post-discovery at a premium: tax treatment of ongoing expenditure commitment	Ongoing expenditure is tax deductible if it satisfies the WEN (wholly, exclusively & necessarily incurred) test. Where it is discovered that the farmor has enjoyed a Capital Gain from the upfront payment at a premium, then Capital Gains Tax at 10% is applied on the difference between sales proceeds (upfront cash) and the cost of the portion farmed out. The farmor reports the overriding royalty received from the farmee as income and it is subject to tax.	The farmee's tax deductible expenditure increases by the amount of the premium where the farmee and farmor file their tax returns separately. The farmee pays an overriding royalty to the farmor on production revenues.

Brazil

Scenario	Tax treatment of farmor	Tax treatment of farmee
Farm-out pre-discovery at cost: tax treatment of upfront cash payment	Upfront cash payment is considered as farmor's taxable revenue.	Upfront cash payment is treated as part of the concession's intangible asset cost.
Farm-out pre-discovery at cost: tax treatment of ongoing expenditure commitment	Brazil does not have a specific law provision for this issue. Ongoing expenditure would be subject to normal tax rules.	The ongoing expenditure commitment is considered cost and is treated as part of the concession's intangible asset cost.
Farm-out post-discovery at a premium: tax treatment of upfront cash payment	Upfront cash payment is considered as farmor's taxable revenue.	It is considered cost and is treated as part of the concession's intangible asset cost.
Farm-out post-discovery at a premium: tax treatment of ongoing expenditure commitment	Brazil does not have a specific law provision for this issue. Ongoing expenditure would be subject to normal tax rules.	The ongoing expenditure commitment is considered cost and is treated as part of the concession's intangible asset cost.

Chapter 10

Indirect Transfer of Assets

10.1   INTRODUCTION

10.1.1   Executive summary

10.1.1.1   The issue of indirect transfers of assets in mining and oil and gas, as well as in other sectors, is receiving increasing attention, particularly in developing countries. The concern often expressed is that by using the principle of separate legal personality, and tax planning through residence of companies and similar entities, multinational enterprises (MNEs) may, in substance, change the ownership of an asset located in a developing country without triggering the corresponding taxation of the economic profits from the ownership change in that developing country.

10.1.1.2   What is often said to amount "in substance" to the sale of an asset in the developing country (which may otherwise attract tax on the profits) is transformed into an offshore sale of a foreign holding company (which may hold the developing-country asset directly or through other foreign companies) usually to an offshore buyer. The claim is then usually made that the developing country may lack the jurisdiction under the domestic law to tax such an "extraterritorial" event not involving its own tax residents and not directly involving assets in that country. The further claim is often made that even if domestic law allowed taxation of indirect transfers of assets, a tax treaty between the developing country and the country of the transferor company might be said to override any domestic taxing right the developing country would otherwise have had.

10.1.1.3   In examining the issues involved in the taxation of indirect transfers, the first consideration should be the basic policy issue of whether the country should tax gains made on the direct transfer of capital assets at the time of the transfer or should only tax the profits over time as income is generated by those assets. Therefore, this chapter first examines the issues involving the taxation of capital gains in the area of extractives, including its pros and cons. If the policy decision is to tax such gains on the *direct* transfer of assets, a further policy decision is whether the country desires also to tax the *indirect* transfer of capital assets. If a country determines, as a general policy matter, to tax indirect transfers, it must also decide on the types of transfers it wishes to tax.

10.1.1.4   For example, certain business reorganizations are often exempt from immediate taxation, even if done directly and within the country. Some transfers of smaller shareholdings are similarly exempted. This chapter will therefore consider factors in deciding if immediate tax should be imposed on certain transfers in the extractive industries, whether indirect or direct.

10.1.1.5   Where a country determines that immediate taxation should be imposed on a particular indirect transfer, the final set of issues relates to how this should be done, given that the transferor and the transferee are often foreign tax residents and the transaction is conducted outside the country where the assets are located. From a policy and administration viewpoint, the issues involved include:

(i)   How to ensure an awareness of such transactions when they occur, by taxpayers and administrations;

(ii)   Who should bear the tax obligation and how it will be collected;

(iii)   How a system of taxing indirect transfers can be achieved fairly but with a degree of certainty that tax will be paid; and

How applicable tax treaties impact the taxing rights over such transfers. In other words, how a tax treaty may interact with either general or specific provisions in domestic law seeking to address perceived abuse in this area, including the issue of "treaty override" rules, also needs to be considered.

10.1.1.6   This chapter gives examples of responses to this issue and practical guidance on other potential responses.

10.1.2   Purpose

10.1.2.1   This chapter is intended to provide options for policymakers and administrators in developing countries on the taxation of indirect transfers of assets within the extractive industries, as well as to offer guidance on the pros and cons of such options which are specific to this type of industry. It also seeks to assist countries in limiting potential negative aspects of options taken.

10.1.2.2   More specifically, the chapter explores the issues involved in deciding whether a tax should apply to capital gains in the extractive industries and, if so, under what circumstances. In cases where there is such a tax, it further explores some of the policy and administration issues involved in covering indirect transfers, whereby extractive assets are not themselves transferred (as in the first example in Figure 10.F.1 below) but companies or other entities (often resident offshore) holding the assets directly or through further entities are transferred, as in the second example in 10.F.1.

10.1.2.3   An issue of concern is that the indirect transfer of assets may be motivated by – and structured primarily around – avoiding capital gains tax by having the transfer occur at the level of a company in a low or no-tax jurisdiction, rather than in a country where the extractive assets are located. On the other hand, there can be circumstances where such indirect transfers are effectively and genuinely motivated by other non-tax business considerations, such as in large merger transactions, or in situations where parties are trying to maintain other corporate attributes that stem from the manner in which assets are directly owned. While such non-tax reasons need to be fairly recognized and taken into account, they should not be used to disguise or give a cover for tax-motivated structuring, of course; the realities of the situation as a whole have to be evaluated. As this chapter shows, taxing indirect transfers can raise difficult issues which may be relevant to policy decisions regarding whether the transfers are taxed at all and, if they are, how that is achieved.

10.1.2.4   In essence, the issues are (i) whether gains from direct transfers of extractive assets should be taxed; (ii) whether gains from *indirect* transfers of the same extractive assets should be treated (by the country where the mine or other extractive assets are located) in the same way as in a direct transfer of extractive assets; and (iii) if so, how a tax on such a gain can be effectively implemented from the perspectives of administrations and taxpayers. It is recognized that, as background to this issue, there are differences between common law and civil law legal systems that should be borne in mind. It has been noted that:

"...the essence of the difference is that civil law countries treat all the income of a commercial company as business profits; the result is that the approach in the case of income earned by a commercial company is based on the type of person, while common law countries make the determination according to the type of income. The most obvious example of this difference in approach is that common law countries make a distinction between capital gains and business profits when taxing companies; civil law countries do not, because capital gains are part of business profits."[1]

10.1.2.5   The term "transfer," whether direct or indirect, is used for convenience in this chapter, and is intended to cover not just sales where money changes hands, but also many other forms of changes in ownership interests relating to extractive assets, e.g., swaps (including asset-for-share transactions) and farm-in sale price to treatment under the developing country's tax arrangements of the type discussed below in this Chapter.[2] Similarly, the reference to extractive "assets" refers not just to physical assets, but also to the rights appertaining to their use, such as exploration and development rights; some countries specifically provide information relating to extraction (such as survey information) to be treated in the same way, because of the value it may have, and the role it plays in the pricing of a transfer.

10.1.2.6   A particular issue for many policymakers and administrators is how a policy decision to tax indirect transfers of valuable extractive industries interests can be effectively implemented in practice. Implementing such a regime involves information and administrative (including enforcement) considerations and requirements for tax authorities. For sellers/transferors, it raises issues of their

---

[1] John F. Avery Jones and others, "Treaty Conflicts in Categorizing Income as Business Profits: Differences in Approach Between Common Law and Civil Law Countries," in *Bulletin for International Fiscal Documentation* (June 2003), pp. 237–248, including footnotes 4 and 5.

[2] See also the discussion in Jack Calder, *Administering Fiscal Regimes for Extractive Industries: a Handbook* (Washington, D.C., International Monetary Fund, 2014), p.87.

liability to taxation in a country that is neither their country of residence nor where a transfer occurred. It also raises issues of whether a seller will be taxed by a country, but the buyer will not be entitled to the treatment under the same country's tax law that the buyer would be accorded in the case of a *direct* transfer of the asset (i.e., where the tax basis of the asset in the hands of the buyer equals its purchase price), even though the tax situation of the seller is likely to be factored into the sale price.

10.1.2.7   There are particular issues for taxpayers and administrations when the indirect transfer or sale concerns a small percentage of an asset, or when an asset is sold to multiple buyers. Keeping track of changes in the indirect ownership of assets imposes an increased burden on tax administrations and can be constrained by its ability to collect and compile information. In this sense, the more capable the information technology systems of an administration are, the more effective its information-gathering powers are; and the more integrated into the international system of exchange of taxpayer information it is, the easier it will be to account for and tax an indirect transfer of assets.

10.1.2.8   A transfer to a single entity with an investment in only one jurisdiction raises fewer complexities, but the same policy considerations apply. If a country determines to tax such indirect transfers, it is particularly important for the source country's domestic legislation to explicitly address the indirect transfer as one that is subject to tax. Provided the seller and buyer both know that the transfer will be subject to a capital gains tax, they can take the tax into account upon sale of the asset and may be able to adjust the price or other contract terms to account for the taxes which will be due in the source state, either by a fixed amount or by reference to some formula based on tax ultimately imposed. In some cases, upfront taxation of indirect transfers may preclude a transfer from taking place, given that the economics of the transaction will be different from ones where the indirect transfer is not a taxable event.

10.1.2.9   Annex I to this chapter shows a "decision tree" of major policy decisions that arise in this area, with an indication of where each of the issues is discussed in this paper. Annex II deals with some symmetry issues that often arise in indirect transfer cases.

10.2   THE ISSUES

10.2.1   Should capital gains be taxed?

10.2.1.1   A threshold policy issue is whether to tax gains made when an asset is disposed of *directly*, such as by sale or other transfer. Such a tax is referred to as a capital gains tax (CGT) in this chapter, although in some countries such gains are subject to a distinct capital gains tax (whether comprehensive[3] or more specific)

---

[3] In practice, no capital gains tax (CGT) is completely comprehensive. The term is used here to mean a relatively comprehensive system of taxation of capital gains.

while in others the gain will be taxed under the general income tax provisions, or as a capital gain specifically brought under those income tax provisions, rather than as a separate tax on capital items only.

10.2.1.2   In a CGT, what is taxed is the *gain* made from the disposal, not the full amount received as proceeds. For a CGT to operate in a particular case, the *person* making the gain will have to be subject to the tax; the *type of asset* disposed of and the *type of disposition* will have to be covered by the tax; and the *type of gain* made will have to be of a type covered by the tax.

Fig. 10.F.1. Direct and Indirect Transfers

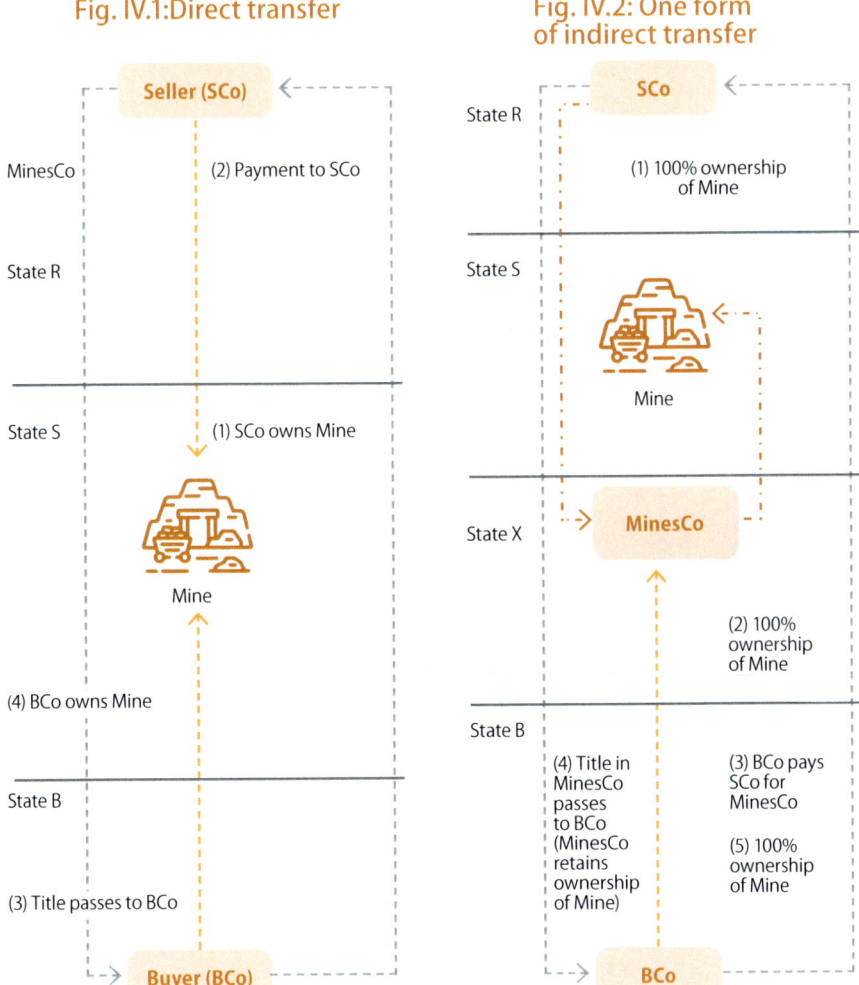

Fig. IV.1:Direct transfer

Fig. IV.2: One form of indirect transfer

10.2.1.3   Policy reasons for or against taxing capital gains comprehensively will inevitably include reasons related in practice to passive assets rather than active assets. While some of these reasons may not be relevant to the extractive sector assets, they are helpful in understanding the wider issues when deciding whether or not a comprehensive tax on capital gains should be introduced. Assuming a capital gain tax is introduced, the reasons assist in assessing whether in the case of certain active assets, there should be an exception.

10.2.2   Arguments for taxing capital gains

10.2.2.1   In policy terms, there are many reasons why capital gains might be taxed, and not all of them will be directly relevant to transfers of extractive assets or even other corporate assets. Reasons commonly given for taxing capital gains when realized are covered in the following paragraphs.

10.2.2.2   The need for base broadening, as part of a trend to widen tax bases and lower tax rates among many countries. The benefits from ownership of property and other forms of capital may not otherwise be as comprehensively taxed as income and consumption, and expanding the tax base in this direction may also have lower economic costs than a rise in tax rates on income items.[4]

10.2.2.3   The concern is that if there is no CGT (or even taxation at a lower rate) taxpayers would rather acquire assets generating capital gains because of the difference in tax treatment between ordinary income and capital gains, thus distorting economic decisions. This leads to a lack of "horizontal equity" between two persons earning the same amounts, one through a capital gain and one through ordinary income, such as wages or business profits. A CGT may reduce the incentive to invest in those assets most likely to produce capital gains.[5]

10.2.2.4   Without CGT, there is a lack of neutrality in the system that prefers capital returns over normal income and creates incentives towards conversion (or the appearance of conversion) of normal income into capital gains. Horizontal equity requires that individuals in similar economic circumstances should bear a similar tax burden irrespective of the form the accretion of the economic benefit takes. In other words, taxpayers should bear similar tax burdens, irrespective of whether their income is received in the form of wages or capital gain. The exclusion of capital gains from the income tax base fundamentally undermines the horizontal equity of the tax system.

10.2.2.5   The concessionary treatment of capital gains as compared to income gains can also lead to speculation and inflation of preferred classes of investments (such as the housing sector). This leads to inefficient allocation of resources, and the waste of human capital in recharacterizing income as capital gains and in combatting such attempts, respectively by taxpayers and tax administrations. The

---

[4] Victoria University of Wellington, *A Tax System for New Zealand's Future, Report of the Victoria University of Wellington Tax Working Group: New Zealand Tax Working Group Report* (2010), p. 16. Available at http://www.victoria.ac.nz/sacl/centres-and-institutes/cagtr/pdf/tax-report-website.pdf.

[5] Ibid, p. 63

application of scarce resources to tax planning and tax avoidance is a dead-weight loss to society.

10.2.2.6   The wealthiest persons (including corporates) will be most likely to make significant capital gains. To tax capital gains reflects their greater ability to pay tax and addresses the conversion of income into capital. Not taxing capital gains results in a lack of horizontal equity that arises because one taxpayer is likely to have proportionately more capital returns, while the other earning the same amount is likely to rely more on normal income. Vertical equity requires that taxpayers with greater ability to pay taxes should bear a greater burden of taxation. It is commonly accepted that capital gains accrue disproportionately to wealthier individuals. Thus, including capital gains in taxable income contributes to the progressivity of the income tax system, while enabling government to pursue other tax policy objectives, premised on widening tax bases and reducing standard tax rates.[6]

10.2.2.7   A comprehensive CGT represents a "safety net" that taxes economic gains that would avoid taxation as normal income. It, thus, implements a more comprehensive concept of taxable "income" than might apply on normal concepts, such as in case law. In some countries, the law might, in fact, already reflect this more comprehensive approach to "income tax."

10.2.2.8   Taxing such gains will speed up the point when tax is paid to the location where the asset is utilized.

10.2.3   Arguments against taxing capital gains

10.2.3.1   A tax on capital gains inappropriately taxes illusory income, since a large component of any gain may be due to inflation on assets held over many years.

10.2.3.2   Not taxing capital gains may encourage investments by allowing them to occur at a lower economic cost, which in turn, creates jobs and encourages economic growth.

10.2.3.3   A comprehensive CGT may be difficult to administer. The potential exceptions, investment distortions and other efficiency implications that may arise from a partial CGT are economically harmful.

10.2.3.4   The complexity (including difficulties in identifying all possible disposal events) of many comprehensive CGT regimes, especially for developing countries, comes with high administration costs (for the revenue administration) and compliance costs (for taxpayers).[7] One senior US Senator stated in 2012 that

---

6 See also Thomas L. Hungerford, "The Economic Effects of Capital Gains Taxation," in *Congressional Research Service* (June 2010). Available at https://fas.org/sgp/crs/misc/R40411.pdf.

7 See, for example, J. Clements, C. Lammam and M. Lo, "The Economic Costs of Capital Gains Taxes in Canada." *in Capital Gains Tax Reform in Canada: Lessons from Abroad* (Canada,

"...we must consider complexity. Experts tell us that about half the US tax code—more than 20,000 pages—exists solely to deal with capital gains..."[8]

10.2.3.5   Taxing business-related capital gains may be purely a timing issue. For example in the case of depreciable assets which are directly acquired, if gains are taxed, the purchaser may obtain a step up in the basis for the acquired assets equal to the price paid, which provides a tax deduction over time against the purchaser's future income. If the gain is not taxed, no such increased tax basis arises and future income and taxes due may be higher. The overall tax paid over time is the same. Given this, and specifically with respect to indirect transfers, the benefit of seeking to tax gains is outweighed by the costs and complexities of doing so, as explained further in this chapter.

10.2.3.6   The deductibility of the stepped-up asset basis referred to above is an issue of particular relevance to taxpayers and one of the main justifications for countries not imposing a CGT on indirect transfers (when the seller might not have the opportunity to further deduct it from his income tax return upon sale of a business or an asset). That is particularly true for those countries concerned with their ability to attract foreign direct investment. In order to make sure that the (direct or indirect) transfer is addressed appropriately by the CGT legislation and that taxpayer is allowed a deduction for the cost incurred, policymakers can adopt approaches such as:

- Taxing the consideration received by the transfer, reduced by the undeducted cost of the transferred right and allowing the acquirer to deduct (over time) the consideration paid for the right (i.e., a stepped-up basis approach); or

- Not taxing the consideration received by the transfer, reduced by the undeducted cost of the transferred right, but likewise not allowing the acquirer to deduct the consideration paid for the right and instead only allowing future deductions equal to the transferor's undeducted costs of the right (i.e., a carryover basis approach).

10.2.3.7   Capital gains taxes are in a sense "voluntary" taxes, unlike taxes on ordinary income. Only when a taxpayer chooses to dispose of assets may tax be payable in respect of those assets. Economic decisions as to disposal of assets will therefore be influenced and potentially distorted by such a tax. This arises since there will be an incentive to retain some investments, even if more profitable or productive opportunities exist, with the result that the economy loses the extra output that would have resulted from the reallocation of capital occurring in the absence of the CGT. This is the so-called lock-in effect of a capital gains tax.[9]

Fraser Institute (2014), p.10. Available at https://www.fraserinstitute.org/sites/default/files/economic-costs-of-capital-gains-taxes-in-canada-chpt.pdf.

[8] US Senate Finance Committee Chairman Max Baucus (2012). Available at http://crfb.org/blogs/capital-gains-and-tax-reform.

[9] See, for example, J. Clements, C. Lammam and M. Lo, "The Economic Costs of Capital Gains Taxes in Canada," *in Capital Gains Tax Reform in Canada: Lessons from Abroad* (Canada,

It follows that, for some, not taxing such gains prevents encouraging these sorts of economic distortions.

10.2.3.8   Not taxing capital gains can keep a country competitive with other countries that do not tax such gains, and create a competitive advantage over those that do.

10.2.3.9   Economic double taxation arises if capital gains on the sale of shares and other interests in entities directly or indirectly owning business assets are taxed. The value of the shares and other interests reflects expected future profits of the extractive activities and the future profits will be taxed as they arise. That would also be the case if the business assets consist of extractive licences, or other extractive assets. In other words, taxes on gains from sales of investment assets are in effect a double tax: the income earned to make the investment was already subject to an income tax and the income from further use of the asset will also be taxed even in the absence of a capital gains tax.

10.2.4   If capital gains are taxed, what should be taxed and how should that be done?

Stand-alone CGT on the gain made through the transfer

10.2.4.1   A country's domestic tax laws could tax capital gains through a comprehensive CGT where the disposal of any kind of assets would be subject to taxation. Alternatively, a specific CGT could be configured, aiming to tax only certain assets or transactions. A comprehensive CGT could have exemptions or "rollovers" delaying the timing of taxation for certain types of assets or upon certain types of events. Such exceptions can distort economic decisions in favour of certain types of assets, but a country may regard that as appropriate to encourage investment in that area.

10.2.4.2   Taxing certain transactions where no cash or other readily marketable property is involved can be harmful to efficient and cost-effective corporate repositioning of assets. In such cases, a country might consider it appropriate, as a means of not discouraging economically beneficial transactions, to exempt or defer tax, where such relief is not seen as abusive of the CGT system. The benefits may be that businesses will be more efficient, and profitable, and therefore able to generate more value over time (including creating additional jobs and additional tax revenues). For example, certain reorganizations between related parties are often exempt, or tax is deferred until there is a disposal to an unrelated party. Even if such an approach is taken, in some cases it may only apply where the restructuring will not lead to reduced tax liability at a later stage.

10.2.4.3   With respect to the extractive industries, it would in practice be very rare for a tax system to exempt all gains from the sale or other transfer of assets

---

Fraser Institute. (2014). p.10. Available at https://www.fraserinstitute.org/sites/default/files/economic-costs-of-capital-gains-taxes-in-canada-chpt.pdf.

used in resource extraction, particularly the exploration and extraction rights and the extractive facilities, from the operation of CGT. However, rules that apply to other businesses, and tax principles that apply to reorganizations or the facilitation of efficient investment, are also highly relevant and important to resource extraction. This issue is specifically considered below in the context of indirect transfers.

10.2.4.4   If there are different tax rates between capital gains and ordinary income, or if the rules operate differently between the two, there will be clear incentives to attempt to earn capital gains rather than ordinary income, or vice versa.

CIT that encompasses capital gains

10.2.4.5   Assuming that the gains from the sale of a capital asset are encompassed within the meaning of taxable income under the regular domestic CIT, they will be taxable as long as the seller is a company considered to be a tax resident or if it is an international company operating through a permanent establishment in the country. Under this scenario, the gain would be integrated into the general income tax base and the corporate income tax rate would apply.

10.2.4.6   Countries wishing to relieve the tax burden—because of the general investment climate, or because they consider that transfers of such assets may encourage more motivated, better-equipped buyers—could allow for tax exemption for certain transactions or tax deductions directly related to the transfers, provided certain requirements are met. These exemptions should be carefully considered since they do reduce the overall tax base in a particular year, although they may not affect the overall tax base over the life of the assets. The current trend in income tax systems is for a wider current year tax base combined with lower rates.

10.2.4.7   The overall fiscal regime that applies in some countries, to a particular extraction activity may be uniquely crafted pursuant to negotiations. In such cases, additional requirements may be imposed by the government, such as specific obligations to construct or improve infrastructure, train workers, or pay surpluses not required from other types of businesses. As a part of the negotiations, a country may also agree to exempt the extractive investment from certain provisions if it feels, in the overall design of the fiscal regime, that such exemptions are warranted and may promote investment. In such cases, one could envision an exemption from capital gains taxes if, as part of an overall negotiation, the country considers it has compensated itself in other ways through the overall fiscal regime it adopts.

10.2.4.8   Whatever approach is taken, transparency and a well thought through policy approach is the best way of encouraging other countries to allow a credit for the tax paid or an exemption, if that is a relevant consideration to the parties. Even under a tax treaty, other countries will only consider themselves bound to allow a credit in view of tax paid in the source country that meets the test of being in accordance with the provisions of the tax treaty. If that is not an issue, there may still be scope for different measurements of the gain. For this reason, openness about the taxation of capital gains, including in treaty negotiations (where a summary of the tax system is often useful and can become an agreed part of the record of the negotiations) and when changes are made to tax rules, is an important component of balancing the need for revenue with the need to have an investment climate encouraging investment for development.

10.2.4.9   Of course, it does not necessarily follow that a transfer involves a gain, and sometimes the transfer outside the country of extractive activities will involve an indirect sale of ownership interests in many countries (such as in the *Zain vs. Uganda Revenue Authority* case in Uganda, noted in box 10.B.4 below). In such cases there will need to be a fair assessment of the amount of the gain connected to/sourced in the particular country and then whether and how the gain is taxable under domestic law.

10.2.4.10   If taxes are imposed on business-related capital gains, it is arguable that, to be even handed, business related capital losses should be deductible against a country's income or capital gains taxes.

10.2.5   Should gains in the extractive industries receive "special" treatment?

10.2.5.1   Countries that tax capital gains do not typically exempt extractive industries from CGT. Arguments that gains from asset sales in the extractive industries should be entirely exempt from capital gains taxation usually relate to their use in an active trade or business as opposed to a passive investment activity.

10.2.5.2   Some countries might consider that unrelieved capital gains taxation might be inappropriate to the class of actively used assets to encourage investments in certain circumstances. For example, Australia has an active assets capital gains tax reduction of 50 per cent, but only for small businesses. Canada also has certain exemptions for certain types of active businesses, but again only for small businesses. South Africa does not tax capital gains on the disposal by individuals or small businesses under certain circumstances.

10.2.5.3   A general exemption might be possible for gains made on extractive industries assets, particularly where returns might, at least in early years, be more marginal, but such exemptions are not at all common in practice. The lack of a wholesale exemption is supported by (i) public expectations that such gains should, in principle, be shared with the country through taxation, and (ii) on the basis that if the main reason for not having a CGT is to encourage investment, that reasoning may not hold for those cases where there is a general perception that the project would go ahead even without this measure. It should be noted, however, that imposition of a tax on a capital gain generally only accelerates tax paid to a country; it does not increase the overall taxes paid over the life of the investment.

10.2.6   Country examples of use of CGT provisions

10.2.6.1   More likely than a special provision exempting the extractive indus-tries from a country's capital gains tax is that countries *without* a general capital gains tax will have a provision bringing gains in that sector into the tax base. Kenya, for example, had been suspending the operation of its CGT since 1985, but in 2012 introduced legislation imposing a 10 per cent final tax on residents (20 per cent non-final on non-residents) for gains on the transfer of shares or property interests in oil and gas, mining or prospecting companies. In 2015, Kenya reintroduced the suspended CGT to tax capital gains generally, but while the general rate is 5 per cent, the rate for the extractive industries is 30 per cent for residents and 37.5 per cent for non-residents with permanent establishments.

10.2.6.2   It should be noted that differential treatment between residents and non-residents may raise tax treaty issues of "non-discrimination," such as under Article 24 of the United Nations Model Convention. The taxable gain is the net gain derived on the disposal of an interest in a "person,"[10] if the interest derived its value from immovable property in Kenya. "Immovable property" in this context meant a mining right, an interest in a petroleum agreement, mining information or petroleum information.[11]

10.2.6.3   Later in the same year, Finance Act 2015 changed the law so that gains from the disposal of shares of a non-local holding company (i.e., an indirect transfer) would not be subject to CGT in Kenya. There is, however, a special rule for oil and gas companies. Paragraph 14(1) of the Ninth Schedule to the Income Tax Act (which deals with taxation of petroleum operations)[12] imposes an obliga-tion to immediately notify (it is not a taxing obligation) the Commissioner if there is a 10 per cent or more change in the underlying ownership[13] of a company operating in the mining, oil and gas sectors.

10.2.6.4   The same paragraph provides that "[i]f the person disposing of the interest to which the notice under subparagraph (1) relates is a non-resident person, the licensee or contractor shall be liable, as agent of the non-resident person, for any tax payable under this Act by the non-resident person in respect of the disposal."

10.2.6.5   The net gain from the indirect disposal of shares in petroleum com-panies is subject to tax in a manner similar to the taxation of transfer of rights, as follows:

---

[10] The term "interest in a person" includes a share or other membership interest in a compa-ny, an interest in a partnership or trust, or any other ownership interest in a person—Section 1(1).

[11] See Kenya Revenue Authority (KRA) CGT Guidelines, Paragraph 13 (January 2015). Avail-able at http://www.revenue.go.ke/notices/pdf2015/Capital-Gains-Tax-Guidelines.pdf. Paragraph 13 of Guidelines dated April 2016, but no longer available on the Internet, indicated the same.

[12] Available at http://kenyalaw.org/lex/actview.xql?actid=CAP.%20470#part_XXVII

[13] "Underlying ownership" is defined as an interest in the person held directly, or indi-rectly through an interposed person or persons, by an individual or by a person not ultimately owned by the individuals.

- Where the interest derived directly or indirectly from immovable property is below 20 per cent of the total value of the interest, the net gain is not taxable;

- Where the interest disposed is between 20 per cent and 50 per cent, the net gain will be taxable using a prescribed formula; and

- Where the interest disposed is above 50 per cent, the net gain will be fully taxable.

- Section 17 of the Ninth Schedule provides that "[a]n amount that is by virtue of this Schedule charged to tax under section 3(2) (a) (i) shall be deemed to be income that accrued in or was derived from Kenya."

10.2.6.6   Other countries which do not have a general tax on capital gains often have special extractive industries legislation, such as New Zealand's provisions that in effect disregard the normal distinction between capital and income returns on asset transfers so that extractives-related capital gains are treated as income. The New Zealand provisions cover, for example, information obtained as a result of exploratory or prospecting activities. However, there are some exceptions in the case of transfers of shares in closely held corporations.

Box 10.B.1: A non-governmental organization's view on the issue of timing of receipts[a]

The view expressed below may be valid based on the assumption that the purchaser in the transaction giving rise to the capital gains tax can deduct the purchase price (including capital gains realized by the seller) from taxable income arising from extractive activities:

It is often argued that it is politically unfeasible in developing countries not to tax billion-dollar sales of the right to exploit national resources. One of the very few ways that a government can extract revenue from extractive sector projects that will not generate a profit for years or even decades is to impose a tax on capital gains. The early injection of substantial revenue from capital gains taxes is obviously very welcome. In some cases, it is seen as a major victory over powerful international companies and a redress to generous tax concessions offered in the original contracts.

The significance of capital gains tax payments is often not well understood. In most countries, the capital gains tax is deductible against future assessments of taxable income. This means that a capital gains tax is not an additional source of government revenue. It does enable the government to bring forward some future revenue. But it also generates additional deductions against company taxable income. Securing early revenue in advance

---

of production delays the onset of profit based taxes (IRPC) and pushes back the date when government revenues will become significant. The resulting offset in medium-term government revenues is considered, if it is even considered at all, a small price to pay for substantial early revenue.

ª Centre fo Public Integrity, Taxing *"Capital Gains" in Mozambique's Extractive Sector* (May 2014). Available at Taxing Capital Gains in Mozambiques Extractive Sector.pdf (acismoz.com)

10.2.6.7   Perhaps one important factor in the general taxation of capital gains in the extractive industries is the widespread public view that transfers of large-scale extractive facilities should bring a return to the government, especially as profits are often seen as coming "a long way down the road" or possibly not materializing at all due to economic circumstances or (sometimes) profit shifting arrangements.

10.2.6.8   In any event, there will be a time value of money advantage for developing countries upon early receipt of consideration for the sale of capital assets, as compared to the later receipts of consideration for outputs from the capital assets. Such an advantage may be especially significant for developing countries. Investors, on the other hand, will see a time value of money disadvantage to such a system, and will build that consideration into their overall investment decision-making and their economic projections.[14] That does not necessarily mean they will not invest because of such a common approach to taxation; it may merely factor into expected profits of an otherwise profitable investment.

10.2.6.9   Rather than a wholesale exemption for the extractive industries from a capital gains tax, far more likely is a tailoring of the application of such a tax to the unique aspects of the industry itself. Thus, as in the instance provided earlier regarding certain corporate restructurings, other transactions and restructuring of asset ownership may also deserve similar exemption or deferral from a potential taxable gain. For example, in many industries, exchanges of assets used in a trade or business that are similar in nature are not taxable immediately. The notion is that each taxpayer has simply continued its investment in the assets of its business, and no cash proceeds have been realized. In such a case, some countries defer the exchange of like-kind assets from taxation until the asset received is ultimately sold.

---

[14] Countries and investors do not always view timing differences equally, since the discount rates they use in determining the present value of an income stream often differ. In many cases, the investor's risk-adjusted discount rates are higher than the country's rate (generally a borrowing rate); where this occurs, the advantage viewed by a country in accelerating a payment to it may be quantitatively less than the disadvantage an investor sees from such an acceleration. In such a case, there is an overall economic loss. "The fact that timing differences are often more valuable to investors than they are costly to countries on a present value basis is an important tool for countries to use to their benefit." See, for example, Karl Schmalz, "Capital Gains Issues in the Extractive Industries," in *Tax Notes International* (October 2016), pp. 91–92.

10.2.6.10   Similarly, most countries encourage investors and businesses to join in conducting a business or making an investment. For example, generally the transfer of assets into a corporation in exchange for an ownership interest (i.e., shares) is not a taxable event. Similarly, the transfer of assets to a partnership to operate a joint business activity is not generally taxable to the partners. Countries examining the scope of taxable events under a tax system that otherwise taxes sales or transfers of assets need to carefully consider application of such taxes to these types of activities.

10.2.7   What are "farm-out" and "farm-in" agreements and how should they be treated?

10.2.7.1   One distinctive characteristic of the extractive industries is that investors often spread their risks (including political, exploration and development risks) by carrying out large natural resource operations jointly.[15] Often these joint ventures are formed after one party has already engaged in substantial activities to acquire licences and conduct exploration activities. As a result of such activities, the value of the initial investment in the extraction project may have substantially increased and, hence, financial exposure has similarly increased. To attract other investors to share in the costs, risks and obligations of developing the project, the initial investor will need to transfer a portion of the project to the new investor, while retaining a smaller portion but with reduced obligations and risks. In most cases, no cash is paid.

10.2.7.2   In the extractive industries, one way to involve additional investors in such a way is through "farm-out" agreements. Particularly common in the oil and gas industry, in these agreements an owner of an oil or gas interest (the "Farmor") agrees to assign part of its interest to another party (the "Farmee") in exchange for certain obligations in connection with development of the oil or gas interest. Sometimes the obligations may include the provision of certain services. More generally, they simply require the new investor to pay a share of all the ongoing costs of exploration and development. In the purely service context (by far the least relevant in large joint venture farm-outs), sometimes these services include drilling a well to a certain depth, in a certain location and in a certain time frame.

10.2.7.3   The agreement also typically stipulates that the well must obtain commercial production. After this contractually agreed service is rendered, the Farmee is said to have "earned" an assignment. This assignment comes after the services are completed, and is sometimes subject to the reservation of an overriding royalty interest in favour of the Farmor.[16] From the Farmee's perspective these are known as "farm-in agreements" (see also Chapter 9, at 9.10 et seq. for

---

[15] Jack Calder, Administering *Fiscal Regimes for Extractive Industries: A Handbook* (Washington, D.C.: International Monetary Fund, 2014), p.87.

[16] Austin W Brister, *Farmout Agreements: The Basics, Negotiations and Motivations* (2013). Available at http://www.Oilandgaslawdigest.Com/Ogagreements/Farmout-Agreements-Basics-Negotiations-Motivations/.

financing aspects of farm in agreements).[17]

10.2.7.4   More typically with respect to extractive industries projects of large scope, the introduction of coventurers simply results in the new investor taking on the responsibility to fund a share of ongoing costs. Generally, these conventional farm-out agreements do not involve cash, or the retention of an overriding royalty. To the extent cash is received, it is generally taxable to the recipient. Where a royalty or overriding royalty is retained, there is no tax due at the time of the farm-out, but tax is paid as income from the royalty, or overriding royalty, is received. The United States of America has long considered the pooling of capital in connection with oil and gas activities as non-taxable under its "pool of capital" doctrine as explained in box 10.B.2 below. Even where the pool of capital doctrine does not apply, tax rules relating to partnerships provide a similar avenue for effecting joint ventures without tax on formation.

10.2.7.5   A major consideration in allowing additional partners to join in the ongoing exploration and/or development of natural resources in a non-taxable fashion is to maximize the chances for full development and provide an efficient way of achieving risk sharing. Given the size and extent of the risks involved in large natural resource developments,[18] policies that facilitate risk sharing will be viewed very favourably by investors. In contrast, policies that in effect place restrictions or additional costs on commonly employed transactions that facilitate risk sharing can make a prospective investment significantly less attractive.[19]

10.2.7.6   The capital gains treatment of farm-outs has great scope for uncertainty, in part because of their frequent complexity, and tax administrations tend to give them increased scrutiny.[20] How they may operate in tax terms needs to be closely considered by administrations and the participants. Of course, how a country's tax system treats the formation of a joint venture to develop an extractive project will inevitably have some consequences as to a potential investor's decision whether or not to go forward with the development opportunity, and if so, how.[21]

---

[17] An example of an actual agreement in the case of coalbed methane resources may be seen at https://www.sec.gov/Archives/edgar/containers/fix045/1124024/0001193125090545 36/dex101.htm.

[18] See, for example, *International Energy Agency Special Report on World Energy Investment Outlook 2014 Special Report*, p. 32, for a list of the risk factors investors face.

[19] Given that over the life of the project, the same amount of taxes should be collected, the timing benefits to the country of receiving some of this revenue at an earlier period must be weighed against a permanent loss of revenue if a project does not go forward, or is not as fully developed as it otherwise could be as a result of these policy choices.

[20] See, for example, Greenwoods and Freehills, "Tax certainty for farm-outs?," in *Tax Brief* (September 2011). Available at http://www.greenwoods.com.au/media/1308/tax_brief_tax_certainty_for_farm-outs.pdf. The Australian Taxation Office Rulings referred to MT 2012/1 and 2012/2 are available, respectively, at http://law.ato.gov.au/atolaw/view.htm?docid=MXR/MT20121/NAT/ATO/00001 and https://www.ato.gov.au/law/view/document?docid=MXR/MT20122/NAT/ATO/00001.

[21] See, for example, the discussion in Denis Kakembo, "How to keep investors' taps flowing as global oil prices head to rock bottom," in The East African (February 2015). Available at http://

Box 10.B.2: Services performed for oil and gas property interests[a]

1. Frequently promoters, accountants, lawyers, geologists, operators, and others receive an interest in an oil and gas drilling venture in return for services rendered. These services may have been rendered in acquiring drilling prospects, evaluating leases, packaging the drilling programme, or, in general, administrative services such as formation of partnerships, filing with Securities and Exchange Commission (SEC) and other functions.

2. It is a common practice for the promoter or sponsor of a drilling package to acquire part or all of the interest in the drilling venture in return for services. GCM 22730, 1941–1 CB 214, provided that the receipt of an interest in a drilling venture in return for capital and services furnished by a driller and equipment supplier was not taxable on receipt. This ruling provided for the "pool of capital" doctrine that is widely quoted in oil and gas tax law. The same reasoning has been extended to geologists, petroleum engineers, lease brokers, accountants, and lawyers who receive an interest in an oil or gas drilling venture in return for services rendered. This doctrine resulted from the court decision in **Palmer vs. Bender,** 287 U.S. 551 (1933); 1933–1 C.B. 235; 11 AFTR 1106; 3 USTC 1026.

3. The "pool of capital doctrine" is widely accepted by accountants and lawyers and is still quoted to justify the tax-free receipt of property for services. Subsequent changes in the tax laws and subsequent court cases have significantly limited the use of GCM 22730. (…)

8. While the pool of capital doctrine is still viable in specific factual circumstances, it does not equate to a special exemption from IRC 83 for the oil and gas industry. Generally, for the pool of capital doctrine to apply all of the following must occur:

> **A.** The contributor of services must receive a share of production, and the share of production is marked by an assignment of an economic interest in return for the contribution of services.

> **B.** The services contributed may not in effect be a substitution of capital.

> **C.** The contribution must perform a function necessary to bring the property into production or augment the pool of capital already invested in the oil and gas in place.

> **D.** The contribution must be specific to the property in which the economic interest is earned.

E. The contribution must be definite and determinable.

F. The contributor must look only to the economic interest for the possibility of profit.

---

[a] Internal Revenue Service, Oil and Gas Handbook, section 4.41.1.2.3.1. Available at www.irs.gov/irm/part4/irm_04-041-001.html.)

10.3 TAXATION OF GAINS FROM INDIRECT TRANSFERS IN DOMESTIC LAW

10.3.1 Tax policy considerations

10.3.1.1 When making policy decisions, each country must consider its own circumstances in determining whether or not it should tax gains made from indirect transfers. If a country decides to tax indirect transfers, the question is how that should be done, taking into account the tax policy aspects addressed in this chapter. There are increasing expectations, including from the broader citizenry, that if direct transfers of a mine or other extractive facilities are subject to taxation on the gains made, an indirect transfer should have the same effect in revenue terms, despite the lack of any change in the direct ownership of the assets, and the separate legal entity status of distinct companies in the chain of ownership.

10.3.1.2 In tax policy terms, the position is often taken that the soundness of the system for taxing direct transfers of interests requires the taxation of indirect transfers that otherwise have the same characteristics; otherwise those with the means to do so will simply structure transfers indirectly. The value of extractive facilities is no doubt one reason for the particular focus on indirect transfers of such facilities, and one of the ways a multinational can extract profits from the extractive industries is through the sale of shares. The issue also arises in other areas also, such as in connection with real estate holdings and telecommunications assets. It is fair to say, however, that the information and other compliance and enforcement issues in taxing indirect transfers are not sufficiently discussed in detail in such debates, even if legislation can be drafted in a way that seeks to deal with these issues, as noted below.

10.3.1.3 Apart from the compliance and enforcement issues, another argument

---

www.theeastafrican.co.ke/OpEd/comment/How-to-keep-investors--taps-flowing-as-global-oil-prices-fall/434750-2616576-item-1-h80dmqz/index.html. For other examples and templates see example https://www.ampla.org/modeldocuments/documents/model-documents52; https://www.otciq.com/otciq/ajax/showFinancialReportById.pdf?id=108854; http://www.okbar.org/members/BarJournal/archive2005/Mayarchive05/obj7615oil.aspx;and Michael L. Covey Jr., Documenting the Oil and Gas Farmout Agreement (2005).

given for not taxing indirect transfers is that the production of income from the domestic mine or oil and gas assets continues to be subject to taxation; thus, no tax revenue is lost to the country. While there is a timing difference on the collection of tax revenues, the absolute amount does not change. This is because if the gain is taxable, in order to avoid double taxation, the domestic asset values need to be increased for tax purposes by the amount of that gain, giving rise to higher ongoing depreciation and depletion deductions and a corresponding reduction in future tax receipts. Given the fact that the total amount of taxes ultimately paid will not change (if the tax value of the domestic asset values is increased) a country needs to balance the revenue timing benefit versus the complexity of compliance and enforcement that arises from seeking to tax such indirect sales.

Box 10.B.3: An example of asset transfer taxation: Norway [a]

As a starting point, capital gains/capital losses arising from the transfer of assets located on the Norwegian continental shelf are taxable/deductible. (…)

However, in practice, most asset deals are exempt from tax based on provisions in section 10 of the PTA. According to section 10, an approval from the MOF [Ministry of Finance] is required with regard to the tax effects of a transfer of assets that are under the petroleum tax regime, provided that consent to the transfer is needed from the MPE [Ministry of Petroleum and Energy]. Consent from the MPE is needed upon a direct or indirect transfer of a licence and where the assets will follow the transfer of the licence. This is applicable if all fixed offshore installations pertaining to a licence are transferred (even if the licence itself is not transferred).

According to regulations adopted based on section 10 of the PTA, capital gains arising from the transfer of assets that are allocated to the petroleum tax regime are not taxable and losses non-deductible (neither when calculating ordinary petroleum tax nor special tax). Moreover, the buyer will take over the seller's tax balances (including the basis for uplift) and other tax positions and stand in the shoes of the vendor.

There are also specific provisions in the regulations dealing with transfers where one of the parties covers future exploration costs, or where the seller covers future abandonment costs pertaining to the assigned interest. Broadly, the regulations state that it will be the party who will eventually bear the costs that may deduct those costs and claim a refund of the tax values of those costs when they accrue (i.e., according to the same system that would apply to the seller if the licence was kept). (…)

The rationale for these rules is that the Norwegian state tax revenues from upstream activities should be unaffected by a transfer. (…)

Consent from the MOF is also required for an indirect transfer such as a share deal implying a change of control. Such deals are, in practice, straightforward from a tax perspective as there are no withholding taxes regardless of where the shareholder is a resident.

_____

ᵃ The text of this box is quoted from: Deloitte Touche Tohmatsu Limited, Oil and Gas Taxation in Norway (Stavanger, Norway, 2014), p. 6. Available at http://www2.deloitte.com/content/dam/Deloitte/global/Documents/Energy-and-Resources/gx-er-oil-and-gas-taxguide-norway.pdf.

10.3.1.4   Another argument commonly made against the taxation of indirect transfers is that it in effect constitutes extraterritorial taxation of foreign economic activity by the source state. Owing to the separate legal entities involved, taxing such transfers occurring in a foreign country does not involve any domestic residents as a party to the transfer. It should also be borne in mind that taxing indirect transfers affects the price of the transaction, as the seller will factor the tax to be paid into the selling price of the shares.

10.3.1.5   The contrary view is that a certain degree of extraterritoriality is well supported in international law and is often explicitly part of domestic law.[22] It is expressed in the Government of India's 2012 Draft Report on Retrospective Amendments Relating to Indirect Transfer Expert Committee, which noted that:

[I]n the case of *Electronics Corporation of India Ltd.* (ECIL) the Supreme Court referred the matter, being of substantial public importance, to a Constitution Bench after making the following observations:

- The operation of the law can extend to persons, things and acts outside the territory of India.

- Reliance was placed on the decision of the Privy Council in the case of *British Columbia Electric Railway Co. Ltd. v. King* [1946] AC 527, 542 (PC) wherein it was stated that "A Legislature which passes a law having extra-territorial operation may find that what it has enacted cannot be directly enforced, but the Act is not invalid on that account, and the courts of its country must enforce the law with the machinery available to them."

_____

[22] See, for example, the influential Statute of Westminster, section 3: "It is hereby declared and enacted that the Parliament of a Dominion has full power to make laws having extra-territorial operation." Although an Act of the United Kingdom of Great Britain and Northern Ireland Parliament, this Act established the legislative independence of what were then the self-governing Dominions of the British Empire. Available at http://www.legislation.gov.uk/ukpga/Geo5/22-23/4/section/3.

- The provocation for the law must be found within India itself. Such a law may have extra-territorial operation in order to subserve the object and that object must be related to something in India. It is inconceivable that a law should be made by Parliament in India which has no relationship with anything in India. However, the matter was not pursued by the applicant, being a public-sector company, and therefore it is still an open issue. The decision did clarify one issue that, on the grounds of non-enforceability in India, a law cannot be held as invalid. The reference was, however, made on the second issue, i.e., whether there was sufficient nexus with India or not.[23]

10.3.1.6   Cameroon amended its legislation in 2014 to deal with the matter quite explicitly. Law No. 2014/026 of 23 December 2014 on the Finance Law, amended existing legislation as follows:

Section 42: The following shall be taxable as (...) net overall capital gains realized in Cameroon or abroad during the transfer, **even indirect**, of stocks, bonds and other capital shares of enterprises governed by Cameroonian law (...).

The indirect transfer of stocks, shares and bonds of enterprises governed by Cameroonian law including notably any transfer made in Cameroon or abroad between two foreign companies under the same consolidation scope when one of the entities of this scope, completely or partially, holds the share capital of an enterprise governed by Cameroonian law.[24]

10.3.1.7   Countries asserting tax jurisdiction over indirect transfers will usually need to explicitly assert jurisdiction over both the transfer and the transferor (even if they also claim jurisdiction over a local entity, such as in an agency capacity or because it has failed to notify of the indirect disposal as required by law) and will also generally need to provide that it is to be treated as a domestically sourced gain. Ecuador provides in Article 8 of its domestic tax law, for example, that the following category of income is deemed to be from an Ecuadorian source:

3.1.   The profits obtained by companies, regardless of whether they are domiciled in Ecuador or not, and Ecuadorian or foreign individuals, regardless of whether they are resident in the country or not, derived from the disposal, be it direct or indirect, of shares, equity participations, other claims to capital or other rights permitting exploration, production, concession or similar activities,

---

23 See paragraph 4.1.1. Available at https://www.incometaxindia.gov.in/Lists/Press%20Releases/Attachments/21/Draft_Report.pdf.

24 Available at http://www.prc.cm/en/multimedia/documents/3310-finance-law-of-the-republic-of-cameroon-for-the-2015-financial-year.

of companies that are domiciled or permanent establishments in Ecuador.[25]

10.3.1.8   Some countries take positions that judicial or legislative anti-abuse rules, such as a general anti-avoidance rule (GAAR), apply to indirect transfers. For example, the People's Republic of China's State Administration of Taxation issued new administrative guidance on application of their GAAR in 2015 to recharacterize an indirect transfer of certain properties as a direct transfer of those properties.[26] Those favouring GAARs point to the need to cover types of conduct (abuses) and discourage them rather than merely addressing specific types of such abusive conduct, providing a possible "road map" for tax avoidance.

10.3.1.9   One issue that may arise when GAARs are relied on in the case of indirect transfers is that of whether there is a "treaty override" occurring. The circumstances when GAARs may or may not be in compliance with tax treaties are discussed in the Commentary to Article 1 of both the United Nations and OECD Models Conventions. By using domestic law to address certain indirect sales as "abusive" it follows of course that the scope of the anti-abuse rules would be necessarily limited to what constitutes abusive transactions in the terms of the relevant legislation (including any requirements of proof that fall upon the tax administration) and this might not always be seen by a country as sufficient for properly achieving the goals of taxing capital gains derived from extractive assets. If officials are not confident that such anti-abuse rules will be applied by courts to indirect transfers in the same way as for direct transfers, more specific domestic legislation would be necessary to achieve this result. Such specific domestic legislation does not necessarily have to be a special anti-abuse (or anti-avoidance) rule (a SAAR) and can be applicable to more types of transactions.

10.3.1.10   Treaty abuse and the use of a GAAR have been the subject of some discussion in recent Indian cases relating to indirect transfer of assets that might otherwise be subject to taxation in India. Such cases include *Vodafone International Holdings B.V. v. UOI & another*[27] and *Sanofi Pasteur S.A v. Dept of Revenue.*[28]

---

[25] SRI (Internal Revenue Service of Ecuador) presentation, Treatment of capital gains in mining projects in Ecuador (September 2015). Available at https://www.imf.org/external/spanish/np/seminars/2015/andean/pdf/sesion2-delgado-en.pdf .

[26] See Baker and McKenzie, Breaking News: China Issues Long Awaited Indirect Transfer Regulation Replacing Notice 698 (February 2015). Available at http://www.lexology.com/library/detail.aspx?g=b8226983-cb9e-4575-8ce8-cb9283a41706.

[27] Vodafone International Holdings B.V. v. UOI & another [2012] 341 ITR 1 (SC). Available at https://indiankanoon.org/doc/115852355.

[28] Sanofi Pasteur Holding SA v. Dept of Revenue [2013] 30 taxmann.com 222 (AP). Available at https://indiankanoon.org/doc/171254621/. See also in this respect, Canada-Mill Investments S.A v. Her Majesty the Queen, Case number 2004-3354 (IT) G, Tax Court of Canada, 19 August 2006, concerning a complex tax reorganization and restructuring in order to (i) avoid the incidence of capital gains tax in Canada (the underlying asset responsible for the capital gain was a deposit of nickel, copper and cobalt in Canada; and (ii) obtain a more favourable jurisdiction from which to invest in mines in Africa. The court found that the Canadian GAAR would not apply in this case because there was no avoidance transaction. There was an underlying issue related to the application of Article 13(4) in the treaty between Canada and Luxembourg, but the court found that there was no abuse in the use of the treaty, and that the Canadian tax

Vodafone addresses the taxability of an offshore transfer of shares with their under-lying value being assets in India. The case concerns the transfer of shares of CGP, a Cayman based subsidiary of HTIL, owned by the Hutchinson group, to Vodafone, a company incorporated in the Netherlands. HTIL owned Hutchinson's operations in India through a series of companies incorporated in Mauritius.[29]

10.3.1.11   The tax authorities notified Vodafone of what they considered its failure to withhold taxes on gains arising to HTIL from the transfer of shares to CGP, based on the argument that the sale of shares resulted in an underlying sale of assets located in India. The case was examined by the Indian Supreme Court and it found for Vodafone, deciding that no taxes were payable in India on the indirect transfer. The Indian Government subsequently enacted retroactive amendments to the Finance Act of 2012, which in effect reversed the effect of the court decision.[30]

10.3.1.12   Soon after the Vodafone case, the Andhra Pradesh High Court had a similar case submitted to its adjudication with a similar result: the *Sanofi Pasteur Holding SA v. The Department of Revenue* case. In *Sanofi,* the issue was whether the gains arising from the offshore transfer of shares of a French company holding substantial interest (80 per cent) in an Indian company, were subject to tax in India. As in *Sanofi*, the revenue authorities contended that the transaction attracted capital gains tax in India because it resulted in an indirect transfer of assets in India. The High Court concluded that the French company could not be disregarded as a legal entity merely because it was regarded as an intermediary holding company. As a result, there was no treaty abuse. The decision was based on the tax treaty between France and India, which gave the taxing rights of the transaction to France. Although the *Vodafone* and the *Sanofi* cases both ruled for taxation by the residence country, these cases go to show that countries which typically hold activities and generate value are becoming ever more vigilant towards indirect asset transfers.

10.3.1.13   Differences will exist among the revenue authorities and the courts of different countries on how these indirect transfer cases should be assessed against the law; the possibility of double taxation, therefore, arises (although many transfers would be structured to also avoid taxes abroad). However, there is also a risk to buyers of an unexpected liability arising in a foreign country and that it might impact the ability to effectively or profitably utilize the purchased asset. This is likely to have an impact on the investment climate of a country.[31]

---

authorities must have had a good reason to allow Luxembourg to retain taxing rights over the transaction.

[29] M. Butani, *Tax Dispute Resolution—Challenges and Opportunities for India*, Lexis Nexis, Crier, (2016) pp. 47–48.

[30] The 2012 Finance Act of India has sought to include specific anti-avoidance rules relating to indirect transfers of capital assets by (i) taxing capital gains even when the transfer price is not ascertainable/determinable and (ii) imposing the onus on the holding company to prove the source of income of a resident shareholder, among others.

[31] Investors seek certainty and the reduction of risks. They highly value legal systems that are predictable and clear. When a country changes its rules after investments have been made

10.3.1.14   As recognized in the Commentaries to Article 1 of both the United Nations and OECD Model Conventions, issues of treaty override may also arise in the case of specific legislation. Countries proposing or having legislative provisions dealing with indirect transfers, therefore, need to at least consider their relationship to treaty obligations; of course, it is always advisable to notify negotiation partners of legislation addressing such issues and to keep treaty partners advised of changes in such legislation. In particular, even if local courts accept that the domestic law must be followed (either because it is compatible with the treaty applying accepted rules of treaty interpretation, or because it must be applied by the court even if inconsistent, i.e., they do not have a constitutional or other provision giving treaties supremacy over legislation) there is no guarantee that the other country will accept this (especially in the latter case) and give credit for the taxes paid as a result of the judgment.

Box 10.B.4: Uganda: *Zain vs. Uganda Revenue Authority* [a]

In September 2014, an appeals court in Uganda ruled in favour of the Uganda Revenue Authority (URA) in the *Zain vs. Uganda Revenue Authority* case. Shares in the Netherlands company Zain Africa BV, that owned 100% of a Ugandan telecommunications provider, were transferred between two Dutch companies (from Zain BV to Bharti A BV) and it was argued that even if taxation was allowed under domestic law, under the Netherlands-Uganda tax treaty, Uganda had no taxing right preserved (there was no equivalent to the United Nations or OECD Article 13(4)) of their respective Models). The URA was able to apply Section 88(5) of Uganda's Income Tax Act to preserve its taxing right. This section provides that:

[W]here an international agreement provides that income derived from sources in Uganda is exempt from Ugandan tax or is subject to a reduction in the rate of Ugandan tax, the benefit of that exemption or reduction is not available to any person who, for the purposes of the agreement, is a resident of the other contracting state where 50 per cent or more of the underlying ownership of that person is held by an individual or individuals who are not residents of that other Contracting State for the purposes of the agreement.

The argument would be that the United Nations and Organization for Economic Cooperation and Development (OECD) Models both give (in their Commentaries to Article 1) some latitude for domestic anti-avoidance rules to operate consistently with a treaty, and that Section 88(5) met that test. The alternative would be that it was inconsistent with the treaty and

---

or transactions have occurred in reliance on then existing statutes or other rulings, uncertainty increases, and future investment will be affected.

could not operate in domestic law in this case. The Court ruling over-turned an earlier High Court decision that Uganda had no jurisdiction to tax. It decided the case on a narrow procedural ground, however: The URA had originally assessed it as an ordinary capital gain, but when challenged by the taxpayer, they revised their assessment to treat the Uganda company that had changed hands via the Netherlands holding company as one deriving most of its value from immovable assets. The taxpayer's challenge was that the revenue authority had not followed the correct process in changing the grounds of its assessment, but the court held that the URA did have the right to reassess the taxpayer. It did not pronounce on whether that revised assessment would be valid. The decision did not finally dispose of the case and the issue of treaty compatibility of Section 88(5) but the matter was sent back to the URA to consider whether and if so what amount of gain was sourced in Uganda and taxable.

---

[a] See, for example, Daniel K. Kalinaki, "Court gives URA nod to seek taxes on sale of Zain assets in Uganda," in *The East African* (September 2014). Available at: HakiPensheni: Court gives URA nod to seek taxes on sale of Zain assets in Uganda

10.3.1.15   There are other reasons often favouring SAARs rather than relying on a GAAR, and in recent years there has been a great deal of such legislation in Africa to attempt to counter indirect transfers in the extractive industries.[32] These reasons include that SAARs can be more precise about who must bear the compliance obligations, and what the obligations are. A SAAR can, for example, focus on related party transfers, minimum shareholdings and off-stock exchange transfers to limit the impact on transactions that are not considered to be high risk. Finally, a SAAR need not depend on a "purpose" test (which can be difficult to prove for whomever bears the onus of proof, create uncertainty for both administrations and taxpayers and can involve a great deal of discretion on the part of officials). Instead, it can more "scientifically" make an indirect transfer taxable irrespective of the purpose of the transfer by, for example, treating it as equal to a direct transfer.

10.3.1.16   Any such legislation needs to be seen (like a GAAR) in the context of a country's tax treaty network. Tax treaties cannot give a taxing power that does not exist in domestic legislation, but they can either allow it to continue to be exercised or can prevent it from being exercised. It is therefore important that a country's tax treaties preserve the right to apply the domestic legislation in that treaty relationship. It is also strongly advisable that all treaties consistently preserve these rights, otherwise, there would be an inducement to use treaty shopping

---

[32] Kennedy Munyandi and others, "*Tax Policy Trends in Africa—Commentary on the Major Tax Developments in 2013 and 2014,*" in *Bulletin for International Taxation* (March 2015), pp. 154, 158–9.

techniques to have a transfer occur in a state against which the domestic legislation of the other state is overridden by treaty rules (i.e., where no taxing right is preserved). This issue is discussed further in the section on symmetry following.

10.3.2   The issue of symmetry

10.3.2.1   Whatever approach is taken to the application of a general or specific capital gains tax provision, one factor in the policy decision is the possibility of asymmetries of treatment.[33] From the revenue perspective, a country would not want to allow a purchaser to take current or future deductions based on the purchase cost of an asset if the country has a capital gains tax but is, for whatever reason, unable to tax capital gains derived by the seller of the asset. This situation could arise where a transfer is either untaxed or concessionally taxed (as compared with income gains). Thus, where a gain is treated as a capital gain and is either untaxed because the country does not have a CGT, or concessionally taxed under the CGT, then there will be asymmetric tax treatment between the transferor and transferee, as the transferee's cost represented by the gain is likely to be deducted at the normal corporate tax rate.

10.3.2.2   On the other hand, it may deter economic activity if the seller's capital gains are taxed but no deductions are available to the purchaser for the cost of acquiring the asset in the form of depreciation or cost-basis in the asset that can be deducted when calculating taxable income (including capital gains) in the future.

10.3.2.3   For example, in a case where an indirect transfer is recharacterized as a direct transfer, the built-in gains in the assets held by the underlying domestic corporation will be essentially taxed to its shareholder-seller. In this case, symmetry may be regarded as being maintained between the seller and the purchaser, since the purchaser's basis in the shares in the domestic corporation would be the purchase price paid to the seller, for which the seller realized capital gain. However, without a specific statutory rule, the basis in the assets owned by the domestic corporation would remain unchanged (i.e., not stepped-up for the amount of capital gains already taxed in the seller) and this can be regarded as an asymmetry.

10.3.2.4   In contrast, some countries address an indirect transfer by deeming a transfer and the subsequent re-acquisition by the underlying domestic corporation of assets owned and liabilities owed by that corporation immediately before the underlying ownership changed,[34] thus, confirming a liability to domestic tax. In those cases, symmetry will be maintained, since the domestic corporation acquires a cost-basis in the assets deemed to be acquired which can be deducted in the future for tax purposes.

---

[33] See Annex III to this Handbook with worked examples illustrating the significance of the issue of symmetry.

[34] See, for example, the United Republic of Tanzania Income Tax Act 2004 (as amended), S.56. Available at http://www.wipo.int/wipolex/en/details.jsp?id=11106

10.3.2.5   If a country deems a transfer and re-acquisition by the underlying domestic corporation, it would not have access to consideration for an actual transfer of shares or other indirect interests with which to pay the tax. The increased future deductions by the corporation would negatively impact taxes payable in future on its reduced taxable income. One possibility would be conditioning the basis "step up" to the purchaser on the revenue authority receiving the tax from (or on behalf of) the seller.

10.3.2.6   Where countries frame their indirect transfers legislation relatively narrowly in order to deal with what are perceived as abusive cases (less likely to involve unsuspecting buyers and sellers and more likely to involve a purpose of avoiding tax on a transfer) they may be less willing to grant symmetrical benefits to the buyer. In such cases, there is probably an intention to bring about the result that the buyer will ensure the right amount of tax is paid on the gain—especially since the buyer may otherwise be a beneficiary from the seller not paying taxes on the transfer—through paying a lower price, albeit with lower deductions over time. The possible imposition of a "double" penalty (i.e., on both buyer and seller) should be recognized and evaluated in policy terms, however, and the impact on any unsuspecting buyers should be borne in mind in framing any legislation. There could possibly be a provision allowing the buyer to obtain symmetrical benefits if the buyer can prove *bona fides* through a demonstrated lack of either (i) awareness of; or (ii) negligence as to, the abusive purpose/lack of reasonable commercial purpose.

10.3.2.7   Countries will also take different views on how to ensure symmetry, since this can be done by either (i) taxing gains to the seller but allowing a deduction for the buyer based on the purchase price; or (ii) not taxing the seller and not granting deductions to the buyer. The former approach might be preferred by those desiring payments as early as possible, and with less concern regarding the budgetary implications of the "lumpiness" of revenues and difficulty in predicting such payments, or the impact on investors or on those having a sense that the impact on investors is reasonable in the context of the agreement as a whole. The latter approach might be preferred by countries who are confident that future profit will be properly recorded and will be taxed in practice, who regard such profits as more predictable over time and who desire to preserve such revenues for future needs.

10.3.3   Indirect transfers and corporate restructuring

10.3.3.1   There are many business reasons unrelated to taxation for corporate restructuring, such as adapting to changes in markets, the way in which a business is conducted, or in management approaches. Restructuring could, for example, be undertaken in preparation for a share market float, to prepare for a transfer of some or all of the business, or to raise capital. Such a restructuring can lead to disposals and could lead to an indirect transfer of an asset in another country.

10.3.3.2   Some countries provide capital gains relief for dispositions arising from certain types of corporate restructuring, such as between related companies. South Africa's rollover relief for asset-for-share transactions, amalgamation transactions and intra-group transactions is an example.[35] One policy issue is whether—and, if so, why—there should be any different result if the same type of exempt direct transfer was done as an indirect transfer.

10.3.3.3   In relation to its Public Notice 7 on indirect transfers (considered below) for example, China addresses these issues by providing relief for internal group restructurings that meet certain specified requirements: (i) a more than 80 per cent equity relationship exists between the transferor and the transferee; (ii) the tax burdens in China for any subsequent indirect transfer would not be less than that for the same or similar indirect transfer were it to be conducted instead of the indirect transfer at issue; and (iii) the consideration paid by the transferee only consists of equity of the transferee or its affiliates.[36] Even in reorganizations or acquisitions involving unrelated parties, a question arises as to whether such transactions should trigger indirect taxation events wherever the acquired entity has subsidiaries or other business operations. For example, when one publicly listed major enterprise combines with another via a merger transaction, clearly not motivated as a means of avoiding local taxation, countries may often decide to limit their indirect transfer jurisdiction.[37]

10.4   BILATERAL TAX TREATY ASPECTS

10.4.1   Taxing rights in tax treaties

10.4.1.1   Tax treaties are generally regarded as not creating taxing rights that do not exist in domestic law, but they can prevent or limit the operation of domestic law where that is for the benefit of taxpayers of the countries entering those treaties. This means that if the domestic law of a country provides for the taxation of offshore indirect transfers, the tax treaty between that country and the country of residence of the seller of the interest will need to be examined to see if it (i) allows the domestic law to operate as intended; or (ii) restricts the operation of the domestic tax law to the advantage of a taxpayer covered by the treaty. The consequences of this relationship between tax treaties and domestic law are that:

(i)   If there is no domestic law in place taxing gains from indirect transfers, the treaty will not address the deficiency by creating a taxing right;

(ii)   Any treaty right conferred to the country of location of the assets

---

[35] See sections 42, 44 and 45 of South Africa's Income Tax Act of 1962.

[36] See Baker and McKenzie, Breaking News: China Issues Long Awaited Indirect Transfer Regulation Replacing Notice 698 (February 2015). Available at http://www.lexology.com/library/detail.aspx?g=b8226983-cb9e-4575-8ce8-cb9283a41706.

[37] See Baker and McKenzie, Breaking News: China Issues Long Awaited Indirect Transfer Regulation Replacing Notice 698 (February 2015). Available at http://www.lexology.com/library/detail.aspx?g=b8226983-cb9e-4575-8ce8-cb9283a41706.

subject to an indirect sale merely represents an unexercised right to taxation unless and until the domestic law is amended to tax indirect transfers;

(iii) A treaty right to tax need not have all the details of the domestic law, but it needs to be broadly expressed if it is to cover all the situations foreseen under domestic law (as in the United Nations and OECD Model Conventions discussed below); and

(iv) The treaty may limit the operation of domestic law to the extent that the right preserved is narrower than domestic law or no taxing right is preserved. Any attempt to change that by amending domestic law may be a treaty override contrary to the terms of the treaty.

10.4.1.2   The relationship between a tax treaty and domestic law was raised in *Resource Capital Fund III LP v. Commissioner of Taxation* (Australia).[38] Resource Capital Fund III LP (RCF) was a limited partnership formed in the Cayman Islands. In 2006, it bought shares in St. Barbara Mines Limited (SBM), an Australian company that conducted gold mining activities in Australia. In 2007, RCF sold some of its shares in SBM to unrelated parties with a gain. RCF's affairs were managed by a Delaware Limited Liability Company (LLC), based in the United States, which is the reason why the US treaty was invoked in this case. Many of the limited partners were also US-based.

10.4.1.3   The issues in RCF were whether (i) the Commissioner was allowed to issue an assessment to RCF or whether the treaty precluded him from doing so; and (ii) if the Commissioner was able to issue the assessment, whether the gain realized by RCF was subject to tax in Australia under the domestic tax law provisions. The Full Federal Court concluded that since the LP is not a US resident for treaty purposes, the Australia-US treaty did not apply to it and, therefore, the treaty could not prevent the operation of the domestic rules that treated the LP as a separate taxpayer making the gain in Australia. Therefore, in this case, the domestic law prevailed, since no applicable treaty existed to limit that law's operation, and the capital gain met the legislative test of taxable Australian property.[39]

10.4.1.4   Assuming that domestic law on taxation of indirect transfers is in place or is being kept open as a possibility, the question is then whether the treaty limits such an exercise of taxing rights and thereby overrules the legislation to some degree. To consider that issue, the provisions on capital gains of a specific tax treaty (often Article 13) have to be studied:

---

38 Case number (3013) FCA 636, Federal Court of Australia—Full Court, 3 April 2014.

39 Leave to appeal was refused by the Australian High Court.

Box 10.B.5: Australia: Lamesa v. Commissioner of Taxation[a]

In *Lamesa v. Commissioner of Taxation*, the issue was whether Lamesa Holdings BV, a Dutch company, was liable to pay income tax under Article 13(2) of the Australia-Netherlands treaty in respect of profits made by it from the sale of shares in a publicly listed Australian company. In 1992, a US business became interested in acquiring an Australian listed mining company. To this end, a US investment vehicle was established which acquired an Australian subsidiary. A Dutch company was interposed. The Australian subsidiary then acquired another Australian company that, in turn, acquired a 100% interest in the listed mining company in a takeover. That mining company owned a subsidiary which held a number of mineral exploration rights. In 1994 and 1996, the Dutch company sold its shares in the first Australian subsidiary, first by way of flotation on the stock exchange and the balance by way of private sale. The Dutch company was assessed to capital gains tax on the profits made from its sale of these shares. Objections against these assessments were allowed. However, further assessments were then issued on the basis that the profits of some $200 million were ordinary income of the company. This time, objections were disallowed and the company appealed.

The company relied on Article 13 of the treaty to argue that the profits were excluded from Australian tax. Article 13 deals with alienation of assets and operates as an exception to the general rule in Article 7 dealing with business profits. Article 7 provides that profits of Dutch enterprises are only taxable in the Netherlands unless the enterprise is carried out in Australia through a permanent establishment. The Australian Taxation Office (ATO) accepted that the company did not have a permanent establishment in Australia. At the time of the conflict, Article 13(2) provided that Australia could tax income from the alienation of real property situated in Australia. "Real property" was defined in the treaty to include direct interests in land, exploration rights and shares in companies with assets principally consisting of interests in land or exploration rights. The Federal Court held that Article 13(2) did not apply to allow Australia to tax the profits made by the Dutch company on the sale of shares in its Australian subsidiary. The company did not acquire direct interests in land or any exploration rights. Note that, despite a frequent analysis of this case, it seems that the reference to direct interests only was not critical ("direct" interests referred to the inherent nature of the interests, not how they were held, i.e., directly as opposed to indirectly held).

> (1) Upon consideration as to whether Article 13(2)(a)(iii) of the treaty should be construed so that the words "the assets of which" extend to assets of various companies down the line of a chain of companies, or should be restricted so that the words

bear their literal meaning, the Court decided that Article 13(2) did not apply to give Australia exclusive taxing rights over the profit on the sale of the shares. Rather, the profits fell to be taxed exclusively under Dutch law (which happened to provide an exemption for these profits).

(2) The words of Article 13(2) are to be given their literal meaning. The assets of the company that were sold could not be taken to extend to the mining interests held through the chain of subsidiaries. When the law speaks of the assets of a company, it invariably does not intend to include the assets belonging to another company, whether or not held in the same ownership group.

In response to this decision, section 3A was inserted into the International Tax Agreements Act 1953 (the Act that incorporates Double Tax Agreements into Australia's domestic tax legislation). This amendment clarified the meaning of terms used in the Alienation of Property Article in Australia's Double Tax Agreements. The intention of this amendment was to ensure that the Alienation of Property Article was read to cover alienations of shares or other interests in companies, and in other entities, whose assets consist principally of Australian real property, whether held directly or indirectly through a chain of interposed companies or other entities.

---

[a] *Lamesa Holdings BV v. Commissioner of Taxation*, 20 August 1997, IBFD Tax Treaty database. With additional United Nations/Department of Economic and Social Affairs (UN/DESA) comments.

10.4.2   Analysis of Model Convention provisions

Box 10.B.6: Capital Gains under the model tax conventions

Capital gains under the 2017 UN Model: Article 13

1. Gains derived by a resident of a Contracting State from the alienation of immovable property referred to in Article 6 and situated in the other Contracting State may be taxed in that other State.

2. Gains from the alienation of movable property forming part of the business property of a permanent establishment which an enterprise of a Contracting State has in the other Contracting State or of movable property pertaining to a fixed base available to a resident of a Contracting State in the other Contracting State for the purpose of performing independent personal services, including such gains from the alienation of such a permanent establishment (alone or with the whole enterprise) or of such fixed base, may be taxed in that other State.

3. Gains that an enterprise of a Contracting State that operates ships or aircraft in international traffic derives from the alienation of such ships or aircraft, or of movable property pertaining to the operation of such ships or aircraft, shall be taxable only in that State.

4. Gains derived by a resident of a Contracting State from the alienation of shares or comparable interests, such as interests in a partnership or trust, may be taxed in the other Contracting State if, at any time during the 365 days preceding the alienation, these shares or comparable interests derived more than 50 per cent of their value directly or indirectly from immovable property, as defined in Article 6, situated in that other State.

5. Gains, other than those to which paragraph 4 applies, derived by a resident of a Contracting State from the alienation of shares of a company, or comparable interests, such as interests in a partnership or trust, which is a resident of the other Contracting State, may be taxed in that other State if the alienator, at any time during the 365 days preceding such alienation, held directly or indirectly at least ___ per cent (the percentage is to be established through bilateral negotiations) of the capital of that company.

6. Gains from the alienation of any property other than that referred to in paragraphs 1, 2, 3, 4 and 5 shall be taxable only in the Contracting State of which the alienator is a resident.

Capital gains under the 2017 OECD Model: Article 13

1. Gains derived by a resident of a Contracting State from the alienation of immovable property referred to in Article 6 and situated in the other Contracting State may be taxed in that other State.

2. Gains from the alienation of movable property forming part of the business property of a permanent establishment which an enterprise of a Contracting State has in the other Contracting State, including such gains from the alienation of such a permanent establishment (alone or with the whole enterprise) may be taxed in that other State.

3. Gains from the alienation of ships or aircraft operated in international traffic, boats engaged in inland waterways transport or movable property pertaining to the operation of such ships, aircraft or boats, shall be taxable only in the Contracting State in which the place of effective management of the enterprise is situated.

4. Gains derived by a resident of a Contracting State from the alienation of shares or comparable interests, such as interests in a partnership or trust, may be taxed in the other Contracting State if, at any time during the 365 days preceding the alienation, these shares or comparable interests derived more than 50 per cent of their value directly or indirectly from immovable property, as defined in Article 6, situated in that other State.

5. Gains from the alienation of any property, other than that referred to in paragraphs 1, 2, 3 and 4, shall be taxable only in the Contracting State of which the alienator is a resident.

Definition of "Immovable Property in Article 6 of the United Nations Model (and in the OECD Model):

2. The term "immovable property" shall have the meaning which it has under the law of the Contracting State in which the property in question is situated. The term shall, in any case, include property accessory to immovable property, livestock and equipment used in agriculture and forestry, rights to which the provisions of general law respecting landed property apply, usufruct of immovable property and rights to variable or fixed payments as consideration for the working of, or the right to work, mineral deposits, sources and other natural resources; ships and aircraft shall not be regarded as immovable property.

10.4.2.1   Assuming the sort of indirect transfer illustrated (at a very basic level) in the second example in Fig. 10.F.1. of this chapter, how will the basic provisions of Article 13 of the United Nations Model addressed in Box 10.B.6 apply?

10.4.2.2   **Paragraph 1** would obviously not apply, as there is no alienation of the immovable property itself, at least directly. The general anti-avoidance rules in tax treaties, as provided for in the Commentaries to Article 1 of the United Nations and OECD Model Conventions, may in some countries allow for coverage of indirect transfers, but this will rarely be clear, and may be regarded as an interpretation no longer open under Article 13 where there is a specific provision on indirect transfers, because of the presence of paragraph 3. This reflects the common legal principle that specific coverage with limitations implies that a more general coverage is not intended. In contrast, where a domestic anti-abuse rule recharacterizes an indirect transfer of an immovable property as a direct transfer of the same, paragraph 1 directly applies, as long as such domestic anti-abuse rule is not in violation of applicable tax treaties.

10.4.2.3   **Paragraph 2** would not apply, as the shares sold are not effectively connected to the permanent establishment, comprised by the extractive facility.

10.4.2.4   **Paragraph 3** would obviously not apply, as it relates to ships and aircraft.

10.4.2.5   **Paragraph 4** specifically applies to address indirect transfers of immovable property. The United Nations version of the paragraph differed until 2017 from the OECD version. Now the two provisions are the same, drawing drafting from both of the previous models. This paragraph (often referred to as the "land-rich entities provision") is considered in more detail below.

10.4.2.6   **Paragraph 5** would only apply to shares in "land-rich" companies that are not covered under paragraph 4. However, the paragraph only applies to shares in a company resident in the country seeking to tax the transfer; in the illustrated indirect transfer, the company whose shares are transferred may have underlying interests in a mine or other facility but is itself located in another country, and it is not at all clear that paragraph 5 refers to the indirect transfer of interests in domestic companies, especially as paragraph 4 is explicit on the point.

10.4.2.7   **Paragraph 6** merely confirms that unless the country where the extractive facility is located has a taxing right preserved by the preceding paragraphs, only the residence state of the seller of the shares can tax profits made, and that will usually be another country.

10.4.3   Importance of the domestic meaning of "immovable property"

10.4.3.1   Countries seeking to tax indirect transfers resulting in capital gains, and having treaty clauses similar to Article 13(4) need to take stock of their domestic law meaning of the term "immovable property." This is especially important because the term "immovable property" is not defined in Article 13. This means that it either (i) looks to domestic law unless the context requires otherwise (in the terms of Article 3(2) of both the United Nations and OECD Model Conventions); or else (ii) follows the definition in Article 6. The definition in Article 6 is not expressed (unlike the Article 3 definitions) to apply for the purposes of the Convention as a whole, but unlike the definitions of dividends, interest and royalties, it is also not expressed to apply only for the purposes of the Article (i.e., Article 6). Therefore, since there is a definition of immovable property in article 6 that is not explicitly confined to article 6, the definition may be considered as a relevant part of the treaty context;

10.4.3.2   Most countries regard the Article 6 definition as applying to Article 13, by inference. This takes us back to the meaning in domestic law, but ensures that—whatever the domestic legislation says—"rights to variable or fixed payments as consideration for the working of, or the right to work, mineral deposits, sources and other natural resources" are covered by the definition;

10.4.3.3   To guard against an interpretation that the term "immovable property" takes its meaning from domestic law only, with no "supplementation" from the Article 6 definition, countries should consider either (i) making specific reference to the Article 6 definition in Article 13; or (ii) reflecting the Article 6 definition coverage, as a minimum, in domestic law. The latter would be an easier option for many countries as they can make it unilaterally. Countries might also consider it helpful to specifically clarify, in domestic law, the tax treatment of rights relating to the mining/oil or gas production, including reconnaissance and/or exploration-related rights as well as the extraction (i.e., development) rights themselves, and possibly surveys and other non-public information pertaining to the immovable property. Rights granted by or on behalf of a government might be covered, whether or not they are expressed to be licences or to be granted as part of licences.

10.4.3.4   It should be noted that the reference is to the domestic law "meaning" of "immovable property" and, in some countries, it might not be considered necessary to specifically define "immovable property" because the meaning of the term is sufficiently clear. In contrast, as noted in box 10.B.8 below, Australia has legislated that the term "immovable property" encompasses the term "real property" more commonly used in Australian law.

10.4.4   Design of an effective land-rich entities regime in Article 13(4) of tax treaties

10.4.4.1   The Final Report on Action 6 of the OECD/Group of Twenty (G20) Base Erosion and Profit Shifting (BEPS) Project considered the operation of Article 13(4) and drew upon aspects of the United Nations and OECD Model Conventions versions of that provision in its suggested changes to the OECD Model.[40] The 2017

---

[40] OECD, *Preventing the Granting of Treaty Benefits in Inappropriate Circumstances*, (Par-

update of that model included these changes:

4. Gains derived by a resident of a Contracting State from the alienation of shares *or comparable interests, such as interests in a partnership or trust, may be taxed in the other Contracting State if, at any time during the 365 days preceding the alienation, these shares or comparable interests derived* more than 50 per cent of their value directly or indirectly from immovable property, *as defined in Article 6,* situated in *that* other State.

10.4.4.2   While this already largely reflects much of what is in the Commentaries to the United Nations and OECD Model Conventions, the importance of this provision, which largely came from a developing country and United Nations Model Convention practice, is increasingly being recognized. The United Nations Committee of Experts on International Cooperation in Tax Matters (United Nations Tax Committee) began consideration of whether Article 13(4) could be clarified or improved as part of the 2017 update of the United Nations Model Convention. Eventually, the same text was adopted as under the OECD Model Convention.

10.4.4.3   There are many choices involved in relation to a specific indirect transfer provision in a tax treaty, and of course the results of those choices will have to be negotiated with other countries, many of which will have different views.

10.4.5   TREATY POLICY OPTIONS AND DESIGN CONSIDERATIONS

10.4.5.1   The following considerations have to be taken into account

10.4.5.2   Whether to have a specific indirect transfers provision at all:

a.   As noted above, unless there are domestic law provisions giving taxing rights or negotiators want to ensure that any such future legislation will not be rendered ineffective in a treaty relationship, there is little point in negotiating for a provision such as this where the other negotiating party does not seek it. The other side will almost inevitably seek some concession in return for a treaty provision that may not advance the policy interests and revenue base of the country;

b.   The advantage of a specific provision is that there is a clear coverage of indirect transfers, unless there are court decisions on the coverage of indirect transfers under paragraph 1 in a country (something that is likely to be very rare). It reduces the risk of an interpretational difference between two countries that leads to both claiming competing taxing jurisdiction under paragraph 1, and possible unresolved double taxation. This could negatively impact the investment climate; and

is, OECD Publishing, 2015), p.71–72. Available at http://dx.doi.org/10.1787/9789264241695-en.

    c.   A potential disadvantage of a special provision is that, because of what is specifically required before it can apply (noted in more detail below) it can reduce the likelihood of a purposive, anti-avoidance approach to paragraph 1 by the courts, and it can also serve as a (not easily amended) road map for tax avoidance by mitigating the effect of the specific requirements.

10.4.5.3   Whether to have traditional wording as in the 2011 United Nations Model Convention (emphasis added)— "property of which **consists** directly or indirectly principally of immovable property situated in a Contracting State may be taxed in that State"; whether to use the pre-2017 OECD Model Convention wording— "Gains derived by a resident of a Contracting State from the alienation of shares deriving more than 50 per cent of their value directly or indirectly from immovable property situated in the other State may be taxed in that other State"; or whether, as in the 2017 version of both the UN and OECD model conventions, to specifically provide that the test need not be satisfied at the time of transfer, but can be met at any time in the 365 days prior to the transfer. Some will see this as potentially unfair on the sellers (and potentially the buyers) while others will see it as a useful way of ensuring the proportion of value comprised by the property in the taxing state is not artificially "watered down" just prior to sale with a view to the negate the provision's operation. The United Nations Tax Committee has not yet decided on this point.

10.4.5.4   Whether gains on such a transfer should be deemed to be sourced locally:

    a.   While some provision (such as Article 13(4)) is needed to preserve the taxing right in a tax treaty, the specific rule deeming such gains as locally sourced should be placed in domestic law. The treaty will not, in the view of most countries, provide a taxing right that does not exist in domestic law;

    b.   Where there is domestic legislation, it should provide that the gains made are sourced locally when the immovable property is located locally. The gains could be taxed or could be limited to the proportion of the gains that reflect the proportion of the value of shares sold corresponding to the proportion of local immovable property to other assets;

    c.   In tax treaty terms, the domestic legislation will not, of course, by itself, ensure that the gain is treated as taxable in the country of t he immovable property asset under the treaty, and require the treaty partner to, for example, give credit for that tax paid. The treaty partner may, for example, regard the gain as sourced in its country and fully taxable under the treaty there, or as sourced in a third country. To avoid double taxation based on source (and double non-taxation, where a taxing right might be claimed by the treaty partner but not exercised) it is, therefore, important to consider specifically addressing such transfers in treaties, such as in some form of Article 13(4) provision which specifically allows the country of the asset a taxing right. Of itself, it will not prevent a third country with which no treaty exists from claiming source taxing rights under its own law.

10.4.5.5 Whether an indirect transfer provision should extend beyond transfers in shares:

a. If the indirect transfers provision is confined to the transfer of company shares, it would be easy to avoid it (such as by using a unit trust, and selling units), although this also may depend on the entity-classification rule of countries (for example, if trusts, partnership or estates are fiscally transparent and thus looked through, such an avoidance attempt may not be successful). The United Nations Model Convention was, thus, revised in 1999 (published in 2001) to extend the rule to trusts, partnerships and estates, although estates might not be relevant, particularly to extractives.

b. The OECD Model Convention had an option at paragraph 28.5 of the Commentary to cover "shares or comparable interests." There seems to be increasing use of these sorts of extensions, and the OECD/ G20, in its 2014 BEPS Deliverable on Action 6, recommended amending Article 13(4) to cover "shares or comparable interests, such as interests in a partnership or trust." This is a clause blending the above United Nations and OECD Model provisions. The Final Report on Action 6 in October 2016 carried through this suggestion. The 2017 Update of the OECD Model made this change.

c. Some will prefer the option under the 2011 United Nations Model Convention, which does not depend on the concept of "comparable interests," although the OECD Model Convention drafting seems designed to state that partnerships and trusts are de facto comparable interests, without the need to look at the domestic laws of one State or another. The 2011 United Nations Model Convention avoided any such issues, if they exist, but some may prefer the OECD Model Convention as allowing coverage of comparable interests even if they are not the partnerships, trusts or estates addressed specifically (and, it seems, as an exhaustive list) by the United Nations Model Convention. As noted, the 2017 United Nations Model Convention uses the same wording as the 2017 OECD Model Convention;

d. The specific rule extending taxing rights beyond transfers of shares to cover other interests would need to be reflected both in the treaty provision preserving the taxing right and in the specific domestic legislation to ensure that the treaty right is implemented in practice.

10.4.5.6 Whether there should be an exception for immovable property used in an extractive business:

a. The United Nations Model Convention until 2017 provided at paragraph 4(a) of Article 13 that:

    Nothing contained in this paragraph shall apply to a company, partnership, trust or estate, other than a company, partnership, trust or estate engaged in the business of management of immovable properties, the property of which consists directly or indirectly principally of immovable property used by such company, partnership, trust or estate in its business activities;[41]

b. It was not entirely clear what the central phrase "used ... in its business activities" meant. On one view, any holdings of mines and other facilities, as well as mining leases and other related immovable property leases would inevitably fall outside the scope of the indirect transfer provision, as they are actively being used in business activities. On another view, however, more is required, since merely holding an asset, for example, is not a use in one's own (as a distinct legal entity) business activities. Further, the fact that Company A owns Company B (which holds a particular asset) does not mean that Company A is using Company B's assets in its (i.e., Company A's) business activities. In this view, there has to be direct active use, not just a passive holding. In other words, indirect holdings are explicitly addressed by this paragraph, but indirect use through the mining operator further down the chain is not treated as a use in the business activities of the company higher up the chain, perhaps several companies removed;

c. The Commentary did not address the interpretation of this provision (added as part of the United Nations Model Convention as amended in 1999 and published in 2001) in any detail, but some support for the latter view could be found in the Commentary:

    [Paragraph 4] is designed to prevent the avoidance of taxes on the gains from the transfer of immovable property. Since it is often relatively easy to avoid taxes on such gains through the incorporation of a company to hold such property, it is necessary to tax the transfer of shares in such a company (...) It also decided to exclude from its scope such entities whose property consists directly or indirectly principally of immovable property used by them in their business activities;[42]

d. On the other hand, those opposed to the latter interpretation would point out that the paragraph may have little meaning if it were the correct interpretation, as a company rarely if ever uses the assets of its subsidiaries in its operations itself. They would also point to the discussion of the same issue in the OECD Commentary at paragraph 28.7:

    Also, some States consider that the paragraph should not apply to gains

---

[41] 2017 United Nations Model Convention.
[42] Ibid.

(…) where the immovable property from which the shares or comparable interests derive their value is immovable property (such as a mine or a hotel) in which a business is carried on. States wishing to provide for one or more of these exceptions are free to do so.

e.   Paragraph 8.4 of the Commentary to the 2017 United Nations Model Convention provides:

In adopting the updated wording from the OECD Model Convention in 2017, the Committee decided to omit paragraph 4(a) from the United Nations Model Convention as it did not reflect common practice. It was found that the provision was very rarely used and was difficult to apply. However, countries may agree during bilateral negotiations to include the words from subparagraph (a) as it appeared prior to the 2017 update, at the end of paragraph 4, as follows: (…)

10.4.6   Computational and administrative considerations

10.4.6.1 What valuation method should be used:

a.   Paragraph 4(b) of Article 13 of the United Nations Model provided until 2017 that "[f]or the purposes of this paragraph, "principally" in relation to ownership of immovable property means the value of such immovable property exceeding fifty per cent of the aggregate value of all assets owned by the company, partnership, trust or estate." This was merely repeated in the Commentary on that article, without elaboration of how it is to be applied in practice;

b.   The OECD Commentary on Article 13 provides at paragraph 28.4 that "paragraph 4 allows the taxation of the entire gain attributable to the shares to which it applies even where part of the value of the share is derived from property other than immovable property located in the source State." The determination of whether shares of a company derive more than 50 per cent of their value directly or indirectly from immovable property situated in a Contracting State will normally be done by comparing the value of such immovable property to the value of all the property owned by the company without taking into account debts or other liabilities of the company (whether or not secured by mortgages on the relevant immovable property). Paragraph 8.3 of the 2017 United Nations Model Convention's Commentary takes the same approach;

c.   It seems that practice on whether countries use fair market value (reflecting current value in the market) or book value (reflecting the price initially paid) as the valuation method is very varied. Some countries have a blended requirement that allows the latter to be used in some circumstances unless there is any reason for a shareholder to suspect that it does not fully reflect the underlying value of the immovable property, as compared with other assets. Many, probably most, countries do not seem to include intangibles in the calculation, perhaps in part because of the difficulty of accurately calculating this. However, such interpretation might be problematic in countries where intangibles are treated as a "property" or "asset" under domestic laws, especially when they use fair market value as the valuation method, since sometimes the fair market value of intangibles can be significant, and exclusions of those intangibles may be regarded as overly broadening taxing rights of such countries contrary to the terms of the applicable treaties.

10.4.6.2 Whether there should be an exception for shares quoted on a stock exchange:

a. This is sometimes used as a mechanism to reduce compliance costs for taxpayers (and administration costs for tax authorities) in cases where there is a genuine share market transaction, since there can be less tax-avoidance risk involved. It would usually be defined to include at least the stock exchanges of the two treaty countries, and in the case of domestic legislation operating even without a treaty, the legislating country's stock exchange(s). As regards stock exchanges in third countries, countries may not be willing to broadly cover all stock exchanges in any countries, and instead may want to confine coverage to certain reputable and reliable stock exchanges. In this regard, tax treaty practices in defining "recognized stock exchange" in limitation on benefits (LOB) clauses may serve as a useful reference. They typically either simply define the term as stock exchanges agreed between the competent authorities or else list certain stock exchanges, usually in the two countries as well as other stock exchanges agreed between the competent authorities.[43] Sometimes the term is used but left undefined[44] and sometimes it may list stock exchanges in countries with which either of two treaty countries have strong economic connections (such as regional stock exchanges or a major international stock exchange).[45]

b. The specific exception for such on-market transfers would only need to be reflected in the domestic legislation if there is a taxing right such as under Article 13(4) since it narrows rather than extends the treaty right. For example, Public Notice 7 of China, although an administrative regulation, exempts transactions through public securities markets. In contrast, Japan sets a higher threshold for percentage of shares that need to be held by the transferor in the case of listed shares, which is 5 per cent, as opposed to 2 per cent for the other

[43] Costa Rica-Mexico Double Tax Treaty (2014) Article 24 (4).

[44] Singapore-Sri Lanka Double Tax Treaty (2014) Article 14(4).

[45] Ethiopia-Netherlands Double Tax Agreement (2012) Article 3(1).

shares;[46] this can also be seen as one variety of this exception. The United States also has a 5 per cent threshold for the same percentages, which is only applicable to listed shares.

10.4.6.3 Should there be a reorganizations clause?

In paragraph 28.7 of the OECD Model Convention Commentary to article 13.4 it is noted (emphasis added) that:

[A]lso, some States consider that the paragraph should not apply to gains derived from the alienation of shares of companies that are listed on an approved stock exchange of one of the States, **to gains derived from the alienation of shares in the course of a corporate reorganization** or where the immovable property from which the shares derive their value is immovable property (such as a mine or a hotel) in which a business is carried on. States wishing to provide for one or more of these exceptions are free to do so.

The rationale behind this type of provision is not to grant an exemption for such transactions, but simply to neutralize, by means of a deferral system, the taxation on the unrealized gains existing at the time the reorganization takes place, and to therefore not discourage more efficient capital allocation. Those not providing such a special treatment in domestic law and in treaties may be concerned about possible abuses. The pros and cons of such domestic law and treaty provisions should both be considered when addressing this policy issue. If it is included in a treaty, its scope of operation, including its relationship to anti-avoidance rules, should be discussed between the negotiating parties.

10.4.6.4 What should be the percentage of the gain taxed?

The provisions in the United Nations and OECD Models Conventions allow, when the company meets the requisite test for domestic immovable property holdings, for taxing of the whole gain, not just the percentage of it relating to immovable property in the taxing jurisdiction, but some countries provide a moderating effect in their domestic laws so that only that percentage is taxed.

10.4.6.5 How can abuses be addressed within Article 13(4):

a. Some countries provide that the gain will be taxable if the percentage test for immovable property was met at any time in the year before transfer. This is to prevent manipulation of indirect assets held temporarily when the transfer occurs. In fact, the OECD 2014 BEPS Deliverable on Action 6 notes this issue and gave a drafting suggestion which was

---

[46] Edwin T. Whatley and Shinichi Kobayashi, "Taxation of Indirect Equity Transfers: Japan," in *17 Asia-Pacific Tax Bulletin*, 2 (2011) p. 138

reaffirmed in the Final Report on Action 6, as follows:[47]

32. Article 13(4) allows the Contracting State in which immovable property is situated to tax capital gains realized by a resident of the other State on shares of companies that derive more than 50 per cent of their value from such immovable property.

33. [omitted]

34. There might also be cases, however, where assets are contributed to an entity shortly before the transfer of the shares or other interests in that entity in order to dilute the proportion of the value of these shares or interests that are derived from immovable property situated in one Contracting State. In order to address such cases, it was agreed that Article 13(4) should be amended to refer to situations where shares or similar interests derive their value primarily from immovable property at any time during a certain period as opposed to at the time of the alienation only.

35. The following revised version of paragraph 4 of Article 13 incorporates these changes:

a. Gains derived by a resident of a Contracting State from the alienation of shares or comparable interests, such as interests in a partnership or trust, may be taxed in the other Contracting State if, at any time during the 365 days preceding the alienation, these shares or comparable interests derived more than 50 per cent of their value directly or indirectly from immovable property, as defined in Article 6, situated in that other State.

b. The question has sometimes arisen about whether Article 13(4) may still apply if the company holding the immovable property borrows money just before the share transfer to dilute the percentage of assets constituted by immovable property. Some countries take the view that, as the OECD Commentary states at paragraph 28.4, debt should not be taken into account in the valuation of the property of the company, that the money borrowed should not be taken into account to dilute the percentage of immovable property interests. Other countries more specifically address this, as many do not see the implication as flowing necessarily from the OECD Commentary. In any case, this part of the OECD Commentary is not quoted in the United Nations Model Convention Commentary.

10.4.6.6 What are the possibilities for limiting the compliance difficulties in taxing capital gains?

---

[47] OECD, BEPS Action 6: 2014 Deliverable, pp. 78–79; cf. BEPS Action 6: 2015 Final Report, pp. 71–72.

a. One of the difficulties is that of how a shareholder will know if the test of indirectly held immovable property subject to taxation on indirect transfers has been met in a particular country. As it is often not clear whether the information could be effectively requested from the company, especially at a particular point in time, and as knowledge of immovable property held is not enough, the taxpayer would need to know where it is held. Even access to balance sheets may not indicate all of the assets of a company, or whether they are properly classed as "immovable" under relevant legislation. For these sorts of reasons, a number of countries such as Australia (10 per cent) and the United States (5 per cent, but only for listed shares) have de *minimis* standards in their domestic law so that small shareholders (portfolio investors) are not burdened by this requirement. South Africa has a 20 per cent threshold test for the taxpayer and related parties' total holdings. These sorts of provisions may be especially relevant in the case of non-corporate vehicles, where less information is usually publicly available, although controlling interests may be more common.

b. As noted above, some countries, such as China, do not apply the laws of the countries where the shares are openly traded on certain stock exchanges (e.g., those in the treaty countries) thus reducing compliance and administration costs.

c. South Africa only applies its legislation to non-residents where 80 per cent or more of the market value of the holdings (shares, in the case of a company) derives from South African immovable property (otherwise held as trading stock) and where the non-resident (together with related parties) holds directly or indirectly 20 per cent or more of the shares in the company or ownership or right to ownership of another entity.

d. What percentage is appropriate as applicable to the extractive industries would have to be determined, by also taking into consideration the practice in the industry. For example, if the industry practice is basically that one single investor wholly or substantially owns one mine, setting a high threshold percentage would still work in terms of effectively taxing an indirect transfer of extractives. If, in contrast, it is the industry practice that several different investors sometimes invest in the same mine by setting up a joint venture, and that they transfer their interest to or among third parties, a high threshold percentage may not suffice. Treatment of farm-out and farm-in agreements may also have to be examined in this context.

e. Recognizing that the percentage of assets may vary over time, some countries allow shareholders to take the proportions from the most recent accounts (i.e., not on the day of the transfer), unless they have reason to believe that those most recent accounts will not reflect the reality on the day of transfer. Malaysia, for example, allows the

397

taxpayer to submit the audited accounts of the company for the financial year that is closest to the date of the transfer. In the United States, if there is a transfer between two balance sheet dates, the US corporation must nevertheless be able to demonstrate whether it is a U.S. Real Property Holding Company (the US legislative term for a "land-rich company") on the date of transfer. A US corporation can rely on the most recent balance sheet (i.e., quarterly, monthly, etc.) and determine whether there was a material shift in value or whether an additional relevant date was triggered in between the balance sheet date and the date of transfer by the foreign taxpayer.

10.4.7   Examples from bilateral treaties in force and domestic provisions

10.4.7.1 Examples of a reorganizations clause can be seen in the following treaties:

Article 13.4 of the Belgium-Democratic Republic of the Congo Double Tax Treaty (2007)

Gains derived by a resident of a Contracting State from the alienation of shares deriving more than 50% of their value from immovable property situated in the other Contracting State may be taxed in that other State. This paragraph shall not, however, apply to gains derived from the alienation:

(a)   Of shares listed on a recognized stock exchange of a Contracting State; or

(b)   Of shares sold or exchanged in the framework of a corporate reorganization, of a merger, of a division or of another similar operation; or

(c)   Of shares deriving more than 50% of their value from immovable property in which the company exercises its activities; or

(d)   Of shares owned by a person who holds directly or indirectly less than 25% of the capital of the company whose shares are alienated.

Article 14.4 of the Hong-Kong—Malaysia Double Tax Treaty (2012)

Gains derived by a resident of a Contracting Party from the alienation of shares of a company deriving more than fifty (50) per cent of its asset value directly or indirectly from immovable property situated in the other Contracting Party may be taxed in that other Party. However, this paragraph does not apply to gains derived from the alienation of shares:

(a)   Quoted on such stock exchange as may be agreed between the Parties; or

(b)   Alienated or exchanged in the framework of a reorganization of a company, a merger, a scission or a similar operation; or

(c)   In a company deriving more than fifty (50) per cent of its asset value from immovable property in which it carries on its business.

Before 2003, reorganization clauses were not so relevant, however, some countries had taken them into account:

Protocol to the Treaty between Spain and Mexico (1992)

(a)   With respect to paragraph 3 of Article 13,[48] gains derived from the alienation of shares in a company that is a resident of Mexico shall be determined without including capital contributions made during the period in which the shares are held and the profits accrued during the same period on which the issuing company has already paid income tax.

(a)   The tax charged, under paragraph 3 of Article 13, in the State of residence of the company the shares of which are alienated shall not exceed 25 per cent of the taxable gains.

(b)   Where, owing to a reorganization of companies which are owned by the same group of shareholders, a resident of a Contracting State alienates property as a consequence of a merger or division of companies of or an exchange of shares, then the recognition of the gain arising on the alienation of such property shall be deferred, for purposes of the income tax in the other Contracting State, to the moment in which a subsequent alienation which does not meet the requirements provided for in this paragraph for the deferment of the gains is affected.

10.4.7.2   Examples of immovable property defined in domestic law

---

Box 10.B.7: The meaning of "immovable property" in South Africa[a]

The capital gains tax provisions inter alia apply to the following assets of a person who is not a resident:

- Immovable property situated in the Republic held by that person;

- Any interest or right of whatever nature of that person to or in immovable property situated in the Republic; and

---

[48] Paragraph 3 states: "Gains from the alienation of shares that represent a participation of at least 25 per cent of the capital of a company resident of a Contracting State and held during at least the 12-month period preceding such alienation, may be taxed in that State."

- Rights to variable or fixed payments as consideration for the working of or the right to work mineral deposits, sources and other natural resources.

An interest in immovable property situated in the Republic includes any equity shares held by a person in a company or ownership or the right to ownership of a person in any other entity or a vested interest of a person in any assets of any trust, if:

(a) 80 per cent or more of the market value of those equity shares, ownership or right to ownership or vested interest, as the case may be, at the time of disposal thereof is attributable directly or indirectly to immovable property held otherwise than as trading stock; and

(b) In the case of a company or other entity, that person (whether alone or together with any connected person in relation to that person) directly or indirectly, holds at least 20 per cent of the equity shares in that company or ownership or right to ownership of that other entity.

---

[a] *South Africa's Income Tax Act 58 of 1962*, Eighth Schedule, paragraph 2. Available at http://www.into-sa.com/uploads/download/file/12/Income_Tax_Act__1962_.pdf.

Box 10.B.8: The meaning of "real property" in Australia[a]

A capital gains tax asset is taxable Australian real property if it is:

(a) Real property situated in Australia (including a lease of land, if the land is situated in Australia); or

(b) A mining, quarrying or prospecting right (to the extent that the right is not real property) if the minerals, petroleum or quarry rights are situated in Australia.

Note: The International Tax Agreements Amendment Bill 2014 was approved by the Australian Parliament on 24 September 2014. It clarifies that the term "immovable property" encompasses "real property" to the extent that an Australian treaty provides that immovable property has the same meaning it has under domestic law.

---

[a] *Australia's Income Tax Assessment Act 1997*, Section 855.20. Available at http://www.austlii.edu.au/au/legis/cth/consol_act/itaa1997240/s855.20.html.

Box 10.B.9:
The meaning of "immovable property" in India[a]

India provides in its legislation that plant and fittings and "other things" transferred with a building are included in the broadly defined term "immovable property" as follows:

(a)   "Immovable property" means -

(i)   Any land or any building or part of a building and includes where any land or any building or part of a building is to be transferred together with any machinery, plant, furniture, fittings or other things such as machinery, plant, furniture, fittings or other things also.

Explanation. For the purposes of this sub-clause, "land, building, part of a building, machinery, plant, furniture, fittings and other things" include any rights therein;

(ii)   Any rights in or with respect to any land or any building or a part of a building (whether or not including any machinery, plant, furniture, fittings or other things therein) which has been constructed or which is to be constructed, accruing or arising from any transaction (whether by way of becoming a member of, or acquiring shares in, a co-operative society, company or other association of persons or by way of any agreement or any arrangement of whatever nature) not being a transaction by way of sale, exchange or lease of such land, building or part of a building.

---

a   *Indian Income Tax Act, 1961-2014,* Section 269UA. Available at http://www. lawzonline. com/bareacts/income-tax-act/section269UA-income-tax-act.htm.

10.4.7.3 Country practice – approach adopted in Peru

Box 10.B.10: A case in point: Peru

Taxing transfer of shares in "land-rich" companies

By Law N°. 29663 of 15 February 2011, capital gains of non-residents of Peru from the indirect transfer of ownership or participation in Peruvian companies is treated as sourced in Peru and taxable in Peru.

The indirect transfer is deemed to occur if shares from a non-resident company are transferred and that company owns shares of a resident company, directly or through other companies, as long as (i) over the 12 months prior to disposal the market value of the domiciled company's shares held by the non-domiciled company directly or through other companies equals 50 per cent or more of the market value of shares of the non-domiciled entity; or (ii) the non-domiciled entity resides in a low-tax jurisdiction.

Peruvian resident companies must report any indirect transfers to the Peruvian Tax Administration by foreign affiliates. If the transferor is not a resident, the domestic company will be jointly and severally liable for any capital gains tax arising from the indirect transfer.

There was criticism that very small transactions would be caught by the legislation, provided that the transfer resulted in a capital gain for a non-resident company owning the shares.

In July of 2011, Law N°. 29757 provided some relief. An indirect transfer would only be taxable if the transaction represented a transfer of 10 per cent or more of the non-resident company's interest in its investment in Peru. The 10 per cent threshold is determined by amalgamating any disposals over a 12-month period (to reduce the chances of transfers done little by little over a 12-month period).

Law N°. 29757 also addressed issues of the *amount* of the taxable capital gain. In general, the basis of shares acquired before the 16 February 2011 effective date of Law No. 29663 would be the greater of (i) the market value of the shares as of 15 February 2011; or (ii) the acquisition cost or the value of the equity if acquired without consideration. Market value, if the shares were listed on a stock exchange, would be the stock exchange **price at the close of February 15, 2011, or the last published quotation.**

For shares not listed on a stock exchange, the value of the shares at the time when they were added to the company's balance sheet is used, based on an audited balance sheet of the non-resident company. The balance sheet could not be dated earlier than 15 February 2010.

Other changes included in Law No. 29757 were new provisions that:

> (i) Limited the deemed Peruvian sourced income to the proportion of the value of the shares sold which represents the indirect Peruvian interests (i.e., the gain on the shares as a whole would not be taxed *where part of the value relates to unrelated investments*); and

> (ii) Considered those who were paying or crediting income as a result of the indirect transfer of shares to be deemed with holding agents, and in such cases the company whose shares are indirectly sold is not jointly or severally liable.

10.4.8   IMF advice on treatment of indirect transfers of interest

10.4.8.1   In a 2012 International Monetary Fund (IMF) Staff Technical Assistance Report on Mongolia, the IMF recommended that the definition of "immovable property" should specifically include depreciable assets used in the extractive operation:

40. Exploration and mining licences are typically regarded as immovable property; depreciable assets used in mining activities are not necessarily covered as such. If the double tax agreement (DTA) provision does not explicitly state that the value of such assets must be taken into account, part of the domestic taxing right is not safeguarded, and consequently, a smaller part of the capital gains can be taxed in Mongolia. Under the DTAs with Canada and France, it could be argued that the Mongolian domestic tax provision is safeguarded as an exploration or mining license can be regarded as "rental property that is used by the taxpayer to carry on its business activities."[49]

10.4.8.2   Ultimately countries will need to ensure that they have a definition that is sufficiently broad to allow the full value of the immovable property to be taxed and makes sense in the context of their domestic law (the concept of "fixtures" can be a very complex one that may be alien to a country's jurisprudence, for example). No less important, the legislation should be consistent with an interpretation resulting from the obligation to interpret the treaty in good faith (see Article 31 of the *Vienna Convention on the Law of Treaties*,[50] regarded as reflecting customary international law).

10.4.8.3   Example of advice in The Philippines

---

[49] International Monetary Fund, "Mongolia: Technical Assistance Report—Safeguarding Domestic Revenue—A Mongolian DTA Model," in *IMF Country Report No. 12/306* (July 2012), paragraph 40. Available at http://www.imf.org/external/pubs/ft/scr/2012/cr12306.pdf.

[50] United Nations, Treaty Series, vol. 1155, p. 331.

Box 10.B.11: IMF recommendations on the Philippines[a]

Transfers of exploration permits, mining agreements, and interests in mining companies

58. **The Mining Act allows for the assignment (transfer) of exploration permits to another person**. Gains realized on the transfer of an exploration permit or mining agreement are subject to income tax as business income or capital gains, most likely as capital gains since a mining company will not hold permits as inventory. Any gain realized on the transfer by a company of an exploration permit or mining agreement will thus likely be subject to a 30 per cent tax. In contrast, if mining rights are held indirectly through an interposed company, the increased value of the rights could be realized by way of a sale of shares in the interposed company with the tax rate on this gain being 10 per cent.

59. A non-resident company is liable to tax on gains realized on the sales of real property in the Philippines and sales of shares in a Philippine company as both are treated as Philippine-source income wherever the sale may be completed. There is no specific rule for mining interests, however, and a sale of mining interests by a non-resident might be able to escape tax if sold directly and almost certainly would escape tax if it were sold indirectly by way of a sale of shares in a foreign upper tier company that owned a Philippine company that owned the mining interests. A solution to this problem commonly used elsewhere is to expand the definition of real property for income tax purposes to include any mining interests or any interests in any trust, company, partnership or any other entity or arrangement where at least 50 per cent of the value of the interest is attributable to direct or indirect interests in real property (included deemed real property in the form of mining rights). If this rule were adopted, gains from the sale of shares in companies that directly or indirectly owned mining rights would be taxed at 30 per cent as gains from the sale of real property rather than at 10 per cent as gains from the sale of shares.

60. Unfortunately, the Philippines has entered into a number of tax treaties that require it to give up its right to tax residents of the treaty partner country on gains from the sale of mining rights where those rights are held via a small chain of companies. The Philippines has a very extensive tax treaty network and it will be almost impossible to renegotiate the treaties to extend Philippines taxing rights over gains related to Philippine mining interests. However, future treaties should adopt a broad definition of real property for purposes of the capital gains article to include all direct and indirect interests in mining rights. If there are opportunities to amend existing treaties, these should be used to address

the definition of real property in existing treaties.

61. Philippines authorities currently have no direct enforcement powers over non-residents with respect to the collection of income tax on gains from direct or indirect sale of Philippine mining rights. However, it is likely that Philippine authorities only learn of any indirect transfers of Philippine mining rights (i.e., selling of interest in the company that owned the company with the mining rights) through international mining industry information channels and not through any government data collection. A simple enforcement mechanism to ensure collection of tax on both direct and indirect sales would be to provide an automatic security interest for the [Bureau of Internal Revenue] in respect of any unpaid tax on gains on the direct or indirect sale of mining interests. If this rule were in place, the parties to the transaction itself would ensure tax is paid to protect the interest of the buyer and the sale price of the seller.

62. An alternative approach that the authorities may want to consider would be taxing the deemed gain of the local company holding the mining rights. Under this approach, if there is a five or 10 per cent or more change in the underlying ownership of the entity holding the mining right, the entity is treated as: (1) disposing of its proportionate interest in its mining right and immediately re-acquiring that interest; (2) receiving for the disposal consideration equal to the market value of the proportion of the mining right treated as disposed of; and (3) incurring a cost in respect of the re-acquisition of an equal amount.

---

a International Monetary Fund, "Philippines: Reform of the Fiscal Regimes for Mining and Petroleum," in *IMF Country Report Nº. 12/219* (Washington, D.C., IMF, 2012), p. 29-30.

10.5   OTHER APPROACHES FOR TAXING INDIRECT TRANSFERS IN COMPLIANCE WITH TAX TREATIES

10.5.1   General anti avoidance rule (GAAR)

10.5.1.1   There are at least two other approaches that can effectively tax indirect transfers without violating tax treaties. First is the use of a GAAR in domestic tax law that recharacterizes, for domestic tax law purposes, an indirect transfer of shares in a domestic corporation as a direct transfer of the same, where only the latter is taxable under the domestic tax law. For example, Public Notice 7 of China is based on a GAAR in its domestic tax law and recharacterizes an indirect transfer as a direct transfer in certain circumstances (see boxes 10.B.12 and 10.B.13 below for more details). Under this approach, countries can effectively tax indirect transfers, regardless of the proportion of values in shares that are derived from immovable properties.

10.5.1.2   Countries that want to tax indirect transfers even in non-extractive industries may prefer this approach for the following reasons:

(i)   As regards the relationship with tax treaties, if such recharacteriza-tion under the domestic tax law is respected for tax treaty purposes as well, Article 13(5) of the United Nations Model Convention will, to the extent permitted thereunder, authorize taxing rights to the coun-try seeking to tax the transfer. As regards GAARs, paragraphs 22 and 22.1 of the OECD Commentary states as follows (**emphasis added**):

22.   Other forms of abuse of tax treaties (e.g., the use of a base company) and possible ways to deal with them, including "substance-over-form," "economic substance" and **general anti-abuse rules** have also been analysed, particularly as concerns the question of whether these rules conflict with tax treaties, which is the second question mentioned in paragraph 9.1 above.

22.1   Such rules are part of the basic domestic rules set by domestic tax laws for determining which facts give rise to a tax liability; these rules are not addressed in tax treaties and are therefore not affected by them. Thus, as a general rule and having regard to paragraph 9.5, **there will be no conflict.** For example, to the extent that the application of the rules referred to in paragraph 22 results in a recharacterization of income or in a redetermination of the taxpayer who is considered to derive such income, **the provisions of the Convention will be applied taking into account these changes.**

(ii)   The guiding principles to qualify as a GAAR under the OECD Commentary are found in paragraph 9.5 of the Commentary on Article 1, being that:

(a)   A main purpose for entering into certain transactions or arrange-ments was to secure a more favourable tax position; and

(b)   Obtaining that more favourable treatment in these circum-stances would be contrary to the object and purpose of the relevant provision.

(iii)   OECD/G20 2014 BEPS Deliverable on Action 6 reinforced this posi-tion and states that if these conditions are satisfied, there would be no conflict with tax treaties; the Final Report on Action 6 reaffirmed this.[51] Paragraphs 20–27 of the United Nations Commentary on Article 1 basically follow the OECD Commentary.

---

[51] OECD, BEPS Action 6: 2014 Deliverable, p. 92; cf. BEPS Action 6: 2015 Final Report, p. 79 ff.

(iv) Hence, as long as the United Nations and OECD Commentaries are followed, and those guiding principles are satisfied, GAARs would be respected for tax treaty purposes.[52] Countries have to make sure that these principles are satisfied, and this would affect the scope of indirect transfers that can be covered by this approach. For example, in order for an indirect transfer to be considered abusive, it would be generally necessary that the percentage of shares transferred be sufficiently high. Furthermore, if countries desire to effectively tax the indirect transfer of shares in domestic corporations the sale of shares to related persons and sales over a period of time may need to be aggregated. Also, industry practices should be examined in order to decide on the level of an appropriate threshold percentage to effectively tax indirect transfers in the extractive industry.

(v) The determination of which circumstances satisfy such guiding principles can largely depend on how strictly the court in each country reviews the conformity of GAARs with those principles; establishing such conformity may be burdensome for tax administrations in some countries. In addition, this GAAR approach may be considered too uncertain for taxpayers due to the subjective standard to be used, particularly if one of the requirements is dependent on a future event (e.g., tax implications of a future transaction) and this may impede otherwise desirable business transactions. For these reasons, countries may prefer other approaches.

10.5.1.3 Where an indirect transfer of shares in a domestic corporation is successfully recharacterized as a direct transfer of the same, attention should be paid to the issue of potential double taxation. While, as a result of recharacterization, the transferor is treated as having directly transferred shares in a domestic corporation, it does not follow that the transferee is treated as directly acquiring and owning those shares for tax purposes in the future as well. As a matter of fact/form, the transferee owns the shares in the offshore holding company, which in turn owns the shares in a domestic corporation, and such fact/form can be respected in deciding the tax consequences of a future transaction. This can be problematic particularly when the offshore holding company sells the shares in the domestic corporation, since in this case, unless the GAAR (or relevant enforcement regulation thereunder) specifically addresses the issue of basis in the shares owned by the offshore holding company, double taxation can potentially arise. This is because the offshore holding company by itself neither owns newly-acquired shares in the domestic corporation nor paid taxes for the transfer in the first transaction, and hence, its basis in the shares may be treated as unchanged, despite the fact that taxes for built-in gains in those shares are effectively already paid by the former shareholder of the offshore holding company. It appears theoretically consistent to give the offshore holding company

---

[52] But see Qiguang Zhou, "The Relationship between China's Tax Treaties and Indirect Transfer Anti-avoidance Rules," in *74 Tax Notes International*, 543 (May 2014), for its criticism of the OECD/United Nations interpretation as too general.

a stepped-up basis in the shares; however, since a GAAR would be generally triggered only in abusive cases under the aforementioned guiding principles, some countries may not be willing to do so.

10.5.1.4 Example of enforcement of indirect transfer rules:

Box 10.B.12: A case in point: China
General anti-abuse rule, with specific enforcement regulation for indirect transfers

Under Article 47 of the Corporate Income Tax Law of China, introduced in 2008, if taxable income is reduced as a result of arrangements with no reasonable commercial purpose, the tax authorities can make adjustments.

According to State Administration of Taxation Order 32, which was published in 2014 as a general administrative guidance on the application of Article 47, two major features of a tax avoidance arrangement are required to justify its denial under Article 47: (a) its sole or main purpose is to obtain tax benefit; and (b) its legal form is not commensurate with its economic substance.

Additionally, Public Notice 7 was released in 2015 as an enforcement regulation to specifically handle indirect transfers. This new regulation replaces previous rules under Circular 698, issued in 2009. Under Public Notice 7, an indirect transfer will be recharacterized as a direct transfer of China Taxable Property if the following requirements are *all* satisfied:

> (a) A non-resident entity transfers equity or other similar interests in an offshore holding entity that directly or indirectly holds China Taxable Property;

> (b) The result of the transfer is, in substance, the same as or similar to the direct transfer of the China Taxable Property;

> (c) The transfer is made by the non-resident entity through arrangements lacking reasonable commercial purpose; and

> (d) The non-resident entity avoids corporate income tax liability.

"China Taxable Property" is defined as (a) property of an "establishment or place"—a domestic concept corresponding to a permanent establishment under treaties—in China; (b) real property in China; (c) equity interests in Chinese resident entities; and (d) other property directly held by a non-resident entity and the transfer of which brings about corporate income tax liability. This definition was expanded from the one in the Circular, under which only equity interests in Chinese resident entities were covered. In the case of (b) and (c) above, buyers owe obligations to withhold 10 per cent from the purchase price.

Box 10.B.13: A case in point: China—Public Notice 7 factors General anti-abuse rule, with specific enforcement regulation for indirect transfers

Public Notice 7 lists the following as factors to be taken into consideration for the purpose of determining the existence of "reasonable commercial purpose":

(a) Whether the value of the offshore holding entity's equity is mainly directly or indirectly derived from China Taxable Property;

(b) Whether the assets of the offshore holding entity mainly comprise direct or indirect investments in China, or whether the revenue of the offshore holding entity is mainly sourced directly or indirectly from China;

(c) Actual functions performed by or actual risks assumed by the offshore holding entity and its affiliates holding directly or indirectly China Taxable Property is sufficient to prove economic substance

(d) Duration of the offshore holding entity's shareholders, business model and relevant organizational structures;

(e) Tax implications of the indirect transfer outside of China;

(f) Whether the investment and transfer of China Taxable Property could have been affected directly, as opposed to indirectly;

(g) Applicable tax treaties or arrangements in China with respect to the indirect transfer; and

(h) Other relevant factors.

The following three categories of transactions are exempted from the recharacterization: (a) intra-group reorganizations satisfying certain requirements; (b) gains that would have been exempt even in the case of a direct transfer; and (c) transactions through public stock exchanges. The categories (a) and (b) above are addressed by Public Notice 7, but not under Circular 698.

Public Notice 7 includes a provision for voluntary reporting of transactions to the tax authority by buyers, sellers and underlying Chinese entities. This is a change from Circular 698, where buyers were required to report transactions. If buyers report transactions, they are potentially entitled to exemption from, or reduction of, future penalties. If sellers report transactions, they can be exempted from additional annual 5 per cent punitive interest. Tax authorities are also specifically authorized to make information requests to buyers, sellers, underlying Chinese entities and advisers.

10.5.2   Deemed gains

10.5.2.1   Another approach to effectively tax an indirect transfer is to impose tax on the underlying domestic corporation that holds immovable properties—instead of the shareholder who transferred the offshore holding company which, in turn, owns the underlying domestic corporation—by deeming all built-in gains in properties of such domestic corporation as realized when there is a change in its shareholding over a certain percentage. The built-in gains to be taxed can be limited to those derived from immovable properties, but countries can also choose to tax all of them. For example, the United Republic of Tanzania taxes an underlying domestic corporation for all of the built-in gains if its ownership changes more than 50 per cent (see box 10.B.14 below for more details).

10.5.2.2   Countries that want to follow this second approach may consider the following:

(i)   Tax treaties are generally applicable to protect only non-residents from taxation. It may be arguable that this domestic legislation is effectively taxing capital gains that are protected under Article 13. However, countries generally have broad discretion as to how to structure realization events for capital gains under their domestic legislation. For example, some developed countries have a fair-market-value based taxation system for listed stock or other financial instruments that have a fair market value. Also, the amount of capital gains can be different between a direct transfer and an indirect transfer since the bases in the assets can be different. Hence, this accelerated realization of built-in gains itself would unlikely cause a conflict with tax treaty obligations.

(ii)   Another tax treaty obligation that countries should pay careful attention to is Article 24 (Non-discrimination) of both the United Nations and OECD Model Conventions. Paragraph 3 forbids taxation of a permanent establishment that an enterprise of a Contracting State has in the other Contracting State that is less favourable than the taxation levied on enterprises of that other State carrying on the same activities. Paragraph 3 *only* relates to the taxation on the permanent establishment itself, however.

(iii) Paragraph 5 of Article 24 forbids giving less favourable treatment to a resident corporation owned by non-residents. Hence, if the domestic legislation under this approach is applicable only to domestic corporations owned by non-residents, it can be considered invalid by violating Article 24(5). In order to avoid this concern, countries subject to such treaty obligations would have to apply this regime regardless of whether shareholders are residents or non-residents.

(iv)   In contrast, paragraph 5 of the United Nations Commentary on Article 24 includes the following alternative provision of Article 24(5) which was developed as part of the 2001 version of that Model in consideration of the tax compliance problems arising from foreign ownership of domestic corporations in developing countries. It was designed to provide "that special measures applicable to foreign-owned enterprises should not be construed as constituting prohibited discrimination as long as all foreign-owned enterprises are treated alike" (emphasis added):

(v)   Enterprises of a Contracting State, the capital of which is wholly or partly owned or controlled, directly or indirectly, by one or more residents of the other Contracting State, shall not be subjected in the first-mentioned State to any taxation or any requirement connected therewith which is other or more burdensome than the taxation and connected requirements to which are subjected other similar enterprises the capital of which is wholly or partly owned or controlled, directly or indirectly, by residents of third countries.

(vi)   Unlike Article 24(5) of the United Nations and OECD Model Conventions, only discrimination between non-residents is prohibited under this alternate provision. There are several treaties that adopt this or similar provisions,[53] and under those treaties, countries that

---

[53] See, for example, the Norway-Qatar Treaty, as well as several treaties signed by Kuwait and the United Arab Emirates (UAE). For example, Article 26(3) of the Mongolia-UAE treaty states: "Enterprises of a Contracting State, the capital of which is wholly or partly owned or which is controlled, directly or indirectly, by one or more residents of the other Contracting State, shall not be subjected in the first-mentioned Contracting State to any taxation or any obligations connected therewith which is other or more burdensome than the taxation and connected obligations to which other similar enterprises the capital of which is wholly or partly owned or which is controlled directly or indirectly by one or more residents of any third state are or may be subjected."

have adopted this alternate provision in their tax treaties can limit the scope of domestic legislation under this approach to cases where foreign ownership is involved. The arguments for and against the alternative provision are addressed in paragraphs 5 to 7 of the United Nations Model Commentary on Article 24.

10.5.2.3   As long as a change in ownership over a specified percentage happens, this approach fully taxes built-in gains regardless of the percentage of shares transferred indirectly, and the amount of tax can be quite burdensome in light of the percentage of shares actually transferred.

10.5.2.4   There are several options to mitigate this problem, which are not necessarily mutually exclusive:

(i)   First, as regards the minimum threshold percentage of shares that need to be transferred, countries may consider setting a relatively high percentage (e.g., 50 per cent in the United Republic of Tanzania or 20 per cent in South Africa, with, in the latter case, at least 80 per cent of the market value of the company's shares being attributable directly or indirectly to immovable property) as compared to those used for domestic legislation pursuant to Article 13(4) of the United Nations and OECD Model Conventions (e.g., 5 per cent for listed shares and 2 per cent for non-listed shares in Japan). Such higher threshold may not be sufficient to deal with indirect transfers where several different shareholders set up a consortium to jointly invest in one project, for example in order to diversify the risks involved, and only some of them indirectly transfer their ownership rights. Again, industry practice should be examined to determine an appropriate threshold percentage.

(ii)   Alternatively, countries may choose to deem built-in gains as realized only to the extent corresponding to the percentage of shares transferred, although this can make the rule too complicated for both tax administrations and taxpayers.

(iii)   Another option is to deem not only built-in gains but also built-in losses as realized, and thereby, reduce the net taxable gains. In order to prevent attempts to avoid taxes by accelerating loss realization, countries may want to limit such deemed loss realization to the extent not exceeding the amount of gains deemed realized.

10.5.2.5   While this approach would make it easier for a tax administration to actually collect taxes, since the taxpayer is a domestic corporation located within its jurisdiction, it can at the same time cause a cash flow problem. The domestic corporation will need to finance the taxes due, even though the corporation itself does not receive any cash or other consideration for the transfer. In some cases, the domestic corporation may be obliged to dispose of some of its assets only to pay taxes, and this can ruin the business rationale of the transaction. In practice, this problem can be avoided if the transferor and transferee agree to reduce the consideration for the share transfer to the extent of taxes due on the domestic corporation and, after the transfer, the transferee contributes cash to the domestic corporation so that it can pay taxes. However, this practical solution may not always work, particularly when less than 100 per cent of the total shares in the domestic corporation are indirectly transferred, in which case the transferor would not be willing to bear all of the tax burden in the form of the reduction in consideration it is entitled to.

10.5.2.6   Double taxation can also arise under this approach, and it can be more problematic here than other approaches. Under this approach, Article 24(5) of the United Nations and OECD Model Conventions would require domestic tax laws to cover domestic corporations owned by residents. As a result, where a resident transfers shares in a domestic corporation, and the requirements for deemed gain recognition are satisfied, both the domestic shareholder and the underlying domestic corporation would have to realize gains immediately. This is different from other approaches where double taxation potentially arises only when the relevant shares/assets are transferred in the future. One solution would be to grant the shareholder a tax credit equivalent to the amount of taxes paid by the underlying domestic corporation as a result of the deemed gain recognition.

Box 10.B.14: A case in point: The United Republic of Tanzania (deemed realization of gains by the underlying entity whose shares are indirectly transferred)[a]

Under the Income Tax Act of the United Republic of Tanzania, an entity will be deemed to have realized gains in its assets, if its ownership changes, directly or indirectly, by more than 50 per cent (change of control) during a three-year period. As a result, if the underlying entity is a *resident*, it has to pay taxes for all of the gains deemed as realized, while a *non-resident* underlying entity is liable for taxes only to the extent derived from "domestic assets," including immovable properties in the United Republic of Tanzania.

This regime effectively triggers taxation by the Government, where domestic assets in the United Republic of Tanzania are indirectly transferred through a transfer of shares in an offshore holding entity. One distinct aspect of this regime as contrasted with the Peruvian approach above is that the underlying entity, not the shareholder who transferred its shares, is treated as realizing gains and thus liable for taxes. This unique nature was introduced by an amendment to the Income Tax Act in 2012. Before this amendment, the transferor, not the underlying entity, had been the taxpayer, and reducing enforcement difficulties and practical challenges by making the underlying entity directly liable for

---

taxes appears to have been the main purpose of this amendment.

The Tanzanian Income Tax Act intentionally has no exemption for intra-group reorganizations, apparently due to concerns about potentially significant tax avoidance risks.

---

[a] Mr. Charles Bajungu, *Capital gains and taxation in indirect sales: experience, challenges and remedial efforts in Tanzanian perspective* (paper presented at the meeting of the Tanzania Revenue Authority and the United Nations Tax Committee, New York, October 2014). Available at http://www.un.org/esa/ffd/wp-content/uploads/2014/11/10STM_PresentationBajungu.pdf.

10.5.3   Issues of identification

10.5.3.1   The first issue is how the country concerned gains information about the indirect transfer in a timely manner, especially a transfer effected in a foreign jurisdiction, as it often will be.

(i)   It is possible that information may come to light in an automatic exchange of information (although developing countries at this stage do not have many such arrangements) or by a spontaneous exchange from another country, but this is not likely to happen often either.[54] Where treaty relationships exist, information could be sought from treaty partners, but that would usually only happen after there was an initial awareness of the transfer, and at least some of its details.

(ii)   Officers in the revenue collection agency should keep up to date with industry news and conduct regular Internet searches for sets of key words such as the names of mines, the word "mine," and the country name have some value, but are necessarily to some extent reliant on the chance to make discoveries of indirect transfers. Commercial databases may assist as might details of foreign takeovers required to be announced under domestic law or notifications of changes required under extractives legislation. In one case in China, a public announcement was found on the website of the buyer, announcing the completion of the acquisition of the Chinese company, but without mention of the intermediate holding company, a Hong Kong special purpose vehicle with little substance.[55] Changes in auditors may also sometimes reflect wider developments.

---

[54] The situation has improved with the information sharing protocols established; see: https://www.oecd.org/tax/automatic-exchange/international-framework-for-the-crs/exchange-relationships/

[55] Cadwalader, Wickersham and Taft LLP, Circular *698: China's Anti-Tax Avoidance Measures for Offshore SPVs* (August 2010). Available at http://www.lexology.com/library/detail.aspx?g=80bb2c3b-c408-4d9a-8880-86f49c8d6fdd.

(iii) Intelligence on developments in the extractive industries, internationally as well as domestically, will often first come to the attention of the resources ministry or some other investment-related ministry. There should be clear reporting arrangements between such ministries and the tax authority on changes in ownership, contractors, other rights holders and the like, matched by strong reporting arrangements within the various parts of the tax authority.

(iv) Other potential pointers to an indirect transfer might include changes in enterprise names, changes in directors and changes in tax auditors.[56] It has been noted that companies that have been listed on international stock exchanges subsequent to structuring are more prone to detection, and that accountants may be required to "provision" for a potential tax liability of the selling entity.[57]

(v) Some countries have imposed reporting obligations (i) on underlying domestic companies to report to authorities when they are indirectly sold or where there are major changes in their shareholding; or (ii) on shareholders of such companies, usually only those in a control situation. The requirements can cast heavy obligations on the shareholder to know what business the company is conducting, and *might* present an issue of extraterritorial exercise of jurisdiction, particularly when imposed too extensively, to report to authorities a transfer indirectly affecting local property. The fact that it is *only* a reporting obligation may be relevant in challenging claims of an extraterritorial exercise of jurisdiction, however.

(vi) To be effective, even requirements to notify major shareholding changes (of those above 10 per cent, for example) would need to provide coverage for multiple changes to shareholdings over a reasonable period of time (12 months or longer in some cases) to prevent several transfers of 9 per cent in a short time span not having to be reported.

(vii) Further, reporting requirements on ownership of interests would need to apply at more than one level, to ensure that the reporting requirements are not avoided by having the changes occur further up a string of companies. The intention of such "indirect" transfers being covered would need to be clear in the legislation.

(viii) Sometimes the approach has been taken that even despite the difficulties identifying indirect disposals, legislation should be put in place (including requiring the local entity to notify any changes of ownership over a certain threshold) that can "provide the administration with a legal arsenal allowing it to take transfers of this type into account when its oversight capacities have advanced."[58]

---

[56] Ibid.

[57] Ibid.

[58] International Monetary Fund, "Mali Technical Assistance Report—Mining and

(ix) More recently, some countries have opted to attribute "joint and several" liability (i.e., each party being independently liable for the full extent of any breach) for the payment of the tax between the purchaser and the entity holding the mining rights. That has been the experience in Mozambique, after the introduction of the new Mining Tax law, which came into effect in early 2015.

10.5.3.2 Examples

Box 10.B.15: Mozambique Law No.28/2014 (the new Mining Tax Law)

On 23 September 2014, Mozambique introduced a new tax regime and incentives for the mining sector. Among other things, the new law established that mining rights are considered as immovable property (within the meaning of Article 13(4) of its bilateral tax treaties) and that all capital gains arising from the direct or indirect transfer of mining rights by non-resident entities, with or without permanent establishment in Mozambique, will be taxable at a fixed rate of 32 per cent. This capital gains tax shall become due and payable by the seller or transferor but the purchaser and the Mozambique entity holding the mining rights has several and joint liability for the payment of the tax. In the case of doubt on the price of the transaction, the tax authorities may refer to the best international practices to determine the price.

The law sets out specific rules relating to the calculation of gains, taxable income, deductible costs and amortization in the framework of mining activities, rules that were previously established under the different concession agreements.

Box 10.B.16: Viet Nam Ministry of Finance Circular N°.36/2016/TT-BTC dated 26 February 2016[a]

Article 21 - Subjects of tax

1. The transfer of interests from participation in a petroleum contract is that the organizations or individuals sell, transfer their investment capital (including the property and money) in the petroleum contract, petroleum enterprises or joint venture enterprises in Vietnam, transfer

---

Petroleum Taxation (Diagnostic Assessment)," in *IMF Country Report No. 15/348*, (December 2015) paragraph 131. Available at https://www.imf.org/external/pubs/ft/scr/2015/cr15348.pdf.

the ownership, change the ownership or control right of one contractor party or determine by other ways the whole or a part of the rights, interests and obligations in the petroleum contract, petroleum enterprises or joint venture enterprises (the transferor) for one or many organizations or individuals (the transferee) except for the financial restructuring or arrangement of the transferor or consolidation of the transferor's parent company. The transferee has the contractor's obligations and interests to conduct the search, exploration and extraction of oil and gas.

Where the enterprise is established in a foreign country (hereafter referred to as a foreign enterprise) transfers its shares or investment capital (including the property or money) or other interests in an enterprise established in a foreign country, but the enterprise whose capital is transferred holds directly or indirectly the property and interests of a participation in petroleum projects in Vietnam, this leads to a change of contractor's owner, the person holding the interests of a participation in petroleum projects in Vietnam. This transfer is also regarded as the transfer of interests of participation in the petroleum contract. The foreign enterprise carrying out the above transfer is regarded as the transferor. (...)

» Article 23. Declaration and payment of corporate income tax for income from the transfer of interests of participation in the petroleum contract

> ***The transferor of interests of participation in the petroleum contract must make a declaration and pay tax for the income from the transfer of interests of the participation in the petroleum contract.***

1. Where the transfer changes the contractor's owner who is holding the interests of participation in the petroleum contract in Vietnam, the contractor named in the petroleum contract in Vietnam must inform the tax agency upon generation of transfer and make a declaration and payment of tax on behalf of the transferor for the generated income pertaining to the petroleum contract in Vietnam in accordance with regulations.

2. The dossier of tax declaration for income from transfer of interests of participation in the petroleum contract:

The Declaration of corporate income tax on transfer of interests of participation in the petroleum contract is the Form N°. 03/TNDN-DK issued with this Circular.

> ***A copy of transfer contract (English copy and the Vietnamese translation).;***

417

> › **Certification of the operators, joint operating companies, parties involved in joint venture enterprises, Vietnam Oil and Gas Group on the total expenses incurred by the transferor in proportion to the prime price of the transferor's transferred interests and the evidencing documents;**
>
> › **The original documents of expenses pertaining to the transfer transaction;**
>
> › **Where the transfer changes the contractor's owner who is holding an interest in participation in the petroleum contract in Vietnam, the foreign contractor directly involved in the petroleum contract in Vietnam must make a report and provide the additional documents as follows:**

• The shareholding structure of the company before and after the transfer.

• The financial statement of two years of foreign enterprises and their subsidiaries/branches directly or indirectly holding the interests of participation in the petroleum contract in Vietnam.

• The report on the valuation of property and other evaluating documents used to determine the value of transfer of stocks and foreign investment capital under contract.

• The report on reality of income tax payment of foreign enterprise pertaining to the transfer leading to the change of contractor's owner who is holding the interests of participation in the petroleum contract in Vietnam.

• The report on relationship between the transferring foreign enterprise and the branches/subsidiaries directly or indirectly holding the interests of participation in the petroleum contract in Vietnam on: contributed capital, business and production, rev¬enues, expenses, accounts, assets, personnel…

• In case of required addition of dossier, the tax agency shall inform the taxpayers within three working days from the date of receipt of dossier.

---

[a] Hệ thống pháp luật Việt Nam. See https://vanbanphapluat.cocircular-no-36-2016-tt-btc-tax-conducting-the-search-exploration-extraction-oil-gas.

Box 10.B.17: India Ministry of Finance Notification S.O. 2226 (E) of 28 June 2016 (extract)[a]

3. In the said rules [the Income Tax Rules, 1962], after rule 114DA, the following rule shall be inserted, namely:

"114DB. Information or documents to be furnished under section 285A."

(1) Every Indian concern referred to in section 285A shall, for the purposes of the said section, maintain and furnish the information and documents in accordance with this rule.

(2) The information shall be furnished in Form No. 49D electronically under digital signature to the Assessing Officer having jurisdiction over the Indian concern within a period of ninety days from the end of the financial year in which any transfer of the share of, or interest in, a company or entity incorporated outside India (hereafter referred to as "foreign company or entity") referred to in Explanation 5 to clause (i) of sub-section (1) of section 9 has taken place: Provided that where the transaction in respect of the share or the interest has the effect of directly or indirectly transferring the rights of management or control in relation to the Indian concern, the information shall be furnished in the said Form within ninety days of the transaction.

(3) The Indian concern shall maintain the following along with its English translation, if the documents originally prepared are in foreign languages and produce the same when called upon to do so by any income-tax authority in the course of any proceeding to substantiate the information furnished under sub-rule (2) namely:

(i) Details of the immediate holding company or entity, intermediate holding company or companies or entity or entities and ultimate holding company or entity of the Indian concern;

(ii) Details of other entities in India of the group of which the Indian concern is a constituent;

(iii) The holding structure of the shares of, or the interest in, the foreign company or entity before and after the transfer;

(iv) Any transfer contract or agreement entered into in respect of the share of, or interest in, any foreign company or entity that holds any asset in India through, or in, the Indian concern;

(v) Financial and accounting statements of the foreign company or entity which directly or indirectly holds the assets in India through, or in, the Indian concern for two years prior to the date of transfer of the share or interest;

(vi) Information relating to the decision or implementation process of the overall arrangement of the transfer;

(vii) Information in respect of the foreign company or entity and its subsidiaries, relating to -

    (a) The business operation;

    (b) Personnel;

    (c) Finance and properties;

    (d) Internal and external audit or the valuation report, if any, forming basis of the consideration in respect of the share, or the interest;

(viii) The asset valuation report and other supporting evidence to determine the place of location of the share or interest being transferred;

(ix) The details of payment of tax outside India, which relates to the transfer of the share or interest;

(x) The valuation report in respect of Indian asset and total assets duly certified by a merchant banker or accountant with supporting evidence;

(xi) Documents which are issued in connection with the transactions under the accounting practice followed.

(4) The information and documents specified in sub-rule (3) shall be kept and maintained for a period of eight years from the end of relevant assessment year.

---

[a] India Ministry of Finance, Notification S.O. 2226(E) (2016). Available at https://www.incometaxindia.gov.in/Communications/Notification/Notification552016.pdf

10.5.4   Enforcement issues

10.5.4.1   If there is a taxable disposition, how can the tax debt be enforced in practice? The indirect transfer generally takes place outside the jurisdiction where the property (such as a mine) is located and usually neither the buyer nor the seller is a resident.

(i)   While both the United Nations and OECD Model Conventions now contain optional Assistance in the Collection of Tax Debt Articles for countries wanting to provide for this in bilateral tax treaties, and there is a multilateral OECD/Council of Europe Convention on Mutual Administrative Assistance in Tax Matters on the subject, this is not something most developing countries have included in their bilateral or multilateral agreements.

(ii) In a report to the G20 proposing, in effect, a framework for further G20-related work on indirect transfers, some of these options, described as "alternative approaches to collection," are briefly noted as follows:[59]

    1. Imposing a withholding obligation on the buyer/transferee;

    2. Treating a resident party as the agent for the non-resident transferor;

    3. Deeming a resident to have made the transfer; or

    4. Introducing regulatory requirements that make approval for transfer conditional on payment of the tax.

(iii) One approach taken has been to deem that, where there is a change in ownership of an underlying domestic corporation holding assets over a certain percentage (50 per cent in the United Republic of Tanzania as seen above; 10 per cent in the case of Peru, as also seen above) there has been a disposal and reacquisition of exploration and development rights by such underlying domestic corporation. This would lead to a domestic capital gain (the responsible taxpayer will have to be made clear) and countries can enforce against a resident taxpayer. Depending on the legislation, reapprovals might be required for exploration, production or export licences, for example (although such reapprovals may not be necessary, if deemed disposals and re-acquisitions are made only for tax purposes). Reapproval may be required after a set period of years, however. Requiring a reapproval of the exploration, production or export licences in the event of a change in underlying ownership might be one mechanism to ensure that the capital gains tax owed on the transaction has been paid to the government of the country where the exploration happens or from where export occurs. This would, of course, have an impact in terms of the investment climate for such activities, and the relevant or otherwise applicable investment treaties would need to be considered. Some preapproval processes may mitigate but will unlikely eliminate these concerns.

---

[59] G20 Development Working Group, *A Report on the Issues Arising from the Indirect Transfer of Assets to Identify Policy Options to Tackle Abusive Cases, with Particular Reference to Developing Countries: Concept Note* (2015). Available at http://g20.org.tr/wp-content/uploads/2015/11/Concept-Note-on-the-Report-on-Issues-Arising-from-the-Indirect-Transfer-of-Assets.pdf.

(iv) Alternatives include "joint and several" liabilities of the seller and buyer for the tax debt, or else a tax obligation on the indirect buyer of the assets (such as withholding obligation to withhold a specified percentage from the purchase price, which may or may not be sufficient to cover all taxes due on the seller). In the 2014 IMF's Mali Technical Assistance Report, when addressing that country's extractive legislation, the IMF noted that (after proposing an indirect transfers treaty provision that unusually focused on Article 13(5) of the United Nations Model—dealing with transfer of shares) rather than Article 13(4)):

> **or tax collection purposes, provisions could be made for the establishment of a withholding mechanism to ensure that taxes are collected.** A company established in Mali, whose rights are being directly or indirectly transferred, should withhold the amount of tax on capital gains realized abroad on the direct or indirect transfer of its rights. The new mechanism should be inserted in the form of an article in the General Tax Code. For reasons of simplicity, in the event that this tax is withheld at source when the transferring company is a non-resident, the mission suggests that the capital gain realized not be included in the IS [corporate income tax] tax base.[60]

(v) The theory is that publicizing an indirect transfer regime will put the buyer (exercising due diligence) on notice so that the buyer takes necessary actions, for example, making sure that the seller pays or reimburses all the taxes due through an indemnity clause.[61] In those cases, where the underlying domestic corporation becomes the taxpayer, the transfer price will reflect that. There may have to be legislation imposing obligations on the operator of, for example, a mine (such as in the capacity of a withholding agent in respect of interest or dividends payable to shareholders/owners of the operating company) and imposing a specific lien upon the facility in the event of non-payment. In a case in Uganda, the revenue authority treated the buyer as the agent for the seller because it was a signatory on an escrow account put aside by the seller for possible tax liabilities, even though the seller disputed the liability, and issued an "agency notice" to pay taxes due on the buyer.[62]

---

[60] Ibid., paragraphs 130–132.

[61] The indemnity clause between a seller, Heritage Oil and Gas, and a buyer, Tullow Uganda, after the latter was treated as an agent by the Ugandan tax authorities was the subject of major litigation. See, for example, Alexander Keepin, Theo Jones, *M&A in emerging markets—don't lose value through the tax indemnity; lessons to learn from Tullow Uganda v Heritage Oil and Gas* (Berwin, Leighton, Paisner, August 2014). Available at http://www.blplaw.com/expert-legal-insights/articles/ma-in-emerging-markets.

[62] Ibid.; see also on this specific point: Alexander Keepin and Theo Jones, The deal risks of a disputed tax bill: *Tullow Uganda v Heritage Oil and Gas* (Berwin, Leighton, Paisner, September 2013). Available at http://www.blplaw.com/expert-legal-insights/articles/the-deal-risks-of-a-disputed-tax-bill-tullow-uganda-v-heritage-oil-and-gas.

(vi) One alternative is allowing non-payment by a certain time after the payment becomes due to be a factor in denying export licences for the minerals, oil, or gas produced by the facility. This sort of provision is a very serious step, and it would need to preserve normal taxpayer rights under domestic law for contesting a tax debt. Its impact on any other owners of the mine or oil and gas facility whose interests were not transferred should also be borne in mind.

(vii) However, this sort of response may not be possible (or only with the risk of substantial damages) because of contractual obligations, including stability (or "stabilization") clauses that may sometimes freeze the applicable law for the life of the project or reimburse for costs resulting from regulatory change or because of governing Investment Protection Agreements with Fair and Equitable Treatment[63] or Umbrella clauses,[64] for example. However, stability clauses typically apply to the fiscal regime of mining operations, rather than the taxes that apply to non-resident indirect owners of shares in mining projects under concession agreements. Any consideration of a regime to address indirect transfers and any risks in relation to meeting Investment Protection Agreement obligations should consider the possible effect of these obligations. As always, addressing potential abuses of the system must be balanced with not creating too much complexity for the country, given the scope of the benefits it perceives and without increasing uncertainty or investment risks for compliant taxpayers. When stability clauses became an issue for Ghana, a seven-person team was set up to review such clauses, renegotiate them where necessary and develop procedures for granting stability clauses in the future.[65]

(viii) One particular aspect of this is that any tax payable in the country of the mine or other facility may not be viewed as properly creditable in a treaty partner; they may view the gain as sourced offshore. Any indirect transfer legislation could specifically indicate that the gain is to be treated as domestically sourced to prevent issues in the courts. However, other countries may not accept that, leading to possible double taxation that will have some impact on the investment climate.

---

[63] See, for example, *United Nations Conference on Trade and Development, Fair and Equitable Treatment. UNCTAD Series on Issues in International Investment Agreements II* (New York, United Nations, 2012). Available at http://unctad.org/en/Docs/unctaddiaeia2011d5_en.pdf.

[64] Umbrella clauses meaning "[e]ach Contracting Party shall observe any obligation it may have assumed with regard to investments," which gives an additional treaty basis to claims that contractual terms have not been abided. See, for example, Katia Yannaca-Small, "Interpretation of the Umbrella Clause in Investment Agreements," in International Investment Law: Understanding Concepts and Tracking Innovations: A Companion Volume to International Investment Perspectives (Paris, OECD Publishing, 2008). Available at http://dx.doi.org/10.1787/9789264042032-3-en.

[65] Ghana Ministry of Finance, Duffuor Inaugurates Team to Review Mining Stability Agreements (February 2012).

ANNEX I: Further information

Charles Bajungu, *Capital gains and taxation in indirect sales: experience, challenges and remedial efforts in Tanzanian perspective* (paper presented at the meeting of the Tanzania Revenue Authority and the United Nations Tax Committee, New York, October 2014). Available at http://www.un.org/esa/ffd/wp-content/uploads/2014/11/10STM_PresentationBajungu.pdf.

Baker & McKenzie, *Breaking News: China Issues Long Awaited Indirect Transfer Regulation Replacing Notice 698* (February 2015). Available at http://www.lexology.com/library/detail.aspx?g=b8226983 -cb9e-4575-8ce8-cb9283a41706.

Cadwalader, Wickersham and Taft LLP, Circular 698: *The China's Anti-tax Avoidance Measures for Offshore SPVs* (August 2010). Available at http://www.lexology.com/library/detail.aspx?g=80bb2c3b -c408-4d9a-8880-86f49c8d6fdd.

Jack Calder, *Administering Fiscal Regimes for Extractive Industries: a Handbook* (Washington, D.C., International Monetary Fund, 2014).

Center for Public Integrity, *Taxing "Capital Gains" in Mozambique's Extractive Sector* (May 2014). Available at http://www.cip.org.mzcipdoc/307_Spinformacao_2014_04_en.pdf.

IMF, OECD, UN, World Bank Group, *A Toolkit for Addressing the Taxation of Offshore Indirect Transfers* (2017).

Jason Clements, Charles Lammam and Matthew Lo, "The Economic Costs of Capital Gains Taxes in Canada," in *Capital gains tax reform in Canada: lessons from abroad,* (Vancouver, Fraser Institute, 2014) p. 17. Available at https://www.fraserinstitute.org/sites/default/files/economic-costs-of-capital-gains-taxes-in-canada-chpt.pdf.

J.J.P. De Goede, "Allocation of Taxing Rights on Income from Cross-border (indirect) Sale of Shares," in *Asia-Pacific Tax Bulletin* (May/June 2012), p. 211.

Ernst and Young, "China released Administrative Measures for General Anti-avoidance Rules (GAAR)," in *China Tax & Investment News* (December 2014). Available at http://www.ey.com/Publication/vwLUAssets/EY-CTIN-2014002-ENG/$FILE/EY-CTIN-2014002-ENG.pdf.

Thomas L. Hungerford, "The Economic Effects of Capital Gains Taxation," in *Congressional Research Service* (June 2010). Available at https://fas.org/sgp/crs/misc/R40411.pdf.

IMF Fiscal Affairs Department, *Fiscal Regimes for Extractive Industries: Design and Implementation* (August 2012). Available at https://www.imf.org/external/np/pp/eng/2012/081512.pdf

Daniel K. Kalinaki, "Court gives URA nod to seek taxes on sale of Zain assets in Uganda," in *The East African* (September 2014).

Kennedy Munyandi and others, "Tax Policy Trends in Africa—Commentary on the Major Tax Developments in 2013 and 2014," in *Bulletin for International Taxation* (March 2015) p.154.

OECD, *Model Tax Convention on Income and on Capital* (15 July 2014). Available at http:www.keepeek.com/Digital-Asset-Managemento/ecd/taxation/model-tax-convention-on-income-and-on-capital-condensed-version-2014_mtc_cond-2014-en#page1.

OECD G20, *Base Erosion and Profit Shifting Project: Preventing the Granting of Treaty Benefits in Inappropriate Circumstances: Action 6: 2014 Deliverable* (Paris, OECD Publishing, September 2014), p. 78–79. Available at http://www.oecd.org/tax/preventing-the-granting-of-treaty-benefits-in-inappropriate-circumstances-9789264219120-en.htm.

Robin Oliver, *Capital Gains Tax—The New Zealand Case* (paper presented at the Fraser Institute 2000 Symposium on Capital Gains Taxation, Vancouver, 15–17 September 2000), p. 5. Available at https://taxpolicy.ird.govt.nz/sites/default/files/news/2000-09-12-speech-oliver-capital-gains.doc.

J. Phan, "Preferential Treatment of Capital Gains," in *Contemporary Tax Journal* (Spring/Summer 2013).

Karl Schmalz, "Capital Gains Issues in the Extractive Industries," in *Tax Notes International*, vol. 84 (October 2016), p. 91. Available at http://iticnet.org/images/84TI0091_Schmlz.pdf.

S. Simontacchi, "Immovable Property Companies as Defined in Paragraph 13(4) of the OECD Model," in *Bulletin of International Taxation* (2006) vol. 60, No. 1, p. 29.

UNCTAD, "Fair and Equitable Treatment," in UNCTAD *Series on Issues in International Investment Agreements II* (New York, United Nations, 2012). Available at http://unctad.org/en/Docs/unctaddiaeia 2011d5_en.pdf.

Edwin T. Whatley and Shinichi Kobayashi, "Taxation of Indirect Equity Transfers: Japan," in *17 Asia-Pacific Tax Bulletin 2* (2011), p. 138.

United Nations, *United Nations Model Double Taxation Convention between Developed and Developing Countries* (2011). Available at http://www.un.org/esa/ffd/documents/UN_Model_2011_Update.pdf.

United Nations, Department of Economic and Social Affairs (2018). *2017 United Nations Model Taxation Convention between Developed and Developing Countries*. Available at http://www.un.org/esa/ffd/ffd-follow-up/tax-committee.html

Victoria University of Wellington Tax Working Group, *A Tax System for New Zealand's Future* (2010). Available at http://www.victoria.ac.nz/sacl/centres-and-institutes/cagtr/pdf/tax-report-website.pdf.

Debra J. Villarreal and Lucas LaVoy, Texas Oil and Gas Exploration and Development Agreements, in *31 Energy & Min. L. Inst.* 10 (2010). Available at https://www.emlf.org/clientuploads/directory/whitepaper/Villarreal_LaVoy_11.pdf.

Katia Yannaca-Small. "Interpretation of the Umbrella Clause in Investment Agreements," in *International Investment Law: Understanding Concepts and*

Tracking Innovations: A Companion Volume to International Investment Perspectives (Paris, OECD Publishing, 2008). Available at http://dx.doi.org/10.1787/9789264042032-3-en.

Qiguang Zhou, "The Relationship between China's Tax Treaties and Indirect Transfer Anti-avoidance Rules", in *Tax Notes International*, vol. 74, No. 6 (May 12), p. 43.

ANNEX II: Flowchart for analysis of indirect Offshore transfers

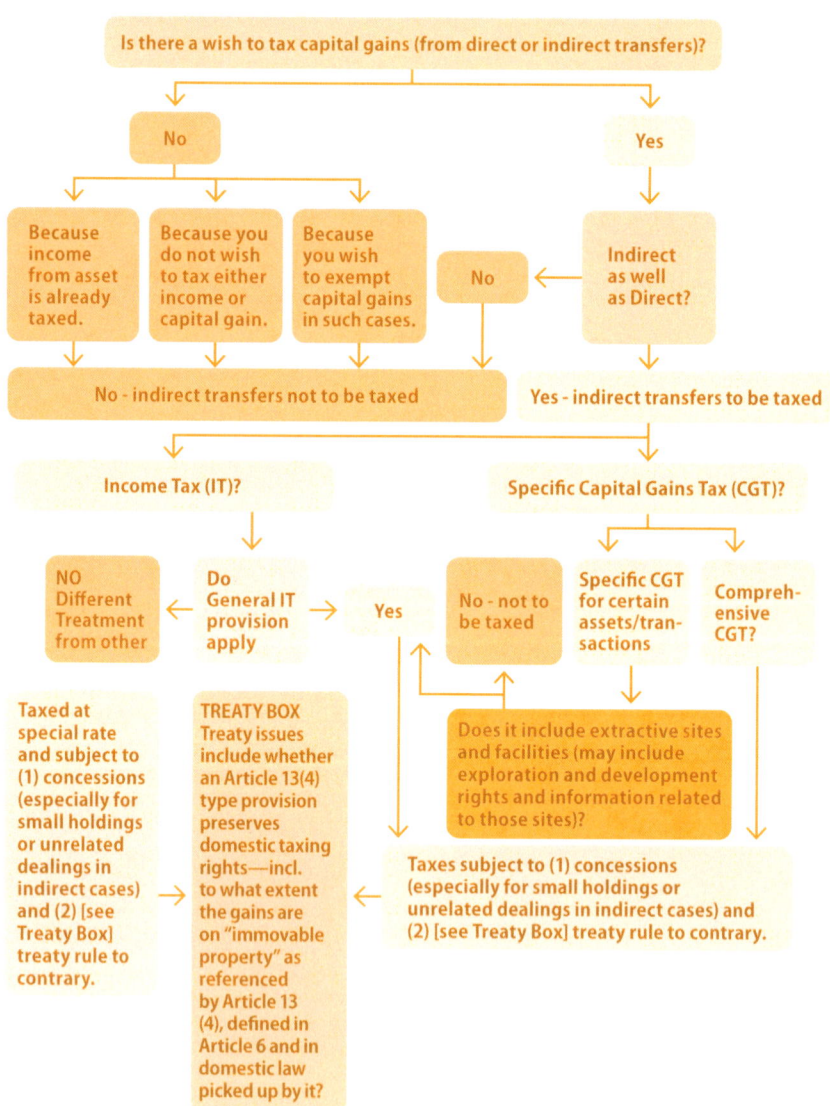

Figure 10.F.2: Taxation of Indirect Offshore Transfers

ANNEX III: Symmetry in capital gains taxation

Capital gains taxation rules are as important to the buyer as they are to the "tax-paying" seller. When a seller is taxable on its gain, measured by its sales price over its remaining cost basis in an asset, the buyer takes as its beginning tax basis the same price (in this case, its purchase price) for measuring future income or capital gains. Unless this occurs, the structure of the tax law itself will impose double taxation, contrary to basic taxation principles. While this "symmetry" is clearly understood as an important principle for in-country direct sales of operating assets, its impact is equally important in the case of indirect sales that may take place outside of the country.

To fully appreciate the importance of symmetry in this context it is critical to understand the economic analysis underlying sales transactions and, in particular for purposes of this chapter, sales transactions involving extractive assets and operations. Consider the following fact pattern. Opco owns and operates an oil well in Country X. Opco is a resident of Country X and is owned by Holdco, which is a resident of country Y.

Opco's well is expected to generate net cash (cash revenues less cash operating/capital expenses) of 100 for each of the next 10 years. For tax purposes, Opco's well is fully depreciated and there are no other differences between net cash and taxable income during the 10-year period. Assuming a Country X tax rate of 50 per cent, Opco expects to generate after-tax net cash of 500 over 10 years (100 x 10 = 1,000 – 50 per cent tax rate = 500). Country X will receive 500 in tax revenues over the same 10-year period.

Assume Buyer has expressed an interest in buying Opco's well. To reach an agreement, Buyer and Opco will have to arrive at a mutually agreeable sales price. Putting aside for the moment financial principles that deal with the present value of money,[66] Opco would demand an after-tax sales price of at least 500, which is the expected after-tax cash from retaining the well. Likewise, Buyer will only be willing to pay a sales price that is, at most, equal to the after-tax cash that it expects to receive from the well. Thus, the tax treatment of the transaction will have a significant impact on whether Opco and Buyer will be able to reach a mutually agreed upon price. In general, if the tax rules of Country X allow for symmetrical treatment, then there would be no tax impediment to Opco and Buyer reaching a deal.

Symmetry: seller's gain taxed/buyer deducts purchase price

Under these rules, assume for simplicity's sake that Buyer is willing to pay 1,000 to Opco for the well. Buyer's economic analysis of this decision would be as follows.

---

[66] These principles are very important and are essential to understanding the impact of tax depreciation rules on the incentives for investors to risk and invest capital.

	Cash	Tax Calculation
Income	1000	1000
Tax Deduction		(1000)
Taxable Income		0
Tax	0	0
After-tax Cash	1000	

Assuming the well generates the same net cash of 100 over 10 years, Buyer's future depreciation deductions (that were not available to Seller) will offset taxable income generated from the well and as a result Buyer's future net after-tax cash generated is 1,000. Under these simplified facts, Buyer "breaks even" on this investment.

Seller, on the other hand, will accept the 1,000 knowing that it is fully taxable at 50 per cent because the after-tax cash to seller will be the same 500 that Seller expected to receive from continuing to own and operate the well. Country X receives the same 500 in revenue that it would have received absent a sale.

Symmetry: seller's gain not taxed/no deduction for buyer (typical offshore indirect sale)

In this case, for Buyer to have a "break-even" investment, it would be willing to pay only 500 for the well because that is the expected after-tax cash generated from the operation of the well. Under these rules, Buyer basically steps into the shoes of Opco and has the same after-tax result that Opco would have had: 1,000 of before-tax cash minus 500 of tax paid nets 500 of after-tax cash. Seller is willing to accept the 500 because it is not subject to tax and therefore Seller's after-tax cash from the sale is also 500. Country X will receive 500 in revenues and is in the same position as before.

These two fact patterns are instructive, because they demonstrate, contrary to assertions frequently made, that a Seller can avoid local country tax through an offshore sale and that such a sale deprives developing countries of tax revenues.[67] Notice that in this case, Opco bears the full brunt of the Country X tax. Buyer's calculation of the sales price it is willing to pay to Opco is based on the *after-tax* cash flow that is expected from the well. In other words, even though the well generates 1,000 of revenues, Buyer is only willing to pay Opco 500 after deducting the expected tax payments of 500. Country X also is kept whole and will still receive 500 of revenue.

Nonsymmetrical treatment: seller's gain taxed/no deduction for buyer

Under these rules, Buyer will only be able to break-even by paying Opco 500 for

---

[67] OECD, *Part 1 of a Report to G20 Development Working Group on the Impact of BEPS In Low Income Countries*, (July 2014). Available at http://www.oecd.org/tax/part-1-of-report-to-g20-dwg-on-the-impact-of-beps-in-low-income-countries.pdf

the well because, as explained above, that is the expected after-tax cash flow from the well. For Opco, a payment of 500 is insufficient because the sale would be subject to 250 of tax by Country X (500 x 50 per cent); therefore, Opco's after-tax cash is only 250 (500–250) which results in an effective tax rate of 75 per cent—i.e., double taxation.

Some may argue that this tax regime is favourable for Country X because it will receive 750 of tax revenues (250 from Opco as a result of the sales transaction plus 500 from Buyer as a result of the ongoing operations of the well). However, it is unlikely that this windfall to Country X will ever materialize. As stated previously, the sales transaction will only take place if Opco and Buyer can arrive at an agreeable price. Under this tax regime, the likelihood of that happening is extremely unlikely. As a result, the sales transaction will not take place and Opco will remain operator of the well. In the long run, this may be detrimental to Country X if Buyer would have been a more efficient operator or would have been more willing to make additional investments.

Nonsymmetrical treatment: seller's gain not taxed/buyer deducts purchase price

Under these rules, Country X would subsidize the sales transaction between Opco and Buyer. For the reasons explained above, Buyer would be willing to pay 1,000 for the well. Seller would receive a windfall in this case because the after-tax cash to Seller would also be 1,000 if the sale is not subject to tax. Country X would receive zero tax revenues under this regime.

In conclusion, a tax regime that provides symmetrical treatment for the Seller and the Buyer will protect the country's revenue and will not present an economic impediment to investors seeking to maximize efficiencies.

Even if a system is designed to create symmetry, there is still a question as to which approach is the best, i.e., tax gains to the Seller but allow a deduction for the Buyer or do not tax gains to the Seller but likewise do not allow deductions based on the purchase price to the Buyer. This ultimately becomes a question of timing. For example, under the Opco example above, if the gains are taxed, then Country X receives a lump sum of 500 in the first year and then nothing in future years. If the gains are not taxed, Country X continues to receive a steady stream of 50 in revenues for the next 10 years. Which is best for Country X? Obviously, many factors come into play but one item that public finance experts may consider is whether Country X's budgeting and spending processes are sufficiently disciplined to account for one-time acceleration of expected revenues. Would one year's spike in revenues be mistaken for a continuing trend or would other pressures force the revenues to be spent, effectively mortgaging the future? Alternatively, would it be better from a budgeting perspective to be able to rely upon a stable income flow in future years? A country will need to weigh these factors in making a policy decision on this significant issue.

Chapter 11

Transfer Pricing Issues

11.1 INTRODUCTION

11.1.1 Executive summary

11.1.1.1   In the course of the work of the "Subcommittee on Extractive Industries Taxation Issues for Developing Countries" for (2013-2017), a need was identified to develop a guidance document containing and analysing some examples of transfer pricing issues in extractive industries, both relating to the production of oil and natural gas and relating to mining and minerals extraction.

11.1.1.2   This chapter responds to that need and highlights some of the transfer pricing issues arising in the extractive industries. The chapter draws on materials that have been published in other forums, including the Platform for Cooperation on Tax (typically referred to as the PCT) reflecting enhanced collaboration between the International Monetary Fund (IMF), Organization for Economic Cooperation and Development (OECD), the United Nations (UN) and the World Bank Group (WBG) for the benefit of developing countries. Reference can be made to the PCT's Toolkit for *Addressing Difficulties in Accessing Comparable Data for Transfer Pricing Analyses.*[1] The Toolkit includes a Supplementary Report on *Addressing the Information Gaps on Prices of Minerals Sold in an Intermediate Form* (the Supplementary Report). Reference can also be made to the WBG Extractive Industries work and materials;[2] the WBG publication *Transfer Pricing in Mining with a Focus on Africa;*[3] and the African Tax Administration Forum (ATAF) *Toolkit for Transfer Pricing Risk in the African Mining Industry.*[4]

11.1.1.3   This chapter focuses specifically on the value chain of mining and mineral extraction and of the production of oil and natural gas. The tables at 11.2.2 et seq. identify the transfer pricing issues that often arise in the extractive

---

[1] Available at https://www.oecd.org/tax/toolkit-on-comparability-and-mineral-pricing.pdf.

[2] Available at http://www.worldbank.org/en/topic/extractiveindustries/overview..

[3] Pietro Guj et al., *Transfer pricing in mining with a focus on Africa: a reference guide for practitioners* (Washington, D.C., World Bank Group, Centre for Exploration Targeting, Minerals and Energy for Development Alliance, 2017). Available at http://documents.worldbank.org/curated/en/801771485941579048/pdf/112346-REVISED-Dated-Transfer-pricing-in-mining-with-a-focus-on-Africa-a-reference-guide-for-practitioners-Web.pdf.

[4] See: https://events.ataftax.org/index.php?page=documents&func=view&document_id=13

---

industries. The tables are organized by reference to the various major stages in the extractive industry value chain. They make some general suggestions on methods and approaches that might be used to address the identified issues.

11.1.1.4   The chapter then provides several case examples, some of which result from discussions with tax inspectors working in developing countries. Taken together, the tables and the examples provide useful background information for developing countries to utilize in addressing transfer pricing issues in extractive industries. The chapter does not aspire to provide comprehensive transfer pricing guidance for the extractive industries and should provide a useful summary and checklist of some of the issues that commonly arise. It is recommended that this extractive industry chapter and the UN Transfer Pricing Manual (see 11.1.2) be consulted together.

11.1.2   Background and relationship with UN Transfer Pricing Manual

11.1.2.1   The first edition of the *United Nations Practical Manual on Transfer Pricing for Developing Countries* (the Manual) was issued in 2013. This responded to a need expressed by developing countries for clearer guidance on the policy and administrative aspects of applying transfer pricing analysis to some of the transactions of multinational enterprises (MNEs) commonly occurring in developing countries. The Manual was updated and revised in 2017 (second edition) and again in 2021 (third edition).[5]

11.1.2.2   The Manual is based on the work of the Subcommittee on Article 9 (Associated Enterprises) pursuant to a mandate with the following requirements:

(i)   That it reflects the operation of Article 9 of the United Nations Model Convention, and the arm's length principle embodied in it, and is consistent with relevant Commentaries of the United Nations Model Convention;

(ii)   That it reflects the realities for, and the needs of, developing countries at their relevant stages of capacity development;

(iii)   That special attention should be paid to the experience of developing countries, and the issues and options of most practical relevance to them; and

(iv)   That it draws upon the work being done in other forums.

11.1.2.3   The 2021 *Transfer Pricing Manual* is organized into four parts:

---

[5] The latest edition of the United Nations Manual on *Transfer Pricing for Developing Countries* is available at https://www.un.org/development/desa/financing/sites/www.un.org.development.desa.financing/files/2021-04/TP_2021_final_web%20%281%29.pdf

(i)   Part A relates to transfer pricing in a global environment;

(ii)   Part B contains guidance on design principles and policy considerations;

(iii) Part C addresses practical implementation of a transfer pricing regime in developing countries; and

(iv)   Part D contains country practices.

11.1.2.4   The third edition of the Manual made improvements in usability and practical relevance, and updated and improved the existing text, including on Country Practices. There is new content, in particular, on financial transactions, profit splits, centralized procurement functions and comparability issues. There is additional material and updated content on areas such as cost sharing arrangements, which are of relevance to the extractive industries.

11.1.2.5   The Manual does not address industry-specific issues, but serves to provide general guidance on technical aspects such as (i) the need for and how to conduct a comparability analysis; (ii) the respective available transfer pricing methods and how they operate; (iii) transfer pricing issues particular to intra-group services; (iv) transfer pricing considerations for intangible property; (v) cost contribution arrangements; (vi) transfer pricing of business restructurings; and (vii) the general legal environment relating to domestic transfer pricing legislation. The Manual also provides guidance on administrative issues such as transfer pricing documentation, audits and risk assessment, dispute avoidance and resolution and establishing transfer pricing capability in developing countries. Finally, the Manual provides an overview of certain country practices and perspectives on transfer pricing.

11.2   TRANSFER PRICING ISSUES THAT MAY ARISE IN THE EXTRACTIVE INDUSTRIES

11.2.1   Breakdown of issues

11.2.1.1   Transfer pricing issues in the extractive industries that in particular may affect developing countries include:

(i)   Fragmentation of the supply chain and ability to relocate functions in order to allocate profits to:

a. Marketing/procurement companies or branches; and

b. Offshore hedging companies.

(ii)   Fragmentation of transactions (i.e., where MNEs enter into convoluted structures involving the inter-positioning of multiple companies, generally in low-tax jurisdictions (splitting out of functions and risks) to shift profits);

(iii) Thin capitalization and other types of financial transactions that may lead to potentially deductible expenses or have other impacts on the tax base;

(iv) Intra-group charges (e.g., technical fees and management fees); and

(v) Taxpayers using offshore marketing companies to shift profits, arguing that they are securing demand through customer relationships, smart contracting and high-quality services—all of which are key to placing product in the market and to overall value creation.

11.2.1.2   Table 11.T.1 below presents the transfer pricing issues that might develop during the course of business for those engaged in the extractive industry. These issues arise in conjunction with the major stages in the life of an extractive industry activity.[6]

11.2.2. Negotiation and bidding

---

[6] With respect to the transfer pricing issues listed in Table 11.T.1, reference is also made to the Toolkit for Transfer Pricing Risk Assessment in the African Mining Industry:https://www.igfmining.org/beps/resources/toolkit-for-transfer-pricing-risk-assessment-in-the-african-mining-industry/.

Table 11.T.1: Transfer pricing issues

Issue	Sector	Description	Guidance
1. Acquisition of data from related parties	Mining Oil and Gas	Where the geological data is acquired from a related party, there is risk of overstatement of the acquisition cost (for deduction or depreciation).	Use traditional transfer pricing (TP) methods (Comparable Uncontrolled Price—CUP—or Cost Plus) to assure reasonability of the price. However, comparability may be a real issue. Transfer of (geological) data might occur directly or indirectly by transferring the shares in the entity holding the data.
2. Acquisition of extraction rights from related parties	Mining Oil and Gas	A difficulty at this stage may be the valuation of the likelihood of success in discovering recoverable resources. Transfer mispricing may be used as a technique to shift profit between parties in this early phase of the process.	Use of a valuation technique may be most appropriate but also consult Chapter VI Section D.4 of the OECD TPG and paragraph 6.190 regarding hard to value intangibles. Comparability may be a real issue. Not applicable in countries where extractive rights are not granted to foreigners. In that case, there is probably no cross-border transfer pricing issue. Transfers of extraction rights might happen directly or indirectly by transferring the shares in the entity holding the rights. For discussion of the issues arising in the indirect transfers of the shares in the entity holding the rights, see Chapter 10 of this Industry Handbook and the dedicated Toolkit issued by the PCT.[7]
3. Advisory, consultancy, managerial and technical services from related parties	Mining Oil and Gas	The costs for services form part of the capital expenditure that can be deducted against extraction income, and a carry forward can be allowed if there is insufficient current income to offset the capital expenditure.	First consider the benefit test to ensure that the services are chargeable (general reference is made to Chapter 5 ("Intra-group services") in the UN Manual). Consider the most appropriate TP method (CUP, Cost Plus or Transactional Net Margin Method (TNMM) based on cost. Focus on verifying how the components of the cost base were established. Reference is also made to Chapter VII Section D of the OECD Transfer Pricing Guidelines (TPG) as regards to the simplified approach for low value adding services and the guidance provided by the EU Joint Transfer Pricing Forum (EUJTPF) on low value adding services.[8] Domestic withholding taxes, that are retained in Double Tax Treaties (i.e., through the Technical Services article) may help to mitigate cost overstatement. Some countries may have reporting obligations for outbound payments of service fees, which can help identify expenses and which may help counter the overstating of expenses. Charging and allocation of costs are discussed in the Manual at 5.3.2 (paragraphs B.4.3.5.to B.4.3.9. of the second edition) and allocation keys are discussed at 5.4.8 (sections B.4.56 to B.4.62 in the second edition).

---

7 PST: The *Taxation of Offshore Indirect Transfers— A Toolkit*; For details see https://www.tax-platform.org/sites/pct/files/publications/PCT_Toolkit_The_Taxation_of_Offshore_Indirect_Transfers.pdf

8 https://ec.europa.eu/taxation_customs/sites/taxation/files/docs/body/jtpf_020_rev3_2009.pdf

Table 11.T.1: Transfer pricing issues (cont'd)

Stage	Industry	Why is it an issue?	How to deal with this?
			In the oil and gas industry, it has been a common and longstanding practice that services to projects, especially in the upstream life cycles, are provided at fees that ensure recovery of costs, without the inclusion of a profit margin or markup for the service provider. There is a tension between the joint venture partners on the one hand, who do not allow a profit markup where on the other hand the jurisdiction of the service providers would like to see and sometimes even demand a markup. Different authorities have different views as to whether this is at arm's length. Potentially, this can be seen as a cost contribution arrangement. For more details see Chapter 7 of the Manual (B.6 in the second edition) or alternatively this issue could be addressed through a bilateral advance pricing agreement (APA).
4. Performance guarantees	Mining Oil and Gas	It is not uncommon for the host country that awards a licence to a company to seek some form of guarantee from or through the parent company regarding the performance of the exploration and development contract. The transfer pricing question here is whether contract-related guarantees require an arm's length charge. Financing guarantees clearly would.	For example, the India Model Production Sharing Contract provides for a full parent company guarantee, as well as a bank performance bond (for 7.5 per cent of the contract obligations at various stages). Article 29.1 of the Contract states that "[e]ach of the Companies constituting the Contractor shall procure and deliver to the Government within thirty (30) days from the Effective Date of this Contract: (a) an irrevocable, unconditional bank guarantee from a reputed bank of good standing in India, acceptable to the Government, in favour of the Government, for the amount specified in Article 29.3 and valid for four (4) years, in a form provided at Appendix-G; (b) financial and performance guarantee in favour of the Government from a Parent Company acceptable to the Government, in the form and substance set out in Appendix-E1, or, where there is no such Parent Company, the financial and performance guarantee from the Company itself in the form and substance set out in Appendix-E2, (c) a legal opinion from its legal advisers, in a form satisfactory to the Government, to the effect that the aforesaid guarantees have been duly signed and delivered on behalf of the guarantors with due authority and is legally valid and enforceable and binding upon them[.]" (Available at http://petroleum.nic.in/sites/default/files/MPSC%20NELP-V.pdf.) Nigeria has similar provisions requiring both parent company guarantees and a bank performance bond. See Production Sharing Contract between Nigerian National Petroleum Corporation and Gas Transmission and Power Limited, Energy 905 Suntera Limited, and Ideal Oil and Gas Limited covering Block 905 Anambra Basin (2007). (Available at http://www.sevenenergy.com/~/media/Files/S/Seven-Energy/documents/opl-905-psc.pdf.)

1.1.3   11.2.3. Exploration and appraisal[9]

Stage	Industry	Why is it an issue?	How to deal with this?
1. Transfer of exploration equipment	Mining Oil and Gas	Transfer of new equipment from a related party may not be at arm's length, especially with "long lead equipment"[9] in a volatile world. Additional considerations may arise, where the new equipment is produced by a related party benefiting from special (tax) incentives. Transfer of existing equipment at a price that is too high may result in a step up in base, which may lead to excessive depreciation charges. Extra attention may be required when the sale is structured through an intermediary related entity with favourable tax treatment.	Look at the proper application of the transfer pricing methods. Consider the application of group synergies at section 6.2.5 of the Manual (paragraphs B.5.2.28 of the second edition) and consider closer cooperation between direct tax and customs authorities and review of customs valuation (section 3.6.6 of the Manual, previously para. B.2.4.7. in the second edition). This risk may be amplified if the jurisdiction has customs exemption for exploration equipment. The original contract should be reviewed considering the facts and circumstances that were available at the time of signing of the contract. From a risk assessment perspective, it may be worthwhile to inquire if any tax or other incentives were available. If necessary, consider using the mechanism of Exchange of Information to collect documents that are not available. For oil and gas, the cost-only practices described in section 3 of the table at 11.2.2 and the required agreement of joint venture partners may reduce these risks for the country whose resources are being developed but might require a buy-in of knowhow and intellectual property (IP) which needs to be valued.
2. Lease of exploration equipment	Mining Oil and Gas	Overstatement of lease rental rates is possible, either because of hiring from related parties or arrangements made by related parties. Additional considerations may derive from the relevance of the particular provisions in domestic law and bilateral DTA, which may require application of withholding tax on the lease payments (i.e., Art 12 UN MTC).	Look at the proper application of the transfer pricing methods. Consider the application of group synergies (section 6.2.5 of the Manual, previously paragraph B.5.2.28 in the second edition of the Manual) and risk assessment in section 3.4.7 of the Manual (previously in paragraph B.2.3.2.23 in the second edition). Challenges may arise in case of long-term contracts, which were concluded at a particular point in the economic cycle. The original contract should be reviewed considering the facts and circumstances that were available at the time of signing the contract. Reference is also made to the comment on the cost-only practices and the joint venture partners in section 1 of this table.

[9] Long lead equipment refers to goods, products or systems that are identified at the earliest stage of a project to have a delivery time long enough to affect directly the overall lead time of the project.

1.1.3   11.2.3. Exploration and appraisal (cont'd)

	Industry	Why is it an issue?	How to deal with this?
3. Exploration services: seismic, drilling, sampling and analyses	Mining Oil and Gas	Related parties' involvement in these activities may lead to overstatement of the value of these services, which creates a high cost base for future depreciation.	See section 2 of the table at 11.2.2. Applicable tax treaties may have specific rules for the extractive industry, e.g., exploration-related permanent establishments. Reference is made to the discussion in Chapter 7 of this Handbook on Permanent Establishments. Reference is also made to the comment on the cost-only practices and the joint venture partners in section 1 of this table.
4. Administrative, managerial and technical services, and legal services from related parties	Mining Oil and Gas	Where the expenses from this stage may be deductible in the future, the company may be motivated to overstate the price for such services to allow for future deductibility in the form of carry-forward losses.	See section 3 of the table at 11.2.2.
5. Financing/ Guarantee/ Funding arrangements	Mining Oil and Gas	Level of possible interest payments which may be deferred (initially interest free loan then later interest bearing). Unrelated parties may not be able to obtain a loan at this risky stage of the project.	This may (or may not) be a transfer pricing issue and may be addressed under domestic law. The transfer pricing issue would typically be the applicable interest rate or guarantee fee.

1.1.4   11.2.4. Development[10]

Stage	Industry	Why is it an issue?	How to deal with this?
1. Sale/lease of extraction rights— (royalty payment/sales value)	Mining Oil and Gas	Assignment of extractive rights to related company or outright transfer of extractive rights to related company can be at a high cost and it may be the case that the proceeds from the transfer of the extractive right may not be taxable in some jurisdictions	See section 2 of the table at 11.2.2. Please note that, at this stage, the value of the rights may have changed as more information on the success of the project is available. For example, there may be more certainty around the development plan and the extent of proven or probable reserves. Farm-in/farm-out considerations may be relevant at this stage of the process. See further Chapter 10 (Indirect Transfer of Assets).
2. Purchase/ lease of plant, equipment and machinery	Mining Oil and Gas	See sections 1 and 2 of the table at 11.2.3.	See sections 1 and 2 of the table at 11.2.3. Reference is also made to the comment on the cost-only practices and the joint venture partners in section 1 of the table at 11.2.3.
3. Advisory, consultancy, managerial and technical services from related parties	Mining Oil and Gas	See section 3 of the table at 11.2.3.	See section 3 of the table at 11.2.3.
4.Financing/ guarantee/ funding arrangements	Mining Oil and Gas	The interest rate or other conditions of the financing agreement could give rise to transfer pricing issues.	See section 4 of the table at 11.2.3. Some countries may address this issue in other legislation that is not part of the transfer pricing rules, e.g. general anti-avoidance rules or in specific interest limitations rules. In this respect see, for example, Action 4 final report of the OECD BEPS Project, which was further elaborated with the focus on Mining Industry in the joint IGF-OECD Paper.[10]

10 Long lead equipment refers to goods, products or systems that are identified at the earliest stage of a project to have a delivery time long enough to affect directly the overall lead time of the project.

1.1.5   11.2.5. Production/extraction stage

Stage	Industry	Why is it an issue?	How to deal with this?
1. Lease of concession rights (royalty payment)	Mining	Concession owner leases the right to exploit to a related company in exchange for remuneration.	There may be a difference between the tax treatment of a sale or a lease. This in itself is not a transfer pricing issue but relates to whether the transaction is a bona fide sale or bona fide lease. The transfer pricing issue is whether the sale price or the lease payments qualify as being at arm's length (comparability analysis process).
2. Payments for purchase or lease of extractive equipment	Mining Oil and Gas	See sections 1 and 2 of the table at 11.2.3.	See sections 1 and 2 of the table at 11.2.3. Reference is also made to the comment on the cost-only practices and the joint venture partners above in section 1 of the table at 11.2.3.
3. Advisory, consultancy, managerial and technical services from related parties	Mining Oil and Gas	See section 3 of the table at 11.2.2. At this stage of the process, the MNE may be earning sales income and subsequently service fees may be charged calculated based on sales.	See section 3 of the table at 11.2.2. A service fee calculated as a percentage of sales may not be appropriate as it may overcompensate the service provider relative to the costs incurred. Typically, payment for services would be calculated by reference to the cost of the actual services provided. This may require an allocation of group costs among operating entities based on allocation keys. For purpose of the allocation of a pool of costs, an appropriate allocation key should be used. Reference is made to paragraph 5.4.8 (previously B.4.4.19) of the Manual for examples of appropriate allocation keys.
4. Payments for use of intellectual property (IP)	Mining Oil and Gas	At the production stage, the use of technology provided by related parties is important. Calculating the appropriate transfer price may be a challenge.	Reference is made to chapter 6 (previously B.5) of the Manual as it contains a comprehensive discussion of this issue. Reference is also made to the comment on the cost-only practices and the joint venture partners in section B.1 of this table. For use of IP in a cost contribution agreement (CCA) setting it will need to be considered if buy-in payments are required.
5. Mining sub-contracting services and special regimes (where tax rates for mining services and production operations are significantly different)	Mining	In cases where there is a lower tax rate for mining services and mining operation compared to the local corporate tax rate, profit shifting through transfer mispricing may offer even more benefits.	This may be a case of shifting profits between different tax regimes within a country. Use traditional TP methods (CUP or Cost Plus) to ensure reasonability of the transfer price of the services provided. However, comparability may be a real issue.

1.1.5   11.2.5. Production/extraction stage (cont'd)

Stage	Industry	Why is it an issue?	How to deal with this?
6. Contract mining services	Mining	In cases where mining services are outsourced to a related offshore entity that purportedly is carrying far more risk, profit may be shifted offshore.	In this case, a proper functional analysis is required to properly delineate transaction and risk allocation. See the Manual, Section 3.3 (paragraph B.2.3.1.4 in the second edition) on delineation of the transaction. Developing countries should be aware of the fact that the OECD BEPS Action 8 to 10 also affect mining and extraction industries and that transfer pricing can be used to shift income and tax base offshore to low-tax jurisdictions. In these scenarios, it is recommended that the step-analysis listed in the Manual at section 3.2 (previously B.2.3.1.4) and the risk analysis in the Manual at section 3.4.4 (paragraph B.2.3.2.3 in the second edition) be considered.
7. Sale of raw minerals and adjustments	Mining	An ore can contain various minerals at its unrefined phase, making it difficult to determine the price.	Considering the actual characteristics of the mineral is important in helping determine the arm's-length price in the sale between related parties. See also the PCT Toolkit for Addressing Difficulties in Accessing Comparable Data for Transfer Pricing Analyses, especially its Supplementary Report, Addressing the Information Gaps on prices of Minerals Sold in an Intermediate Form (the "Supplementary Report").[11]
8. Interest income/ interest expenses	Mining Oil and Gas	Both the interest income and interest expense need to be priced at arm's length. The fact that a company is highly capitalized and at this stage of the extraction process may be cash rich, it may prefer to issue a loan to a related party over making a dividend distribution. It is debated in some jurisdictions whether this is a transfer pricing issue or not.	See section 4 of the table at 11.2.3. Reference can be made to the Transfer Pricing Guidance on Financial Transactions of the Inclusive Framework on BEPS: Actions 4, 8-10, which also contains discussions on cash pooling and other relevant financial transactions.[12]

---

11 https://www.oecd.org/ctp/toolkit-on-comparability-and-mineral-pricing.pdf

12 For details see: http://www.oecd.org/tax/beps/transfer-pricing-guidance-on-financial-trans-actions-inclusive-framework-on-beps-actions-4-8-10.htm

1.1.6   11.2.6. Processing (refining and smelting)

Stage	Industry	Why is it an issue?	How to deal with this?
1. Tolling fee for contract processing	Mining Oil and Gas	At issue is the appropriateness of the tolling fee where tolling is done by a related party to the concentrate producer. There is a risk that the fee may not be at arm's length. In cases where mining services are outsourced to a related offshore entity purportedly carrying far more risk, iprofit may be shifted offshore.	See section 6 of this table.
2. Adjustments to the reference price (treatment charges, refining charges, penalties and price participation clause)	Mining Oil and Gas	Payments for the concentrates are often based on reference pricing. The treatment charges, refining charges and other payments can be used to shift profits where the parties involved in the process implementing these charges are related parties, if they are not priced at arm's length. In the mining industry, credits for recoverable metals (e.g. precious metals in a copper or cobalt concentrate) may be under-priced. Similarly, penalties for impurities in the concentrates may be overpriced. In the mining industry smelters sometimes enter into a price participation agreement where the price of the commodity is adjusted based on the fluctuation of the market price of the commodity. They may receive an additional fee or get an additional charge. In oil and gas, the acquisition and sale of crude oil and natural gas (LNG) from upstream producers to the midstream and downstream sector may be to related or third parties. Normally, these transactions are priced "at index" which means that such transactions are based upon market prices, generally referring the price of a barrel of crude oil to oil benchmarks.	The price of the commodity is based on a reference price adjusted by items such as treatment charges, logistics, refining charges, credits for recoverable metals, or penalties for impurities. Such adjustments are often calculated by reference to industry averages and a transfer pricing issue can arise if a company departs arbitrarily from the industry practice. Reference is made to the Platform's Supplementary Report. In the situation of the price participation agreement in the mining industry, if the smelter is a related party, it needs to be determined whether any price adjustments are arm's length. Therefore, industry know-how is crucial. Reference is made to the pricing practices paragraph of the Platform's Supplementary Report. As regards oil and gas, many different oil benchmarks exist, with each one representing crude oil from a particular part of the world. However, most of them are referred to one of three primary benchmarks that serve as a reference price for buyers and sellers of crude oil: the West Texas Intermediate (WTI), Brent Blend and Dubai/Oman. Depending on the type of crude oil, these benchmarks are generally adjusted depending on crude density (e.g. American Petroleum Institute (API) gravity), location or other factors different from the referenced index. These benchmark prices are published by reliable international organizations such as Platts, Oil Price Information Service (OPIS) Argus or the New York Mercantile Exchange (NYMEX) and are widely used by the public and private sector. To calculate the taxable income of oil and gas companies, most producing countries have set tax reference prices (also known as norm

1.1.6 11.2.6. Processing (refining and smelting) (cont'd)

Stage	Industry	Why is it an issue?	How to deal with this?
		It needs to be considered whether the right benchmark is used and if the price used for the intercompany transaction may need to be adjusted depending on crude density (e.g., API.[13] gravity) location, sulphur content or other factors different from the referenced index.	prices) for given time periods. These reference prices are established by the government (e.g., a Petroleum Council) or the National Oil Company (NOC) in order to provide oil and gas prices that best represent the market conditions. These reference prices are normally determined from the assessment of the crude oil international benchmarks mentioned above (e.g., Platt's market indicators) generally adjusted to the specific gravity API of the actual crude produced, resulting in a valid comparable for oil and gas transactions performed in the country. In some countries, the body in charge of setting the reference prices also takes into account the market indicators presented by the companies operating in their jurisdiction (based on price quotations from official publications and their own observations)
3. Advisory, consultancy, managerial and technical services from related parties	Mining Oil and Gas	See section 3 of the table at 11.2.2.	See section 3 of the table at 11.2.2.
4. Payments for use of IP	Mining Oil and Gas	See section 4 of the table at 11.2.5.	See section 4 of the table at 11.2.5.
5. Transportation	Mining Oil and Gas	The calculation of prices of transportation is generally based on comparables and Incoterms are relevant in this industry. The question is whether the Incoterms are appropriately applied within related party transactions. In the oil and gas industry, long-term commitments are common and present risks if short-term conditions change. In the event payments are made between related parties based on changed conditions or transportation risks materializing, it should be determined whether these payments (penalties, fees) are at arm's length.	Comparability factors need to be checked. Double check if the risks allocated to a related party can be managed and controlled by that party. The original contract should be reviewed considering the facts and circumstances that were available at the time of the signing of the contract.

13 API stands for the American Petroleum Institute, which is the major United States trade association for the oil and natural gas industry. The API gravity is used to classify oils as light, medium, heavy, or extra heavy.

1.1.6   11.2.6. Processing (refining and smelting) (cont'd)

Stage	Industry	Why is it an issue?	How to deal with this?
6. Transfer pricing where different tax regimes are applicable	Mining Oil and Gas	The risk of profit shifting may arise in case there are different tax regimes available in a country. The processing and refining activities are often subject to lower tax rates than the extractive tax regimes. Considering domestic law, a transfer pricing analysis may be required, also when one company shifts value between two different tax regimes. (i.e., net-back calculations).	Reference is made to the United Nations Handbook on Selected Issues in Protecting the Tax Base of Developing Countries and to the issue of safe harbours, discussed in the Manual at section 10.2 (previously B.8.8). It should be considered whether domestic laws even allow transfer pricing rules to apply in domestic transactions or, where (in the case of the same enterprise) the activity takes place within the same legal entity but with a different tax regime, the transfer pricing rules should also apply for the intra-company transaction, between the ring-fenced regimes.

1.1.7   11.2.7. Sales and marketing

Stage	Industry	Why is it an issue?	How to deal with this?
1. Marketing hubs	Mining Oil and Gas	The issue is to determine whether a related marketing hub is remunerated at arm's length, considering there are several remuneration models available. A company may be paid commissions under an off-take agreement that it has with producer. The commission needs to be reviewed as to whether the fee is at arm's length.	This can vary, and therefore, arrangements must be properly investigated. It is important to consider the delineation of the transaction and, from that, the basis for payments for sales/marketing and their relationship to value creation in the industry. For instance, it is commonly argued that a marketing hub is analogous to a "distributor" of goods and hence should be rewarded by way of a percentage of sales. Consider whether the FAR of the marketing entity are in fact analogous to a typical distributor or whether they are rather routine support services. Consider also the value-add of the marketing entity to the commodity product and the potential impact that may have on the arm's-length remuneration for the transaction. Reference is also made to the Manual, section 3.3 (para. B.2.3.1.4. in the second edition) on delineation of the transaction. Access to information on the actual activities of the marketing entity will be critical for such analysis. This reinforces the point on obligations of the taxpayer to obtain and provide the relevant information as well as the rules on information requests and/or Exchange of Information upon request.

1.1.7   11.2.7. Sales and marketing (cont'd)

Stage	Industry	Why is it an issue?	How to deal with this?
2. Hedging gains and losses	Mining Oil and Gas	There is an issue when the related party party is the buyer of the commodity and is also the one doing the hedging for the producer.	It needs to be determined who manages and controls the risks and whether the hedging gains and losses are allocated at arm's length. Issues to consider are whether hindsight is being used or if the hedge is asymmetric. Some countries under domestic laws have a regime in place that separates hedging gains and losses from extractive activities.
3. Payment terms such as credit interest on advance payments	Mining Oil and Gas	Determination of arm's-length prices should take into account the relevant payment terms.	Various types of payment terms may be introduced in related party situations, which may potentially lead to (significant) adjustments to the transaction value. These adjustments may need to be carefully analysed both from the perspective of their nature and also their quantum.

Payments made before or after the time when an unrelated party would have made payment may need to be adjusted for the time value of money, while some of the general considerations related to the appropriate treatment of financial transactions referred to above remain relevant.

Consideration could be given to whether the payment terms have an inappropriate impact on the fiscal take (e.g. royalties). |
| **4. Transportation** | Mining Oil and Gas | See section 5 of the table at 11.2.6. | See section 5 of the table at 11.2.6. |
| **5. Sales price of commodities** | Mining Oil and Gas | The key risk is undervaluation of the commodity value in sales to related parties. By undervaluing the price of the commodity, not only the income tax revenue but also revenue in the form of royalties and other mineral taxes (additional profit tax, mining taxes) can be significantly reduced. Reference pricing may be used for spot sales. Long-term customers generally pay a premium above the quoted reference price at the time the long-term contract is executed. | Use of traditional TP Methods—CUP Method. Also see the Manual. at section 4.2 (previously B.3.4.2.).

Some countries use reference prices, replacing the transaction value with a reference price. Some countries may allow the reference price to be reasonably adjusted to reflect the specifics of the mineral.

Pricing must be properly evaluated before it can be said that the reference price is the answer. |
| **6. Abusive structures** | Mining Oil and Gas | There are structures where an intermediary service provider is interposed to purchase the commodity, often below the market price, and sell it to independent parties at a profit. | Tax abuse provisions may be needed to tackle this issue or it should be considered whether the transfer pricing rules could be applied also to transactions of parties who are not fall within the definition of associated enterprises under domestic law. |

1.1.7   11.2.7. Sales and marketing (cont'd)

Stage	Industry	Why is it an issue?	How to deal with this?
		This profit may then be made available to the principal, who instructed the agent to carry out the transactions for a commission fee. Most countries' transfer pricing rules do not seem to apply in this situation.	For example, Tanzania has a definition of related party/associate worded as follows: "in any case not covered by paragraphs (a) to (c) such that one may reasonably be expected to act, other than as employee, in accordance with the intentions of the other."[14]
			Where reference prices have been introduced, ensure that they apply to all transactions—related party transactions and unrelated party transactions.
			An alternative approach could be introducing and applying controlled foreign corporation rules (CFC rules) or to have legislation which allows for a review of a series of consecutive transactions.

14 Tanzania. Income Tax Act. S. 3(d).

1.1.8   11.2.8. Decommissioning

Stage	Industry	Why is it an issue?	How to deal with this?
1. decommissioning services	Mining Oil and Gas	The price for Decommissioning services provided by related parties may be overstated.	See section 3 of the table at 11.2.2. See Chapter 14 on the Tax Treatment of Decommissioning.
2. Sale or transfer of equipment	Mining Oil and Gas	The equipment and infrastructure developed or purchased during the different stages of the project may still be functioning even though fully depreciated and having zero or close to zero value. The company may seek to sell or transfer this property close to the scrap or nominal value, rather than market price.	Use traditional TP Methods—CUP or alternative valuation. It should be considered whether alternative valuations can be used as an indicator for the arm's length price. See at 11.2.3, particularly the comment on the cost-only practices and the joint venture partners.

11.2.9   Generic case examples

11.2.9.1   The following case examples are generic in nature for the extractive industry, meaning that the same facts and circumstances may arise in the extraction of minerals and in the oil and gas industry.

Example 1: Marketing hub

Facts

11.2.9.2   Parent company A established marketing entity B in a low-tax jurisdiction. Company B is described by the taxpayer as a fully-fledged marketing/distribution company responsible for servicing demand for a specific commodity and growing the business for the entire MNE group.

11.2.9.3   The operations are staffed by a very limited number of management and administrative employees. Company B maintains that its operations perform a strategic and vital role, are fully risk taking (entrepreneurial risk) by buying and selling the refined product and that it performs value added functions that warrant a high return.

Findings

11.2.9.4   After examining the activities and functions performed by Company B, a tax audit reveals that Company B actually provides management and marketing support services rather than being a full risk marketing/distribution company as purported. The functions actually performed only warrant a routine return.

Considerations

11.2.9.5   Fundamental to these findings is the fact that customers consisted of a number of long-term customers that were procured decades before by Parent company A, and that no additional customers were established and no other value is being created by Company B. All subsequent activities performed by Company B are of a management and marketing support nature.

11.2.9.6   The accounting flow of the transaction was different from the physical movement of the refined mineral.

11.2.9.7   As a result of the above determination, the profits attributed to Company B are not in line with the actual activities and need to be adjusted and reduced by applying the relevant provisions in the domestic law, in order to compensate Company B in a way that is commensurate with the activities it performs. See also the table at 11.2.7, row 1 above.

Example 2: Information challenges

Facts

11.2.9.8   Company A is engaged in mining activities and being audited by the tax authorities in Country A, where the mining activities take place. The tax authorities of Country A wish to review the company's transfer pricing practices. Part of the audit questions by the Country A tax inspector include information regarding Company A's foreign related parties (e.g., taxpayer identification numbers, their functional profiles, etc.). In response to the latter question, Company A informs the local tax inspector that the requested foreign information is unobtainable by the domestic tax authorities and confidential.

Findings

11.2.9.9   When pressed further as to why Company A believes that the foreign information does not have to be submitted, Company A mentions that because the obligation to provide the information is not explicitly included as required in domestic law, there is no legal requirement for Company A to submit that information.

Considerations

11.2.9.10   In many cases, there might not be an agreement for the exchange of information (EOI) or a double tax treaty in place between Country A and the respective jurisdictions where Company A's related parties are located. Alternatively, if Country A participates in the Country-by-Country (CbC) reporting requirements under the OECD Base Erosion and Profit Shifting (BEPS) Action 13 regarding transfer pricing documentation, it may receive access to relevant foreign information. For further guidance on effective implementation of TP Documentation requirements, see the PCT Toolkit dealing with this matter.[15]

11.2.9.11   Without these international instruments in place, the tax authorities need to make sure domestic law clearly allows for the request of such information and that taxpayers are obliged to provide such information. Tax authorities may also consider having rules in place that allow for presumptive taxation, where competitor information may be treated as indicative using Resale Price or Cost Plus Methods (see paragraph B.8.7. of the Manual). They may also consider taxation on a gross basis, if domestic companies cannot disclose information on payments made to related parties that under domestic law would otherwise qualify as deductible expenses.

---

[15] For details see: https://www.tax-platform.org/sites/pct/files/publications/PCT_Toolkit_TP_Documentation.pdf

Example 3: Management services

Facts

11.2.9.12   Company A conducts mining activities in a developing country and receives management services from related Company C, which is located in a low-tax jurisdiction. Company C charges its services out to the entire mining group, including Company A.

11.2.9.13   The tax authorities of Country A audit Company A as regards its related party transactions, in particular as regards the (price for) services rendered by Company C to Company A.

Findings

11.2.9.14   During the audit of Company A by the tax authorities of Country A, the management of Company A is being interviewed, and after a benefit test is applied for the services from Company C by the tax authorities of Country A, they conclude as follows:

Company A did not request any services from Company C; no meetings were held to review the services requested and supposedly received from Company C; no records were provided of the respective services to Company A; and Company A arguably performed these services themselves internally (i.e., the services may be duplicative).

Considerations

11.2.9.15   To determine the arm's-length nature of such charges, first the benefit test should be applied to ensure that the services are chargeable. Next, the most appropriate TP method (CUP, Cost Plus or TNMM based on cost) ought to be considered, while focusing on verifying how the components of the cost base were established. To the extent the service charge consists of allocated costs, the allocation key for charging the costs needs to be reviewed. See also section 5.4.8 of the Manual (paragraphs B.4.3.5–B 4.3.9 in the second edition). A service fee calculated as a percentage of sales may not be appropriate as it may overcompensate Company C relative to the cost of providing the service. Typically, payment for services would be calculated by reference to the cost of the actual services provided. This may require an allocation of group costs among operating entities based on allocation keys.

11.2.9.16   For the purpose of the allocation of a pool of costs, an appropriate allocation key should be used. Reference is made to section 5.4.8 of the Manual (paragraph B.4.4.19 of the second edition) for examples of appropriate allocation keys.

11.3 VALUE CHAIN FOR MINING AND MINERALS EXTRACTION

11.3.1 Introduction

11.3.1.1   The value chain of mining and minerals extraction depends on the specific mineral commodity involved and the type of mining needed to extract the mineral depending on whether it is available above ground or underground.[16]

11.3.1.2   The transformation of minerals from the exploitation phase to the eventual trade, marketing and sale thereof typically follows a series of consecutive steps:

(i)   Acquisition of the mining rights and exploration;

(ii)   Construction and mine development;

(iii)   Mining, processing and concentration;

(iv)   Transportation;

(v)   Smelting and refining; and

(vi)   Trade, marketing and sales.

11.3.2 Functions

11.3.2.1   To undertake mining activities, companies will generally perform the following relevant functions:

(a)   Exploration for minerals;

b)   Research and Development related to exploration and to provide related technical assistance services;

(c)   Financing of activities;[17] and

(d)   Marketing and trading of commodity products, which may or may not include shipping and distribution.

---

[16] Reference can be made to the PCT "Supplementary Report—Addressing the Information Gaps on Prices of Minerals Sold in an Intermediate Form," in *The Platform for Cooperation on Tax, which was released as part of the Platform's Toolkit for Addressing Difficulties in Accessing Comparables Data for Transfer Pricing Analyses* (June 2017). The Supplementary Report provides guidance on identifying the types of mine and production methods. Available at http://www.oecd.org/tax/toolkit-on-comparability-and-mineral-pricing.pdf.

[17] Ibid. The document also provides guidance on financing arrangements affecting transacted product prices.

11.3.2.2   Usual functions, like headquarter functions, insurance, and other services (such as those related to information technology and human resource management) will also be performed by (some of the) separate entities of the MNE.

11.3.2.3   It should be noted that countries that grant licences for mining and extraction of minerals usually have a requirement that different activities performed by the mining company are treated as separate taxable objects and as separate taxpayers. They are ring-fenced, which means that for tax purposes the income and expenses and tax base of the activities are determined separately for separate projects (horizontal ring-fencing) or that different types of activities (e.g., extraction, processing, etc.) are treated differently from other types of activities (vertical ring-fencing). The legal form in which the mining or mineral extraction activities are performed in the host country is more often that of a local subsidiary/corporate body, rather than through a branch of a foreign company. The shares of the local entity may or may not be partially owned by the local authorities.

11.3.2.4   To perform a transfer pricing analysis of companies engaged in mining and minerals extraction, tax authorities need to develop a thorough understanding of the functions performed, the assets used, and risks borne by the respective MNE entities involved. For more details on conducting a functional analysis, reference can be made to section 3.4.4 of the Manual (paragraph B.2.3.2.7. in the second edition) on functional analysis.

Figure 11.F.1:[a] Diagram of vertically integrated mining operation, including relationship with service provider hubs.[b]

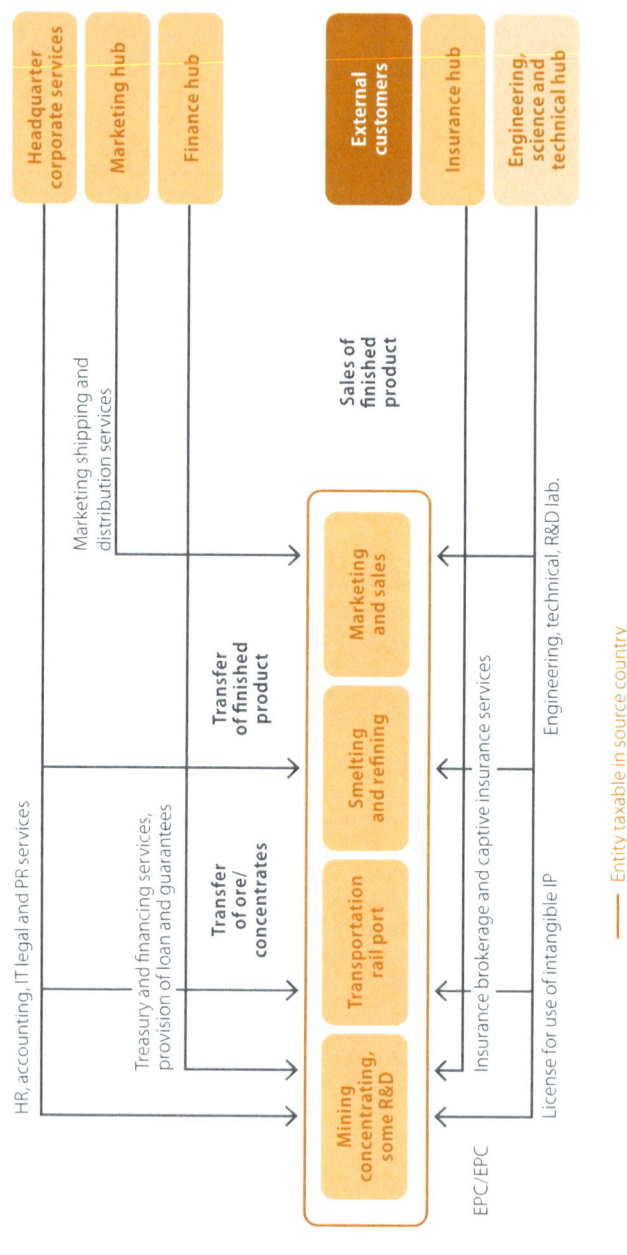

[a] Pietro et al.. Transfer pricing in mining with a focus on Africa

[b] Modified from the Transfer Pricing Handbook for the Mining Industry (Transfer Pricing Associates, 2012).

11.3.2.5   The form within which a fully vertically integrated mining operation is conducted may be fairly straightforward, but the allocation of functions, assets and risks relevant to operating in the mining and mineral extractive industry within an MNE may be diverse. To get a better understanding of the step-by-step process pursuant to which copper, iron ore, thermal coal and gold are mined, reference is made to the Platform for Collaboration on Tax Toolkit.[18]

11.3.2.6   An MNE is likely to obtain services and products both from related parties and unrelated suppliers. Getting a proper understanding of whether parties with which the MNE conducts business are associated, and therefore, subject to the arm's-length standard of Article 9 (Associated Enterprises) of the United Nations Model Convention may present a challenge. Furthermore, through location of functions in the supply chain outside of the country where extraction takes place, MNEs may be able to allocate profits abroad.

11.3.3   Assets

11.3.3.1   Assets that can be considered and used by an MNE operating in mining and minerals extraction are listed in the table below. For more details on the importance of assets within an MNE for transfer pricing purposes, reference can be made to section 3.4.4 (paragraph B.2.3.2.17 in the second edition) of the Manual.

Table 11.T.1: Typical assets of a mining company[19]

Exploration Discovery	Mine Development and Construction	Mine Exploitation	Beneficiation, Smelting and Refining	Trading, Marketing and Sales
Exploration and mining licenses and rights, (I)	Engineering design (I)	Exploitation techniques (I)	Beneficiation processes (I)	Customer lists and relationships (I)
Access and surface rights (I)	Engineering machinery (T)	Exploitation plant and equipment and infrastructure (T)	Beneficiation plant and equipment (T)	Marketing and distribution activities (I+T)
Drilling rights	Engineering, procurement and project management know-how (I)	Logistics management and infrastructure (I+T)	Logistics management and infrastructure (I+T)	Logistics management and infrastructure (I+T)
Exploration and laboratory equipment and machinery (T)	Construction, drilling and excavation plant and equipment (T)	Transportation plant and equipment and infrastructure (T)	IP relative to the smelting/refining processes and protocols (I)	Shipping and warehousing (T)

---

[18] Available at https://www.oecd.org/tax/toolkit-on-comparability-and-mineral-pricing.pdf.

[19] Pietro Guj, Stephanie Martin and Alexandra Readhead, *Transfer pricing in mining with a focus on Africa: a briefing note* (Washington, D.C., World Bank Group, German Cooperation Deutsche Zusammenarbeit, Centre for Exploration Targeting, 2017). Available at http://documents.worldbank.org/curated/en/213881485941701316/pdf/112344-REVISED-Transfer-pricing-in-mining-with-a-focus-on-Africa-a-briefing-note-Web.pdf.

Table 11.T.1: Typical assets of a mining company (cont'd)

	Mine Development and Construction	Mine Exploitation	Beneficiation, Smelting and Refining	Trading, Marketing and Sales
Topographical surveys (I)	Construction camp and logistic infrastructure (T)	Value of mineral resources and reserves included in price of acquisition of mining rights from a third party (not by means of discovery) (I)	Smelting and refining plant and equipment (T)	Product stocks (T)
Geological surveys (I)	Mine development (T)	Broken ore stockpiles and inventory (T)	Ore, concentrate and metal stockpiles and inventories (T)	Marketing know-how (I)
Geochemical surveys (I)				Trading software/ platforms (I)
Geophysical surveys				Specialized aspects of supply chain management (I)
Transport, communication and camp facilities (T)				Product innovation processes (I)
Exploration techniques and know-how (I)				Distribution rights (I)
IP related to remote sensing and GIS techniques and related data bases (I)				Pricing negotiations know-how for unusual commodities (I)
IP related to negotiation, contract structuring and management of joint ventures (I)	IP related to negotiation, contract structuring and management of joint ventures (I)			

11.3.4   Risks

11.3.4.1   Some of the relevant risks that an MNE operating in the mining and minerals extraction industry may incur can be external or internal and are summarized in the table below.

11.3.4.2   For more details on the importance of risks within an MNE for transfer pricing purposes, reference can be made to section 3.4.4. (paragraph B.2.3.2.22 and onward in the second edition) of the Manual.

Table 11.T.2: Risks typically encountered by a mining company

X= Limited risk, X = Moderate risk, X = High risk

Risks	Acquisition/ Exploration	Mining	Ore Processing	Trade	Marketing/ Sales
Exogenous					
Market risk	–	X	X	X	X
Currency/foreign exchange risk	X	X	X	X	X
Social/political sovereign/ legal risk	X	X	X	–	–
Natural disaster risk	X	X	X	–	–
Environmental risk	X	X	X	–	–
Endogenous					
Exploration risk	X	–	–	–	–
Operating risk	X	X	X	X	X
Processing risk	–	X	X	–	–
Capacity underutilization and availability risk	–	X	X	X	–
Transportation risk	–	X	X	X	X
Inventory risk	–	X	X	X	X
Product liability risk	–	X	X	X	X
Credit risk	–	X	X	X	X

Source: TPA Global

11.3.5   Industry-related case examples

11.3.5.1   The following is a compilation and series of case examples regarding issues and facts encountered in practice with respect to mining and mineral extractive industries.

Example 1: Export of low value minerals to an intermediary distribution company

Facts

11.3.5.2   Physical commodities are shipped directly from the Mining Company to the third-party customer. However, the invoice flow is from the Mining Company to an intermediary group Distribution Company C located in a low-tax jurisdiction and then on towards the third-party customer.

11.3.5.3   The transfer price between the Mining Company and intermediary Distribution Company C is determined with reference to an index price or reference price for the commodity, less a distribution/marketing margin for the functions performed by the intermediary group Distribution Company C.

11.3.5.4   In this scenario there are two pricing issues to evaluate:

(a)   The point in time the reference price is determined compared to when it is calculated in an arm's-length situation;

(b)   Whether the distribution/marketing margin is arm's length. The CUP method may be appropriate for the purposes of determining whether the reference price applied in the transfer pricing between Mining Company and intermediary Distribution Company C is arm's length. However, for the purpose of the distribution/marketing margin the CUP Method may not be appropriate if the intermediary Distribution Company C performs substantial marketing/distribution functions. In that case, another method may be considered to determine the remuneration for Distribution Company C, which will depend on the facts and circumstances.

Findings

11.3.5.5   Although the sale of the commodity was on a back-to-back free-on-board (FOB)/cost, insurance and freight (CIF) (or "flash title") basis from the Mining Company to the intermediary Distribution Company C and to the end customer, the pricing between the parties in the supply chain was determined at different points in time. The production sale price from Mining Company to related party intermediary Distribution Company C was determined at the index price of the month prior to shipment, while the related party intermediary sales price to end customer was determined at the index price at the month of shipment (i.e., later in time).

Considerations

11.3.5.6   The difficulty faced in this scenario is to get documentation/benchmarking data that can assist in the evaluation of whether, in a back-to-back (flash title) sales transaction, the producer's sale price (at index price prior to shipment) is at arm's length.

For more information on pricing practices, also consult the Supplementary Report.

Example 2: Coal group marketing activities

Facts

11.3.5.7   The Coal group is involved in the mining, production and distribution of coal. The entities within the group perform research, development, marketing, sales, shipping and distribution of coal.

11.3.5.8   Coal Company is a tax resident of a developing country. The company owns several mines and is involved in the exploration, development and mining of coal. The coal that is produced by the Coal Company is used for electricity generation and more than 90 per cent of the Coal Company's revenue relates to coal that is exported.

11.3.5.9   Marketing Company is incorporated under the laws of a low-tax juris-diction. Marketing Company entered into a distribution agreement with Coal Company for all coal produced by Coal Company that is suitable for export.

11.3.5.10   According to a legal agreement between Coal Company and Marketing Company, Marketing Company is responsible for sourcing customers, contract negotiations, delivery of coal to end customers and exploiting the market for coal. It also bears inventory, credit, quality, price, foreign exchange and delivery risk. As consideration for the functions and risks borne, Marketing Company earned a gross margin of 7 per cent. Marketing Company is described as a fully-fledged distributor.

11.3.5.11   The key value drivers in this industry are considered to be: Ability to blend different coal qualities to match customer requirements; coal specifications, for example, the higher the calorific value and lower the impurities, the higher the expected price per ton; prompt delivery to end customers; and freight rates.

11.3.5.12   Marketing Company does not have any technical sales personnel. Coal Company is responsible for blending coal according to customer specifications. Customers inform Marketing Company of their need for blending and it passes the request to Coal Company to do the actual blending. Marketing Company does not hold inventory and takes flash title to the goods. At Marketing Company's request, Coal Company can liaise directly with the end customer to organize delivery of coal.

11.3.5.13   The market has changed drastically over the years. There has been a change in the grade of coal required by customers due to an economic downturn, environmental laws, availability of substitutes and increased number of sellers in the market. This has put pressure on coal suppliers to come up with innovative ways to retain their position in the market. The expertise of Coal Company's tech-nical team is required to evaluate the changes to coal specifications and ensure that the group achieves high margins.

11.3.5.14   Marketing Company has four employees. Based on the documenta-tion reviewed and interviews conducted, only two of these employees are respon-sible for marketing the coal. Marketing Company entered into an agreement with Advisory Company, a related party marketing agent, located in the same country as Marketing Company. According to this agreement, Marketing Company out-sourced all of its marketing functions to Advisory Company as it did not have the necessary skills and resources to fully market the coal bought from Coal Company. For the service it provides, Advisory Company receives a commission of 3 per cent on all sales by Marketing Company to third parties. A Resale Price Method was used in determining a margin of 7 per cent for Marketing Company.

Findings

11.3.5.15   The Revenue Authority in Country A is of the view that seven per cent is excessive and Marketing Company should have been classified as a limited risk distributor. According to the benchmarking study performed by the Revenue

Authority in Country A, comparable entities earn gross margins between two and four per cent.

Considerations

11.3.5.16   From the background information presented above, the following should be considered:

(a)   What factors influence the sale of coal? Obtain an understanding of the coal industry and the economic environment in which the taxpayer is operating;[20]

(b)   The terms of the distribution agreements: Are they comparable to third-party distribution agreements? If they are not, this forms a basis for a transfer pricing adjustment;

(c)   Obtain a clear structure of the group and an understanding of the supply chain (what are the roles and functional profiles of each of the companies – Coal Company, Marketing Company as well as the Advisory Company). Understand the transactional flow of invoices and physical flow of goods;

(d)   The above step should be followed by delineating the actual transaction and allocating functions, assets and risks to each company in the supply chain. Does the conduct of parties differ from the legal agreement?;

(e)   Who manages the risk and has the financial capacity to bear the risk? Which entity in the supply chain is ultimately liable to third parties? It is important to understand where value adding activities are conducted and managed as this is where economic functions should be allocated;

(f)   Review internal comparables, and if they exist, consider whether reasonable adjustments can be made; and

(g)   What is the appropriate transfer pricing method to select? Does external data exist? If it does, perform a benchmarking study where comparable entities are identified.

Example 3: Price fluctuations and intermediary sales of uranium

Facts

11.3.5.17   Company A operates a uranium mine in developing Country A. Upon extraction, Company A sells the mined uranium to a related Swiss marketing

---

[20] Please note that the *Platform's Supplementary Report* includes an extensive example explaining thermal coal mining, markets and trading, pricing and contractual arrangements.

entity at an output kilogram price that reflects the long-term commodity price, which is agreed to in the related party distribution agreement.

11.3.5.18   Because of external developments, the uranium price decreased to 30 per cent of the price agreed between the related mining company and its intermediary sales company.

Findings

11.3.5.19   Upon audit, the tax authorities in Country A question the use of the long-term commodity price between the related parties, as it does not seem to consider who carries the risk of loss when commodity prices fluctuate and (as in this case) drop. There is no benchmark made available to help substantiate the income allocation between the related parties.

Considerations

11.3.5.20   At issue is whether the price set between the related parties qualifies as being at arm's length, considering the facts and circumstances at the time the contract was entered into. Would independent parties have agreed on an adjustment clause in case of changing market circumstances? What is the custom in the business? Tax authorities have to be careful in using a hindsight analysis. Is the risk of loss (or gains) upon price fluctuations allocated to the party that can best handle, manage and control the risks, when market conditions change? For example, did any of the parties enter into hedging agreements to mitigate price fluctuations?

11.3.5.21   To analyse these facts, it is important to consider the market environment. For example, in this particular industry, if there is a shortage of smelting services, a price participation agreement may be appropriate.

Example 4: Market off-taker function

Facts

11.3.5.22   Company B is located in Country B, a low-tax jurisdiction. Pursuant to an off-take agreement with related Company A in developing Country A, Company B is obliged to buy 100 per cent of the coal produced by Company A.

11.3.5.23   The off-take agreement between Company A and Company B does not include a guarantee on price. The pricing is based on current market prices minus a discount reflecting the risk assumed by Company B for the (100 per cent) off-take obligation. Company B takes flash title to the coal it off-takes from Company A, and therefore, does not carry inventory risk.

Findings

11.3.5.24   The tax authorities of Country A challenge the discount to the market price that Company B receives when buying coal from Company A, as Company A is in a position to adjust its production based on market supply and demand conditions.

11.3.5.25   The mining group takes the position that the discount ought to be higher than that given to independent, fully fledged distributors, to reflect the risk it takes in the off-take agreement.

Considerations

11.3.5.26   The tax authorities should review whether the market off-taker (Company B) really assumed these additional market risks, in particular considering that Company A adjusts its production based on supply conditions in the market. Furthermore, the pricing is based on the current market price and volume risk is managed by Company A.

Example 5: Buying and selling of iron

Facts

11.3.5.27   The taxpayer is resident in a developing country that has a relatively low corporate tax rate, and is engaged in the business of buying and selling raw materials (iron). The taxpayer has an associated Headquarters company in Europe and a direct Parent company, which is a holding company in the Middle East.

11.3.5.28   The taxpayer buys iron from associated enterprises in South America and sells the iron to associated enterprises in Asia and the United States of America. About 80 per cent of the buying and selling of ore is being conducted in Asia. Getting information on the technicalities of this particular business has proven to be very difficult.

11.3.5.29   The taxpayer reports a markup of 0.5 per cent on cost on its intercompany buy-sell transactions. A comparison of companies that operate more or less in the same line of business shows margins between 1 and 1.5 per cent. Research also shows that the country of source of the iron provides a six-year tax holiday.

11.3.5.30   Additional challenges encountered in this case regard getting information on the margins obtained from buying and selling that specific iron.

Findings

11.3.5.31   Even though the corporate tax rate in the developing country where the taxpayer is operating its buy-sell activities is 15 per cent, which is lower than the tax rates in many other countries, the MNE of which the taxpayer is a part would have a benefit in leaving taxable profit at the source of the location where the iron originates. This case scenario shows that a corporate tax rate of 15 per cent does not necessarily mean no transfer pricing irregularities will take place.

Example 6: Intercompany financing

Facts

11.3.5.32   The taxpayer is engaged in the exploration of minerals and mining.

460

11.3.5.33   The Parent company is located in a developing country and owns a mining company and an operations company, both in Africa.

11.3.5.34   The Parent company has issued loans to its African subsidiaries, which bear no interest.

11.3.5.35   On the other hand, the Parent company borrows funds denominated in US dollars from associated enterprises for which it pays a London Interbank Offered Rate (LIBOR) plus 2.5 per cent interest rate.

11.3.5.36   Furthermore, the developing country-based Parent company pays a technical assistance fee to the two Africa-based companies, based on the respective companies' salary cost, consulting costs, moving expenses of employees, and for providing technical services. The technical assistance fee is at a cost plus five per cent level.

11.3.5.37   Considering the absence of interest income yet the incurrence of interest costs and technical assistance fee costs, the developing country-based Parent company consistently operates at a loss.

11.3.5.38   The African mining company enjoys a tax holiday and other companies in the same industry normally report earnings at cost plus four per cent.

Findings

11.3.5.39   This example presents the difficulty of associated enterprises reporting ongoing losses, and the fact that it is a challenge to obtain data on intercompany financing activities and the conditions of intercompany financing.

11.3.5.40   The developing country in issue has signed the Agreement on Mutual Administrative Assistance in Tax Matters, but collecting relevant information from abroad remains very time-consuming, in particular as transactions tend to involve several jurisdictions.

Example 7: Copper JV

Facts

11.3.5.41   A copper mine in Country M is owned and operated by a joint venture company, JV, organized under the laws of Country M. 45 per cent of the equity interests in JV are owned by Company A, a Country X subsidiary of a large mining conglomerate based in Country Y. 40 per cent of the equity interests in JV are owned by Company B, a Country X subsidiary of another large mining conglomerate that is based in Country Z. The remaining 15 per cent of the equity interests in JV are owned by Company C, an entity wholly owned by the Government of Country M.

11.3.5.42   JV has entered into service agreements with Companies A, B and C pursuant to which JV agrees to pay an annual fee equal to five per cent of its revenues to Companies A, B and C as compensation for any technical services that may be required to support the operation of JV from time to time. Under the agreements, the service fee payments are to be divided among the three recipients of the payments in proportion to the equity interests of Companies A, B and C in JV. Country M imposes a 10 per cent withholding tax on dividends but has a double tax treaty with Country X that exempts service fees from withholding tax.

11.3.5.43   The Country M tax authorities audit the services arrangements between JV and Companies A, B, and C. They learn that Companies A and B each provide occasional services of a technical nature to JV. The services are provided by a combination of employees of Companies A and B and employees of their respective parent companies. The amount and nature of the services provided varies substantially from year to year, but the tax authorities are told that JV has no available information regarding the costs incurred by Companies A and B in providing the services and that no specific invoices for particular services are provided. Instead, there is merely a single annual invoice for the five per cent of revenue payment. The Country M tax authorities learn further that Company C has never provided services of any kind to JV.

Analysis

11.3.5.44   The first step in conducting a transfer pricing analysis of the relationships between Companies A, B, and C and JV is to accurately delineate the transactions. In doing so, the Country M tax authorities determine that there is a service arrangement between Company A and Company B and JV. However, the amount and nature of services provided cannot be determined based on the available information. The Country M tax authorities determine that no services arrangement actually exists between Company C and JV.

11.3.5.45   Since there is no evidence of the type and amount of services provided, the Country M tax authorities decide that without further information they are unable to determine whether the actual services provided by Companies A and B satisfy the requirements of the benefits test described in section 5.2.2 (previously paragraph B.4.10) of the Manual. They therefore conclude that, unless further information regarding the nature of the specific services is provided, no deduction should be allowed for the five per cent fee and that it should be properly characterized as a distribution of profits to the holders of equity interests in JV.

Example 8: Sale and leaseback of equipment

Facts

11.3.5.46   Five years ago, Mining Company in Country G acquired a fleet of dump trucks to transport the ore it mined from the mine site to its nearby beneficiation plant. In accordance with Country G's accelerated depreciation provisions, Mining Company depreciated the capital costs of the trucks over five years. At the end of the five-year period, Mining Company sells the fleet of trucks to Equipment Company, an associated enterprise of Mining Company, located in Country X, a low-tax jurisdiction. The sales price received by Mining Company from Equipment Company is equal to the written down value of the trucks, which is nil as the trucks have been fully depreciated.

11.3.5.47   Immediately after the sale, Mining Company enters into a five-year operating lease with Equipment Company to lease back the fleet of trucks. Mining Company pays an arm's-length rent to Equipment Company for the use of the trucks.

Findings

11.3.5.48   Mining Company has recorded depreciation deductions against the acquisition costs of the fleet of trucks. The sale of the fleet at their written-down value means that Mining Company records no recoupment of depreciation or capital gains upon the transfer of the asset. Under the lease arrangement, Mining Company can record deductible rent payments for the use of the same fleet of trucks it owned earlier and depreciated.

Considerations

11.3.5.49   The hiring or acquisition of equipment can be problematic. Here, Mining Company has mining equipment. It depreciates the asset and then sells it to related party Equipment Company in Country B at a price of nil. Country B records it as a new asset as opposed to a second-hand asset and if depreciation is based on the value of the trucks they may be re-depreciated all over again in Country B. This form of tax planning may in itself not be a transfer pricing issue, but there is a need to consider whether the transaction is a bona fide sale, a donation or bona fide lease. In this respect, reference is made to section 3.3.3 of the Manual (paragraphs B2.3.1.4–B2.3.1.9 of the second edition). It should be considered for transfer pricing purposes whether the sale value is understated (if so, there will be a recoupment in Country A). Also, the customs value may be under-declared to avoid high tariffs (the shipping value is not always checked against the sale value); this creates room for arbitrage and generates tax benefits.

11.4   VALUE CHAIN FOR THE PRODUCTION OF OIL AND NATURAL GAS[21]

11.4.1   Introduction

11.4.1.1   The oil and gas exploration business is a high-risk global industry, but when particular projects are successful the reward is potentially very high. In most countries, governments own the subsurface oil and gas. Rather than trying to extract these natural resources themselves, governments see value in bringing in specialized oil and gas companies to perform those activities. The main reason for this is to balance risks and rewards. Exploration and Production

---

[21] For more information, see Silvana Tordo, Brandon S. Tracy and Noora Arfaa, "National Oil Companies and Value Creation: Study and Results," in *World Bank Working Paper 218* (Washington, D.C., World Bank, 2011). Available at: https://documents1.worldbank.org/curated/en/650771468331276655/pdf/National-oil-companies-and-value-creation.pdf.

(E&P) contracts describe the rights and responsibilities of the investor and also entail the share of production and/or revenues that have to be paid to the government. These contracts are usually in the form of either concessions or production sharing contracts.

11.4.1.2   E&P contracts reflect a fine balance between International Oil Companies (IOCs) and developing-country governments, their aspirations and expectations. In collaboration with natural resource owners, IOCs are prepared to accept numerous risks associated with a project, such as (i) exploration risks (i.e., whether oil and gas reserves can be found in commercial quantities); (ii) development risks (i.e., the technical risks associated with the physical investment needed to produce and transport production to market); (iii) economic risks (the upfront capital outlays required prior to production and the ongoing operating costs of the project); and (iv) market risks (the price and supply/demand risks over a very long project life).[22] In return, the IOCs expect (a) a fair risk/reward relationship; (b) a fair rate of return on capital; and (c) as much certainty as governments can provide with respect to fiscal and legal terms. Content of the contracts can vary depending on the prevailing energy prices, demand for hydrocarbons and availability of funds for investments.

11.4.2   Upstream, midstream and downstream activities

11.4.2.1   The value chain of production of oil and natural gas commences with identifying suitable areas to conduct exploration for oil and/or gas, and continues with upstream activities, consisting of exploration, development and production of crude oil and natural gas (this may include oilfield-related activities such as seismic surveys, well drilling and equipment supply or engineering). As with mining, the oil and gas industry requires significant upfront capital investments, but the upstream activity (i.e., the exploration risk in the oil and gas industry) tends to be riskier than in the mining industry.

11.4.2.2   So-called midstream activities in this industry include those related to the necessary infrastructure and storage to be able to refine the oil and process the gas. Processed products are subsequently distributed towards wholesale and retail; this part of the business is described as consisting of "downstream" activities. This includes the transport of the product via pipelines or oil tankers, refining and wholesale and retail sales. Midstream activities are often included in the downstream processes.

11.4.2.3   The figure below presents an overview of the respective upstream to downstream activities:

---

[22] A more complete discussion of risks, including references, can be found in Chapter 1 (Overview) of this Handbook.

Figure 11.F.2: Upstream, midstream and downstream activities in the extractive industries

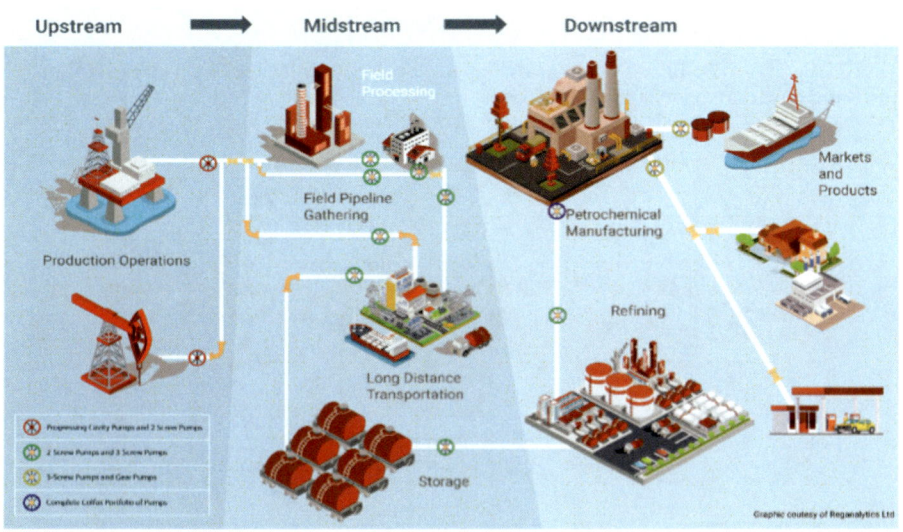

Source: Reganalytics Ltd

11.4.2.4   The functions performed, assets used and risk exposure of companies engaged in the oil and gas industry are different depending on the type of system or contract that the company has entered into with the host country where the oil and gas reserves are located. The types of system or contract are as follows:

(i)   In a concessionary system, the oil company, as licensee, obtains a lease for a fixed period of time from the government, is responsible for all investment and generally owns all exploration output and production equipment subject to making royalty, tax and other licence payments to the government;

(ii)   Under a production sharing contract, the production and reserves in the ground usually are owned by the State (or the national oil companies) with which the company has contracted, whereas the company (fully) funds the development of the oil and gas production. Part of the produced oil and gas serves as reimbursement for the company's investments and part of the produced oil and gas will be shared between the State and the contracting company;

(iii)   Under a service contract, the contracting company is usually paid a service fee for providing the service of producing oil and gas on behalf of the host State. The contracting company usually provides all capital associated with exploration and development without any claim to ownership of reserves or production. However, part of the sales revenue of the oil and gas will be applied to reimburse the contractor's costs and pay its service fee.

11.4.2.5   The figure below provides for a generic overview of the upstream oil and gas industry value chain:

Figure 11.F.3: Upstream oil and gas industry value chain

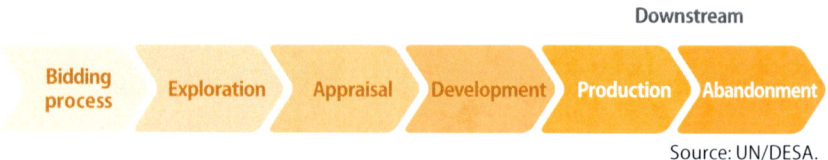

Source: UN/DESA.

A more detailed overview is provided below.[23]

---

[23] Silvana Tordo, Brandon S. Tracy and Noora Arfaa, "National Oil Companies and Value Creation: Study and Results" in *World Bank Working Paper 218* (Washington, D.C., World Bank, 2011). Available at: World Bank Document.

Figure 11.F.4: Petroleum value chain[24]

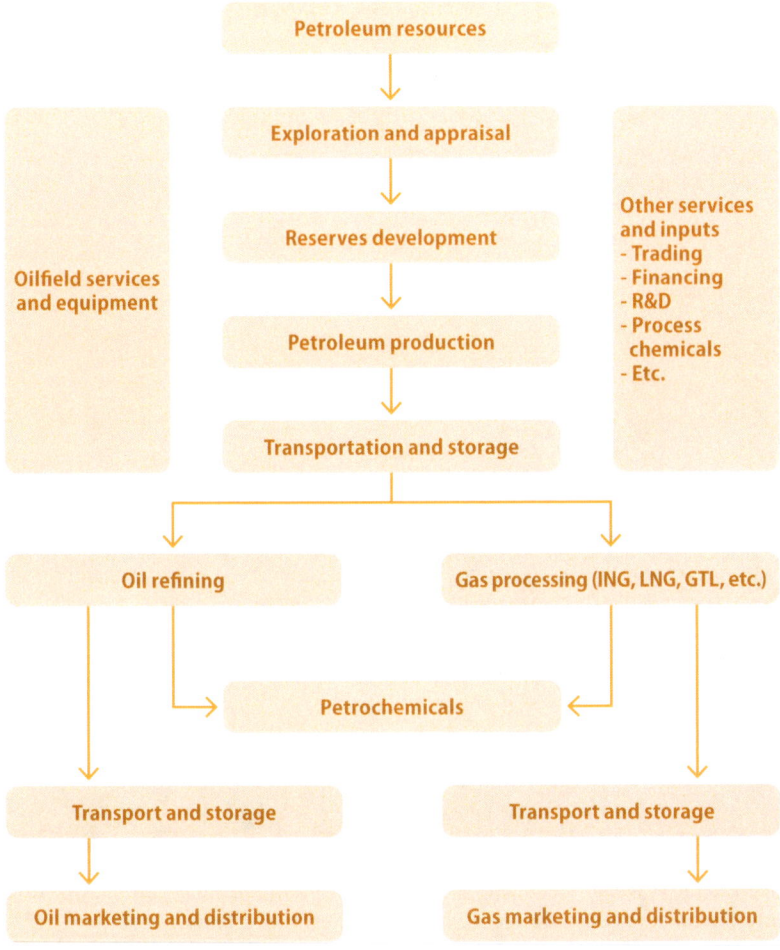

11.4.2.6   The valuation of crude has been an area of contention in the past, when many IOCs traded the produced crude with their downstream organizations often at low transfer prices. Host governments in the producing countries assumed that the price was kept artificially low to reduce upstream taxation, and therefore, they introduced a posted price or a tax reference price. As there are now clear indices on international crude prices, this hand-off point to downstream business can be benchmarked.

---

[24] C. Wolf, Does Ownership Matter (2009)

11.4.3 Industry-related case examples

11.4.3.1   Due to its nature, the oil and gas industry presents specific transfer pricing issues. Some of these industry-specific aspects are shared with the mining and extractives industry and are identified in Table 11.T.1, listing consecutive phases that extraction of minerals may involve. Other oil and gas industry issues that may be relevant from a transfer pricing perspective include:

- Central operating model;

- Financing cost;

- Intra-group guarantees;

- Cost sharing;

- Group synergies;

- Charging at cost; and

- Ring-fencing.

11.4.3.2   Table 11.T.1 addresses the consecutive phases that may be involved in the extraction of minerals. That analysis uses the same structure listed/identified above for the hydrocarbons sector to the extent possible,.

11.4.3.3   The following is a compilation and series of real-life case examples regarding issues and facts encountered in practice with respect to the oil and gas industry.

Example 1: Oil acquired from related companies

Facts

11.4.3.4   Fuel Company is engaged in the blending and refining of crude oil to produce fuel that is sold to consumers in Country A. Imported crude oil is a very important element required to produce fuel sold by Fuel Company.

11.4.3.5   Fuel Company purchases crude oil from its wholly owned subsidiary, Shipping Company, which is incorporated in, and tax resident of Country B. Shipping Company purchases crude oil from Sourcing Company, incorporated and tax resident in Country C (a low-tax jurisdiction).

11.4.3.6   Sourcing Company acquires crude oil from unrelated third parties in Countries D and E.

11.4.3.7   Shipping Company and Sourcing Company are both wholly owned subsidiaries of Fuel Company.

Findings

11.4.3.8   Upon review of the facts and intercompany agreements, it becomes clear that Sourcing Company has long-term contracts for the purchase of crude oil from unrelated parties in Countries D and E. Sourcing Company sells the crude oil to the related Shipping Company on an FOB basis. Shipping Company is responsible for all freight and related activities and sells the crude oil to related Fuel Company on a CIF basis. Crude oil is loaded at the ports in Countries D and E and delivered in Country A at the port near Fuel Company's facilities. In the past, Fuel Company used to acquire crude oil directly from third parties in Countries D and E.

Considerations

11.4.3.9   As Sourcing Company is resident in and operates from a low-tax jurisdiction, there is an inherent risk that the group profits may be diverted to that jurisdiction with the effect of reducing the tax liability of the group and eroding the tax base of the Fuel Company.

11.4.3.10   It is assumed that the price paid by Sourcing Company to the unrelated third parties for the purchases of crude oil is a market price. Should the terms and conditions of the contracts between Sourcing Company and Shipping Company, and between Shipping Company and Fuel Company, not reflect terms and conditions that would have been agreed upon in a contract between independent unrelated parties, Fuel Company could end up paying an inflated price for the purchase of crude oil from the related Shipping Company.

11.4.3.11   The result is that the tax base of the country in which Fuel Company is resident is eroded by the inflated price paid for the crude oil purchases. Controlled foreign company (CFC) rules could be applied to tax the profits made by Sourcing and Shipping companies as a result of mispricing of the transactions between Sourcing Company and Shipping Company, as well as between Shipping Company and Fuel Company.

11.4.3.12   As Sourcing Company and Shipping Company are subsidiaries of Fuel Company, they are controlled companies and should be within the scope of domestic CFC rules, if those are in place. If applicable, CFC rules cover situations where goods are purchased from third parties located in third countries for on-sale to the resident country, then the profits arising from those transactions could be imputed to Fuel Company and included in the taxable income of Fuel Company. These diversionary rules would tax the full profit of the CFC from the diversionary activities performed by the CFC.

Example 2: Market volatility issues

Facts

11.4.3.13   Oil and Gas (O&G) Company decides to lease drilling equipment from a related party for several years at a time when drilling equipment is scarcely available due to a high-demand market caused by high oil prices. The drilling equipment is to be used globally to realize activities in diverse countries where Exploration & Processing (E&P) campaigns are (expected) to be performed during these years of high oil prices.

11.4.3.14   Later, the oil price drops significantly. A consequence of this unexpected drop in price is that drilling equipment becomes available in the market at very competitive fees, and considering the impact on profitability of high cost and reduced earnings, several planned E&P projects are cancelled by the O&G Company.

Findings

11.4.3.15   The O&G Company that entered into the drilling equipment lease continues to pay a recurrent fee to the owner of the drilling equipment that was previously hired, even if the drilling equipment is on standby and not currently in use.

11.4.3.16   At issue is whether the price paid for the drilling equipment between related parties—consistent with the intercompany agreement which is not adjusted for current market prices—qualifies as being at arm's length.

Considerations

11.4.3.17   The price paid is a consequence of the contract entered into between the parties and the fact that it is difficult to quantify the cost of the risk of not having the equipment available at the time a drilling campaign approaches its commencement of drilling (sometimes referred to as the "spud date") in a certain country against the cost of the risk of oil prices dropping.

11.4.3.18   The related party that invested in the long-term lease arrangement in the drilling equipment still requests the agreed price, whereas the related operating company is currently not able to use the drilling equipment and may request price adjustments.

11.4.3.19   To determine if the price is at arm's length, it is valid to consider all available information as well as the options realistically available to both of the parties to the transaction at the time the contract was concluded. Well-prepared transfer pricing documentation that records the relevant economic conditions and other relevant facts contemporaneously may offer support and evidence for the business decision that will help clarify if the pricing is at arm's length.

Example 3: Financing costs

Facts

11.4.3.20   O&G Parent Company is based in Country A. O&G Operating Company develops a block in developing Country B. The condition of the concession to conduct E&P activities limits the amount of interest expense that may be deducted from the tax base.

11.4.3.21   In the exploration phase it is usually not feasible to obtain loan financing given the exploration activities are capital intensive and high risk. Once the project advanced from the exploration stage to the development stage, O&G Parent Company switched to project finance (loans). Therefore, Parent Company grants an intercompany loan to O&G Operating Company.

11.4.3.22   Because of the concession conditions, developing Country B disallows a portion of the interest costs incurred by oil and gas Operating Company while Country A includes the full interest in the tax base of oil and gas Parent Company resulting in double taxation.

Considerations

11.4.3.23   In essence, this is not a transfer pricing issue, but more a conflict between the concession agreement and the tax legislation of the Parent Company. Transfer pricing considerations would relate to determination of an arm's-length interest rate or reclassification of the loan into equity.

Example 4: Horizontal ring-fencing

Facts

11.4.3.24   MNE Group D consists of three taxpayer entities: Principal Company D, Company A and Company B. Company A and Company B are each special purpose vehicles whose sole business consists of the exploration and, if successful, development and operation of Blocks A and B respectively. Principal Company D acts as group coordinator in Country M. In this role, Principal Company D contracts with an arm's-length service provider to undertake exploratory drilling in blocks A and B. The fee for this service is 100 per block.

11.4.3.25   Assume that in the area of Blocks A and B and given the stage of exploration, it is anticipated that 50 per cent of exploratory drilling will be successful such that it will lead to development of the block and production of oil.

11.4.3.26   Company A and Company B each initially pay a fee of 50 to Principal Company D for the drilling work undertaken by the service provider. A further 150 is payable to Principal Company D if the drilling is successful.

Findings

11.4.3.27   In this example, it turns out that Block A is successful and Block B is not. Furthermore, the oil produced by Block A results in 1,000 of income. Company A's accounts will show an initial loss of 200 (the 50 initial fee and the 150 success fee) but this loss can be offset against its future income of 1,000. Company A's net taxable income is therefore 800. Company B's accounts will show a loss of 50 (the initial fee). As Company B has no income and the ring-fence does not allow Company B's loss to be transferred elsewhere, the 50 of costs are effectively stranded costs and can never be deducted against income. Principal Company D's accounts will show total income of 250, consisting of 50 from Company B and 50 plus 150 from Company A. Principal Company D's costs of 200 (100 x 2) are paid to the service provider. Principal Company D's net income therefore is 50. The total Group taxable income is 800 + 50 = 850.

Considerations

11.4.3.28   These arrangements may lead to shifting of costs between ring-fenced blocks and effectively overriding the ring-fencing. If Company B makes a successful discovery and receives its success fee, that fee constitutes costs of the successful block, which may be used to offset against future taxable income from that Block. Company B is facilitating the override of the ring-fencing for Company A. It would be relevant to look for unrelated party comparables.

11.4.3.29   Without the interposition of Principal Company D between Company A and Company B, and without making use of the success fee that Principal Company D demands, the accounts would show a different picture. Company A's accounts would show a tax loss of 100 (the service fee paid for exploratory drilling) which can be offset against its income of 1000. Company A's net income would be 900. Company B's accounts would also show a tax loss of 100 (the service fee paid for exploratory drilling) but this amount would constitute stranded costs. The total group taxable income would therefore be 900.

11.4.3.30   Some questions arise on whether the pricing between Company A and Company B and Principal Company D—and making use of a success fee—is at arm's length, and it should be determined what an arm's length fee would be for the services rendered by Principal Company D.

Example 5: Cost contribution arrangement

Facts

11.4.3.31   O&G Company has a development cost contribution arrangement in which all the operating entities participate. Under the cost contribution arrangement, costs of R&D development are shared among the participants on a projected benefit basis. The participating operating entities have access to all the developed technology and jointly own the intellectual property (IP).

11.4.3.32   The O&G Company is rolling out a multi-year project to deploy a new information technology (IT) system across the world. The cost of this project is included in the cost base of the cost sharing arrangement and is allocated based on the number of personal computers in the respective operating entities. In year one, the programme is rolled out in Countries A and B, but not yet in Countries C and D. Still the operating companies in Countries C and D need to bear their proportionately allocated costs under the cost sharing arrangement. In year two, the programme is rolled out to Countries C and D.

Findings

11.4.3.33   In year one, Country C and Country D treat the cost sharing as a cafeteria-style arrangement, implying that the operating entities should only share the costs in which they have a current-year benefit (cherry picking) and therefore not receive a proportionate charge of the new IT system costs.

11.4.3.34   Under the cost sharing arrangements, all participants are entitled to IP resulting from pooled R&D. Country C disallows a deduction for the operating entity in its country of the proportionate charge of the R&D activities as they do not see current benefits.

Considerations

11.4.3.35   Cost sharing arrangements generally consider anticipated benefits and not only current-year benefits (reference is made to the Manual, Chapter 7 (previously part B.6). A bona fide cost sharing arrangement requires consistent use of allocation keys among the participants. The applied allocation key should reflect a reasonable allocation of anticipated (future) benefits. Where countries would prefer cost sharing for services to cost sharing for R&D, it should be considered that the latter may reduce future royalty discussions for IP used by the cost sharing participants operating in their countries.

Example 6: Intercompany charges at cost

Facts

11.4.3.36   Under a production sharing agreement, a consortium of three independent parties is established. From among the participating companies, an operator is appointed. The operator runs the project on behalf of the consortium and provides all technical and functional services, ensuring that costs and risks are shared with the consortium members. Pursuant to the consortium agreement, the operator is not allowed to benefit or be disadvantaged by its position, compared to the non-operating consortium members. As such, the consortium agreement stipulates that the operator and its affiliates may not earn a profit from undertaking activities for the benefit of the consortium.

Findings

11.4.3.37   The tax authority of the country where the related service company of the operator is located requires a markup on the services provided to the consortium.

11.4.3.38   The operator takes the position that the consortium agreement does not allow the associated service provider to charge a markup on its services provided. In case a markup on costs was to be charged due to commercial and legal arrangements, the consequences would include cost rejection by partners to the production sharing agreement and joint operating agreement and double taxation.

Considerations

11.4.3.39   The issue to be resolved is whether the consortium arrangement provides a comparable basis for asserting that charging at-cost is appropriate.

11.4.3.40   Figure 11.F.5 below depicts how the at-cost restriction for services rendered by all consortium members is passed on to the operator or service company:

Figure 11.F.5: Flow of at-cost restrictions

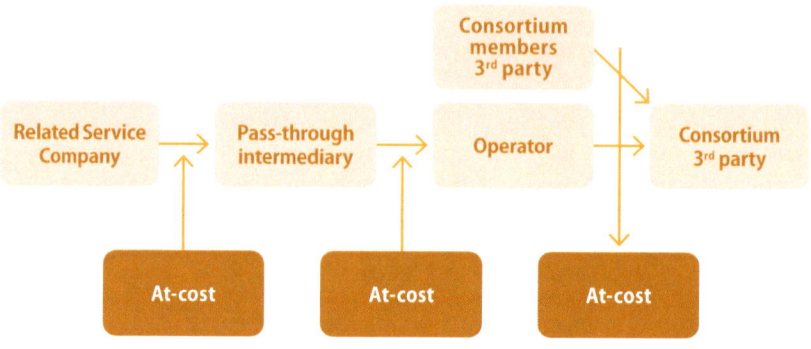

Example 7: Performance guarantees and bonds

Facts

11.4.3.41   Country A awards an oil and gas exploration and development licence to Operating Company X. Operating Company X is incorporated in developing Country A and is a subsidiary of Company Y. Company Y is incorporated in Country B. Country A, as a condition for awarding the licence, requires two types of guarantees with respect to Company X's obligations. First, Country A insists that Parent Company Y guarantees in full the obligations Company X has agreed to under the licence contract throughout the contract life. Second, in addition to the parent company guarantee, Country A requires a more limited but third-party provided performance bond granted in favour of host Country A. Under this bank performance bond, an unrelated third party, Bank Z, guarantees 7.5 per cent of the total obligation value under the contract for the first four years of the agreement.[25]

---

[25] See, for example, Article 29.1 of India Model Production Sharing Contract at http://petroleum.nic.in/sites/default/files/MPSC%20NELP-V.pdf as quoted in Table 11.T.1 at part 4 of the table: "Each of the Companies constituting the Contractor shall procure and deliver to the Government within thirty (30) days from the Effective Date of this Contract: (a) an irrevocable, unconditional bank guarantee from a reputed bank of good standing in India, acceptable to the Government, in favour of the Government, for the amount specified in Article 29.3 and valid for four (4) years, in a form provided at Appendix-G; (b) financial and performance guarantee in favour of the Government from a Parent Company acceptable to the Government, in the form and substance set out in Appendix-E1, or, where there is no such Parent Company, the financial and performance guarantee from the Company itself in the form and substance set out in Appendix-E2; (c) a legal opinion from its legal advisors, in a form satisfactory to the Government, to the effect that the aforesaid guarantees have been duly signed and delivered on behalf

Findings

11.4.3.42   Country A's tax authorities review the performance guarantee provided by Parent Company Y and find that no charge has been made to its subsidiary, Company X. They further note that in the case of the performance bond provided by independent Bank Z, a fee has in fact been charged. After further researching the bank guarantee, it is determined that the capitalization of Company X is sufficient to satisfy the coverage requirements of the bank for its level of exposure, but if the exposures were materially higher, Bank Z would not issue the performance bond without additional capital or further security.

Considerations

11.4.3.43   The issue involved is whether Parent Company Y should charge a fee for providing its performance guarantee for Company X's obligations and, if so, how should the appropriate level of the fee be determined.

11.4.3.44   One approach to be explored is whether the third-party Bank Z's fee for its guarantee can be used as a comparable to determine what an arm's length fee for Company Y's guarantee should be. In evaluating this, a key difference can be observed—i.e., that the level and timeframe for Bank Z's exposure is different from that of Company Y. This difference is clearly material, and the tax authorities will need to assess whether some type of "multiplier" to that fee can be made. They will also need to consider what additional security a third-party bank would seek.

11.4.3.45   An additional consideration could be a finding that for related party contract guarantees (such as the parent company guarantee in the example) prevailing practice is that there is generally no charge to the in-country affiliate for a parent company guarantee.[26] The basis for not charging a fee in these circumstances is that the guarantee is often viewed as a requirement for the affiliate (and indirectly, the parent) to qualify for the contract, and is thus just as much a benefit to the parent as to the affiliate. Alternatively, the parent guarantee is often viewed as simply the equivalent of an agreement to further capitalize the subsidiary if needed to meet its obligations, and generally not something for which a fee is charged. [27]

---

of the guarantors with due authority and is legally valid and enforceable and binding upon them (…) Available at http://www.dghindia.gov.in/assets/downloads/56ce986044a31ModelCBM.pdf. Also, see *Sharing Contract between Nigerian National Petroleum Corporation and (i) Gas Transmission and Power Limited, (ii) Energy 905 Suntera Limited and (iii) Ideal Oil and Gas Limited, covering Block 905 Anambra Basin* (2007). Available at http://www.sevenenergy.com/~/media/Files/S/Seven-Energy/documents/opl-905-psc.pdf.

[26] See Shepherd and Wedderburn LLP, Parent company guarantees and performance bonds (2010): which notes that "(…) a parent company guarantee should be provided at no cost to the developer, whereas there will be [a] charge for [third party] performance bonds…" Available at http://www.shepwedd.co.uk/knowledge/parent-company-guarantees-and-performance-bonds.

[27] See the United Nations Manual on Transfer Pricing for Developing Countries and the OECD Transfer Pricing Guidelines regarding intra-group services and when a charge may be appropriate. The former provides:

"5.2.6.2   Shareholder activities are activities undertaken to provide an economic benefit

Example 8: Transfer Pricing Issues of Loan Pricing

The facts

11.4.3.46   MiningCo, HoldCo and FinCo are 100% subsidiaries of HeadCo. FinCo is the group's treasury company. HeadCo's rating is A+, the rating of the three subsidiaries is BBB. MiningCo is a mining company. On 30 January 2018, MiningCo signed a loan contract with HoldCo for an amount of EUR 200 million at a fixed rate of 12.5%. The aim of the loan is the purchase of a mine in MiningCo's country. The loan's term is 5 years. According to the contract, interest will not be paid annually but only at the request of HoldCo, based on MiningCo's financial performance. For the documentation of the loan, following a request of information from tax authorities, MiningCo provided a transfer pricing study related to a loan of USD 800 million contracted by HoldCo with the internal bank of the group, FinCo. The term of this loan is 10 years (2017-2027). This study shows that HoldCo's cost of financing is 3.5%, i.e., an interest rate of 2.5% (the median interest rate from the comparability analysis) plus 1% of the guarantee fee paid by HoldCo to the parent company, HeadCo. The credit risk premium applied on this loan, based on MiningCo's rating (BBB) and the country risk is 9%.

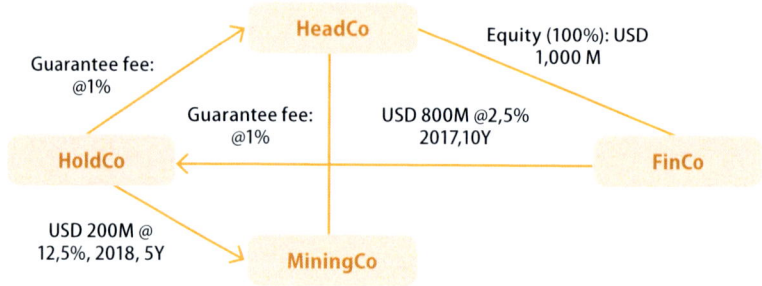

---

only to the shareholder company (ultimate parent company or any other shareholder such as an intermediary holding company, depending on the facts of the case) in its capacity as shareholder. Accordingly, the cost of shareholder activities should be borne exclusively by the shareholder. Shareholder activities performed by an associated enterprise on behalf of its parent company should be charged to the parent company on an arm's length basis.

    5.2.6.3 Shareholder activities may include the following:

    • The preparation and filing of reports required to meet the juridical structure of the parent company;

        • The appointment and remuneration of parent company directors;
        • The meetings of the parent company's board of directors and of the parent company's shareholders;

        • The parent company's preparation and filing of consolidated financial reports, reports for regulatory purposes and tax returns;

        • The activities of the parent company for raising funds used to acquire share capital in subsidiary companies; and

        • The activities of the parent company to protect its capital investment in subsidiary companies."

11.4.3.47   In addition, within the framework of a group services agreement signed with the parent company HeadCo, MiningCo has to pay a 1% guarantee fee. This guarantee is required by HoldCo, the lender, as a condition for accepting the loan application. Following this payment, the total interest rate of this loan is 14.5%.

What is the concern?

11.4.3.48   This loan arrangement raises several questions for the tax authorities in MiningCo's country:

(i)   The implied credit risk premium of 9% may not be arm's length. A credit risk premium is the interest rate charged by banks on loans to private sector customers minus the "risk free" treasury bill interest rate at which short-term government securities are issued or traded in the market. This risk premium should be checked against the risk premium in MiningCo's country. The transfer pricing analysis does not contain any additional evidence to support the view that this particular loan instrument attracted additional risk at the time it was issued.

(ii)   The guarantee granted by HeadCo is a written explicit financial guarantee, however there is no evidence that MiningCo received a real economic benefit from entering into the financial guarantee. It does not appear MiningCo was able to access a larger amount of borrowing and/or at a reduced interest rate.

(iii)   Consideration of parental support is an important element in assessing the arm's length nature of the interest rate. Undertaking an assessment of the strategic importance of MiningCo to HeadCo to understand if the subsidiary is considered in the core portfolio of key assets of HeadCo will assist in determining if the credit rating of BBB needs to be notched up due to implicit support provided by HeadCo. Global credit rating agencies publish information which can assist with determining an appropriate notching adjustment.

(iv)   The interest rate paid by HoldCo on the loan from FinCo is based on a benchmark of bonds whose principal amounts are significantly larger than the MiningCo loan and that have longer terms. There is an issue of comparability. The amount and period until maturity have an impact on the risk, and therefore, on the risk premium. No adjustments have been made to account for these differences. The tax authority should seek to identify any other third party debt arrangements that may have been entered into by the HeadCo group in January 2018 as this loan may be traceable to the acquisition of MiningCo and assist with undertaking a pricing analysis.

(v)   An upfront fee is a fee paid to a lender by a borrower as consideration for making a new loan to reflect specific types of costs or activities that may be related to the origination of the loan. Those costs/activities may not have been present in this case.

(vi) Interest will be paid at the request of HoldCo based on MiningCo's financial performance. First, this condition could indicate that in substance, it is not really a loan but a contribution of equity, as the yield is similar to a dividend. The tax authority should review the local country's debt/equity rules as there may be legal grounds to deny interest deductions where the amount is deemed to be equity under the local country tax rules. Second, with this condition, HoldCo can only request the payment of interest when MiningCo has generated profits, which ultimately delays collection of tax to a later date.

(vii) Determining the commercial purpose of the basis of interest payments would be important. E.g., it is not uncommon for payments of interest to be deferred until there is positive cash flow to repay debts, otherwise additional debt would be required to make interest payments. However, as HoldCo can control to some degree when interest is paid, if the local country tax rules allow interest deductions only when payments are made, rather than when interest accrues, then it may be possible to circumvent the interest limitation rule if it is based on an earnings before interest, tax, depreciation and amortization (EBITDA) test (refer to Chapter 9 on Tax Treatment of Financial Transactions in the Extractive Industries for further information).

Example 10: Currency Hedge

Facts

11.4.3.49 Extractive Parent Company X is a large multinational company based in Country A and operates in several countries around the world. Like most extractive companies, Parent Company X has a functional currency of US dollars.

11.4.3.50 Subsidiary Company Z is a subsidiary company of Parent Company X that operates in Country B. It is one of several production entities within the Company X MNE group. Company Z is producing extractive materials and is selling the material to an unrelated third party buyer. Company Z is paid by the unrelated third party buyer in US Dollars. Company Z has an accounting functional currency of US Dollars and has elected under the domestic tax regime of Country B to have tax functional currency of US Dollars.

11.4.3.51 Company Z is also undertaking significant expansion in its operations which requires large capital expenditure investment and a moderate short term increase in operating expenses. The capital expenditure comes from a third party supplier and is paid to a third party supplier in US Dollars. The operating expenses are mostly denominated in the local currency of Country B, however, a small proportion of specialised consultants and engineers are paid in foreign currencies such as US Dollars and Euros.

11.4.3.52 Company Z requires additional financing to fund the expansion of the operations and is granted a related party loan by Parent Company X. The loan is priced at arm's length terms and is denominated in US Dollars.

11.4.3.53   Company Z is of the view that because most of its operating expenses are in a local currency, it requires funding in the local currency of Country B. Company Z enters into a cross currency interest rate swap (CCIRS) with a related party SwapCo, which swaps the exposure to the US Dollar loan into the domestic currency.

11.4.3.54   The cash consequences of the CCIRS are as follows:

- The initial principal is exchanged from US Dollars into Country B's local currency.

- Periodic interest payments are exchanged so that Company Z pays in local currency.

- At the swap contract maturity, the principal will be re-exchanged.

- The total borrowing cost of the financing is the interest expense in local currency plus the hedging expenses.

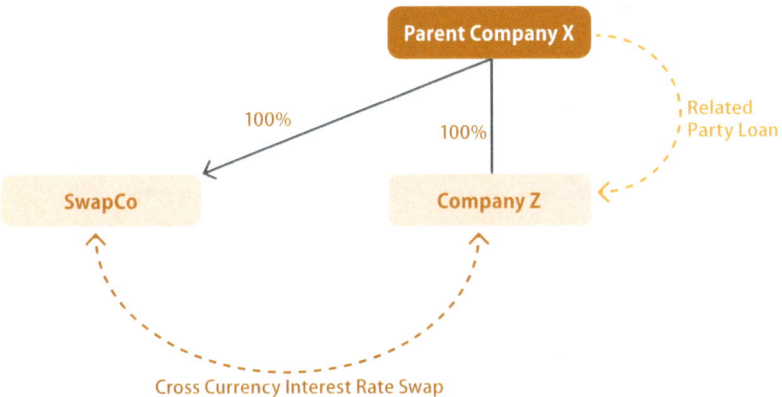

Financial outcomes

11.4.3.55   The cash consequences of the CCIRS are as follows:

1.   The initial principal is exchanged from US Dollars into Country B's local currency.

2.   Periodic interest payments are exchanged so that Company Z pays in local currency.

3.   At the swap contract maturity, the principal will be re-exchanged.

4.   The total borrowing cost of the financing is the interest expense in local currency plus the hedging expenses.

Tax outcomes

11.4.3.56   Subject to laws of Country B:

1.   There is a tax deduction for the interest incurred.

2.   There is withholding tax on the interest payment to Parent Company X (a related non-resident company).

3.   There is a realized tax gain or loss on the periodic interest payments, depending on the difference between the swap obligations and the actual spot exchange rate at the time the interest payments are made.

4.   There is generally no withholding tax on the swap payments.

5.   There is a crystallised tax gain or loss at maturity when the principal is re-exchanged, depending on the amount agreed under the CCIRS and the actual spot exchange rate at the date of maturity of the CCIRS.

Considerations

11.4.3.57   What type of foreign exchange (FX) risk is Company Z seeking to manage? In this example, Company Z faces a general operational FX risk as it generates income in US Dollars but incurs operational costs in another currency (Country B local currency). This is not uncommon in the extractive industries as commodities are almost exclusively sold on a US Dollar basis but most of the resources are located outside of the United States. Owing to its economic FX risk, Company Z decided to enter into a CCIRS.

11.4.3.58   What are the options available for Company Z to manage its FX risk? Foreign exchange risk is typically managed through natural hedging or hedging with financial instruments. Natural hedging refers to operational actions in certain currencies that mitigate or eliminate FX risk without the use of financial instruments. Alternatively, an MNE may choose to use financial instruments that are negotiated privately or through a public exchange to mitigate the FX exposures.

11.4.3.59   Were the actions taken by Company Z economically rational given the options available? Company Z earns income in US Dollars, and therefore, has a natural hedge against a US Dollar borrowing. In the absence of a CCIRS, there is a transactional FX exposure if the loan funding is required to pay for operational expenses. By entering into a CCIRS to swap the exposure to the US Dollar loan into the local Country B currency, Company Z is able to mitigate FX risk on the financing of operational expenses.

11.4.3.60   However, a loan denominated in the local currency has created new FX exposures:

- To service the interest on the loan, Company Z will need to exchange its US Dollar income into the local currency. This creates a translation risk every time the periodic payments are due on the CCIRS.

- There is a significant FX exposure once the CCIRS matures, when Company Z will be required to re-exchange the principal amount into US Dollars.

- From the MNE group's perspective, unless SwapCo entered into a back-to-back arrangement with a third party, the FX risk the CCIRS purports to mitigate remains within the group and is unhedged.

11.4.3.61   In this example, the additional FX risk created by the CCIRS is likely to exceed the risks it purports to mitigate and the commercial rationale to enter into a hedging arrangement is questionable.

11.4.3.62   Is the transaction priced on an arm's length basis? Asymmetrical hedging arrangements create a transfer pricing risk and need to be benchmarked against publicly traded derivatives to determine whether they are priced on an arm's length basis.

Chapter 12

Value Added Tax

12.1   INTRODUCTION

12.1.1   Executive summary

12.1.1.1   This chapter covers the key issues relevant to the application of value added tax (VAT) in the extractive industries. The VAT, also commonly referred to as the goods and services tax (GST), is the broad-based consumption tax of choice in more than 160 countries worldwide, including those countries with large extractive industries.[1] Ideally, VAT should not operate differently for extractive industries as compared to any other industry. Developing countries with limited administrative capacity may however experience challenges in following this ideal, and may consider, or have already implemented, alternative policy or administrative measures.

12.1.1.2   Due to their predominantly export-orientated nature, governments should not expect large amounts of VAT revenue from the extractive industries operating in their country. The VAT treatment of the extractive industries could, however, be a barrier to investment, which could ultimately lead to decreases in tax revenues from other taxes. There are also neutrality, efficiency and other potential costs to consider when deciding on the desired VAT system to apply to the extractive industries.

12.1.1.3   As VAT is applied to both extractive industry inputs and outputs—and also taking into account the long lead times in extractive industry investments—VAT affects the industry at every phase in its typical life cycle. The typical VAT treatment of expenditure and key issues related to the relevant life cycle phase are set out in Table 12.T.1. below.

---

[1] One exception to this generalization is the United States of America which has no national level broad-based consumption tax, although most states have adopted retail sales taxes.

Table 12.T.1: Value added tax in the life cycle of the extractive industries

Life cycle phase	Key activities undertaken[a]	Input VAT deduction	Output VAT charged	Key issues
Exploration	Locating deposits; assessing commercial and economic viability; and typical 3–10 year period	Yes	No	Surplus input VAT refunds due; opportunity cost on cash flow; and exposure to exchange rate depreciation
Development	Preparation of site for production; establishment of infrastructure; typical 2–4 year period	Yes	No	Surplus input VAT refunds due; opportunity cost on cash flow; and exposure to exchange rate depreciation
Production	Production and commercial processing and typical 15–20+year period	Yes	Yes—Often at a zero-rate as output is largely exported	Generally, 0% VAT on export of outputs; recovery of input VAT; opportunity cost on cash flow; exposure to exchange rate depreciation; and compliance costs for documentary requirements accompanying export
Decommissioning /rehabilitation	Removal of infrastructure; and restoration of site	Yes	Limited amount and often zero-rated as output and infrastructure is exported	Surplus input VAT refunds due; opportunity cost on cash flow; and exposure to exchange rate depreciation

[a] These activities may take longer in practice than the typical period provided in this table.

12.1.1.4   Both the exploration and development phases require considerable direct investment, with the development phase alone often accounting for 40 to 50 per cent of the total cost of the project.[2] Large capital goods are generally imported and other goods and services are also imported or supplied by the local economy. During these periods there is no commercial production/sales of output. This means that extractive industries may have difficulty in being allowed to register for VAT and that there is little or no output VAT on domestic sales against which input VAT can be deducted. Typically, input VAT refunds will arise that can only be claimed when registration is allowed. Therefore, it is important that registration for VAT is made available for entities undertaking early stage activities such as exploration and development.

---

[2] United Nations, "Extractive industries: optimizing value retention in host countries" in *The United Nations Conference on Trade and Development* (2012). Available at http://unctadxiii.org/ en/SessionDocument/suc2012d1_en.pdf.

12.1.1.5   The refund policy of the host country, thus, becomes critical to investment decisions as it affects the cash flow position of the investor and could become a cost to the investor. The delay of input VAT refunds can act as a barrier to investment during the exploration and development phases.[3] Further, the adopted VAT policy applicable to the extractive industries and related administration can have spill-over effects into the local economy, whether positive as a result of increased economic activity or negative as a result of decreased economic activity or non-neutrality of treatment.

12.1.1.6   During the production phase, produced goods are often predominantly exported,[4] meaning the destination principle will apply to these exports— the destination principle allows for VAT only to be collected in the country of consumption of goods and services. This is achieved by zero-rating exports and charging import VAT on imports, so that in the case of exports during this phase, the supply[5] will be zero-rated.[6] Due to the majority of output being exported and therefore zero-rated, the amount of output VAT against which input VAT can be deducted is limited, creating the need to obtain refunds of input VAT from the government. During this phase, the delay of input VAT refunds could create VAT policy and related administration challenges and be a barrier to investment.

12.1.1.7   During the decommissioning/rehabilitation phase, services that relate to decommissioning are often supplied by businesses in a different jurisdiction than that of the extractive site. This is as a result of an expert level of these services often not being obtainable in the country of the extractive site. Since production has ceased and generally few supplies are made during this phase, challenges regarding the refund of input VAT may again arise. This is because there is no output VAT against which input VAT (primarily on services) can be claimed, and extractive industries may be required to deregister for VAT purposes before completing the decommissioning/rehabilitation phase.

12.1.1.8   From an extractive industries perspective, the key issues to note therefore relate to:

- A stable, neutral and efficient VAT framework applicable to the industry;

- The timely recovery of input VAT, to (i) mitigate opportunity costs on cash flow, and (ii) protect against exchange rate depreciation which would erode the value of the refunds due;

---

[3] It can also be argued that the timely refund of input VAT can create a competitive advantage to a country in relation to other potential investment countries.

[4] It should be noted that this is not always the case (e.g., in the case of gas in Brazil).

[5] VAT is usually described as being imposed on "supplies" rather than "sales" of goods or services, since the term "supplies" includes sales as well as other forms of providing goods and services to a customer (refer to terms used).

[6] All countries with a VAT apply the destination principle. The destination principle ensures neutrality in trade and protects the legal base of the VAT (consumption).

- Being allowed to register before making any taxable supplies and not being forced to deregister during the decommissioning/ rehabilitation phase; and

- Efficiency regarding the administrative requirements when exporting goods.

From a host country perspective, the key issues to note would relate to:

- A stable, neutral and efficient VAT framework ensuring that VAT refunds due are administered in a timely manner and minimize distortions;

- Demonstrating that the host country is a suitable location for long-term, stable investments;

- Developing the local economy as a result of the increased investment in the country;

- A robust set of rules relating to the VAT treatment of decommissioning; and

- Limiting evasion under the VAT to the extent it applies to the extractive industry and industries supplying to this industry.

12.1.2   Purpose

12.1.2.1   The purpose of this chapter is to provide an overview of VAT policy and administration measures that countries have implemented or could consider as they relate to the life cycle of the typical extractive industry activities. The potential impact on investment decisions and spillover effects into the local economy are also discussed. Place of supply and consumption rules, as they relate to the extractive industries, are also suggested.

12.1.2.2   This chapter is for information purposes only. It is intended to identify VAT issues related to the extractive industries and identify and discuss all potential policy and administrative initiatives that countries have implemented or could consider implementing. It should be understood that the discussion of a policy or administrative initiative does not mean that this initiative is recommended. On the contrary, some initiatives are not recommended, but are discussed since some countries have implemented these initiatives and others may consider doing so in the future.

12.2   VAT POLICY AND ADMINISTRATION IN THE EXTRACTIVE INDUSTRIES

12.2.1   An overview of the VAT

12.2.1.1   The VAT is a tax on final consumption of goods and services charged on value added at multiple stages of production. Table 12.T.2 illustrates this process.

12.2.1.2   From Table 12.T.2 it can be seen that the total value added in the production-distribution chain (20,000) multiplied by the tax rate (10 per cent) is equal to the net amount received by government (2,000) which is paid by the consumer. This amount is, however, collected from registered businesses in the production-distribution chain based on their value added. This is achieved by having registered suppliers charge output VAT on their supplies and allowing registered purchasers an input VAT deduction of the tax paid to the supplier. The tax is, therefore, not borne by registered businesses since the tax paid by them to their suppliers is either deducted or refunded (where their input VAT deductions exceed their output VAT charged).

Table 12.T.2: Workings of a VAT (assumed rate of 10 per cent)[a]

Workings of a VAT (assumed rate of 10 per cent)

BASIC TRANSACTIONS, EXCLUDING VAT		
Production-distribution chain	**Purchases**	**Sales**
Producer	0	4 000
Manufacturer	4 000	12 000
Wholesaler	12 000	14 000
Retailer	14 000	20 000
Consumer	20 000	-
VAT PAYMENTS TO SUPPLIERS AND BUYERS		
Production-distribution chain	**VAT paid to supplier**	**VAT paid by buyer**
Producer	0	400
Manufacturer	400	1 200
Wholesaler	1 200	1 400
Retailer	1 400	2 000
Consumer	2 000	-
FRACTIONAL COLLECTION OF VAT PAID BY CONSUMER		
Distribution-production chain	**Tax paid to supplier**	**Tax paid to government**
Consumer	2 000	-
Retailer	1 400	600
Wholesaler	1 200	200
Manufacturer	400	800
Producer	0	400

[a] Adjusted from Sijbren Cnossen, "A VAT primer for lawyers, economists, and accountants," Tax Notes 124(7) (2009), p. 687–98.

12.2.1.3   An input VAT deduction is, however, only allowed if the registered purchaser will use the goods or services purchased to make taxable supplies (e.g., supplies that are charged with VAT). Since a consumer is a final recipient of the product (i.e., it does not make taxable supplies) no input VAT can be deducted by the consumer and the consumer pays all the tax. The consumer—as opposed to a producer—paying the VAT is central to ensuring the neutrality and economic efficiency[7] of the VAT.

---

[7] For this purpose, economic efficiency means that the VAT does not influence the behaviours

12.2.1.4   A key feature of all VAT systems is the destination principle, which ensures neutrality in trade and protects the legal base of VAT. Neutrality in trade can be taken to mean that foreign businesses are not advantaged or disadvantaged in respect of the level of VAT applied to a supply of goods or services in a jurisdiction. As noted above, in essence, the destination principle allows for VAT only being collected in the country of consumption of goods and services. This is achieved by zero-rating exports and charging import VAT on imports. Table 12.T.3 illustrates the workings of the same transactions as in table 12.T.2, but where the manufacturer makes a zero-rated supply by exporting goods.

12.2.1.5   From Table 12.T.3 it can be seen that as a result of exporting the goods or services, the government receives no VAT revenue (400–400). It is further important to see that this will only be the case where the manufacturer is allowed to deduct input VAT on the VAT paid to the producer (400). Where the manufacturer makes other standard rated taxable supplies, this input VAT can be offset against those supplies. If, however, the manufacturer does not have sufficient supplies against which to offset the input VAT, the government needs to provide the manufacturer with a VAT refund. Failure to do so, or do so in a timely manner, results in many distortions, some of which are discussed later in the chapter, and incorrectly taxes production rather than consumption.[8]

Table 12.T.3: Basic transactions, excluding VAT

Basic transactions, excluding VAT		
BASIC TRANSACTIONS, EXCLUDING VAT		
Production-distribution chain	**Purchases**	**Sales**
Producer	0	4 000
Manufacturer	4 000	12 000
VAT PAYMENTS TO SUPPLIERS AND BUYERS		
Production-distribution chain	**VAT paid to supplier**	**VAT paid by buyer**
Producer	0	400
Manufacturer	400	0 (in country of origin)
FRACTIONAL COLLECTION OF VAT PAID BY CONSUMER		
Distribution-production chain	**Tax paid to supplier**	**Tax paid to government**
Manufacturer	400	400
Producer	0	(400)

12.2.2   VAT registration

12.2.2.1   Due to the extensive periods during the exploration, development and

---

and decisions of producers.

[8] If a government does not plan on providing input VAT refunds to extractive industry suppliers, it should make that clear during negotiations. It should further understand that this is entirely inconsistent with the nature of a VAT and creates an entirely different type of cost.

decommissioning/rehabilitation phases when extractive industries often do not make taxable supplies, registration issues may arise. Many countries impose a voluntary registration threshold, requiring suppliers to make taxable supplies in excess of a certain amount within, generally, a 12-month period before being able to register. There may also be other requirements that need to be met before allowing a supplier to register for VAT, for example a requirement that the supplier is carrying on an enterprise for VAT purposes. Further, when a supplier no longer makes a sufficient amount[9] of taxable supplies, that supplier may be required to deregister.

12.2.2.2   It is important to note that an extractive industries supplier should be considered to be conducting an enterprise for VAT purposes from when, and for as long as, that supplier is carrying on the activities of the enterprise. The classification as a "VAT enterprise" should not be artificially limited only to periods when it is making taxable supplies. In other words, an extractive industries supplier should be viewed as constituting a VAT enterprise during the whole life cycle of the business, including all the phases, not only the production phase.

12.2.2.3   To enable an extractive industries supplier to deduct the input VAT and import VAT paid (and to claim a refund) the supplier should be allowed to register when its activities relating to the extractive industries commence (exploration phase) and should not be deregistered until after its activities cease. This means that the decommissioning/rehabilitation phase should be considered an integral part of the exploration venture, and the supplier should only be made to deregister after this phase is complete. Not doing so might result in an investor not being able to claim VAT refunds.

12.2.3   Issues relating to VAT policy and administration in the extractive industries

12.2.3.1   As a result of the destination principle, VAT should, in theory, have little impact on the extractive industries, since its supplies are generally exported and VAT on inputs is creditable/refundable for extractive businesses. Further, due to its export orientation, government should not expect to raise much VAT revenue from this sector, as revenue is typically raised on domestic consumption. A government's revenue generation from the VAT is, therefore, limited to the amount of VAT on the product consumed domestically, less any VAT deductions on inputs. However, it is notable that, in practice, challenges with VAT remain—particularly in relation to refunds—as explained in this chapter.

12.2.3.2   The exploration and development stages do pose particular challenges for VAT; there is significant capital and other investment (input VAT including reverse charge on imports) but little or no production (output VAT). This ultimately creates a surplus input VAT position which, if not refunded in a timely fashion, will impact cash flow, foreign exchange fluctuations, the cost of investment and associated investment decisions.[10] Refer to box 12.B.1 for some relevant country examples.

---

[9] This is generally the amount of the voluntary registration threshold.

[10] This is, of course, an issue in other industries besides the extractive industries.

12.2.4   Application of VAT to the extractive industries

12.2.4.1   Ideally, a VAT policy for the extractive industries should not be any different from the policy governing any other industry. The key focus should be an efficient and robust VAT framework, which favours government, as well as the investor, and does not leave the investor or government in a position where the payment of funds is delayed.

12.2.4.2   A standard rate of VAT is charged on all inputs, and corresponding outputs are charged at the standard VAT rate on domestic supplies and a zero-rate on exports. Excess input VAT would be refunded at the end of the requisite period. Extractive industries suppliers would be allowed to register at the exploration phase so that the typical VAT input/output mechanism would function. This approach would ensure that domestic consumption attracts VAT while production, once exported, would not attract VAT in that jurisdiction.

Figure 12.F.1:
VAT Policy Options: standard rated inputs

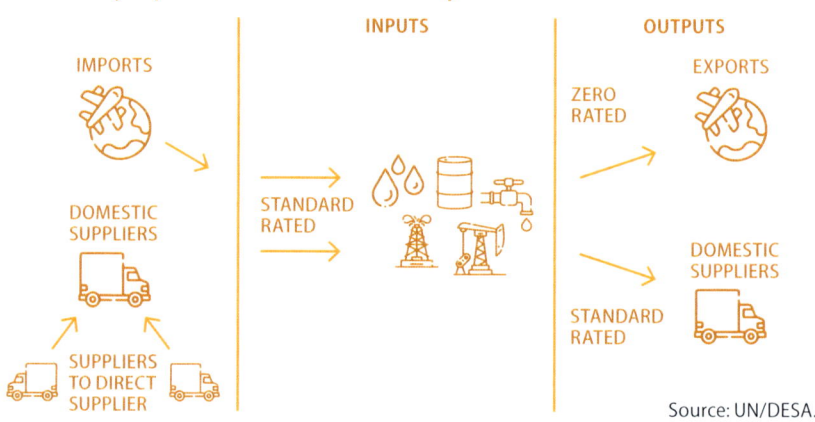

Source: UN/DESA.

12.2.4.3   Although this best practice policy approach is ideal, unless there is a robust system that works to efficiently refund surplus input VAT, it may create cash flow issues for the extractive industries, especially at the early stage of projects where there are no revenues. The administrative requirements in successfully implementing this approach (specifically, the timely payment of VAT refunds) may suggest that alternative policies may be preferable for governments and investors. These alternative policies, together with their advantages and disadvantages, are discussed in the remainder of this section.

12.2.5   Exempt goods and services supplied to the extractive industries

12.2.5.1   One approach to mitigate the issues regarding the timely payment of input VAT refunds is to exempt goods and services typically supplied to the extractive industries. This means that a careful selection of goods and services would be required to mitigate the risk of this exemption being used for goods and services not specific to the extractive industries. Strict audit and enforcement rules would also be required to limit the abusive use of these exemptions.

Figure 12.F.2:
VAT Policy Options: exempt inputs

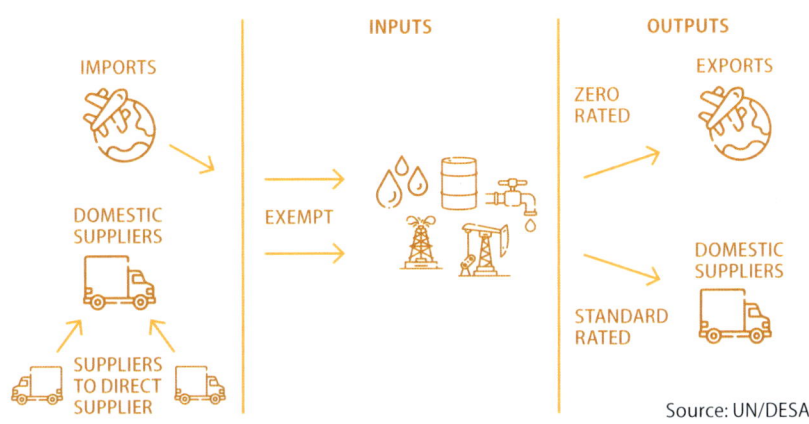

Source: UN/DESA.

12.2.5.2   In the case of imported exempt goods or services, import VAT would not be imposed, meaning no entitlement to an input VAT deduction. Similarly, specific locally sourced goods would be exempt from VAT, and as such there would be no input VAT deduction on the locally sourced goods. The issues regarding the timely payment of input VAT refunds should, with this approach, be largely resolved.[11] It should be noted, however, that a full VAT exemption regime could result in economic distortions. Local suppliers to the extractives would continue to have input VAT on their inputs, which they would not be able to fully offset by charging output VAT on their supplies to the extractive industries. This may result in local suppliers attempting to pass such irrecoverable costs to the extractive industries. There would also be a theoretical risk of creating a pro-import bias in the sense that supplies imported free of VAT could ultimately be cheaper than local supplies with inflated prices. Such a consequence could negatively impact the local economy beyond the extractive industries.

12.2.5.3   Compliance burdens for local suppliers would further increase to the extent that they would be required for distinguishing between exempt supplies and standard-rated supplies. The local supplier would then be required to do an input VAT apportionment, which might give rise to significant compliance costs to the local supplier. The non-neutrality and the non-symmetrical compliance burden, and the accompanying economic distortions that result because of implementing

---

[11] It may be that there are certain types of goods or services used by many industries that are standard rated and an input VAT refund may still potentially arise. It can, however, be expected that this refund would be significantly less.

the exemption, are most likely to constitute detriments that exceed the benefit of resolving the refund problem.

12.2.6 Treatment of zero-rated goods and services in the extractive industries

12.2.6.1   Another approach to avoiding the issues regarding the timely pay-ment of input VAT refunds is to zero-rate the goods and services predominantly supplied to the extractive industries. Similar to the exemption regime discussed at below, there is a high risk, especially in less developed economies, that the zero-rated goods and services would in practice not be used only by the extractive industries. This risk is likely to be higher under this option, when compared to the exemption regime, since locally sourced goods and services of these types would not be subjected to any VAT.

Figure 12.F.3:
VAT Policy Options: zero-rated inputs

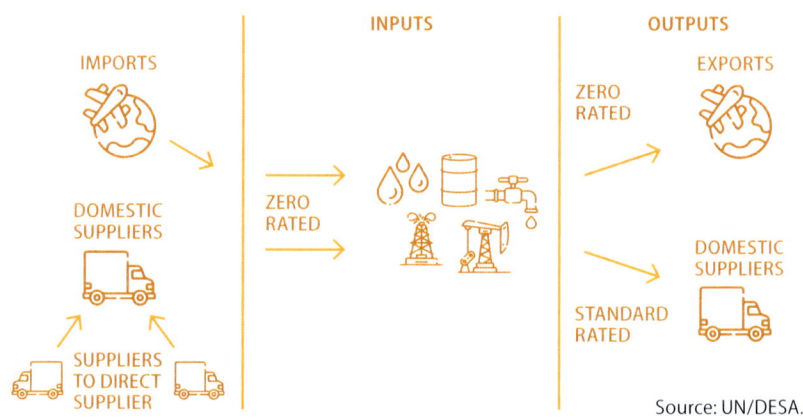

Source: UN/DESA.

12.2.6.2   An issue to consider under this approach is that recovery of any input VAT would effectively be shifted towards suppliers to the extractive industries (they would ultimately be in a refund position). This means the accompanying issues in obtaining a VAT refund within a reasonable period are also shifted towards these suppliers. This would particularly occur in instances where the supplier was not making other standard-rated supplies.

12.2.6.3   In summary, the following issues are likely to arise when goods and services supplied to the extractive industries are zero-rated or exempted:

- A decrease in the neutrality and economic efficiency of the VAT due to the differentiated treatment of goods;

- Non-symmetrical compliance burdens between local registered businesses and extractive industries suppliers;

- An increase in administration and compliance costs of the VAT, without any additional revenue being generated from extractive businesses;

- A decrease in total revenue, due to goods that were previously standard rated and consumed by households now being zero-rated or exempt;

- Bargaining to expand the goods that are zero-rated or exempt by extractive industries suppliers or by other industries to obtain preferential treatment; and

- Increased opportunity for fraud and evasion.

12.2.7   Policies similar to selective zero rating of supplies to the extractive industries

12.2.7.1   In attempting to resolve or address issues connected to the timely payment of VAT refunds, countries may adopt policies in the form of accounting measures that have a similar result to applying a selective zero rating of supplies to the extractive industries.[12]

12.2.7.2   The purpose of such policies would be to promote the effective administration of VAT such that VAT refund positions, should they arise, would not be unduly delayed. Further, such policies would be expected to limit economic distortions and the possible risk of using zero-rated supplies in other industries besides the extractive industries.

12.2.8   VAT on imported services: application of the reverse charge

12.2.8.1   A reverse charge mechanism provides that the responsibility for reporting a VAT transaction moves from the provider to the recipient of a good or service, with the latter required to report both their purchase (input VAT) and the supplier's sale (output VAT) in their VAT return.

12.2.8.2   The reverse charge could also be applied to import services, whereby the requirement to pay and later request a refund could be lifted. The extractives industries would be required to self-assess the amount of import VAT that needs to be paid and claim an input credit in the same VAT return. Similar approaches can be applied to the importation of goods.

---

[12] It may be that there are certain types of goods or services used by many industries that are standard rated and an input VAT refund may still potentially arise. It can, however, be expected that this refund would be significantly less.

Figure 12.F. 4:
VAT Policy Options: the reverse charge mechanism

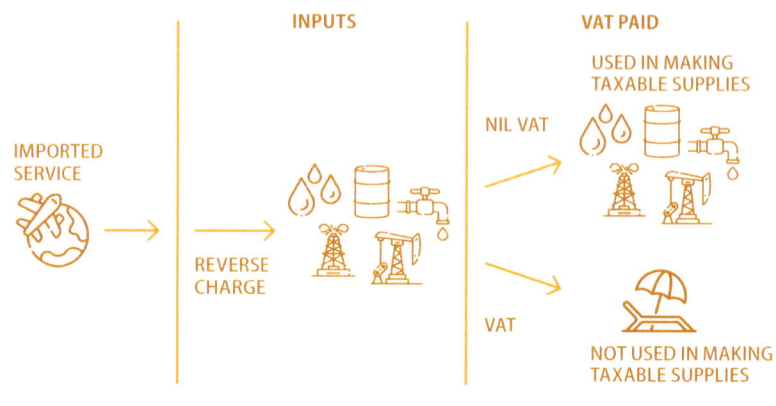

Source: UN/DESA.

12.3 SPECIAL VAT REGIMES FOR THE EXTRACTIVE INDUSTRIES

12.3.1 Deferral of VAT on imported goods: payment time lag

12.3.1.1   A payment time lag would allow deferral of payment of import VAT for a specific period of time by not requiring import VAT upon importation, but providing for a payment of output VAT in a later VAT return. The aim of this approach is to allow registered suppliers to make taxable supplies from the use or supply of the imported goods for a limited time before ultimately being accountable to pay the VAT, thereby easing cash flow constraints.

12.3.1.2   Ideally, this mechanism allows registered suppliers to charge output VAT and then account for the VAT on imports. It should be noted, however, that where the taxable supplies of the importer are zero-rated (as would often be the case in the extractive industries due to exporting their supplies) there would be no output VAT against which the input VAT deduction can be claimed and the issues regarding the timely payment of VAT refunds would remain. Further, if the period of deferral is too short, the cash flow issues would remain.

Figure 12.F.5:
VAT Policy Options: payment time lag

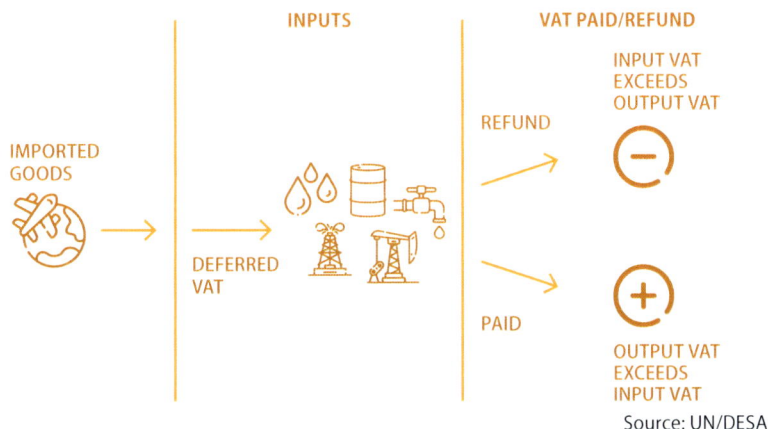

INPUTS   VAT PAID/REFUND

IMPORTED
GOODS

DEFERRED
VAT

REFUND

INPUT VAT
EXCEEDS
OUTPUT VAT

PAID

OUTPUT VAT
EXCEEDS
INPUT VAT

Source: UN/DESA.

12.3.2   Deferral of VAT on imported goods: accounting only, no payment[13]

12.3.2.1   Another, perhaps more preferred, method of deferral of import VAT is to require the importing supplier to simply account for the import VAT on its VAT returns as an "in" and "out." The supplier would show the import VAT as output VAT with an immediate input VAT deduction for the output VAT shown on the return, meaning that a net nil VAT position would arise on the importation of goods.

12.3.2.2   This approach would, however, require robust administration and liaison between domestic tax collection services and customs services, and therefore might only be suitable for experienced tax administrations. Further, good tracking mechanisms would be required to ensure that only eligible items are included within the scope of this provision. It may also be possible to allow the deferral not on specific goods, but rather on all goods imported by a specific entity.[14]

---

[13] This approach is currently adopted by the European Union for all supplies of goods between countries in the Union.

[14] It should be noted that for temporary importation of goods (typically for temporary extractive industry missions) alternative approaches may be preferred to defer the import VAT.

Figure 12.F.6:
VAT Policy Options: netting inputs and outputs

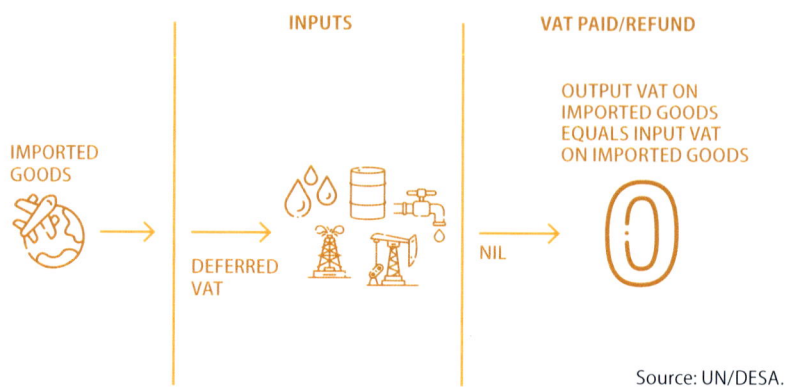

Source: UN/DESA.

12.3.3   Exempt status to the extractive industries suppliers

12.3.3.1   It would also be possible to provide exempt status in relation to certain imported goods to suppliers in the extractive industries. This approach is therefore different to the one discussed in section 12.2.5.1 on exempt goods and services (above) as it does not involve a change in legislation. Upon the importation of those specific goods, a supplier would provide proof of its exempt status to the customs office to relieve the imposition of import VAT. There is, however, an obvious risk of fraud in this approach from importers who falsify their proof of exempt status or import goods under the exempt status of another supplier.[15]

Figure 12.F.7:
VAT Policy Options: exemption for extractive inputs

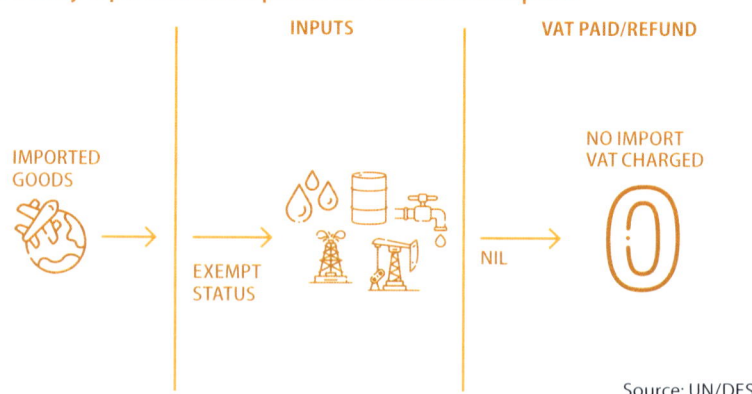

Source: UN/DESA.

_____

[15] Similar risks of evasion that are present under a retail sales tax could arise under this approach. Goods may be removed from the VAT chain and it may be difficult to track this type of fraud.

496

12.3.4   Pure administrative approaches for the extractive industries

12.3.4.1   It should be understood that the majority of issues regarding input VAT refunds to the extractive industries are administrative. These issues can be associated with compliance costs in claiming VAT refunds, administrative costs in auditing VAT refunds, sufficiently budgeting for VAT refunds, and the physical payment of VAT refunds.

12.3.4.2   The following paragraphs outline administrative approaches that could be implemented if a country has the administrative capacity to resolve the issues arising from VAT refunds by administrative measures (rather than policy or accounting) the following:

12.3.4.3   Review of the documentation required to claim an input VAT refund as well as the time it takes suppliers to prepare and submit applications for input VAT refunds and attempt to decrease these documentary requirements. The risk of fraud should also be considered in this process.

12.3.4.4   In budgeting for input VAT refunds, refund forecasting and monitoring tools could play an important role in ensuring sufficient funds are allocated and made available to pay refunds. Such tools would forecast the expected amount of refunds that need to be budgeted for, based on patterns of past refund claims. A dedicated VAT refund account at the Central Bank of a country may also address cash flow problems faced by government in relation to paying input VAT refunds.

12.3.4.5   Ensure that there are extractive industries taxation experts within the general VAT tax administration unit. Not fragmenting the administration of extractive industries allows for harmonized and consolidating procedures in terms of risk management, assessment, payment, appeals and collection, while still recognizing and addressing unique issues of the extractive industries.

12.3.4.6   Offsetting input VAT refunds against other tax liabilities:

(i)   It is possible to allow extractive industries to offset input VAT refunds owed against other tax liabilities. This approach would, however, require that a unified taxpayer accounting debt management system be in place;

(ii)   It is important to note that allowing offsetting of input VAT refunds against other debts besides tax liabilities owed to government may provide for significant administrative challenges. Further, input VAT refunds should not be offset against future tax liabilities, which cannot be accurately established.

12.3.4.7   Implementing a risk-based approach to VAT administration which could see targeted audits and potentially more refunds being paid and with less delay:

i.   Following a risk channeling approach (often referred to as a "green and red channel" approach)[16] that could assist tax compliant suppliers ("green channel") receiving refunds in a timely manner. This could further provide an incentive for "red channel" taxpayers towards increasing compliance in an attempt to be moved to the "green channel." The only significant issue with risk channeling is that the treatment of established and newer VAT suppliers may not be neutral and may favour established VAT suppliers. However, this can also be an effective benefit to government, since new vendors will have an incentive to demonstrate their compliance with VAT requirements as soon as possible;

ii. Post VAT refund audits for lower risk refund claims, meaning that such refunds can be paid more often and with less delay; and such audits could be conducted with support from a team with specific expertise in the extractives industry (see chapter 13 for further information on audits).

12.3.4.8   The country examples in Box 12.B.1 highlight some of the challenges related to VAT policy and administration.

Box 12.B.1

Country examples

Ghana

In 2008, Ghana introduced an administrative measure called the VAT Relief Purchase Order (VRPO) applicable only to the extractive industries. Extractive companies could issue VRPOs instead of paying VAT for certain goods that were specific to the industry. The VRPO system effectively resolved the refund issue for these goods and was similar to providing an exempt status to the extractive industries for these goods.

The VRPO system, however, required additional monitoring to ensure it was not misused. To manage fraud under this system, the Ghanaian tax authority promptly withdrew eligibility to use VRPOs whenever any misuse arose.

The Ghanaian tax authorities stated that they would in due course withdraw the use of VRPOs. This was as a result of systematic and fundamental changes made to the VAT refund system, which allowed quick and efficient processing of refund claims, so that the VRPO system would no longer be required. It has since been replaced by a General Refund

---

[16] This is also sometimes referred to as the "gold and silver status" approach

scheme where investors and beneficiaries who are granted exemptions on domestic taxes, particularly VAT, will pay VAT to their suppliers and apply for refund.[a]

Democratic Republic of the Congo

In 2016, in an attempt to reduce pressure on the domestic currency, the Government of the Democratic Republic of the Congo directed that VAT refunds should no longer be paid until further notice. This saw a significant growth in the amount of refunds due to the extractive industries. In an attempt to decrease the growth in refunds owed, the country temporarily exempted imported goods to the mining industry. The view has been expressed that such an instability in the tax system could have a negative impact on investors' sentiment.[b]

Zambia

In 2014, due to strict export documentary requirements, a large amount of refunds due by the Zambian Government accumulated. The Chamber of Mines of Zambia appealed in a media statement to the Government to refund VAT owed to mines. According to this statement, failure to pay VAT refunds would force the already cash-constrained mining industry to cut back on capital projects, lower production, make suppliers wait longer for their money, interrupt certain corporate social investment projects and diminish the collection of revenue by the Zambia Revenue Authority. This has been commented on as an example of the often unforeseen distortions and negative consequences of not paying VAT refunds in a timely manner.[c]

---

[a] Government of Ghana, *Ghana: Letter of Intent, Memorandum of Economic and Financial Policies, and Technical Memorandum of Understanding* (September 2016), paragraph. 41, available at https://www.imf.org/external/np/loi/2016/gha/091616.pdf

[b] Tom Wilson, "DR Congo's Government Drops VAT on Imports for Mining Companies," in *Mining News Magazine*, available at http://www.miningnewsmagazine.org/?p=992.external/np/loi/2016/gha/091616.pdf

[c] Lusaka Times, *Chamber of Mines urges Resolution of VAT Rule 18*, (September 2014), available at https://www.lusakatimes.com/2014/09/24/chamber-mines-urges-resolution-vat-rule-18/.org/?p=992.external/np/loi/2016/gha/091616.pdf

Table 12.T.3: Value added tax in the life cycle of the extractive industries

Life cycle phase	Key activities undertaken[a]	Input VAT deduction	Output VAT charged	Key issues
Exploration	Locating deposits; assessing commercial and economic viability; and typical 3–10 year period	Yes	No	Surplus input VAT refunds due; opportunity cost on cash flow; and exposure to exchange rate depreciation
Development	Preparation of site for production; establishment of infrastructure; typical 2–4 year period.	Yes	No	Surplus input VAT refunds due opportunity cost on cash flow; and exposure to exchange rate depreciation
Production	Production and commercial processing typical 15–20+ year period	Yes	Yes—Often at a zero-rate as output is largely exported	Generally, 0% VAT on export of outputs; Recovery of input VAT; opportunity cost on cash flow; exposure to exchange rate depreciation; and compliance costs for documentary requirements accompanying export
Decommissioning /rehabilitation	Removal of infrastructure; restoration of site	Yes	Limited amount and often zero-rated as output and infrastructure is exported	Surplus input VAT refunds due; opportunity cost on cash flow; and exposure to exchange rate depreciation

[a] These activities may take longer in practice than the typical period provided in this table.

12.4   PLACE OF SUPPLY AND CONSUMPTION AS APPLICABLE TO THE EXTRACTIVE INDUSTRIES

12.4.1   Issues regarding services

12.4.1.1   Registered businesses in the extractive industries often make use of service suppliers located in other jurisdictions than the extractive site. Further, an extractive site can be located offshore and outside the scope of a country's VAT. This section considers these issues and how to potentially treat them for VAT purposes.

12.4.1.2   Applying the destination principle to services has been problematic due to difficulties in determining the place of supply and consumption of services. Before the recent growth in globalization and technology, there was little need to establish rules relating to the place of consumption of services, as most services were consumed in the country where they were physically performed.

Globalization and technology has resulted in many different proxies used by different jurisdictions in determining the place of supply and consumption of services. These different proxies can create problems such as double taxation, non-taxation and increased administrative and compliance burdens.

12.4.1.3   In the extractive industries, services are often supplied by suppliers located in other jurisdictions. It is therefore important to determine the place of supply and consumption of these services.

12.4.2   General rules relating to the place of consumption of services

12.4.2.1   To avoid double or non-taxation for the supply of interjurisdictional services, VAT taxing rights are granted to a single jurisdiction. This generally means that the services will be exported services and zero-rated in other jurisdictions and charged with VAT in the jurisdiction which holds the taxing rights. Of course, it is first necessary to determine whether a supply of services is interjurisdictional before determining taxing rights.

12.4.2.2   The OECD has set out guidelines that apply the destination principle to internationally traded services.[17] These guidelines as they relate to business-to-business supplies are:

- For consumption tax purposes, internationally traded services and intangibles should be taxed according to the rules of the jurisdiction of consumption;

- The jurisdiction in which the customer is located has the taxing rights over internationally traded services or intangibles;

- The identity of the customer is normally determined by reference to the business agreement; and

- When the customer has establishments in more than one jurisdiction, the taxing rights accrue to the jurisdiction(s) where the establishment(s) using the service or intangible is (are) located.

12.4.2.3   It should be noted that the aim of these guidelines is to allocate the taxing rights to ensure that the value added by these services is taxed in the jurisdiction where the goods and services that ultimately arise as a result of the supply of services will be consumed.

12.4.3   Place of supply of services

12.4.3.1   A further issue is the place of supply of services. Services could either

---

[17] See the *OECD International VAT/GST Guidelines* (November 2015). Available at http://www.oecd.org/tax/consumption/international-vat-gst-guidelines.pdf.

be supplied in another jurisdiction and, therefore, be imported services subject to import VAT, or be supplied in the same jurisdiction as the extractive site and, therefore, potentially be subject to output VAT.

12.4.3.2   Whether the services supplied are imported or domestically provided could also be important for the extractive industries, especially if the reverse-charge rule on imported services is applied. If the reverse-charge rule applies to imported services, the extractive industries supplier may well prefer that the services be regarded as imported services. In the case where the services are regarded as domestically supplied, the extractive industries supplier would be entitled to an input VAT deduction on these services, and issues regarding the timely payment of input VAT refunds may arise.

12.4.3.3   The place of supply is also of importance to the supplier. Generally, if the place of supply of services is in another jurisdiction to that of the supplier, that supplier may be required to register for VAT in the other jurisdiction. This would of course result in a large compliance cost for the supplier.

12.4.3.4   Based on the above, it may be preferable to allow services provided to the extractive industries from other jurisdictions to be treated as imported services.

12.4.4   Place of consumption and supply of decommissioning/ rehabilitation services

12.4.4.1   Services supplied during the decommissioning/rehabilitation phase often give rise to particular issues relating to the place of consumption and supply, since these services are supplied in multiple jurisdictions. These services often involve a planning stage and an execution stage. The planning stage will generally take place at the supplier's place of operation or fixed establishment, often in a different jurisdiction to the extractive site. The execution stage would take place at the extractive site.

12.4.4.2   With reference to the section above on general rules, it is evident that the jurisdiction in which the extractive site is located will have the taxing rights for decommissioning/rehabilitation purposes. Although the customer may have establishments in more than one jurisdiction, the taxing right should accrue to the jurisdiction where the decommissioning/rehabilitation will take place (where the applicable extractive site is located). Due to the service possibly being supplied in two jurisdictions, it may be preferred to treat the entire service as an imported service.

12.4.5   Place of consumption and supply of offshore extractive activities out of the scope of the VAT[18]

12.4.5.1   Some extractive industries activities may be performed outside of the

---

[18] If the extractive site is situated within the scope of the VAT, then no special consideration is required.

territory of a country and may, as a result, occur outside that country's VAT geographical scope.[19] Goods may be imported or locally purchased to be used at an offshore site located outside the scope of a country's VAT and there may also be services supplied at this offshore site. Some goods may also be moved in and out of the scope of a country's VAT, within a short-time period.

12.4.5.2   Once goods are removed beyond the scope of a country's VAT, the removal of such goods would constitute an exported supply and be zero-rated. If goods are imported and thereafter exported to an offshore site situated outside of the scope of a country's VAT, the issue of VAT refunds may again arise and a country may consider the policy and administrative approaches discussed in the section on VAT policy and administration (above). This would also be the case where goods move in and out of the VAT scope within a short-time period.

12.4.5.3   For services physically performed at the offshore site, which is outside of the scope of a country's VAT, the place of supply of the services will not be in any country. The place of consumption of the services would depend on whether the supply of services is directly connected with immovable property situated at the offshore site. If this is the case, the place of consumption would be at the offshore site and no country would have taxing rights on the service supplied.

12.4.5.4   Where the supply of services is not directly connected with immovable property situated at the offshore site, the place of consumption of the services may be argued to be within the country where the customer is located (the extractive industries' onshore establishment). The services will therefore be imported services and the reverse-charge rule should be applied to these services.[20]

12.5   CONCLUSION

12.5.1.1   From a developing-country perspective, while the benefits of having a VAT mechanism in place are clear, the effects of the system not working effectively should not be understated. Investment decisions and cash flow could be affected, and spillover effects on local content could also be a consequence. While the extractive industries should generally not be seen as different to other industries, given their predominant export character, an efficient VAT mechanism along with supporting administration is especially important to these industries. An inefficient system can increase project costs and discourage investment. In particular, VAT for the extractive industries should not be seen as merely a revenue generation tool.

12.5.1.2   Finding the right balance between providing VAT policy and related administration that is attractive to extractive industry investors and also supports growth of the domestic economy would ease perceived barriers to investment. As noted, VAT revenue from the extractives industries is likely to be

---

[19] This is generally 12 nautical miles from the shore of a country.

[20] Refer to the *OECD International VAT/GST Guidelines* for further discussion regarding the place of consumption of interjurisdictional services.

minimal in countries where the industry is largely export-oriented, but inefficient administration of the VAT could provide challenges for continued investment in the industry.

12.5.1.3   From a policy perspective, the ideal approach would be to apply full taxation to this industry. If the full taxation approach is not administratively feasible, deferring the import VAT on capital goods by requiring suppliers to report the VAT in their subsequent VAT return may be preferable. Generally, to protect the domestic market, exemption or zero-rating of goods and services supplied to the extractive industries is less preferred.

12.5.1.4   From an administrative perspective, measures should be put in place to decrease the delay in paying input VAT refunds. These could include an improved risk-based auditing approach and post-refund audits of low risk input VAT refunds. Further, forecasting tools can assist in ensuring sufficient revenue is allocated and available for input VAT refunds. If a taxpayer accounting and debt management system is in place, it may also be beneficial to allow taxpayers to offset input VAT refunds against other tax liabilities.

12.5.1.5   Structured dialogue between government and the extractive industries could also provide for solutions to the issues discussed in this chapter that are tailored to each country's specific context.

Chapter 13

Issues and Generally Acceptable Practices in Auditing Oil, Gas and Mining Activities

13.1   INTRODUCTION[1]

13.1.1   Executive summary

13.1.1.1   The purpose of this chapter is to provide developing countries with an overview of the issues that are encountered in relation to tax audits and to provide insights on generally acceptable practices that can be used by officials in developing countries when auditing the extractive sector. The chapter provides practical illustrations employed by countries in dealing with issues arising from the audit of the extractive industry.

13.1.1.2   The chapter discusses the entire audit process: preparation, planning, execution and finalization and discusses the intricacies of extractive sector audits. The pros and cons of different tax administration organisational approaches are discussed in addition to staff expertise and experience arrangements, as well as the extent of governmental agency cross collaboration that could add value to extractive industry audits.

13.1.1.3   Determining the nature and scope of an extractive industry audit from the outset is important as each stage of the extraction process has its own associated peculiarities and tax issues. A site visit could enhance understanding of the operations being audited and could inform the planning choices and extent of involvement by non-tax office stakeholders such as technical experts. The chapter discusses the typical audit approach as well as providing a non-exhaustive summary of the typical costs encountered at each stage of the extraction process and signposts to various information depositories for comparative information.

13.1.1.4   This chapter also discusses other compliance approaches that can be applied in parallel to audits, including capacity building possibilities, which could, in the appropriate tax environment, improve overall taxpayer compliance.

---

[1] The publishers would like to thank Dr. John Abrahamson and colleagues at the Australian Tax Office for their input to this chapter

13.1.1.5   Finally, this chapter addresses the issue of trade mispricing or actions that could be regarded as deliberate fraudulent/illegal manipulation of revenue and expenditure to evade taxes. Strategies to detect such mispricing activities and any mitigation methods are discussed. The issues discussed are not intended to be exhaustive and will require detailed and extensive analysis in practice given the nature of the extractive industry.

13.1.2   Purpose

13.1.2.1   The aim of this chapter is to provide developing countries with an overview of the issues that are typically encountered during planning and execution of tax audits in the extractive industry. The chapter also provides insights on administrative practices that can be used by tax officials in countries when auditing the extractive sector.

13.1.2.2   The issues discussed in this chapter are not intended to be exhaustive. They will require detailed and extensive analysis in practice given the complex nature of the extractive industry.

13.1.2.3   Although the Chapter predominately focuses on domestic audit practices, Section 13.6 describes bilateral and multilateral audit approaches in recognition of the growing international use of joint audits and simultaneous audits. Section 13.9 further describes audit capacity building programs, such as Tax Inspectors Without Borders (TIWB),[2] that are available for developing countries.

13.1.2.4   Determining the nature of an audit from the outset is important (general vs specific audit scope) as it informs the planning choices and extent of involvement from non-tax office stakeholders such as technical experts or representatives from other Governmental agencies. This paper discusses the typical audit approach.

13.1.2.5   For completeness, Section 13.8 briefly discusses other compliance approaches that can be applied in parallel to audits, which could in the appropriate tax environment, improve overall taxpayer compliance.

13.2   TAX ADMINISTRATION - INSTITUTIONAL AND ORGANISATION STRUCTURES

13.2.1   Overview

13.2.1.1   Traditionally, many countries operated a decentralized model due to the physical proximity requirements that were needed to carry out audits. However, many tax administrations are now moving towards a centralized

---

[2] TIWB is a joint initiative of the UNDP and OECD, designed to support developing countries in building tax audit capacity

model to better implement a shift in compliance strategies towards an integrated compliance risk management model.[3]

13.2.1.2   Functional structures within tax administrations can vary from country to country. Two types of functional structures are discussed below with each having its own merits:

- Hub and spoke model: is a centralized operational model where communication and information are passed from a functional line team (such as auditors) to a centralized "hub" for response coordination and intelligence gathering. The hub can be formalized through reporting lines or operate through internal procedural directives. In practice, the model is adaptive and can be applied in many different contexts such as a main office in a regional capital with several provincial offices in locations across the region. Another application of this model is where tax technical specialists are grouped together (the 'hub') and provide expert advice to generalist tax officials (the 'spoke').

- Matrix model: is an operational management approach where a tax official may have more than one management reporting relationship. For example, a tax official can be a member of a large business audit team and also be recruited into a special project or taskforce team to deliver on unique assignments. This approach allows officers of different expertise and skill sets to be grouped together on a project by project basis depending on the intricacies of the audit work to be undertaken.

13.2.1.3   For specialized industries such as the extractive sector, a dedicated sector specific compliance team is beneficial due to the complexities associated with the interaction between sector-specific tax laws and the commercial operations of extractive companies. For example, it is not uncommon for extractive audits to consider how Petroleum Agreements, Development Investment Agreements and other specific contracts may interact. These agreements may contain specific tax rules or may stabilize tax laws at a particular date which may take precedence over general domestic tax laws and regulations. It is therefore necessary for tax auditors to consider, at the outset of any audit, the relevant tax laws and regulations that are applicable.

13.2.1.4   A dedicated extractives tax unit enables tax officers to develop specific expertise and a thorough understanding of the extractives sector, thereby developing an exhaustive understanding of the interaction of tax and non-tax levies applicable to the sector, including commercial arrangements or any peculiarities associated with specific commodities which are extracted in the specific jurisdiction. For example, the tax provisions associated with gold mining may differ from other minerals such as copper or silver. Officials assigned to an extractives unit acquire skills to manage such differences and assess the deductibility

---

[3] Forum on Tax Administration Information Note – *Working Smarter in Structuring the Administration in Compliance, and through Legislation*, Organisation for Economic Co-operation and Development, p.15

or otherwise of costs reported as incurred (a non-exhaustive summary of some of the typical costs incurred is shown in Table 13.T.3 below).

13.2.1.5   To manage resourcing and ensure a consistent approach to technical issues the dedicated team would typically be able to call on subject matter experts outside the audit team who may be within the tax authority or other Governmental agencies (e.g., experts in financing arrangements, transfer pricing, international tax, technical accounting, etc.). Taking confidentiality and management of sensitive information into account, this allows subject matter experts to support multiple teams and multiple audits.

13.2.1.6   The benefits of a dedicated team to address the unique features of the extractives industry cannot be understated. By way of an example, Table 13.T.1 below sets out, in relation to fiscal depreciation (capital allowances), potential differences between general tax provisions, sector-specific tax rules and fiscal terms in project specific agreements. A dedicated team that is focused on mining and/or oil and gas could help bridge the gap in the application of relevant tax laws and regulations.

Table 13.T.1: Country examples of general vs. specific tax rules relating to fiscal depreciation[4]

Country	Ghana	Zambia	South Africa
General tax rules	Tax depreciation generally on a reducing balance basis with specific rates highlighted in the tax law	Tax depreciation generally on straight line basis with specific rates highlighted in tax law	Tax depreciation (wear and tear) allowance for items not of a permanent nature, on a straight-line basis, with specific rates set out in a South African Revenue Service (SARS) Interpretation Note.
Oil and Gas	5-year straight line basis	Oil and gas follows general tax rules as Zambia is not an oil producing country	100% deduction irrespective of whether the company is in a taxable income or assessed loss situation. An additional deduction is granted for expenditure of a capital nature equal to 100% for exploration and 50% for post-exploration (but preliminary to refining).
Mining	5-year straight line basis	100% deduction for exploration expenditure; 5-year straight line basis for mining operations	100% deduction for exploration expenditure subject to the discretion of the Commissioner for SARS. Mining capital expenditure is fully deductible but limited to taxable income from a mining source. The capital expenditure deduction cannot create or increase an assessed tax loss. The amount of unredeemed capital expenditure is carried forward to the next tax year, when it is deemed to be capital expenditure incurred in that year.

---

[4] For further detailed discussion on the overlay of the various taxes, regulations and agreements, reference can be made to Chapters 2 and 4 respectively on the Fiscal Take and Production Sharing Contracts.

Country	Ghana	Zambia	South Africa
Agreements	Depending on the type of agreement, there are different bases of tax depreciation which may supersede local laws.	None in place	Not applicable

13.2.2   The right staff mix

13.2.2.1   Many tax administrations have a dedicated team dealing with the extractive industry with a mixture of tax officials who have competencies and qualifications, including but not limited to accounting, economics, law, mining engineering and geology backgrounds. Specifically, the tax administration needs officials on the team with industry relevant and applicable professional or academic backgrounds which can provide a strong basis for understanding industry-specific terms. People with experience in the industry are familiar with such terms but the terms may seem foreign to new entrants or those who are not familiar with the industry. This approach helps set up a platform for constructive dialogue, continuous education, and improvement of communication between the taxpayers and tax administrators. Another benefit of this approach is that it is easier to identify potential risk issues and areas to focus on.

13.2.2.2   The digitalization of tax filing systems and use of data in increasing size and volume has also increased the relevance of technology and data analysis skills as complementary competencies to audit planning and implementation.

13.2.2.3   Officials with industry experience of many years often bring invaluable tax memory in terms of understanding the rationale for and background for changes in laws and regulations as well as in tax regimes as set out in specific agreements. This is especially beneficial in tax administrations that have limited experience in dealing with the sector.

13.2.2.4   Finally, it is important to manage long term staff retention and movement, with tax administrations needing to balance benefits that come with staff stability against an over reliance on the experience and knowledge of a small number of tax officials. Therefore, it is critical that tax administrations have processes in place to ensure that the long-term preservation of corporate memory and knowledge sharing practices are established as a priority. Reliance may also be placed on robust information depositories (such as secure electronic databases) for preservation and retention of historical information.

13.2.3   Government agency collaboration

13.2.3.1   Extractive industry participants are often regulated and scrutinized by different government agencies, ranging from and including:

- An industry regulator (overseeing the issue of permits, compliance with laws and reporting)

- Tax administrator (collection of tax and administration of tax rules)

- Ministry of Finance (tax policy development and implementation)

- National Oil or Mining Company (which may exercise oversight but no operational responsibilities. In some jurisdictions, National Oil or National Mining Companies have a stake in operational activities and do not play an oversight role).

    ➢ The oversight role may encompass administration of joint sharing arrangements, administration and distribution of royalties and other non-tax levies.

- Ministry of Mineral Resources/Lands/Mines/Petroleum (licensing and regulation)

    ➢ In some jurisdictions, agencies are in place that are dedicated to specific aspects of extractive operations to the extent that the expenditure on those aspects is considered to be public expenditure.

    ➢ In others, the Supreme Audit Institution may have oversight of cost recovery where the expenditure involved is considered to be public expenditure.

- Any other Ministries or offices that may have oversight of other relevant areas specific to extractives.

13.2.3.2   Within the above main agencies are several subsets that are also in charge of (or have oversight of) the same industry participants. These include for example: forestry resources, water resources, fisheries, sanitation, shipping, customs and excise. In many jurisdictions, these agencies operate within the boundaries of their established objectives and specific governing laws and there could be limited sharing of information to avoid breaching strict privacy and taxpayer confidentiality laws.

> **Box 13.B.1:**
> **An example of inter-agency extractive industry taskforces in Sierra Leone**
>
> Inter-Agency Collaboration in Sierra Leone[5]
>
> Coordination of mining sector policy at the technical level improved considerably following the establishment of the Extractive Industries Revenue Taskforce (EIRT) in Sierra Leone. The EIRT is hosted by the section responsible for Tax Revenue Policy at the Ministry of Finance and Economic Development and includes the Ministry of Finance, National Revenue Authority, National Minerals Agency, Petroleum Directorate and the Extractive Industries Transparency Initiative (EITI) Secretariat.
>
> The EIRT began informally to troubleshoot various issues relating to EITI reconciliation reports. Members of the group found it so useful in terms of sharing information and solving problems that they decided to formalize it and extend its mandate beyond EITI challenges. One achievement of the EIRT was to reduce the export duty on gold to levels more comparable to the other Mano River Union (MRU) countries (Guinea, Liberia, Ivory Coast), which is seen to be the main factor in recent decreases in smuggling and increases in official gold exports.

13.2.3.3   In some jurisdictions, there could be an overlap in information requests to industry participants by each of the oversight agencies, albeit in different forms and using different templates. Where it is legally permissible, cross-agency sharing of previously requested information could improve compliance efficiencies for both the tax administration and taxpayer alike, and is therefore encouraged.

13.2.3.4   In some jurisdictions such as Zambia, this potential overlap has been bridged by the establishment of a central information collation portal whereby taxpayers upload information in pre-determined templates, following which relevant Government stakeholders have access to this portal to download information relevant to their remit. Such an approach could reduce any duplication of information requests or overlap of issues.

---

[5] Natural Resource Governance Institute, Preventing Tax Base Erosion *in Africa: a regional study of transfer pricing challenges in the mining sector.* p23: https://resourcegovernance.org/sites/default/files/documents/nrgi_transfer-pricing-study.pdf

13.2.3.5   Apart from the advantage of reducing the duplication of audits conducted on the extractive industry by each oversight agency collecting the same information, a collaborative approach to information gathering and planning would be of assistance to building and widening the tax office's internal knowledge capabilities, whilst building industry expertise and leveraging from knowledge in other departments.

13.2.3.6   Table 13.T.2 below sets out an overview of Zambia's central information collation portal, known as the mineral value chain monitoring system.

Table 13.T.2 - Overview of Zambia's mineral value chain monitoring system relating to fiscal depreciation

Mineral Value Chain Monitoring System – Case of Zambia				
An Integrated and transparent multi-stakeholder electronic mineral monitoring framework providing consistent data relevant to various government departments and agencies.				
Agencies	System Modules	Input	Output	Benefits
Tax Administration; Mining Department; National Statistics Office; Company and Business Registration Office; Bureau of Standards; Roads Department; Road Transport and Safety Department	• Mineral production • Export permit	• Monthly quantity of minerals produced (own and third party) • Monthly quantities of minerals purchased from third parties • Monthly quantity of minerals sold • Government Mineral Laboratory Assay Reports • Mine Gate and inland weigh bridge quantities	• Production reports specific mineral type • Sold production quantities • Export permits	• Detection of any mineral misclassification by exporters • Improved stakeholder collaboration • Source of third party information for cross checking completeness of information in relation to tax audit reviews • Realtime access to mineral production (including sold quantities) reports • Ease of crosschecking information submitted to Customs Authorities and that submitted in relation to application for export permits • Acts as deterrence to under-reporting/declaration for tax purposes • Quicker compilation of national statistics

13.3 INDUSTRY KNOWLEDGE OF THE EXTRACTIVE INDUSTRY IN THE CONTEXT OF AUDITS

13.3.1 Overview

13.3.1.1   The extractive industry has unique technical and commercial factors and developing specific knowledge is highly beneficial for tax administrations. Understanding the commercial drivers and operations of the business, including each stage of the extractives value chain[6] (exploration, development, production, transport, marketing, selling, and decommissioning/rehabilitation) can help auditors identify accounting anomalies and separate true commercial drivers from tax driven schemes.

13.3.1.2   The extractive industry is particularly sensitive to capital and operating costs. These are the main variables that are largely within the control of the extractive company. Extractive sales are largely dictated by regional or global prices that are outside the control of the extractive company. In this regard, most extractive companies would be considered to be 'price takers'. For these reasons, one of the key commercial imperatives for an extractive company is to be a low cost producer.

13.3.1.3   Each stage of the extractive process is unique in approach and cost base as well as in the tax rules that apply to it. Whilst a basic technical appreciation would be important, understanding the nature and purpose of each stage from a business strategy perspective would also help provide appreciation of the type of commercial costs that can be expected and costs which may otherwise be characterized as uncommercial or tax driven.[7] This may involve gaining an appreciation of:

    a.   Supply chain management and the processes and costs involved in sourcing raw materials, equipment and other inputs.

    b.   The processes involved in refining the mineral and ultimately selling to end customers and where to obtain contemporaneous market benchmarks on those costs.[8]

    c.   How the group funds and manages its financing risk can be informative as to how it would be expected to fund and mitigate financial exposures at a subsidiary level, particularly for transfer pricing risks associated with financing arrangements.[9]

---

[6] Refer to the Introduction Chapter in this manual for an overview of typical extractive industry processes

[7] For example, see section 1.3.3 of the UN Transfer Pricing Handbook

[8] For example, treatment and refining costs for copper concentrate follow industry benchmarks and exact rates can be found in commercial databases.

[9] The Introductory Chapter to this manual and Chapter 9 on financing transactions contain detailed supporting summaries.

d. Familiarity with how extractive material is priced would be advantageous as minerals and hydrocarbons are often traded on public commodity exchanges.[10] A good understanding of the functioning of these markets and the quotation methods is very useful for auditing intra-group prices within multinational enterprises.

13.3.1.4 Industry or subject matter experts in other units within the tax authority could be good sources of reference or background information. In addition, government agencies and other non-governmental agencies provide useful reference points to have a balanced and targeted approach to understanding the extractive industry.

13.3.2   The relevance of site visits in tax audits

13.3.2.1 Undertaking regular site or field information visits is recommended as a means of engaging with the industry and promoting dialogue with field operations. In addition to building an informed awareness of the industry, such site visits, particularly for large and complex taxpayers, enable tax officials to contextualize the scale and size of operations. Further site visits could be useful after a company employs a new business strategy or process (such as investment in, or installation of new equipment), to discuss and understand the associated tax issues.

13.3.2.2 In addition to visiting operations, meeting with staff in corporate office locations is also useful and relevant.

13.3.2.3 Such visits may be undertaken on an information only basis (e.g., to understand any updates or changes in business circumstances), on a relationship building basis or as part of formal tax audits during which auditors verify costs and activities.

• When visits are undertaken in the context of information gathering and learning, and not in a formal audit setting, it helps to promote trust from both taxpayer and administrator perspectives by providing a means of dialogue for understanding differing perspectives and approaches of all stakeholders.

13.3.2.4 Through the site visits and meetings, tax auditors would have an opportunity to, amongst others:

a. Discuss the company's strategic objectives and the potential impact they would have on financials and tax;

b. Enhance taxpayer relationships based on mutual trust and transparency;

c. Understand the size and scale of operations;

---

[10] These include: the Intercontinental Exchange or the Chicago Mercantile Exchange for oil and gas as well as minerals, including gold, silver, copper, and aluminum.

d.   View and verify the capital and other industrial equipment of the company;

e.   Identify key sources of information in advance of commencing audit procedures.

13.3.2.5   Where due to remoteness or other circumstances, physical site visits are not possible, virtual meetings and virtual site walk throughs would be encouraged. Reviewing historic site visit reports that are on the taxpayer's file would be a good alternative in the absence of a physical visit.

13.3.2.6   The tax administration should plan for the site visit and be prepared in advance, having the benefit of the historical information sources and repositories discussed earlier in this chapter. Preparation is key to enable targeted and focused discussions and information gathering. For example, a detailed internal checklist prepared in advance of the meetings would serve as a useful guideline. Similarly, the tax administration may share a checklist with the taxpayer for provision of information. In the same vein, taxpayers could be notified in advance and helped to prepare for site visits and meetings. The tax administration could provide the taxpayer with an overview of their operations, safety and other logistical protocols and requirements. For example, protocols related to underground mines may differ from surface mines.

13.3.2.7   The table below provides a non-exhaustive summary of the types of costs that are typically encountered at each stage of the extractive value chain and are complementary to the summaries in Chapter 1: Overview, the introductory chapter of this manual as well as Chapter 5 of the United Nations Practical Manual on Transfer Pricing for Developing Countries.

Table 13.T.3 Overview of typical costs across the extractives industry value chain

	Mining	Oil and Gas
Exploration	• Applying for licenses • Obtaining/reviewing geological & geophysical data • Surveys • Explosives • Equipment • Technical fees (e.g., geologists) • Study costs • Drilling • Other exploration costs	• Bidding/applying for licenses and contracts • Obtaining/reviewing geological and geophysical data • Seismic surveys • Exploration drilling • Study costs • Other exploration costs
Development	• Community relocation (including compensation) • Freight costs • Infrastructure development • Equipment (e.g., trucks, loaders, dozers) • Surface stripping • Crushing • Chemicals and extraction infrastructure • Other development costs	• Appraisal and development drilling • Downhole and wellhead engineering • Well completion • Production and storage facilities • Evacuation infrastructure (pipelines, vessels, terminals) • Other development costs

	Mining	Oil and Gas
Production	• Infrastructure development • Freight costs • Equipment (trucks, loaders, dozers) • Crushing • Milling • Chemicals and extraction materials • Technical, managerial and administrative services • Refining • Marketing/selling • Other production costs	• Supplies and services • Repairs and maintenance • Secondary and tertiary recovery • Marketing/selling • Other production costs
Decommissioning/ Rehabilitation[11]	• Restoration • Rehabilitation • Other rehabilitation and restoration costs	• Plugging wells • Dismantling wellhead and evacuation facilities • Restoration of the site • Other decommissioning costs

13.3.3 Use of price reporting agency market data

13.3.3.1 In the extractives industry, market information pertaining to commodity prices, quantities, supply and demand data among other information is published by price reporting agencies and extractive sector market research service providers at a fee through subscription, and in some circumstances, limited data can be accessed at no cost.[12]

13.3.3.2 This information can be of great value for undertaking risk and trend analysis or to serve as a basis for audit adjustments as the information represents third party market data on historical and current commodity prices.

13.4 TAX AUDIT PROCESS AND ISSUES

13.4.1 Overview

13.4.1.1 Whilst tax audits of extractive industries can often be lengthy due to the complex nature of the industry, tax officials play a critical role in administering laws, regulations and agreements in a balanced and objective manner. Through tax audits, officials can ensure that correct and fair tax is collected. In the same vein, taxpayers receive tax education where aspects of the law are incorrectly applied and are also assured following an audit, that their tax records are satisfactory and acceptable.

---

[11] Refer to Chapter 14: The tax treatment of decommissioning for detail on tax issues associated with decommissioning/rehabilitation

[12] An example of a cost free repository: https://www.oecd.org/tax/toolkit-on-comparability-and-mineral-pricing.pdf. See Annex 2, starting pg.227 for a summary list of pricing databases.

13.4.1.2   Typical audit processes, i.e., the annual comprehensive risk based audit plan, would differ from jurisdiction to jurisdiction and would depend on the provisions in respective tax laws or tax provisions in specific agreements, as well as on the supporting information and documents to be reviewed. Nevertheless typical audit processes are summarized below and these may be modified to suit specific circumstances:

- Conduct an initial risk assessment or overview of the industry and company/group to be audited. This would help determine the scope and extent of the audit procedures to be undertaken. The outcome of the risk assessment would also bring into scope the number of officers to be assigned, as well as the specific backgrounds and experience that would add value to the audit.

- Review of internal processes and documentation to ensure legislation, supporting regulations and specific agreements are applied. In this regard, it is necessary to determine which specific tax laws are applicable for the audit – i.e., general or specific domestic law, or fiscal terms/laws stabilized by, or set out in, specific agreements.

- Review of taxpayer's reporting and other related compliance to determine taxpayer compliance level.

- Structure of audit routines and work plan for the sector and the benefits of having a well-structured audit process (including step by step guidance on the audit approach). This would include an overview of:

- Agreed audit timelines: start dates and anticipated duration of audit.

- Process for providing information and templates.

- Templates for acknowledging receipt of information and requests for further information.

- Awareness of information and data collection (powers to collect, and impose penalties to mitigate or prevent delays and non-provision of audit information).

- Approach to post audit reporting and conclusions.

- Mechanisms to agree extensions of time for audit reports and/or tax collection (for the taxpayer or the tax authority as necessary).

13.4.1.3   Advance planning is essential for a successful audit. Below is a general overview of a typical audit planning process.

13.4.2   Planning/risk analysis

13.4.2.1   It is recommended that an audit plan and timing of certain field audit activities should be agreed with the taxpayer. This would include the areas of audit, nature of information requests to undertake the audit, personnel at the taxpayer company to assist, and timelines for each stage to ensure the audit is undertaken within a reasonable time frame agreeable to both tax authorities and taxpayers. To ensure a planned approach, comprehensive preparatory work is required and is likely to involve:

- Undertaking a comprehensive risk assessment which aims to identify key risk areas and areas of focus, including potential materiality;

- Identifying an approach to examining evidence (e.g., sampling high value transactions rather than reviewing each transaction). Supporting documents in the working/official language of the operating jurisdiction (or jurisdiction under audit) are beneficial to avoid misunderstanding in application/documentation;

- Reviewing financial statements, and prior year audit reports including past information relevant to the audit that is on file;

- Reviewing submitted compliance returns (monthly, quarterly and annual tax filings);

- Requesting preparatory information from the taxpayer for desk audit review purposes and to augment information already gathered.[13] This may include:

    ➤ A summary of the ownership and funding structure of the taxpayer;

    ➤ Key related party transactions;

    ➤ Detailed Trial Balance and General Ledger;

    ➤ Sales and other agreements;

    ➤ High value imports and local purchases;

    ➤ Other supporting information or questions raised during the audit preparation.

13.4.2.2   Where possible and permissible, auditors are encouraged to liaise with other agencies to ascertain their understanding of the taxpayer's operations

---

[13] Taxpayers should also be encouraged to adopt best practices in dealing with tax authorities. Business at OECD has published suggestions to improve taxpayer engagement with developing countries: https://biac.org/wp-content/uploads/2020/11/Statement-of-Tax-Best-Practices-for-Engaging-with-Tax-Authorities-in-Developing-Countries-Original-release-Sep-2013-1.pdf

and processes and to obtain further information which may help in the planning process. To the extent available, Country by Country reports would be a useful source of information.[14] The OECD's International Compliance Assurance Program (ICAP) and the applicable database could serve as a source for understanding what other countries have identified as audit risks.

13.4.3 Field audit recommendations

13.4.3.1   For conducting an efficient audit in a timely manner, a focused approach, borne out of careful and detailed planning is key.

13.4.3.2   The steps recommended in a field audit, irrespective whether it is undertaken in person or remotely, are laid out in the following paragraphs.

13.4.3.3   An introductory meeting:

- Hold a preliminary interview with key staff to have a high-level understanding of the business operations;

- Introduce the audit team and team leader and also confirm the nature of the audit and expectations;

- Identify staff members who would be involved and would be providing pertinent information;

- Indicate any outstanding information that was requested prior to the site audit and agree on timelines for its submission;

- Take all supporting documents and information, so as not to be dependent on the company and establish professional conduct rules for the field audit (i.e., not to live in company quarters, to avoid conflict of interest).

13.4.3.4   Provide a clear and comprehensive audit information request, based on planning/risk analysis done prior to embarking on field audit. The information request may be regularly updated (keeping duplication of requests at a minimum) to promote efficiency and transparency and to mitigate delays in management decisions; it is recommended that updates are kept to a minimum and should be based on the discovery of new information, not necessarily gathered during planning.

13.4.3.5   Ensure there are regular meetings with the appointed management liaison person to provide progress updates and to discuss and identify information gaps.

---

[14] Some extractive companies publish Country by Country Reports on their websites for ease of reference. Further reference could also be made to the OECD International Compliance Assurance Programme (ICAP), as a potential source of understanding what other countries have identified as audit risks.

13.4.3.6   Ensure that an audit debrief session is undertaken prior to leaving the site. Whilst not necessary, this could include providing an initial overview of key issues noted for discussion and highlighting any key issues that need clarification, including any additional or outstanding information that is required by the tax auditors. The debrief would at a minimum include agreeing next steps and timelines, but may not necessarily involve communicating audit findings (auditors generally need time to review materials and submit them for review within the tax authority). The audit team may also use the debrief to offer the taxpayer some education on issues misunderstood or considered to be incorrectly applied.

13.4.4   Post audit reporting and issuance of audit reports/findings

13.4.4.1   Tax auditors should produce an initial draft report. After an internal review, the tax authority should provide detailed preliminary audit findings to the taxpayer management, including the audit report if necessary. The taxpayer is given a reasonable time frame in which to respond to the preliminary audit findings and also provide further information where necessary before the audit is finalized. Providing the audit findings helps promote transparency and fairness in the audit process. This ensures that a correct tax assessment is issued (if any) at the conclusion of the audit, thereby avoiding unnecessary tax disputes.

13.4.4.2   The response to audit findings by the taxpayer is internally reviewed and in the absence of any disagreement on the explanations and further information provided by the taxpayer, a revised audit findings letter is issued reflecting adjustments made to the preliminary audit findings and initial draft report.

13.4.4.3   In a case where the audit leads to adjustments to the tax calculation, tax assessments are issued after the revised audit letter is issued, or in some cases after an audit settlement is agreed with the taxpayer.

13.4.4.4   Other useful references from the United Nations Tax Committee Handbooks which provide reference points for audit related issues include:

    i.   Chapter 14 on Auditing in the TP Manual;

    ii.   Chapter 2 on Approaches to Avoiding Disputes in the Handbook on Avoidance and Resolution of Tax Disputes;

    iii.   The chapter on transfer pricing issues in this Handbook.

13.5   ROLE OF JOINT VENTURE PARTNERS

13.5.1   Auditors may consider whether costs of a venture are reviewed by a partner in a resources joint venture arrangement and may also consider the terms that govern that review process. If the joint venture terms provide for robust reviews, this may potentially provide support for the basis of pricing used, or the level of shared costs arising. For example, it is a common term of many joint venture agreements that shared costs do not have a mark-up. Other costs may not be audited by the joint venture partners and may require increased focus in an audit.

13.5.2   Where the national oil, national mining company or government agency holds interests in the joint venture, and runs its own audits to protect government interests, the tax administration may rely on audits already undertaken.

13.5.3   In an unincorporated joint venture, one of the partners is chosen as the operator. The operator carries out day-to-day operations and allocates costs to its non-operator JV partners, known as 'shared costs.' Non-operator partners have an incentive to closely scrutinize the shared costs to avoid being overcharged by the operator. Partner-level costs are those that each joint venture partner incurs separately. For example, in most joint ventures, each partner is expected to access finance independently, which means the payment of interest on loans is not cost recoverable. The risk of cost overstatement is higher because these costs are not policed by the joint venture and are likely to be incurred with related parties, which raises the possibility of transfer mispricing. Consequently, governments should prioritise tax audits of separate partner-level costs in addition to reviewing the operator's cost records centrally.[15]

13.6   External assistance in tax audits

13.6.1   Generally, a tax administration's audit function is undertaken by dedicated audit teams charged with the task of auditing the extractive industry. However, in recognition of the varying audit capacity levels and information asymmetries, a number of cooperative initiatives have been developed internationally and at regional levels. These initiatives offer opportunities for collaborative administrative assistance aimed at strengthening the efficiency and effectiveness of audit capacities in respective tax administrations. At the same time, they can enhance international cooperation to tackle tax evasion and avoidance schemes. These initiatives are legally made possible by countries entering into bilateral or multilateral agreements or contractual arrangements depending on the type of audit initiative adopted by the country or tax authorities.[16] The implementation of these initiatives is usually supported by enabling legal provisions for appointing auditors, exchanging information and keeping information confidential. The various audit options that countries can adopt, and their objectives, are highlighted in Table 13.T.4 below.

13.6.2   In addition to audits by local tax authorities, alternative or additional audit approaches that can be employed by the tax authorities include:

---

[15] *Examining the Crude Details, Government Audits of Oil & Gas Project Costs to Maximize Revenue Collection,* OXFAM Briefing Paper, November 2018, p.36.

[16] Reference may be made to the following UN Manuals for further information: UN Model Double Taxation Convention between Developed and Developing Countries and UN Manual for the Negotiation of Bilateral Tax Treaties between Developed and Developing Countries.

- Joint audits;

- Simultaneous audits;

- Outsourcing audits to private audit firms engaged as consultants to the tax authority. This could also include engagement of external subject matter expert consultants as part of tax audit teams;

- UNDP/OECD Tax Inspectors Without Borders (TIWB).

An overview of each audit approach is summarized below:

Table 13.T.4 Examples of external assistance in tax audits

Audit Type	Definition/ Description	Legal Basis	Objective
Joint Audit	The joint undertaking of a tax audit on a specific taxpayer in a country where it is resident/ domiciled by the local tax administration with either a foreign tax administration or any expert personnel that are not employees of the local tax administration. A single audit team is formed under this arrangement.	• DTA • MAAC • TIEA • AMATM • Domestic Legislation • Memorandum of Understanding supported by Domestic Law	To audit specific issues of common interest with the goal of sharing information at the end of the domestic law audits on the matter. The information shared is used to confirm compliance or non-compliance
Simultaneous Audit	The undertaking of simultaneous audits by tax administrations, each in their own countries on affairs of taxpayers where there is common interest on those tax affairs	• DTA • MAAC • TIEA • AMATM • Domestic legislation	
Outsourcing Audit*	Engaging an audit firm or independent auditors on a fixed term contract/arrangement with a specified scope of work. Engaging external subject matter expert consultants as part of tax audit teams.	• Contract/ agreement • Domestic legislation to appoint or delegate powers of the tax administration	• To build audit capacity through on the job training • Deal with specific audit risks which require specialised industry or tax expertise
Developmental Agencies	The assistance provided by tax experts from a different tax administration or former tax officials to a tax administration in dealing with specific tax issue(s) for a given period and scope.	• Memorandum of understanding • Terms of reference • Domestic legislation to appoint or delegate	Enhance capacity building and share experience in dealing with specific audit matters or challenges that a tax administration is facing

Box 13.B.2:
A Practical Spotlight on Outsourcing

Historically, a number of tax administrations in Africa have engaged external consultants to provide audit support. These include the tax authorities in Ghana, Sierra Leone, Zambia, Mozambique and Burundi.

These arrangements have been on a fixed basis with a pre-determined contract length and scope of work. In many cases, these consultants have been from external audit firms, such as the Big 4, or from specialist technical firms. The objective of such outsourcing arrangements is to address a variety of issues which include:

- Expert input into complex business arrangements;

- Capacity building for tax administration staff;

- Independent assessment of key risks and objectives;

- Adding efficiency to audits;

- Access to external databases and resources.

Fee arrangements for outsourced audits have included fixed term fees or a negotiated percentage of additional taxes collected. However, tax authorities should limit the percentage of tax agreements as they risk creating unwarranted disagreements between the government and taxpayers resulting in unnecessary work and delayed results.

With many such arrangements, there are associated downsides, and the ability of the tax administration to limit risks is important to achieving the initial objectives of outsourcing. The consultant should at a minimum have the requisite understanding and experience of extractive industry audits to enable a value-added audit.

The potential downsides such as access to classified taxpayer data by non-tax administration staff could be managed by putting into place specific engagement terms and conditions which include pre-set audit objectives, a mechanism for data collection and management, access to taxpayer files and associated confidentiality limitations as well as post audit handover arrangements.

Whilst the outsourced audit, if planned carefully, may generate gains in the short term for the tax administration, the impact on the taxpayer and long-term tax administration objectives should be managed carefully, especially in audits where consultants are engaged on a percentage of tax collected basis and are motivated as such, to the potential detriment of the long term relationship with the taxpayer. As there is potentially no downside to raising issues, unintended consequences may include disagreements between the government and taxpayers resulting in additional work and delayed results.

It may also be possible to request assistance from other tax authorities, including the provision of temporary secondees. Examples include France providing assistance to Gabon, Australia to Papua New Guinea, and Nigeria to Liberia.

13.7   Audit tools

13.7.1.1   The audit of large enterprises in the extractive industry usually poses a challenge of auditing voluminous and bulk information relating to operations. In order to enhance effectiveness and efficiency in handling bulk data, it is ideal for tax administrations to invest in appropriate audit tools. A non exhaustive list is provided in the following paragraphs.

13.7.1.2   Use of computers/laptops that have large storage size and higher processing speeds.

13.7.1.3   Consider the use of cloud storage to store data for ease of access. Given that taxpayer data is involved, management of the potential for security breaches would be critical. Robust firewalls and other data loss prevention mechanisms are essential.

13.7.1.4   Electronic Audit Software - Use of audit software to extract and analyze large quantities of data; cross checking data reported to tax administrations through various tax returns (VAT/GST, Customs, Royalties); cross checking with data in Country by Country reporting.

13.7.1.5   Data analytics - Tax authorities are increasingly using data analytics to identify anomalies or to conduct exception testing. Examples would include determining an industry trend and identifying outliers as a result; or, determining historical trends and understanding reasons for variances or departures.

13.7.1.6   Use of portable scanners, cameras, and smart phones for gathering audit evidence when conducting site audits.

13.7.1.7   Subscriptions to extractives industry and other databases and institutions providing industry information on costs and commodity prices.[17]

---

[17] An example of a cost free database: https://www.oecd.org/tax/toolkit-on-comparability-and-mineral-pricing.pdf. See Annex 2, starting at p.227 for a summary list of pricing databases.

13.8   Alternative compliance approaches

13.8.1.1   Audits are but one compliance tool that is available to a tax administration. Other tools and approaches that are available to a tax administration to improve compliance in the extractives industry are outlined in Chapter 2 of the UN's Dispute Avoidance and Resolution Handbook[18], including:

- Binding and non-binding guidance and advice provided by the tax administration;

- Advance agreements or forward compliance products that provide certainty for future tax filings of a taxpayer on a particular transaction;

- Cooperative compliance approaches that encourage greater transparency and voluntary compliance;

- Transnational compliance initiatives such as Joint Audits and the International Compliance Assurance Programme (ICAP);

- Enforcement of the tax laws and regulations.

13.8.1.2   Utilising some or all of these compliance approaches can help provide greater certainty, improve engagement and allow a more efficient use of compliance resources for both taxpayer and tax administration.

13.9   Capacity building possibilities

13.9.1.1   In some jurisdictions, a lack of both audit and industry expertise as well as human resources can hinder the effectiveness of tax compliance activities introduced by tax administrations in the extractives sector. This includes compliance programmes ranging from risk assessment, case selection, audit and dispute resolution. Each of these areas requires sector-specific knowledge, experience, as well as information from companies, government agencies, and other jurisdictions.

13.9.1.2   Given limited resources, it is common for tax officials to take a selective and risk-based approach to auditing to direct the use of resources into areas that have the highest risk of non-compliance. Notwithstanding this, many developing countries continue to face shortfalls in capacity to adequately address potential tax risk in the extractives sector. One effective means to close the capacity gap has been to take advantage of capacity building initiatives offered by a number of international organisations and development agencies. Examples[19] include:

---

[18] Dispute Avoidance and Resolution Handbook (Projected Framework): Chapter 1: Introduction and Overview | Financing for Sustainable Development Office (un.org)

[19] Active programs as at the time of publication

a. The UNDP-OECD Tax Inspectors Without Borders initiative;

b. The Base Erosion and Profit Shifting in Mining joint programme offered by the African Tax Administration Forum (ATAF), the Intergovernmental Forum on Mining, Metals and Sustainable Development (IGF) and the Organisation for Economic Development and Co-operation (OECD);

c. The Extractives and Development programme run by Deutsche Gesellschaft für Internationale Zusammenarbeit (GIZ); and

d. The tax authority education programmes run by the International Tax and Investment Center, particularly in countries that are new to the extractives industry.

13.9.1.3   The summary below provides an overview of development areas that may be employed for capacity building, related to improving audit skills and strengthening the understanding and knowledge of the extractive sector, many of which have been discussed in preceding sections of this chapter:

a. Enhancing interviewing skills;

b. Enhancing negotiating skills;

c. Developing data analysis skills;

d. Developing project management skills;

e. Accounting and audit skills – including refresher and possibly certification courses and updates on recent changes;

f. Regular engagements with industry through industry associates – this allows tax authorities to highlight areas of developing concern and hear updates about issues relevant to the industry;

g. Independent industry-led training by industry experts (which may be cost effective for multiple personnel); and

h. Hiring personnel with different experiences and backgrounds (e.g., advisory firms, government departments, private sector).

13.10   TRADE MISPRICING

13.10.1   Overview

13.10.1.1   This section addresses the deliberate fraudulent/illegal manipulation of revenue and expenditure pricing in order to evade taxes. However, trade mispricing can have other motives apart from tax evasion that are beyond the scope of this chapter (examples include money laundering and avoiding capital controls). It should be noted that much of the business of the extractives industry is to produce commodities and sell them at an arm's length price which can be readily determined by reference to externally published sources.

13.10.1.2   Trade mispricing is the deliberate and fraudulent practice of understating exported products - by price, volume, content or all three - and conversely overstating imported products. Trade mispricing occurs not only in domestic markets but also in international trade. Mispricing within a country, referred to as domestic trade mispricing, concerns both developing and developed countries. Whether in developing or developed economies, trade mispricing on the local market is the result of fraudulent behavior by companies to deliberately evade taxes, especially indirect taxes such as VAT or GST. It can range from under/over invoicing of goods sold, to sales that are not reported for tax purposes at all, to fictitious import invoices and/or contracts.

13.10.1.3   This section will focus on mispricing for cross-border transactions related to extractive industries.

13.10.1.4   In the extractive industries, trade mispricing often seeks to minimize the payments of taxes such as excise taxes, export subsidies, VAT/GST, corporate income tax, etc. or to exploit tax incentives offered to particular economic zones and/or industries. This applies to transactions among related parties as well as to deals between unrelated parties.

13.10.1.5   For cross-border transactions, trade mispricing for exports happens in the form of export undervaluation. This usually has a significant negative impact on tax revenue in the form of diminished corporate income tax and *ad valorem* royalties assessed on sales prices. Conversely, imports can be overstated for the purpose of lowering the taxable revenue and/or illegally transferring income out of the country. This is even more so in the case of restrictive control of foreign currencies. In general, mispricing can occur for various reasons and take different forms, including but not limited to, misquoting prices, excessive deductions, or misrepresenting the quantity or type of valuable elements in products.

13.10.2   What are the reasons for international trade mispricing?

13.10.2.1   As noted above, trade mispricing can occur in relation to third party transactions or between related parties or within an MNE. For related party transactions, trade mispricing can be contrasted with transfer pricing where there is a requirement that transactions with related parties apply arm's length prices and where there is potential for genuine disagreements to arise between tax authorities and taxpayers in relation to the price of related party transactions. This is an issue of transfer pricing dealt with in chapter 11 of this Handbook.

13.10.2.2   This section will focus on trade mispricing with non-related parties. Such schemes will involve the use of unreported accounts or other forms of compensation. Although trade mispricing has some similarities with abusive transfer pricing, it is distinctly different in the following manner:

- Trade mispricing involves fraudulent and criminal behavior;

- Trade mispricing does not require the involvement of related parties;

- Trade mispricing can take the form of forged invoices or sales contracts to and from third parties, as well as the undocumented cross-border movements of goods.

13.10.2.3   Motives a company may have to overprice imports or under-price exports or vice versa may include:

- Paying less VAT/GST on imports in the case of misquoting the price (undervaluing) of imports;

- Lowering the taxable profit and payment of income tax in the case of misquoting the price (overvaluing) imports; or

- Transferring revenue out of the country in the case of undervalued exports.

13.10.2.4   The latter case can happen in a country where foreign reserve restrictions are in place and as such would most likely have a twofold impact: i) non-payment of taxes, and ii) deterioration of the balance of payments with excessive outflows of foreign currencies. The consequence of the latter is particularly damaging where trade mispricing occurs in the extractive sector, as developing countries are highly reliant on the extractive sector to contribute to their foreign currency reserves. The foreign currency reserves are in turn used to pay government debts that are typically denominated in foreign currency. The illicit erosion of foreign reserves through trade mispricing therefore can place significant pressure on the solvency of a country's treasury. Table 13.T.5 below summarizes the different scenarios.[20]

13.10.2.5   Another aspect of concern is sometimes classified as a case of mispricing relates to the deliberate non-declaration of the presence of by-products or the deliberate misrepresentation of the content of a certain mineral.

Table 13.T.5 Impact of trade mispricing

Trade	Overinvoicing	Underinvoicing
Exports	Gains for export subsidies	Capital flight, avoiding export tax
Imports	Capital flight, lowering profit tax	Evading import duties

---

[20] Reproduced from Volker Nitsch. 2012. "Trade Mispricing and Illicit Flows." in World Bank: Draining Development: Controlling Flows of Illicit Funds from Developing Countries

13.10.3   Impact of trade mispricing on country revenue

13.10.3.1   The impact of trade mispricing on revenue may be better explained by a simple numeric example.

13.10.3.2   Company C operating in Country X exports a type of mineral valued at US$ 100 million to Company A and receives US$ 100 million; but it declares US$ 85 million in its invoice and accounts, which is 15% less than the actual/real value received by Company C. In other words, Company C officially receives US$ 85 million, and Company A receiving the merchandize will transfer the difference (US$ 15 million) to another unreported account held by Company C. Company C on evidence has deliberately under reported US$ 15 million by deliberately mis-quoting the price of its export. At the end of the year, Company C realizes a profit of US$ 10 million recorded in its filing with Country X's tax authorities for tax declaration purposes. With a tax rate of 30% on income Company C is required to pay US$ 3 million in taxes. If Company C had declared the true value of its exports for US$ 100 million, it would have been required to pay income tax of US$ 7.5 million. This shows that with exports 15% undervalued, Country X loses 60% of its tax revenue (US$ 4.5 million over 7.5 million).

13.10.3.3   This example illustrates the magnitude of revenue loss a country may face when a company fraudulently manipulates the price of its exports by misquoting the price. A comparable effect would occur if the price of its imports (machinery or services) were to be overstated. The potential effect on tax collection and country foreign reserves is detrimental. This demonstrates the negative impact of trade mispricing in extractives industries in developing countries.

13.10.3.4   Whilst the issue occurs in practice, issues arise as to how to value the resulting impact. More important is the issue of how to prevent its occurrence from a front office compliance and an audit perspective. Some experts have argued that there is no single variable more important in determining the revenue of a mineral producing country than the price of the mineral.

13.10.3.5   Tax authorities are encouraged to closely monitor price data on global commodity market exchanges to detect changes in price that may help benchmark the price paid for the local production and to strengthen the technical skills of their compliance officers.

13.10.4   Detecting, identifying and auditing trade mispricing

13.10.4.1   With regard to mispricing with non-related parties, broader initiatives are required such as improving the exchange of information and cooperation between customs authorities and other authorities in different jurisdictions.

13.10.5   Use of benchmark and reference prices for tax collection purposes

13.10.5.1   Tax administrations in many countries, developing and developed alike, have used quoted prices from reputable agencies to adjust the value of export volume for tax calculation purposes. Some difficulties can arise, however. Often minerals are traded in intermediary forms such as blister copper, pig iron and ore concentrate, but the quoted price is for the refined metal (quoted metal). In such cases, the reference price needs to be adjusted by deducting treatment and refining costs. Other elements to consider while computing the benchmark price include the quality or grade of the mineral, delivery dates, currencies, freight costs, among other things. It is important to use renowned sources for reference prices.

13.10.5.2   Understandably, this is by no means an easy task, as the price index may not reflect the grade/content of the raw mineral extracted. This may involve some technical testing. For a country endowed with substantial natural resources, it may be worthwhile to develop the required expertise within the tax administration. Selected consultancy firm expertise or recourse to advisory services from some development agencies may be an option. The exchange of information clause, especially between countries with a Double Tax Convention can be a useful tool to detect suspected cases of mispricing.

13.10.5.3   In Norway for instance, the Petroleum Price Board (PPB) sets the reference oil price to be used in calculation of taxable income. The PPB meets every quarter and sets a daily norm price for each oil field to be applicable to the calculation of taxable income for the previous quarter. Companies may appeal the set norm price within 30 days. Some other oil producing countries, including Angola and Indonesia, have also adopted measures to value oil at a price set by government agency for tax valuation.

13.10.5.4   In instances where the commodities are sold below market prices, it is necessary to document all data and inputs that account for such low value. For instance, this may happen when a producer sells to a trader at a deep discount to account for other aspects of the mining business such as prior provision of capital, production risk, processing functions, etc. Long term contracts with price included also exist and, in many cases, the price may be defined or pegged against variables such as exchange rates or content of metal. Such deals need to be scrutinized by the tax authority to make sure they are economically justified.

13.10.5.5   In Laos PDR, to prevent mispricing the Ministry of Energy and Mines sets a reference price based on the London Metal Exchange (LME) price for copper to assess royalties payable to the government on copper production. The reference price is based on the determination of the content of the metal in the mineral, the transport, insurance, and handling costs and other inputs.

13.10.6   Source of data for monitoring and price adjustment in extractive industry transactions

13.10.6.1   Another challenge for tax authorities auditing and identifying trade mispricing in the extractives industries is the development and maintenance of a reliable database of prices, marketing costs, level of royalties, across the value chain. For countries substantially endowed in natural resources a long-term strategy to build a national repository of strategic information may be worth the cost. This can start by collecting and assembling already existing information from various national resources such as the Ministry of Mining and Oil and Gas, the Customs and Revenue Services and environmental agencies.

13.10.6.2   One of the hurdles in this endeavour might be the aggregated nature of official statistics. For instance, the export of a given metal might be recorded as one category without any distinction according to the grade (purity or content percentage) of the metal, rendering comparisons almost impossible. However, at a national level, the major players (for 80% of export of a given mineral) are always well known but few. Therefore, their transactions can be identified and recorded at a granular level. Some ethical issues on how to handle and protect individual company data will need to be addressed.

13.10.6.3   Regional Economic Blocs and other international organizations can also be another source for comparability data. For long term strategy, those regional and global institutions may assess the potential for building a global database for shared usage.

Chapter 14

The Tax Treatment of Decommissioning

14.1   INTRODUCTION

14.1.1   Executive summary

14.1.1.1   This chapter covers the tax treatment of decommissioning, remediation, closure, and rehabilitation[1] costs for mining and oil & gas projects. Such decommissioning is required under a wide range of domestic laws, international agreements, and voluntary guidelines. Decommissioning requirements may be mandated by law or by the agreement under which the extraction activity has taken place and may be intended to meet a number of goals.

14.1.1.2   To consider the tax treatment of decommissioning costs, it is necessary to understand the environment in which those costs will be accrued and incurred. This chapter therefore first addresses the broad principles behind a government's regime for decommissioning and considers the actual work that needs to be done to achieve local, national, and international requirements. It then discusses methods by which responsibilities to carry out such work are assigned, and the different contractual and legal frameworks which govern the relationship between the host state/resource owner and the investor involved with the extractive activity.

14.1.1.3   Building on this legal and commercial background, the chapter then examines different models for funding decommissioning work, and the methods by which costs can be estimated. It examines three key models and the direct tax treatment of each such model. The models represent choices that can be made by a country in designing its tax regime for the extractive sector, and each model could potentially distort the decisions made in relation to decommissioning. These potential distortions are identified and methods to address adverse distortions under each model are discussed.

14.1.1.4   The two main extractive industries are mining and oil & gas; within each of these categories, there is a range of technology requirements depending on the resource to be extracted, its location (e.g., onshore or offshore) and the facilities needed to process the extracted resource. Such facilities may require large multi-year capital investments in infrastructure or access to additional inputs for processing the output of natural resource projects. As the mines and the oil and gas fields become depleted, the associated facilities require decommissioning.

---

[1] Hereafter referred to as "decommissioning costs" for ease of reference.

14.1.2   Purpose

14.1.2.1   Decommissioning is a complex multi-disciplined process with an overall timescale normally lasting several years, requiring the management of diverse issues, and involving international and government agencies, mining or oil & gas producing companies, third party contractors, local communities, and non-governmental organizations. The purpose of this chapter is to outline the processes involved and the tax implications of these processes.

14.1.2.2   There are many thousands of mines and oil & gas fields in operation worldwide which will need to be decommissioned, including 8,000 offshore oil and gas installations. The Oil and Gas Authority in the UK has indicated that the decommissioning cost on the United Kingdom continental shelf is around GBP 49 billion.[2] The very high costs to decommission such facilities will reduce the net profits of the private sector. Governments will correspondingly collect less income and/or profit taxes as a result of decommissioning obligations.

Decommissioning is part of the life cycle of an installation, as illustrated here in the case of mining and below for oil & gas. Within that life cycle, the financial and technical planning of decommissioning often receives insufficient consideration during the planning, design, and operation phases of these facilities. This has led to many unforeseen issues and challenges, as mines and oil & gas fields reach the end of their economic life.

Fig. 14.F.1. Mine closure framework

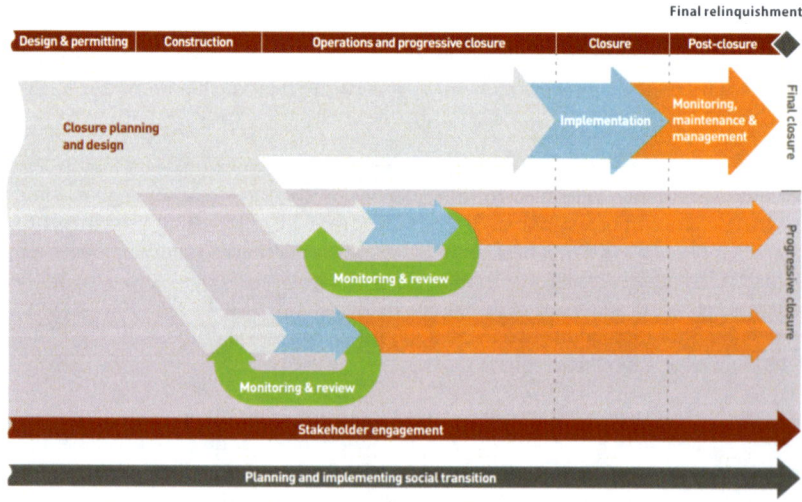

Source: OGUK

---

[2] The UKCS Decommissioning 2019 Cost Estimate Report, available at https://www.ogau-thority.co.uk/media/5906/decommissioning-estimate-cost-report-2019.pdf

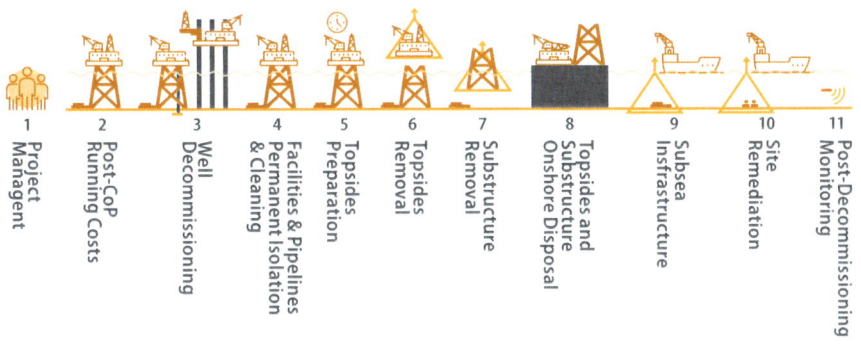

1. Project Managent
2. Post-CoP Running Costs
3. Well Decommissioning
4. Facilities & Pipelines Permanent Isolation & Cleaning
5. Topsides Preparation
6. Topsides Removal
7. Substructure Removal
8. Topsides and Substructure Onshore Disposal
9. Subsea Insfrastructure
10. Site Remediation
11. Post-Decommissioning Monitoring

Source: ICMM

14.1.2.3   There is also a legacy of mines and oil & gas fields that have already been closed and decommissioned in the last century but were not properly remediated and which as a result today are creating environmental and risk issues, as there are no clearly responsible parties and/or no funds reserved to address the decommissioning issues. Furthermore, these issues can foster a negative opinion and reputation of the industry and cause communities to oppose plans for new extractive industry operations.

14.1.2.4   The decommissioning phase must comply with sector law and regulations, both national and local, and/or the terms in the lease or contract. Consultation with impacted local communities will also be necessary. Typical steps to comply with these requirements are:

- Clarification of the laws, regulations and guidelines applicable to the decommissioning of the facility;

- The removal or conversion of infrastructure and rehabilitation of land;

- In the case of mining, the stabilization of open pit or underground workings (foundations, mine shafts, buried pipelines, etc.);

- Rehabilitation of tailings, rock stock-piles, etc. from the mines, and removal of drill cuttings, shell mounds, wells, etc. from the oil & gas operations;

- Management of surface and groundwater and air quality during decommissioning activities;

- Post-decommissioning monitoring to ensure that potential environmental issues are effectively managed;

- Transfer of liability, for example on reversion of ownership to the state or as a result of repurposing of land to its next use; and

- Recognition of residual liabilities.

14.2   DETERMINING DECOMMISSIONING PRINCIPLES

14.2.1   Key drivers

14.2.1.1   The key drivers which affect the decommissioning of mines and oil & gas facilities include:

1. Politics, public concern, and reputation at a local, regional and national level;

2. National and international legal requirements;

3. Contractual obligations assumed by the investor or licence holder (hereafter referred to as the investor);

4. Cost and economics;

5. Taxation framework;

6. Technical feasibility;

7. Health, risk, safety, and security;

8. Environmental impact;

9. Socio-economic transition of the land to its next use, including impacted community aspects; and

10. Requirements of next users of the land plus users of adjacent land and the sea.

14.2.1.2   The above listed elements are not ranked in order of importance, and policymakers should decide the weight to be given to each element based on the economic conditions and policy priorities of their own country for an overall decommissioning regime. Further, within that national approach, it is recommended that the ranking of each facility in the country against these criteria should be carried out on a case-by-case basis.

14.2.1.3   The political and community impacts of the decommissioning of facilities of significance in a community make decommissioning more difficult. There are often profound economic consequences on local communities or host nations in association with mine shutdown and the decommissioning of oil & gas facilities. Environment, sustainability, health, and security (ESHS) issues may be especially complex in the social context and provisions may have to be made for retraining of the workforce and the development of sustainable economic alternatives to mining and oil & gas activities, or the management of reduced-scale and downsized facilities. This also triggers intense and detailed scrutiny of the decommissioning process by the affected communities and by the local and national government.

14.2.2   Decommissioning issues in mining vs. hydrocarbon operations

14.2.2.1   Mining operations tend to impact significant areas of land and hence the decommissioning work needed can be extensive, particularly in open pit mines.[3] For example, once mining finishes, the following, as well as other activities, might be undertaken:

- Waste dumps profiled to further stabilize them against erosion;

- The tailings storage facilities and waste rock dumps covered with a layer of clay to prevent access of rain and oxygen from the air, which can oxidize the sulphides to produce sulphuric acid;

- Landfills covered with topsoil, and vegetation planted;

- Dumps fenced off to prevent livestock denuding them of vegetation;

- The open pit surrounded with a fence, to prevent access, and allowed to fill up with groundwater; and

- Supernatant water on tailings storage facilities (including dams) left to evaporate, then the facility is capped to stabilize it.

14.2.2.2   The nature of the above activities can, depending on the nature of the mine, require that these activities be undertaken at the end of the useful life of the mine, rather than in stages as the mined resource is depleting.

14.2.2.3   Oil & gas operations may have an impact on areas of sea as well as land and, as with mining, require proper assessment and decommissioning needs to be executed.

14.2.2.4   The nature of traditional onshore and offshore upstream exploration and production ("E&P") i.e., oil & gas operations, results in a smaller footprint than that of most mining operations. Hence, the scale of land rehabilitation, re-vegetation and other reclamation activities associated with mining does not typically apply to upstream hydrocarbon operations. Furthermore, part of the decommissioning can be undertaken in stages, rather than waiting for the end of the life of the field. Notwithstanding these generalisations, it should be noted that some unconventional oil & gas projects have characteristics which bear closer resemblance to mining projects in terms of their economic profile and, in some cases, arguably, the environmental footprint (e.g., oil sands).

---

[3] For underground mines, decommissioning work may be significantly less due to lower volumes of waste rock and tailings. Furthermore, the removal of plant and infrastructure is not always part of a rehabilitation programme, as many old mine plants have cultural heritage and value.

14.2.3 Decommissioning phases

14.2.3.1   Decommissioning phases of mines and oil & gas fields comprise numerous complex and costly activities such as:

- Clarification of the sector and national law, regulation, and guidelines applicable to the decommissioning of oil & gas facilities (onshore or offshore);

- Interpretation of law and regulations to produce environmental, safety and technical "Rules for Decommissioning";

- Development of the case-specific decommissioning option, evaluation and selection process, typically in consultation with regulators and impacted communities;

- Execution of a formal public and government review of the decommissioning option selection process and outcomes, where not already provided for under statute;

- Preparation of decommissioning engineering, permitting, project execution and dismantling, and removal of structures used during resource exploitation;

- Implementation of remedial measures to manage ESHS issues remaining from operations or resulting from cessation of operations and decommissioning activities;

- Restoration of the site to an agreed-upon use and quality in line with the expectations of government authorities, relevant stakeholders, and nearby communities;

- Final survey and verification;

- Achieving project signoff by government; and

- Assessment of any future liability, considering any agreed transfer of liability to the next user of the land (in the case of mining).

14.2.3.2   A number of the above workstreams are ongoing over the life of an operation, as the decommissioning plan is regularly refined and updated to ensure regulatory and legal requirements are taken into account. These then assume greater prominence during the decommissioning studies phase of an operation (i.e., 0-10 years before cessation of operations) as detailed health, safety, environmental and technical regulations would need to be considered.

14.2.3.3   As many of the existing mines are nearing depletion or the economic limits of extractability, and oil & gas fields are in decline, decommissioning activities are expected to increase. This decommissioning process will result in a complex sustainability issue which is part of the natural life cycle of a mine or an oil & gas field.

14.2.3.4   Planning for the decommissioning process should begin during the early phases of the project life cycle, incorporating environmental concerns as well as health and safety issues and the socioeconomic needs of the nearby population. Starting the planning requires clarity over who will be responsible for what. In the best cases, there are laws, regulations, and contracts available that clarify this; however, this is not always the case. Engaging bilaterally to agree on these issues as early as possible will help improve clarity and support a clear environment for investment decisions.

14.2.4   Approach to a tax policy framework for decommissioning

14.2.4.1   This chapter recommends that policy makers utilize the following approach in determining decommissioning policy:

1. Establish principles of decommissioning from a governmental perspective;

2. Design the regimes for delivering decommissioning principles;

3. Understand and manage the risks from the interaction between the tax regime and decommissioning; and

4. Consider the recommendations made in this chapter on mechanisms to resolve tax issues.

14.3   CONTRACT STRUCTURES AND FISCAL REGIME DESIGN

14.3.1   Legal frameworks

14.3.1.1   There are many different legal frameworks which govern the relationship between the host state/resource owner and the investor tasked with developing the natural resource. These include concession agreements/licensing regimes, production sharing contract (PSC) type regimes and service contracts.

14.3.1.2   Conceptually these frameworks can each offer a variety of different fiscal 'levers' which can operate to share the risks and rewards of projects between the parties. These levers include, but are by no means limited to:

•   Signature bonuses;

•   Production bonuses;

- Royalties;

- Profit based taxes; and

- Profit sharing with cost recovery **mechanisms.**

14.3.1.3   In this chapter, references to 'tax' and 'taxation' should be taken as references to all forms of payments received by the host state/owner of the resource in return for the development of its natural resources, including production sharing, and references to the "fiscal regime" are to the legal and economic framework which determines the taxes and other forms of government share due. However, since taxes under revenue-based mechanisms do not commonly respond to costs, this chapter necessarily focusses on the way decommissioning expenditure is reflected (i.e., deducted) in the calculation of profit-based taxes/ profit sharing and cost recovery calculations.

14.3.2   The broad decommissioning regime and decommissioning principles

14.3.2.1   This chapter sets out the principles behind a government's regime for the funding of decommissioning into which the taxation rules will need to fit. These are included since the taxation rules that are best for adoption will depend critically on the mechanism by which governments choose to fund decommissioning.

14.3.2.2   The following guiding principles are used within this chapter when considering the precise design of the tax regime—i.e., that the tax regime should not undermine any of the principles below.

- Governments should recognize the decommissioning liabilities of a resource project, which should be explicit and visible at the start of the project life cycle, and the corresponding decommissioning plan and cost estimates should be updated regularly during the project life. These include both discrete liabilities and residual liabilities.

14.3.2.3   The reason why this is important is that the costs (and risks of uncertainty) relating to the decommissioning liability will be factored into the decision-making of the investor(s) and hence the government will have lost value unnecessarily if the liabilities it ultimately imposes are significantly different from the prudent assumptions of the investor. Investors may be expected to seek reassurances from governments in this regard. In the UK for example this is done in the form of a Decommissioning Relief Deed, which is a contract between the government and companies operating in the UK and UK Continental Shelf, to provide confidence on the tax relief they will receive when decommissioning assets. This is further discussed under Model 1 below.

14.3.2.4   Where the liability for decommissioning lies should be the choice of the government of the resource state—the government should not unwittingly be left with the liability to perform decommissioning. Roles and responsibilities for decommissioning should be clearly defined at the inception phase of extractive projects, i.e., at the time the lease or contract is originally awarded. These should include:

    a.   Responsibility for execution;

    b.   Responsibility for costs;

    c.   Stewardship of decommissioning; and

    d.   Rules for transfer of liabilities on transfer of ownership of projects or assets (including relinquishment of land to government).

14.3.2.5   This will allow all parties to understand their roles and to plan accordingly.

- Rules should have enough flexibility to enable a range of technology choices and be responsive to project needs, recognising that technology choices can change over time. The overall decommissioning regime should not constrain the opportunity to take advantage of improvements in technology. Rules that lock participants into technologies early are likely to result in a sub-optimal choice of decommissioning outcomes once the decommissioning starts.

- Governments should develop decommissioning policies bearing in mind national socio-economic, environmental, finance and governance impacts. Management of the regime should encourage a "whole of government approach" (which should include the national oil company where present)—as the agreement of regulators on the policy approach is essential for efficient oversight and management of the decommissioning process. Government and the extractive company should also have a clear strategy for managing conflicts in priorities (e.g., between costs of full removal versus alternative solutions).

14.3.2.6   The choices for decommissioning will have a wide range of impacts so it is important that the decisions are coordinated across the relevant government departments.

14.3.2.7   As an associated point, developing countries and regional and international organisations should strive to build capacity on decommissioning matters and share knowledge among countries.

14.3.3   Choosing who is responsible and who should pay

14.3.3.1   There are two key decisions that are needed in determining the decommissioning regime and these will critically impact the tax rules applicable to decommissioning expenses. These are:

- Who has responsibility for decommissioning, such as:

  - ➤ The government;

  - ➤ The investor; or

  - ➤ Shared between the investor and the government.

- Who pays for the decommissioning, such as:

  - ➤ The government pays for it all;

  - ➤ The investor pays an agreed amount;

  - ➤ The investor pays an agreed fraction; and

  - ➤ The investor pays for it all.

14.3.3.2   Typically, the investor will pay for the decommissioning. However, a secondary effect can arise in two circumstances. First, where the profits from the licence activities are subject to a profit-based tax, the costs of decommissioning, as expenses of the business, will reduce the overall taxable profit as compared to a case where such costs are not required to be incurred, but it should be noted that tax relief may not be effective if costs are incurred after the operation has ceased and losses cannot be carried back or otherwise offset. Similar considerations may apply in relation to cost oil under a PSC, depending on its terms.

14.3.4   Funding decommissioning

14.3.4.1   The next question arising is how the decommissioning is going to be funded. For an investor's share, in essence, there are three key options:

1.   Decommissioning costs funded as the underlying activity occurs, without any security provided by the investor;

2.   Decommissioning costs funded as the underlying activity occurs, with security, in the form of:

   • Assets pledged (including cash);

   • A parent company guarantee; or

   • A letter of credit from a bank.

3.   De-commissioning costs pre-funded during the operation phase via contributions into a fund owned by the government:

   • Funds earmarked for decommissioning activity (i.e., ring-fenced from the general budget); or

• Funds not earmarked (become part of the general budget);

• Independent fund per project; or

• Independent fund per investor;

• Held outside the investor (e.g., in escrow);

• Within the investor (not ring-fenced).

14.3.4.2   These options can combine with the options set out in this chapter to create a complex environment, such that the options chosen by two countries can differ significantly. They raise a number of operational challenges.

14.3.4.3   The government will also need to consider how it would fund its share of those liabilities which could arise through state participation in decommissioning and/or national oil company participation in the investment. In addition, and as noted earlier, even without direct participation, income-based taxes to the government will be reduced given higher costs, and lower or no production, during periods of decommissioning. In many cases, losses will be incurred during such periods, and thus refunds of prior taxes paid may be due, triggered by the carrying back of losses from the decommissioning. Broadly, this may be met out of current period tax receipts or reserves which the government may hypothecate or commit into a specially designed fund.

14.3.4.4   Similar questions arise in relation to accounting and tax provisions. Given the above, the fiscal regime will need to consider:

•   Whether contributions to the fund are tax deductible when made, or at some other time (e.g., when the fund spends the money);

•   Whether tax is imposed on drawings from the fund and/or any return of surplus and release; and

•   How earnings on the fund itself **are taxed (or exempt from tax).**

14.3.4.5   These and other tax issues are discussed in the next section.

14.3.4.6   In relation to funds, the following questions arise:

a.   How much should be contributed into the fund?

b.   What is the mechanism for withdrawals from the fund?

c.   On what basis should the obligation to fund be imposed?

d.   When should companies pay into the fund?

e.   What companies should pay into the fund? (is this just the investor?)

f.   What can be contributed into the fund (e.g., profit oil rather than just cash)?

g.   What happens in the event of a:

• Funding shortfall; or

• Funding surplus; and

• What currency is the fund?

14.4   TAX POLICY CHOICES: COMMON MODELS

14.4.1   Overview

14.4.1.1   The basic choices for providing a tax deduction for decommissioning costs are as follows:

• Provide a tax deduction when cash is expended on decommissioning;

• Provide a tax deduction when decommissioning is accrued; or

• Provide a tax deduction when decommissioning is pre-funded.

14.4.1.2   These options are considered in more detail below. They are all seen in practice, as shown by the examples in the chart below. Sometimes the choice of Model 1 or 3 may be at the option of the taxpayer, as seen below.

Table 14.T.1: Examples of countries adopting models 1 to 3

Tax treatment/ model	Deduction upon	Example countries
1	Expenditure	*Oil & gas:* Australia, Denmark, Norway, South Africa, and the United Kingdom. *Mining:* Australia, Canada, Chile, Peru, South Africa, USA and Zambia.
2	Accrual	*Oil & gas:* Netherlands and Spain (by election). *Mining:* United States and Spain (both by election).
3	Contribution to fund	*Oil & gas:* Ghana, India and Mozambique and South Africa. *Mining:* Canada, South Africa and Zambia.

14.4.1.3   Additional tax questions arise in relation to payments for security (e.g., letters of credit) such as how/when to:

• Provide a tax deduction for costs of obtaining security; or

- Provide a tax deduction if security is used (requiring the security issuer to obtain reimbursement from the taxpayer).

14.4.1.4   Again, the answers to these questions are likely to vary depending on the type of security.

14.4.1.5   In addition to the questions of the timing of deductions for decommissioning costs, there is also the valuation of the costs of decommissioning. The relevance of this will again depend on the model used, since estimates of costs will of course be harder to establish than costs that have been incurred.

14.4.1.6   In considering any of the options, the assumption has been made that if the tax treatment is understood by all parties upon entering into the licence/contractual agreement, then the overall "government tax share" (i.e., the overall amount of tax and other amounts payable to the state) will adjust to offset differences in tax treatment. Hence the key concern should be to ensure that any regime that is chosen does not create incentives that run counter to the decommissioning principles. Choices that merely change the timing of tax deductibility for decommissioning costs do not need to affect the overall amount of government take. On the contrary, as noted above, a well-designed fiscal and decommissioning regime should optimise the level of government share in the context of the appropriate sharing of risks for the exploration and development (including decommissioning) of a particular resource between the state and a company.

14.4.2   Model 1 — providing a tax deduction upon expenditure

14.4.2.1   Under this system, a tax deduction is only provided on a cash basis, leaving no tax incentive for the taxpayer to pre-fund its decommissioning. This means that there will be a greater need for government to ensure that funds are available at the time of decommissioning. This therefore encourages the use of security.

14.4.2.2   This is the simplest mechanism as the expenditure incurred on decommissioning can be verified against an agreed decommissioning plan or where such a programme has not been prepared and/or agreed (i.e., due to the decommissioning works being undertaken *mid-life*, at which point it may not be customary to have a fully developed decommissioning plan in place), potentially by reference to some other form of government test, condition, or established process. Expenditure should only be allowable when it is clear that the work has been performed and the costs actually incurred. There will be other questions that need to be addressed, such as whether costs are general expenditure rather than decommissioning costs and to which project the particular element of decommissioning expenditure relates (which is particularly important if the projects are taxed at different tax rates).

14.4.2.3   This also provides a cash flow advantage to the government since it will receive all taxes/receipts from the extraction of the resources but will only permit tax deductibility for costs at (or near) the end of life of the project.[4]

---

[4] Of course, the cash flow impact on the taxpayer will be the opposite.

One important direct consequence of providing tax deductibility at the end of project life is that investors in the extractive industries may apply some level of risk premium to their investment opportunities due to the potential for a territory to adversely change the investor's decommissioning tax relief terms late in a project's life cycle when decommissioning activity is more relevant. Naturally, this perceived risk may impact some territories more than others and will to a degree depend upon how confident investors are in a territory's likelihood of honouring its fiscal terms.

14.4.2.4   In the UK for example, the maturing of the United Kingdom continental shelf elevated this investor risk regarding, inter alia, confidence around levels of decommissioning tax relief. The result was that the UK Government introduced a legal instrument *(the Decommissioning Relief Deed)*[5] which could be entered into between the investor and the UK Treasury to provide more investor confidence versus protection under general UK tax statute.

14.4.2.5   The choice of timing can also be linked to the choice of tax regime more generally—if the rest of the regime is effectively a cash flow tax (e.g., providing immediate relief for capital expenditure) then allowing relief only on a cash flow basis is consistent.

14.4.2.6   From a tax perspective, this means that the project will be paying tax once the project has repaid investment and will carry on doing so through to the end of project life. At that point (or slightly beforehand) the taxpayer will incur decommissioning costs which will crystallise a large loss once the project has entered the decommissioning phase.

14.4.2.7   In most tax systems, tax losses are carried forward to the next tax year and allowed as a deduction in that year. However, the use of a loss carry-back will be needed as a way to provide an effective tax deduction for such costs unless there are other ways to offset the loss. A special provision can be made in the corporate income tax law to allow loss carry-backs in the case of a terminal loss arising from the decommissioning of mining or oil & gas operations. In turn, this may involve reviewing the income taxes paid for previous years and will typically result in refunds of taxes paid for such years.

14.4.2.8   Policymakers will need to be conscious of the government budgetary implications and availability of funds for refunds. Investors may be expected to seek reassurance that any refunds due will actually be made. Further, consideration will need to be given to the administration of the carry-back.

14.4.2.9   Assuming the budgetary and administrative issues can be resolved, the use of loss carry-backs can be an effective means of providing a tax deduction for such costs. This is particularly true when ring-fencing applies; also, it allows for accurate deduction of the actual costs incurred and avoids the issues of recapture of excess deductions taken or allowance of further costs inherent in other mechanisms.

---

[5] Example of UK's *Decommissioning Relief Deed* (DRD) at: https://assets.publishing.service. gov.uk/government/uploads/system/uploads/attachment_data/file/255650/Decommissioning_ Relief_Deed.DOC

14.4.2.10   Rules are needed to cover how that loss is deducted, such as allowing offset against profits made earlier in the project life. If this is achieved through a carry-back of the loss against the most recent periods first (i.e., on a last-in-first-out or "LIFO" basis) then the effective tax rate will be the rate that applied near the end of the project life rather than at the start of project life. Where the tax rate has varied in line with the profitability of the project, this may be considerably less than the peak tax rate on the project or indeed the average rate. Significant uncertainty may arise due to the risk of law changes and this is exacerbated by the long period before effective tax deductibility is obtained.

14.4.3   Model 2 — providing a tax deduction upon accrual

14.4.3.1   Under this model, a tax deduction is taken as the decommissioning expense is charged to the profit and loss account. Where the expenditure has not yet been incurred, this will create a provision for future expenditure. The taxpayer will get the tax deduction earlier in the life of the project than under Model 1.

14.4.3.2   The provision method enables the taxpayer to deploy its capital most efficiently. It may be argued that, without the obligation of an actual cash outlay, tax-deductible provisioning can increase the expected rate of return from the project since it provides improved cash flows over Models 1 and 3. It, thus, could also result in greater returns to the state given the different discount rates used.

14.4.3.3   On the other hand, policymakers should be conscious that an unfunded provision requires the tax authority to have the capacity to implement appropriate and robust controls and monitoring processes to ensure that excessive amounts are not being provided for.[6] In some countries, the decommissioning provision accrued in the year will only be tax deductible when it corresponds to a decommissioning plan formulated by the taxpayer and expressly accepted by the relevant authority. Further, it may be prudent to ensure that, while a provision is being made, there is some corporate backing provided by the operator, in the form of one or more financial guarantees (discussed in the section above) that the investor will perform its decommissioning obligations.

14.4.3.4   Finally, it will also be necessary to develop rules to deal with excess or inadequate provisions made. Where excess sums have been provided for, there should be explicit provision in the tax law to recapture the excess. A further consideration here is whether the recapture should be at the tax rate of the excess provision year(s) or the year in which recapture takes place, and whether interest should be charged. Again, policymakers will have to consider the trade-offs in view of their need to attract additional investment to the extractive sector, their revenue goals and the need to have a simple, practical, and clear decommissioning regime.

14.4.3.5   This model has the following characteristics which need particular attention:

---

[6] The use of the accounting provision for decommissioning costs can operate as a constraint on over-accruals.

- Estimate of costs: The estimate will be based on the decommissioning plan or equivalent documentation, where the associated costs will have to be estimated and agreed with the relevant sector ministry in advance.

- Accruing the costs: It will be necessary to have detailed rules on how the provision should be calculated and how much can be provided for each year. The investor may also be given a choice of different methods of accruing the provision, e.g., provide for the estimated cost over the life of the field or based on each unit of production (i.e., a certain fixed amount is provided for against each ton of ore or barrel of oil produced). The government could also determine a specific provision schedule as part of the negotiations with the investor(s) in relation to the concession.

14.4.3.6   It will also be necessary to consider the tax treatment of foreign exchange gains and losses relevant to the accumulated provision. Typically, the deductions will be allowed in the currency in which the investor submits the accounts, which in most cases will be in an internationally recognized currency (e.g., USD) and/or the national currency. However, the actual decommissioning costs will typically have to be paid in other currencies, and the conversion rate of such costs to the national currency may be different from when such costs were accrued. Therefore, in making interim or final adjustments to the provision, it will be necessary to consider currency movements. If amounts are accrued and deducted based on local currency, devaluation of the currency will mean that additional contributions will need to be made to the accumulated provision. Hence a current year deduction could consist of the accrual for that year plus an additional accrual for prior year amounts that have appreciated or depreciated in value.

14.4.4   Model 3 — providing a tax deduction upon pre-funding

14.4.4.1   Some governments require or allow companies to contribute to a decommissioning fund out of which the decommissioning liability is settled.

14.4.4.2   This model provides a tax deduction for contributions made to a dedicated and protected decommissioning fund. Typically, contributions would be made by an investor who is liable for decommissioning costs under the extractive contract, or a share of such costs in the event that more than one investor constitutes the contract group, their relationship being governed by a joint operating agreement. Decommissioning expenditure met directly or indirectly by the fund would not receive further tax deductibility. The fund would be outside of the sole control of the company or the government and, once committed, funds could only be released to pay for decommissioning expenditure.

14.4.4.3   The fund would be "insolvency remote," such that it could not be accessed by, for example, a liquidator should a licencee be put into liquidation. Once contributed, funds could only be used for legitimate decommissioning expenditure (whether before or after cessation of production) or refunded if the fund were in surplus once all decommissioning has been carried out.

14.4.4.4   Under this approach the taxpayer obtains a tax deduction for the costs before cessation of production and there is a shorter period during which the taxpayer is exposed to the risk of law change.

14.4.4.5   A practical issue for investors and governments is ensuring there is clear agreement as to when payments to the fund are triggered, especially where those triggers are based on certain milestones being reached, as projections can change. The use of decommissioning funds raises questions addressed in the following paragraphs.

14.4.4.6   The timing of a tax deduction will have cash flow implications for the government. The options include providing relief upon contribution of the cash to the fund. Tax deductibility can take place on an "as-funded" basis—i.e., when an actual payment is made into a decommissioning fund or trust fund established for this purpose. This is an established practice in a few countries, including India, Mozambique, Zambia, and South Africa. Examples of the rules applicable in the last two countries are provided in Annexes A and B of this Chapter.

14.4.4.7   These contributions are made during the development and/or operations phases of the project. It is important to clarify when to start the contributions to the fund. The fund (or other holding mechanism) is then used for project decommissioning costs at the end of the useful life. Under this approach, the deduction is allowed well in advance of the date that the decommissioning expenditure is actually incurred, but at the time the investor makes a cash payment to the fund and loses control of that cash. The project investor's deduction occurs when it is earning income from mining or oil & gas operations against which the deduction can be offset. The financial and tax treatment, and therefore budgetary impact for the government, is settled at the time of contribution to the fund—rather than the implications only becoming apparent later, when the provision is used for decommissioning.

14.4.4.8   The ability to take the tax deduction upon contribution mitigates the timing disadvantage to the investor of contributing to the fund but may, from a cash flow perspective, be less attractive to the investor as compared with Model 2. It does provide greater visibility and assurance to the government concerned that funds will be available at the end of project life than Model 2, unless some additional security is provided under that Model.

14.4.4.9   Upon accrual of the expenditure by the fund: For funds that remain close to the control of the taxpayer, deduction may only be given once it is clear that the funds will be spent on tax-deductible decommissioning activity. Hence, deductions could be delayed until the fund contracts for such activity. Given the difficulties in verifying the contractual relationships, this option should be used with caution.

14.4.4.10   Upon expenditure by the fund: This provides the same tax effect as Model 1 above but has a far more onerous commercial implication since the investor is required to provide the funds early but is entitled to the tax deduction only at the later date of actual expenditure on decommissioning costs.

14.4.4.11   Note that the independent fund per company model could in some cases give the company the possibility to deduct a surplus from other fields or activities. This will depend on the specific agreement/legal framework.

14.4.4.12   Treatment of surplus: The treatment of the surplus will determine the attractiveness to the taxpayer of contributing to a fund. In almost all cases, if contributions are tax deductible on the way in then, to the extent the surplus is repaid to the company, it should be taxable at that time of repayment.

14.4.4.13   Taxation of deficit funding: The tax system can be used to provide an incentive for the taxpayer to finance the decommissioning fund, for example, by allowing a lower rate of deduction on any contributions that are made towards the end of project life. However, this will complicate the tax system and, hence, may not be the most efficient way in which to provide the incentive.

14.4.4.14   Taxation within the fund: The taxation of the fund (i.e., whether the income of the fund can roll up free of tax, or exemption from any wealth/capital taxes) will materially affect the quantum of the funds available for decommissioning. However, this can be considered in determining the levels of contribution required.

14.4.4.15   The following table elaborates on some considerations to be taken into account in determining which Model to adopt.

Table 14.T.2: Types of decommissioning fund and tax treatment

	At contribution	Upon amortisation	When spent
Government	Deduction can be justified at this time, since the funds are out of the control of the taxpayer	N/A	N/A
Independent per field	Deduction can be justified at this time, since the funds are out of the control of the taxpayer.	N/A	N/A
Independent per company	Since the fund relates only to one company and it might receive a refund of any surplus, caution should be taken in relation to deduction.	Once the fund has contracted for the decommissioning, deduction could be provided to the taxpayer.	N/A
Company	This is equivalent to an accrual. No deduction since there has been no setting aside of funds.	Deduction should be given on the same basis as if there was no fund. May be a stronger case for accrual relief.	

14.5   COMPUTATION ISSUES IN DECOMMISSIONING

14.5.1   Overview

14.5.1.1   A fundamental question in relation to providing deductions for decommissioning costs is what costs are properly considered to be decommissioning costs. This involves both the determination of what qualifies as such, and the mechanism for estimating the costs that will be incurred in the future.

14.5.1.2   It is typically the mining and oil & gas companies that generate the decommissioning cost estimates and the provision for such decommissioning, since they are operating the facilities.

14.5.1.3   In a relevant international accounting standard (IAS 37 on Provisions, Contingent Liabilities and Contingent Assets)[7] the annual accounts must have a provision for the liability for the decommissioning of redundant facilities.

14.5.2   Framework of quantification

14.5.2.1   International and regional legal frameworks drive the cost of decommissioning, assuming that the country has ratified the relevant treaties and agreements. This international legal framework defines what must be removed, when it must be removed, to what degree the sites need to be reclaimed and rehabilitated. But these laws and regulations are at a very high level and rely on, when available, the more detailed national and state laws, regulations, and guidelines.

14.5.2.2   These country-specific laws, regulations and guidelines are used to define the decommissioning and rehabilitation specifications in technical and environmental terms. These specifications are the basis of the final engineering and environmental solutions, which generate the decommissioning cost estimates. Accurate decommissioning costs are critical as, if there is a shortfall in accrued provision at the end of the life of the oil & gas field or mine, the state and the other partners will have to fund this shortfall.

14.5.3   Costs

General

14.5.3.1   Decommissioning cost in the oil & gas industry worldwide is estimated to be in the billions of dollars and the trend is increasing. Planned costs have often been lower than actual costs, especially for the bigger operations.

14.5.3.2   The costs have risen in recent years due to stricter sectoral, national, and international legal frameworks; higher HSE scrutiny; increased focus on well operations and plug and abandonment (P&A) activities; and limited experience

---

7   See, for example, https://www.ifrs.org/issued-standards/list-of-standards/ias-37-provisions-contingent-liabilities-and-contingent-assets/.

in complicated operations, final disposal and requirements to recycle more. Subject to important environmental considerations, decommissioning costs can be reduced by the application of an appropriate national and international legal framework, new technology and more cost-effective ways to organize the removal process. Decommissioning should be included in the early planning phase of a project, so that life cycle perspectives, economies of scale and bundling of projects can be taken into account.

14.5.3.3   Potential charge of costs incurred for staff utilisation and know-how developed elsewhere should also be considered when assessing specific fields or projects.

Cost estimation in the oil & gas industry

14.5.3.4   Sources of data on estimating decommissioning costs in the oil & gas sector describe the possibilities and limitations of using the various available sources for cost savings estimates.

14.5.3.5   Oil & gas investors make periodic assessments on their expected decommissioning costs as a basis for their provision requirements. These are generally calculated for individual platforms using a *quantity x resource x time-method.* The quantity (jacket and top side weight) is calculated once while the rate (price per unit) and time (heavy lift vessels duration in days) are updated on a regular basis. Some investors make these calculations in-house with their own cost models that might be based on benchmark data. Other investors use external engineering consultants to make cost estimates. For structures where decommissioning is expected to occur on a medium to long-term basis, these calculations tend to be based on a cost per unit. For structures where the decommissioning date lies closer to the present, the calculations will be more detailed.

14.5.3.6   There is no agreed standard established by the industry.

Cost estimation in the mining industry

14.5.3.7   Practice in the mining industry differs considerably. Chilean law[8] requires that mining companies provide financial guarantees for the decommissioning of currently active and future mining operations. The value of the guarantee is to be based on the present value of the estimated decommissioning cost for the mine (presented in the decommissioning plan) and the planned operating life of the mine. The responsibility for reviewing and approving both the decommissioning plan and the estimate of decommissioning costs falls to the Chilean government mining and geology agency, called *Servicio Nacional de Geología y Minería* (SERNAGEOMIN).

---

[8] Law 20.551 on the Closure of Mines: Available in Spanish at https://www.leychile.cl/Navegar?idNorma=1032158.

14.5.3.8   A national guide for the estimation of decommissioning costs in Chile has been developed. The core of the guide is a cost estimation model that calculates costs based on a breakdown of the mine into a limited number of costing components and takes into account key modifying factors that are used to adjust costs, such as local geography, accessibility, and elevation.

14.5.3.9   The value of the guarantee is based on the estimated decommissioning cost for the project, including both the execution of decommissioning measures at the end of mine life, and a fund for the execution of post-decommissioning measures after the completion of major decommissioning works.

14.5.3.10   International practice differs in relation to the determination of the quantum of the financial provision for mine rehabilitation and decommissioning.

14.5.3.11   The practices and methodologies from the selected countries can be categorized as follows:

- Area-based, that is the quantum for the financial provision is calculated by multiplying the area of the mining operations by a fixed standardised unit rehabilitation cost; and/or

- Project-based, where the costs of each component of rehabilitation of the mine site are determined and totalled for the life of the mine.

14.5.4   Accurate estimation of costs/prudent provision reporting

14.5.4.1   Specific decommissioning plans and associated cost estimates are generally set out in regulations that have their basis in national legislation. Which of the associated costs should be included in the decommissioning cost estimate is governed by the legal and administrative framework that defines the scope of decommissioning under the relevant regulatory scheme. However, specification in the national law and regulations varies among countries, from cases where it is clearly defined to cases where these issues are hardly included in the legislation.

14.5.4.2   The cost estimates are important for ascertaining that the necessary funds are available to cover the actual costs of decommissioning the installations.

14.5.4.3   There is a considerable difference in the format, content, and practice of cost estimates, which makes it challenging to compare estimates, even for similar types of installations. The reasons are largely differing legal requirements in various countries and established practices.

14.5.4.4   Owners/licensees are generally responsible for developing cost estimates and funding mechanisms. They are required to submit the estimates to the regulator for review or approval.

14.5.4.5   The types and extent of assumptions and boundary conditions typically applied in cost estimates have a major effect on the overall costs. Regulators can specify boundary assumptions as a way of ensuring completeness in the coverage of the cost estimates, as well as the quality of the analysis. This could limit cost underestimation and over-provision, given that the regulator has the right knowledge and competence. Where needed National Authorities can seek the service of an external expert.

14.5.4.6   Standard definitions of cost items should be established. Development of an international guideline, or a standard list of items for cost estimation, could establish more consistency and comparability if countries used common or comparable definitions of cost elements and cost groups.

14.5.4.7   Developing valid cost estimates requires not only good definitions and specific assumptions, but also good data; hence, the accuracy of cost estimates depends both on the methods used and quality of the data.

14.5.4.8   In some industries, quality control by the regulator is established as an important reference point for validation of cost estimates: regular tracking of costs, benchmarking of actual experience against the cost estimates and requiring full documentation from the investor of how the cost estimate was developed.

14.5.4.9   The aim should be to develop a standard tool or procedure by which national cost estimates could be mapped for the purpose of comparison primarily nationally, but also internationally. One advantage of such comparison is to create more transparency of cost estimates and build confidence in the estimating basis.

14.5.5   Measuring the costs of decommissioning

14.5.5.1   Specific decommissioning plans are generally set out in regulations that have their basis in national legislation. The determination as to which of the associated costs should be included in the decommissioning cost estimate should be governed by the legal, contractual, and administrative framework that defines the scope of decommissioning under the relevant regulatory scheme. However, specification in the national law and regulations varies, from being clearly defined in some countries to hardly being mentioned at all in the legislation of some others. Local legislators do have the flexibility to decide exactly how decommissioning costs should be determined and dealt with, and thereafter it is the responsibility of the tax authority to apply the law.

14.5.5.2   It is recommended that the costs recognised for tax purposes are reconciled with those available elsewhere in government, such as the authority that approves the decommissioning plan, so that there is no opportunity for disparity in the numbers. See Annex G in relation to the current mechanisms by which decommissioning costs are estimated for non-tax purposes.

14.5.5.3   It is recommended that, where costs are deductible, there is clarity in the rules as to:

1.   Which expenditure is allowable and which costs are disallowed; and

2.   At what rate those costs are deductible (as countries may apply
     different tax rates to different streams of income).

14.5.5.4   In addition, there should be confidence that effective tax relief for
allowable costs will be available.

14.5.6   Estimating the costs of decommissioning

14.5.6.1   In addition to agreeing on the actual costs, Model 2 (and potentially
Model 3, depending on how payments made into or out of the fund and income
earned by the fund are taxed) will provide a tax deduction based upon the estimation of the costs of future decommissioning. Determination of the estimated costs
of decommissioning is a technical matter, for which the best expertise is likely to
reside within the investor and/or appropriate resource ministry (mining or oil &
gas). It is recommended that the tax deductibility be conditional upon approval
of the estimated costs by the resource ministry and the notification by it to the
tax administration. Governments may choose to address this matter through
regulation.

14.5.6.2   It is also important for policy makers to recognize that the decommissioning costs estimate is only an estimate. The actual decommissioning costs at
the end of the project life may be quite different due to a wide range of factors,
including changes in technology, increases or decreases in labour or material costs,
currency valuation changes, and the development of more innovative solutions and
different environmental standards at the end of project life compared to the start.
There needs to be a degree of flexibility built into the cost estimation process and
in the consequent deductibility of such costs for adjustment of the estimate over the
life of the project, and at the end of the decommissioning process.

14.5.7   Implications of financial security requirements

14.5.7.1   In addition to the taxation treatment of the decommissioning, a common
factor in many regimes will be the requirement to provide security. Furthermore,
given that requiring the setting up of funds can lead to capital being left idle and
unavailable for investment, some governments have instead sought to address the
risk by merely making sure that the funds are available to be called upon if needed.

14.5.7.2   This results in the taxpayer obtaining security from:

- A bank, through a letter of credit;

- The parent company or an affiliated company, through a guarantee on
  arm's length conditions; or

- A charge over assets.

14.5.7.3   Since the costs of obtaining these securities are effectively costs of
decommissioning, these costs should be tax deductible in the same manner as
costs for decommissioning or current costs, whichever is most appropriate. If tax
relief is available on either a cash or an accrual basis, fees charged by the banks

for letters of credit will be deductible as they are incurred.

14.5.7.4   In the case of a parent or affiliate guarantee, where a fee is involved, it may or may not be deductible depending on the law of the country.

14.5.7.5   If the security is called upon and the bank then calls on the resources of the taxpayer, the calling by the bank should be treated in the same way as if the expenditure had been made by the taxpayer. If the security is called, care needs to be taken to avoid tax deductibility being given twice, i.e., once to the company and once to the bank.

14.6   TAX POLICY DESIGN ISSUES

14.6.1   Legislative issues

14.6.1.1   In common with other areas of tax treatment of the extractive sector, an initial issue to be decided is the location of the income tax provisions for the sector. There are various options, including:

- A separate omnibus law that is applicable to extractive industries, covering both tax and non-tax subjects;

- A chapter (or part) in the corporate income tax legislation that covers the extractive sector, and includes decommissioning related provisions;

- The sector legislation, meaning that the mining law and/or the oil & gas law, as appropriate, would have a tax chapter; or

- A contractual obligation between the government and the licensee.

14.6.1.2   The key consideration in the location of any legislation is that duplication should be avoided, and definitions harmonized to the largest extent possible. This will particularly be the case where the country chooses to place the tax rules in the tax legislation, and the general decommissioning requirements in the sector legislation. Care needs to be taken to ensure that the tax law follows the definitions and tests used in the sector legislation and does not seek to duplicate or create alternative tests for tax purposes, whether by statute or by regulations. There also needs to be clarity in relation to the ordering of precedent for legislation, including the status of specific agreements, sector specific tax laws and the general tax law.

14.6.2   Potential impact of various tax policy choices on decommissioning

14.6.2.1   By taxing the profits from extraction, there is the natural consequence that a tax deduction is provided against the income for the costs incurred in earning that income, including those of decommissioning. Given that the decommissioning costs may only be payable late in the project life, there is a risk that governments may not plan appropriately or adequately recognise these costs. Tax policy can also be employed to enhance rehabilitation programs, for example through additional deductions for rehabilitating throughout the project life or putting cash into rehabilitation funds plus tax advantages for investing in technologies that improve outcomes. Further, tax rules may have the following behavioural impacts:

1. Influence or even impede the choice of who actually does the decommissioning;

2. Prevent "time being your friend"—i.e., prevent future developments (such as technological breakthroughs) positively influencing decommissioning outcomes;

3. Encourage the removal of more equipment due to the future application of the precautionary principle ultimately requiring removal of equipment by the investor;

4. Promote premature decommissioning, e.g., through:

   a. Restrictions on loss carry-backs; transfers; or

   b. Entity segregation for tax purposes, thus, restricting loss

   c. Restrictions of transfer of the resource asset to late life developers.

5. Promote only a standard decommissioning approach rather than a specifically designed approach;

6. Influence the selection of the method of developing resource projects, thus, influencing the ultimate decommissioning method and approach;

7. Influence the premature shutdown of the infrastructure which will result in premature decommissioning of assets and potential lost value;

8. Stop alternative uses of resource fields and therefore promote premature or delayed decommissioning; and

9. Advantage multi-field investors over single field investors, which will reduce the investor pool.

14.6.2.2   In the case of Joint Development Areas (JDAs), different tax rules in the partner jurisdictions will add to the risk that incentives and obligations are misaligned, e.g., that costs are split disproportionately among the countries involved.

14.6.2.3   This section considers the incentives that the tax system can create. These are considered for the three models.

14.6.3   Application to Model 1

14.6.3.1   As noted above, for many mining projects, particularly open pit mines, it can be very difficult to start decommissioning except at the end of the mine's life. This means that the vast majority of decommissioning costs will occur after the mine has stopped producing income. The position is similar for oil & gas projects, although some elements of decommissioning can be undertaken during project life.

14.6.3.2   Consequently, the impact of Model 1 is the creation of a large tax loss once the mine or oil & gas field has stopped producing taxable income. At the most fundamental, the costs of decommissioning may not receive an effective tax deduction, even if the project has been profitable and the intention of the government has been that the project would be taxable on its overall profits (i.e., after all costs including decommissioning). Most tax systems will seek to mitigate this through allowing the decommissioning loss to be set off against profits elsewhere in the group or against the profits of a certain number of years before cessation.

14.6.3.3   However, this is not wholly effective, as follows:

- The ability to offset the decommissioning costs against profits elsewhere in the group can reduce the impact for those groups with additional mining or oil & gas facilities that are profit-making at the time of decommissioning. For these groups, the issue remains important, but generally only for the last asset. However, this option is not available for those companies with only one asset;

- The ability to carry decommissioning tax losses back against the taxable profits of the previous few years can reduce the impact, but this requires that there be sufficient profits in the years prior to cessation of production that are covered by the loss carry-back provisions. Ignoring any tax incentive, it can be expected that the last few years of ownership would be generating far less profit than earlier in the project and hence may not be sufficient to absorb the whole of the decommissioning costs.

14.6.3.4   As well as potentially meaning that the method is frustrating the government's intention to provide relief, this can also create the following key risks:

1. Constraining the sale of late life assets:

- The use of loss carry-back as the mechanism for relieving decommissioning costs requires the taxpayer to have a history of taxable profits. This means that the sale of an asset to a new entrant could be impeded, as the new entrant would not inherit the profit history and might not generate sufficient profits in the remaining period of ownership to offset the decommissioning costs. In practice, an incumbent owner might be willing to pay a new entrant to relieve it of the asset, but the potential denial or reduction of a tax deduction for decommissioning costs would impede such a transaction. During 2019 and after several years of constructive discussion with UK investors, the UK introduced "Transferable Tax History (TTH)"[9] legislation to address the concern that the lack of access to tax history of profits by potential UK continental shelf asset buyers (particularly new entrants) was creating a fiscal barrier to promoting UK continental shelf asset trading, an essential component required to support the extension of asset lives and the longevity of the associated UK continental shelf infrastructure whilst helping to reduce the risk of UK continental shelf assets being prematurely decommissioned.

- To some extent, this can be overcome by selling the company that operates the project, rather than the asset itself. However, this may be difficult to achieve commercially since this involves the purchaser taking on the risks inherent in the past, rather than just the asset. Furthermore, this can be constrained by legal restrictions on the sale of such companies and the involvement of minority shareholders.

- A further example of this could be where a taxpayer transfers the asset but retains the obligation for decommissioning. In that case, the ability to carry-back losses may be lost or may give rise to an odd result. For example, if the decommissioning is carried out by the seller and the losses offset against profits far earlier in the ownership history (due to the recent history being in the hands of the buyer) the tax rate applicable to the deduction for decommissioning costs could be considerably higher or lower than that applied to the profit when earned.

2. Promoting premature decommissioning:

- If the period over which the loss can be carried back is not long enough, the taxpayer can be incentivised to decommission early—i.e., before the historic profits become insufficient to absorb the decommissioning costs or the tax rate applicable to the deduction reduces.

3. Disadvantaging single mine/field investors:

- The ability for multi-field investors to offset decommissioning costs incurred on one field against profits arising in other fields will provide an inherent disadvantage for single mine/field investors.

4. Restricting change of use:

- If the project is sold to a third party to use the mine or field for a different use (e.g., carbon capture and storage) then the new party may not have sufficient taxable profits to absorb the decommissioning costs. Further, the profits from any new activity in which the asset is used may be taxed at a different (lower) tax rate to the extraction activity.

---

[9] https://www.gov.uk/government/publications/an-outline-of-transferrable-tax-history

The decommissioning costs will be deductible at a rate lower than the rate at which the extraction profits were taxed. Whilst the tax deductibility would be deferred, this would also defer the decommissioning costs and therefore could provide a cash flow benefit.

14.6.3.5   Furthermore, as the majority of mines or fields in a particular jurisdiction reach the end of their life, a concern will arise in the investor community that the tax provisions may be changed to restrict the carrying back of losses. Since no tax deduction has yet been provided, the amount of tax to be repaid may be considerable. In this environment, it will be important that it is generally accepted that the current government will honour the commitments of the government that provided the licence. If that is not accepted, then investors may be incentivised, for example, to decommission early so that those decommission activities are undertaken before any change of law. This will generally lead to a poor outcome for the country and hence care is needed to reinforce confidence that the law will not be changed.

14.6.3.6   The extent to which these concerns need to be addressed depends critically on the facts and circumstances of the jurisdiction. Options for addressing these concerns include:

1. Longer periods for loss carry-back:

- Some countries will provide a longer period for carrying back of decommissioning losses than elsewhere in the tax system. This will help to address the concerns that a single mine/field investor would otherwise not be able to obtain appropriate deductibility for decommissioning costs and, thus, risking premature decommissioning, as it ensures that more of the mine/field's profits are available to offset the losses. However, this does not in itself address the constraint on sale of late life assets and may not address the restriction in change of use.

2. Loss histories that follow the asset:

- Some of the taxes operating in oil & gas apply on a field basis, rather than a company basis, such that the losses incurred will result in the repayment of tax to whomever was the owner at the time. In this case, contractual arrangements can be entered into between buyers and sellers to ensure that repayments are suitably allocated. It can be possible to deliver the same result in relation to taxes that are not on a field basis.

14.6.3.7   The precise options that are relevant depend critically on the nature of the tax regime and require specific consideration. Care will need to be taken to ensure that this does not result in the jurisdiction refunding more tax than has been paid on the field.

14.6.4   Application to Model 2

14.6.4.1   The provision of a tax deduction on an accruals basis should address many of the risks inherent in Model 1, in that it provides effective deductibility to single mine/field investors; allows for transfer of the field since the tax effect to date will already have been provided; and reduces the change of law risk as there is less tax to be repaid at the end of life.

14.6.4.2   However, the following risks arise:

1. Securing that decommissioning will occur and be funded:

- Providing deductibility before the decommissioning has been undertaken creates the risk that the government will ultimately have provided a deduction for decommissioning that is not undertaken. This, however, is not a tax issue and should be addressed within the wider consideration of security over decommissioning obligations.

- In order to ensure that liquidity is available to undertake the decommissioning of the mines or fields at the time of decommissioning, some countries include a tax incentive in their regulations - a so-called "depletion factor" consisting of an additional reduction of the taxable base during the life of the mines or fields, due to the fact that mineral or hydrocarbon resources are consumed when exploited, with the burden of maintaining said reserves and reinvesting the reduced amount in mining or oil activities that meet certain conditions, such as the activity of decommissioning. In this way, taxpayers would have the necessary liquidity to accommodate the decommissioning of the assets since they will have created their own internal reserves with the benefits generated by the mine/field activities that have benefited from the depletion factor.

2. Constraint on the use of funds:

- In determining the use of the funds that have been reserved, it will be important that the decommissioning techniques available at the time of decommissioning govern, to avoid undermining any advances in technology. Hence, when the funds are utilised, the tax effects for any expenses previously accrued for decommissioning that are not required should be "recaptured."

14.6.4.3   These risks can be addressed, depending on the nature of the tax system. Some systems[10] also provide for the increase in the funds arising through interest. Where the interest is not taxed, the costs covered by such amounts are not deductible. This effectively addresses the concern, in part, that tax deductibility

---

[10] For example, the United States mining regime under section 468 of the Code on Closure and Restoration (reclamation).

is provided early.

14.6.5   Application to Model 3

14.6.5.1   Again, the provision of a tax deduction upon contribution to the fund addresses many of the concerns highlighted in Model 1. The issues in relation to payments into and out of the fund, and the taxation of the fund itself have already been addressed. It will be important that the fund suffers no tax on expenditure that is incurred in relation to the decommissioning for which the fund has been set up.

14.6.5.2   As with Model 2, it will be important that the qualifying decommissioning costs are those determined when the decommissioning is undertaken, not at the time the fund was financed. Otherwise, the creation of the fund may require decommissioning techniques that are outdated.

14.7   APPLIED TAX TREATMENT ISSUES IN DECOMMISSIONING

14.7.1   Accounting for costs

14.7.1.1   In accounting for decommissioning costs, it will be necessary to consider the general rules for accounting for costs. It is of course logical that the approach taken by the country in handling project related costs, e.g., in a cost sharing contract, be followed for the sake of consistency.

14.7.1.2   Further, policymakers should also consider whether decommissioning costs should be deductible on an entity or a project basis, especially where a deductible provision solution is opted for, or in cases where the overall natural resource extraction regime is based on ring-fencing of reserves. The guidance provided on accounting of costs in Chapter 2 of this Handbook (the Government's Fiscal Take) also needs to be borne in mind.

14.7.1.3   The accounting currency for decommissioning costs may be a specific challenge, as they will typically be in hard currency, while the accounting currency will usually be the national currency of the project country. This will not be a significant issue where a tax deduction is available and is made on an ongoing basis, or even in the use of funded mechanisms, especially if the fund is managed in hard currency. However, there may be a significant mismatch where accruals-based provision is made, and policymakers will have to decide, in cases where the actual cost in hard currency exceeds the provision made, whether to allow the excess relief in the year of disbursement or over the life of the project. The same consideration should then apply to all recapture of excess provision made.

14.7.1.4   It is recommended that any foreign exchange gains and losses on disbursements from a fund set up under a funded deduction mechanism be explicitly kept out of the capital gains tax regime. Any such gains and losses will be reflected in the net balance of the fund, which would be subject to the recapture provisions in cases of excess deduction.

14.7.1.5   To the extent that a company has set up a decommissioning provision and is expecting to receive tax deductibility at a future date, such as in Model 1, the accounts will recognise a deferred tax asset which represents the tax effect that will arise from the deduction for qualifying decommissioning expenditure that has been accrued.

14.7.2   Allowability of costs

General principles

14.7.2.1   In general, deductibility will follow the tax policy approach chosen. However, there needs to be provision for allowance for excess costs over the planned and agreed costs if such costs occur, and for recapture of excess provision allowed.

Complex cases

14.7.2.2   The tax deductibility of decommissioning costs, and the recapture of excess provisions in accrual provision regimes, will be particularly complex in the case of single block/field investors. In this situation, the investor will have no operating income in the country and will have little incentive to fulfil its obligations, beyond the risk to its general reputation. It may be useful to consider a mix of instruments as a solution, e.g., the availability of loss carry-backs for such investors, subject to approval by the tax authority.

14.7.2.3   Another possible area of complexity will be deductibility of costs for decommissioning of ancillary and supplementary equipment that is not the investor's property, e.g., those owned by subcontractors or partners. It is necessary to take a flexible approach to these issues and to leave scope to permit deductibility on a case by case, where the expense is actually incurred.

14.7.2.4   A further challenge may come from costs incurred that are strictly speaking not for decommissioning, e.g., for repurposing of fields, something which is not uncommon for the mining sector. It is possible that, in some cases, good planning can lead to continued use of an extractive sector project for some completely different purpose, e.g., the conversion of open pit mines into a lake with fisheries or tourism potential. The technical argument here will be whether such expenditure is of a revenue nature (i.e., for decommissioning) or a capital cost (development of a new facility), especially if the same owner or a related company continues to operate the facility. It is recommended that a flexible approach be taken, and the tax treatment decided in a manner that balances the need to encourage more efficient use of sites with the need to raise revenue.

Multiple investor cases/combined fields

14.7.2.5   Another complex area can be that of multiple investors who partner in a single field area. One investor may have other income from the jurisdiction while the other investor may only have one project. The first investor may wish to see ongoing deduction of decommissioning costs, while the latter would probably prefer an accrued provision. Again, a flexible approach, based on the accurate estimation of costs, and controls to ensure that both investors will perform their obligations, can enable policymakers to create a "win-win" situation that will allow both investors to make the most efficient use of their resources.

14.7.2.6   A related challenge can be multiple investors who manage contiguous fields but utilize common facilities such as pipelines. The problem can be particularly aggravated if the fields in question have different expected lives, as the investor in the field with the lower expected life have less time to provide for its share of decommissioning costs of common facilities, and more importantly, will probably be absent from the country when the pipeline needs to be decommissioned. In such cases, the decommissioning plan needs to be agreed with both (or multiple) parties and respective shares allocated. A funded mechanism with oversight from both parties is probably the best solution.

14.7.3   VAT/GST and services tax issues around decommissioning

14.7.3.1   VAT/GST and other indirect taxes on services will also impact decommissioning. See Chapter 12 of this Handbook (Value Added Tax) for further information.

14.7.4   International tax issues[11]

14.7.4.1   The tax regimes for Joint Operating Areas and contiguous fields need to be considered by the jurisdictions concerned. There can be a situation where a single field falls in two jurisdictions, which are exploited by a single investor, or two or more investors exploit contiguous offshore fields that fall within two separate jurisdictions but share facilities.

14.7.4.2   There is a need to design a holistic decommissioning regime wherever possible within the auspices of the joint operating agreement (JOA)/joint development area (JDA) authority where applicable, or by consultation between the parties, in line with the recommendations of this chapter, and then proceed to the estimation of plans and costs. The partner jurisdictions should then consider a consultation between their tax authorities to deal with the tax consequences that arise for the costs that are allocable to their jurisdiction.

14.7.5   Tax treatment of contractors undertaking decommissioning work

14.7.5.1   The overall tax treatment of contractors performing decommissioning work should be on the same basis as those providing any other form of technical

---

[11] To ensure that decommissioning tax relief arrangements provided for in local legislation are fully effective, see also Chapter 5 on Tax Incentives, section 5.7 (Interaction with Investor and Other Tax Regimes).

services in the country. The extension of deemed permanent establishment (PE) treatment to offshore projects under decommissioning should resolve any issues regarding work done on offshore platforms. Such subcontractors should be subject to the normal regime for withholding taxes and VAT.

ANNEX A: Tax treatment of decommissioning expenses in Zambia

A.1   Introduction

This Annex provides insights on the tax treatment of environmental restoration and rehabilitation costs in Zambia. It also provides a historical background to the current legislation.

The mining industry is an economic and social backbone of Zambia. The major minerals produced include copper, cobalt, nickel, manganese, coal, emeralds, amethyst, beryl, limestone, talc, and uranium (though uranium is currently being stockpiled only). The major by-products from copper extraction are gold, platinum, palladium, selenium, and silver.

The mining methods include both open pit and underground mining as well as retreatment of historic tailings and waste rock via leaching, solvent extraction, and electrowinning.

A.2   Case study — environmental restoration costs

Mining companies in Zambia, as in most countries, are required[12] to undertake environmental impact assessment studies and make binding commitments through an environmental management plan to conserve and protect natural resources during and after cessation of mining activities.

Whilst this legislation had been in place under the Mines and Minerals Act since 1995, Zambia had until April 2006 no specific provisions in the Income Tax Act (ITA) that dealt with the environmental restoration and rehabilitation costs. Nonetheless, the ITA had two general provisions that dealt with environmental restoration expenses, namely:

General deduction provision

Section 29(1)(a) of the ITA is the general deduction provision and provides that: "in ascertaining business gains or profits in any charge year, there shall be deducted the losses and expenditure, other than of a capital nature incurred in that year wholly and exclusively for the purposes of the business."

---

[12] Under the Mines and Minerals Development Act (2015).

The above provision requires that the environmental restoration and rehabilitation costs:

> a.   Should *not* be of a capital nature; and
>
> b.   Should be incurred in the relevant year to qualify for tax deduction.

Whilst the decision whether the outgoing is revenue or capital in nature is a debatable one, under Zambian tax cases, environmental restoration and rehabilitation costs were determined to be of a capital nature, and thus, not deductible under section 29(1)(a). Accordingly, one had to look at the provisions in the ITA applicable to capital expenditure deductions for mining companies.

Capital expenditure deduction

Section 33(b) of the ITA is the principal provision for capital expenditure deductions incurred by Mining Companies. This Section provides that: "Capital allowances are deducted in ascertaining the gains or profit of a business and the emoluments of any employment or office for each charge year – (...) (b) for capital expenditure in relation to mining operations, according to the provisions of Parts I to VI inclusive of the Fifth Schedule. Part VI of the Fifth Schedule (Paragraph 19) defines qualifying capital expenditure as "expenditure, in relation to mining or prospecting operations (...) on buildings, works, railway lines or equipment (...)".

The ITA does not have a definition of "works" and thus taking the ordinary meaning, the term includes environmental restoration and rehabilitation works. Whilst the above definition of capital expenditure was sufficient, the complication in allowing deductions on environmental costs came in through paragraph 22(1) of the Fifth Schedule which provided that: "a deduction shall be allowed in determining the gains or profits from carrying on of mining operations by any person in a charge year in respect of the capital expenditure incurred by the person on a mine which is in regular production in the charge year."

Therefore, from the foregoing, environmental restoration and rehabilitation costs were deductible as capital expenditure provided that the expenditure had been incurred; and it had been incurred on a mine which was in regular production.

These two conditions were at the heart of concerns from the mining sector as it was not practical to commence environmental restoration and rehabilitation works on a mine that was in regular production. It was therefore contended that the legislation as it stood prior to the Tax Amendment of April 2006, effectively barred the right to deduct environmental restoration and rehabilitation expenditure.

Current tax treatment (tax deduction provisions after 1 April 2006)

To address the undesirable effects of the Tax Law, amendments were made effective April 2006. The following is the current law. A deduction is allowed in ascertaining the gains or profits of a person involved in mining operations in respect of actual costs incurred by way of restoration and rehabilitation works or amounts paid into the Environmental Protection Fund, (this fund is administered and managed by the Environmental Protection Fund Committee that is appointed by the Minister Responsible for Mines). Only actual costs are deductible and therefore provisions are not allowable in determining taxable profits.

Additionally, amounts refunded from the Environmental Protection Fund to any person carrying on mining operations are recognised as income in the year the refund is made and hence qualify to be taxed.

The extracts of relevant provisions under the Income Tax Act are given below.

First schedule to the income tax act (further classification of income)

Paragraph 9

Amounts refunded to any person carrying on mining operations pursuant to paragraph (a) of subsection eighty-six of the Mines and Minerals Development Act, 2015 shall be deemed to be income in the year that the refund is made.

Fifth schedule to the income tax act (mining expenditure deductions)

Paragraph 22(3)

A deduction shall be allowed in ascertaining gains or profits of a person involved in mining operations in respect of actual costs incurred by way of restoration and rehabilitation works or amounts paid into the Environmental Protection Fund pursuant to section eight-six of the Mines and Mines Minerals Development Act, 2015.

ANNEX B: Tax treatment of decommissioning expenses in South Africa

B.1   Income tax rules relating to rehabilitation of the environment

Mining rehabilitation expenditure consists of two components, ongoing environmental rehabilitation expenses and expenses in respect of the decommissioning of mining projects. Although both components are required to be expended in terms of National legislation (NEMA[13] and MPRDA[14]) the tax effects are not the same.

In the case of ongoing rehabilitation expenses, a tax deduction is normally allowed under the general deduction formula in the Income Tax Act[15] (IT Act) in the year

---

[13] National Environmental Management Act (Act 107 of 1998) (NEMA).

[14] Mineral and Petroleum Resources Development Act (Act 28 of 2002) (MPRDA).

[15] Section 11(a) of the Income Tax Act (Act 58 of 1962) allows a deduction from the income derived, by a person from carrying on a trade, of expenditure and losses actually incurred in the production of the income if the expenditure and losses are not of a capital nature.

the expenditure is actually incurred. Decommissioning costs quantified and provided for in accordance with the requirements of MPRDA and NEMA relate to expenditure to be incurred in the future and cannot be claimed for income tax purposes until they have been actually incurred. The IT Act specifically prohibits the deduction of provisioning for future expenses.[16] A further aspect to be noted is that expenditure on decommissioning and environmental rehabilitation incurred after an extractive company ceases its mining activities may not be deductible for income tax purposes. The reasons are that trading activities may have ceased, and the general deduction formula does not allow a deduction if trade is not carried on or the expenditure is not incurred in the production of income. Closer to the end of the life of a mine or oil & gas field the expenses (including decommissioning and rehabilitation) would exceed income earned and even if expenditure can be deducted the benefit of assessed losses is forfeited. The South African tax system does not allow the carry-back of tax losses by a taxpayer and tax losses cannot be carried forward to future tax years if the company is no longer trading.[17]

Mining and oil & gas extractive companies have the option of utilising funding vehicles described in section 37A of the IT Act to earmark assets for all or part of the required *financial provision* for decommissioning of latent or residual environmental impacts. The use of these funding vehicles enables extractive companies to comply with their *financial provision* obligations under MPRDA and NEMA in a tax efficient manner.

B.2   Closure rehabilitation trusts and companies

To encourage and facilitate preservation of funds for environmental rehabilitation and decommissioning activities, the tax system provides tax benefits in relation to a 'closure rehabilitation trust' or company.[18] A qualifying trust or a company used as a funding vehicle results in tax deductible contributions to the vehicle and a tax exemption of receipts and accruals of the vehicle.[19]

Legislative requirements are set on the type of contribution, the type of funding vehicle, the persons that may make deductible contributions, assets that may be owned, utilisation of assets, excess assets after decommissioning and contravention of legislative provisions.

Type of contribution

Only amounts in cash may be paid to the funding vehicle. Therefore, the transfer of assets such as shares, financial instruments or tangible property is not allowed. This could conceivably still occur, but the donor or transferee will not be able to deduct the value of such donation or transfer in terms of section 37A of the IT Act.

---

[16] Section 23(e) of the Income Tax Act provides that no deduction shall be made of income carried to any reserve fund or capitalized in any way.

[17] Section 20(1) of the Income Tax Act.

[18] Section 37A of the Income Tax Act.

[19] Section 10(1)(c) of the Income Tax Act.

Type of funding vehicle

Only a trust[20] or a company may qualify as a funding vehicle. The sole object of the trust or company must be to apply its property solely for rehabilitation upon premature and final decommissioning, and post decommissioning coverage of any latent and residual environmental impacts on the area covered in terms of any permit or right in respect of prospecting, exploration, mining or production, or reservation or permission for or right to the use of the surface of land as contemplated in paragraph 9 of Schedule II to the MPRDA to restore one or more areas to their natural or predetermined state, or to a land use which conforms to the generally accepted principle of sustainable development.[21]

Any distributions by the trust or company must be solely for purposes described in its sole object or in certain circumstances to a similar trust or company.[22] The constitution of the company or the instrument establishing the trust must incorporate the provisions of section 37A.[23]

Persons that may make deductible contributions[24]

Mining and oil & gas extractive companies that hold a permit or right in respect of prospecting, exploration, mining or production, or reservation or permission for or right to the use of the surface of land as contemplated in paragraph 9 of Schedule II to the MPRDA; or are engaged in prospecting, exploration, mining, or production in terms of any permit, right, reservation or permission referred to above.

After approval by the Commissioner for the South African Revenue Service, the extractive company may pay an amount in cash to the closure trust or company on condition that the payment was not part of any transaction, operation or scheme designed solely or mainly for purposes of shifting the tax deduction from another person to the extractive company making the payment.

Assets that may be owned

The closure trust or company may only own permitted assets. These permitted assets are limited to financial instruments issued by South African regulated

---

[20] A trust is not a legal person as it is not an independent entity. Any property held in trust is held by the trustee in his/her capacity as trustee. The Income Tax Act specifically includes a trust in the definition of a person.

[21] Section 37A(1)(a) of the Income Tax Act.

[22] Section 37A(1)(c) of the Income Tax Act.

[23] Section 37A(5) of the Income Tax Act.

[24] Section 37A(1)(d) of the Income Tax Act.

collective investment schemes, long-term insurers, banks, and mutual banks; financial instruments in listed companies,[25] unless the company is making contributions to the closure trust or company or the company is a connected person[26] in relation to the company making contributions to the closure trust or company; and financial instruments issued by any sphere of government of South Africa.

The tax policy objective is to limit permitted asset to assets that are relatively liquid and easy to value (for the benefit of regulatory oversight).

Utilisation of assets

The closure trust or company must use all of its assets solely for purposes of its sole objective of rehabilitation upon premature and final decommissioning, and post decommissioning coverage of any latent and residual environmental impacts on the area covered in terms of any permit or right in respect of prospecting, exploration, mining or production, or reservation or permission for or right to the use of the surface of land as contemplated in paragraph 9 of Schedule II to the MPRDA to restore one or more areas to their natural or predetermined state, or to a land use which conforms to the generally accepted principle of sustainable development of mining rehabilitation upon decommissioning.[27]

Excess assets after decommissioning rehabilitation

When the Minister of Mineral Resources is satisfied that all of the areas relating to any permit, right, reservation or permission of the persons contributing to the closure trust or company have been rehabilitated as set out on the object of the trust or company, the company or trust in respect of those areas must be wound up or liquidated and its assets remaining after the satisfaction of its liabilities must be transferred to another closure trust or company as approved by the Commissioner for the South African Revenue Service or to an account or trust prescribed by the Minister of Mineral Resources and subject to approval by the Commissioner for the South African Revenue Service.[28]

Excess assets held by closure trusts or companies (i.e., amounts exceeding the anticipated mining rehabilitation liability) can also be transferred to other similar closure trusts or companies before termination if the Minister of Mineral Resources is satisfied that the closure trust or company will be able to satisfy all of its rehabilitation liabilities and it has sufficient assets to rehabilitate and restore all of the areas relating to any permit, right, reservation or permission of the persons contributing to the closure trust or company as set out on the object

---

[25] The definition of listed company in section 1(1) of the Income Tax Act refers to companies listed on the JSE (previously the JSE Securities Exchange and the Johannesburg Stock Exchange) or a recognised offshore exchange.

[26] Connected person is defined in section 1(1) of the Income Tax Act.

[27] Section 37A(1)(b) of the Income Tax Act.

[28] Section 37A(3) of the Income Tax Act.

of the trust or company and the Commissioner for the South African Revenue Service approves the transfer.[29]

Contravention of legislative provisions

If a closure trust or company owns any impermissible assets, an amount of taxable income equal to 50 per cent of the market value of the impermissible assets becomes taxable for the mining or oil & gas extractive company contributing to the closure trust or company to the extent that the impermissible assets are (directly or indirectly) derived from cash paid by that extractive company.[30]

If a closure trust or company:

(a) Distributes assets for a purpose other than:

- Rehabilitation upon premature closure;

- Decommissioning and final closure;

- Post closure coverage of any latent or residual environmental impacts; or

- Transfer to another closure trust or company; or

(b) Uses property as security for any debt for a purpose other than for rehabilitation upon premature closure or decommissioning and final closure, an amount equal to 50 per cent of the market value of assets that were so distributed or used is deemed to be an amount of tax payable by the mining or oil & gas extractive company contributing to the closure trust or company.[31]

If tax imposed for contraventions cannot be paid by the mining or oil & gas extractive company, the tax must be paid by the closure trust or company.[32]

B.3   Deduction of expenditure of oil & gas companies

An oil & gas company[33] may deduct environmental rehabilitation expenditure

---

[29] Section 37A(4) of the Income Tax Act.

[30] Section 37A(6) of the Income Tax Act.

[31] Section 37A(7) of the Income Tax Act.

[32] Section 37A(8) of the Income Tax Act.

[33] An oil and gas company is defined in paragraph 1 to mean any company that holds any specified oil and gas right granted under the MPRDA, or engages in exploration or post-exploration in terms of any oil and gas right.

incurred in respect of exploration[34] or post-exploration[35] activities against its oil & gas income.[36] The deduction of exploration or post-exploration expenditure[37] is limited to oil & gas income derived during the tax year, or future tax years if the deductions result in assessed losses. Therefore, environmental rehabilitation and decommissioning expenditure incurred after cessation of production will not be deductible as no oil & gas income is derived.

The benefit of a deduction under paragraph 5 of the Tenth Schedule to the Income Tax Act is that an additional deduction[38] is allowed against oil & gas income based on:

a)   100 per cent of all expenditure of a capital nature actually incurred in that year of assessment in respect of exploration in terms of an oil & gas right; and

b)   50 per cent of all expenditure of a capital nature actually incurred in that year of assessment in respect of post-exploration in respect of an oil & gas right.

ANNEX C: National and international legal requirements

C.1   International oil & gas legal requirements for decommissioning

Since 1958, international conventions have stated that all offshore platforms must be decommissioned at the end of the field life. As the complexity of the offshore oil & gas facilities has evolved, the challenge to balance the total removal with environment, safety, technical feasibility, cost, etc. has forced an evolution in the decommissioning law and regulations.

---

[34] Exploration is defined in paragraph 1 to mean the acquisition, processing and analysis of geological and geophysical data or the undertaking of activities in verifying the presence or absence of hydrocarbons (up to and including the appraisal phase) conducted for the purpose of determining whether a reservoir is economically feasible to develop.

[35] Post-exploration is defined in paragraph 1 to mean any activity carried out after the completion of the appraisal phase, including:
(a) the separation of oil and gas condensates;
(b) the drying of gas; and
(c) the removal of non-hydrocarbon constituents, to the extent that these processes are preliminary to refining.

[36] Oil and gas income is defined in paragraph 1 to mean the receipts and accruals derived by an oil and gas company from:
(a) exploration in terms of any oil and gas right;
(b) post-exploration in respect of any oil and gas right; or
(c) the leasing or disposal of any oil and gas right.

[37] Paragraph 5 of the Tenth Schedule to the Income Tax Act read with section 26B of that Act.

[38] Paragraph 5(2) of the Tenth Schedule to the Income Tax Act.

The optimal solution may not be the total removal of a specific oil & gas facility, but a carefully balanced compromise within the relevant legal framework. It is important that governments incorporate flexibility into their national legal framework. The current international laws and conventions, listed below, are applicable in most of the countries and have built in such flexibility:

- United Nations Convention on the Continental Shelf, 1958.

- United Nations Convention on the Law of the Sea, 1982, UNCLOS III.

- "The International Maritime Organisation Guidelines and Standards for the Removal of Offshore Installations and Structures on the Continental Shelf and in the Exclusive Economic Zone," 1989 (a.k.a. IMO Guidelines).

- "Convention on the Prevention of Marine Pollution by Dumping of Wastes and Other Matter," 1972 (a.k.a. London Dumping Convention-LDC).

- "1996 Protocol to the Convention on the Prevention of Marine Pollution by Dumping of Wastes and Other Matters" (a.k.a. London Protocol).

A list of the relevant treaties currently in force and the signatory countries can be found on the Law of the Sea section XXI of the UN Treaty Collection website here: https://treaties.un.org/Pages/Treaties.aspx?id=21&subid=A&clang=_en

These international conventions and regulations are supplemented by relevant national and state legalisation. The national and state legalisation can impact on decommissioning of oil & gas facilities, under environmental, safety, waste management, socio-economic and tax and customs laws, etc. Furthermore, due to the potential socio-economic impacts, the decommissioning of redundant oil & gas facilities may often become a regional issue.

The decommissioning of pipelines in the oil & gas industry is not covered in international law and usually this issue is managed in national legalisation. But for pipelines there are two clear principles in international law:[39] No interference with navigation, fishing, and other users of the sea; and all appropriate measures must be taken for the protection of the living resources of the sea from harmful agents.

These are the guiding principles of the countries' national law regimens, which cover pipelines. For installations located onshore, sectoral, regional, and national laws and regulations are applicable.

---

[39] *Geneva Conventions on the Law of the Sea* (1958). Available at http://legal.un.org/avl/ha/gclos/gclos.html. *United Nations Convention on the Law of the Sea*—UNCLOS (1982). Available at http://www.un.org/depts/los/convention_agreements/convention_overview_convention.htm; *International Maritime Organization—International Convention on Salvage* (1989). Available at http://www.imo.org/en/About/Conventions/ListOfConventions/Pages/International-Convention-on-Salvage.aspx.

C.2   International best practices for mine decommissioning

National mine decommissioning policy is usually dictated in its national constitution that mandates a healthy environment for its citizens or by requirements of international treaties and agreements. At the national level, individual national sectoral policies and legislation (other than those for the environment and mining), various Executive Decrees and specific Local Government Agreements (often with industry), all must be provided for as part of an overall national programme for acceptable mine decommissioning. These are in addition to specific instruments under Environmental and Mining legislation that require putting in place policy and legislation for Environmental Impact Assessments, Social Impact Assessments, Mining Plans, Standard Mining Agreements, bonding procedures and providing for Inter-Ministerial Agreements to achieve comprehensive mine decommissioning and sustainable development.

Many countries do not have provisions for mine decommissioning in their mining laws. Few governments have actual mine decommissioning legislation. Where mine decommissioning legislation is enacted, it is primarily with respect to reclamation and rehabilitation. Countries with mining interests are encouraged to enact clear and comprehensive legislation to clarify requirements well before actual decommissioning takes place.

Comprehensive mine decommissioning and all that it entails would simply be part of any mining planning and design if the life cycle of a mine was fully considered before establishing the mine. However, history and present practices in many countries clearly demonstrate that this is not the case.

Countries which have enacted a national mining decommissioning law typically do so by including it directly in the national Mining Law or indirectly within the national Environmental Law but also within their Foreign Investment Laws for comprehensive mine decommissioning. Compliance with these provisions is often a pre-condition of acquiring a mining licence, which is a better approach than simply requiring "best practices" to be adopted. In some countries, their legislation contains only general statements with respect to "appropriate" or "reasonable" reclamation and rehabilitation with the specific issues related to mine decommissioning normally being dealt with on an "ad hoc" basis.

In practice, however, rehabilitation, reclamation and mine decommissioning plans vary greatly among and within individual countries, as do the requirements for bonding or other surety instruments to ensure that the plans are carried out.

The level of provision for mine decommissioning within the mining laws and regulations of the developing countries is largely dependent on three factors, i.e.:

- The age of the country's mining law and regulations;

- The activities of past mining enterprises; and

- Related policy and legislation, in particular, environmental policy and legislation.

Many developing countries in Africa, Latin and South America and Asia, each with a long mining history of private sector mineral development, are characterized by having:

- A very general policy and legislation for mine decommissioning;

- A high degree of state responsibility for both abandoned and some operational mines; and

- Few, if any, bonding procedures to ensure comprehensive mine decommissioning and provision for mine decommissioning on a negotiated "mine-by-mine" basis.

However, some developing countries, such as Bolivia, Mali, Namibia, and Zambia can be said to have comprehensive policy and legislation that provides for comprehensive mine decommissioning and for post-mining sustainable development. It is often the case that inadequate and unproven fiscal regimes exist in countries where post-decommissioning sustainable development presents the greatest challenge for the government. One of the key fiscal regimes is a taxation system which facilitates this process.

In summary, the sector law and regulations for decommissioning provide the overall framework within which the taxation rules for decommissioning must be designed.

ANNEX D: Political issues, public concern and reputation

As discussed above, the effects resulting from the political and community reaction to the decommissioning of major facilities in a community can heavily influence the decommissioning process. If not properly managed, a destructive distrust can develop between the principal players. If any indication of non-disclosure emerges, this can lead to catastrophic outcomes, such as the Brent Spar incident.[40]

It is advised that the selection of the decommissioning option must be managed in a transparent process with a fully developed public audit trail. The three major components that need to be managed are: national and local political issues; public concern; and reputation.

The development of a proper decommissioning process includes guidance from stakeholder groups representing all national and local interests including representatives from impacted communities, the oil & gas and mining industries, fishing industries, environmental non-governmental organisations, government officials in the areas of mining/oil & gas regulation, mining/oil & gas safety,

---

[40] Brent Spar was an oil tanker loading buoy in the North Sea. After the end of its useful life, in 1991 Shell researched options for disposal and decided to dispose of it in a deep part of the Atlantic. As a result of public and political opposition in Europe, in 1995 Shell scrapped its disposal plans but still insisted that this was the safest option for health and safety, and for the environment. Later, much of the structure was re-used to construct harbour facilities in Norway.

fishing, navigation and all affected users of the land and the sea in the region.

The objectives of a stakeholder policy development process usually are:

- To develop:

  ➢ Principles/guidelines to apply to the decommissioning of existing facilities;

  ➢ Principles/guidelines to apply to the design, operation, and future decommissioning of new facilities; and to the extent possible, consensus between stakeholders.

- To provide:

  ➢ Regulators (both Designated Authorities, the Department of the Environment and Water Resources and others) with guidance on how applications for decommissioning are to be assessed;

  ➢ Industry with guidance as to what will be expected of them in respect of decommissioning, with the aim of reducing risk and uncertainty; and

  ➢ An opportunity for public comment and involvement in the development of government policy.

There should also be recognition of possible future liabilities and how they could be managed.

Annex E: Stakeholders

E.1. Stakeholder identification and engagement

Decommissioning is expected to attract increasing interest from parties both within and outside the industry, particularly regarding issues on environmental, social, and economic impact. The industry operates within a regulated legal framework overseen by national regulator(s).

The framework seeks to achieve effective and balanced solutions for decommissioning activities. These solutions need to be consistent with each nation's international obligation (treaties) and have a proper regard for safety, environment, other legitimate users of the land and/or sea, and economic as well as social considerations.

An important part of the decommissioning process is the identification and mapping of issues for key stakeholders, and to provide general advice on future stakeholder engagement. Stakeholders will have a specific and defined interest in the decommissioning activities, either because they could be impacted by the decision, and/or they can have an impact or influence on the planned activity.

Involving or engaging stakeholders can take a range of different forms, including provision of information, consultation or dialogue. The design of a stakeholder engagement plan or guidelines could be a useful tool to demonstrate how engagement is an integral part of achieving a robust, sustainable, and acceptable decommissioning programme. The guidelines set out the benefits of good engagement for the investors and stakeholders alike.

Key questions in a stakeholder engagement process are:

- Which stakeholders to engage?

- How to engage?

- When to engage?

Well managed stakeholder engagement can improve decommissioning plans and make the whole process more efficient. Stakeholder engagement can make the outcomes of the decommissioning project more sustainable. It can be cost efficient and reduce the potential for conflict when done properly. The essential characteristic of stakeholder engagement is that it seeks an effective and balanced decommissioning solution.

E.2. Indicative list of stakeholders

The key stakeholders are the governments of resource-rich countries, specifically the regulatory authorities, institutions, and ministries responsible for administering mineral resource and oil & gas extraction contracts; issuing environmental permits for exploration, exploitation, and decommissioning; and ensuring that legal, financial, and technical measures are in place to address temporary shutdowns as well as complete decommissioning at the end of the productive life of oil & gas and mining operations.

A list of stakeholders would include traditional owners, other impacted local communities, government authorities, representatives and legislators, including:

- National (Ministries and Agencies);

- Regional/District Authorities;

- Local (Port Authorities, Local communities);

- International and Regional Regulators;

- Commercial Interest Groups including:

  - Decommissioning Supply Industry;

  - Local Industry;

> ➤ Investors; and

> ➤ Unions/Employee Organizations;

Stakeholders also include the public and the wider citizenry, including:

> ➤ NGO Groups;

> ➤ Environmental Groups;

> ➤ Marine Life;

> ➤ Other Users of the Sea;

> ➤ Shipping & Navigation;

> ➤ Fishing Industry;

> ➤ Tourist Industry;

> ➤ Navy and other defence actors;

> ➤ Media; and

> ➤ Universities and Research Organizations.

Some of these interests would be less relevant for land-based activities such as onshore mining, and other interests and interest groups would be relevant in their place.

ANNEX F: Impact assessment

Once decommissioning strategies have been decided upon, it will be necessary to develop Impact Assessments for the relevant options, rank the options and communicate the outcome to various stakeholders. No mine shutdown or decommissioning study would be complete without a proper impact assessment.

The purpose of an impact assessment is to clarify the effects of measures that may have significant consequences for the environment, natural resources, and society. The impact should ensure that these effects are taken into account when the measure is planned and when decisions are reached regarding whether, and on what conditions, the measure may be carried out. Key issues include the impact on the environment and the local community. For on-shore activities, a key consideration is social transition, which involves planning and preparation to help manage the impacts of social and economic change for the workforce and communities connected to the extractives site and improving the legacy and benefits from the extractive activities. For example, social transition for mine closure recognises risks associated with local dependence on the mine and consequently creates opportunities to encourage the development of sustainable post-closure options. In mining, post closure land use is another key consideration.[41]

Examples of impact drivers in the extractives industry include:

- ➢ Protection of the environment;

- ➢ Precautionary Principle;

- ➢ Definition of the end state (e.g., how much cleaning/rehabilitation is required);

- ➢ Preserving prior legal positions (grandfathering);

- ➢ Understanding and managing emission paths and receptors;

- ➢ Characterization and management of waste; and

- ➢ Decommissioning plan and valuation of impacts.

The inclusion of all stakeholder groups is essential in the environmental impact assessment. The groups can consider the balancing of different policy priorities and set the standard for the assessment that is appropriate to national needs, and in line with national policy priorities. It is important to recognize that there is a trade-off to be achieved, and ultimately sovereign countries must determine the standard to be achieved, while bearing in mind international standards. The more clarity that can be provided up front on what will be considered and who will be responsible, the better. The impact assessment needs to consider compliance with any relevant laws applicable to decommissioning, as discussed in Annex C.

---

[41] Further information on social transition and post closure land use, as well as other relevant issues can be found in the ICMM Integrated Mine Closure Good Practice Guide, 2nd Edition https://www.icmm.com/website/publications/pdfs/closure/190107_good_practice_guide_web.pdf

Glossary

Abandon in Place: A disposal option category in which all or part of an installation is left in its position for controlled, natural deterioration and where the marking of the installation can be maintained.

AMATM: Agreement on Mutual Assistance in Tax Matters.

Arm's Length Principle/Standard: The arm's length principle is an international standard that compares the transfer pricing charged between related entities with the price of similar transactions carried out between independent entities at arm's length. An adjustment may be made to the extent that profits of a related party differ from those that would be agreed between independent entities in similar circumstances.

Artificial reef: A structure placed on the seabed to provide anchorage and shelter for marine life.

Associated enterprises: Enterprises under common control. This will generally be the case where the same persons participate directly or indirectly in the management, control or capital of both enterprises.

ATAD: The EU's Anti-Tax Avoidance Directive (ATAD) contains a rule on hybrid mismatches to prevent companies from using hybrid instruments or entities to exploit mismatches between national rules; a controlled foreign companies (CFC) rule; a switchover rule to prevent double taxation of some income; a rule on exit tax to prevent companies avoiding tax when moving assets across borders; an interest imitation rule; and a general anti-abuse rule.

BEPS (Base erosion and profit shifting): The OECD's plan to combat base erosion and profit shifting involves 15 actions aiming to end tax avoidance strategies that exploit gaps and mismatches in tax rules.

Best practical option: The disposal option which both for the licensees and the authorities is considered as the most cost-effective solution without compromising internal and external regulations on health, environmental, safety and emergency preparedness issues.

Bonuses: Lump sum (or sometimes staged) payments made to a government upon award of a natural resource licence or some other project event. Bonuses can come in a number of forms, depending on the contract negotiated.

Capital Gain Tax (CGT): Generally used (especially in chapter 10 of this publication) to include taxation of a capital gain either through a separate specific capital gains tax regime or through the general income tax system.

Cessation plan: A "close-down" plan containing the licensees' proposal for disposing of the installations and associated interconnecting pipelines.

Cold installation: Installation without presence of hydrocarbon/inflammable liquids (class A or B) or inflammable gas.

Cold phase: Any period of time during which an installation is "cold," cf. definition of "Cold installation" above.

Comparable data: In the transfer pricing context, these may be internal comparables, i.e., transactions between the tested party and independent parties, or external comparables, i.e., transactions between two independent entities that are not a party to the controlled transaction.

Comparable Uncontrolled Price (CUP) Method: A transfer pricing method comparing the price of the property or services transferred in the controlled transaction with the price charged in comparable transactions in similar property or services in similar circumstances.

Concession regimes: Structures involving government grants to an entity of the rights to exploration, development, and extraction of natural resources at the grantee's sole risk. Grants generally cover a fixed area and impose certain time limits for the activities. These regimes are sometimes also known as "tax and royalty" regimes and are common in both the petroleum and mining industries.

Concrete installation: A reinforced concrete structure founded on the seabed, and supporting topside structures over the wave zone.

Consortium or joint venture: An arrangement of several investors who may pool capital and expertise to jointly exploit and share the risks connected with exploiting a particular extractive project.

Continued use: A disposal option category in which it has been decided to continue use of all or part of an installation in the petroleum industry or a mine.

Contract regimes: Structures involving government appointment of an entity as a contractor who agrees to bear exploration, development and other costs at its sole risk in return for a share of production in the case of a success; more common in the petroleum industry and can be structured as a production sharing contract/agreement (PSC or PSA) or a risk service contract.

Contractual area: Oil and gas activities are related to the geographical areas delineated in the petroleum contract. They could also be identified, in general and depending on the country, as the "field" or "block."

Controlled foreign corporation (CFC): A corporation normally located in a low tax jurisdiction and controlled by shareholders resident in another country. A CFC legislation normally combats the sheltering of income in such corporations in low tax jurisdictions by attributing a proportion of the income sheltered in the corporation to the shareholders in the country where they are resident.

Controlled transaction: Transaction between associated enterprises for the transfer of property or services. The term may also be used to denote a transaction between related enterprises which is the subject of a transfer pricing analysis.

Cost contribution arrangement (CCA): It is an arrangement between enterprises to share the costs and risks of developing, producing or obtaining assets, services or rights. The arrangement sets out the responsibilities and risks of the participants and the nature and extent of the interest of each participant in the assets, services or rights resulting from the arrangement.

Cost oil: Portion of produced oil that the operator applies on an annual basis to recover defined costs specified by a product sharing contract.

Cost Plus Method: A transfer pricing method that evaluates the arm's length nature of an intercompany charge for tangible property or services by reference to the gross profit markup on costs incurred by the supplier of the property or services. It compares the gross profit markup earned by the tested party with the gross profit mark-ups earned by comparable companies.

Cost sharing arrangement (CSA): The term used in the United States to describe a cost contribution arrangement between enterprises to share the costs and risks of developing intangible assets. The arrangement would normally set out the contributions of the participants and define their share in the results of the assets resulting from the arrangement.

583

Cost stop: A limitation set to the amount, types or proportion of cost oil that can be considered as cost oil. When defined in a product sharing contract, the cost stop is generally set per reporting period.

Country-by-Country Report: The final Organisation for Economic Co-operation and Development's (OECD) Base Erosion and Profit Shifting report on Action 13 (2015) on transfer pricing documentation included a Country-by-Country (CbC) reporting requirement for multinational groups that meet a specified turnover threshold to provide aggregate information on an annual basis covering the jurisdictions in which they operate giving details of entities, income and taxes paid in each jurisdiction and indicators of economic activity and substance.

Creaming mechanism: A mechanism or provision that allows for the proportion of government revenue to increase if certain aspects of the extraction or relevant financials improve. Such mechanisms can depend on things such as the commodity price, volumes produced or even overall profitability of the project. In general, these mechanisms will also ratchet down and decrease government revenue in case the price, volume produced or overall profitability decreases.

DD&A: Depreciation, depletion, and amortization.

Decommissioning: Prepare a hot installation for a disposal option or a cold phase to be followed by disposal (deferred disposal).

Deferred disposal: Disposal after a cold phase, or after continued/other use under the current licence, whereby the economical or technological advantages of delayed disposal may be realized.

Disposal: An agreement or a process of deconstruction/dismantling/modification and/or transportation, which brings an installation to its final destination.

Double Tax Agreement (DTA): An agreement negotiated by two (or more) countries to ensure the avoidance of double taxation.

Double tax treaty (DTT): See DTA.

Downstream: The term refers to activities related to the transportation of crude oil and natural gas and to the refining, storage, distribution and marketing of crude oil and its derived products.

DTA: Double Taxation Agreement

Environmental impact assessment (EIA): A process of evaluating the likely environmental impacts of a proposed project or development, taking into account inter-related socio-economic, cultural and human-health impacts, both beneficial and adverse.

"EPC" means engineering, procurement, and construction.

"EPCM" means engineering, procurement and construction management.

Euribor: Euribor, the Euro Interbank Offer Rate, is a reference rate representing the average interest rate offered by eurozone banks for unsecured short-term lending in the inter-bank market.

Exclusive Economic Zone: An Exclusive Economic Zone (EEZ) is an area of the sea under the territorial ownership of a coastal state, guaranteed by the UN Convention on the Law of the Sea (UNCLOS). The coastal state has the right to explore and exploit, and the responsibility to conserve and manage, the living and non-living resources.

Exemption: An exemption means that no VAT is charged on a supply of goods and services and no input VAT deduction can be claimed.

Extractive industries: Those industries engaged in finding, developing, producing, and selling non-renewable resources such as crude oil, natural gas, and hard minerals and their products.

Farmee: A party in a farm-out agreement who receives part of an oil and gas interest as an assignment from the Farmor.

Farmor: The owner of an oil or gas interest and a party in a farm-out agreement who assigns part of its interest to another party (Farmee).

Farm-out/Farm-in agreements: Common oil and industry farm-out agreements, where the owner of an oil or gas interest (the Farmor) agrees to assign part of its interest to another party (the Farmee), in exchange for certain obligations relating to the development of the oil or gas interest.

FDP: Field Development Plans include activities and processes required to optimally develop a natural resources field.

Fiscal systems: The general economic framework governing natural resource activities, generally falling into two broader categories: concession regimes or contract regimes.

Fiscal terms: Specific economic elements relating to extractive industries activities within a particular country including taxation, other payments such as bonuses and royalties, legal framework, and state participation.

585

Flow through shares (FTS): A type of share issued by a corporation to a tax-payer, pursuant to an agreement under which the issuing corporation incurs eligible exploration expenses in an amount up to the consideration paid by the taxpayer for the shares. The corporation "renounces" to the taxpayer an amount in respect of the expenditure; and the exploration and development expenses are then considered to be the taxpayer's expenses for tax purposes. The shareholder can deduct the expenses as if they were incurred directly.

FTA: Forum on Tax Administration: The OECD's Forum on Tax Administration (FTA) brings together Commissioners from more than 50 advanced and emerging country tax administrations including all OECD and G20 member countries.

Full taxation: In relation to VAT, full taxation means that a single rate is applied to all goods and services in the economy, i.e., there are no exemptions, no zero ratings (except for exported supplies) no reduced ratings or other alternative policies applicable to the VAT.

General Anti-Avoidance Rule or General Anti-Abuse Rule (GAAR): A rule in tax statutes or sometimes as evolved through judicial decisions (such as "substance-over-form" approaches) empowering a revenue authority to deny taxpayers the benefit of an arrangement that they have entered into for an impermissible tax-related purpose (usually only where this is a main purpose or the sole purpose, differentiated for example from non-tax business or commercial purposes). It is general in nature and descriptive, because it is meant to be able to address abuses not specifically identified in law.

Government Share: The total amount of direct revenue that a host government receives from the project. This amount can include taxes, royalties, bonuses, share of profit, hydrocarbons and government participation, and is generally expressed as a percentage of divisible income generated by the project.

Grandfathering: A grandfather clause is an exemption that allows persons or entities to continue with activities or operations that were approved before the implementation of new rules, regulations or laws.

GST: Goods & Services Tax.

Import VAT: VAT paid by a recipient of imported goods or services. Import VAT is generally paid to a customs or similar office on the importation of goods and to a branch of the tax administration or post office on the importation of services.

Inclusive Framework: Acting through the OECD/G20 Inclusive Framework on

BEPS, more than 135 countries and jurisdictions are collaborating to put an end to tax avoidance strategies that exploit gaps and mismatches in tax rules to avoid paying tax.

Input VAT apportionment: An input VAT apportionment will generally need to be made where a registered supplier acquires goods or services partly for making taxable supplies and partly not for making taxable supplies.

Input VAT: VAT charged on a supply of goods or services to a purchaser, where the VAT may be deducted or reclaimed by the purchaser. The VAT will in most cases be deductible if the purchaser is registered for VAT and acquires the goods or services for the purpose of making taxable supplies. Note that the terms "input credit" or "VAT credit" are often used to mean the same as "input VAT deduction."

Installation: Fixed platform and associated systems, inventory, bridges, tripods and risers.

Internal rate of return (IRR):   Metric used to measure the profitability of (potential) investments. The higher an investment's internal rate of return, the more profitable it is expected to be and the more desirable it will be to undertake. The internal rate of return is the discount rate that makes the net present value of all cash flows from a particular project equal to zero.

International oil company (IOC):   Largely publicly traded, an internationally operating company involved in the oil and gas industry.

Jacket installation: A tubular steel structure founded on the seabed, and supporting a topside structure over the wave zone.

Joint Operating Agreement (JOA):   An association or consortium of two or more oil and gas companies engaged in a business enterprise regarding a contractual area without actual partnership or incorporation. The JOA regulates the management of the operation and decision-making.

Licence holder: Person obtaining the licence to explore and extract the natural resource from the State, often through a process of competitive bidding.

LTU/LTO   Means a Large Taxpayer Unit/Large Taxpayer Office, i.e., a tax administration department or function focused on large taxpayers, typically defined by turnover levels, capitalization/capital employed, employee numbers, etc.

MAAC: Convention on Mutual Administrative Assistance in Tax Matters.

MNE: Multinational Enterprise.

Module support structure (MSS): A generic term used to describe the structures whose purpose is to transfer loads from the modules to the jacket.

National oil company (NOC): A largely government-owned company, predominantly involved in oil and gas industry in that country.

Netback: Benchmark used in the oil and gas industry to assess the profitability and efficiency of a project based on the price, production, transportation, and selling of the hydrocarbon volumes produced. Netback is calculated by taking the revenues from the oil, less all costs associated with getting the oil to a market, including transportation, royalties, and production costs.

Non-operator: In the joint operating agreement, the participating oil and gas companies, other than the operator.

Operator: The entity in charge of performing the actual extractive industries activities with respect to a particular project. It can be the licence holder, or one of the licence holders if the licence was granted to a consortium or joint venture. In a joint operating agreement, the operator is in charge of the current and ordinary activities and of implementing the decisions made by the parties through the management committee. Normally, the operator can act with some freedom in all areas not specifically falling under the decision-making powers of the committee formed by the partners.

Output VAT: VAT charged on the supply of goods or services by a registered supplier.

Parent company guarantee: A parent company guarantee is a guarantee by a parent company of a contractor's performance under its contract with its client, where the contractor is a subsidiary of the parent company.

"PE" Means permanent establishment.

Permanent establishment (PE): Term used in double taxation agreements to refer to a situation where a non-resident entrepreneur is taxable in a country—that is, an enterprise in one country will not be liable to the income tax of the other country unless it has a "permanent establishment" through which it conducts business in that other country. Even if it has a PE, the income subject to taxation will generally only be taxed to the extent that it is "attributable" to the PE.

Petroleum contract: Legal document signed between the government and the contractor giving title (mining domain) and exploration and production rights to the contractually assigned area. There are several configurations, even in the same country, in terms of the rights and obligations assigned to the parties. These contracts can be classified as follows: (i) concession or licence contracts; (ii) production sharing agreements or contracts (PSCs); or (iii) service contracts.

Piece small: Reducing, in the case of steel structures, the installation material into pieces no larger than 1.5m x 0.6m, thus making them suitable for inserting in a steel mill furnace. For concrete structures, reducing the concrete to rubble, or to lift able sections.

Plug and abandonment (P&A) operations: Localization and securing of well zones where flow of oil or gas may occur between zones or to the surface.

Precautionary principle: If an action or policy has a suspected risk of causing harm to the public, or to the environment, in the absence of scientific consensus (that the action or policy is not harmful) the burden of proof that it is not harmful falls on those taking that action.

Production sharing contract (PSC) (or Production Sharing Agreement, PSA): A term used in the hydrocarbon industry which refers to an agreement between a contractor and a government, with regard to the exploration and production of hydrocarbons, whereby the contractor bears all exploration risks, production and development costs in return for its stipulated share of (profit from) production resulting from this effort. The costs incurred by the contractor are recoverable in the event of a commercial discovery. Thus, a PSC is a fiscal regime for the exploration and production of hydrocarbons.

Profit oil: The amount of production, after deducting cost oil, allocated to costs and expenses that will be divided between the participating parties and the host government under the product sharing contract.

Provision: An amount set aside from a company's profits for an expected liability or for the decreasing value of an asset, though the specific amount might be unknown.

Registered supplier: A person that is registered or required to be registered for value added tax.

Related parties: Entities under common management, control or ownership, or where one entity controls the other entity.

Relinquishment: The return of part or all of a lease or concession geographical area to a lessor, farmor or host government. The return may be vol-

589

untary or compelled contractually or by law.

Removal: A disposal option in which all or part of an installation is moved completely or partially from its present position, and deposited, or further dismantled, in order to recycle, reuse, or deposit its constituent materials and components.

Resale Price Method: A transfer pricing method that analyses the price of a product that a related sales company charges to an unrelated customer, i.e., the resale price, to determine an arm's length gross margin that the sales company retains to cover its sales, general and administrative expenses and still make an appropriate profit. The remainder of the product's price is regarded as the arm's length price for the transactions between the sales company and a related party.

Reserves replacement ratio (RRR): A performance metric which indicates to what extent entities are able to find and prove new hydrocarbon reserves in comparison to the hydrocarbon reserves produced. The RRR indicates to what extent future resource production equals current resource output from existing sites.

"Resource Company" Means the concessionaire/licence holder to the resource extracted.

"Resource State" Means the jurisdiction who granted the exploration or extraction licence. While this term is used in the chapter to provide context in the extractive sector, it may be understood to be interchangeable with the term "source state" as used in discourse regarding international tax matters.

Reuse: Further use of an installation, its parts, systems or inventory in a new or existing location.

Reverse-charge rule: A rule that is often applied to imported services. The recipient of the imported services would be required to self-assess the VAT on such services.

R-factor: A profitability ratio defined by a contractor's cumulative revenues to the contractor's cumulative costs.

Ring-fence: Tax treatment attributed to some contracts whereby each contract is treated as an independent and autonomous unit. As a result, in general, losses from one contractual area cannot be offset against profits from another contractual area, even if both contractual areas are using the same contractor.

Risk assessment: Analysis including a systematic identification and categorisation of risk to people, the environment, assets and financial interests.

Royalty: In the extractive industries, the term "royalty" refers to the obligatory payment made by the operator of the extraction project to the country as compensation for the extraction rights. Royalties are generally calculated with reference to the type, quantity, quality, and/or value of the extracted mineral resource as a percentage of the gross volume or value of the production (i.e., costs generally do not reduce the base) and are due once production commences. The term "royalties" as defined under Article 12 of the United Nations Model Convention has a different meaning and refers to the payment for the right to use property (in the case of the United Nations Model, both tangible and intangible).

Service provider or subcontractor: A company or individual providing various types of services and other supplies in the framework of the extractive industries.

Severance taxes: Severance taxes are volume or value-related payments due when non-renewable natural resources are extracted. Resources that typically incur severance taxes when extracted are oil, natural gas, coal, uranium and timber. Where the resources are publicly owned to begin with a resource royalty is paid instead of a tax.

Sliding scales: A mechanism with a more flexible share scale of fees, taxes, wages, etc. that varies in accordance with the variation of a particular standard or parameters.

Specific Anti-Avoidance Rule (SAAR): A rule in tax statutes empowering a revenue authority to deny taxpayers the benefit of a particular known and defined arrangement. It has a very limited scope of application and allows only limited discretion to the tax authorities compared to a GAAR. Like most GAARs, however, some specific rules have a purpose test, rather than relying purely on objective factors such as publicly quoted market prices.

State participation: Direct government ownership or shareholding in a portion of a project and or extractives company (beyond its ownership of the underlying resource reserves); also known as "equity participation."

Streaming arrangements: These are contracts for the ongoing supply of mineral production whereby, upon advance payment of a premium, the buyer agrees to purchase, at a fixed, discounted and predetermined price, all or part of the mineral production to be extracted by a mining company during a certain period. The arrangement would provide the funding necessary for a mining company to develop, construct and operate or expand the mine.

Structure: A part or whole of an installation.

Subcontractor Means a service provider to a resource company, limited to the type of services discussed in this chapter.

Supply: The term "supply" has a wider meaning than the term "sale" in normal usage and also includes, for example, rental agreements, instalment credit agreements, involuntary disposals and compulsory disposals.

Surface fee: Regular fee paid to the host government for the use of a piece of land or surface (e.g., area of a block or field).

Tax oil: Tax oil is the part of the profit oil that is used to actually pay income taxes owed by the investors on their profit oil. This is not always defined in the production sharing contract.

Taxable supplies: Supplies of goods or services by a registered supplier that are charged with VAT. This will include supplies that are charged with the standard VAT rate, a reduced VAT rate in the case of a country that applies multiple VAT rates, or a zero-rated supply.

TIEA: Tax Information and Exchange Agreement.

TIWB: Tax Inspectors without Borders. A joint initiative of the OECD and UNDP to support countries in tax audit capacity building, and extended to other areas including tax administration capacity in dealing with the extractive sector.

Toppling: Controlled rotation of an installation (with or without topsides) from a vertical to a horizontal position resting on the seabed.

Transactional Net Margin Method (TNMM): A transfer pricing method (TNMM) that examines the net profit margin relative to an appropriate base (e.g., costs, sales, assets) that a taxpayer realises from a controlled transaction. This is compared to the net profit margins earned in comparable uncontrolled transactions.

Transfer pricing adjustment: An adjustment made by the tax authorities to the profits of an enterprise after determining that the transfer price of a transaction with a related party does not conform to the arm's length principle.

Transfer pricing: The general term for the pricing of cross-border, intragroup transactions in goods, intangibles or services.

Treaty Shopping: The practice of structuring an investment/business activity so as to take advantage of a particular tax treaty. The term is normally applied to a situation where a person not resident of either of the treaty countries establishes an entity in one of the treaty countries in order to obtain treaty benefits.

Uncontrolled transaction: A transaction between independent and unrelated enterprises.

Unconventional oil and gas: Unconventional oil is petroleum produced or extracted using techniques other than the conventional (oil well) method. Oil industries and governments across the globe are investing in unconventional oil sources due to the increasing scarcity of conventional oil reserves.

UNDP: United Nations Development Programme.

"UNMC" Means the United Nations Model Convention.

Upstream: The term refers to activities related to the exploration and production of crude oil and natural gas, the beginning stages of the life cycle of an extractive industry project, and which involve large upfront capital investment that carries significant risks in terms of achieving commercially successful results.

Value added tax (VAT): A general, broad based tax on final consumption, assessed on the value added to goods and services. A VAT generally allows for the deduction of tax paid on inputs; a similar tax may be referred to as GST in some jurisdictions.

Zero-rate: A zero-rate for the purpose of VAT means that a supply will be charged with VAT at zero per cent and a registered supplier would remain entitled to an input VAT deduction.